Institutions and European Trade

What was the role of merchant guilds in the medieval and early modern economy? Does their wide prevalence and long survival mean they were efficient institutions that benefited the whole economy? Or did merchant guilds simply offer an effective way for the rich and powerful to increase their wealth, at the expense of outsiders, customers and society as a whole? These privileged associations of businessmen were key institutions in the European economy from 1000 to 1800. Historians debate merchant guilds' role in the Commercial Revolution, economists use them to support theories about institutions and development, and policymakers view them as prime examples of social capital, with important lessons for modern economies. Sheilagh Ogilvie's magisterial new history of commercial institutions shows how scrutinizing merchant guilds can help us understand which types of institution made trade grow, why institutions exist and how corporate privileges affect economic efficiency and human well-being.

SHEILAGH OGILVIE is Professor of Economic History at the University of Cambridge, and a Fellow of the British Academy. Her prizewinning publications include *State Corporatism and Proto-Industry: The Württemberg Black Forest 1590–1797* (Cambridge, 1997, winner of the Gyorgy Ranki Prize 1999), and *A Bitter Living: Women, Markets, and Social Capital in Early Modern Germany* (2003, winner of the René Kuczynski Prize 2004).

Cambridge Studies in Economic History

Cambridge Studies in Economic History comprises stimulating and accessible economic history which actively builds bridges to other disciplines. Books in the series will illuminate why the issues they address are important and interesting, place their findings in a comparative context, and relate their research to wider debates and controversies. The series will combine innovative and exciting new research by younger researchers with new approaches to major issues by senior scholars. It will publish distinguished work regardless of chronological period or geographical location

Institutions and European Trade

Merchant Guilds, 1000–1800

Sheilagh Ogilvie

University of Cambridge

CAMBRIDGE
UNIVERSITY PRESS

CAMBRIDGE
UNIVERSITY PRESS

University Printing House, Cambridge CB2 8BS, United Kingdom

Published in the United States of America by Cambridge University Press, New York

Cambridge University Press is part of the University of Cambridge.

It furthers the University's mission by disseminating knowledge in the pursuit of education, learning and research at the highest international levels of excellence.

www.cambridge.org
Information on this title: www.cambridge.org/9780521747929

First published 2011

A catalogue record for this publication is available from the British Library

Library of Congress Cataloguing in Publication data
Ogilvie, Sheilagh C.
Institutions and European Trade : Merchant Guilds, 1000–1800 /
Sheilagh Ogilvie.
    p.   cm. – (Cambridge Studies in Economic History. Second Series)
Includes bibliographical references and index.
ISBN 978-0-521-76417-9 (hardback) – ISBN 978-0-521-74792-9 (paperback)
1. Europe – Commerce – History.   2. Merchants – Europe – History.   I. Title.
HF3495.O45   2011
382.094 – dc22   2010052617

ISBN 978-0-521-76417-9 Hardback
ISBN 978-0-521-74792-9 Paperback

Contents

Acknowledgements

I have been exceptionally fortunate to have so many colleagues and friends who gave their energy, ideas and time to help improve this book. Jeremy Edwards read several very different drafts, provided detailed comments, and encouraged me to say when I thought an emperor had no clothes. André Carus, Tracy Dennison, Erik Lindberg, Tom Scott, Danielle van den Heuvel, and several anonymous readers all made extremely helpful comments on the whole manuscript. In addition, the following provided stimulating advice on particular aspects of the book and reactions to some of its arguments: David Abulafia, Jörg Baten, Marco Belfanti, Ian Blanchard, Chris Briggs, Montse Cachero, D'Maris Coffman, Partha Dasgupta, Kent Deng, Roberta Dessì, Steven Durlauf, Ann Fender, Oscar Gelderblom, Jessica Goldberg, Regina Grafe, Oliver Grant, Tim Guinnane, Donald Harreld, John Henderson, Ajit Karnik, Timur Kuran, Paola Lanaro, Joe Manning, Chris Meissner, Leos Müller, Klas Nyberg, Geoffrey Parker, Maarten Prak, Tom Safley, Paul Seabright, Joel Sobel, Mark Spörer, Peter Spufford, Peter Stabel, James Thomson, Michael Toch, Francesca Trivellato, Allan Tulchin, Klaus Weber, Ralph Woodward and Hillay Zmora. I would also like to thank participants in the lively and well-attended session on 'The Costs and Benefits of Merchant Guilds, 1300–1800' at the Fifth European Social Science History Conference in Berlin in March 2004, for eloquently demonstrating that economic history can arouse inspiration and passion.

1   Merchant guilds, efficiency and social capital

Merchant guilds – privileged, corporate associations of wholesale traders – were important institutions in the European economy from the eleventh to the nineteenth century, and scholars are still arguing about them now. Historians debate their economic, social and political roles. Economists draw lessons from merchant guilds to support their theories about the institutions that support economic development. Social scientists view merchant guilds as prime historical examples of 'social capital', with important lessons for the present day.

But why did merchant guilds exist? Does their wide prevalence and long survival mean they were efficient institutions that benefited the entire economy? Or did they simply offer an effective way for rich and powerful men to grab a bigger slice of the pie, at the expense of outsiders, customers and society as a whole? These questions are controversial. This book shows that the answers to them can help us understand how economies grow, why institutions exist and what are the real effects of social capital.

Privileged associations of merchants have been widespread since ancient times. They existed not just in Europe but also in North Africa, the Near East, Central and South America, India and China. Merchant associations were active in Egyptian, Greek and Roman antiquity, and survived in European and Mediterranean trading centres during the five centuries after the fall of Rome. They became a salient institution in much of Europe during the medieval Commercial Revolution, between c. 1000 and c. 1500. Although merchant guilds declined in some societies – particularly the Low Countries and England – from the sixteenth century on, they survived in many parts of southern, central, Nordic and eastern Europe into the eighteenth or early nineteenth centuries. New merchant guilds (and privileged merchant 'companies' that often resembled guilds) formed in emerging sectors such as proto-industrial exporting and the intercontinental trade until around 1800. Merchant guilds also spread to European colonies, especially to Spanish

America, where typically they were only abolished with independence in the early nineteenth century.

1.1   Merchant guilds and theories of institutions

Any institution that exists so widely over such long periods raises fundamental questions. Why did this institution arise? Why did it survive? Why did it ultimately decline? And what was its long-term impact? In recent decades many scholars have been attracted by the idea that institutions arise and survive because they are 'efficient'. An institution is efficient if it solves economic problems better than any other – if there is no feasible alternative institution such that the gains of those who would benefit from the alternative exceed the losses of those who would be harmed by it.[1] So an efficiency view would argue that merchant guilds existed so widely and survived for so long because they made the whole pre-industrial economy work better – their aggregate economic benefits outweighed their costs.[2]

Efficiency views of historical institutions have become very popular in the last few decades. This started with North and Thomas's theory of European serfdom, and soon spread to peasant communes, craft guilds and a colourful array of other pre-modern social arrangements including feuds and vigilantism.[3] The merchant guild alone has been portrayed as a socially beneficial solution to at least six serious economic problems: state extortion, commercial insecurity, contract enforcement, principal-agent relationships, imperfect information and economic

---

[1] A set of economic arrangements is *Pareto-efficient* if there is no feasible alternative set of arrangements that can make some individual better off without another being made worse off. A Pareto-improvement involves a change that benefits at least one individual without harming any others. Since this concept of efficiency relates only to changes in which there are no losers, it is silent about distributional trade-offs. In practice, it is difficult to make changes in economic arrangements that do not involve both gainers and losers, so the concept of efficiency is often interpreted in terms of the gainers being able *in principle* to compensate the losers and still be better off after the change. In this interpretation, an institution is efficient if there is no feasible alternative institution such that the gains of those who would benefit from the alternative exceed the losses of those who would be harmed by it. It is important to note that minimizing the *costs* of economic activity (of producing and transacting) is a necessary, but not sufficient, condition for economic efficiency. For example, a monopoly may produce its output at *minimum cost*, but the outcome is not *efficient* because the price charged to consumers exceeds the marginal cost of production. Ending the monopoly would increase efficiency because the gains to consumers would exceed the losses of the monopolist, and thus in principle the consumers could compensate the monopolist for the lost monopoly profits and still be better off. On the concept of efficiency as applied to pre-industrial economic institutions, see Ogilvie (2007b), 651–8; Ogilvie (2007a), 4–5.

[2] This is the simplified definition of efficiency suggested by Acemoglu (2006), 516.

[3] For a survey, see Ogilvie (2007b), 652–5.

volatility.[4] By solving these problems, merchant guilds are supposed to have fuelled the medieval Commercial Revolution – the substantial and sustained quickening of exchange from the eleventh century on, first in the Italian maritime cities, later in other coastal areas (Flanders and the German Hanseatic towns), reaching most of Europe by the fifteenth century. Regulated or chartered merchant companies which closely resembled guilds are held to have solved a resurgence of these problems during a second, 'early modern' Commercial Revolution when Europe began trading extensively with other continents in the sixteenth century. Merchant guilds facilitated these two great bursts of long-distance trade, the argument goes, thereby powering the long-term development of the European economy between the Dark Ages and factory industrialization.

But this is not the only way to look at merchant guilds. Merchant guilds secured legal privileges which gave their members the sole right to trade in particular sectors. Merchant guilds excluded most people from membership: they barred trade by women, Jews, immigrants, peasants, the poor, particular ethnic groups, different religions and people their members simply didn't like. Merchant guilds regulated how their own members could do business, limiting competition, so customers had to pay higher prices. Guilds bribed and lobbied officials and rulers to enforce their privileged position. They engaged in bitter conflict – even violence – against individuals and other guilds who tried to infringe on their trading privileges. Merchant guilds thus had a dark side – they used their social capital to seek 'rents' (monopoly profits) and distort markets in favour of their members. Monopolies, market distortions and rent-seeking are not efficient: they reduce aggregate well-being and economic growth. Nor are they socially just: they redistribute resources from outsiders to insiders.

This means we have to look at *everything* merchant guilds did – the dark side as well as the bright side – before we conclude that they favoured economic development. It also means we have to think differently about institutions in general. In particular, we have to question the idea that institutions exist and survive because they are efficient. After all, institutions affect not just *efficiency* – the aggregate size of the economic pie – but *distribution* – how this pie is shared out. So an institution can emerge and survive not because it serves the interests of the whole economy, but because it benefits powerful interest-groups, who use the benefits that

---

[4] Some but not all of these efficiency theories of merchant guilds are referred to in Gelderblom and Grafe (2004), 1–2. Each of these theories is explored in detail in a separate chapter of the present book.

the institution creates to keep it in being.[5] Merchant guilds provide an excellent illustration of this principle, as we shall see, since their efforts to redistribute resources towards their own members were unrelenting, and this in turn affected almost every aspect of pre-modern exchange.

We must also approach the evidence critically. Merchant guilds were most prevalent in Europe between *c.* 1000 and *c.* 1500, a time before economic activity was fully documented, especially in quantitative form. Evidence on merchant guilds comes mainly from qualitative sources: rulers' edicts, municipal legislation, guild charters, court minutes, subjects' petitions, merchant letters and account-books. These sources must be carefully scrutinized. Normative legal documents such as edicts, laws and charters reflect what princes, town councils and guilds believed was desirable, but not how the economy actually worked. Even sources closer to actual economic activity such as court minutes, petitions and letters must be used critically, with careful attention to their rhetorical purposes. Few qualitative sources, moreover, contain evidence of how prevalent were the practices which they record.[6] So we must often formulate hypotheses in such a way that they can be refuted with counter-examples, since they cannot be either rejected or 'confirmed' by statistical processing of large volumes of data.

Analysing a pan-European institution such as the merchant guild inevitably means relying on secondary literature. While many secondary works reliably reflect the content of the documentary or archaeological sources, some are influenced by the assumptions of their authors and the fashions of their time. Three major sources of potential distortion are particularly worrying.

First, there is the 'legislative history' approach. This is based on the (justified) recognition that legal monopolies are harmful combined with the (unjustified) belief that laws and ordinances accurately reflect economic reality. This has given rise to negative evaluations of merchant guilds based solely on their legal entitlements to exercise monopolies. Such assessments must be subjected to deeper examination, and legislative sources compared with evidence on what actually happened. Chapters 3 and 4 do precisely this, first asking whether merchant guilds got legal monopolies and then assessing the evidence on whether they enforced them.

---

[5] For an exposition of this approach to economic institutions, see Ogilvie (2007b), 662–7.

[6] The exception are those qualitative sources which can be transformed into quantitative meta-sources through the 'micro-exemplary' method discussed in Carus and Ogilvie (2009); hitherto this approach has not been applied to the study of merchant guilds.

A second way of looking at merchant guilds is the 'institutional advocacy' approach. A scholar studying a particular institution may come to identify with it, either for its own sake or because it is associated with a modern institution which that scholar values. This gives rise to studies of historical institutions which defend them against all criticisms and manufacture ingenious theoretical mechanisms by which their apparently abusive practices actually generated socio-economic benefits. A notable example is that strand of traditional scholarship which sees the German Hanse as a precursor of German national unity, a standard-bearer for German developmental superiority to other mercantile systems, or even a precursor of the modern European Union.[7] But the same tendency can be found in most national and municipal historiographies. Such cases, too, must be explored more deeply to separate facts from advocacy.

Finally, there is the 'efficiency' stance we have already discussed. This approach is based on the (justified) recognition that all institutions exist for a reason, combined with the (unjustified) belief that this reason is that they are economically efficient. Such claims are sometimes also buttressed by statements made by merchant guilds or their advocates at the time, concerning the supposed benefits of establishing or strengthening guild privileges. This approach has given rise to excessively positive evaluations of merchant guilds, even ones that devoted most of their efforts to redistributing resources towards their own members at the expense of the wider economy. The putative benefits of merchant guilds, whether claimed by contemporary apologists or elaborated by modern theorists, must be subjected to empirical examination. Chapters 6 through 10 try to do just that.

This book seeks a middle course between the drily negative assessment of merchant guilds applied by the 'legislative history' approach, and the enthusiastically positive views advanced by the 'institutional advocacy' and 'efficiency' approaches. It tries to show how forming and using merchant guilds were good, rational choices for their individual beneficiaries even while guilds could have bad effects for their victims and the wider economy. To do so, it focuses in turn on each major activity of merchant guilds: monopolizing trade, interacting with rulers, providing security, enforcing contracts, regulating agency relations, conveying information and manipulating prices. The result is a radical reassessment of both merchant guilds in economic history and institutions in economic theory.

Not only do we unveil a more complex picture of this central historical institution. We also discover a more differentiated analytical approach to

---

[7] See the careful discussion of Hanse historiography in Selzer and Ewert (2005), 8–18.

economic institutions. A given institution does many things, it turns out, and all its activities must be taken into account before we declare that it is efficient or inefficient. Moreover, no institution exists in isolation, and we cannot evaluate one without examining its interactions with surrounding institutions in that society. Most crucially, few institutions are distributionally neutral, and their redistributive activities often affect efficiency. Any adequate economic theory of institutions must incorporate these lessons from the history of merchant guilds.

1.2   Merchant guilds and social capital

The history of European merchant guilds also shines a searchlight on the economic role of 'social capital'. Social capital is the name given by modern social scientists to the stock of shared norms, information, mutual sanctions and collective action which are created by closely knit, multistranded social networks, and are supposed to have far-reaching benefits for economic development. The merchant guild is widely portrayed as a prime example of a network that created this kind of beneficial social capital. Although both social capital theories and efficiency theories adopt favourable views of merchant guilds, they are conceptually quite distinct. Social capital theories claim not that all institutions are efficient, but that those institutions that generate social capital are superior to those that do not. This is a strong and interesting theory. One aim of this book is to test it, by investigating the social capital generated by merchant guilds, assessing its economic impact and exploring its implications for social capital in developing economies more generally.

Economic institutions are generally divided into three types, according to how they organize transactions: hierarchical governance, market exchange and horizontal contracting.[8] Merchant guilds are viewed as an example of horizontal contracting, in which repeated interactions within a closely knit network create a social capital of shared norms, information, sanctions and collective action. This social capital, it is argued, reduces transaction costs below those that prevail under hierarchical governance or market exchange, thereby benefiting not just members of the network itself, but also the wider economy.[9]

Merchant guilds are adduced as prime historical examples of how social capital is supposed to have favoured economic development, and are

---

[8] North (1981), 37, 45–58; North (1990), 27–35, 61–3.

[9] For definitions and discussion of the concept of social capital, see Bourdieu (1986); J. S. Coleman (1989); Dasgupta and Serageldin (2000); Glaeser, Laibson and Sacerdote (2002); Lin (2001); Ogilvie (2003); Putnam (2000); Putnam, Leonardi and Nanetti (1993); Sobel (2002).

frequently used to support arguments advocating investment in social capital to solve modern economic problems. Thus, for instance, Putnam has argued that the social capital created by northern Italy's medieval guild tradition was a major determinant of its modern economic success, and claims that social capital in general fosters 'aggregate economic growth'.[10] In a 1999 speech, the Chief Economist of the World Bank listed 'guilds' among those institutions which, by generating social capital, could 'support entrepreneurial efforts' in Eastern European transition economies.[11] Bardhan argues that merchant guilds benefited European commerce in history, and urges more studies of how social capital of this sort can benefit developing economies in the present.[12] Surveys of social capital and economic development commonly refer to merchant guilds as networks whose social capital facilitated European commercial growth in the past and hold positive lessons for developing economies now.[13]

Can we view European merchant guilds as a test case for social capital? Merchant guilds certainly possessed the required institutional features – multiplex links and closure. Multiplex links are important because social capital is more likely to be generated when members of a social network transact with one another in a range of different spheres – economic, social, political, religious, cultural, demographic. This is because multi-stranded ties among network members make relationships within the network 'appropriable': the resources of one relationship can be brought into play in other relationships with the same person. Multiplex links mean that members have multiple means to reinforce shared norms, convey and receive information about one another, inflict penalties on network members who violate norms and efficiently organize collective action.[14]

Relationships within merchant guilds were certainly multi-stranded – so much so that some historians have argued that guilds were not primarily economic institutions at all: 'it is cultural identity and sociability, rather than commercial networking and economic security, that decided the merchant guild's activities'.[15] As this book shows, the evidence does

---

[10] Putnam, Leonardi and Nanetti (1993), 163–85; Putnam (2000), 319, 322–3 (quotation), 325, 346–7. On merchant associations in the modern diamond trade as an example of beneficial social capital, see J. S. Coleman (1989), S97–S99.

[11] Stiglitz (1999); Stiglitz and Ellerman (2000), 63 (quotation). On the relevance of merchant guilds and social capital to modern transition economies, see also Raiser (2001), 231.

[12] Bardhan (1996), 6–7.   [13] E.g. Narayan and Pritchett (2000).

[14] J. S. Coleman (1989), S104–S110.

[15] Lambert and Stabel (2005), 15, 22 (quotation). Harreld (2004a), by contrast, while acknowledging merchant guilds' role in social solidarity (46–50), portrays their economic role as dominant (41–2, 47).

not support the view that merchant guilds primarily focused on sociability and cultural identity. They were formed around shared occupations and, until their declining phases, focused mainly on furthering the economic interests of their members.[16] But in so doing, they also engaged in non-economic activities.

Obligatory participation in corporate social gatherings, for instance, was an important shared norm in many merchant guilds.[17] One of the earliest surviving records of a post-antiquity merchant guild dates from 1024, and describes how members of the merchant guild of the Dutch city of Tiel

begin their drinking bouts at the crack of dawn, and the one who tells dirty jokes with the loudest voice and raises laughter and induces the vulgar folk to drink gains high praise among them. For this purpose they pool their money and finance carouses at special times of the year where they, at higher feasts, get drunk quasi solemnly.[18]

Another early merchant guild, that of St Omer in France around 1100, is also recorded as fostering norms of collective sociability and penalizing members who violated them.[19] The thirteenth-century merchant guild of the German city of Stendal fined members for missing its thrice-yearly assemblies.[20] A major article in the first Brabant charter issued to the Merchant Adventurers of England in 1296 'allowed the merchants their assemblies', and the Adventurers regularly held full meetings of their members both in England and abroad.[21] Sociable gatherings made up such an important aspect of the various guilds of German long-distance merchants in Riga in the fifteenth century that the guilds kept registers of attendance.[22]

Sociability fostered the multi-stranded relationships by which guild members conveyed information about one another and penalized violations of guild norms. The importance attached to social gatherings by merchant guilds is illustrated by a conflict which arose in 1449 over guild finances between the mercer and the fishmonger factions of the English Merchant Adventurers, in which harmony was restored through corporate sociability between their local merchant guilds at home in London:

---

[16] For similar conclusions, see Selzer and Ewert (2005), 8–18, on the German Hanse; and De Smedt (1950–4) on the 'English nation' (Merchant Adventurers) in Antwerp.

[17] Gross (1890), I: 32–4; Kohn (2003a), 42–3; Lambert and Stabel (2005), 15.

[18] Pertz (1925), 118–19; quoted in Volckart and Mangels (1999), 438. For more detail on the economic component of this guild's collective norms, see also Dilcher (1984), 69–70.

[19] Dilcher (1984), 70.   [20] Schulze (1985), 379–80.

[21] Sutton (2002), 31–3 (quotation on 31).   [22] Brück (1999), 113–16.

for as much as that great discord and variance fell between the gatherers of the conduits of the Mercery and the wardens of the Fishmongers, therefore a supper was made at the King's Head on Cheap at the desire and request of the said wardens for continuance of good love betwixt both parties . . .[23]

Guild sociability was thus not only practised for its own sake, but mobilized to serve other purposes. De Roover goes so far as to argue that the main purpose of sociability within a merchant guild 'was not to provide entertainment, but to bring social pressure to bear upon the members of the group'.[24] Likewise, Brück argues that participation in the festivities of the German merchant guild in medieval Riga was partly to introduce new guild officials to the assembled merchantry.[25] A number of scholars have argued that the parties held by the Artusbruderschaft, a drinking society in Danzig (Gdańsk) whose members were mainly long-distance merchants, enabled traders to form contacts and learn about the reputations of third parties, reducing transaction costs[26] – a theory explored more deeply when we investigate contract enforcement in Chapter 6 and commercial information in Chapter 9.

Religious observance constituted a second set of multi-stranded relationships fostered inside merchant guilds. A merchant guild often focused its activities around a particular church or chapel, in which members not only worshipped, but also held assemblies, archived records or stored wares.[27] In medieval Novgorod, the church of St Peter's, dating from c. 1200, was located in the German merchants' compound and was known as des kopmans kerke ('the merchants' church').[28] In medieval England, some merchant guilds bore the name of a patron saint, employed a chaplain or priest, and engaged in good works and devotional observance, although religious activities were probably less important for merchant guilds than for other types of guild.[29] In medieval Lyons, the Florentine merchant guild worshipped and kept its archives at the church of the convent of the Franciscans.[30] In medieval Bruges, the alien merchant guilds of Venice, Genoa and Lucca used the chapels of the Augustinian friars.[31] In medieval Constantinople, too, a merchant church was an indispensable appurtenance of a fully fledged alien merchant guild, and specific churches have been identified for the Venetian, Amalfitan, Pisan and

---

[23] Sutton (2002), 35.   [24] R. De Roover (1948a), 20.   [25] Brück (1999), 116.

[26] Selzer (2003), 77–94; Link and Kapfenberger (2005), 165.

[27] For an overview, see Slessarev (1967), who goes so far as to suggest that merchant churches were the forerunners of alien merchant guilds in the Mediterranean.

[28] Slessarev (1967), 178–9.   [29] Gross (1890) I: 34–5.   [30] Mauro (1990), 264.

[31] Lambert and Stabel (2005), 14–15; Paravicini (1992), 110; Gelderblom (2005a), 14–15 with n. 73; Henn (1999), 136; W. D. Phillips (1986), 42–4.

Genoese merchant colonies in the city.[32] Similarly, in the mid-twelfth century the Venetian merchant guild in Rodosto (present-day Tekirdağ, in European Turkey) was linked both religiously and commercially to the local priory of St George.[33]

Guild churches served secular as well as religious purposes. According to De Roover, the 1478 charter of the Lucca merchant guild in Bruges (based on an earlier charter of 1369) shows it to have been

> at the same time a trade association, a social club, and a religious brotherhood formed to promote the devotion to the *Volto Santo*, the national cult of Lucca. As always in the Middle Ages, the religious and mystical element was closely interwoven with political, social and other activities.[34]

Maréchal describes how the members of the Spanish merchant guilds in Bruges remained assembled after their shared religious services to discuss their business.[35] Monasteries of St Nicholas were used by medieval Venetian merchant colonies in Corinth, Thebes, Sparta and Abydos as clearing houses, banks and sometimes goods-depositories, as well as places of worship.[36] The Merchants' Church in medieval Novgorod was used by the German merchant colony not just for religious purposes but to store merchandise.[37]

Such multiplex interlinkage of commercial and religious ties within alien merchant colonies continued into the early modern period. In the sixteenth century, nearly all important merchant colonies maintained by traders from Ragusa (Dubrovnik) in Ottoman Balkan cities had their own Catholic churches, whose clergy ministered to merchants, educated traders' offspring and even sometimes themselves operated merchant businesses. The religious institutions of the Ragusan merchant guild in Belgrade were so important to its members that struggles for religious control sparked decades of internal conflict between Ragusan and Bosnian factions within the colony, endangering its commercial privileges.[38]

Multi-stranded relationships were also fostered by norms of religious oath-taking, collective funeral attendance, participation in civic parades and festivals, donations to charity and even the wearing of special clothing.[39] A number of Lucca merchants trading in Bruges were fined between 1377 and 1404 for missing 'the mass of the Holy Cross, the

---

[32] Slessarev (1967), 183–9.   [33] *Ibid.*, 186.   [34] R. De Roover (1948a), 18.
[35] Maréchal (1953), 31.   [36] Slessarev (1967), 186–7.   [37] *Ibid.*, 178–9.
[38] For a detailed discussion of these conflicts, see Molnár (2007).
[39] Gelderblom (2005a), 14–15 n. 73; Blockmans and Prevenier (1999), 139; Henn (1999), 136.

central festival day of the Lucchese community in Bruges'.[40] German merchant guilds in fifteenth-century Riga formally required members to participate in carnival processions.[41] Merchant guilds used religious oaths to strengthen and reaffirm internal ties among members, as in 1278 when Pietro Rondana wished to be readmitted to a Piacenzan merchant firm in Montpellier, and was required to swear the oath required of members of the 'community of merchants of Tuscany and Lombardy' in the city.[42] Religious observance thus constituted an important component of the multiplex ties within merchant guilds that helped generate guild-specific social capital.

Multiplex ties inside guilds were further enhanced by kinship links. Demographic studies often show high endogamy within merchant guilds. In the Hanse city of Thorn, for instance, leading families of the local merchant guild in the fourteenth and fifteenth centuries were linked through joint trading ventures, political office-holding and intermarriage.[43] The occasional south German or Italian merchant who gained acceptance to the German Hanse typically managed it through a strategic marriage into an existing Hanse family.[44] Members of Italian merchant guilds in medieval Bruges rarely married local women but rather sought brides from Italy.[45] Members of Italian merchant guilds in Paris and Bruges almost always married women from their home cities.[46] In sixteenth-century Lyons, likewise, only a few members of alien merchant guilds were integrated into Lyonese society.[47] Members of the Lucca merchant guild rented dwellings in Lyons but did not buy them, and married within the circle of Italian merchants.[48] Members of the Portuguese merchant guild in early modern Rouen did not intermarry with townspeople and seldom entered into business ventures with them, instead intermarrying primarily with other members of the Portuguese colony.[49] Members of the Bohemian merchant guild in eighteenth-century Cadiz did not intermarry with locals but instead selected brides from their home communities in Bohemia.[50] Members of eighteenth-century Armenian merchant communities throughout Europe and Asia typically travelled 'home' to find brides in New Julfa, the Armenian colony in the Persian city of Isfahan.[51] Members of the legally privileged network of foreign wholesale merchants in eighteenth-century Stockholm, the so-called Skeppsbronn Nobility, married frequently inside the network, and did not seek marriage partners either among Swedes or outside

---

[40] Lambert and Stabel (2005), 5.   [41] E. Thomson (1994); Redlich (1934).
[42] Bautier (1987), 224 n. 98.   [43] Sarnowsky (1999), esp. 230–1.
[44] Selzer and Ewert (2001), 156–7.   [45] R. De Roover (1948a), 22.   [46] Esch (1992).
[47] Mauro (1990), 265.   [48] *Ibid.*; Mirot (1927), 78–81.   [49] Brunelle (2003), 297.
[50] K. Weber (2004), 136–7, 352–61.   [51] Aslanian (2004), 43.

Sweden in their own places of origin.[52] Members of the Maltese merchant guilds in eighteenth-century Spanish cities enforced internal endogamy by 'exclud[ing] from their companies those who marry in Spain'.[53]

But guild endogamy varied. In places and times when merchant guilds wielded fewer legal privileges and economic powers, their members often married outside their own communities. In sixteenth-century Antwerp, for instance, foreign merchants were numerous but their guilds were not very powerful: their members often married Antwerp women rather than seeking brides back home.[54] Thus, for instance, Lodovico Guicciardini wrote in 1576 that 'There are mor *Spaniards* in *Andwerpe* than of anie other Nation, because divers of them are married & dwell there.'[55] In Bruges, by contrast, alien merchant guilds retained many privileges until the mid-sixteenth century, and their members continued to practise endogamy until then.[56] As late as 1558, the son of a member of the Castilian consulado in Bruges who had married a Flemish wife obtained a royal decree from the king of Spain declaring that he was to be considered 'as a member of the [kingdom and lordships of Castile] and as such can have and hold and enjoy in them all the things which those who are natives enjoy and can enjoy'.[57] In 1559 the merchant Diego Pardo wrote that 'I am not a Brugeois of this town of Bruges but a member of the Nation of Spain and as such I can make my will according to the custom of Spain and no one can contradict me.'[58]

So merchant guilds, at least in the periods and places where they were economically important, manifested the first feature social scientists deem essential for generating social capital – multiplex internal relationships. Norms of compulsory sociability, religious observance and endogamy can be replicated for almost every economically important merchant guild in pre-modern Europe. These norms reinforced the multiplex links that made relationships appropriable, giving guild members multiple means to convey information about one another, to inflict penalties on those who violated guild norms and to organize collective action.[59] In this sense, therefore, European merchant guilds qualify as a good test case for the economic impact of social capital.

---

[52] Hasselberg, Müller and Stenlås (1997), 16–17.   [53] Quoted in Vassallo (2002), 12.
[54] On the lack of economic power of alien merchant guilds in early modern Antwerp, see Harreld (2004b), 21; on intermarriage between alien merchants and locals in early modern Antwerp, see Blondé, Gelderblom and Stabel (2007), 168; Subacchi (1995), 83–7.
[55] Quoted in C. R. Phillips (1983), 268.
[56] Mollat (1970); W. D. Phillips (1986), 33, 35–6, 39.
[57] Quoted in W. D. Phillips (1986), 45–6.   [58] Quoted in *ibid.*, 36.
[59] J. S. Coleman (1989), S104–S110.

A second key institutional feature regarded as essential for creating social capital is 'closure' – a clear definition of who is a member of the network and who is not. Careful demarcation of network membership increases the density of interactions between members, thereby intensifying the quality and reliability of the information sharing and third-party monitoring needed to enforce cooperation.[60] European merchant guilds also manifested this feature. As we shall see in Chapters 3 and 4, they restricted admission to men who satisfied certain conditions and they carefully monitored who participated in activities reserved for guild members.[61] Merchant guilds enjoyed their special economic and political position by virtue of claiming certain privileges for their members, conveying information among their members, creating norms that were shared by their members, punishing members who violated these norms and organizing collective action among their members. This entailed defining everyone outside the guild as a *non*-member – an outsider who could *not* enjoy the privileges of membership.

European merchant guilds thus possessed the second key institutional feature for generating social capital – network closure. Guilds focused on making clear who was and was not a member. But such institutional closure, although crucial for *generating* social capital, raises interesting questions about who *benefits* from it. Social capital theorists typically concur with efficiency theorists in arguing that merchant guilds were economically beneficial. But closure by its nature means that outsiders are excluded and important activities are reserved for network members. As this book will show, in assessing social capital we have to look at its effects not just on network insiders, but on outsiders and the wider economy.

1.3 Merchant guilds and economic development

This book lays bare the myth and the reality of merchant guilds by using a rich international literature to address important questions. First, did merchant guilds favour or hinder the long-term development of the European economy from the medieval Commercial Revolution to the late-eighteenth-century Industrial Revolution? Second, do merchant guilds' widespread existence and long survival mean they were efficient institutions that benefited the whole economy or simply effective ways of redistributing resources to the rich and powerful – do they support an

---

[60] For the original insight, see *ibid.*, S104–S110. For a more rigorous development, see Sobel (2002), esp. 151.

[61] Ogilvie (1997), 72–9, 127–80; Ogilvie (2003), 21–2, 329–31.

efficiency or a distributional approach to economic institutions? Finally, what light do merchant guilds shed on the economic role of social capital?

Answering these questions inevitably requires generalizing – identifying common features across a wide and colourful array of merchant organizations that differed in other ways. As we shall see in Chapter 2, there was a lot of variation among different types of merchant 'guild' – the post-antiquity *collegia* of the tenth or eleventh centuries, the classic merchant guilds of the high Middle Ages, the surviving merchant guilds of early modern Iberia or Germany, the proto-industrial merchant associations, the regulated and chartered companies. There was variation across time, with merchant guilds changing gradually during the medieval period, and then more rapidly (at least in some European economies) after about 1500. There were important regional variations, with differences between the north Atlantic maritime economies (the Low Countries, England, northern France), eastern and central Europe (Germany and the Slavic lands), the Nordic countries, the Iberian peninsula, the western Mediterranean of Italy and Provence, and the eastern Mediterranean of the Balkan, Levantine, Byzantine and Ottoman economies. There were variations among different types of trade – between the regional wholesaling of the local merchant guilds, the international wholesaling of alien merchant colonies and hanses, the single-branch wholesaling of the proto-industrial merchant associations, and the intercontinental and colonial wholesaling of the regulated and chartered companies. Not all merchant guilds engaged in the same activities, whether because of their members' specialization, the characteristics of the surrounding economy, or the politics of the realms where they had to secure their privileged position. But, as Chapter 2 demonstrates, there were also institutional and economic resemblances between all these merchant guilds, colonies, hanses and 'companies'. This justifies subjecting them to common scrutiny in order to analyse their effects on efficiency and distribution.

Chapter 3 begins this process by probing more deeply into the economic activities of local merchant guilds. These came into view after about 1000, became nearly universal in European towns in the thirteenth and fourteenth centuries, declined in some parts of the continent after *c.* 1500, but flourished in others into the late eighteenth century. Chapter 3 examines the privileges local merchant guilds claimed over trade, the advantages they offered to their members and their powers in the wider society. It analyses how local merchant guilds mobilized the multistranded relationships among their members to generate a social capital that exercised far-reaching effects which extended, as we shall see, to their colonies in foreign trading centres. The chapter asks whether local merchant guilds sought or obtained monopolies from rulers, whether they managed to enforce them, and what impact this had on the wider economy.

Chapter 4 shifts the focus to alien merchant guilds, hanses and privileged companies. Most pre-modern European trading cities contained one or more guilds of foreign merchants. The traders from one specific foreign town typically formed an exclusive guild, although sometimes they admitted traders from neighbouring or allied towns, and occasionally merchants from a group of towns would form a hanse to represent their interests in foreign trading centres. Chapter 4 examines the privileges alien merchant guilds and hanses secured for their members, and how these privileges affected commerce as a whole. It investigates the extent to which the monopoly privileges obtained by alien merchant guilds and hanses enabled them to shape trade in their members' interests, and asks what impact this had on the economy at large.

Chapter 5 focuses on why merchant guilds were able to exist and survive for so long, even though they enjoyed monopolies that imposed costs on outsiders. It finds the answer in their distributional activities, which benefited two powerful parties – merchants and rulers. Merchant guilds provided a set of mechanisms enabling traders and rulers to collaborate in extracting resources for themselves at the expense of the wider economy. Through their guilds, merchants negotiated with rulers to grant them exclusive rights to trade. This gave them economic rents (monopoly profits), which their guilds enabled them to commit themselves to share with rulers by making cash transfers, facilitating tax collection, supplying favourable loans, assisting in military and naval expeditions and providing political support. This two-way flow of benefits, organized through merchant guilds, benefited both rulers and guilded merchants, but had effects on the wider economy that were far-reaching and malign.

Did merchant guilds generate countervailing benefits, however, which might have compensated for the costs they inflicted on outsiders, consumers and the economy at large? Chapter 6 examines one type of benefit merchant guilds are supposed to have generated: commercial security. Efficiency theorists have argued that merchant guilds solved security problems, in an era before effective states, either by providing collective protection to their members or by using trade boycotts to press rulers into providing security. This, it is argued, justified guilds' monopoly privileges and facilitated long-distance trade. To investigate this theory, Chapter 6 examines pre-modern commercial insecurity and the role merchant guilds played in it. To the extent that merchant guilds reduced commercial insecurity at all, it finds, they did so only for their own members. They did not help outsiders, however. Indeed, merchant guilds were probably a net source of *insecurity* in the pre-modern trading system as a whole. This was because their exclusive legal privileges created an incentive for outsiders to attack them and guild members to fight back. The competing legal privileges of different merchant guilds created a quasi-legitimate basis for inter-corporate conflict, which spilled over into riots, privateering, piracy and acts of war. While a superficial view might suggest that merchant guilds increased commercial security by protecting their members, deeper analysis shows that their privileges may have exported insecurity to the wider pre-modern trading system.

Chapter 7 turns to another way in which merchant guilds are sometimes claimed to have generated economic benefits – by enforcing commercial contracts. Merchant guilds substituted for legal contract enforcement, it is often argued, whether through autonomous guild jurisdictions or through collective reprisals against entire guilds if one member defaulted on a contract. Chapter 7 examines how contracts were enforced in pre-modern Europe and the role played by merchant guilds. Guild jurisdictions, it finds, were common but not universal. The system of collective reprisals against entire guilds was widely disliked by both merchants and rulers, and cannot be regarded as beneficial for commerce. Pre-modern contract enforcement was profoundly imperfect, and did improve in the course of the medieval and early modern period. But it did so through institutional innovations unrelated to merchant groups. Even though these new mechanisms were imperfect, they were often preferred to guilds by merchants themselves. The contract-enforcement activities of merchant guilds, however, cast illuminating light on the transition from particularized to generalized commercial institutions which, this book argues, was central to European economic development.

Chapter 8 examines a further economic benefit sometimes claimed for merchant guilds – the solution of principal-agent problems. Long-distance trade required merchants to employ agents in distant trading centres. But how did they monitor and control these agents? Merchant guilds are supposed to have been the efficient solution, controlling fraudulent agents by internal employment contracts, performance bonds and collective penalties including ostracism. Chapter 8 scrutinizes these ideas by examining the various mechanisms available to pre-modern merchants to solve principal-agent problems. It finds that these problems were real, but merchant guilds played only a minor role in solving them. The true innovations which contributed to the solution of such problems lay in legal forms of enterprise within merchant trading houses and in public jurisdictions – again, generalized rather than particularized institutional solutions.

To explore this theory, Chapter 9 directs attention to another important problem which merchant guilds are sometimes claimed to have solved – obtaining commercial information. Because information is non-rival (one person can use it without diminishing it for others) and non-excludable (once information has been provided to one person it is hard to prevent it from being communicated to others), markets may under-provide it because its costs are hard to recoup. Merchant guilds are supposed to have solved this market failure by gathering information and disseminating it to their members. Chapter 9 finds that merchant guilds played a minor role in collecting information for their members, while restricting its diffusion to non-members. Merchants devised a wide array of mechanisms for collecting and diffusing commercial information, and these gradually improved across the medieval period. Such mechanisms contrasted with merchant guilds, however, in being impersonal, accessible to all and not dependent on the social capital of exclusive networks.

Chapter 10 turns to a final sphere in which merchant guilds are thought to have created economic benefits – reducing economic volatility. Merchant guilds are sometimes claimed to have stabilized pre-modern economies by maintaining prices at a legally fixed and predictable level. Chapter 10 examines the role played by merchant guilds in the price fluctuations that often afflicted pre-modern trade. It shows that where merchant guilds were able to affect prices, or the underlying economic factors determining prices, they probably decreased stability by seeking to restrict participation and erecting trade barriers. Price volatility continued to be a problem throughout the medieval period, the heyday of merchant guilds. Stability only increased after about 1500, beginning in those economies of north-west Europe – the Netherlands, Flanders, England – where the privileges of merchant guilds declined earliest.

Merchant guilds and privileged merchant companies were a central institution of European economies, societies and polities from the end of antiquity to the beginning of industrialization. They are also the prime historical exemplar of social capital adduced by modern social scientists, and are often used to draw broad implications for modern developing economies. Academics and policymakers routinely refer to merchant guilds as the solution to problems of state extortion, security, contract enforcement, principal-agent problems, information and stability, and as important contributors to the development of the European economy. The final chapter of this book draws together the findings of earlier chapters to cast empirical light on these influential claims. It shows that the benefits of merchant guilds have been exaggerated and their costs under-estimated. The Commercial Revolutions of medieval and early modern Europe took place despite the social capital generated by merchant guilds, not because of it. The benefits that merchant guilds are supposed to have generated through their particularized social capital prove illusory on closer examination. Instead, it was the gradual, uneven and imperfect growth of generalized institutions, impartially facilitating transactions for all, that created the basis for economic growth in the centuries leading up to industrialization.[62]

[62] On the dark side of social capital more widely, see Ogilvie (2003); Ogilvie (2004a); Ogilvie (2004b); Ogilvie (2004c); Ogilvie (2005); Dennison and Ogilvie (2007).

2   What was a merchant guild?

What was a merchant guild? A guild – in its most general form – is an association of people who share some common characteristic and pursue some common purpose. The shared characteristic can be anything: religion, nationality, neighbourhood, cultural interests, military service, good works, political convictions. But by far the commonest is occupation.

Medieval and early modern Europe had a few religious guilds (more often called fraternities), but most guilds were formed around shared economic activities.[1] Guilds were *least* prevalent in the primary sector, although guilds of farmers, gardeners, winegrowers, shepherds and fishermen formed in some medieval and early modern European societies.[2] Guilds were *most* prevalent in industrial occupations, with a majority of urban craftsmen and even many rural proto-industrial workers forming guilds.[3] But guilds were also widespread in tertiary production, with service professionals such as barber-surgeons, musicians, artists and chimney sweeps organizing guilds in some European economies.[4]

By far the commonest tertiary-sector guilds were formed by merchants. Narrowly defined, merchants were wholesale traders. They specialized in trading for profit, dealing in goods that they did not produce themselves and selling them to other wholesalers, to retailers or to industrial, commercial, institutional or other business users, but not directly to consumers. Some merchant guilds contested the precise definition of a

---

[1] Maréchal (1953), 13; Vander Linden (1896), 1–11.

[2] For examples of primary-sector occupational guilds, see Götz (1976); Marsh (2006); Ogilvie (1997), 74–5; Schuster (1913); Van den Heuvel (2007), 92, 103–4, 107–10, 133–4; F. M. Weber (1955), 178.

[3] 'Proto-industrial' is the term given to workers in cottage industries who produced for export markets outside the immediate region; they are contrasted with traditional 'craftsmen' who produced mainly for local consumers. On guilds in proto-industries, see Ogilvie (1996a), 30–3; Ogilvie (2007a), 1, 5, 9, 14–15, 38–9, 44.

[4] On guilds in various sectors of the pre-industrial European economy, see Ogilvie (1996a), 30–3; Ogilvie (1996b), 285–90; Ogilvie (1997), 412–37; Ogilvie (2004c); Ogilvie (2007a).

'merchant' in order to justify imposing barriers to entry, for instance by excluding craftsmen and farmers (who produced as well as traded), retailers (shopkeepers, stallholders, hawkers, peddlers), and even other wholesalers (small-scale merchants, brokers, shippers).[5] But other merchant guilds incorporated *all* commercial occupations in a particular territory, including retailers, brokers and even shippers, alongside wholesale 'merchants'. This book concerns itself with all corporative associations formed by merchants (i.e. wholesalers), while paying heed to possible differences between guilds of 'pure' wholesalers and those of 'mixed' traders.

2.1   Local merchant guilds

The basic European merchant guild was a *local* association among the merchants of a particular town or city, which obtained privileges from a local ruler, giving its members exclusive rights to practise certain commercial activities. As we shall see in Chapter 6, long-distance trade that crossed international boundaries was much less important than local and regional trade, and was only practised by a minority of merchants – at least until the nineteenth century. So guilds of *alien* merchants doing business in distant trading centres (discussed in the next section) were less numerous, arose later and almost always established themselves as branches or colonies of their members' local guilds back home. Occasionally, as we shall see, the long-distance merchants of several neighbouring or allied cities trading abroad would form a multi-city association or 'hanse' – the German Hanse being the most famous example. But hanses, too, depended on the local guilds of their member merchants, and membership of the hanse was conditional on home membership in one of those local guilds.

What was the origin, then, of merchant guilds? European merchant guilds saw their heyday in the later Middle Ages – from about 1000 to about 1500. But their roots, though obscured by lack of documentation, reach back into antiquity. We know that ancient Greek city-states had merchant guilds, but there is very little information about what these organizations actually did.[6] We know a little more about the merchant *collegia* of the ancient Roman empire. In the Roman West, everyday records were kept on wax tablets which do not survive, so we rely on

---

[5] On disputes within and between guilds about demarcations between different commercial activities, see Chapters 3 and 4.

[6] Ziebarth (1896); Waltzing (1895–1900); Francotte (1900–1); Stöckle (1894); Flambard (1987); Van Nijf (1997).

formal or pictorial evidence from inscriptions and mosaics, with a few bursts of light from guild graffiti on the walls of buried Pompeii.[7] More is known about ordinary economic life in ancient Roman Egypt, where everyday information was recorded on papyrus. These records show that merchant guilds in Roman Egyptian towns excluded outsiders, arrogated to their members exclusive rights to sell in particular localities, fixed minimum prices for merchandise, set maximum sales quotas and restricted competition[8] – in fact, they did most of the things we shall see medieval and early modern merchant guilds doing in Chapters 3 and 4.

After the fall of the western Roman empire in the fifth century, the quality of record-keeping in Europe declined catastrophically. We have sporadic references to merchant organizations called *collegia*, *schola* and *ministeria* in a number of European cities over the five centuries of the so-called Dark Ages (*c.* 500–*c.* 1000). But we do not know much about what they did. This makes it hard to be sure whether the merchant guilds that come into view after about 1000 – often still called *collegia* – were indeed lineal descendants of the merchant *collegia* of antiquity, or constituted a fundamentally new departure.[9] As later chapters will show, medieval merchant guilds bore at least some resemblance to ancient ones, notably in lobbying rulers for monopolies and offering them favours in return.

Merchant guilds as they are best known – and as we shall discuss them in this book – come into view after about 1000, with the resurgence of princely and municipal record-keeping in Europe. Some historians have gone so far as to date the emergence of merchant guilds to precise centuries – in England to the tenth; in northern France, the Low Countries and northern Germany to the eleventh; in Italy to the twelfth; and in Iberia to the thirteenth.[10] In fact, the timing was probably much messier, and was further confused by the accident of which documents survived where. But like their ancient and Dark Age predecessors, medieval merchant guilds were associations among the traders of a particular locality, which initially obtained privileges from their local rulers, giving them exclusive rights to practise certain types of trade.[11]

Some medieval towns had already existed in antiquity. Here, a local merchant guild is often mentioned in the earliest surviving records,

---

[7] Liebenam (1890), 35–7; Waltzing (1895–1900), I: 12, 169–74; Seland (1996), 114; Meiggs (1960), 311–12; Ausbüttel (1982), 20, 85, 94–6.

[8] Alston (1998), 175; Cotter (1996), 83–4; Van Nijf (1997), 13–14.

[9] For the view that there was such continuity between ancient Roman *collegia* and medieval guilds, see Waltzing (1895–1900); for criticisms, see Racine (1985), 127–8, 143–9.

[10] Dilcher (1984), 72–6; Kohn (2003a), 3; S. Reynolds (1997), ch. 4; Woodward (2005), 631–3.

[11] Bernard (1972), 304; Dilcher (1984), 72–6; Ehrbrecht (1985), 430, 449; Schütt (1980), 79; Racine (1985), 131–2, 134–8.

implying that it may indeed be the lineal descendant of a Roman merchant *collegium* in that town. But many new towns sprang up in central and western Europe during a spate of urban foundations after *c.* 1000. In these, a merchant guild often appears in the earliest records. However, the older theory that these new urban foundations were an entirely new type of town, deliberately established by guilds of long-distance merchants, is no longer accepted.[12] Modern archaeological and documentary analyses suggest, instead, that the new towns were an amalgamation of a feudal nucleus (under a lay or an ecclesiastical overlord) with a merchants' quarter. The people living in the merchants' quarter might sometimes take the initiative in this amalgamation, but typically as an association of men claiming exclusive rights to trade *locally* – in the town and surrounding countryside.[13] After that, the town was dominated by this association of merchants or commercially privileged citizens, who were distinguished from the rest of the local population by their special privileges over *local* trade.[14]

As European trade revived in the eleventh and twelfth centuries, these local merchant guilds became more elaborate. Some towns had just a single 'mixed' merchant guild which claimed exclusive privileges over all wholesaling (whether local, regional or international), retailing, brokerage and sometimes even shipping. But others had multiple local traders' guilds, each with privileges over different activities, wares or destinations. In Florence, for example, by 1218 there were separate guilds of the wool merchants, the silk merchants and the merchants specializing in money changing, and a further guild of the leather merchants had sprung up by 1267.[15] The medieval Flemish town of Oudenaarde had separate guilds of merchants and of shopkeepers.[16] Large medieval German cities often had an over-arching guild of all wholesalers, and then sub-guilds of merchants trading with particular foreign destinations.[17] Thus Cologne in 1246 had the *fraternitas danica* comprising all the merchants trading to the Baltic, by 1324 a separate association of merchants trading to England, and in the fifteenth century the *Fenedierverder* comprising those trading to Venice.[18] Lübeck had an over-arching merchant guild which included both wholesalers and retailers, a separate association of long-distance merchants (from which retailers were excluded), and sub-associations

---

[12] For the clearest statements of the idea that the new medieval towns were deliberately formed by guilds of long-distance traders, see Rörig (1922); Rörig (1928). For criticisms, see Winterfeld (1955); Mayer (1956); Brandt (1956). For a survey of the debate, see Dollinger (1970), 20–1.

[13] Dollinger (1970), 14–15.   [14] *Ibid.*, 14.   [15] Green (2000), 483, 487.

[16] Stabel (1997), 157.   [17] Mauro (1990), 258.   [18] Dollinger (1970), 162.

of long-distance merchants trading to different destinations (who often excluded each other's members).[19]

Guilds' internal differentiation often intensified over time. In places where merchant guilds survived for longest, such as Germany and Scandinavia, demarcations among different traders' guilds proliferated. Thus in 1533 the German town of Lemgo had separate guilds for merchants, shopkeepers and *Höcker* (hucksters); the merchants constantly sought to prevent the shopkeepers and hucksters from encroaching on the activities they claimed as 'theirs'.[20] Seventeenth-century Stockholm had separate guilds of general wholesale merchants, silk merchants, shopkeepers and fishmongers.[21]

The typical pattern, however, was for the earliest surviving documents in a medieval town to refer to a single local merchant guild (or commercially privileged citizenry) with exclusive rights to practise wholesale and retail trade in the town and its hinterland. Only later might this guild establish local sub-associations for particular branches of commerce, or colonies abroad for long-distance trade.

2.2   Alien merchant guilds

Such merchant colonies abroad made up a second type of merchant grouping, which – following the literature – we shall term *alien merchant guilds*. These were much less common than local merchant guilds because, as we shall see, only a minority of merchants ever traded abroad, and not all long-distance traders formed foreign guilds.

Long-distance merchants had always obtained privileges – which could include legal permits to trade, safe-conducts, tax reductions, exclusive monopolies and other special favours – from rulers through whose territories they travelled.[22] Initially, rulers tended to grant such privileges on an ad hoc basis to individual merchants. But as European trade expanded after *c.* 1000, and larger numbers of traders from particular cities became active in alien trading centres, rulers increasingly granted such privileges to entire groups. Early examples were the numerous Latin trading colonies established with commercial privileges, consuls, and hostels or compounds, in Near Eastern trading centres during the Crusades (1095–1291).[23] Nonetheless, as we shall see in later chapters, individual

---

[19] *Ibid.*, 159–62; Lindberg (2004), 8; Lindberg (2009), 612.
[20] Nitzsch (1892), 19.   [21] Müller (1998), 51.
[22] Sprandel (1985), 11–13, 27–8; Racine (1985), 131–2, 134–5; Planitz (1940), 19–20.
[23] J. Day (2002), 808.

traders continued to obtain individual privileges from rulers to the very end of the medieval period. Moreover, even the most important trading centres – such as Bruges or the Champagne fair-towns – contained foreign merchants who did not belong to any merchant colony, although they did belong to their own local merchant guilds back home.[24]

Paucity of documentation in medieval Europe makes it hard to state categorically that a particular institution came into being in a particular year. But the first *local* merchant guilds in Europe after the Dark Ages are thought to have arisen (or re-emerged) in the eleventh century, while the first *alien* merchant guilds followed later. Thus according to Kohn, the first alien merchant colonies were established in the early twelfth century in eastern Mediterranean trading centres such as Acre, Antioch, Alexandria and Constantinople. Slightly later, alien merchant colonies arose in south Italian cities such as Rome, Naples and Palermo. By the end of the thirteenth century, associations of alien merchants were found in almost every major European trading city.[25]

Individual towns confirm the typical chronology – local merchant guild first, foreign colonies later. In Cologne, 'the mother of the German towns', a local merchant guild existed by 1074, after which date the town was governed not by its archbishop but by the *Richerzeche* ('Rich men's guild') whose membership consisted exclusively of great wholesale merchants and property owners. It was only around 1130 that the Cologne merchant guild established its first foreign offshoot, in London.[26] In Pisa, merchants established their local guild with its own consular court in 1075, but did not start forming branches abroad until the following century.[27] In another large group of Italian cities, the earliest records of merchant consuls date from the period 1154–83, and refer to local organizations formed to regulate local trade; only later did these local guilds form branches abroad.[28] Spanish merchants, likewise, first formed local merchant guilds (*consulados*) or regional hanse-like federations (*hermandades, universidades*) in Spain itself, and only later formed organizations in foreign trading centres such as Bruges which 'were not independent entities, but branches'.[29] It was only for cities such as Venice and Genoa, which were distinctive in not having local merchant guilds at all but rather

[24] Schütt (1980), 79; Racine (1985), 134–5; Planitz (1940), 19.

[25] Kohn (2003a), 6–7. This is also the chronology given by Lopez (1987), 347; Nitzsch (1892), 3; Spufford (1988), 137, 146, 252.

[26] Dollinger (1970), 6, 14 (quotation).   [27] Woodward (2005), 631.

[28] Racine (1985), 142, 146, points out that the first merchant consuls are mentioned for Piacenza in 1154, Milan in 1159, Pisa in 1162, Verceil in 1165, Verona in 1178 and Brescia in 1183.

[29] Maréchal (1953), 15.

letting anyone trade who had full town citizenship, that the first recorded merchant guilds are alien ones. So exuberantly did Genoese merchants establish overseas colonies – at Antioch in 1097, at Jerusalem in 1099, at Acre in 1104, at Tripoli in 1109, at Bougie in 1152, at Ceuta in 1160, at Tunis in 1179, at Léon de Castille in 1146 – that one anonymous twelfth-century Genoese poet was moved to write, 'So many are the Genoese, so scattered world wide – that they build other Genoas wherever they reside.'[30]

Alien merchant guilds not only arose later than local ones, but continued to depend on them, as we shall see in Chapters 5 and 6. Rulers abroad only recognized an alien merchant guild by virtue of the fact that it was recognized by its own local authorities. An alien merchant guild depended on political support from its home government, and its negotiating power with a ruler abroad was strongly influenced by the power of the home city. For all these reasons, alien merchant guilds cannot be understood separately from the local merchant guilds that gave rise to them – an analytical point to which we shall return.

2.3   Merchant hanses

A third type of merchant guild was a 'hanse' – a federation of the merchant guilds of a whole group of towns for the purposes of foreign trade, often led by one dominant town.[31] Debate rages over whether a hanse was a guild of merchants, a commercial association of guilds, a political association of independent towns or some different type of institution altogether. 'Hanse' is an ancient German term originally meaning a warrior band. By the twelfth century it was used to refer to 'a tribute paid by merchants, sometimes a group of merchants abroad'. At the beginning of the thirteenth century, the term first appears in its modern form, referring to an association of merchants from different Flemish towns. By 1267 it was being used to refer to an association of merchants from different north German towns trading in England. Soon afterwards, one finds hanse used for small groups of merchants from Hamburg and Lübeck trading in various Dutch towns. But it was not until 1343 that the word 'hanse' was applied to what would ultimately become the most famous

---

[30] Doehaerd (1941), 76, 87–8; Lopez (1987), 347. The original quotation reads: 'E Tanti sun li Zenoexi / E per lo mondo si distexi, / Che und'eli van o stan / Un'atra Zenoa ge fan' (Briys and De ter Beerst (2006), 36–7).

[31] Kohn (2003a), 7–8; Planitz (1940), 20–1; Reyerson (2000), 68; R. De Roover (1965), 111; Stabel (1997), 139; Volckart and Mangels (1999), 441. On a hanse as a 'federation of guilds', see Laurent (1935a), 81.

hanse of all, 'the entire community of north German merchants' or the 'German Hanse'.[32]

The German Hanse is believed to have had its roots in the *universi mercatores imperii Romani Gotlandiam frequentantes* ('Community of Merchants from the Holy Roman Empire Regularly Visiting Gotland'), an association of guilded merchants from Lübeck and several other north German towns first recorded in 1161 at Visby on the island of Gotland.[33] An older scholarship sometimes portrayed the Gotland Community as a purely private association with no formal legal status. We now know otherwise: Henry the Lion, Duke of Saxony, encouraged merchants from newly founded Lübeck and neighbouring towns to form the Gotland Community, and endowed it from the beginning with official privileges.[34] The Gotland Community expanded rapidly over the following years, with support from its member merchants' home towns.[35] Around 1200, merchants from Lübeck and other German towns set up a branch colony in Novgorod.[36] Around 1230 the guilded merchants of Lübeck and Hamburg formally allied for the purpose of overseas trade,[37] and in 1252–3 they were granted privileges in Flanders.[38] In 1267, a hanse of north German merchants was trading in London.[39] By 1298, German merchants in Gotland 'no longer operated as individual traders but were organized under the representation of their towns of origin . . . Merchants were forbidden to operate through private organizations.'[40] By the end of the thirteenth century, the German Hanse was operating – although still not usually under that name – as an association of guilded merchants from various north German, Dutch and Baltic towns. The core group comprised the approximately seventy 'towns of the Hanse', with a varying penumbra of as many as one hundred smaller 'Hanseatic towns' that enjoyed membership at different periods.[41] It was not until 1356 that the first general Hanseatic diet (assembly) was held, initiating the German Hanseatic League, and not until the later fourteenth century that the German Hanse took on its secondary, political meaning of a 'league of cities'.[42] Even then, the German Hanse retained its primary, mercantile meaning of a 'community of merchants' – as shown, among other things, by the fact that citizens of Hanseatic towns were not 'Hanse members' unless they were guilded wholesale merchants in their own home towns.[43]

---

[32] Dollinger (1970), xix–xx (quotation xix).

[33] Angermann (1987), 57; Spruyt (1994), 120–1; Dollinger (1970), 24–6.

[34] Dollinger (1970), 24.   [35] *Ibid.*, 25.   [36] *Ibid.*, xi.   [37] *Ibid.*   [38] *Ibid.*

[39] *Ibid.*, xix–xx.   [40] Spruyt (1994), 122.

[41] Angermann (1987), 57; Bernard (1972), 299; Daenell (1905); Dollinger (1970), ix–x, 87–9; Spruyt (1994), 125.

[42] Dollinger (1970), xii.   [43] See the discussion in Chapter 4 below.

The German Hanse, although the most important, was not the only hanse. Other hanse-like organizations existed at various points in the Middle Ages. One was the 'Flemish Hanse of London', which is thought to have been organized in the twelfth or thirteenth century by the merchant guilds of the towns of coastal Flanders to represent those of their members who traded with England and Scotland.[44] The Flemish Hanse of London was directed (at least in principle) by a council of five towns (Bruges, Ypres, Diksmuide, Aardenburg and Lille), but was dominated by Bruges.[45] It was oriented towards the littoral of maritime Flanders and commerce with the British Isles, and was basically Flemish in composition.[46] Its main purpose was to organize the trade in wool out of England to supply the cloth industries of the Flemish textile cities.[47] The big problem is that it is so sparsely documented that there is massive doubt about whether it existed, when it existed and what it did. It is mentioned in two sets of ordinances in Flanders which may date from any period between 1187 and c. 1300: scholars disagree. It is unclear whether these ordinances refer to a real organization or a proposed one. And there is absolutely no mention of the organization in any English documentary sources, even though it was supposed to organize Flemish trade with England: the king of England dealt with the count of Flanders, individual Flemish towns or individual Flemish merchants trading in England. This suggests that the Flemish Hanse of London was at most a very loose and informal organization – if it existed at all.[48]

Flanders also gave rise to another, somewhat better documented medieval hanse – the 'Hanse of the Seventeen Towns'. This organization was formed in the thirteenth century by the merchant guilds of various Flemish and French textile-producing towns, already twenty-two in number by the time of the earliest surviving list. By contrast with the Flemish Hanse of London, whose ordinances show it being oriented to the maritime west of Flanders, the Hanse of the Seventeen Towns was oriented towards the immediate south – Champagne and the Île-de-France.[49] It was supposed to represent those merchants from its member towns who exported cloth to Mediterranean Europe via the Champagne fairs. The earliest document mentioning the Hanse of the Seventeen Towns dates from 1230 (referring to events of 1213) and the organization flourished for about three-quarters of a century, before declining in the fourteenth century and completely disappearing by the beginning of

[44] Laurent (1935a), 81; Bautier (1970), 55–7; Stabel (1997), 139; Postan (1987), 273, 286; Häpke (1908), 53–8, 128–9; Carolus-Barré (1965), 27.
[45] Stabel (1997), 140; Häpke (1908), 54–6, 128–9; Carolus-Barré (1965), 26.
[46] Laurent (1935a), 87.   [47] *Ibid.*   [48] Lloyd (1977), 23–4.
[49] Laurent (1935a), 87.

the fifteenth.[50] Its leading cities were Ypres, Douai, Arras, Saint-Quentin and Cambrai, which probably constituted its governing council. But the Seventeen Towns is otherwise quite mysterious and formed, at most, a fairly loose merchant organization.[51]

The specific term 'hanse' was restricted to Germany and the Low Countries. But we can see hanse-like organizations in other parts of medieval Europe. They were quite rare among Italian merchants, possibly because of the early development of the north Italian city-states and their long-distance merchants. The major forum where Italian hanse-like associations can be seen is at the Champagne fairs between c. 1278 and c. 1318.[52] Since these six fairs, first documented in the twelfth century, formed an almost continuous cycle throughout the year as they moved from one Champagne town to the next, the merchant associations formed at them must be regarded as permanent associations rather than merely temporary and short-lived ones.[53] By 1278, the merchants of the 'Lombard and Tuscan' towns (Rome, Genoa, Venice, Piacenza, Lucca, Bologna, Pistoia, Asti, Alba, Florence, Siena and Milan) formed a *universitas* at the Champagne fairs, headed by a *capitaneus*.[54] Occasionally the Italian merchants frequenting the Paris and Champagne fairs formed common cause (possibly even a joint organization) with those of Provence, e.g. in 1286 and 1299.[55] The only other Italian hanse was recorded in 1277 when the king of France persuaded Italian merchants to change their seat of operations from non-French Montpellier to French Nîmes by granting them the privilege of forming 'a *universitas* of merchants just like they have at the Champagne fairs'.[56] In general, however, hanse-like associations were rare among Italian merchants.

They were more common among Provençal merchants, possibly because of the smaller size of each urban centre, with only Montpellier playing in the major league. After 1246, the Provençal merchants formed a distinct *universitas* at the Champagne fairs, headed by its own *capitaneus* who was usually from Montpellier.[57] As we have seen, sometimes the

[50] Bernard (1972), 301; Blockmans (2000), 412–13; Carolus-Barré (1965), 26–7; Laurent (1935a), 81, 87–8; Stabel (1997), 139–40; Verlinden (1965), 127, 132; Häpke (1908), 128–9.
[51] Carolus-Barré (1965), 26.   [52] Bourquelot (1865), I: 151, 167–9.
[53] Goldschmidt (1891), 195.
[54] Bourquelot (1865), I: 151–3, 167–9; Bassermann (1911), 4–6; Goldschmidt (1891), 194–5; Verlinden (1965), 128; Bautier (1987), 196–7.
[55] Goldschmidt (1891), 194, 198 with n. 186.
[56] Bourquelot (1865), I: 168–9; Goldschmidt (1891), 195–6 with nn. 175, 177 (quotation 196 n. 177).
[57] Bourquelot (1865), I: 151–3, 167–9; Bassermann (1911), 4–6; Goldschmidt (1891), 194–5; Verlinden (1965), 128.

Provençal merchants acted in combination with the Italian merchants at the Champagne fairs, and may even have formed temporary joint organizations with them in the later thirteenth century.[58] On other occasions, merchants from the dominant Provençal trading city of Montpellier formed joint organizations with Catalan or Aragonese towns, as in 1259 when the leather merchants of Montpellier, Barcelona, Valencia and Lérida were operating collectively at the Champagne fairs.[59] Provençal and Catalan towns also formed hanse-type associations in other trading centres, outside Champagne. Thus in the Lebanese town of Tyre at the end of the twelfth century the four towns of St Gilles, Montpellier, Marseille and Barcelona formed a collective merchant community under the unified headship of half a dozen consuls, with a common jurisdiction.[60] Likewise, Marseille, Montpellier and the other Provençal merchants signed a collective commercial treaty in Cyprus in 1236.[61]

Spanish merchants also formed hanse-like associations. In 1267, the merchants of various towns of Christian Spain (including some that are now part of southern France) formed a collective group at the fair of Lille, and in 1280–2 they appeared collectively in Bruges.[62] In 1346, Castilian, Portuguese and Aragonese merchants – but also, remarkably, German ones – appeared as a collective entity in the Hainaut town of Maubeuge to demand redress of common grievances.[63] In 1494, all the Spanish merchants trading at the fair of Medina del Campo elected a joint commission, consisting of two members from Burgos and two from the other Spanish towns, to check the accounts of the external factors of Spanish merchant houses trading there.[64]

French merchants also appear to have favoured the hanse type of association. In 1262, the allied merchantries of La Rochelle, St Jean d'Angely, Niort and other towns of western France – 'all other merchants of Poitou, Gascony and elsewhere in those parts there who are and will be of their company' – were granted a special legal basis for their trade in Flanders and Hainaut by the countess of Flanders.[65] France also contained smaller-scale 'regional' hanse-type associations, such as the 'community of merchants frequenting the Loire river and the rivers flowing into it', which incorporated the merchants of some twenty-two French towns, existed from at least 1344 and was only formally abolished in 1773.[66]

[58] Goldschmidt (1891), 194, 198 with n. 186.   [59] *Ibid.*, 193 n. 169.
[60] *Ibid.*, 194.   [61] *Ibid.*   [62] Häpke (1908), 148–9.
[63] Goldschmidt (1891), 194 n. 169.   [64] *Ibid.*   [65] Häpke (1908), 140.
[66] Goldschmidt (1891), 218.

Hanse-type associations can even sometimes be found under special circumstances in economies where they were otherwise unusual. Something close to the hanse model appears to have been used by the 'Merchant Adventurers of England', an association of merchants from different English towns who engaged in trade overseas, initially in the Low Countries but subsequently elsewhere in northern Europe.[67] Similarly, although south German trading cities were not part of the German Hanse and did not generally form hanse-like associations, they did trade through a joint organization in Venice, the Fondaco dei Tedeschi, headed by its own merchant consuls, although this may have been as much through Venetian pressure as voluntary choice.[68]

Hanses, like alien merchant guilds, were pre-dated by *local* merchant guilds (or town citizenries with similar exclusive privileges) in their member cities.[69] They tended to be formed when the absolute number of merchants from each individual town travelling to a particular foreign destination was too small to constitute an effective pressure group: 'by acting together overseas, they found they could obtain better privileges'.[70] Like an alien merchant guild, a hanse derived its legitimacy abroad from the recognition of its members as guilded merchants by their home governments.[71] The original Gotland Community, as we have seen, was formed at the instigation of the duke of Saxony; it relied on this prince's recognition of its leader Olderic; it subsequently developed with the support of the municipal governments of the interested towns; and, as Chapter 6 shows, it was seldom able to act independently of its members' towns of origin.[72] Other hanses, too, as we shall see, always depended heavily on the political support of their constituent town governments, and referred back to them for legal decisions, diplomatic support and military protection – another way in which they resembled the individual merchant guilds that constituted them. Consequently, we regard them, as does recent analytical literature, as a type of merchant guild.[73]

---

[67] For a recent discussion placing the Merchant Adventurers in the context of other medieval merchant hanses or 'federations', see Sutton (2002), 27–8, 38.

[68] On the geographical sphere from which its member merchants were drawn, see Heyd (1874), 199–200.

[69] Mauro (1990), 258.   [70] Spruyt (1994), 120–1.

[71] See Daenell (1905), 6, 9, 19. According to Planitz (1940), 19, the term 'hanse' dates only from the beginning of the twelfth century.

[72] Dollinger (1970), 24–5; Spruyt (1994), 122.

[73] For examples of literature treating the German Hanse as a merchant guild for analytical purposes, see, e.g., Dam (2006), 5; Fehr and Harbord (2007), 8, 12, 19; Volckart and Mangels (1999), 437, 441; Grafe and Gelderblom (2010a), 481, 483 n. 10, 484 n. 12, 486 n. 15, 492, 494, 497, 505; Greif, Milgrom and Weingast (1994), 758–62, 773; Greif (2006b), 225; Lindberg (2008), 645–7, 649–50; Lindberg (2009), 605–6.

2.4   Early modern merchant associations

Merchant guilds are often portrayed as institutions specific to the medieval economy. But they did not, in fact, disappear after 1500. In some parts of Europe, some types of merchant guild weakened from the early sixteenth century on. But in many European economies, merchant guilds remained strong long after 1500. And new types of merchant association arose in emerging sectors such as proto-industrial exporting and the intercontinental trade well into the eighteenth century. These associations were given various names, the most common being 'merchant company'.

This has led some scholars to treat the privileged merchant 'companies' of the post-1500 period as the progenitors of modern 'firms'. But merchant firms – such as the famous house of Medici – had already arisen in the medieval period, and continued to develop into the early modern period. The post-1500 privileged companies were quite different. Some of them resembled modern firms in selling shares, paying salaries to employees, holding core capital in common or providing for periodic reorganization so as to survive the death of individual partners; some even had forms of limited liability.[74] But they also shared key features with merchant guilds. In particular, almost all the post-1500 privileged companies obtained legal monopolies over particular branches of trade, and erected barriers to entry. Furthermore, many of the putative economic benefits of merchant guilds are also ascribed to these privileged companies. So this book also discusses the privileged merchant companies where appropriate, while paying due respect to differences between them and traditional merchant guilds.

Local merchant guilds on the medieval pattern gradually began to decline after about 1500, although for a long time this decline was largely restricted to two areas of Europe – the Low Countries (modern Belgium and the Netherlands) and England. In those two economies, the later fifteenth and early sixteenth centuries saw the emergence of a new type of merchant trading, dominated by 'individual entrepreneurs who did not belong to any formal kind of associations'.[75]

Lively debate rages about why this should have happened, and Chapter 5 examines this question closely. One factor emphasized by Dutch and Belgian historians is the sheer density of urban centres in the Low Countries and the intensity of economic and political competition among them, which made it increasingly difficult for the local merchant guild of

---

[74] See the discussion in Harris (2000), 40–5, 142–4; Kuran (2003), 426–8.
[75] Gelderblom and Grafe (2004), 1 (quotation); Grafe and Gelderblom (2010a), 485.

any given city to enforce exclusive privileges. Trade moved to the countryside where no individual city could thoroughly implement its guild regulations because of competition and political objections from the many other cities whose merchants also wanted to trade there. In Antwerp, merchant guilds began to decline around 1500, with 'a shift away from dominance by the merchant guild toward one in which individual merchants could conduct trade without the restrictions often imposed by guilds'.[76] Amsterdam, which rose in the early modern period to be 'the warehouse of the world, the seat of opulence, the rendezvous of riches, and the darling of gods', never had an over-arching local merchant guild and prohibited alien merchant guilds, although it did have some local guilds with special privileges over particular branches of commerce.[77] In most other Dutch and Flemish cities, traditional merchant guilds gradually lost their powers during the sixteenth century. After the foundation of the Dutch Republic in 1581, as we shall see when we look at the early modern privileged companies, the only groups of Dutch merchants that got corporative state charters were those in the colonial and whaling trades. Attempts to form Dutch merchant associations with privileges over the Russian grain trade and the Levant trade failed.[78] In local trade in the Low Countries, while merchant guilds did not break down altogether, many branches of commerce became effectively open to all participants. Local merchant guilds remained formally in existence, and continued to exercise religious, charitable, cultural and social functions, but lost many of their economic powers in the course of the sixteenth century.

England was the other European economy where local merchant guilds gradually lost economic power after *c.* 1500, while still formally staying in existence. Thus in the medieval period Ipswich had a powerful merchant guild, but by the later fifteenth century this had diminished into a social and cultural club: 'judging from the financial account of the Gild for 1478/79, the celebrations on Corpus Christi day – including a large feast – may have been the sole significant function of the Merchant Gild'.[79] The London livery companies (guilds of merchants and craftsmen) also found it increasingly difficult to enforce their economic privileges as the sixteenth century progressed, and by the mid-seventeenth century were

---

[76] Harreld (2004b), 3, 7 (quotation); see also Harreld (2004a), 5–6.

[77] Braudel (1979), III: 153 (quotation); Gelderblom (2005a), 32; De Vries and Van der Woude (1997), 407–8.

[78] Gelderblom (2005a), 38. By 'Levant' is meant the territories (mainly Muslim and Greek) surrounding the eastern Medterranean and the Black Sea; for this definition, see J. Day (2002), 807.

[79] Alsford (2003), 'History of medieval Ipswich', www.trytel.com/~tristan/towns/ipswic13. html, s.v. 'Economy'.

concentrating increasingly on sociability.[80] Claims that the livery companies remained economically significant until the late seventeenth century appear questionable in the light of the evidence. Thus only about half of a sample of 850 merchants active in London in the 1690s took up the 'freedom' of the City (i.e. obtained municipal citizenship, necessary for livery company membership), and only 38 per cent actually joined such companies: 'membership of a livery company was clearly not a prerequisite for prominence within the trading world'. The minority of merchants who did join livery companies did so from motives of sociability and 'informal personal influence'.[81] Some London merchants even paid heavy fines to stay *out* of any livery company, expecting membership to bring little commercial advantage.[82] The London livery companies also played little role in commercial lobbying, accounting for 'less than 6% of the 1,174 petitions submitted to the Commons concerning mercantile matters in the 1690–1714 period'.[83] Membership of local merchant guilds thus gradually became economically unimportant in London and certain other important English trading centres in the course of the sixteenth and seventeenth centuries.

But England and the Low Countries were exceptional. In most other European economies, local merchant guilds retained important powers for much longer, often only breaking down in the late eighteenth or early nineteenth century[84] – as we shall see in later chapters. Traditional merchant guilds continued to dominate local and regional trade, and new merchant 'companies' arose in emerging sectors such as proto-industries.

'Proto-industries' were dense cottage industries, often located in rural areas, producing large volumes of wares destined for markets outside the local region.[85] In most proto-industries outside the Low Countries and England, rulers issued charters to existing merchant guilds or new merchant companies, granting their members exclusive rights to buy up the products of a particular industry and export them internationally. Case studies document merchant guilds or privileged merchant companies in the proto-industrial sectors of Bologna,[86] Florence,[87] Catalonia,[88] France,[89] French Flanders,[90]

---

[80] Kellett (1958).   [81] Gauci (2002), 130, 134.

[82] Example cited in *ibid.*, 131.   [83] *Ibid.*, 138 n. 28.

[84] On the chronology, see also Gelderblom and Grafe (2004), 1; Lindberg (2004), 2; Lindberg (2009), 606.

[85] See Ogilvie (1993); Ogilvie and Cerman (1996).   [86] Poni (1982a), 5, 7–9, 17.

[87] Litchfield (1969), 699, 704, 712–13, 717–18.

[88] Torras (1986), 8–9; Torras (1991), 99–100, 105–6, 108.

[89] Poni (1985), 313; G. Lewis (1993), 61–3, 90, 101; J. K. J. Thomson (1982), 318–22, 341–2, 364–5, 454–5; Johnson (1982); Gullickson (1986), 64; Bottin (1988), 981, 983–4, 987, 990.

[90] Guignet (1979), 28–30; Terrier (1983), 539.

Switzerland,[91] Austria,[92] Saxony,[93] Silesia,[94] the Rhineland[95] and Württemberg.[96] Proto-industries in which trade was not the exclusive domain of a merchant guild or privileged merchant company were the exception rather than the rule in early modern Europe.[97]

Alien merchant guilds and hanses, which needed to get legal recognition from foreign rulers as well as their own home ruler, found it more difficult to survive on the international trading scene after 1500 – at least within Europe itself. In some parts of the European continent, alien merchant guilds survived, particularly in the Iberian peninsula, German-speaking central Europe, Russia, the Balkans and the Ottoman empire.[98] But in the most dynamic European trading economies, particularly the Low Countries and England, foreign merchants gradually shifted towards trading as individuals or forming firms with distinct legal personalities, and membership in alien merchant guilds became less important. Already in the late Middle Ages, as we shall see in Chapter 7, individual merchants had begun to set up multi-branch firms for long-distance trade, though they were still legally obliged to join both the local merchant guild in their home town and that guild's branches abroad. In the sixteenth century most Flemish, Dutch and English towns ceased to require foreign merchants to belong to a corporate body in order to trade there – indeed, many of them, such as Bruges, Antwerp, Amsterdam and London had never made such membership compulsory in any case.[99] In early modern London, overseas merchants had no livery company, alien merchant guilds lost significance after c. 1500, and the only corporative organizations formed by long-distance traders were regulated and chartered companies (discussed below) and 'the fluid associations of the unregulated mercantile sector'.[100] Amsterdam rose to prominence as a centre of long-distance international trade in the sixteenth century, and had no alien merchant guilds at all. Indeed, Amsterdam repeatedly refused demands for special privileges by any alien merchant colony, even large and important ones such as the German Hanse or the English Merchant Adventurers. Although the Portuguese merchants in Amsterdam referred to themselves as a 'natie' (alien merchant 'nation' or guild), they did not enjoy any formal jurisdiction, and their seventeenth-century Amsterdam

[91] Braun (1978), 294–6; Pfister (1992), 210–17.
[92] Cerman (1993), 289; Freudenberger (1966); Freudenberger (1979); Grüll (1974); Hofmann (1920); Ogris (2004).
[93] K. H. Wolff (1979), 38.   [94] Boldorf (1999).   [95] Kisch (1972).
[96] Flik (1990); Troeltsch (1897); Ogilvie (1997).
[97] For a survey, see Ogilvie (1996a), 30–3; Ogilvie (1997), 412–37.
[98] Molnár (2007); K. Weber (2004), 104; Gecsényi (2007), 58; Gelderblom (2005a), 4.
[99] Ibid., 2–3.   [100] Gauci (2002), 128.

ordinances merely regulated religion, marriage and charity, with no reference to economic privileges or rules.[101]

In one branch of the European long-distance trade, however, corporative merchant associations survived and proliferated after *c.* 1500 – the intercontinental trade between European countries and extra-European destinations. Almost every early modern European state granted exclusive privileges over commerce between its own polity and key non-European destinations to privileged merchant associations called regulated or chartered companies. In this, the Low Countries and England were no exception. England saw the formation of the Muscovy (or Russia) Company (1555), the Spanish Company (1577), the Eastland (or North Sea) Company (1579), the Turkey (or Levant) Company (1581), the Morocco Company (1588), the English East India Company (1600), the Providence Island Company (1629), the Hudson's Bay Company (1670) and the Royal African Company (1672).[102] Most of these English merchant companies retained legal privileges well into the eighteenth century, and the Hudson's Bay Company kept its official entitlements into the nineteenth.[103] However, the English government rejected a proposal in 1662 for regulated companies to be formed to govern commerce with Spain, Portugal, France and Italy.[104]

The Dutch state was even less willing than the English one to grant monopoly privileges to merchant companies for Dutch trade within Europe or its near abroad, rejecting a proposal in 1629 for a 'Compagnie van Assurantie' with monopolistic privileges over commerce with North Africa and the Levant, on the grounds that 'commerce exists by virtue of industry, diligence and activity. By means of the "Compagnie van Assurantie" the slack and clumsy would have the same advantage as the bold and active merchants.'[105] Although the Dutch States-General (parliament) did grant monopolies over the Dutch trade with Russia and West Africa, the merchant companies that obtained these legal privileges soon collapsed under the pressure of internal competition among their constituent merchant firms.[106] Much longer-lived were the monopolies the government granted over the Dutch intercontinental trade: to the Verenigde Oost-Indische Compagnie (Dutch East India Company or VOC) (1602), the New Netherland Company (1614) and the Dutch West India Company (1621).[107]

Nearly every European state issued legal privileges to at least one intercontinental 'company'. Thus the Portuguese government granted

---

[101] Gelderblom (2005a), 31–4.   [102] S. R. H. Jones and Ville (1996), 898.
[103] Fender (2004).   [104] Riemersma (1950), 35.   [105] Quoted in *ibid.*, 36.
[106] *Ibid.*, 36.   [107] Gelderblom (2005a), 38.

monopolies to the Guinea Company (1482) and the Portuguese East India Company (1628). The French government granted monopolies to the Company of One Hundred Associates to trade in North America (1613), the Company of American Islands (1635), the French East India Company (1664) and the French West India Company (1664). The Danish government granted monopolies to the Danish East India Company (1616), the Danish Africa Company (1659), the Danish West India Company (1671) and the Danish Asiatic Company (1730). The Swedish government granted monopolies to the Swedish Africa Company (1649–67), the Swedish East India Company (1731), the Swedish Levant Company (1738) and the Swedish West India Company (1738). There was even one German intercontinental merchant company, the Brandenburg African Company which got state privileges over trade with the Gold Coast in 1682.

These early modern merchant companies were not all identical. One crucial distinction was between the 'regulated' companies and the 'chartered' (or 'joint-stock') companies. A regulated company was very similar to a traditional merchant guild: the company's governing body negotiated monopolies and other legal privileges from rulers (usually over trade from the home polity to particular distant destinations) and established warehouse facilities abroad; the company controlled entry through an admission fee; and members then traded independently on their own accounts. A chartered company, by contrast, resembled a modern firm in selling shares and trading collectively. Whereas a regulated company controlled participation in its trading activities the same way a merchant guild did, by requiring would-be participants to apply for admission as individuals (which the company could deny), participation in a chartered company was obtained through a purchase of shares (which was in principle open to anyone).[108] In a regulated company, only members could participate in the profits of trade; in a chartered company, even non-members could participate, simply by purchasing shares in the company. The ability to sell shares gave chartered companies their 'joint-stock' nature, enabling them to raise larger quantities of capital, and causing them to be favoured in the intercontinental trade across vast distances, whereas the regulated companies tended to trade within Europe or, at furthest, the Levant.[109] Members of a merchant guild or regulated company traded individually on their own accounts (although regulated by a set of common rules), whereas a chartered company traded collectively as a single entity with shareholders, managers and salaried employees,

---

[108] Rabb (1964), 662.   [109] Riemersma (1950), 34–5.

in that way resembling a modern (or medieval) firm.[110] But a chartered company retained one key similarity with a merchant guild or a regulated company: it, too, typically got the political authorities to issue it with legal monopolies and other commercial privileges over particular trade goods, routes or destinations.[111]

The 'private' merchant companies – whether regulated or chartered – of the Netherlands and England in turn differed from the 'state' companies of Portugal, France or Denmark. The private type of merchant company was established, constituted and managed by a group of private merchants. The government had no share in the company, so much so that in 1624 the directors of the English East India Company refused to admit King James I as a member, arguing that a monarch could not enter into a fellowship with his subjects.[112] This did not mean that the private type of merchant company had no ties to the state, as shown by the fact that English and Dutch merchant companies made gifts and loans to governments in return for confirming or extending their monopolies, as we shall see in Chapter 5. But this was a lesser degree of state involvement than in many other European privileged companies. In most of the Portuguese and Spanish privileged companies, and to a lesser extent the French and Danish ones as well, the crown itself had a direct financial interest and considerable influence on commercial decisions. All the European intercontinental merchant companies had monopolies over trade between the home country and overseas destinations, but the 'state' companies of Portugal and Spain also enjoyed monopolies over trade in these products within Europe, whereas the 'private' English and Dutch companies generally had to compete with others in the European trade.[113]

The privileged merchant companies of the sixteenth and seventeenth centuries are sometimes portrayed as forerunners of modern joint-stock companies and corporations, as we have mentioned. This is because their internal organization and financing display certain innovations in that direction: paying salaries to employees, holding some capital in common and outliving the death of individual participants. The chartered (joint-stock) type of merchant company also resembled a modern firm in selling shares and trading as a single entity.[114] Some scholars have gone so far as

---

[110] The differences are expounded in A. Smith (1776), Book 5, ch. 1, part 3, section a, para. 6; S. R. H. Jones and Ville (1996), 898; Carlos and Nicholas (1990), 853–4; Riemersma (1950), 33–4; Moodie and Lehr (1981), 267–8.

[111] Riemersma (1950), 33–4.   [112] *Ibid.*, 38.

[113] Rei (2007), 6, 21–6; Riemersma (1950), 33.

[114] Truitt (2006), 3: the English Muscovy Company, founded in 1555, is regarded as 'the first corporation' because it sold shares that could be traded and limited the liability of

to argue that European economic development surpassed that of Islamic societies after the medieval period precisely because Europe developed merchant corporations of this type, permitting business partnerships to reorganize and outlive their individual members, in ways not permitted under Islamic law.[115] However that may be, both regulated and chartered companies in Europe had one important feature that linked them more closely with merchant guilds than with most modern (or medieval) firms: they secured and exploited exclusive trading monopolies from rulers. No citizen of the state could legally participate in that branch of foreign trade except as a member, shareholder, manager or employee of that merchant association. These monopolies enjoyed by chartered and regulated companies are often described as benefiting efficiency in similar ways to traditional merchant guilds. This book therefore considers the privileged merchant companies alongside the merchant guilds which they coexisted with and so closely resembled.

2.5   The decline of merchant guilds

Merchant guilds did slowly break down in Europe between *c.* 1500 and *c.* 1800. But they did so gradually and unevenly. In the main trading cities of the Low Countries and England, as we have seen, local merchant guilds lost economic power in the sixteenth century and new trading cities arose which wholly lacked such organizations. In Scotland, merchant guilds began to weaken in the late seventeenth century. In Switzerland and France, the same process can be traced across the eighteenth century. But in many central and southern European economies, notably in Iberia, Italy, Germany, Austria and Russia, privileged local merchant associations continued to exercise power over retailing, regional trade and proto-industrial exporting into the late eighteenth century or even the early nineteenth. And most European states – including England and the Netherlands – set up privileged merchant companies with monopolies over the colonial and intercontinental trade.

Both in their heyday and during their gradual decline, merchant guilds were sometimes evaded. A typical European merchant guild or privileged company created a whole penumbra of black-market commercial activities which its privileges rendered illegal. The existence of the guild created an incentive for non-members – those who could not gain

---

shareholders to the amount of their investment; this pattern was followed on a much larger scale by the Dutch East India Company, founded in 1602.

[115] The main statement of this argument is in Kuran (2003), esp. 425–8; and Kuran (2004), 71, 73, 77–9. It has been taken up subsequently, e.g., in Greif (2006c), 308.

admission – to trade illegally. It also created incentives for its own members to evade guild regulations for individual profit. Together, such activities made up an 'informal sector' whose participants tried to circumvent the privileges of merchant guilds. Analyses of the informal sectors of modern less-developed economies suggest that their development potential is very different from that of the formal economy with its public scrutiny, public services, open flow of information and legal enforcement of contracts. Thus even when merchant guilds were evaded – even as they gradually declined – they still affected how the economy worked, how it could grow and how its members could improve their own well-being.[116]

Why did merchant guilds decline? Efficiency approaches give a simple answer. An institution disappears when it stops being efficient. So those who argue merchant guilds existed to provide commercial security claim that guilds declined because the growth of the state enabled rulers to provide policing, diplomacy and military intervention to guarantee commercial security – although different scholars regard this as happening at different times.[117] Those who argue that merchant guilds existed to guarantee contract enforcement claim that guilds declined when governments began to provide public enforcement of commercial contracts – although, again, different scholars think this happened in different centuries.[118] Those who argue that merchant guilds existed to solve principal-agent problems claim that guilds decline when alternative mechanisms for detecting and punishing defaulting agents became available – although different variants of this theory evoke differing chronologies.[119] Those who argue that merchant guilds existed to solve imperfections in information markets claim that guilds declined as new technologies emerged for providing commercial information.[120] Those who hold that merchant guilds existed to stabilize prices and business cycles would argue that

[116] On the informal sector, see Batini et al. (2010); Todaro (1989), 270–1; ILO (1989); Ogilvie (2007b), 671–4. For illustrations from the Peruvian informal sector, see De Soto (1989).

[117] For the version of this argument that regards merchant guilds as being replaced by the state in providing security after c. 1500, see Greif, Milgrom and Weingast (1994); North (1991); Pearson (1991). For a version which regards this development as happening in the course of the early modern period, perhaps as late as the end of the eighteenth century, see Gelderblom (2005a), 41, Grafe and Gelderblom (2010a), 478–9.

[118] There are several variants of this argument. Greif (2002a) thinks this happened in the late thirteenth century. Gelderblom (2005a), 5, 41, and Grafe and Gelderblom (2010a), 478–9, portray it as taking place in the early sixteenth century.

[119] Greif (2002a), 197–200, portrays merchant guilds as being replaced by more efficient institutions for solving such problems in the late medieval period or, at latest, by the sixteenth century; Carlos and Nicholas (1990), by contrast, view privileged merchant companies as the efficient solution for agency problems well into the later eighteenth century.

[120] Gelderblom (2005a), 4, 41; Kohn (2003b), 30; Lambert and Stabel (2005), 13.

they declined with urbanization and the emergence of permanent town markets.[121]

This book questions these arguments. Merchant guilds did not disappear with the emergence of new techniques and practices governing commercial security, contract enforcement, principal-agent relations, information provision or price stabilization. Such techniques were already available in many medieval economies well before 1500, and coexisted with merchant guilds. This is not to say that these other commercial techniques worked perfectly. Even in the most 'advanced' centres of medieval and early modern international trade, these techniques were often inadequate to solve all the problems faced by pre-modern merchants, arising from both market failures and state failures. In more 'backward' European economies these techniques arrived even later and functioned even less well. But, as we shall see, these techniques, imperfect though they were, were much more widely used than guild mechanisms to address most commercial problems in long-distance trade. The fact that there were alternative mechanisms for solving commercial problems, mechanisms that coexisted with merchant guilds and were preferred by individual traders, casts doubt on efficiency theories claiming that merchant guilds arose and persisted because they were efficient solutions to such problems.

Efficiency theorists are right in saying that state and market solutions to commercial problems improved after *c.* 1500. But they are wrong in claiming that this accounts for the decline of merchant guilds after that date. On the contrary: merchant guilds continued to exist and proliferate into new sectors long past 1500 in most European economies, including those with strong states and lively markets – at least markets that were lively outside the guilded sectors of the economy. This survival of merchant guilds into the era of the growth of the state and the market poses serious problems for efficiency explanations. Why, then, did merchant guilds exist? A first strand of any explanation must be sought in the complex of commercial privileges they secured from rulers, to which we now turn.

---

[121] Gelderblom and Grafe (2004), 1; Van der Kooy (1970); Klein (1982); although cf. Harreld (2004b), 1–2.

3   Local merchant guilds

> . . . the profit arising [from the Gild Merchant] does not accrue to the advantage of the community of the borough, but only to the advantage of those who are of the said society.
>
> (Twelve jurors of Derby, 1330)[1]

The commonest merchant guild was an association of men – women were normally excluded – who claimed exclusive rights over trade in a particular locality. To secure its claims, a local merchant guild got legal privileges from the political authorities: the town government, ecclesiastical ruler, noble overlord, territorial prince or emperor. Every merchant guild we know about today enjoyed such privileges, usually enshrined in a foundation charter and enhanced by subsequent edicts. No merchant guild could exist without government privileges.[2]

Merchant guild privileges varied in detail. But they typically granted guild members three core entitlements: the exclusive right to practise particular types of trade, the right to decide who could become a guild member and the right to regulate members' commercial activities. Together, these gave the guild the legal right to act as a monopolist – or the guild's members the right to act as a cartel.

Cartels affect two aspects of economic well-being – equity and efficiency. They affect equity – the distribution of income – because they transfer income from outsiders to cartel members. Successful cartels earn unusually high profits by increasing prices above the level that can be charged when suppliers compete. This means that customers pay more and the cartel members get higher profits. Cartels are also often not just monopolists but monopsonists – sole buyers. This means they can pay suppliers, including employees, less than the prices or wages they would earn if there were competition. This transfers income from suppliers and employees to members of the cartel. Cartels also exclude non-members

---

[1] Quoted in Gross (1890), I: 42.
[2] See, e.g., Frölich (1972), 16–17; Kuske (1939), 4–5; Choroškevic (1996), 78–9; Schütt (1985), 266; R. De Roover (1948a), 13.

41

from trading, forcing them to work in less profitable activities. In so far as a merchant guild was able to behave cartellistically in markets for its outputs and inputs, it transferred income from customers, suppliers, employees and potential competitors to its own members.

But cartels also affect efficiency. That is, they do not just transfer income between different groups in society, making cartel members better off and others worse off by an equal amount. They actually reduce the overall gains from economic activity in the whole society, relative to what could be obtained if the cartel did not exist. This is because when the cartel raises prices above marginal cost in order to extort monopoly profits, some quantity of output that customers value more than it would cost to produce is no longer produced and exchanged. The economy as a whole is worse off. In so far as a merchant guild was able to behave cartellistically, it reduced aggregate well-being in that economy.

The cartels enjoyed by merchant guilds have been recognized since they were first granted, beginning with the protests of contemporaries against being excluded from trade, charged extortionate prices or attacked by guilds as interlopers. The importance of guilds' monopoly rights was also reflected in their expensive lobbying campaigns to get and keep their privileges, bitter conflicts among guilds over demarcations between their monopolies, guilds' elaborate systems to detect and punish encroachers, outsiders' willingness to pay for exemptions from guild rules, black-market trade by interlopers, and the influx of new traders and new trade when merchant guilds weakened. The overwhelming majority of evidence-based studies consequently conclude, as we shall see, that merchant guilds acted as monopolists – both in law and in practice.

But some scholars seek to rehabilitate merchant guilds, claiming that they were not monopolists after all – and thus neither inequitable nor inefficient. These scholars advance five main arguments. The first is to deny that merchant guilds even *tried* to obtain commercial monopolies; instead, it is claimed, guilds pursued some other purpose entirely – mutual security, religious observance, political influence, social solidarity.[3] A second is to admit that although a local merchant guild usually did enjoy exclusive trading privileges, this did not actually amount to a monopoly since 'entry into the guild was permitted'.[4] A third approach is to acknowledge that merchant guilds both sought and captured commercial monopolies, but to dispute guilds' ability to enforce them in practice.[5] A fourth line of argument is to claim that, no matter what

---

[3] E.g. Lambert and Stabel (2005).
[4] E.g. Greif, Milgrom and Weingast (1994), 757 with n. 12.
[5] E.g. Jenks (2005), 31–4.

the evidence shows, economic theory demonstrates that merchant guilds *cannot* have been monopolistic because they survived for so long, and inefficiency means that 'all monopolies collapse in the short or the long term'.[6] A fifth argument is to admit that merchant guilds did enjoy monopolies on paper, were able to enforce them in practice and did not permit free entry, but that this was actually efficient since it enabled guilds to engage in collective activities that benefited the wider economy: 'monopoly rights generated a stream of rents that depended on the support of other members and so served as a bond, allowing members to commit themselves to collective action'.[7]

Although some studies advance all five arguments at once,[8] they are mutually incompatible. Either merchant guilds did or did not seek commercial monopolies. Either merchant guilds did or did not limit entry. Either merchant guild monopolies were or were not enforced in practice. Either inefficiency makes all monopolies collapse in time, or the benefits they create for powerful interests can keep even inefficient monopolists in business. Either merchant guilds did enjoy legal monopolies that were enforced in practice, generating significant rents for their members, enabling them to commit themselves to collective action (but also to harm outsiders and reduce efficiency in the economy at large); or merchant guilds did not enjoy legal monopolies that could be enforced in practice, hence did not generate significant rents for their members, and thus did not enable their members to commit themselves to beneficial collective action (but also did not enable them to use their monopolies to harm others and reduce efficiency in the wider economy).

So we need to analyse exactly what commercial privileges merchant guilds got and how they used them in practice. This chapter begins by addressing the first two arguments. Did merchant guilds seek legal monopolies, or not? And were merchant guilds indeed 'open to entry' so that no legal monopoly could have been effective, or did they try to impose barriers to entry?

What would we expect to observe empirically if a merchant guild had sought to exercise a monopoly? The theory of industrial organization predicts that a monopolist will engage in six specific forms of behaviour. First, a monopolist will try to become the only entity to engage in particular economic activities. Second, a monopolist will seek to exclude new entrants. Third, a monopolist will try to increase prices above the

---

[6] As argued for the German Hanse by Jenks (2005), 33 (quotation); Selzer and Ewert (2001), 136.

[7] E.g. Greif, Milgrom and Weingast (1994), 749 (quotation), 758.

[8] E.g., see Greif, Milgrom and Weingast (1994), 749, 757–8.

competitive level. Fourth (and closely related to the third), a monopolist will attempt to restrict trade volumes. Fifth, a monopolist will seek to lower the costs of its own inputs below the competitive level. Sixth, a monopolist will try to increase the costs faced by competitors. All of these activities (especially raising prices above the competitive level and restricting trade volumes) are closely related analytically. But they generate different types of evidence in the historical sources, so we shall examine them separately.

The first section of this chapter finds plentiful examples of merchant guilds seeking the legal right to engage in all six activities which economic theory predicts of monopolists. In itself, this constitutes suggestive *indirect* evidence that merchant guilds did act as monopolists, since otherwise one must devise an explanation for why these guilds so universally sought and obtained entitlements in law which they then refrained from enforcing in practice.

But perhaps merchant guilds were unable to enforce their legal monopolies, or (for some reason) were uninterested in doing so? The second section of the chapter investigates this question. Even in modern economies, it is often hard to get direct evidence of anti-competitive activity, since monopolists conceal their actions to avoid adverse attention from governments and the public. In historical economies, the difficulty is compounded by the lower frequency of written records and their scattered survival. In past economies as in modern ones, monopolists leave much richer evidence of *imposing barriers to entry* than of what exactly they do *behind* such barriers. They also leave much more evidence of their willingness to pay to obtain and defend monopoly privileges than of how they exploit these privileges on a daily basis. But enough evidence survives to demonstrate that many European merchant guilds between *c.* 1000 and *c.* 1800 enforced their monopolies sufficiently to exercise real economic effects.

This leads to a final question. Were the monopoly privileges enjoyed by merchant guilds actually beneficial because they enabled guilds to created efficiencies elsewhere in the economy? Did the economic 'rents' (monopoly profits) generated by guild privileges give guild members incentives to commit themselves to forms of collective action – to invest in social capital – that benefited society at large? This argument is taken up in later chapters.

3.1   Did local merchant guilds seek legal monopolies?

Merchant guilds are sometimes described as 'voluntary associations' or 'private-order institutions' – that is, organizations formed through voluntary, collective action on the part of private agents rather than being based on any formal steps taken by the public authorities. Putnam, for instance, includes guilds among the 'voluntary associations' that, he argues, generated beneficial social capital.[9] Greif describes merchant guilds as 'intentionally created, voluntary, interest-based, and self-governed permanent associations'.[10] 'Voluntary' invites analogies with social clubs, parent–teacher associations, user networks or programmer communities – a type of group that anyone might join (or decide not to join), not an exclusive cartel.[11]

But these analogies are quite misleading. Merchant guilds were neither voluntary associations nor private-order institutions. North recognizes part of the problem when he characterizes merchant guilds as only 'quasi-voluntary', since they were frequently 'endowed, empowered, and sometimes delegated by the state to have coercive force'.[12] The coercive force North has in mind, however, is merely the licence to engage in violence towards rivals. Merchant guilds indeed often engaged in such violence, as we shall see in Chapters 5 and 6. But merchant guilds were non-voluntary in a deeper way – they had the legal right to require membership of anyone who wanted to trade, to exclude applicants for membership, to force non-members out of trade and to compel their own members to do business in particular ways. A merchant guild enjoyed, in short, the coercive entitlements of a legal monopolist.

3.1.1   Exclusive right to trade

A merchant guild's first coercive entitlement was its members' sole right to do particular things. A local merchant guild's members had the exclusive right to practise most types of local trade. Local farmers and craftsmen were allowed to sell what they themselves produced, but not to buy wares for resale. Foreign merchants were allowed to bring in wares from abroad (within limits), but not – as we shall see – to sell them freely. Apart from that, trade in a locality was typically reserved for members of the local merchant guild. Guild members had exclusive rights over

---

[9] Putnam, Leonardi and Nanetti (1993).   [10] Greif (2006c), 308.

[11] The terminology of 'voluntarism' can be found in North (1991), 25, 30, 33, who describes pre-modern merchant associations as 'voluntaristic'; in Benson (2002), 128, who describes merchant guilds as creating an autonomous legal code that was 'voluntarily produced, voluntarily adjudicated, and voluntarily enforced'; and in Nye (2003), 218–19, who compares merchant guilds to communities of software programmers and technology companies 'developing the code and norms of the Internet partly outside the control of formal political institutions'. For further examples, see Black (1984), 149; Harreld (2004a), 40.

[12] North (1991), 25.

particular *types of transaction* (especially intermediation); particular *wares* (usually local staples, but sometimes a whole list of 'merchants' wares'); and particular *routes* and *destinations* (usually those most important for that town).

Local merchant guild charters sometimes just declared that guild members were exclusively entitled to engage in 'merchant trading' or 'merchandising', but left the specific transaction types, wares and destinations to be defined by local custom or by-law.[13] In twelfth-century Ghent, for instance, only a member of the merchant guild was allowed to 'trade as a merchant'.[14] A typical English royal charter read: 'We grant a Gild Merchant with a hanse and other customs belonging to the Gild, so that no one who is not of the Gild may merchandise in the said town, except with the consent of the burgesses.'[15] Merchant guild charters from medieval Italy, Spain and Germany also endowed members with exclusive privileges over 'merchant trading' or 'merchandising'.[16] But in many cases, richer documentary sources provide more detail about the specific activities defined as 'merchandising' and hence reserved for members of the local merchant guild.

3.1.1.1 Types of transaction reserved for merchant guild members
The local merchant guild almost always monopolized intermediation, prohibiting non-local merchants from trading directly with one another or with local customers except during periodic fairs, obliging them instead to trade on commission through local guilded merchants or brokers.[17] The local merchant guild also normally enjoyed rights of compulsory 'staple' or 'transit', requiring foreign merchants to unload their wares in municipal warehouses where local guild members had rights of prior purchase at prices fixed under guild influence.[18]

In most medieval European towns, non-local merchants could trade with local residents only through members of the local merchant guild. To give just a few examples, in 1157 the Danish crown granted privileges establishing the local merchant guild as 'the sole privileged guild'

---

[13] Postan (1973), 189–91; Schütt (1980), 121.   [14] Planitz (1940), 27–8.
[15] Gross (1890), I: 8.
[16] On Italy, see Racine (1985), 142, 148. On Spain, see Grafe (2001), 13. On Germany, see Dilcher (1985), 88–9; Frölich (1972), 26–33, 40, 50–1; Irsigler (1985a), 64.
[17] Bernard (1972), 302; Choroškevic (1996), 84–6; Gelderblom (2005a), 11 with n. 54; Hibbert (1963), 169–74; Irsigler (1985a), 59; Leguay (2000), 121; Postan (1973), 189–91; Reyerson (2000), 59–60; Schultze (1908), 498–502, 506, 523, 526–7; Spufford (2000), 177.
[18] Volckart and Mangels (1999), 444; Reyerson (2000), 58; Bernard (1972), 302; Kuske (1939); Schultze (1908), 500.

in Roskilde, giving its members exclusive rights to intermediate all local trade by non-local merchants.[19] In the fourteenth century the English crown granted the Lynn merchant guild exclusive legal rights over wholesaling and trading with non-local merchants except on official market days.[20] Around 1370, local merchant guilds in southern Transylvania got exclusive rights to intermediate in the trade of all non-local merchants.[21]

The local merchant guild's monopoly usually extended to transactions among different non-local merchants. The 'guest law' of German Hanseatic towns, for instance, required visiting merchants who wanted to trade with one another to pay local guilded merchants to intermediate among them.[22] The Finnish town of Turku permitted non-local merchants to sell goods only to the town's own full burghers, who constituted the local merchant guild.[23] The Russian towns of Pskov (Pleskau) and Novogorod obliged visiting merchants to trade with each other only via local merchant guild members.[24]

Retailing was a second type of transaction typically reserved for the local merchant guild, as in eleventh-century Worms,[25] twelfth-century St Omer,[26] thirteenth-century English towns,[27] fourteenth-century Novogorod,[28] Norway[29] and Upper Austria,[30] and fifteenth-century Transylvania[31] and Germany.[32] Only in towns where retailers formed separate guilds did the local merchant guild not monopolize retailing. In medieval Bruges, for example, retailing 'was completely in the hands of the mercers, the grocers, and the local gilds', excluding both foreign merchants and local non-guild-members.[33] In thirteenth-century London, different branches of retailing were monopolized by different livery companies, with the mercers' company having the most extensive privileges.[34]

Trade with the surrounding countryside was a third type of transaction usually reserved for local merchant guild members. This entitled them to be the sole intermediaries in trade within the town's rural dominions or a particular 'ban' around the town. Local merchant guild privileges over rural trade are recorded throughout medieval Europe – from

[19] Schütt (1980), 108–9.
[20] Alsford (2003), www.trytel.com/~tristan/towns/lynn7.html.
[21] Pakucs (2003) (abstract).
[22] Bulst (2002); Dollinger (1970), 73–4; Federowicz 1979, 221; Jenks (1996); Pearson (1991), 76; Pelus-Kaplan (2007), 132–3.
[23] Kallioinen (1998), para. 32.   [24] Angermann (1974), 80; Angermann (1987), 69.
[25] Seider (2005), 49.   [26] Kemble (1876), II: 533.
[27] N. Fryde (1985), 220, 225; Hibbert (1963), 194–6, 200–1; Postan (1972), 240.
[28] Angermann (1987), 69.   [29] Riis (2005), 37.   [30] Wilflingseder (1969), 298–300.
[31] Pach (2007), 17–18.   [32] Dollinger (1970), 162, 196.
[33] R. De Roover (1948a), 16 (quotation); Häpke (1908), 255–7.   [34] Moore (1985), 92.

eleventh-century Valenciennes with its one-mile 'ban',[35] to thirteenth-century England[36] and Norway,[37] to fourteenth-century Elbląg (Elbing), Gdańsk (Danzig) and Stralsund,[38] to fifteenth-century West Prussian towns.[39] By regulating transactions between town and country, the local merchant guild could extract monopoly profits from a large share of economic activity, since the rural economy produced a majority of output in most European economies until at least 1800.[40]

3.1.1.2 Wares reserved for merchant guild members   Local merchants also enjoyed sole legal rights to trade in certain goods. Which goods these were varied from one town to another: wine in twelfth-century Paris,[41] salt in the thirteenth-century Austrian town of Laufen,[42] millstones and marble in the medieval Norfolk town of Lynn,[43] malt, grain and butter in fourteenth-century Norway,[44] herring in fifteenth-century Göttingen,[45] lead in fifteenth-century York,[46] iron in fifteenth-century Bilbao,[47] Tokay wine and 'Turkish goods' in sixteenth- and seventeenth-century Košice,[48] tar in seventeenth-century Sweden,[49] silk in eighteenth-century Florence.[50] In cities with multiple merchant guilds, each guild monopolized a different set of goods. So in tenth-century Constantinople five different merchant guilds monopolized trade in raw silk, linen, bullion, manufactures imported from the Muslim world and general merchants' wares,[51] while in thirteenth-century Florence three different merchant guilds monopolized trade in woollen textiles, silk and leather.[52]

But most towns had a single local merchant guild with exclusive rights to trade in the major local export wares.[53] So in Alexandria, where spices were the main export, the powerful merchant association of the Karīmi legally monopolized the spice trade from the mid-twelfth to the mid-fifteenth century.[54] In medieval England and Spain, where raw wool was

---

[35] Planitz (1940), 25.   [36] Postan (1972), 240.   [37] Riis (2005), 34–6.
[38] Sarnowsky (2002), 68–9; Dollinger (1970), 73, 195.
[39] Sarnowsky (2002), 69–71.   [40] Crafts (1985), 48–69; Ogilvie (2000a), 94.
[41] Goldschmidt (1891), 217 n. 94.   [42] Störmer (1985), 366.
[43] Alsford (2003), www.trytel.com/~tristan/towns/lynn7.html.   [44] Riis (2005), 36.
[45] Nitzsch (1892), 34–5.   [46] Kermode (1998), 196.   [47] C. R. Phillips (1983), 261.
[48] Demonet and Granasztói (1982), 523; Gecsényi (2007), 61.
[49] Müller (1998), 113.   [50] Litchfield (1969), 699, 704, 712–13, 717–18.
[51] Freshfield (1938), 16–17, 20, 28–9, 44–5; Dagron (2002), 407, 439–41; Laiou (2002), 718; Lopez (1945), 15–20.
[52] Green (2000), 483, 487.   [53] Gross (1890), I: 45.
[54] Ashtor (1983), 53. Whether the Karīmi association was a merchant guild in the European sense is debated, but it shared many of the key economic characteristics of a merchant guild – common warehouses, a central directing body to administer them, a 'chief' (equivalent to the consul of a European merchant guild), formal membership

a major export, local merchant guilds typically claimed a monopoly over trading in it. In 1281, for instance, the Leicester merchant guild had exclusive rights over the wool trade in the surrounding countryside.[55] In the first half of the fourteenth century, the local guilded merchants of various English towns formed the 'English Company of the Staple' which got exclusive rights to export wool from England. The Staplers set up branches in northern European trading centres as an 'alien merchant guild' or hanse (discussed in Chapter 4), a vivid illustration of how local merchant guilds could parlay their exclusive privileges over local export wares into broader monopolies in international trading centres.[56] After the development of merino sheep made Spanish wool exports worth monopolizing in the late medieval period, the local merchant guild of Burgos claimed a legal monopoly over the Spanish wool trade – and also set up branches abroad in key trading centres such as Bruges.[57]

The single largest branch of manufacturing in pre-industrial Europe was textiles, and wherever textiles were important, local merchant guilds typically obtained legal monopolies over their export. Thus the local merchant guild monopolized wholesale trade in all finished and dyed cloths in most twelfth-century English towns;[58] high-quality woollen broadcloth in twelfth-century Magdeburg;[59] woollen broadcloth in thirteenth-century Goslar[60] and Stendal;[61] woollen cloth in the fourteenth-century Austrian town of Enns;[62] wool and silk textiles in fifteenth-century Göttingen;[63] and all sorts of textiles in most medieval Flemish towns.[64] In the late medieval period, the Merchant Adventurers enjoyed the monopoly right to export English cloth to the European continent.[65]

In some parts of Europe, traditional local merchant guilds with their roots in the medieval period continued to enjoy legal monopolies over the textile trade well into the early modern period. In the north German town of Menden, for instance, the local merchant guild obtained a new charter in 1667 providing 'that no foreigners can trade or peddle white or dyed woollen cloths in the district'.[66] In eighteenth-century Florence, the silk

(a merchant could be described as 'belonging' to the Karīmi, implying that there were others who did not belong), entry restrictions (e.g. on grounds of religion), endogamy and lobbying as a group for commercial privileges that accrued only to its own members. See the thoughtful consideration of this question in Abulafia (1987b), 439–41.

[55] Bateson (1899), 205–7; Lloyd (1977), 303.
[56] Postan (1987), 292; Lloyd (1977), 193–224.
[57] Grafe (2001), 13–14; C. R. Phillips (1983), 261; R. S. Smith (1940), 68–9.
[58] N. Fryde (1985), 220, 225; Hibbert (1963), 194–6, 200–1.
[59] Dilcher (1984), 71; Dilcher (1985), 88–9; Höhlbaum (1876), 19, document no. 32 dated 1183.
[60] Dilcher (1984), 71; Dilcher (1985), 88–9.   [61] Schulze (1985), 379–81.
[62] Wilflingseder (1969), 299.   [63] Nitzsch (1892), 34.   [64] Stabel (1997), 162.
[65] De Vries and Van der Woude (1997), 355.   [66] Quoted in Nitzsch (1892), 44.

merchants' guild still enjoyed a far-reaching monopoly over exporting Florentine silks.[67]

In other parts of early modern Europe, merchants formed new, guild-like companies to monopolize the new textile 'proto-industries' springing up in the countryside. From the sixteenth through to the late eighteenth century, such associations legally monopolized exports from many proto-industrial textile regions – the Wuppertaler Garnnahrung south of the Ruhr,[68] the Calwer Zeughandlungskompagnie in the Württemberg Black Forest,[69] the Uracher Leinwandhandlungskompagnie on the Swabian Jura,[70] the Schwechater Kompagnie in Lower Austria,[71] the Linzer Wollzeugfabrik in Upper Austria.[72] Indeed, the vast majority of continental European textile proto-industries saw their exports legally monopolized by a merchant guild or 'company'.[73] Even when a merchant guild or privileged company monopolized trade only in a single good, it could control a significant share of trade when that was the most important export ware for the local economy. As a result, its foreign branches could exercise monopoly or oligopoly power over supplies of that good abroad – as we shall see in Chapter 4.

3.1.1.3 Routes and destinations reserved for merchant guild members

The local merchant guild also often had a legal monopoly over exporting goods from the town along particular routes or to particular destinations. Again, this typically included the routes and destinations most important for that town's trade. Around 1100, for instance, the merchant guild of St Omer had a legal monopoly over the long-distance trade from that town to France south of the Somme and to England.[74] In the 1150s, the merchant guild of Rouen enjoyed the exclusive right to trade by ship along the lower Seine.[75] A charter of 1190 gave the Paris guild of the *Marchands de l'Eau* a monopoly over trade on the upper Seine, a monopoly that decayed in the fifteenth century but was only formally abolished in 1672.[76] Until 1202, Byzantine rulers granted local Greek merchant guilds a monopoly over all trade beyond Constantinople to the Black Sea, and even thereafter only relaxed it slightly for favoured guilds of foreign merchants.[77] After c. 1300, all trade in Norway north of Bergen was monopolized by local merchant guilds (or town citizenries

---

[67] Litchfield (1969), 699, 704, 712–13, 717–18.   [68] Kisch (1972), 308.
[69] Ogilvie (1997); Troeltsch (1897).   [70] Karr (1930); Medick (1996).
[71] Cerman (1993), 289.   [72] Gutkas (1983), 93.   [73] Ogilvie (1996a), 30–3.
[74] Irsigler (1985a), 57–8; Planitz (1940), 21; Dilcher (1984), 70.
[75] Planitz (1940), 27.   [76] Goldschmidt (1891), 217 n 94.
[77] Lopez (1987), 349, 351.

with similar exclusive privileges).[78] For much of the fifteenth century, the York merchant guild insisted on staple rights over the rural trade in lead, including with settlements over 30 km distant.[79] From the sixteenth to the eighteenth century, the local merchant guilds of Lübeck, Gdańsk (Danzig), Riga, Königsberg and Stockholm legally monopolized all trade between their towns and the Northern Netherlands.[80]

Local merchant guilds thus satisfy the first prediction the theory of industrial organization makes for monopolists – they sought rights for their members to be sole practitioners of particular activities. They got legal monopolies over certain transactions, wares, routes and destinations – typically, those most important for their town. The universality of such exclusive rights in different European societies and time periods suggests that they were a defining feature of the merchant guild as an institution.

3.1.2   Restricting entry

A second characteristic of a monopolist is that it tries to restrict entry. As we have seen, some scholars claim that exclusive trading rights did not amount to a monopoly since 'entry into the guild was permitted'.[81] This claim is not supported with further detail. But it is straightforward to test it. A market is competitive if there is free entry into it. The test is thus not whether there was *some* entry, but whether entry was completely free. So one need only ask whether merchant guilds permitted free entry to anyone who wanted to become a member. The simple answer is no. Every recorded merchant guild enjoyed the legal right to decide who could and could not become a member – to impose what economists term 'barriers to entry' and social capital theorists term 'closure'.

3.1.2.1 Local citizenship   The most liberal merchant guilds, as far as membership was concerned, were those open to everyone with full town citizenship privileges. Some (though not all) of the new towns that arose in Europe after *c.* 1000 initially endowed all their citizens with full merchant trading rights. Although most gradually restricted them after *c.* 1150, a few exceptional cities retained this relatively open arrangement into the later medieval period.

---

[78] Helle (2005), 24–7; Wubs-Mrozewicz (2005), 208–9, 218–19; Blom (1984), 19.
[79] Kermode (1998), 196.
[80] Lindberg (2004), 2; Lindberg (2009), 612, 616–18, 620–1, 626.
[81] Greif, Milgrom and Weingast (1994), 757 with n. 12.

Venice, for instance, permitted any man with full Venetian citizenship privileges to trade as a merchant. Consequently it was sometimes remarked that Venetian merchants did not need a local merchant guild 'because they all lived in one guild'.[82] Genoa, too, differed from most other medieval cities in not having a local merchant guild before the fourteenth century: Genoese law let anyone set up almost any kind of commercial activity in Genoa – hence the famous saying *civis ianuensis, ergo mercator* ('a Genoese citizen, therefore a merchant').[83] This comparative openness of Venice and Genoa may have been one source of their striking commercial dynamism – indeed, their dominance of Mediterranean commerce – during the medieval Commercial Revolution.

But in England, too, which only became a major trading nation towards the end of the medieval period, a number of towns permitted any man with the legal status of citizen (also called 'peer', 'burgher' or 'freeman') to trade as a merchant.[84] In thirteenth-century London, for instance, the wholesale trade in most commodities, including important ones such as raw wool, were open to members of all the crafts – to anyone holding the 'freedom' or citizenship of the city.[85] The 1308 custumal for Norwich, too, permitted any resident to engage in commerce if he had been admitted as a 'peer' of the town.[86]

It might seem that at least in towns like Venice, Genoa or London, the local merchant guild did not have a monopoly since every citizen was a member. But this is to project modern notions of citizenship onto the past. In medieval and early modern Europe, citizenship was local and limited.[87] It was local in that it was community-based rather than state-based. And it was limited in that not every community inhabitant was a citizen, and not every applicant was admitted.[88] Full citizenship was an exclusive set of privileges held only by a subset of community residents; in practice, it was often dominated by merchant families.[89] Citizenship

---

[82] Mauro (1990), 259.

[83] Lopez (1958), 505, 512; Briys and De ter Beerst (2006), 70; Jehel (1978), 246; Tai (1996), 41 with n. 89.

[84] Irsigler (1985a), 56; Kedar (1976), 58; N. Fryde (1985), 220–1; Mauro (1990), 259.

[85] Lloyd (1977), 55, 303.

[86] On this, see Liber Consuetudinum (Book of Customs), Norwich, 1308, Cap. 36, abstracted by Alsford (2003), www.trytel.com/~tristan/towns/norlaws.html, s.v. Cap. 36 'Entrances to the franchise'.

[87] On the medieval (and early modern) concept of citizenship as involving membership in the community rather than the nation, and the implications for privileged access to permission to engage in economic activity, see R. De Roover (1948a), 172–3.

[88] Riesenberg (1992); on Flanders, see Lefebvre (1997); on the Netherlands, see Van Zanden and Prak (2006); on Perpignan, see Daileader (2000).

[89] Schütt (1980), 131; Dilcher (1985), 88–9, 110; Schultze (1908), 475, 490–3; Schulz (1985), 316; S. R. Epstein (2000), 35; Van Zanden and Prak (2006), esp. 115–17; Wubs-Mrozewicz (2004), 56.

was obtained either through inheritance (usually in the male line) or by application, which involved satisfying conditions such as property ownership, occupation, residency, religion, ethnicity, payment of admission fees, sitting out a waiting period and acceptability to the existing citizenry. According to one estimate, consequently, fewer than half the inhabitants of a typical medieval European town held citizenship, although the percentage varied geographically and chronologically.[90] In many cases the share was much lower. In medieval and early modern Dutch and Flemish towns, for instance, between a quarter and a half of inhabitants had formal citizenship rights.[91] In sixteenth-century Venice, 3.5 to 5 per cent of inhabitants were patricians (with the full range of civic privileges), another 5 to 10 per cent held ordinary citizenship (with a restricted set of privileges), and the remainder were non-citizens and hence could not trade as merchants.[92] In medieval Italy, even the republican city-states did not grant citizenship to more than 2 to 3 per cent of their inhabitants, and social mobility into the ranks of the citizenry was low.[93]

Town citizenship was exclusive almost everywhere in medieval Europe. Most of the great Italian trading cities rationed it carefully. The dynamic trading city of Genoa was unusual in being exceptionally open to outside applicants.[94] Indeed, a fourteenth-century Venetian senator characterized Genoa's open citizenship policy as being one of the most important instruments of its commercial and political power.[95] Even in 1404, when Genoa imposed a residency condition for citizenship, it only required the applicant to have lived in Genoa for at least three years; the requirement was soon abolished and the previous liberal citizenship rules restored.[96]

Venice, by contrast, excluded not just foreigners but an increasing majority of local inhabitants, and 'identifying who was really Venetian became a preoccupation of public policy'.[97] In 1315, the city established a new authority, the *provveditori di comun*, which required every merchant to prove his Venetian citizenship and forbade him to trade if he could not do so.[98] The city defined three types of citizenship, explicitly differentiated according to trading privileges. *Cittadini originari* could trade freely at home and abroad with all the privileges accorded to Venetians, but had to prove that their fathers and grandfathers had been citizens. Those with

---

[90] Talarico (2007), www.the-orb.net/textbooks/westciv/medievalsoc.html, s.v. 'Citizenship'.
[91] Van Zanden and Prak (2006), 122, 140.   [92] Dursteler (2006), 48.
[93] Spruyt (1994), 144.
[94] Lopez (1958), 505, 512; Briys and De ter Beerst (2006), 70; Jehel (1978), 246; Tai (1996), 41 with n. 89.
[95] Lopez (1958), 513.
[96] Briys and De ter Beerst (2006), 23 n. 58; Lopez (1958), 512–13.
[97] Mueller (1997), 256.   [98] Rösch (2000), 82–3.

de intus et de extra status could trade between Venice and foreign locations and enjoy the privileges of Venetian merchants, but had to prove they had resided and paid taxes in the city for twenty-five years. Those with *de intus* status could only trade within the city, and even then had to prove they had resided and paid taxes in the city for at least fifteen years. Those without citizenship could not trade legally at all.[99] The majority of inhabitants of Venice itself, let alone its wider Mediterranean empire, were Venetian 'subjects', not 'citizens', and thus could not legally trade as merchants at home or as members of any Venetian merchant guild abroad unless they obtained a special permit.[100]

Other Italian towns were hardly less severe: 'Migration was discouraged by tough citizenship requirements. New arrivals only obtained citizenship rights after many years of residence, and they had to meet certain requirements, such as owning property in the city.'[101] Pisa, for example, imposed a residency requirement of thirty years before an outsider could obtain citizenship.[102]

Spanish towns were also very exclusive in granting citizenship or even residence rights. In 1269, for instance, Barcelona banned foreigners from settling, let alone obtaining citizenship in the city.[103] In the sixteenth century, Seville restricted naturalization, and thus permission to trade as a long-distance merchant, to men who were subjects of the Holy Roman empire or one of its allies, or those who could prove twenty years' residence in Castile and fulfil a property requirement.[104]

The same was true in the towns of German-speaking central Europe, where it was difficult to become a citizen unless one had been born there as the son of an existing citizen.[105] Owning property was another common precondition in German towns, which excluded entire social strata from citizenship and thus from the right to trade as merchants.[106] Most of the new towns established during the German eastward colonization of the lands between the Elbe and the Oder rivers from the twelfth century onwards reserved citizenship for ethnic Germans, excluding indigenous Slavic or Finnic inhabitants.[107] Medieval Bohemian towns set high minimum property-requirements for citizenship, and were often dominated by a German-speaking oligarchy, so much so that shortly after 1350 Emperor Charles IV ordered that half the councillors in the central

[99] Schmitter (2004), 910; Dursteler (2006), 48–50; Fusaro (2002), 8 n. 28; Rösch (2000), 83; Lopez (1958), 512–13.
[100] Dursteler (2006), 16, 23–4, 27, 43–4, 52, 78.   [101] Spruyt (1994), 144.
[102] Waley (1969), 106.   [103] Congdon (2003), 214.   [104] Mauro (1990), 281–2.
[105] Spruyt (1994), 126.   [106] Schultze (1908), 490.
[107] Dollinger (1970), 31. Thus the charter granted in 1257 to the German colonists founding Cracow denied citizenship to Poles until 1316; see *ibid.*, 31, 127.

Bohemian town of Beroun were to be Czechs.[108] After 1350, the German Hanse restricted enjoyment of its privileges to citizens of Hanse towns. In 1417, it sought to prevent non-Hanseatics from gaining such citizenship by banning the acquisition of nominal citizenship in a Hanse town or possession of citizenship in two towns at once. In 1434, it restricted Hanse privileges to those who were *born* with citizenship in a Hanse town.[109] Even applicants who satisfied all other requirements often had to undergo a 'waiting period' of between ten and twenty-five years before qualifying for admission.[110]

In many central European towns, restrictions on citizenship lasted long after 1500. In the sixteenth century, Gdańsk (Danzig) permitted merchant trading to all its 'burghers', but then excluded any foreigners – 'Nurembergers, Lombardians, English, Dutch, Flemish, Jews, or any other nationality' – from living or trading in the town (let alone obtaining burgher rights) without the agreement of the existing burghers.[111] From the sixteenth to the early nineteenth century, even the smallest towns in Württemberg rigorously rationed citizenship, and thus merchant guild membership, according to birth, marriage, occupation, wealth, religion, ethnicity, legitimate birth, serf status, gender, and 'reputation'.[112] Until the early nineteenth century, German Hanse cities such as Lübeck absolutely excluded Jews and Calvinists from dwelling inside the city, let alone obtaining citizenship;[113] even Lutheran immigrants were denied citizenship – and thus Hanse membership – if they practised 'mechanical' trades.[114]

Medieval French towns also restricted citizenship to a subset of residents. The conditions varied from one town to the next, but often included residential requirements, ranging from a liberal one year plus one day to a more stringent ten years. Other conditions included high entrance fees, marriage into a citizen family, minimum property ownership or a minimum annual period of residence. In the mid-thirteenth century the French crown devised a lucrative source of revenues in selling 'letters of bourgeoisie' which declared the recipient to hold rights of citizenship in a particular royal town, even when he did not actually reside there, at a stroke endowing him with rights to trade as a merchant of that town. In the early fourteenth century, foreign (especially Italian) merchants were required to purchase 'letters of bourgeoisie' in French

[108] Heymann (1955), 333 with n. 35.   [109] Dollinger (1970), 200.
[110] Weinryb (1950), 5 with n. 21.   [111] Lindberg (2004), 12.
[112] Ogilvie (1997), 42–57.
[113] Kellenbenz (1958), 77; Grassmann (1988), 509–10; Guttkuhn (1999), 11–25.
[114] Asch (1961), 13–20.

royal towns for a sum equal to 5 per cent of their wealth, if they wanted to go on trading in France.[115]

English towns were relatively open by European standards, yet even there citizenship could be hard to obtain. In Norwich, a 1308 custumal restricted citizenship to those who were born or apprenticed locally, were able to pay high admission fees, could prove their freedom from serfdom, fulfilled property requirements and obtained character references from existing citizens.[116] The 1309 customs of Ipswich ordained that 'no foreign merchant may be accorded the status of a burgess of the town unless he has inherited a tenement there'.[117] A Yarmouth by-law of 1491 required new burgesses either to be sons of existing ones or to pay a fee of twenty shillings, adding that 'those who have the means are to be asked to pay more'.[118] Because English town citizenship often brought full merchandising rights, getting it became extremely important, and a number of Flemish, Italian and German merchants were willing to pay high entrance fees and satisfy other preconditions in order to obtain it.[119] John Lylling, a York mercer, valued his 'freedom' (i.e. York citizenship) so highly that he was willing to pay 540 marks in 1428 to be readmitted after being expelled for adulterating wares.[120]

In the Low Countries, citizenship privileges varied both chronologically and regionally, but also tended to be liberal by European standards. Thus, for instance, foreign merchants managed by deception to sneak themselves in as citizens in medieval Damme, near Bruges, so as to enjoy merchandising privileges there, as shown by the fact that an Italian and four French merchants were discovered and ejected from the registers in 1427.[121] By the early modern period, the commercially dynamic western cities of the Low Countries had developed relatively liberal citizenship regulations, while towns in the Dutch interior tenaciously excluded non-Calvinists from citizenship 'and thus from the guilds'.[122]

In most medieval European towns and many early modern ones, such entry restrictions created significant groups of inhabitants – immigrants, peasants, labourers, women, Jews, servants, serfs, slaves – who were

---

[115] Henneman (1995).

[116] Liber Consuetudinum (Book of Customs), Norwich, 1308, Cap. 36, abstracted by Alsford (2003), www.trytel.com/~tristan/towns/norlaws.html, s.v. Cap. 36 'Entrances to the franchise'.

[117] Calendar of usages and customs of Ipswich, 1309, abstracted by Alsford (2003), www.trytel.com/~tristan/towns/ipswich5.html, s.v. Cap. 63 'no foreign merchant to be a burgess'.

[118] Alsford (2003), www.trytel.com/~tristan/towns/yarmlaws.html, s.v. 'Admission fee for new burgesses' (August 1491) and 'Admission by patrimony' (August 1491).

[119] Dollinger (1970), 56; Lloyd (1977), 30, 41, 46, 49, 55.   [120] Kermode (1998), 195.

[121] Häpke (1908), 227.   [122] Van Zanden and Prak (2006), 123.

excluded from citizenship and hence merchant guild membership.[123] Even in the minority of European towns where the local merchant guild was open to all citizens, therefore, barriers to attaining citizenship meant that only a subset of inhabitants could legally trade as merchants.

But in most European towns the local merchant guild was not even open to all citizens. Most merchant guilds enforced far stricter entry barriers, imposing conditions relating to group affiliation, economic characteristics, personal attributes and acceptability to existing members.[124] This meant that only a minority even of local *citizens* were legally permitted to trade as merchants.

3.1.2.2 Group affiliation One way merchant guilds limited entry was by excluding certain groups: foreigners, members of certain ethnicities, adherents of certain religious confessions or those stained with the hereditary status of serfdom.

'Foreigners' – meaning non-locals – were excluded by most local merchant guilds, unless they managed to buy themselves into community citizenship. In the early phases of commercial growth in Europe after *c.* 1000, some merchant guilds initially defined their membership loosely enough to admit some non-locals who did business in the town. But gradually most local merchant guilds excluded any outsider unless he made a special case and paid for a special permit.[125] In the medieval and early modern Netherlands, those who did not hold local citizenship – including locals who were mere *ingezetenen* (inhabitants) – were barred from the guilds; only those who bought local citizenship rights could then apply for guild membership.[126] Medieval English merchant guilds offered membership to non-citizens only 'on payment of a hefty entrance fee'. Since many 'foreign' applicants came from market centres in the surrounding countryside, this excluded (or increased costs for) many traders whose geographical proximity offered them greatest benefit from trading in that town.[127] In many European towns, merchant guilds excluded non-locals totally – as in eleventh-century Valenciennes[128] or fourteenth-century Barcelona, Mallorca and Perpignan.[129] In fifteenth-century German Hanseatic towns, certain nationalities (especially the English and Dutch) were excluded even if they fulfilled all other preconditions, including obtaining town citizenship.[130] Even within a hanse, the constituent local merchant

---

[123] Leguay (2000), 110–11, 121–2; Schütt (1980), 131; Dilcher (1985), 88–9; S. R. Epstein (2000), 35–6.
[124] Kohn (2003a), 3.   [125] Kohn (2003a), 3.   [126] Van Zanden and Prak (2006), 124.
[127] Basile et al. (1998), 40–1 (quotation); Gross (1890), I: 54, 66–8.
[128] Planitz (1940), 25.   [129] R. S. Smith (1940), 38.   [130] Dollinger (1970), 200.

guilds excluded each other's members as 'foreigners', as in the case of the German Hanse, where

> Each town remained mistress of her own commercial organisation and was only interested in furthering the interests of her own merchants. It was not uncommon for a town to offer special advantages to the merchants of a neighbouring one, but there was no question of extending these favours to all Hanseatics... Discrimination of this kind increased with the passage of time. In the fifteenth century the staple regulations were continually being tightened up in every town, and were often used as much against merchants from other Hanseatic towns as against non-Hanseatics.[131]

Merchant guilds also excluded entrants according to other group affiliations. In the towns of the Teutonic Order from 1309 onwards, local merchant guilds were entitled to exclude all Slavs – even locals.[132] In Riga after 1354, all non-Germans – whether local or foreign – were excluded from the 'great guild' of the merchants, and after 1376 German merchants were forbidden to trade with *Undeutschen* (non-Germans).[133] The Polish city of Poznań excluded Jewish, German, Scottish, Italian, Greek, Dutch, Swiss and other non-Polish traders from the merchant guild, and constantly threatened to eject them from the city altogether.[134] Medieval Catalonian merchant guilds restricted entry to candidates who were Christian by birth, thereby excluding local Jewish and Muslim converts.[135] The merchant guilds of medieval north German towns refused admission to anyone who could not demonstrate that he was free of the 'stain' of serfdom or hereditary servility.[136] Every merchant guild in Europe absolutely excluded Jews – even ones born and brought up in the town.[137]

3.1.2.3 Economic characteristics   Merchant guilds also excluded entrants according to economic attributes. Occupational demarcations played a major role. In tenth-century Constantinople, for instance, a merchant trading in one product was not allowed to become a member

---

[131] *Ibid.*, 191. Gdańsk (Danzig), for instance, 'ended by excluding even the other Hanseatics from its local trade' (Postan (1987), 271).

[132] Dollinger (1970), 132; Postan (1973), 198.

[133] Misāns (2008), 470–2; Dollinger (1970), 132.   [134] Weinryb (1945), 99–100.

[135] R. S. Smith (1940), 38.   [136] Nitzsch (1892), 72.

[137] Abulafia (1987b), 418; Lopez (1945), 24; Weinryb (1945), 97–9. An exception was where Jewish communities were permitted to set up their own merchant guilds, as in the Lithuanian city of Włodawa (a guild of Jewish shopkeepers) or the Polish cities of Cracow, Przemyśl, Brody, Lwów and Bolechów (guilds of merchants); on this, see Rabinowitz (1938a), esp. 182–4; Rabinowitz (1938b), esp. 217–18; Weinryb (1950), 102 with n. 23.

of any of the other three merchant guilds.[138] Guilds of wholesalers often sedulously excluded retailers, as in the Flemish city of Middelburg whose 1271 merchant guild statutes drew a sharp distinction between 'merchants' (who were eligible to join the guild) and 'Höker' or retailers (who were not).[139] Medieval Catalonian merchant guilds required applicants to prove that they were 'active merchants'.[140] Sometimes a merchant guild would specify a particular occupation whose members were excluded, usually because they had recently been seeking to trade in competition with guilded merchants – thus the Skanör merchant guild in thirteenth-century Sweden excluded bakers,[141] while the Stendal guild in fourteenth-century Germany excluded clergymen.[142]

Most merchant guilds imposed a blanket ban on any craftsman, as in tenth-century Constantinople,[143] eleventh-century Valenciennes,[144] twelfth-century English towns,[145] thirteenth-century Middelburg,[146] fourteenth-century Stendal[147] or fifteenth-century Lemgo.[148] This nearly universal exclusion suggests that craftsmen would otherwise have wanted to trade wholesale – and thus that by excluding craftsmen, merchant guilds were preventing profitable activity. The size of the impact was considerable, since craftsmen made up a large share of inhabitants even in highly commercial cities. To give just one example, craftsmen comprised 62 per cent of inhabitants in the Hanse city of Hamburg in 1379, but were excluded from the merchant guild because of their occupations alone.[149]

Merchant guilds also imposed barriers of wealth and property. Some explicitly imposed property qualifications, as in eleventh-century Valenciennes,[150] thirteenth-century Barcelona and Valencia,[151] fourteenth-century Perpignan[152] or fifteenth-century San Feliú de Guixols.[153] Even the 'new consulados' established in the later eighteenth century in peripheral Spanish American trading centres, which were supposed to be more open than the 'old consulados' of Mexico City and Lima, limited membership to merchants and planters who were 'property-owners of sufficient status'.[154]

Entrance fees added an indirect wealth requirement. Merchant guilds charged admission fees in most documented cases – as in

---

[138] Racine (1985), 139; Freshfield (1938), 16, 19, 21–3, 28; Lopez (1945), 15–20; Dagron (2002), 413, 440.
[139] Häpke (1908), 43.   [140] R. S. Smith (1940), 38.   [141] Nitzsch (1892), 9.
[142] Schulze (1985), 379–81.   [143] Dagron (2002), 413.   [144] Planitz (1940), 25.
[145] N. Fryde (1985), 220, 225; Hibbert (1963), 194–6, 200–1.
[146] Häpke (1908), 43.   [147] Nitzsch (1892), 13; Schulze (1985), 379–81.
[148] Nitzsch (1892), 19.   [149] Dollinger (1970), 137.   [150] Planitz (1940), 25.
[151] Woodward (2005), 631, 633.   [152] *Ibid.*, 633.   [153] *Ibid.*
[154] Paquette (2007), 274, 277.

tenth-century Constantinople,[155] medieval England,[156] Italy[157] and northern Germany,[158] or early modern Rome,[159] Plauen[160] and Lodève.[161] Not only did contemporaries complain that admission fees excluded them (as we shall see shortly), but comparisons suggest that merchant guilds charged higher fees than other guilds. In Goslar in 1290, for instance, the merchant guild charged 8 marks, compared to 3 marks for richer craft guilds and 1 1/2 marks for poorer ones.[162] Available calculations suggest that merchant guilds' entrance fees were high enough to constitute a barrier to entry. In medieval Prato, for instance, the merchant guild's admission fee was beyond the means of many inhabitants,[163] and in thirteenth-century Stendal, it was 'such a high sum that this provision meant the practical exclusion of all former craftsmen'.[164]

Imposing economic conditions on entry excluded anyone who could not afford to give up a craft occupation, buy sufficient local property or pay the admission fee. It also deterred anyone who *might* afford these charges but was uncertain about his prospects as a merchant. It thus discouraged both competition and risk-taking.

3.1.2.4 Personal characteristics
Merchant guilds also excluded entrants according to their personal characteristics: gender, age, family descent and marital status. Most merchant guilds excluded females or restricted their participation in trade. Some admitted a few, but only immediate relatives (usually widows) of deceased male members. Others admitted female members but denied them trading privileges, as in medieval Lynn where mothers, wives and widows of members could buy merchant guild membership, but were limited to 'the spiritual and socio-religious benefits'.[165] Most merchant guilds excluded women altogether. Consequently many women whose financial, physical and human capital suited them for merchant trading were barred from doing so.

Many merchant guilds also imposed additional personal requirements. Medieval north German merchant guilds, for instance, excluded anyone who was not of legitimate birth himself, and who could not prove that his mother and father had also been born in wedlock.[166] Most merchant guilds favoured the sons of existing members, either granting them priority in being admitted at all or charging them significantly lower fees – as

---

[155] Dagron (2002), 409.   [156] Gross (1890), I: 29.   [157] Origo (1986), 44.
[158] Nitzsch (1892), 19, 84.   [159] Piola Caselli (1998), 135–6.
[160] K. H. Wolff (1979), 39.   [161] Johnson (1982), 7; J. K. J. Thomson (1982), 318.
[162] Ehbrecht (1985), 445.   [163] Origo (1986), 44.
[164] Nitzsch (1892), 21; Schulze (1985), 379–81 (quotation).
[165] Alsford (2003), www.trytel.com/~tristan/towns/lynn7.html.
[166] Nitzsch (1892), 72–3.

in twelfth-century Worms,[167] thirteenth-century Lübeck,[168] thirteenth-century Andover,[169] and an array of other towns in medieval England[170] and Germany.[171] Age qualifications were imposed by thirteenth-century Catalonian and Aragonian towns,[172] and married status was demanded by local merchant guilds in all Hanseatic cities.[173]

The proto-industrial merchant companies often acted very like traditional guilds, excluding entrants according to personal characteristics such as gender and family descent. The Wuppertaler Garnnahrung, for instance, which legally monopolized proto-industrial linen exports from the Wupper Valley between the sixteenth and the late eighteenth century, was 'a close knit oligarchy, entry into which became increasingly difficult'.[174] The Calwer Zeughandlungskompagnie, which legally monopolized Württemberg's worsted export trade from 1650 to 1797, had 23 founding members, coming from 13 families. Over the 147 years of its existence the number of members never exceeded 43 and only one new family was ever added. In practice, this guild-like company restricted its admissions to male relatives of existing members. It excluded all women: even where a merchant's wife had participated in the business, once he died she had to cease trading.[175]

3.1.2.5 Collective acceptability

Even if an applicant met all other formal requirements, some merchant guilds imposed additional catch-all clauses of 'good reputation' and 'collective approval'. Merchant guilds in thirteenth-century Germany[176] and in fourteenth-century Catalonia[177] and Aragon[178] required applicants to demonstrate 'good reputation'. Many merchant guilds required applicants to get the approval of existing members. In tenth-century Constantinople, for instance, admission to the guilds of the money changers, silk-cloth merchants and raw-silk merchants all required testimony concerning the applicant's integrity or pledges from 'five honourable persons' or existing 'members of the guild'.[179] In 1350 the mayor and burgesses of the English town of Macclesfield declared that no one was entitled to trade as a merchant in the town except burgesses of the Gild Merchant, and 'no one may be admitted as a burgess in the said town except with the assent and concurrence of the aforesaid mayor and burgesses'.[180] Likewise, the merchant guilds

---

[167] Seider (2005), 49.　　[168] Asch (1961), 13–20.　　[169] Gross (1890), I: 31–2.
[170] Ibid., I: 29.　　[171] Nitzsch (1892), 83–4.　　[172] Woodward (2005), 633.
[173] Dollinger (1970), 152.　　[174] Kisch (1972), 308–9, 387.
[175] Ogilvie (1997), 106–10; Troeltsch (1897), 55–6, 64–7.
[176] Schulze (1985), 379–81.　　[177] Woodward (2005), 633.　　[178] Ibid.
[179] Dagron (2002), 409.　　[180] Quoted in Gross (1890), I: 39.

of fourteenth-century Barcelona, Mallorca and Perpignan could refuse entry to any candidate who failed to secure approval from two-thirds of existing members. As a result, 'the matriculation committee often failed to admit merchants who considered themselves eligible. It is undeniable that the merchant class sought to take advantage of a restricted guild membership.'[181]

Merchant guilds left plentiful evidence, therefore, of the second form of behaviour economic theory predicts of a monopolist: restricting entry. This evidence discredits the claim that merchant guilds' exclusive trading rights did not actually amount to a monopoly since 'entry into the guild was permitted'. What is required is not just entry, but *free* entry. Although merchant guilds did admit some new members, they imposed limits both on their numbers and their characteristics, deliberately excluding large swathes of the population. No merchant guild allowed free entry.

3.1.3   Fixing prices

A third form of behaviour which economic theory predicts of monopolists is the attempt to fix prices – either directly, by imposing price regulations (discussed in this section), or indirectly, by restricting supplies (discussed in the next). Like any monopolist, a merchant guild had an incentive to conceal or disguise blatant over-pricing so as to deflect public protests and political pressure. Surviving documents thus probably under-record such activities. Nonetheless, many merchant guilds clearly sought – and obtained – the legal entitlement to set prices and prohibit price competition.[182]

Attempts to issue rules on the prices merchants could charge for their wares can be observed in a wide range of medieval merchant guilds – in tenth-century Constantinople,[183] eleventh- and twelfth-century Sweden,[184] thirteenth-century Alexandria[185] and Denmark,[186] fourteenth- and fifteenth-century Catalonia,[187] fifteenth-century

---

[181] R. S. Smith (1940), 38.   [182] Bernard (1972), 320.
[183] Dagron (2002), 413, 439.   [184] E. Hoffman (1980), 38, 51.
[185] Ashtor (1983), 73–4, 168, 218, 250, 271–83.
[186] According to Jahnke (2008), 182, the merchants of Schleswig and Flensburg responded to competitive threats from the German Hanse by forming a guild in 1282 which behaved similarly to the Hanse, including imposing prohibitions against *Vorkauf*, competitive purchases of wares by merchants operating as middlemen, outside the regulated urban markets.
[187] According to R. S. Smith (1940), 51–6, Catalonian merchant guilds had the legal right to fix freight rates and thus indirectly set the prices for freighted goods.

Castile[188] and medieval southern Germany.[189] In tenth-century Constantinople, the raw-silk merchants' guild operated a 'buying consortium' which internally agreed the prices at which its members would purchase raw silk from rural producers and sell it on to the silk-dressers.[190] If an individual guild member purchased silk from outsiders, he was obliged to sell it to poorer guild members at their request, at a legally fixed profit of 8.33 per cent.[191] Prices were set, therefore, neither by the market nor by the state, but through collective bargaining within and between guilds.[192] Early modern proto-industrial merchant associations were also legally entitled to fix prices – the Calwer Zeughandlungkompagnie in early modern Württemberg,[193] the Lyon silk merchants' guild,[194] the Wuppertaler Garnnahrung in the Wupper Valley,[195] the proto-industrial merchant guilds of the Saxon Vogtland,[196] the Linzer Wollzeugfabrik in Austria[197] and the Bologna silk merchants' guild.[198]

Even if merchant guilds were not always able to *enforce* their attempts to set prices – a question to be discussed shortly – the fact that they sought to do so suggests that they believed there was some probability of success. This is understandable, since setting artificially high prices was good for guilded merchants, increasing their profits. But it was bad for customers – downstream producers and consumers – who paid higher prices and thus enjoyed lower real incomes. It was also inefficient for the economy as a whole because it reduced the amount that was exchanged, thereby diminishing the gains from trade compared to what they would have been in the absence of price-fixing.

3.1.4　Restricting supply

A monopolist can also keep prices artificially high by *indirect* means – through restricting supplies. Monopolists typically seek to limit supplies because demand curves slope downwards: the lower the quantity supplied for sale, the higher the price consumers are willing to pay. If a monopolist can restrict the quantity supplied, consumers will have to pay a higher price, or not consume that good at all. Even when evidence on *prices* is not available – as in many pre-modern economies – deliberate restrictions

---

[188] C. R. Phillips (1983), 261, discusses how the Burgos merchant guild had a legal monopoly over foreign trade from the Cantabrian coast and the right to set freight charges in the ports.
[189] Lopez (1987), 359–60.　　[190] Dagron (2002), 439.
[191] Laiou (2002), 719; Lopez (1945), 16, 18.
[192] Laiou (2002), 719; Lopez (1945), 18.　　[193] Ogilvie (1997); Troeltsch (1897).
[194] Kriedte (1982), 48.　　[195] Kisch (1972), 352.　　[196] Wolff (1979), 39.
[197] Gutkas (1983), 93.　　[198] Poni (1982b); Poni (1982a).

on trade *volume* signal the attempt of a monopolist to exploit its position as sole supplier.

It is therefore striking how universally merchant guilds required their members to submit to common rules on trading quantities.[199] Some did this directly, by imposing trading quotas, as with the fifteenth-century English privileged companies which explicitly laid down the volume of goods to be traded by each member.[200] Others did it indirectly: the merchant guilds of tenth-century Constantinople by prohibiting transactions above a certain value without official permits;[201] those in late-medieval English towns by rationing allotments of shipping space;[202] the river merchants' guild in thirteenth-century Laufen by limiting each member to a maximum of three ships.[203] Early modern proto-industrial merchant associations behaved similarly, and the Calwer Zeughandlungkompagnie,[204] the Wuppertaler Garnnahrung[205] and the Swedish Tar-Merchants' Company[206] all imposed sales quotas on their members in order to keep prices high.

Supply restrictions were enforced by requiring guild members to trade publicly in the presence of other members, as in the tenth century when the raw-silk merchants' guild forbade members to travel outside Constantinople to negotiate individually with silk producers, requiring them instead to participate in the 'buying consortium' of the guild under official supervision.[207] The same pattern can be observed in 1258 when the Leicester merchant guild ordered all members to report to the shops in which the Leicester merchandise was usually deposited at particular trade fairs, where all wares were to be 'opened in the presence of the neighbours'.[208]

Limiting supplies created incentives for illegal interlopers to violate merchant guild monopolies and for customers to buy on the black market. But merchant guilds' charters gave them legal and political support from rulers, and some even had their own officials and security forces, as we shall see. Illegality increased the risks and costs of black-market trading. So customers, whether they bought from the limited quota of goods released onto markets by guilded merchants (at high monopoly prices) or from the black marketeers (whose prices, though lower, were still

---

[199] Bernard (1972), 320.   [200] R. De Roover (1965), 118.
[201] Racine (1985), 139; Freshfield (1938), 17, 19–22, 28; Dagron (2002), 441.
[202] R. De Roover (1965), 118.   [203] Störmer (1985), 366.
[204] For detailed discussions, see Ogilvie (1997), 186–8; Troeltsch (1897), 35–7, 163–5, 172–3, 175–7, 179, 181–4, 186, 194–9.
[205] Kisch (1972), 352.   [206] Müller (1998), 113.
[207] Dagron (2002), 439; Lopez (1945), 15, 18; Laiou (2002), 723, 732.
[208] Moore (1985), 95.

inflated by the risks of prosecution), paid higher prices than if supply had not been capped by merchant guilds. This not only harmed consumers and non-guilded interlopers, but also reduced gains from trade in the economy as a whole.

3.1.5 Dictating input costs

Theory also predicts a fifth form of behaviour of monopolists – exploitation of their position as sole legal *buyers* in particular markets by dictating lower than competitive purchasing prices. That is, a cartel of merchants is not only a monopolist but also, potentially, a monopsonist, artificially depressing its own input costs.

Most medieval merchant guilds pursued this strategy by claiming 'prerogative rights' over local markets – rights of prior purchase over certain wares, often at artificially low prices. Merchant guilds throughout medieval Europe enjoyed such prerogative rights – in twelfth-century St Omer over all merchant goods,[209] in medieval Flemish towns over grain from the countryside,[210] in medieval French towns over raw wool supplies[211] and in Dutch towns such as Dordrecht over rural foodstuffs.[212] In early-thirteenth-century England, visiting Lotharingian merchants were legally compelled to offer their goods first to the merchants of London, then those of Oxford, and finally those of Winchester, and 'it was the merchants of London who were responsible for setting the price'.[213]

Many merchant guilds also imposed regulations outlawing competition among their members for inputs such as labour and real estate, as in tenth-century Constantinople where merchant guilds forbade members to compete with one another on shop rents and employees' wages,[214] or in medieval Brabant where merchant guilds were entitled to fix craft prices and labourers' wages.[215]

Proto-industrial merchant associations also acted as monopsonists, using an array of legal privileges to reduce their own input costs below the competitive level. The Calwer Zeughandlungkompagnie in seventeenth-century Württemberg did not have to pay competitive prices to local weavers, but instead fixed purchase prices through periodic collective negotiations with weavers' guilds under state arbitration, in which the

---

[209] Irsigler (1985a), 57–8; Planitz (1940), 21; Dilcher (1984), 70.
[210] Stabel (1997), 166. [211] Lopez (1987), 359.
[212] De Vries and Van der Woude (1997), 354. [213] Middleton (2005), 340–1.
[214] Racine (1985), 139; Freshfield (1938), 17, 19–22, 28; Dagron (2002), 408 with n. 65, 412.
[215] Prevenier (2000), 575.

merchant association enjoyed advantages by virtue of kinship links with officials and strategic loans to the prince.[216] This merchant company also allied with its usual foe, the weavers' guilds, to cap prices paid for spun yarn, condemning thousands of female spinners to lives of desperate privation.[217] Similar price capping was practised in the seventeenth and eighteenth centuries by the Lodève merchant guild of Languedoc over woollen broadcloth prices and weavers' wage rates,[218] by the Wuppertaler Garnnahrung over weaving piece-rates and linen yarn prices,[219] by the Linzer Wollzeugfabrik over textile raw materials and labour,[220] and by proto-industrial merchant guilds in Catalonia over woollen and worsted purchase prices.[221]

Local merchant guilds in a wide variety of European economies and time periods thus show clear evidence of seeking to exercise legal monopsonies. They obtained 'prerogative rights' entitling them to prior right of purchase of wares at favourable prices. They enjoyed legal entitlements to dictate the prices of the wares they bought for onward trading. They even had the right to cap the prices of inputs such as shop rents, prices of manufactures in which they traded and wages of those they employed. Finally, it was basic to the regulatory strategy of merchant guilds to prohibit members from competing with one another in purchasing, which would have pushed up input prices.

3.1.6   Compulsory staple rights

Merchant guilds also exhibit a sixth form of behaviour predicted of monopolists – seeking to impose costs on potential competitors. A local merchant guild typically had not only the exclusive entitlement to trade freely in the town but also the right 'to impose payments and restrictions upon others who desired to exercise that privilege'.[222] Merchant guilds were entitled to alter costs and conditions, not only in their 'own' market but also in adjacent markets – thereby affecting suppliers, employees and customers. Even where guilds failed to enforce their privileges fully, those infringing on them were obliged to operate, at higher cost and risk, in the black market.

Potential competitors among local residents were relatively easy to deal with, as they could be coerced by the local authorities. Non-local merchants were a greater challenge, since their financial and human capital

---

[216] Ogilvie (1997), esp. ch. 7; Troeltsch (1897).
[217] Ogilvie (2003), esp. ch. 6; Ogilvie (2004a); Ogilvie (2004b).
[218] Johnson (1982), 7.   [219] Kisch (1972), 325, 352.   [220] Gutkas (1983), 93.
[221] J. K. J. Thomson (1996), 93; Torras (1991), 105–6, 108, 113 with nn. 56–7.
[222] Mauro (1990), 259.

enabled them to compete with local guild members and they enjoyed political backing from foreign governments. Non-local merchants also often offered payments and favours to local rulers in return for trading rights, as we shall see in Chapters 4 and 5. So local merchant guilds directed greatest effort at increasing costs for non-local merchants. In the great trading cities of medieval Italy, for instance, foreign traders were 'forced to call [visit the city], forced to pay taxes, forced to trade, forced to use local merchants to sell their goods, and the role of foreigners was very closely regulated so that the natives would make the profits'.[223] Attempts by local merchant guilds to increase the costs of foreign traders, by forcing them to unload their goods in local storehouses and sell them through the sole intermediation of local guild members, are observed in a wide variety of medieval European economies – southern Germany,[224] Denmark,[225] Lübeck,[226] Mallorca,[227] to give only a few examples. Even though no city's local merchants could achieve such ends perfectly, they defended their legal privileges strenuously, often with the backing of the law or even with military force.

Merchant guilds' most important device for imposing costs on outsiders was an institution called the 'staple'. The term 'staple' was used in a variety of different ways in medieval trade: for a locality where merchants *voluntarily* centralized their trade in particular wares (the modern term would be 'entrepôt'); for a locality where merchants were *obliged* to centralize such trade and where a particular body of merchants enjoyed exclusive privileges over that trade; for the complex of corporative *privileges* a particular body of merchants exercised over trade in a compulsory staple location; and for the core *commodities* (wool, grain, wine) that were often the object of staple privileges.[228] The confusion between the voluntary entrepôt and the compulsory staple location existed in medieval usage and has dogged subsequent scholarship, as we shall see in Chapter 10. For merchant guilds (or privileged town citizenries), what mattered were compulsory staple *privileges*, which were obtained by most European merchant guilds from the twelfth century on.[229] Such staple privileges appertained in principle to the entire town or place, but in practice they were specific to a particular body of merchants, usually the local merchant guild (although a few alien merchant guilds also got them).

Typically, staple privileges entitled the merchants of a particular town to compel non-local merchants travelling within a particular distance

---

[223] Pearson (1991), 75.   [224] Lopez (1987), 359.   [225] Schütt (1985), 253.
[226] Volckart and Mangels (1999), 444.   [227] Congdon (2003), 217.
[228] See the discussion in Häpke (1908), 222–4; and *Oxford English Dictionary*, 2nd edn (1989), online version, 'staple, n.²'.
[229] On the origins of the staple, see Kuske (1939); Kohn (2003a), 16.

(often a mile, the so-called ban-mile) to unload their wares in municipal warehouses for a specified period (often three days, though sometimes longer).[230] During this period, locals (particularly local merchant guild members, but sometimes also members of craft guilds with their own 'prerogative' over particular craft inputs) enjoyed exclusive legal rights to purchase the goods at privileged prices, and to take over their onward transport and sale.[231]

Most compulsory staple rights applied to all wares passing within the town's 'ban', but some applied only to specific goods. Thus, for instance, the medieval Flemish cities of Lille, Douai, Bruges and Damme had compulsory staple rights over the wine trade; Biervliet and Dendermonde over beer imports from Germany; Damme over cured herring; Monnikerede over salted fish; and Aalst and Lille over fabric dyes.[232] Indeed, towns in the medieval Low Countries made constant efforts to claim the exclusive privilege of marketing certain classes of goods and to become the regional or national 'staple market' for those wares.[233]

As we shall see in Chapter 4, *alien* merchant guilds could also enjoy compulsory staple rights over particular goods in particular localities. Examples of these alien staple rights are the privileges enjoyed by members of the English Company of the Staple in different Flemish and French localities after *c.* 1313,[234] and those of the German Hanse at its various staple locations in Europe.[235] In fact, the English wool staple oscillated in the fourteenth century between being an alien staple (located in a continental town such as Bruges or Antwerp and administered by the privileged company of English merchants exporting wool to the Low Countries) and being a dispersed local staple in England.[236] In 1326–7 and again in the early 1330s, for instance, the English wool staple enjoyed by the alien merchant guild of the English 'staplers' in the Low Countries was temporarily replaced by a number of local English staples enjoyed by local merchant guilds in fourteen English and Irish towns.[237] Foreign merchants were prohibited from purchasing from wool producers, and instead were required to trade via the

---

[230] Kuske (1939), 15–16, 33–5; Daenell (1905), 16; R. De Roover (1948a), 16; Congdon (2003), 217. This use of 'staple' to refer to legal privileges entitling a city to force travelling merchants to trade there should not be confused with the more neutral meaning of a staple market as 'a place where commerce in a particular commodity was concentrated' (whether institutionally or otherwise); on this, see the lucid discussion in Harreld (2004a), 20–1 (quotation 21).

[231] On Bruges, see Bernard (1972), 302; on Cologne, see Kuske (1939).

[232] Stabel (1997), 164.   [233] Tracy (1991), 14.   [234] Lloyd (1977), 101ff.

[235] See Irsigler (2002), 40, on the initially economic but increasingly coercive character of the Hanse's Bruges staple.

[236] Lloyd (1977), 115, 205; Power (1941), 90–3.   [237] Lloyd (1977), 115.

intermediation of members of local English merchant guilds in the staple towns.[238]

Non-members of the body of merchants holding staple rights were forbidden to participate in those rights or to evade them. The Cologne merchant guild, for instance, enjoyed rights of prior purchase over the goods of non-local merchants and the exclusive right to take over their onward transportation. From the late twelfth century into the early nineteenth century, it used these privileges to block non-local (especially Flemish) merchants from trading in the Cologne hinterland.[239] In 1221, the Viennese merchant guild used its compulsory staple rights to stop merchants from Swabia, Regensburg and Passau from passing through with goods destined for Hungary.[240] In the thirteenth century, the Riga merchant guild used its staple rights to block Russian traders and even other Hanseatic merchants, so that local merchants could monopolize the Russia trade along the Daugava (Dvina) River.[241]

Compulsory staple rights were an attempt to exploit what economists call 'geographical rents' – monopoly profits arising from a town's special location. Important trading centres often occupied advantageous locations which made it costly for long-distance merchants to avoid passing through them.[242] Many compulsory staple privileges were only workable because a particular town dominated a key river or confluence, such as Cologne's strategic location on the Rhine,[243] Ghent's domination of the Flemish river system,[244] Dordrecht's pivotal position at the mouth of the rivers Rhine and Maas,[245] the position of Gdańsk (Danzig) at the mouth of the Vistula river opening into the Baltic,[246] Smolensk's favourable position on the Dnjepr River in the middle of a fertile agricultural region,[247] or Poznań's strategic position on the navigable Warta river, spanning major commercial routes between western Europe and Russia.[248] Other compulsory staple privileges arose from possessing a key harbour, as with Lübeck's critical position controlling the land passage to Hamburg,[249] Lynn's position as the natural harbour for the

---

[238] Power (1941), 91; Lloyd (1977), 116–17.
[239] Kuske (1939), 40–1; Van Houtte (1966), 32–3; Häpke (1908), 81–2.
[240] Störmer (1985), 346–7, 359.
[241] Angermann (1987), 83–4; Dollinger (1970), 294.
[242] On how Cologne, Venice, London, Bergen, Novgorod and other medieval European cities (including most of the towns located on the Rhine) exploited their geographical advantages to attract foreign merchants while still enforcing staple rights for local merchant and craft guilds, see Kuske (1939), 16, 25, 28, 31–3.
[243] Kuske (1939), 16, 25, 28, 31–3; Häpke (1908), 81–2.
[244] Stabel (1997), 168; Bigwood (1906), 411–21.
[245] De Vries and Van der Woude (1997), 354.   [246] Wernicke (1999), 196.
[247] Angermann (1987), 82–3.   [248] Weinryb (1950), 22–3.
[249] Spruyt (1994), 126; Dollinger (1970), 19.

East Midlands grain trade,[250] Riga's key location as the harbour outlet
of the Daugava (Dvina) River running from Russia into the Baltic,[251]
or Bruges' possession of the best harbour on the Flemish coast after
the great storm-tide of 1134 which created a new estuary on the river
Zwin.[252] Venice was able to maintain its compulsory staple privileges
partly because 'its unique harbor facilities and its sheltered location
at the end of the long Adriatic Sea were complemented by excellent
Alpine routes, such as the Brenner Pass, which provided the easiest overland access from Italy to the vast "hinterland" of central and eastern
Europe'.[253]

To protect their geographical rents and increase the costs of competitors, local merchant guilds often secured regulations forbidding foreign
merchants to avoid their staple by travelling on 'prohibited' roads. In
the fourteenth century, for instance, the Saxon towns of southern Transylvania required non-local merchants to travel on 'mandatory roads' as
opposed to the '*vias falsas*', compelling them to bring goods into the
towns where they were subject to mandatory deposit and right of prior
purchase by local merchants.[254] Some local merchant guilds went further,
as in Dordrecht where, as late as the sixteenth century, the local merchant guild actually seized ships from merchants who sought to avoid
the compulsory staple, and even sent warships to threaten their home
towns.[255]

Compulsory staple rights gradually weakened in some European
economies after around 1500, notably in England and the Low Countries. In 1527, Niklaas Everaerts, president of the Council of Holland,
declared that the Dordrecht staple privileges were 'contrary to all natural
right, and therefore null', although this did not prevent their surviving
for a few more decades.[256]

Most other European economies maintained compulsory staple privileges for much longer, and even strengthened them. In the sixteenth
century, Hanse cities such as Cologne, Riga and Lübeck, in an effort to
increase the costs of unguilded Dutch and English competitors, 'tightened up their staple regulations, enforced the "guest law" more strictly,
and forbade their burgesses to enter into partnership with foreigners'.[257]
Cologne enforced its merchant guild's staple until staple rights were
abolished by the Congress of Vienna in 1815.[258] In Spain, local merchant guilds such as those of Burgos and Bilbao used staple privileges to

---

[250] Unwin (1918), ch. 4 para. 4.   [251] Angermann (1987), 83.
[252] Paravicini (1992), 100; Stabel (1999), 31; Henn (1999), 131.
[253] Van der Wee (1990), 21.   [254] Pakucs (2003) (abstract).
[255] Tracy (1990b), 54–5.   [256] Quoted in *ibid.*, 55.   [257] Dollinger (1970), 352.
[258] Kuske (1939), 46.

impose costs on foreign traders throughout the early modern period.[259] In the Swedish monarchy, until the mid-eighteenth century only the privileged merchants of a few staple towns were allowed to engage in foreign trade.[260] On the frontiers with Russia, the Swedish government granted monopoly rights over trade with western merchants to Narva, but monopoly rights over trade with Russia to Ivangorod, giving rise to constant struggles between the merchant guilds of these neighbouring towns.[261] Until 1765, in areas of the Swedish monarchy that are now Finland, almost all towns were compelled to take all their merchandise (including, for instance, tens of thousands of barrels of tar annually) to Stockholm and export it through the privileged merchants of that town.[262] Such policies meant that large swathes of Swedish commerce were divided up into corporative monopolies for different sets of merchant guilds well into the early modern period.

Compulsory staple rights existed so widely and for such a long time because they not only gave advantages to local guilded merchants by increasing competitors' costs, but also benefited rulers by facilitating tax collection, as we shall see in Chapter 5.[263] Compelling non-local merchants to unload their goods in local warehouses and have them inspected by local merchants with their own incentives to monitor rivals closely made it easier for rulers to tax trade.[264] Rulers sometimes even got the local merchant guild to collect trade taxes, as in Cologne where the local brokers' guild was obliged to collect a 1 per cent tax on the value of goods deposited at the staple,[265] or in Sweden where the crown established staple rights for local merchant guilds in the sixteenth century precisely because 'the concentration of foreign trade to a few staple towns would, it was thought, positively affect the efficiency of extraction of revenues (customs duties) from trade'.[266] Other rulers collected a tax directly from foreign merchants in return for *exempting* them from the compulsory staple of the local merchant guild.[267] So rulers had strong incentives to grant compulsory staple rights in order to ease tax collection and secure fiscal and political support from local merchant guilds as powerful domestic interest-groups. But the reason local merchant guilds demanded compulsory staple privileges so universally was because they increased the costs of potential competitors, enabling local guild members to reap higher profits.

---

[259] Grafe (2001), 24; C. R. Phillips (1983), 261.   [260] Müller (1998), 43–4.
[261] Kotilaine (2009), 3–4.   [262] Ojala (1997), 323, 327.
[263] Kuske (1939), 41–5; Kohn (2003a), 16.   [264] On Cologne, see Kuske (1939), 38.
[265] *Ibid.*, 41.   [266] Müller (1998), 44.   [267] For some examples, see Kuske (1939), 37.

3.1.7   Other strategies for imposing costs on competitors

Local merchant guilds also got a wide array of other miscellaneous privileges enabling them to impose costs on competitors. One was the right of brokerage. A merchant guild usually had a legal monopoly over intermediation, as we have seen. This not only gave its members exclusive rights over an important line of business but also imposed costs on potential competitors, particularly non-local merchants, who were obliged to employ local merchants as brokers and pay them a commission on every transaction.[268]

A few major trading centres – notably Bruges, Amsterdam, Venice and some other Italian cities – deviated from the common pattern, and made the intermediary trade a monopoly of separate brokers' guilds. Venice appointed brokers directly from among the citizen-merchantry of the town: non-local merchants were allowed to trade with other non-local merchants only through Venetian brokers, paying a brokerage tax and presenting a broker's certificate at point of export, which increased their costs. But until 1497, there was no brokers' guild, and brokers reported to the Venetian state, not to their own self-governing body.[269] From the thirteenth century, Bruges granted its powerful brokers' guild the right to compel even local citizens to use its members' intermediation in all commercial dealings.[270] This raises the possibility that having separate brokers' guilds rather than reserving brokerage for local merchants had some relationship with the exceptional economic dynamism of Venice and Bruges – whether as cause or consequence.[271] However that may be, Venice and Bruges were exceptional: the European norm was for brokerage to be a legal monopoly of the local merchant guild, which used it to increase the costs of foreign rivals.

Another tactic was for local merchant guilds to force foreign merchants to purchase shipping services from locals. Medieval Catalan merchant guilds prohibited anyone from chartering foreign ships locally if native ships were available, and obliged foreign merchants to use Catalan ships to re-export their wares.[272] In 1400, one of the major demands of the local merchant guilds of Valencia, Mallorca and Barcelona was that

---

[268] Lieber (1968), 238–9; Stabel (1997), 142.
[269] Mueller (1997), 89–90, 266–7; Ashtor (1983), 71; Choroškevic (1996), 84–6; Lieber (1968), 237–8. On the changes that took place after the formation of the Venetian brokers' guild in 1497, see Rothman (2006), 50–7.
[270] Daenell (1905), 16.
[271] This argument is advanced for Bruges by Häpke (1908), e.g. 260. On the variety of patterns of brokerage in different regions of the medieval Low Countries, see Laurent (1935b), 233–4.
[272] Congdon (2003), 228; R. S. Smith (1940), 51–6.

foreign shipping should be taxed or banned entirely, in order to protect local merchants against Italian competitors.[273] In medieval Lübeck the foreman of the 'company' (guild) of merchants trading to Bergen 'collected all requests for cargo to be shipped to that port and distributed the merchandise among the ships available, giving priority to members of his company'.[274] Local merchant guilds thus tried to inflate competitors' costs by making them use shipping services controlled by the guild.

An additional tactic was to limit how long foreign merchants could stay in the town, preventing them from reaping the full benefits of their costly journey. Many local merchant guilds imposed time limits on foreign traders – three months for non-local merchants in tenth-century Constantinople,[275] forty days for Lotharingian and Gascon wine- and woad-merchants in eleventh-century London,[276] six weeks for foreign merchants in Norway in 1316,[277] and forty days for foreign traders in fourteenth-century Lynn and other English boroughs.[278] When Venetian merchants were granted exceptionally liberal trading privileges by the count of Flanders in 1322, the municipal authorities of Bruges blunted the competitive threat by allowing Venetians only forty days during which they could exercise them before having to leave.[279]

A further, widely practised tactic was to restrict competitors to particular locations and limit their movements. Local merchant guilds often constrained foreign merchants' business by obliging them to live and trade in a special building or compound called a *fondaco*.[280] The *fondaco* (from the Arabic *funduq*) probably originated in the Islamic world where early medieval Muslim rulers confined foreigners to *funduqs* 'for taxing mercantile transactions, controlling the storage and distribution of certain goods and, in some cases, regulating the movement of particular groups of merchants'.[281] By the tenth or eleventh century the *fondaco* system was imposed on foreign traders in nearly every European trading centre – in tenth-century Constantinople,[282] eleventh-century Italy[283] and London,[284] thirteenth-century Seville,[285] fourteenth-century Saxon

[273] Fullana Ferré et al. (1998), 9.   [274] Dollinger (1970), 156.

[275] Johanek (1999), 72–3; Slessarev (1967), 181; Dagron (2002), 441; Lopez (1945), 22, 28; Laiou (2002), 732.

[276] Middleton (2005), 336; Bateson (1902), 725; Lloyd (1982), 24–6.

[277] Riis (2005), 36.

[278] See the by-law for King's Lynn, published in Alsford (2003) on www.trytel.com/~tristan/towns/lynnlaws.html, s.v. 'Aliens'.

[279] R. De Roover (1948a), 15.   [280] Lopez (1987), 347.

[281] Constable (2003), 64 (quotation); J. W. Hoffmann (1932), 245.

[282] For a discussion of the Byzantine *mitata* system, see Johanek (1999), 72–3; Lopez (1945), 25–30; Laiou (2002), 732.

[283] Lopez (1987), 347.   [284] Middleton (2005), 341–2.   [285] Lopez (1987), 354.

Transylvania[286] and fifteenth-century southern Germany.[287] Perhaps the best-known example of this system at work was the Venetian Fondaco dei Tedeschi, founded sometime before 1228: German merchants in Venice were obliged to live and trade in a particular building, so that their competitive threat to local merchants could be monitored and controlled.[288]

Local merchant guilds also denied foreign competitors access to local infrastructure. Some limited foreign merchants' access to port facilities – in the German Hanseatic ports,[289] the Norfolk port of Lynn,[290] the Spanish ports of Valencia, Barcelona and Mallorca.[291] Others imposed costs on foreign merchants by denying them access to shipping. The merchant guilds of fourteenth-century Elbląg (Elbing), Gdańsk (Danzig) and Stralsund prohibited English merchants from chartering Hanseatic ships locally.[292] The merchant guild of fifteenth-century Florence prevented non-local merchants from loading goods in the period preceding the embarkation of the Florentine galley fleet to England, with the aim of enabling the Florentine merchant guild in London to fix prices when the fleet arrived there.[293] Still other local merchant guilds forbade foreign merchants from selling in local market locations: thus in 1365 the West Prussian town of Marienburg forbade foreign merchants from doing business in salt or herring below the Lauben (arbours where merchant business was done in the town), requiring them to sell solely from their own carts or ships.[294]

Another tactic was for the local merchant guild to compel foreigners to use local infrastructure by prohibiting neighbouring towns from offering such infrastructure. Thus, for instance, in the thirteenth and fourteenth century, Bruges sought to secure legal sanctions against nearby Aardenburg, preventing it from operating scales over the weight of sixty pounds. This was explicitly in order to compel foreign merchants to use the scales – and merchant intermediaries – of Bruges instead.[295]

A final tactic to increase competitors' costs was to limit the volume of wares they were allowed to trade locally. In tenth-century Constantinople the local merchant guilds prohibited Russian merchants from exporting more than ten lengths of silk per trading trip or total goods exceeding a value of 50 solidi.[296] In medieval Venice, foreign merchants, even ones

[286] Pakucs (2003) (abstract).   [287] Lopez (1987), 347.
[288] Choroškevic (1996); Simonsfeld (1887); J. W. Hoffmann (1932).
[289] Spruyt (1994), 123; A. R. Lewis and Runyan (1985), 152.
[290] Alsford (2003), 'History of medieval Lynn', www.trytel.com/~tristan/towns/lynn7.html, s.v. 'Economy'.
[291] Congdon (2003), 222.   [292] Dollinger (1970), 73.
[293] Mallett (1962), 250–1, 253–4, 256–7.   [294] Sarnowsky (2002), 67.
[295] Häpke (1908), 229.   [296] Gieysztor (1987), 490; Laiou (2002), 724.

who obtained local citizenship, were not permitted to invest above a certain sum in maritime commerce.[297] In thirteenth-century Alexandria, the Karīmi merchant association restricted how much merchandise each Italian merchant could sell.[298] In fifteenth-century German Hanseatic towns, Nürnberg merchants were forbidden to sell wares not manufactured in Nürnberg itself.[299] In seventeenth-century Russia, local merchant guild charters forbade foreign merchants from trading in grain and other goods without a special privilege from the czar.[300]

Local merchant guilds thus secured the precise legal privileges one would predict of would-be monopolists – exclusive rights to do particular types of business, exclude entrants, fix prices, restrict supplies, depress input costs and burden competitors. In law, at least, local merchant guilds were monopolists.

3.2   Did local merchant guilds enforce their monopolies in practice?

But merchant guilds might still have been unable or unwilling to enforce these monopolies. How can we test this hypothesis? A first test is to ask for an alternative explanation of the facts. Why else would merchant guilds so universally have sought and obtained the legal rights to do precisely what a monopolist would want to do? And, having obtained these monopoly rights, why refrain from enforcing them?

A second test is to look at the evidence. What would we expect to observe empirically, if merchant guilds did not enforce their monopolies? First, contemporaries should not complain about being harmed by guild monopolies. Second, merchant guilds should not invest in lobbying to get and keep legal monopolies. Third, conflict should not arise between merchant guilds over monopolies. Fourth, merchant guilds should not bother to penalize encroachers and free-riders on their monopolies. Fifth, outsiders should not pay to circumvent or share merchant guilds' monopolies. Finally, trade should not expand when guild monopolies disappeared. What does the evidence show?

3.2.1   Contemporary complaints

If merchant guilds did not enforce their monopolies, contemporaries should not have complained about them. But they did. Every medieval European society left rich documentary testimony from contemporaries,

---

[297] Mueller (1997), 265–6.   [298] Ashtor (1983), 73–4, 168, 218, 250, 271–83.
[299] Dollinger (1970), 196–7.   [300] Angermann (1974), 82.

reporting – indeed often lamenting – merchant guilds' monopolistic activities.

In medieval England, ordinary consumers, small-scale traders, commodity producers, local officials, outside merchants and parliamentarians condemned merchant guilds, describing them as levying exactions 'after their own sinister mind and pleasure', subjecting the public to 'outrageous hardships' and imposing unreasonable ordinances 'for ther owne singler profite and to the comen hurte and damage of the people'.[301]

Wool producers in the East Riding of Yorkshire complained in 1327, for instance, that members of the merchant guilds of York, Beverley and other towns had been using staple regulations to act as a cartel: they had, it was argued, 'confederated "by writings and oaths" not to pay more than a certain price agreed between themselves'.[302] That same year saw 'numerous complaints from magnates of the realm and others' that the privileges of merchant guilds in the fourteen staple towns were deterring foreign merchants from attending the Boston fair to buy wool, harming English wool producers.[303]

In 1330, a crown attorney described how the burgesses of Derby, 'under cover of this Gild Merchant... have been accustomed to oppress the people coming to the said town with vendible wares'.[304] The Derby guild, he claimed, excluded local citizens from membership by charging high entrance fees, charged double tolls to outsiders wanting to sell goods in Derby, forbade non-local merchants from trading with each other, stopped them from selling wholesale to anyone outside the guild, fixed prices, and intimidated non-guild members – 'which usages redound to the injury, oppression, and pauperization of the people'.[305] According to twelve jurors from Derby itself, 'the profit arising therefrom does not accrue to the advantage of the community of the borough, but only to the advantage of those who are of the said society'.[306]

In 1335, the inhabitants of Ely and other places in Cambridgeshire complained to Parliament that the Lynn merchant guild was preventing them from selling beer and foodstuffs freely in Lynn, instead forcing them to sell through the intermediation of Lynn guild members.[307] In 1355, the 'poor burgesses' of Newcastle upon Tyne complained that the 'rich burgesses' of the Gild Merchant were preventing them from trading in cloth, herrings, wine, groceries and wool.[308] In 1387, a Northleach merchant reported that the merchant guild of Chipping Camden had

---

[301] Quoted in Gross (1890), I: 36.   [302] Quoted in Lloyd (1977), 117.
[303] Quoted in *ibid.*, 118.   [304] Quoted in Gross (1890), I: 41.
[305] Unwin (1918), ch. 4 para. 3; Gross (1890), I: 41 (quotation), II: 51–3.
[306] Quoted in Gross (1890), I: 42.   [307] Unwin (1918), ch. 4 para. 4.
[308] Hilton (1984), 145, 149.

threatened him with violence for infringing on its exclusive privilege to trade in the surrounding countryside.[309] When the fourteenth-century Scarborough merchant William Lovesdale sold fish and other victuals in Yaxley at a lower price than the guilded Yaxley merchants, the Yaxley guild 'laid in wait in ambush with force and arms to kill the said William Lovesdale, and there they wounded, beat, and evilly treated him, and left him there as if dead, so that the said William Lovesdale was in despair of his life'.[310] In 1499, the captain of the Venetian fleet recommended that it sail to Flanders rather than London, 'because the English merchants were starting to abuse their monopoly and kept prices high'.[311]

In Germany merchant guilds attracted similar complaints. In 1315, for instance, the citizens of the New Town of Lemgo complained 'against the claims of the Old Town merchant guild' and sought a protection letter entitling them 'to visit the Old Town and its market every day for buying, selling, and other needs without any compulsion by any guild'.[312] In 1485, the inhabitants of the Prussian town of Thorn complained that the Gdańsk (Danzig) merchants interrupted sea transport and prevented other Prussian merchants from trading with foreign merchants there.[313] In 1492, the inhabitants of Braunsberg accused the Gdańsk merchants of refusing them access to their market and confiscating their wares.[314]

The Low Countries saw similar grievances against merchant guilds. Throughout the fourteenth and fifteenth centuries, Bruges constantly complained of grain shortages and high prices caused by the grain staple of the Ghent merchant guild.[315] In the 1430s and 1440s merchant guilds in several Flemish towns were accused of 'monopolising trade in alum and spices with the aim of raising prices'.[316]

Similar charges were levelled against merchant guilds in Italian cities. In periods of 'popular' government in medieval Florence (e.g. in 1293, 1343 and 1378), consumers brought legal accusations against the merchant guilds, which had temporarily lost their immunity from prosecution for 'monopolistic practices'.[317] In the fifteenth century, the Florentine government criticized the monopoly of the local wool merchants' guild over the galley trade between Florence's subject city Pisa and England on the grounds that the merchant guild never operated enough galleys

---

[309] N. Fryde (1985), 224.
[310] Document reproduced and translated in Landman (1998), Appendix B3, 422–3, no date given.
[311] Stabel (1999), 34.   [312] Nitzsch (1892), 18.   [313] Sarnowsky (2002), 70–1.
[314] *Ibid.*, 71.   [315] Stabel (1997), 166, 169.   [316] Dollinger (1970), 300.
[317] Becker (1960b), 426 n. 27 (quotation); Becker (1966), 17.

on the route, so that supply was restricted, and the Florentine citizenry suffered a 'rise in the cost of all imported commodities as a result of the partial monopolies'.[318] As late as the mid-seventeenth century, the Milan merchant guild was excluding small-scale travelling Piedmontese merchants even though, as one Milan citizen observed, 'the sales of certain goods made by these merchants are very useful to this State because here the same goods are not produced and even when they are produced, they are more expensive'.[319]

The monopolies of the privileged merchant companies of the early modern period evoked similar accusations. In the late seventeenth and early eighteenth centuries, rural people in Upper Austria protested against the state privileges legally obliging them to purchase cloths from the Linzer Wollzeugfabrik and excluding everyone else from the woollen textile trade. A wave of popular opposition greeted the extension of the Linz company's monopoly privileges to Lower and Inner Austria. In Carinthia, open rebellion against the company's monopoly was only calmed when the ruler relaxed it to let peasants make woollen textiles for their own use, though sales and exports were still reserved for the Linz company.[320]

The bitter resentment evoked by the monopolies of proto-industrial merchant companies is vividly illustrated by popular grievances against the Calwer Zeughandlungkompagnie – the guild-like merchant-dyers' company that monopolized the Württemberg worsted trade from 1650 to 1797. In 1650, worsted weavers lamented that the company's monopoly meant it could treat them as its 'slaves and serfs'. A year later, the weavers complained that 'formerly, dyeing and merchant commerce was an entirely free and uncoerced trade, but recently the dyers have employed all sorts of self-seeking petitions, and have compelled the worsted-weavers to them in various ways, so that the weavers must now in every matter live to their will and command'. In the century and a half that followed, the weavers repeatedly lamented that the merchant company treated them with 'coercion', 'compulsion', 'force' and 'hard treatment'. The prices and quotas imposed by the company were 'impossible for the poor weavers to live with', prevented the weavers from 'attaining to their maker's wage', forced weavers to 'work for absolutely nothing' and made it impossible for the weavers 'to co-exist with the company'. Local officials openly acknowledged that the monopoly enjoyed by this merchant association had disastrous economic effects, in 1740 complaining in a lengthy report that

[318] Mallett (1962), 250–1, 253–4, 256–7 (quotation from 254).
[319] Quoted in D'Amico (2001), 715.   [320] Ogris (2004), 377–8, 381–4.

with the increase in the number of poor households, the general *inopia* [poverty] is getting so much out of hand that in the end no-one can help anyone else, and nothing other than desperate thoughts, words and deeds must break out, which we have already experienced several times; certainly, the misery of the poor residents here has so much got out of hand that it cannot be so deplorable in any locality in the whole country, and the greatest contributory factor to it has been that the merchant company in Calw treats our impoverished worsted-weavership so excessively severely, with purchasing- and price-reductions on the worsted wares, so that if this is not changed the weavers will have to leave the craft altogether and go begging in hordes.[321]

Contemporary complaints about the monopolies of proto-industrial merchant associations continued up to the beginning of factory industrialization. As late as 1784, in a famous case, the German linen merchant Johann Gottfried Brügelmann complained about the legal obstacles that his merchant guild, the Wuppertaler Garnnahrung, was placing in the way of his project to build a spinning factory using English machines.[322]

Contemporaries in medieval and early modern Europe thus had no doubt that merchant guilds enforced their monopolies in practice. Consumers, suppliers, outside traders, local officials, parliamentary representatives and state bureaucrats all explicitly criticized the damage inflicted by merchant guild monopolies. Such contemporary testimony comes from so many people, so many different economies, so many different guilds and so many different time periods that it cannot be dismissed as exceptional. Any attempt to claim that the legal monopolies enjoyed by merchant guilds were ineffectual in practice must provide an explanation for why contemporaries, who had to live with these monopolies, saw them as effective – and harmful.

3.2.2   Lobbying

If merchant guilds were not actually able to enforce their monopolies, then they should not have bothered to lobby rulers to grant, maintain or extend them. But the documents record merchant guilds eagerly investing resources in persuading rulers to guarantee their monopolies. Guilds spent time and money on lobbying campaigns, gifts to rulers, bribes to officials, favourable loans to the state, military backup and political support – all in explicit exchange for sole rights over particular branches of trade. Would they have done so had they not regarded these rights as valuable?

---

[321] For this quotation, precise archival references, additional contemporary complaints and detailed analysis of the economic effects of this guild-like merchant 'company', see Ogilvie (1997), esp. 379–83.

[322] Kisch (1972), 400–1.

Guilds made payments to rulers in exchange for trade monopolies throughout Europe, from the tenth through to the later eighteenth century. The silk merchants' guild in tenth-century Constantinople enjoyed a broad monopoly and in return transferred fees levied from its members directly to the emperor.[323] The eleventh-century Pavia merchant *collegium* obtained legal monopolies and reciprocated by paying a tax directly into the royal exchequer.[324] In 1330, the merchant guild of Derby paid 40 marks to the crown to maintain its right to charge high entrance fees, levy double tolls from non-local merchants, exclude outsiders from trade and compel local inhabitants to sell solely to guild members.[325]

Merchant guilds also invested in lobbying to defend their privileges against competitors. In the twelfth century, the Roskilde merchant guild organized vehement protests when the Danish crown threatened to grant normal alien trading rights to German merchants.[326] In 1229 the merchant guilds of Smolensk and Polozk lobbied Prince Mstislav Davidovitsch to limit German merchants' trading rights 'in order to secure for the local merchantry the profits of the brokerage trade'.[327] So effective was the long-standing lobbying campaign of the Polozk merchant guild that it succeeded in keeping Hanseatic merchants out of the Daugava (Dvina) river trade with Russia, severely restricted their business within the town itself and ultimately created such a difficult commercial environment that German traders abandoned the town altogether.[328] In the 1260s, the Barcelona merchant guild lobbied so strongly against the presence of Italian competitors that the king issued a decree expelling merchants from Genoa, Florence and Siena.[329] In the fourteenth century the merchant guilds of Gdańsk (Danzig) and Stralsund mounted repeated lobbying campaigns to maintain their monopoly over trade with their rural hinterlands, specifically to keep out the Dutch.[330] In 1397, the merchant guild of Elbląg (Elbing) lobbied the Prussian state to prevent English merchants from selling cloth at Prussian fairs, and in 1402 got the English restricted to the port towns.[331] In the same period, merchant guilds in the Saxon towns of southern Transylvania invested in lobbying their ruler to exclude competition from Wallachian traders.[332] In 1396, the Barcelona merchant guild secured the prosecution and imprisonment of the great Catalan humanist Bernat Metge, who as a royal councillor had supported the presence of Italian merchants in Barcelona.[333]

---

[323] Racine (1985), 139; Freshfield (1938), 17.   [324] Racine (1985), 135–6.
[325] Unwin (1918), ch. 4 para. 3; Gross (1890), II: 51–3.   [326] Schütt (1980), 108–9.
[327] Angermann (1987), 83 (quotation); Dollinger (1970), 30.
[328] Angermann (1987), 57–8, 84.   [329] Fullana Ferré et al. (1998), 8.
[330] Dollinger (1970), 73, 195.   [331] Sarnowsky (2002), 68–9.
[332] Pakucs (2003) (abstract).   [333] Fullana Ferré et al. (1998), 8.

Medieval French merchant guilds constantly lobbied the crown for 'protectionist measures' to prevent foreign merchants from offering higher prices to wool producers.[334] Medieval Flemish merchant guilds lobbied against villages' attempts to gain market rights which would encroach on urban guild monopolies over the grain trade.[335] When the prince of Burgundy limited the purchasing prerogatives of the Rupelmonde merchant guild to a radius of only two miles around the town, the guild mobilized the town council for vigorous protests.[336]

In some parts of Europe, local merchant guilds and merchant associations continued to lobby for monopoly privileges into the early modern period. In 1508, for instance, the local merchant guilds of Oslo and Tönsberg put enormous pressure on the Norwegian crown to exclude Germans from the intermediary and rural trade.[337] From 1650 to 1797 the Calwer Zeughandlungkompagnie paid regular *honoraria* (bribes) to Württemberg state officials and made favourable loans to the prince in return for confirmation of its monopoly privileges.[338] It also constantly lobbied for state enforcement of trading quotas, explicitly arguing that this enabled it to keep export prices high, profiting both the merchant association and, through it, the Württemberg state.[339] The Lodève woollen merchants' guild in Languedoc campaigned constantly throughout the eighteenth century to secure its monopoly privileges and spent substantial resources maintaining a lobbying presence in Paris.[340]

Members of merchant guilds throughout Europe thus had no doubt that their guilds could enforce their monopolies in practice. They were willing to spend time and money lobbying, to make favourable loans to rulers, and to offer bribes and *honoraria* to officials in order to secure, maintain and extend their monopolies. Such lobbying was undertaken by so many different guilds, in so many European societies and across so many time periods that it cannot be dismissed as exceptional. People and organizations do not expend resources to obtain monopolies that they do not value. If merchant guilds could not enforce their monopolies, then why were they so willing to pay to get and keep such monopolies?

3.2.3 Inter-guild conflict

If merchant guild monopolies were unenforceable, guilds should have had no reason to engage in conflict over them. But historical records

---

[334] Lopez (1987), 359.   [335] Stabel (1997), 159–60.   [336] *Ibid.*, 166 with n. 86.
[337] Dollinger (1970), 313.   [338] Troeltsch (1897), 85.
[339] For a detailed discussion, see Ogilvie (1997), 186–8; Troeltsch (1897), 35–7, 163–5, 172–3, 175–7, 179, 181–4, 186, 194–9.
[340] Johnson (1982), 5ff.

reveal constant struggles between different guilds over their respective monopoly rights.

Local merchant guild monopolies evoked conflict all over medieval Europe. In 1198 the monopoly of local Byzantine merchant guilds over the Black Sea trade was one of the factors inducing Venice to provide financial and military support for the Fourth Crusade in order to put pressure on Byzantine rulers to open up trade to Venetian merchants.[341] In France from the twelfth century on, the rival merchant guilds of Rouen and Paris 'watched and fought jealously over their fields of operations', particularly control over trade on the river Seine.[342] In the early fourteenth century, local merchant guilds in Pisa, Verona and Piacenza waged conflicts against innkeepers who they claimed were illegitimately engaging in merchandising.[343] Fourteenth-century London merchant guilds disputed constantly with Italian merchant guilds, each seeking 'to exclude the other from the wool and the spice trades'.[344] In 1356–8, local merchant guilds in Catalonian and Aragonese towns attacked the 'nations' (guilds) of Venetian merchants who were trying to exercise their new legal privileges to trade.[345] In 1398–9, the Valencian merchant guild prevailed upon the town governors to expel all Italian merchants, who then used their own 'nations' to appeal to the crown to enforce the commercial privileges for which they had paid; during this conflict, the Valencian merchant guild violently attacked the remaining Italian merchants, including Venetians who had been exempted from the expulsion.[346]

Even within the German Hanse, the local merchant guilds of different Hanseatic towns constantly squabbled over demarcating their monopolies. Thus when a subgroup of the Lübeck merchant guild tried to force all Hanseatic merchants to go through Lübeck if they wanted to trade to Bergen, the merchant guilds of all the Wendish Hanse towns on the Baltic Sea mounted concerted opposition.[347]

In some European economies – eastern-central Europe, Iberia, Italy – inter-guild struggles testify to the real economic traction of local merchant guild monopolies long past 1500. In seventeenth-century Poland, for instance, the Poznań merchant guild sought to defend its monopoly over 'all wholesale as well as retail trade' by engaging in continual aggression against local Jews and foreign merchants, culminating in a series of violent attacks and public riots.[348] In seventeenth-century Cantabria, the merchant guilds of Burgos and Bilbao engaged in perpetual struggles to

---

[341] Lopez (1987), 349, 351.
[342] Postan (1987), 271 (quotation); Goldschmidt (1891), 217.
[343] Szabó (1983), 85.   [344] R. De Roover (1965), 102.   [345] Congdon (2003), 217.
[346] *Ibid.*, 221–2.   [347] Dollinger (1970), 156–7.
[348] Weinryb (1945), 93 (quotation), 98–100, 115–16.

expand their monopoly privileges at each other's expense.[349] In early modern Bologna, the monopoly of the guild of silk *brokers* evoked continual opposition from the guild of silk *merchants*.[350] As late as the 1730s, the Bologna hemp producers' guild described the privileges of the hemp brokers' guild as an 'abuse' and a 'monopoly'.[351]

The early modern privileged companies also evoked inter-guild conflict. Guilds of merchants and weavers in Clermont-de-Lodève and other French proto-industrial centres engaged in bitter struggles throughout the seventeenth and eighteenth centuries over who was allowed to engage in which aspects of the textile trade.[352] In the Catalonian town of Igualada, guilds of merchants and proto-industrial weavers pursued costly court cases over each other's monopolies throughout the eighteenth century.[353] The Württemberg worsted industry saw prolonged conflicts between the Calwer Zeughandlungkompagnie and the proto-industrial weavers' guilds over each other's monopoly rights between 1650 and 1797.[354]

Both local merchant guilds and their rivals had no doubt that guild monopolies mattered. They were willing to spend time and money defending the monopolies of their own guilds and attacking those of others. This strongly suggests that these monopolies were enforced. People do not undertake costly conflict over privileges that have no economic effects. Again, such examples of inter-guild struggles over monopoly privileges were not exceptional – they can be found for all parts of Europe from the twelfth century on. Why would so many guilded merchants have engaged in costly conflict over monopolies that were economically irrelevant?

3.2.4   Systems of detection and punishment

If merchant guilds had no expectation of enforcing their monopolies, they should have had no incentive to spend resources setting up systems to detect and punish violators. But everywhere in Europe, local merchant guilds invested in systems to penalize outside competitors who encroached on their monopolies and guild members who broke cartel rules.

Eleventh- and twelfth-century Swedish merchant guilds, for instance, took the trouble to penalize 'unfair commercial competition between

---

[349] Grafe (2001), 25; C. R. Phillips (1983), 261, 276.   [350] Farolfi (1998), 310–11.
[351] *Ibid.*, 311.
[352] Johnson (1982), 5–7; Gayot (1981), 108; G. Lewis (1993), 63–4.
[353] J. K. J. Thomson (1996), 93; Torras (1991), 105–6, 108, 113 with nn. 56–7.
[354] Ogilvie (1997), ch. 10.

guild members'.[355] The merchant guild of thirteenth-century Leicester prosecuted its own members for forming partnerships with outsiders so as to sell the latter's wool, and indicted outsiders for purchasing wool in the town illegally.[356] The merchant guild of thirteenth-century Newcastle under Lyme established a system for confiscating wool traded by outsiders.[357] In 1327, the York merchant guild was enforcing its compulsory staple privileges by issuing certificates authenticated with the staple seal, which were evidently regarded as essential, judging by traders' complaints over delays in certification.[358] The merchant guild of fourteenth-century Ipswich had a system for 'disfranchising' a member who violated its cartel rules, by depriving him of guild privileges for a year and a day.[359] The merchant guild of fourteenth-century Dunwich went to the trouble and expense of reporting the villagers of Walberswick to the royal authorities for buying merchandise 'contrary to the franchise of the merchant guild of Dunwich'.[360] In medieval Cologne the merchant guild drew up blacklists of merchants who sought to evade the compulsory staple, posted the lists in prominent commercial locations and denied violators access to freight cranes, purchasing halls and brokerage.[361] The merchant guild of fifteenth-century Dubrovnik (Ragusa) arranged with Bosnian feudal lords to imprison any Bosnian merchants who sought to circumvent the Dubrovnik guild's monopoly over direct trade with western Europe and the Levant.[362] The merchant guild of fifteenth-century Gdańsk (Danzig) set up a system to confiscate the wares of traders from other Prussian towns who sought to do business in 'their' market.[363] The merchant guild of seventeenth-century Lübeck established a complex system of penalties for monopoly breakers, including a schedule of fines and confiscations.[364]

The proto-industrial merchant companies also regarded their monopolies as worth enforcing. The Calwer Zeughandlungkompagnie, for instance, regularly sent inspectors out to weaving communities in the eighteenth century, confiscated smuggled cloths and penalized any of its own members who violated cartel quotas and prices.[365] The famous Austrian proto-industrial merchant company, the Linzer Wollzeugfabrik,

---

[355] E. Hoffman (1980), 38, 51.   [356] Lloyd (1977), 302–3.
[357] Gross (1890), I: 39.   [358] Lloyd (1977), 118.
[359] Calendar of usages and customs of Ipswich, 1309, abstracted by Alsford (2003), www.trytel.com/~tristan/towns/ipswich5.html, s.v. Cap. 36 'failure to pay for goods bought from strangers'.
[360] UK National Archives, Kew, PRO SC 8/258/12864, Petition from 'the People of Dunwich' to the King and Council [www.nationalarchives.gov.uk/catalogue/display cataloguedetails.asp?CATLN=7&CATID=-4735002].
[361] Kuske (1939), 38.   [362] Carter (1971), 389–90.   [363] Sarnowsky (2002), 71.
[364] Dollinger (1970), 361–2.   [365] Ogilvie (1997); Troeltsch (1897).

appointed inspectors in the eighteenth century to prevent the import and sale of worsted cloths produced by competitors, and imposed confiscation and incarceration on craftsmen selling textiles in violation of its monopoly.[366] Why would merchant guilds have expended resources on setting up elaborate systems of detection and punishment to prevent violations of monopolies which they had no desire or expectation of enforcing?

3.2.5 Legal exemptions and shares

If merchant guild monopolies were not enforced, then people should not have been willing to spend resources to circumvent them or obtain a share of them. But outsiders frequently paid for exemptions from the monopoly privileges of merchant guilds.

Woad merchants from Amiens, Corbie and Nesle, for instance, were willing to pay 50 marks annually from 1275 onwards, in order to be exempted from the various burdens placed on them by the monopoly of the London merchant guild.[367] In 1327, likewise, foreign merchants were willing to lend the English king 13s. 4d. on every sack of wool and 20s. on every last of hides in return for his exempting them from the ordinance requiring them to export via the English staple towns.[368]

Even more frequently, people were willing to pay money to obtain a share of the monopoly profits of local merchant guilds. In tenth-century Constantinople, for instance, the *archontes* (nobles or magnates) were willing to pay members of the raw-silk merchants' guild to act as their 'front men' to gain access to the market in raw silk, otherwise reserved for guild members.[369] In eleventh-century Valenciennes, non-local merchants paid to form commercial partnerships with local merchant guild members so as to share their legal monopoly over trading within a one-mile circumference of the city.[370] In thirteenth-century England and Flanders, foreign merchants illegally entered into partnerships with members of local merchant guilds 'because it constituted a means for aliens to circumvent the disabilities placed upon them by the local gild merchant'.[371] In 1235–6, the abbot and monks of Buckfastleigh agreed to pay the merchant guild of Totnes 22 pence annually in return for sharing in a subset of their trading privileges.[372] In medieval Venice, foreign merchants were willing to pay high prices for naturalization in order to circumvent the merchandising monopoly of Venetian citizens.[373] In Aragon

---

[366] Ogris (2004), 378, 381. [367] Middleton (2005), 341–2. [368] Lloyd (1977), 118.
[369] Dagron (2002), 442. [370] Planitz (1940), 25. [371] Moore (1985), 107.
[372] Gross (1890), I: 40. [373] Mueller (1997), 257, 266–7.

and Catalonia around 1400, Italian merchants were willing to pay for local citizenship in port cities in order to circumvent the discriminatory regulations of local merchant guilds.[374] Conversely, the merchant guilds of Valencia, Mallorca and Barcelona prohibited joint ventures with Italian merchants in order to prevent Italians from using Catalans as 'front men' to circumvent local guild monopolies.[375] In 1401, Venetian merchants expelled from Valencia, Barcelona and Mallorca through pressure from the local merchant guild were willing to pay fees to 'consign' their goods to one of the privileged Genoese or Pisan merchants who had been allowed to remain.[376] In the early sixteenth century, 'Greek' merchants (from Serbia, Armenia, Dalmatia, Macedonia and Albania) were willing to pay to obtain local citizenship rights in Transylvanian towns in order to evade restrictions imposed by local merchant guilds.[377]

All over medieval Europe, foreign merchants paid taxes or tolls to rulers in return for exemptions from the compulsory staple prerogatives of local merchant guilds – indicating that these monopoly prerogatives were enforced.[378]

3.2.6 Guilds limited merchant numbers and trade volumes

Finally, if local merchant guilds had not been able to enforce their monopolies, their existence should not have affected the size of the sector they claimed as their own. Guilds should not have been able to limit the number of practitioners; the emergence of new guilds or the strengthening of existing ones should not have caused trade to shrink; and the weakening or abolition of merchant guilds should not have caused it to expand.

But many local merchant guilds did succeeded in limiting entry, some even imposing a numerus clausus. Thus the fish merchants' guild established in Worms around 1100 fixed total membership at twenty-three. When one merchant died he was replaced by his next male heir, failing which the town council nominated one man so as to restore the number of members to twenty-three.[379] In the thirteenth-century Austrian town of Laufen, the salt merchants' guild fixed total membership at forty merchants in perpetuity.[380] Even when no numerus clausus was explicitly imposed, merchant guilds always restricted entry, as we have seen. This mean that they had fewer members than they would have had if entry had been open.

[374] Congdon (2003), 225 with n. 39.   [375] Fullana Ferré et al. (1998), 9.
[376] Congdon (2003), 226–7.   [377] Gecsényi (2007), 63.
[378] For examples, see Kuske (1939), 37.   [379] Seider (2005), 49.
[380] Störmer (1985), 366.

When merchant guild privileges were introduced or strengthened, trade declined. The privileges obtained by the local merchant guilds of Oslo and Tönsberg in 1508 were enforced so strictly that the volume of trade from Rostock, whose merchants were now excluded, 'diminished noticeably'.[381] Conversely, when merchant guild privileges were relaxed, previously excluded traders entered and the trade expanded. In medieval Venice, the participation of foreigners in trade increased noticeably immediately after the Black Death when the legal monopoly of the privileged Venetian citizenry was temporarily relaxed.[382] After the Florentine merchant guild lost its legal monopoly over the galley trade between its subject-city Pisa and England in 1465, there was a large influx of English, Venetian and Spanish traders, showing that the monopoly had been a binding constraint.[383] In 1621, the Venetian Senate prohibited Dubrovnik (Ragusa) merchants from exporting goods from Venice to Dubrovnik, in order to protect the monopoly of its own merchants in Split. This caused trade through Dubrovnik to slump catastrophically. In the 1640s, when the Candian War with Turkey forced Venice to relax the privileges of its own merchant colonies, trade through Dubrovnik expanded hugely.[384]

In places and periods where the German Hanse tightened its monopoly, trade shrank, and where it was relaxed, trade expanded. In the sixteenth century, the small Livonian port of Narva enjoyed an enormous – if brief – commercial expansion when it temporarily came under Russian rule and let foreign merchants trade with Russians directly instead of having to employ Hanse intermediaries.[385] In the same period, Hamburg repealed the monopolies of its local merchant guild, and permitted non-locals to trade freely among themselves and form partnerships with locals. From that point on, Hamburg, previously a relatively minor trading centre, grew rapidly, surpassing other Hanse cities that maintained their local merchant guild monopolies.[386] Lübeck was one of these, tightening the monopoly of its local merchant guild in a vain attempt to stifle unguilded Dutch and English competition, and consequently stagnating.[387] Had merchant guilds not been able to enforce their monopoly privileges, relaxing such privileges should not have made trade expand and tightening them should not have made it contract.

---

[381] Dollinger (1970), 313.   [382] Mueller (1997), 257, 266–7.
[383] Mallett (1962), 250–1, 253–4, 256–7.
[384] Carter (1971), 386–7, 393 (see esp. Figure 9 for the quantitative impact of the relaxation of the Venetian monopoly during the Candian War).
[385] Attman (1973), 73–84.   [386] Dollinger (1970), 355–6.   [387] Ibid., 355.

3.2.7   Empirical studies of local merchant guilds

This wealth of evidence has led most empirical studies to conclude that local merchant guilds enforced their monopolies. Contemporaries' complaints against guild monopolies, guilds' investment in lobbying for monopolies, guilds' demarcation conflicts with other guilds, guilds' investment in enforcement, outsiders' willingness to pay to circumvent or share guild monopolies, and the expansion of commerce when guilds lost their legal monopolies – all point towards the same conclusion: merchant guild monopolies were enforceable.

The response of some efficiency theorists in recent years has been to claim that studies adjudging guilds to be monopolists have been carried out by uncritical adherents of an outmoded ideological tradition based on eighteenth-century liberal guild critics, notably Adam Smith.[388] But the rich scholarship on the monopolies of merchant guilds cannot be so sanguinely dismissed. Studies of merchant guilds have been carried out by highly heterogeneous scholars covering the whole range of historiographical traditions and ideological approaches. They date from many eras of scholarship from the nineteenth to the twenty-first century. They include detailed micro-studies of nearly every region of pre-modern Europe – from the Mediterranean to the Baltic, from the Byzantine empire to the Low Countries and England – and cover nearly eight centuries – from c. 1000 to c. 1800. And, as we have seen, this scholarship bases its conclusion on a wide array of detailed empirical findings, for which the only coherent explanation is that merchant guilds' legal monopolies often had real, and harmful, economic effects.

Trade in the medieval Mediterranean, for instance, is described by scholars of the most various eras and traditions as involving local merchant guilds that enforced monopoly rights sufficiently to exert real effects on commerce.[389] Historians studying medieval and early modern Iberian trade also conclude that local merchant guild monopolies had an observable economic impact.[390] For England, as well, historians from many different traditions and time periods, including scholars writing in the present day, regard local merchant guilds as having enforced their monopoly rights in practice.[391] The same conclusion emerges from the historiography of the medieval Low Countries, where

---

[388] See, e.g., S. R. Epstein and Prak (2008), 1–2.

[389] Lopez (1945), 30; Ashtor (1983), 53; Lopez (1987), 349; Hunt (1994), 63; Johanek (1999), 72–3.

[390] R. S. Smith (1940), 68–9; C. R. Phillips (1983), 261; Grafe (2001), 13–14, 24; Woodward (2005); Woodward (2007).

[391] Gross (1890), I: 43; Alsford (2003); Pedersen (2006), 164–5.

local merchant guilds are described as monopolizing particular branches of trade and forming price-setting cartels.[392] Studies of merchants in the pre-modern North Sea and Baltic, too, find that local merchant guilds claimed monopoly privileges and enforced them.[393] Historians of German-speaking Central Europe writing from the late nineteenth to the late twentieth century also widely conclude that merchant guilds enforced their legal monopolies.[394] Scholars studying the proto-industrial merchant companies also find that they enforced their monopolies.[395] Consequently, most syntheses of the past six decades of scholarship also conclude that merchant guilds enforced their legal monopolies.[396]

Throughout pre-modern Europe, therefore, a huge array of empirical studies have reached the conclusion that local merchant guilds often enforced their legal monopolies in practice. This rich scholarship cannot be dismissed as mere uncritical acceptance of outmoded opposition to guilds in the tradition of Adam Smith. It represents the research of historians writing from the nineteenth century straight through to the first decade of the twenty-first century, and derives from a wide array of historiographical traditions and approaches. Many of these studies explicitly consider whether and how merchant guilds were able to enforce their monopolies, and conclude that in many contexts they were able to do so. Theories claiming that merchant guilds were not monopolists must address the heavy weight of empirical evidence – only some of it presented in this chapter – that merchant guilds enforced their monopolies in practice.

3.3   Conclusion

What do these findings say about the economic role of local merchant guilds? Were they efficient institutions established to solve problems in ways that benefited the entire economy – that increased the size of the economic pie? Or were they distributional institutions – ones set up to enable their members to get larger slices, even if they kept the pie itself smaller?

---

[392] Nitzsch (1892), 25; R. De Roover (1948a), 16; Lopez (1987), 375.
[393] Dollinger (1970), 291; Angermann (1974), 80–2; Lindberg (2004), 2; Lindberg (2009), 612, 616–18, 620–1, 626.
[394] Schultze (1908), 493; Störmer (1985), 366.
[395] Troeltsch (1897); Kisch (1972), 308; Ogilvie (1997); Boldorf (1999), esp. 9; Ogris (2004), 381; Boldorf (2006), e.g. 58–91, 100, 107–13, 150.
[396] R. L. Reynolds (1952), 361; Hibbert (1963), 211; Postan (1987), 270–1; Schütt (1980), 121; Mauro (1990), 259.

If merchant guilds enjoyed monopolies, they were not efficient institutions, since a monopoly imposes deadweight losses on the whole economy.[397] Merchant guilds might have been efficient if they did not have monopolies, and this is what efficiency theorists argue, claiming variously that merchant guilds did not even seek monopolies, that they could not have been monopolists because they permitted entry or that they enjoyed legal monopolies but did not enforce them. The evidence in this chapter makes it possible to reach a conclusion about these arguments.

First, did merchant guilds seek commercial monopolies? They did. Every merchant guild for which we have evidence obtained legal privileges granting its members exclusive rights over particular types of transaction, wares, routes or destinations. Wherever documents give detail, these privileges included rights to do all the things the theory of industrial organization predicts of a monopolist – excluding entrants, fixing artificially high selling prices, controlling supply, fixing artificially low purchase prices and imposing costs on competitors. The very existence of these legal entitlements in itself constitutes suggestive evidence that merchant guilds were monopolists. Otherwise why would they so universally have sought these precise rights?

Second, did merchant guilds permit free entry? They did not. Even the few cities where every citizen was a member of the merchant guild restricted citizenship rights to a minority of inhabitants – sometimes as few as 2 or 3 per cent. In most cities, not even everyone with citizenship could get membership in the merchant guild. Instead, merchant guilds limited admission, imposing a wide range of conditions to restrict entry. They excluded certain groups outright – foreigners, members of certain ethnic groups, adherents of certain religious confessions (especially Jews), and those hereditarily 'stained' with serfdom. They imposed economic conditions, excluding practitioners of certain occupations (such as craftsmen), those with not enough wealth, those who did not own property locally, those who could not afford high admission fees. Merchant guilds also excluded people according to their personal characteristics – gender (most excluded women), age, parental background and marital status. Finally, to limit entry even when applicants met all other requirements, merchant guilds imposed catch-all clauses of 'good reputation' or 'collective approval' by existing members. So while a merchant guild might admit particular individuals, especially if they were related to

---

[397] It is theoretically possible that merchant guilds, though not first-best efficient, were efficient in a second-best way. This possibility is explored exhaustively in Chapters 5–10.

existing members or paid high fees, no merchant guild was freely open
to all entrants. The only exceptions were guilds still formally in existence
but gradually relaxing their economic regulations and shifting towards
cultural display and sociability, as in many Dutch and English towns
after c. 1500. The vast majority of economically active merchant guilds
did not permit free entry.

Third, did merchant guilds enforce their monopolies? They did.
Although data are scarce and not all guilds have yet been investigated in
detail, where documents survive they show clearly that many merchant
guild enforced their monopolies sufficiently to have real economic effects.
Contemporaries complained about being harmed by merchant guild
monopolies. Merchant guilds themselves invested resources in lobbying governments to grant, confirm and extend their exclusive privileges.
Merchant guilds spent resources defending their monopolies against
attacks from other guilds, which in turn spent resources on attacking
those monopolies. Rival merchants protested against the exclusive rights
enjoyed by merchant guilds and invested resources in lobbying for their
diminution. Craftsmen engaged in bitter socio-political struggle with
merchant guilds, and used their own craft guilds to attack merchant
monopolies. Merchant guild members fined for violating guild regulations appealed to rulers against penalties imposed by their guilds. Suppliers compelled to sell wares to merchant guilds or accept guild-fixed
prices protested and lobbied. Outside merchants objected to merchant
guild regulations that increased their own costs. Such conflict strongly
implies that merchant guild monopolies were effective, since people do
not expend resources to attack valueless privileges.

Merchant guilds established elaborate systems for detecting and punishing violations of their monopolies, showing that they intended to
enforce them. Merchant guilds enforced their monopolies through their
own members and officers, but also mobilized enforcement from the legal
system, town governments and rulers. Non-guild members who sought to
participate in forms of trade reserved to guild members were prosecuted
and punished. Guild members who illegally undercut the monopolistic
prices set by the guild, or sought to free-ride on the guild's cartel regulations, were reported and penalized by fines, confiscation, imprisonment,
ostracism and ejection.

Outsiders spent resources circumventing merchant guild monopolies
or sub-contracting into them, revealing their belief that these monopolies
had economic value. Non-guild members were willing to pay a premium
for permission to trade in the wares and routes reserved for merchant
guilds.

It would have been senseless for so many economic agents in medieval and early modern economies to have invested such large amounts of time and money in lobbying to obtain, defend, attack, circumvent or sub-contract into valueless privileges. Their willingness to do so constitutes strong evidence that the economic privileges enjoyed by merchant guilds profited their members and imposed costs on non-members.

No enforcement regime is perfect. Merchant guild regulations were violated both by free-riding insiders and interloping outsiders. But this simply created an informal sector within which transactions were illegal, risky and high-cost.[398] It did not mean that the merchant guild had *no* economic effects, just that these effects consisted partly of excluding potential competitors altogether and partly of pushing them into the black market. Even where a particular guild's monopoly was not perfectly enforced, at best it created an informal sector of illegal trade by non-guild members whose costs and risks were higher because of the threat of prosecution. Even imperfectly enforced monopolies can exercise real economic effects. Furthermore, when merchant guild monopolies were abolished, hitherto excluded traders flowed into the trade and commerce expanded.

This evidence has led the overwhelming weight of empirical studies to conclude that merchant guilds implemented their monopolies in practice. These studies cannot be dismissed as unrepresentative: they cover the entire cross section of European economies from the tenth century through to the early nineteenth. Nor can they be written off as actu-ated by outmoded prejudices: they are carried out by historians from a wide range of national historiographies and ideological traditions, writing across a wide variety of periods from the nineteenth century through to the twenty-first. Nor can these studies be dismissed as uncritical, since most of them explicitly consider the question of whether merchant guild monopolies were enforced, and, based on a wide variety of empirical indicators, conclude that they were.

This leads to a final question. Merchant guilds did exercise monopo-lies, and these had real effects on the economy. Did these monopolies, real as they were, nonetheless bring economic benefits in their train? Was it true, as some have argued, that the monopoly profits enjoyed by mer-chant guilds provided incentives for their members to commit themselves to beneficial forms of collective action that increased economic efficiency

---

[398] On these characteristics of the informal sector, see Batini et al. (2010); Todaro (1989), 270–1; ILO (1989); Ogilvie (2007b), 671–4.

in other ways?[399] Did merchant guilds and their social capital solve market imperfections that would otherwise have stifled trade and economic growth?

This is a question that can only be answered by examining the particular types of market in which merchants and their guilds operated, assessing the extent of the imperfections in these markets, investigating what merchant guilds did about them and exploring the feasible institutional alternatives. This book undertakes this project – but first it turns its attention to the other main type of merchant guild, the alien merchant guilds, hanses privileged and companies formed as offshoots of local merchant guilds to operate in the polities of rulers other than their own. As we shall see in the next chapter, the two types of merchant guild – local and alien – were closely interdependent and must be analysed in tandem.

---

[399] If this was the case, then merchant guilds might have been second-best efficient, even though the evidence of this chapter makes clear that they were not first-best efficient.

4   Alien merchant guilds and companies

> All the Trade of the Merchants of the Staple, of the merchant Strangers, and of all other English Merchants, concerning th'exportation of all the Commodities of Wooll into those Countries where the same are especially to bee vented, is in the Power of the Merchants Aduenturours only...
>
> (Gerard de Malynes, 1622)[1]

Most merchant guilds were formed by local traders who got privileges from their home rulers. But some local merchant guilds formed branches abroad, where they also got privileges from foreign rulers. Contemporaries gave groups of foreign merchants living abroad various names: colony, community, nation, consulate, consulado, guild, corporation, *universitas*, *societas*,[2] *fondaco*, *massaria*, *Hof*. An alien merchant colony, community or nation might (or might not) include other people from that place of origin alongside merchants, and the merchants it included might (or might not) organize themselves into a corporate group and obtain commercial privileges from the foreign ruler. By contrast, a consulate, consulado, guild, corporation, *universitas* or *societas* typically consisted specifically of merchants who had formed a corporate group and secured commercial privileges from a ruler.[3] A *fondaco*, *massaria* or *Hof* was a dwelling or compound in which a group of foreign merchants chose to reside – or was obliged to do so. Once that happened, they were often (though not always) formally constituted as a corporate entity with commercial privileges.[4] For simplicity and ease of reference to the literature,

---

[1] Quoted in Gross (1890), I: 151.

[2] *Societas* was also used to refer to a merchant firm, so close attention to context is required to distinguish guilds from firms.

[3] On the distinction between the looser 'nation' and the more specific 'consulate', with particular application to Spanish merchant groups in medieval Bruges, see Maréchal (1953), 6.

[4] For a discussion of this issue, with particular application to the Genoese merchant community in medieval Bruges, see Henn (1999), 134–5.

we shall use a single term, 'alien merchant guild', while remaining alert to differences among these variants.[5]

Occasionally, as Chapter 2 discussed, the merchant guilds of a group of towns formed a 'hanse' – a joint organization representing all their members. Some joint associations were temporary and opportunistic, while others were formally constituted as hanses – notably what was to become the best-known of them all, the German Hanse. Since both the economics and the history literature routinely refers to the German Hanse as a 'merchant guild', this book follows that practice, while pointing out how a hanse differed from a simple guild representing the merchants of only a single home city.[6]

The early modern period saw the survival of some traditional alien merchant guilds and hanses – the most obvious being the German Hanse and the Spanish consulados. The Hanse continued to hold its periodic Diets until 1669 and did not close its last main Kontor (counting house or branch office), the one in the Norwegian town of Bergen, until 1776.[7] The Spanish consulados did not begin to break down until the final decades of the eighteenth century, and the last ones survived in Spain itself until 1829 and in most Spanish American colonies until independence in the 1820s. In parts of Latin America, merchant consulados were restored after independence, surviving in Argentina until 1862, Guatemala until 1871, Chile until 1875 and Peru until 1887.[8]

But the early modern period also saw a new type of organization formed by long-distance merchants – the regulated or chartered company. These privileged merchant companies differed from traditional alien merchant guilds and hanses in obtaining privileges mainly from their home governments, although they often also secured them from foreign rulers. In this, they resembled the alien merchant guilds and hanses of the medieval period. To provide a full account of long-distance merchant organizations, we also examine these privileged merchant companies, while paying due heed to their distinctive characteristics.

---

[5] The literature on corporate organizations formed by merchants in alien trading centres uses the term 'merchant guild' for both hanses and single-city merchant groupings; see, e.g., Greif, Milgrom and Weingast (1994), 758; Grafe and Gelderblom (2010a), 481. On some of the penumbra of meanings attached to different terms for corporative merchant organizations, see, on *nationes*, Kahl (1978), esp. 63–5, and Maréchal (1953), 6; and on *societates* and *universitates*, Michaud-Quantin (1970), esp. 11–15.

[6] The German Hanse, for instance, is treated as a merchant guild for analytical purposes in Dam (2006), 5; Fehr and Harbord (2007), 8, 12, 19; Volckart and Mangels (1999), 437, 441; Grafe and Gelderblom (2010a), 481, 483 n. 10, 484 n. 12, 486 n. 15, 492, 494, 497, 505; Greif, Milgrom and Weingast (1994), 758–62, 773; Greif (2006b), 225; Lindberg (2008), 645–7, 649–50; Lindberg (2009), 605–6.

[7] Burckhardt (2005), 69.   [8] Woodward (2007), 1579.

Alien merchant guilds, hanses and privileged companies were much less widespread than local merchant guilds. As we shall see in Chapter 5, only a tiny fraction of pre-modern trade crossed political frontiers. Many European towns had no long-distance traders and thus no occasion to form foreign branches of local merchant guilds.[9] But alien merchant guilds, hanses and privileged companies attract a lot of scholarly attention. Because they were often *associated* with international trade, they are thought to have *encouraged* it by solving problems posed by trading in foreign lands.

Proponents of this efficiency view dismiss the idea that alien merchant guilds were monopolists, variously claiming that they did not seek monopolies at all,[10] that they weren't monopolists since entry into the guild was permitted,[11] that they enjoyed monopolies in law but couldn't enforce them in practice,[12] or that their longevity shows they weren't monopolists since inefficiency causes all monopolies to collapse in time.[13]

On the other hand, alien merchant guilds did erect barriers to entry in foreign trade. To trade as a merchant in a medieval European city, you had to qualify under one of three headings. (1) If you were a local inhabitant, you had to be a member of the local merchant guild (or citizenry with merchant trading privileges). (2) If you were non-local and your home city had an alien merchant guild in the place where you wanted to trade, you had to be a member of that guild. This meant (as we shall see shortly) that you had to be a member of your local merchant guild back home. (3) If you were non-local and your home city did *not* have an alien merchant guild in the place where you wanted to trade, you had to apply either to the alien guild of an allied city for associate membership, or to the ruler of the trading centre for a trading privilege as an individual. Neither was typically granted unless you were a member of your local merchant guild back home. Only members of merchant guilds, therefore, were entitled to trade as foreign merchants in a medieval European city. At periodic fairs and markets, permission to trade was often less regulated. Liberal fair authorities often let foreign merchants trade at fairs without forming alien guilds or proving their home guild membership. This was the practice at the Champagne fairs until the first alien merchant guilds appeared in 1245, and even after that date many merchants

---

[9] Chapter 6 provides a detailed discussion of the relative importance of short- and long-distance trade and its implications for understanding merchant guilds.

[10] As claimed for medieval Flemish merchant guilds by Lambert and Stabel (2005).

[11] As argued for medieval merchant guilds in general by Greif, Milgrom and Weingast (1994), 757 with n. 12.

[12] E.g. in Jenks (2005), 31–4.

[13] As argued for the German Hanse by Selzer and Ewert (2001), 136; and Jenks (2005), 33.

frequented the fairs without guild representation there.[14] But to trade in a foreign place when the special freedoms of a periodic fair or market were not in force typically meant proving guild membership, privileges from a ruler or both. So entry to long-distance merchant trading was not free.

On top of this, an alien merchant guild often enjoyed additional legal privileges over specific lines of trade. For one thing, as we saw in Chapter 3, any local merchant guild enjoyed a legal monopoly over many aspects of trade from that locality. So members of its foreign branches also enjoyed exclusive rights over particular lines of trade emanating from the home town. Such exclusive rights were commercially important, since long-distance merchants often 'specialised in commodities closely linked to their mother-city's economic fortunes'.[15]

Furthermore, many alien merchant guilds also got rulers of international trading centres to grant them monopolies over particular lines of trade, excluding other merchants, even members of local merchant guilds. Notable examples are the Venetian merchant guild's monopolies in medieval Constantinople and the German Hanse's monopolies in medieval England.

Finally, an alien merchant guild might enjoy, by virtue of a legal monopoly granted by a foreign ruler to one of its *other* branches abroad, an exclusive right over a particular line of trade. So the German Hanse Kontor in Bruges might monopolize supplies of Russian goods because of the monopolies enjoyed by the Hanse Kontor in Novgorod. Or the Genoese merchant guild in Valencia might monopolize supplies of Black Sea exotica because of the monopoly enjoyed by the Genoese merchant colony in the Black Sea port of Caffa.

An alien merchant guild's legal monopoly over a particular good from its home town (or some other source) would not matter so much if that good was available from lots of other sources. Even if the guild was a sole supplier and its members were forbidden to compete with one another, members of *other* merchant guilds would provide competition, as long as they could obtain a supply of the good and get permission to trade. So an alien merchant guild's monopolies were most effective where its members' merchandise had no good substitutes available in a particular place. If an alien merchant guild came from a home town with a favourable geographical position – which Chapter 3 showed many major trading cities

---

[14] Bourquelot (1865), I: 151, 164–5, 174; 1245 saw the first references to consuls at the fairs (for Siena and for Montpellier); from 1278 dates the first reference to a *universitas* (joint association) of Italian merchants at the fairs; additional Italian and Provençal merchant consuls were also recorded between 1250 and 1300; but other merchants never formed guilds at the fairs.

[15] Abulafia (1987a), 55.

had – its members could enjoy cost advantages, making them the sole viable suppliers of certain goods abroad. Non-members could not compete with guild members because of cost disadvantages, and members could not compete with one another because of guild rules, so the guild was a monopolist. Likewise, if a merchant guild's home town enjoyed low transport costs to a given foreign trading centre this could create cost advantages, making that guild the sole viable supplier of certain goods to that destination. Together with guild rules preventing competition among members, this enabled the guild to act as a monopolist. Or if resource endowments meant that a guild's home territory was the lowest-cost producer of a good, its members might be the sole viable suppliers of that good in many trading centres, barred by guild rules from competing with each other. If political enmities, warfare or customs barriers increased the risks and costs of alternative supplies, a particular alien merchant guild could find itself the sole feasible supplier of certain goods to certain destinations, and its internal rules would ensure that its members did not compete with one another. Finally, if a particular alien merchant guild obtained a monopoly abroad over a good available from a single source, then its branches in every international trading centre might become the only viable suppliers of that good, and guild rules would ensure that its members did not compete these monopoly profits away.

A number of important internationally traded goods were affected by these factors – geographical advantages, transport costs, resource endowments, warfare, customs barriers and monopolies granted to merchant guilds by distant rulers. In combination with such factors, rules outlawing competition among guild members could create monopolies or oligopolies, in which particular goods were handled by few traders and thus not traded competitively. The favourable geographical position of a city like Venice, for instance, could create advantages enabling its merchant guilds abroad to be effective monopolists in certain goods because merchants from no other town could compete on cost and the internal rules of Venetian merchant colonies prevented their members from competing with each other.[16] The unusual cheapness or fineness of English or Spanish wool could create cost advantages enabling the legal monopoly (and anti-competitive rules) of the Merchant Adventurers or the Burgos consulado over wool exports from England or Spain to translate into an effective monopoly abroad.[17] The legal privileges the Venetian merchant guild in Constantinople got from the Byzantine emperor could make

---

[16] On dominance over markets for particular wares by the Venetian merchant guild in Bruges, see Stabel (1999), 34.
[17] On dominance over wool markets created by the English wool staple in Antwerp and the Spanish wool staple in Bruges, see Harreld (2004a), 21–2, 57.

the Venetian merchant guild in Bruges a monopolist in exotic Levantine merchandise, while the privileges the German Hanse got in Novgorod could turn its Kontor in London into a monopolist in Russian furs and wax. The legal rights the Teutonic Order (a Hanse member) enjoyed over amber combined with the rich amber deposits in its territory to turn Hanse merchants into monopolists of amber in many trading centres.[18] Even in such a highly competitive forum as fifteenth-century Antwerp, Brulez describes spices, copper and alum as being 'products which were parts of monopolies in the hands of a few traders only', in contrast to butter and fish in which 'a great many people and in particular many small merchants traded'.[19]

Even on goods not susceptible to geographical monopolies or legal privileges, the entirety of merchant guilds in a particular city could still exercise a collective near-monopoly, especially if no unguilded merchants were allowed to trade there. Since merchant guilds limited entry and restricted internal competition, the only type of competition that could arise was between different merchant guilds. If only a small number of different merchant guilds was involved in supplying a particular good – for instance, because of geography, transportation costs, resource endowments, war, customs barriers and so on – the outcome would be an oligopoly and it is likely, though not certain, that there would still be monopoly profits. If a very large number of different merchant guilds was involved in supplying a particular good, the outcome might come quite close to competition. Theory alone does not state where the line can be drawn between oligopoly and competition. So we need evidence about whether, in international trading centres with multiple merchant guilds, monopoly profits could be gained by an alien merchant guild, either on goods subject to its own specific legal monopoly or on goods subject to the legal oligopoly enjoyed by all local and alien guilded merchants in that city.

This chapter analyses the evidence available to answer these questions. It begins by addressing the first two arguments advanced by efficiency views of merchant guilds. Did alien merchant guilds seek legal monopolies, or not? And were guilds open to entry so that no legal monopoly could have been effective? It finds a wealth of evidence that alien merchant guilds, just like the local ones of which they were branches, sought legal monopolies and enjoyed the right to exclude entrants. This in itself is suggestive evidence that alien merchant guilds were monopolists, since otherwise one must explain why they universally sought entitlements in law which they then refrained from enforcing in practice.

---

[18] Wernicke (1999), 197. [19] Brulez (1973), 11.

Some scholars nonetheless claim that merchant guilds did not enforce their legal monopolies. The second section of the chapter therefore examines the direct evidence bearing upon this question. Although alien merchant guilds could not always implement their monopolies perfectly, we find that they were able to do so in enough places and time periods to generate monopoly profits for their members and impose costs on outsiders.

This finding provides the first step towards an alternative explanation for alien merchant guilds' longevity – they *redistributed* benefits to their members and other powerful people. This redistributive activity was inefficient: alien merchant guild monopolies transferred resources from outsiders and the economy at large to guild members and the politically powerful. But those harmed by guilds' redistributive activities were too numerous, diffused and powerless to organize to eliminate the inefficiency. Those benefiting from guilds' redistributive activities, by contrast, were few, well-organized and powerful, with strong incentives to act collectively to keep alien merchant guilds in existence for centuries. Chapter 5 will explore these incentives in depth.

4.1   Did alien merchant guilds seek legal monopolies?

The theory of industrial organization predicts that a monopolist should engage in certain activities – the same ones Chapter 3 examined for local merchant guilds. Did alien merchant guilds do the same things?

4.1.1   *Exclusive rights to trade*

First, legal monopolists claim exclusive entitlements to engage in particular economic activities. Alien merchant guilds certainly did this. As we saw in Chapter 3, someone could only trade in a pre-modern European town if he got a legal permit from the local ruler. For a local, this meant being a member of the local merchant guild (or merchant-privileged citizenry on the Venetian model). For a non-local, it meant being a member of the appropriate alien merchant guild – unless one's home town had no merchant guild in that trading centre, in which case one applied for an individual 'guest' privilege by virtue of one's local merchant guild membership back home.

An alien merchant guild was not a 'voluntary organization', any more than a local merchant guild was.[20] If you wanted to trade as a merchant,

---

[20] Contrary to its portrayal in North (1991), e.g., 25, 30, 33; or Greif, Milgrom and Weingast (1994), 759.

you had to join; if it wouldn't let you in (or kicked you out), you couldn't trade: 'The [merchant] firm could not function unless one or more members belonged . . . to the "nation" or like body in any foreign center where it had an agent or partner.'[21] The alien merchant guild had the exclusive right to represent and regulate merchants from its home territory in a particular international trading centre.

As De Roover summarizes it for the Lucca merchant guild in Bruges,

Membership in the 'university' [merchant guild] was not optional, but compulsory for every Lucchese resident in Bruges. Those who refused to join were ostracized and exposed themselves to commercial boycott. The same fate was held in store for those who disobeyed the orders of the consul and were expelled from the 'university'.[22]

In medieval Antwerp, likewise, 'identification with a merchant nation was necessary if a foreign merchant was to operate'. As soon as a foreign merchant came to Antwerp, he had to get a high-status member of the relevant alien merchant 'nation' (sometimes supported by a member of the local Antwerp merchant guild) to vouch for him to the city alderman, who issued a certificate permitting him to trade as a member of that alien merchant guild.[23] Likewise, any merchant from a German Hanseatic city who visited Bruges, Novogorod, Bergen or London was obliged to prove his Hanse membership, register with the local Hanse Kontor, lodge within its walled precinct (except in Bruges), and submit to its prices, quotas and trading regulations.[24]

Similar involuntary procedures prevailed in the great Mediterranean trading centres. Among German merchants in medieval Venice,

It was not left up to the discretion of the individual whether or not he wished to live in the Fondaco [dei Tedeschi]. Rather, the Republic required of each German merchant that he alight there and make use of no other hostel; it obliged the boatmen to deliver new German arrivals to no other location than at the Fondaco. Only thus did the Signoria believe it could properly monitor the trade and conduct of these merchants, collect tolls securely, and prevent harm to indigenous industry.[25]

The same applied to Italian merchant guilds in medieval Provence. In order to be readmitted to a Piacenzan firm in Montpellier in 1278, Pietro Rondana was required to swear the oath required of the 'community of merchants of Tuscany and Lombardy' (the Italian merchant guild in Montpellier).[26] In fourteenth- and fifteenth-century Egypt and Syria,

[21] R. L. Reynolds (1952), 361.
[22] R. De Roover (1948a), 18; see also Mirot (1927), 65–6.
[23] Harreld (2004a), 45–6 (quotation 45); Grafe and Gelderblom (2010a), 492.
[24] Dollinger (1970), 99.   [25] Heyd (1874), 200.   [26] Bautier (1987), 224 n. 98.

likewise, Venetian merchant factors were obliged to register at the office of the consul of the relevant Venetian merchant colony, and indicate which Venetian merchants they represented.[27]

Some medieval towns compelled their merchants not only to *join* the relevant merchant guild abroad, but to *establish* such a guild. Medieval Cologne and Lübeck, for instance, commanded that 'as soon as four merchants found themselves together in a foreign town, they were to elect an alderman and obey him'.[28] A 1255 statute ordered that if more than twenty Marseille citizens found themselves in a foreign locality, they were to elect a consul.[29] A 1258 ordinance obliged any group of Barcelona merchants sailing abroad to elect two *proceres* (or 'consules') to exercise authority over the group's commercial decisions during the voyage and at the destination.[30] A 1274 law required that if three or more Amalfitan merchants were in a locality they had to elect a consul.[31] The medieval Piacenza statutes provided that if more than three of its merchants (or ten of its citizens) appeared in a foreign place, a consul must be appointed.[32] Medieval Florentine ordinances fixed at twelve the number of merchants whose presence triggered compulsory appointment of a consul in a foreign trading centre; for Ancona, it was six merchants; for Pisa, five.[33] Appointing a consul over a group of merchants typically implied forming a corporative association to regulate economic decisions internally and seek privileges externally.[34]

An alien merchant guild claimed the sole right to represent merchants from the home town, and hence to wield all the monopoly privileges the local merchant guild back home enjoyed from its ruler. But many alien merchant guilds also got *foreign* rulers to grant them exclusive rights over particular branches of trade. This created monopoly profits not just for that particular branch of the merchant guild, but for its other international offshoots.

The Mediterranean was the first seat of the medieval Commercial Revolution, and shows clear evidence of legal monopolies for alien merchant guilds. By the early twelfth century, for instance, the Venetian merchant guild in Constantinople enjoyed a special licence from the Byzantine emperor to buy and export silk fabrics, a licence still denied to the Genoese merchant guild as late as 1170.[35] Then, in 1204, the Venetian merchant colony in Constantinople got a monopoly from the Fourth Crusade administration over all trade onwards to the Black Sea, enabling

---

[27] Ashtor (1983), 403.   [28] Dollinger (1970), 105.
[29] Goldschmidt (1891), 183 n. 146.   [30] Hibbert (1949), 354–5.
[31] Goldschmidt (1891), 183 n. 146.   [32] *Ibid.*   [33] *Ibid.*   [34] *Ibid.*, 183–94.
[35] Lopez (1945), 40.

Venetian merchant guilds throughout Europe to monopolize supplies of many eastern exotica.[36] Half a century later, the newly reinstated Byzantine emperor transferred this monopoly to the Genoese merchant guild, whose branches all over Europe rejoiced in the resulting dominance over markets in particular trade goods.[37] From the late thirteenth to the mid-fourteenth century,'Genoese merchants enjoyed a monopoly from the Byzantine emperor over exports of alum, enabling them to reap monopoly profits in western European markets where that chemical compound was crucial for textile production. In 1455, when the Ottomans took over the Byzantine alum mines, they granted the monopoly to the Venetian merchant guild, which profited from it until 1463.[38] In the fourteenth and fifteenth centuries, the crown of Cyprus granted the Genoese merchant community a legal monopoly over exports of 'Orient camelots' (angora textiles of camel's or goat's hair), giving them market power over these rare and costly textiles in western markets.[39] In the Iberian peninsula, trade between Christian and Muslim territories was characterized by legal monopolies for alien merchant groups, as in 1417 when a group of six Christian merchants from Valencia signed an agreement with the Muslim king of Granada 'to gain a monopoly on all the silk, that is, so that no other merchants, Christian, Moors and Jews, and others, can buy any silk or silk cloth in the kingdom of Granada except from the above mentioned'.[40]

Medieval north-west Europe also saw alien merchant guilds seeking legal monopolies. The Flemish 'Seventeen Towns' was a hanse of textile-producing cities that claimed exclusive rights to export cloth from Flanders to France and the Mediterranean in the thirteenth century.[41] The 'Hanse of Ghent' had the exclusive legal right to trade between Ghent and the Rhineland in the same period, giving its German branches monopoly power over goods for which Ghent was the sole supplier.[42] The German Hanse got monopoly rights from rulers in England, Scandinavia and Russia over specific routes and destinations from the twelfth century on.[43] In 1366, its privileges from Russian rulers enabled it to declare explicitly that 'nobody shall visit Novgorod who does not share in the privileges

---

[36] Spruyt (1994), 146.   [37] *Ibid.*
[38] Hunt and Murray (1999), 183; Briys and De ter Beerst (2006), 21, 47, 51, 53–4.
[39] Heers (1971), 1107.
[40] Quoted in Salicrú i Lluch (2001), 296 n. 32. It is unclear whether the merchants in question consisted of the entire Valencian merchant community in Granada or only a privileged sub-group. The fact that several of the group acted as official diplomatic emissaries between the king of Aragon and the king of Granada (*ibid.*, 298–300) may indicate that they held official positions in the Catalo-Aragonese colony in Granada, in which Valencians formed the most numerous faction (*ibid.*, 302).
[41] Stabel (1997), 139–40.   [42] *Ibid.*, 140.   [43] Spruyt (1994), 112.

or [sic] the Hanse of the Germans'.[44] In turn, the Hanse's privileges
from Novgorod rulers gave its other European branches a monopoly
over Russian furs, wax and other primary products.[45] Its privileges from
the Norwegian crown gave all the Hanse's European branches the legal
right to monopolize supplies of goods from Norway.[46] On the peninsula
of Skåne (Scania), the Danish crown granted a series of German, Danish and Dutch merchant guilds the exclusive 'concession' to process and
export herring, giving other European branches of these guilds monopolies over this key comestible for Christian fast days.[47] Ultimately, the
German Hanse induced the Danish crown to grant it exclusive control
over the Skåne fair, enabling it to exclude merchants from Scotland,
England, Flanders and France and to entrench its monopoly over Baltic
products in western Europe.[48]

Another variant was the English wool staple on the European continent. This was a set of exclusive legal privileges for English wool
merchants, originally granted by the king of England, although also confirmed by rulers of the continental localities successively designated as
the staple centres.[49] In the later thirteenth century, for fiscal reasons,
the English crown encouraged English merchants to export wool to a
particular continental town (sequentially Abbeville, St Omer, Antwerp
and Dordrecht), and many merchants did so, but there was no legal
obligation.[50] In the 1290s, the staple town was Antwerp, and English
merchants trading there received a charter from the duke of Brabant
allowing them to hold assemblies and courts and later to elect a 'mayor';
but this emerging merchant body appears to have remained open and not
yet to have enjoyed any legal monopoly.[51] In 1305, the English merchants
trading in Brabant formed a 'semi-corporate' community, elected a leader
called the 'mayor of the merchants' and may have begun using the word
'staple' to refer to their centre of operations in Antwerp.[52] This turned
into a 'compulsory' staple in 1313, when the king of England ordered
all merchants wishing to export wool to Brabant, Flanders and Artois
to send their wares to a particular locality on the continent, to become
members of a corporate group called the 'Staplers' or the 'Company of
the Staple', and to submit to the regulation of 'the mayor and common-
alty of the staple'.[53] The compulsory staple locality was designated as St
Omer in 1314, moving subsequently to different centres such as Antwerp

---

[44] Dollinger (1970), 404, document 19.   [45] *Ibid.*   [46] Postan (1987), 271.
[47] Irsigler (2002), 48; Dollinger (1970), 239–40; Christensen (1953), 249–52.
[48] Rowell (2000), 726; Irsigler (2002), 48.   [49] Häpke (1908), 223–4.
[50] Power (1941), 95–6; Häpke (1908), 67–9; Lloyd (1977), 58, 101ff.
[51] Power (1941), 96.   [52] Lloyd (1977), 102.
[53] Power (1941), 96; Lloyd (1977), 102 (quotation).

and Bruges according to geopolitical and commercial interests of English monarchs, foreign rulers and factions within the Staplers.[54]

At first the compulsory English wool staple was implemented inconsistently, but by the 1320s it was being enforced strictly enough to cause conflict inside and outside the Company.[55] The key issue was the Company's desire for a monopoly over selling English wool on the continent, which

> would enable them to oust the competition of foreign exporters by making these bring their wool from England to the staple instead of taking it straight to customers in Flanders, Holland, Brabant or Italy... They... wanted a merchant company composed of themselves in order to get the most possible out of the buyers on the continent. The company of the staple would enable them to squeeze the buyers by means of concerted prices...[56]

The privileges granted to the Company made its members the sole legal suppliers of English wool to the continent during long phases of the fourteenth and fifteenth century, except for a few non-Staplers who bought costly exemptions from the crown. The Staplers' monopoly rights only dissolved in the second half of the sixteenth century, as the Company progressively lost the support of both the English and the Dutch governments.[57]

In some branches of trade, European rulers continued to grant monopolies to alien merchant guilds into the early modern period. In the late fifteenth and early sixteenth century, for instance, the Portuguese merchant guild in Antwerp enjoyed a legal monopoly over pepper and spices from Portuguese colonies.[58] In 1619, the Shah of Persia auctioned off the monopoly over exporting Persian silk, with the Armenian merchant guild in New Julfa and the English East India Company as the top bidders. The Armenian merchant guild won the export right and combined it with transit privileges from foreign (e.g. Russian) rulers to monopolize Persian silk supplies in many European trading centres for the rest of the seventeenth century.[59] In 1665, the Habsburg governor of Hungary granted 'Greek' merchants a monopoly over trade beyond the river Tisza, excluding all other merchants.[60] Thus even after 1500 when international trade within Europe, at least, was becoming more competitive due to the gradual expansion of legal interstices where unguilded merchants could trade, some alien merchant guilds still managed to secure extensive monopolies from foreign and home rulers.

---

[54] Häpke (1908), 67–9; Lloyd (1977), 102, 108; Power (1941), 92–3, 96.
[55] Lloyd (1977), 111–20. [56] Power (1941), 89. [57] Willan (1959), ch. 2.
[58] Mauro (1990), 263. [59] Aslanian (2004), 42, 49. [60] Gecsényi (2007), 68.

The rise of the European intercontinental trade after *c*. 1500 also saw the emergence of new merchant bodies with exclusive privileges over particular goods, routes and destinations. Sometimes existing merchant guilds just expanded their privileges. The Spanish crown, for instance, granted exclusive rights over trade with America to the consulado (merchant guild) of Seville in 1550, and transferred them to the Cádiz consulado in 1680.[61] But it also devised new monopolistic instruments such as the *asiento*, a monopoly over supplying Spanish America with slave labour, which it sold to a series of Dutch and English merchant associations in the seventeenth and eighteenth centuries.[62]

Most other European economies saw the rise after *c*. 1500 of a new type of merchant organization, the regulated or chartered company, which got exclusive rights over trade between the homeland and specific overseas destinations. In 1555, for instance, the English Muscovy Company got a royal monopoly over trade between England and Russia.[63] In 1600 the English East India Company got a royal monopoly over trade between England and the East, initially for fifteen years but then renewed periodically until 1858.[64] In 1672, the Hudson's Bay Company got a royal charter giving it 'a monopoly position within England to carry on a fur trade in Hudson Bay', which was renewed periodically until 1870.[65]

The Dutch Republic granted similar monopolies to privileged merchant companies to trade overseas. The Dutch East India Company, for instance, enjoyed a legal monopoly over trade between the Netherlands and Asia from 1602 to 1798.[66] In 1621, the Dutch West India Company got a monopoly over trade with the west coast of Africa below the Tropic of Cancer and the entire New World; after its re-establishment in 1674 it renewed its legal monopoly periodically until 1791.[67]

The Portuguese government granted monopolies over trade with Brazil to a series of privileged companies. The Companhia Geral de Comércio do Brasil was founded in 1649 with a colonial monopoly over wine, flour, olive oil and salt cod trading. The Companhia do Grão-Pará e Maranhão was founded in 1755 with a twenty-year renewable monopoly over all commerce between Portugal, Africa and Brazil's Amazon captaincies.[68] In establishing the Companhia do Grão-Pará e Maranhão, the Portuguese prime minister explicitly aimed 'to restore [to] the merchant places of Portugal and Brazil the commissions of which they were

---

[61] K. Weber (2004), 104.   [62] Schnurmann (2003), 492; K. Weber (2004), 105 n. 72.
[63] Truitt (2006), 3.
[64] Hejeebu (2005), 515–16; Pearson (1991), 90; Truitt (2006), 4–5.
[65] Carlos and Nicholas (1990), 860.
[66] De Vries and Van der Woude (1997), 384–5; Truitt (2006), 3.
[67] De Vries and Van der Woude (1997), 399, 465.   [68] Maxwell (2001), 172–3.

deprived, and which are the principle substance of commerce, and the means by which there could be established the great merchant houses which had been lacking in Portugal'.[69]

Alien merchant guilds, hanses and privileged companies therefore satisfy the first theoretical prediction for a monopolist. They obtained exclusive rights for their members to practise particular commercial activities. The minimum content of these privileges was an exclusive entitlement for an alien merchant guild's members to trade as merchants from a particular mother city or territory in a particular foreign location, and thus to exercise all the legal monopoly rights of their local merchant guild back home – as far as they could enforce them. On top of that, many alien merchant guilds also obtained *additional* legal monopolies from rulers abroad. Even in a large trading centre where an alien merchant guild faced rival merchant guilds, whose members were legally entitled to compete with it, its monopoly privileges could be made effectual in so far as it enjoyed geographical or political advantages restricting supplies of equivalent substitutes, since merchant guilds typically forbade competition among their own members – as we shall see.

4.1.2 Restricting entry

A second thing monopolists do is to impose entry barriers. As we saw in Chapter 3, efficiency theorists argue that a merchant guild's exclusive trading rights did not amount to a monopoly since entry into the guild was permitted.[70] Greif, Milgrom and Weingast, for instance, claim that the Hanse was so open that 'any German merchant who arrived in a non-German city could join the local [Hanse] Kontor'.[71] This view has inspired the literature on 'private-order institutions' – ones formed through the voluntary collective action of private agents rather than involving any formal action by the public authorities – to describe merchant guilds as 'open', in the sense that there were 'no significant restrictions to becoming a member of the institution'.[72] Other scholars, by contrast, have argued that merchant guilds *required* entry restrictions in order to generate benefits. Gelderblom, for instance, describes alien merchant guilds as a 'means to solve the fundamental problems of exchange' because 'the credible threat of exclusion reduced the risks of default by guild members'.[73] Even scholars who view merchant guilds favourably, therefore, disagree about whether they restricted entry.

---

[69] Quoted in *ibid.*, 173. [70] Greif, Milgrom and Weingast (1994), 757 with n. 12.
[71] *Ibid.*, 759. [72] McMillan and Woodruff (2000), 2444.
[73] Gelderblom (2005a), 2.

Theory alone cannot decide between these incommensurate positions; we need empirical findings. Once we examine these, it becomes clear that alien merchant guilds did not permit free entry.

There were two ways to become a member of an alien merchant guild. The first was to be a member of the local merchant guild of which it was a branch. As Chapter 3 showed, local merchant guilds universally imposed entry restrictions, first by rationing admission to citizenship privileges in the town and then, usually, by rationing admission to the merchant guild as well. This was the only pathway to admission to a particular alien merchant guild if one came from that particular mother city.

A second way was to apply for associate membership. This path was *not* open to someone who had failed to get into the guild back home. But it might be open to someone from an allied city as long as he was a member of its merchant guild. Associate membership was typically limited to certain situations: the time period immediately after an alien merchant guild was set up; trading centres with comparatively few foreign merchants; and circumstances of particular risk or conflict.

In these situations, an alien merchant guild had three incentives to allow associate membership. First, admitting more members could raise the profile of the guild and hence its bargaining power vis-à-vis foreign rulers and rival guilds. Second, admitting additional members increased the guild's revenues and hence the size of transfers it could offer to rulers in exchange for privileges, as we shall see in Chapter 5. Third, admitting merchants of allied cities ensured that they would not compete with the guild's existing members but would instead be obliged to comply with the restraints on trade mandated by the guild, discussed in detail shortly.[74] But there were also countervailing incentives for merchant guilds to *refuse* to admit associate members and in normal times these predominated, as we shall see.

Unaffiliated merchants without an alien merchant guild of their own also sometimes had an incentive to seek guest membership in the alien merchant guild of another city. Guest membership could let them enjoy that guild's privileges from the foreign ruler and avoid aggression by the guild's members.[75] But these incentives were not overwhelming. Long-distance merchants whose mother city had no alien merchant guild in a particular city often did *not* seek associate membership in any other guild and voluntarily remained unaffiliated.[76]

Associate membership in alien merchant guilds was most frequently observed when trade was just beginning in a particular location. The

---

[74] Abulafia (1978), 68.   [75] For examples of such aggression, see Chapter 6 below.
[76] Abulafia (1986b), 201.

early-eleventh-century rise of trade between the continent and England, for instance, saw associate membership in Dutch and German merchant colonies in London, as shown by privileges granted by King Ethelred II to *homines imperii* from Tiel, Cologne and Bremen.[77] The earliest Italian, Catalan and French merchant colonies in the Levant were also open to associate members, although only in some cases.[78] Thus the Genoese readily granted citizenship in their Levantine merchant colonies to Latins, Greeks, Armenians, Turks and Jews, 'but the Venetians jealously excluded all outsiders'.[79] The twelfth-century rise of western European trade with Russia also saw associate membership of alien merchant guilds, with Scandinavian and German merchants initially forming a joint colony in Novgorod, although by 1250 the German merchants had broken away and founded the independent, purely German Petershof.[80] Similarly, during the early phase of the Skåne herring fairs in the thirteenth century, traders from more remote regions set up shared compounds: the Danzig (Gdańsk) compound was used by merchants from all six Prussian towns, the Briel compound by merchants from the whole Netherlandish province of Voorne and the Amsterdam compound by merchants from the entirety of north Holland.[81] Likewise, around 1300 when Italian merchants began voyaging up the Atlantic coast to north-west Europe, Genoa opened a merchant consulate in Seville which admitted associate members from Piacenza, although by 1350 Piacenza had set up its own independent merchant organization in Seville.[82]

Associate membership was also sometimes observed in contexts of conflict and threat, when a particular alien merchant guild felt a need for extra numbers or support. Venice usually required merchants to prove full Venetian citizenship before they could to become members of Venetian merchant guilds abroad, but in the later fourteenth century the Senate exceptionally permitted the Venetian consulate at Tana on the Black Sea to create new 'associate' Venetian citizens in order to establish a more substantial presence in the face of mounting aggression from the Golden Horde and the rival Genoese merchant colony at Caffa.[83] But 'associate' rights were strictly limited to fifty applicants who had to prove

---

[77] Dollinger (1970), 5–6.

[78] Ashtor (1983), 68, 135, 138, 142, 145–6, 148, 237–8; Abulafia (1986b), 211–12.

[79] Lopez (1987), 351.   [80] Angermann (1987), 62; Dollinger (1970), 7.

[81] Christensen (1953), 249.   [82] Bautier (1987), 209.

[83] The Golden Horde (also known as the Mongol Khanate) was a dynasty that ruled much of Eastern Europe from the 1240s until it began to disintegrate in 1359, finally collapsing in 1396. Its territory extended from the Danube to the Urals and from Siberia to the Black Sea and the Caucasus Mountains.

they were merchants, had 'Latin' origins and knew the Latin language; their associate membership was valid only in the territory controlled by the Golden Horde and not transferrable to other Venetian merchant colonies, let alone Venice itself.[84] Likewise, the Venetian merchant guild in Constantinople began in the sixteenth century to permit associate membership in order to keep Venice's Levantine trade alive in the face of growing French, English, Dutch, Ottoman and Jewish competition.[85] External threats also made Hanseatic merchants willing to share a colony in Pskov (Pleskau) with White Russian and Dutch merchants immediately after the Livonian War ended in 1583, although three years later Lübeck merchants broke away to form their own exclusive guild.[86]

Alien merchant guilds thus did grant associate membership in special circumstances. But they typically ceased to do so as time passed. Rulers of international trading centres preferred the merchants of each foreign city to establish their own separate guild, so as to increase the number of corporate entities offering payments in exchange for commercial privileges, as well as to decrease the bargaining power of any one guild, in a spirit of 'divide and rule'. In medieval Constantinople, for instance, the Byzantine regency permitted a mixed colony of Russian merchants to settle in 944, but required merchants from each Russian town to register separately.[87] In 992, the Golden Bull issued by the Byzantine emperors granted special trading privileges to the Venetian merchant guild in Constantinople but forbade it to admit associates from Amalfi or Bari.[88] In Acre in 1257, rulers ordered the Anconitan merchant guild 'to search out and remove from their midst all pseudo-Anconitans' and henceforth to restrict membership to men of Ancona and its surrounding area.[89] European rulers were always demanding that the German Hanse provide a precise list of member towns, 'so that the benefits might be strictly limited to those entitled to them'.[90] By 1130, the joint London colony of the *homines imperii* had split into a Cologne guild granted special rights of residence while the Tiel and Bremen merchants were excluded.[91] In Novgorod, likewise, the German–Scandinavian colony of 1189 split into separate guilds by 1205.[92] In mid-fifteenth-century Bruges, divergent regional interests split the Spanish merchant guild into the 'nation of Vizcaya' (comprising merchants from the Cantabrian coast and other north Spanish port towns) and the 'nation of Castile' (comprising

---

[84] Doumerc (1987), 6.   [85] Dursteler (2006), 23–4, 27, 43–4, 48, 52–60, 78.
[86] Angermann (1979), 228–9.   [87] Gieysztor (1987), 489.   [88] Citarella (1968), 548.
[89] Abulafia (1986a), 539–40 (quotation); Abulafia (1997), 54–5.
[90] Dollinger (1970), 73, 87.   [91] *Ibid.*, 6.
[92] Angermann (1987), 62, 68, 74; Dollinger (1970), 26.

merchants from towns in the interior of Castile) – although the latter persisted in calling itself 'the nation of Spain in Bruges'.[93]

Most alien merchant guilds either prohibited associate membership from the start or soon came to do so. One reason was the dread – discussed in Chapter 7 – of reprisals against an entire guild when one member committed an offence. Associate members' conduct was harder to monitor and control because they were not members of the home guild.[94] The merchant colonies of Spanish cities abroad, for instance, excluded many other Spanish applicants from membership because of the 'constant fear of being embroiled in the damaging actions of a merchant of one's own nationality'.[95]

A second reason was that local merchant guilds increasingly wanted their foreign branches to deny trading privileges to competitors from rival cities with few incentives to comply with guild rules. Venice always regarded non-Venetians as potential competitors and rarely let merchants from other cities join its colonies abroad; it required its merchants to trade as part of Venetian colonies that were controlled by the home city and represented its interests exclusively.[96] The Hanse adopted a similar stance. Its precursor, the Gotland Community, included both German and Scandinavian merchants, but declined after 1200 because of rivalry between the Lübeck and Visby factions.[97] In the early thirteenth century, German merchant colonies in Novgorod and London began to exclude Scandinavian and Dutch members and strove to negotiate purely 'Hanseatic' privileges.[98] Counter to the efficiency theorists' claim that any German merchant who arrived in a foreign city could join the local Hanse Kontor,[99] by the fourteenth century at latest, the Hanse restricted admission first to those who could demonstrate their membership of a local merchant guild in a Hanse member town, and then to those who could prove they were also *born* in a Hanse town.[100] In 1365 when the aldermen of the German Hanse in Bergen asked if they might be allowed to elect to its council the best man, regardless of his citizenship status, Hanse central office decisively refused.[101]

Most alien merchant guilds did not permit associate membership at all after their formative years.[102] It swiftly became the norm for an alien

---

[93] W. D. Phillips (1986), 35.
[94] Abulafia (1988), 189–91; Abulafia (1987a), 55–6; Ashtor (1983), 411.
[95] Flórez (2003), 48.
[96] Lopez (1987), 351; Constable (2003), 117; Ashtor (1983), 240.
[97] Dollinger (1970), 43.   [98] *Ibid.*, 26.
[99] Greif, Milgrom and Weingast (1994), 759.
[100] Burckhardt (2005), 62; Dollinger (1970), 85–7.   [101] Burckhardt (2005), 62.
[102] Dollinger (1970), 85–7.

merchant guild to limit membership and thus trading rights to guilded merchants from the home city and its dominions. An alien merchant guild thus excluded most applicants via the entry restrictions of its local merchant guild at home. A man from Ghent who failed to obtain admission to his local merchant guild, for example, could not be a member of any Ghent merchant colony in any foreign trading centre, and hence could not trade there legally. Membership in the English Merchant Adventurers was contingent on membership in one of its component local guilds in English towns.[103] Such legal obligations even applied to merchants desiring to trade in a different city within the same country. In fourteenth- and fifteenth-century England, for example, citizens of Winchester had to prove they were members of the Winchester local merchant guild before they could trade as members of the 'alien' (i.e. non-local) Winchester merchant body in London.[104]

The entry barriers imposed by local merchant guilds were often stringent, as we saw in Chapter 3, and meant that men without the required characteristics could not become members of any alien merchant colony from that town. Lacking recognition by the appropriate merchant body prevented them from obtaining a licence to trade in a foreign city, since many rulers granted trading privileges only to members of the appropriate alien merchant guild.

Alien merchant guilds explicitly made use of local guild entry restrictions to exclude applicants. Expulsion from one's local merchant guild meant exclusion from any of its alien branches. In the late thirteenth century, for instance, the St Omer woollen merchants' guild declared that if anyone acted counter to the regulations of the guild he would be fined 60 libres, banished from the town for ever and 'would not be able to work in the Hanse of the Seventeen Towns'.[105] In the German Hanseatic League, as well, a town's application for membership always 'laid great stress upon the fact that the town's merchants had in former times enjoyed the privileges of the "common merchant"' – i.e. that they had always had a proper merchant guild.[106] Since all local merchant guilds in Hanseatic towns excluded craftsmen, this meant that no craftsman could become a member of a Hanseatic merchant colony abroad.[107] When Braunschweig overthrew its merchant-dominated town council in 1374, the town was expelled from the Hanse for five years. When Stralsund overthrew its patrician (i.e. merchant-guild-dominated)

---

[103] Sutton (2002), 43.   [104] Bird (1925), 11, 23.
[105] Quoted in Laurent (1935a), 93 n. 1.   [106] Dollinger (1970), 89.
[107] Hibbert (1963), 201–2.

government in 1384, the threat of expulsion from the Hanse led the town to eject and execute the leader of the revolt.[108]

But alien merchant guilds also imposed additional entry restrictions, on top of those set by the mother guild. In thirteenth-century Ghent and St Omer, the hanse of long-distance merchants was 'a purely economic, monopolistic organization for the furthering of trade in particular foreign regions' and severely excluded all small-scale traders and craftsmen.[109] In thirteenth-century England, the Flemish merchant guild denied newcomers, small-scale drapers, middlemen and 'upstarts' permission to trade.[110] In medieval Bruges, most alien merchant guilds restricted full membership to men who had resided in the city for at least a year.[111] As early as 1260 the German Hanse colony in London was placing limits on the numbers and personal characteristics of those admitted to enjoy its privileges, on top of the entry barriers already imposed by the merchant guilds of its constituent towns.[112] Throughout Europe, the German Hanse sedulously excluded anyone who married a citizen of a non-Hanseatic town[113] and anyone who engaged in retailing.[114]

Many alien merchant guilds and hanses charged additional admission fees on top of the fees charged by their mother guilds back home – as in the cases of the Groningen *hense*,[115] the Catalan merchant guild in Bruges[116] and the English Merchant Adventurers.[117] The hanses formed by long-distance merchants in Ghent and St Omer in the thirteenth century imposed entrance fees in which 'differential tariffs favoured the admission of offspring of members and made much more difficult that of craftsmen'.[118] The Venetian merchant colony at Tana on the Black Sea made merchant residence conditional on paying a fixed annual fee plus percentage tolls on imports and exports, as well as on obtaining authorization from a specially appointed official.[119]

Alien merchant guilds excluded women to an even greater extent than did their constituent local merchant guilds. The Hanse, for instance, excluded all women even though many of its constituent *local* guilds did permit members' widows to continue in business.[120] The Artushof merchant drinking societies in Hanseatic trading centres were completely barred to women except at the great annual feasts – again, even though

---

[108] Ennen (1979), 177; Dollinger (1970), 138–9.
[109] Blockmans (1993), 11–13 (quotation from 11).
[110] Moore (1985), 97, 108, 298–301.   [111] Blondé, Gelderblom and Stabel (2007), 157.
[112] R. De Roover (1965), 113.   [113] Spruyt (1994), 126; Wubs-Mrozewicz (2005), 227.
[114] Dollinger (1970), 161.   [115] Nitzsch (1892), 26.
[116] See the case of 25 September 1458, published in Gilliodts-van Severen (1901–2), 79.
[117] Sellers (1918).   [118] Blockmans (1993), 12.   [119] Doumerc (1987), 6.
[120] Dollinger (1970), 240.

merchants' widows might hold associate memberships in these towns' local merchant guilds.[121] Guilds of medieval Dutch merchants were exceptional in permitting females to be members: the Amsterdam guild of the *bergenvaarders* (merchants trading to Bergen) distinguished itself from its Hanse counterpart, the Bergenfahrer, by apparently admitting women.[122]

The early modern regulated companies also imposed barriers to entry such as occupational prerequisites and admission fees. The English Turkey Company, for instance, charged entrance fees and excluded anyone engaged in retailing.[123] As Adam Smith pointed out, even when the fee was not wholly prohibitive, it could deter the marginal entrant, thereby maintaining monopoly profits for existing members:

A fine [fee] even of twenty pounds, besides, though it may not perhaps be sufficient to discourage any man from entering into the Turkey trade with an intention to continue in it, may be enough to discourage a speculative merchant from hazarding a single adventure in it. In all trades, the regular established traders, even though not incorporated, naturally combine to raise profits, which are no-way [*sic*] so likely to be kept, at all times, down to their proper level, as by the occasional competition of speculative adventure.[124]

Similar entry barriers were imposed by the Seville merchant consulado, which progressively increased the amount of capital one needed to demonstrate owning before one was allowed to participate in the Spanish American trade. The consequence was 'before many decades the consulado became practically a closed corporation of a few great Sevillian commercial houses, enjoying a monopoly of the traffic between Spain and America'.[125] Imposing economic conditions on entry deterred anyone who *might* afford the charges but was uncertain about his prospects as a merchant. It thus discouraged both competition and risk-taking.

It is sometimes argued that the early modern chartered companies were not really monopolists because some – though not all – were open to outsiders who wished to *invest* in them. The Dutch East India Company (VOC) had a legal monopoly over certain trade routes, but differed from a traditional merchant guild in that 'each citizen was allowed to get involved in the company, and many citizens, merchants, manual workers, academics, teachers and clergymen became investors, making contributions from 50 to 85,000 guilders'.[126] Even foreigners were allowed to invest, unlike the English East India Company, which excluded foreign stockholders until 1709.[127] But 'involvement' was limited to *investing*: no

---

[121] Selzer (2003), 79 with n. 28.   [122] Wubs-Mrozewicz (2005), 223.
[123] A. Smith (1776), Book 5, ch. 1, part 3, section a, para. 10.   [124] *Ibid.*
[125] Hussey (1929), 5.   [126] Schnurmann (2003), 478–80.   [127] Neal (1990), 200.

one but a member, manager or employee of the VOC was allowed to *trade* east of the Cape of Good Hope and west of the Strait of Magellan.[128] The same was true of other chartered companies: outsiders could invest in them but not *trade* within the sector any company legally monopolized. In this respect, chartered companies were no different from merchant guilds. A traditional guilded merchant could also borrow capital from someone outside his guild, but this did not amount to permitting that outsider to trade as a merchant.

So alien merchant guilds, hanses and privileged companies provide rich evidence of the second form of behaviour predicted of a monopolist: restricting entry in order to limit competition. The claim that their exclusive trading rights did not constitute a monopoly since entry into the guild was permitted has no empirical support. This claim would only be true if a guild permitted *free* entry. Alien merchant guilds did admit some new members, but imposed limits both on their numbers and on their characteristics, deliberately excluding most inhabitants even of their own home towns. If anything, alien merchant guilds were even more closed than local ones, adding tougher entry barriers on top of obstacles already imposed by the mother guilds. No alien merchant guild permitted free entry. This in itself constitutes indirect evidence that alien merchant guilds were monopolists. Otherwise why restrict entry? Even if one constructed an alternative explanation for entry restrictions, one would then have to explain why an organization would refrain from using such restrictions (once in place) to get monopoly profits for its members.

4.1.3   Fixing prices

Price-fixing is a third form of behaviour distinguishing a monopolist from a competitive trader. As Chapter 3 discussed, fixing prices is blatantly harmful to consumers and difficult to defend to rulers and public opinion, so it leaves few written traces. Furthermore, the precise internal regulations of merchant guilds seldom survive in documents. Nonetheless, Postan argues that alien merchant guilds were 'able to regulate the scale and the methods of individual enterprise and to lay down rigid rules for prices and credit [and] for terms of sales'.[129] Well-documented alien merchant guilds – such as the Venetian merchant colonies in the Levant, the German Hanse, the English Merchant Staplers and many of the early modern privileged companies – left clear evidence that they fixed prices.

The English Company of the Staple, which secured compulsory staple privileges over English wool exporting from 1313 on, explicitly stated

---

[128] Bruijn (1990), 184.   [129] Postan (1987), 270.

that its aim was to fix prices. In 1343, for instance, all English wool merchants were ordered to take their wool to the compulsory staple at Bruges,

and there be at the orders of the mayor and Company of merchants . . . so that all those who pass wool are of one condition and agreement to keep the wool at a high price and receive such payment as shall be agreed by the King and his Council and the said merchants.[130]

In 1363 a Parliamentary petition explicitly described the arrangements of the Company of the Staple as involving the fixing of prices.[131] From 1429 to 1443, the Company operated the so-called Partition Ordinance whereby each member pooled his revenues with all other members dealing in the same grade of wool, and the total revenues were distributed according to the quantity of wool brought to the staple, not the quantity actually sold.[132] This created an incentive to refrain both from circumventing the staple and from lowering prices to attract customers, since one received a share of the revenues irrespective of the amount one sold.

The medieval German Hanse, too, is documented prohibiting members from competing on transport costs from Novgorod[133] and on sales prices for Baltic products in London.[134] The Hanse bought up the entire cloth output of particular Flemish towns and fixed its sales price.[135] It obliged its members to sail in convoy on particular dates in the Baltic so as to prevent price competition.[136] The ordinances of its Kontor in Bergen forbade any Hanse merchant to compete with another by making business contacts with another Hanse merchant's business partner, obtaining individual commercial privileges from rulers or buying wares that had not yet been delivered; the aim was 'to minimize losses through internal and external competition'.[137]

Spruyt ascribes the Hanseatic practice of price collusion to the low profit margins of the North Sea and Baltic bulk trades, and argues that alien merchant guilds acted more competitively in the high-profit-margin luxury trades of the Mediterranean.[138] In fact, however, price collusion within alien merchant guilds was also widespread in the luxury trades – both in southern central Europe and in the Mediterranean markets. In 1289, for instance, the merchant guild of the non-Hanseatic town of Konstanz on Lake Constance formed an association of those of its members

---

[130] Quoted in Power (1941), 89.   [131] *Ibid.*   [132] *Ibid.*, 89–90.
[133] Choroškevic (1996), 72, 75, 79, 83. See also Daenell (1905), 10; and Angermann (1987), 63.
[134] Pedersen (2006), 164–5; Dollinger (1970), 245.   [135] Dollinger (1970), 248–9.
[136] *Ibid.*, 147.   [137] Burckhardt (2005), 66 (quotation); Henn (2005), 241.
[138] Spruyt (1994), 134.

trading luxury linen cloths to the Champagne fairs, with the aim of 'abolishing the competition of the Konstanz sellers among one another' by restricting entry, prohibiting intermediation, obliging everyone to begin selling at the same time in the common hall at each fair and requiring each member to announce to all other members the price at which he was selling.[139]

In the Mediterranean, the Venetian merchant guilds in Alexandria and Acre ruled in 1278 that members arriving earlier than the annual August convoy were not to sell certain goods and that no member was to depart for Venice before mid-September, so that merchants travelling in the official convoy would not face price competition.[140] In 1283 the Venetian merchant guild in Acre required all members to pool their funds and purchase cotton and pepper jointly, to prevent competition among them from driving up prices.[141] The Venetian guild in Alexandria forbade its members to make purchases in Cairo, firstly 'because there was no Venetian consul in the capital who could control the activities of the merchants and, secondly, because that would have resulted in dishonest competition since the spices were sold in Cairo at lower prices than in Alexandria'.[142] Italian merchant guilds in Levantine cities forbade any European merchant to apply for alien resident status since that would enable him to undercut the prices set by the European merchant guilds.[143]

Guild price-fixing did vary across Europe. But the variation resulted not so much from the nature of the wares (bulk vs. luxury) or the size of profit margins (low vs. high) as from whether the guild was politically strong or weak. This is illustrated by comparisons *within* the low-margin North Sea and Baltic bulk trade. In the fifteenth century, German Hanseatic merchants charged much higher freight prices than Dutch merchants trading in the same wares over the same routes. This arose from the strong guild institutions which stifled internal competition among the Hanseatics compared to the lively competition within the ranks of Dutch merchants which their guild institutions were too weak to stamp out. While the weakly guilded Dutch merchants continued to offer low and competitive freight tariffs, the Hanse responded by strengthening its own regulations, banning use of Dutch ships in the Baltic and prohibiting 'unfair' competition on freight tariffs among its own members.[144]

In both the northern and the southern European trade, therefore, the most powerful alien merchant guilds deliberately engaged in

---

[139] Schulte (1900), 163–4.   [140] Ashtor (1983), 10.
[141] Lopez (1987), 375; Lopez (1945), 30 n. 2.   [142] Ashtor (1983), 398.
[143] *Ibid.*, 400.   [144] Dollinger (1970), 158.

price-fixing. Whether a body of merchants tried to fix prices was a function not so much of the technical characteristics of its merchandise or the profit margins of its business, as of the institutional features of its guild organization, in particular whether its guild was powerful enough to prevent competition.

The privileged merchant companies of the early modern period also sought to fix prices, although 'generally speaking, they were better able to influence the prices at which they sold goods at home than the prices at which they purchased goods at home and abroad'.[145] The Dutch East India Company (VOC) has left a particularly clear record of pursuing monopoly profits by fixing prices. For one thing, it sought forcibly to drive Portuguese and English merchants out of the main Asian spice-producing areas, with the explicit aim of enabling itself 'to buy cheap in Asia and sell dear in Europe'.[146] The VOC became the monopoly supplier of cinnamon to Europe after it took Sri Lanka from the Portuguese in the 1650s, and immediately increased the price from 15 stuivers a Dutch pond to 50, and later to 60.[147] In the European pepper market, by contrast, the VOC 'became the low-cost supplier ... but never a true monopoly supplier', so its strategy was 'to slightly oversupply the market, so as to keep the price low enough to discourage rivals while compensating through high volume for the low profit per unit of sale'.[148] This sounds remarkably like what economists call 'limit pricing' – a strategy pursued by the incumbent firm in a sector, which involves setting a lower price than would otherwise be profitable, with the aim of inhibiting or slowing entry by competitors.[149] A further monopoly pricing strategy of the VOC was to fix minimum selling prices for spices in Asia itself.[150] Similar tactics were adopted by the second Dutch West India Company, which compelled Surinam to import food, household goods, luxuries and slave labour exclusively from the Company 'and with graceful acceptance of Dutch prices, although they could have been purchased much cheaper elsewhere in the West Indies'.[151]

Alien merchant guilds, hanses and privileged companies did therefore seek to fix prices. Even if they did not always succeed perfectly, the attempt shows their belief that there was some probability of success. Setting artificially high sales prices was clearly good for members of these guilds, since it gave them supra-normal profits, at least in the short

---

[145] S. R. H. Jones and Ville (1996), 911.
[146] De Vries and Van der Woude (1997), 386.
[147] Pearson (1991), 107; De Vries and Van der Woude (1997), 429–30.
[148] De Vries and Van der Woude (1997), 430.
[149] See the discussion in Grimm, Lee and Smith (2006), 88–9, 158–64.
[150] De Vries and Van der Woude (1997), 430.   [151] Schnurmann (2003), 491.

term. In the longer term, it is possible that behaving more competitively would have increased their trade, but few monopolists up to the present day resist the lure of supra-normal profits when they can get away with charging monopoly prices. The effects on the wider economy were more malign. High monopoly prices were bad for consumers and intermediate producers, who incurred higher expenses and thus enjoyed lower real incomes. High prices also harmed the economy as a whole by reducing the amount exchanged, diminishing the gains from trade.

4.1.4   Restricting supply

If a monopolist can restrict supplies of a particular good, it will not have to dictate prices directly. Consumers will *have* to pay a higher price, and the monopolist will reap supra-normal profits. The fact that alien merchant guilds typically sought to restrict supplies is thus another indication that they sought to act as monopolists.

The German Hanse is one of the best-documented of the organizations referred to in the literature as 'alien merchant guilds', so its tactics for restricting supplies are instructive. In the twelfth century, its Kontor in Novgorod imposed strict limits on the value and type of wares each of its member merchants could sell, the number of times he could visit Novgorod annually and the length of time he could stay.[152] The Kontor rule that no merchant was allowed to bring wares worth over 1,000 marks to Novgorod in any given year was explicitly put in place 'to prevent any over-supply of wares, which would have spoiled the prices'.[153]

In Bergen, too, from the thirteenth century on the Hanse Kontor periodically restricted purchases of wares and imports of grain, flour, vegetables and beer, in order to keep supplies short and prices high.[154] The Bergen Kontor openly penalized members who brought in 'excessive' imports of groceries and general shop goods (silver, silk, linen, yarn, Mediterranean fruits, etc.) as they spoiled the market for other Hanse merchants.[155] The Bergen Kontor also pushed for penalties against foreign merchants buying fish in Iceland and its tributary islands because Icelandic fish were considerably cheaper and undercut the prices of Bergen fish over which the Hanse had control. According to some accounts, the Icelandic fish were so cheap that when they were brought in illegally no one would buy the Bergen fish the Hanse monopolized.[156]

---

[152] Angermann (1987), 64; Choroškevic (1996), 72, 75, 79, 83; Daenell (1905), 10; Dollinger (1970), 218.
[153] Burckhardt (2005), 72.   [154] Spruyt (1994), 127; Dollinger (1970), 49.
[155] Henn (2005), 241.   [156] Wubs-Mrozewicz (2005), 219 with n. 78, 220.

In Bruges, as well, the Hanse Kontor sought to restrict supply through various tactics:

> costly goods and goods which constituted the monopoly of the Hanse, i.e. wax, furs, metals, Skania herring, had to be imported to Bruges before they could be sold elsewhere in Flanders or the Low Countries. In addition, all cloth, whether it was produced in Flanders or in Holland, had to be brought to Bruges before it could be exported to the east. At one time an attempt was even made to exclude Dutch cloth altogether . . . [157]

Through such regulations, the Hanse sought to impose a compulsory 'staple' in its four Kontor locations (Novgorod, Bergen, Bruges and London), as well as branch staples in important supply areas, so that all Hanse merchants would be obliged to centralize trade in all wares through the staple location, under staple rules, before they could be sold onwards.[158]

Some scholars have tried to claim that the Hanse staple was in fact an efficient institution – that it reduced transaction costs in an economy shifting from periodic fairs to permanent markets after *c.* 1300 and that it centralized quality control, thereby overcoming asymmetries of information between suppliers and consumers. In support of such arguments, they adduce the justifications put forward by the Hanse itself when it demanded (or unilaterally imposed) compulsory staple regulations.[159]

But claims made by exclusive bodies of merchants to justify market regulations should not be taken at face value. This efficiency view of Hanseatic staple regulations does not explain a number of findings. First, if a staple had been efficient for reducing transaction costs in an economy increasingly dependent on permanent markets, then surely the Hanse would have found that staple centres arose *voluntarily* in commercially appropriate locations such as Bruges. The fact that the Hanse had to enforce a *compulsory* staple at Bruges as a legal obligation indicates that its own members did not regard the staple as reducing transaction costs, or at least not sufficiently to outweigh the perceived costs of the staple.[160] Second, the efficiency view does not explain why non-Hanseatic merchants from Italy, the Low Countries and England, who did *not* impose a centralized collective staple, not only stayed in business but out-competed Hanse members, except on routes and in goods over which the Hanse was

---

[157] Postan (1987), 305 (quotation); on Dutch cloth, see also Dollinger (1970), 250–1.

[158] See Irsigler (2002), 40, on the initially voluntary but increasingly coercive character of the Hanse staple at Bruges.

[159] Jenks (2005), 38–9; for a similar claim concerning the Hanse Kontore (branch offices) in Prussia, see Link and Kapfenberger (2005), 163–4.

[160] Irsigler (2002), 40.

able to enforce its legal monopoly (often militarily, as we shall see shortly). Third, the efficiency view does not explain why buyers were willing to buy the same goods from interlopers who encroached illegally on the Hanse monopoly. Finally, the efficiency argument justifying the Hanseatic cod staple (for instance) in terms of quality control does not explain why, as late as the mid-fifteenth century, customers from Strasbourg, Frankfurt and Mainz were complaining about the low quality and inadequate packing of dried cod supplied by the Hanse, despite the fact that the Hanse had for generations conducted staples in all the cod-supplying locations, through which its members were obliged to trade. Attempts by the Hanse central office in 1446 to address the problem by imposing an even more centralized cod staple in Lübeck were also a failure.[161] In theory, therefore, staple regulations might have reduced transaction costs and facilitated quality control, but in practice there is no evidence that they did so. Staple regulations did, however, make it possible for the Hanse to control market participation, trading volumes and prices.

Restrictions on supply were practised not just by the well-documented German Hanse, but by many other alien merchant guilds throughout Europe. In 1261, for instance, the Flemish merchant guild in England limited supply not only *indirectly* by excluding newcomers, small-scale drapers and middlemen from selling Flemish cloths, but also *directly* by restricting the number of junior traders a given merchant or firm might employ and the number of cloths each could sell.[162]

Around the same period, as we have seen, the Venetian merchant guilds in Acre and Alexandria forbade their members to sell certain commodities before the annual convoy arrived so as to limit supplies of western goods, and prohibited any member from sailing for Venice before any other so as to keep supplies restricted and prices high.[163] In each Venetian merchant colony throughout the medieval Mediterranean, the consul decided on the number of galleys that would be made available in each sailing, explicitly with the aim of preventing too many goods being sent to Venice at the same time which might drag down prices on the Rialto.[164]

The Fondaco dei Tedeschi (German merchant colony in Venice) required all members to reveal everything they intended to sell in the city to the directors and officials of the Fondaco, so that the total volume of German wares selling in the city could be controlled.[165] An attempt in 1458 to set up a storehouse to sell linen outside the Fondaco in the

[161] Burckhardt (2005), 63.   [162] Moore (1985), 97, 298–301.
[163] Ashtor (1983), 10.   [164] Stöckly (1995), 184–5.
[165] Choroškevic (1996), 84–6; J. W. Hoffmann (1932), 248–9; Heyd (1874), 211–12.

Casa Ruzzini, in violation of these supply controls, was immediately quashed.[166]

In the Low Countries, the English Merchant Adventurers allocated each member an export quota, which was enforced by requiring members to ship collectively and display wares publicly at the guild's staple.[167] In the fifteenth century, the Burgos merchant guild in the Low Countries controlled the volume of Spanish wool supplied to northern Europe by supervising the loading of all wool ships.[168]

Early modern merchant consulados and chartered companies also restricted supplies, both to and from extra-European destinations. The Spanish consulados restricted the supply of trade goods to Spanish colonies such as Hispaniola to keep prices up.[169] The English Bermuda Company restricted supplies to the English colony of Bermuda for the same reason.[170] The Dutch East India Company (VOC) restricted supplies in both directions – to overseas Dutch colonies and to European markets. In the outbound direction, the VOC restricted supplies of goods to the Spice Islands to maintain artificially high sales prices.[171] In the inbound direction, the VOC systematically destroyed production capacity in Asian spice plantations and 'deliberately kept the European market undersupplied in order to raise prices'.[172]

In a wide array of different economies and time periods, therefore, alien merchant guilds and privileged companies had the right to control supply streams. They imposed quotas, prohibited sales at certain periods, dictated places and times of selling, and sought privileges from rulers excluding alternative sources of supply. Of course, all these regulations created incentives for outside interlopers and internal free-riders to break the monopoly. But guilds' monopoly privileges were enshrined in legal charters, so they could enforce their regulations themselves and appeal for support from rulers. This increased the risks and costs of monopoly breakers and their customers, in turn keeping supplies short and prices high even on the black market, helping to sustain the guild monopoly.

4.1.5   Fixing input costs

A monopolist may also be a monopsonist – the sole *buyer* in certain markets – and may impose lower than competitive purchasing prices. Alien merchant guilds often did enjoy monopsony rights. Their main

---

[166] Heyd (1874), 213.   [167] Sellers (1918); Kohn (2003a), 19; Ramsey (1994), 488.
[168] Mathers (1988), 368–70.   [169] Pérotin-Dumon (1991), 208.
[170] *Ibid.*, 222.   [171] Tracy (1991), 7.
[172] Steensgaard (1990), 121 (quotation); De Vries and Van der Woude (1997), 430.

tactic was to agree internally that guild members would not compete when buying particular goods in particular locations. Venetian and Genoese merchant guilds in the Levant, for example, fixed collective prices for spice purchases and forbade their members to offer higher ones.[173] The Venetian merchant guild in thirteenth-century Egypt agreed that its members would purchase pepper collectively, to prevent competition among its members from driving up purchase prices.[174] The Hanse Kontor in Novgorod prohibited its members from competing with each other in buying wares from Russians, so as to keep purchase prices low.[175] The Hanse Kontor in Bergen forbade Hanse merchants to compete with one another in trading with the *nordfarer* (Norwegian merchants who supplied fish in return for grain and other wares).[176] In the sixteenth century, Portuguese merchant guilds outlawed internal competition among their members so as to impose low prices on Asian spice suppliers.[177] The Hudson's Bay Company used its legal monopsony over the Canadian fur market to impose low prices on indigenous fur trappers.[178] The English East India Company used its legal monopsony to impose low prices for goods it purchased in India.[179]

Alien merchant guilds also used their institutional powers to depress their input costs by agreeing not to bid up prices of other inputs such as real estate and labour. The Hanse Kontor in London forbade its merchants to compete with one another in bidding up rents for residential or business premises.[180] To suppress the rising pay demands of sailors on merchant ships, the Hanse forbade its members to compete in offering better wages and threatened recalcitrant employees with imprisonment or branding.[181] At least in the market for maritime labour in the Baltic region, where the Hanse was a large – in some ports the sole – employer of sailors' labour, it used its monopsony powers to keep down its own input costs at the expense of its workers.

Alien merchant guilds, hanses and privileged companies did, therefore, try to exercise monopsonies. They imposed maximum legal purchasing prices for wares, business premises and labour, so as artificially to depress their input costs, and they prohibited their members from competing with one another in ways that would have pushed these prices up.

---

[173] Ashtor (1983), 415.   [174] *Ibid.*, 398.
[175] Choroškevic (1996), 72, 75, 79, 83. See also Daenell (1905), 10; Angermann (1987), 63.
[176] Wubs-Mrozewicz (2005), 224–5.   [177] Pérotin-Dumon (1991), 224.
[178] Carlos and Nicholas (1990), 867–8.
[179] A. Smith (1776), Book 5, ch. 1, part 3, section a, para. 26.
[180] Burckhardt (2005), 72–3.   [181] Dollinger (1970), 154.

4.1.6   Imposing costs on competitors

Monopolists, as we saw in Chapter 3, often try to maintain their exclusive position by increasing costs for potential competitors. Alien merchant guilds unsurprisingly pursued similar tactics by manipulating their legal privileges, their internal regulations and their bargaining position vis-à-vis rulers in such a way as artificially to increase the trading costs of rivals.

One frequent tactic was to threaten competitors with violence if they tried to trade. In the twelfth century, for instance, the Pisan merchant guild attacked the Genoese merchant guild in Constantinople, destroying so much merchandise that major Genoese merchant firms collapsed.[182] In the thirteenth and fourteenth centuries, the German Hanse 'went so far as to stop the Gotlanders passing westwards through the Danish straits, and the Frisians, Flemings, and English eastwards'.[183] In the fourteenth century, the Genoese merchant guild in Caffa physically prevented other western merchants from trading in the Crimea, arresting them and confiscating their goods.[184] In 1397, the Prussian members of the Hanse put pressure on the Grand Master of the Teutonic Order to refuse 'Lombards' (north Italian merchants) entry into the territory.[185] In fifteenth-century Bergen, the Hanse Kontor threatened Amsterdam merchants with violence when they sought to encroach on branches of trade which the Hanse viewed as its exclusive preserve.[186] In the sixteenth and seventeenth centuries, Bosnian merchant colonies took legal steps against Dubrovnik (Ragusa) merchant colonies in Belgrade, Sarajevo and various Hungarian and Slavonian towns, impeding their commerce, restricting their freedom of movement and ultimately seeking their ejection.[187] So frequently did merchant guilds use violence to hinder rivals' trade that it had implications for commercial security in the wider economy, as we shall see in Chapter 6.

Alien merchant guilds also sought to increase competitors' costs by denying them access to shipping and harbours. In 1158, Genoese merchant colonies in Sicily sought to make themselves the sole intermediaries of trade between that island and northern Europe by getting the king of Sicily to exclude Provençal merchants from Sicilian harbours and prevent Sicilian ships from sailing to Provence.[188] In the mid-fifteenth century, the Venetian merchant colony on Crete secured privileges prohibiting any merchant from hiring foreign ships to export wine to England,

---

[182] G. W. Day (1988), 95.   [183] Dollinger (1970), 42–3.   [184] Abulafia (1986b), 205.
[185] Dollinger (1970), 191.   [186] Wubs-Mrozewicz (2005), 219–20.
[187] Molnár (2007), 104–5.   [188] S. A. Epstein (1996), 74.

Flanders or the Baltic ports, obliging all wine exporters to use Venetian vessels.[189]

Privileged merchant companies used similar strategies. In the sixteenth century, for instance, anyone exporting English manufactures to Turkey had to use the ships of the English Levant Company, and since 'the time for the loading and sailing of those general ships depended altogether upon the [Company's] directors, they could easily fill them with their own goods and those of their particular friends, to the exclusion of others, who, they might pretend, had made their proposals too late'.[190] In the seventeenth century, the Dutch East India Company forcibly restricted the movement by ship of foreign merchants' cargoes.[191]

Such tactics – threatening violence, excluding ships from harbours, denying access to shipping – were more likely to be effective where an alien merchant guild was a substantial player in an international trading centre and enjoyed strong support from its ruler. As we shall see in Chapter 5, alien merchant guilds often gave rulers cash payments, favourable loans and military help, precisely in order to secure such support. This benefited members of the guilds but increased competitors' costs, harmed third parties and increased the risks of commerce.

4.2   Did alien merchant guilds enforce their monopolies in practice?

We have seen that virtually all organizations that can be called alien merchant guilds negotiated with rulers to obtain the legal rights to do all the things one would expect of monopolists. They got exclusive rights to engage in particular lines of trade. They were entitled to exclude entrants. They had the right to fix prices and prohibit undercutting. Their privileges let them restrict the supply of wares. They agreed internally to fix input costs below the competitive level. And they set rules imposing discriminatory costs on competitors.

The existence of these legal rights is in itself indirect evidence that alien merchant guilds were monopolists. After all, why would these guilds have sought the legal entitlement to engage in precisely these forms of behaviour, had they not intended to use them to monopolize particular lines of trade? But there is also plentiful *direct* evidence that alien merchant guilds enforced their legal monopolies in practice – seldom perfectly, of course, but enough to exercise baneful economic effects.

---

[189] Fusaro (2002), 11 with n. 42.
[190] A. Smith (1776), Book 5, ch. 1, part 3, section a, para. 735.
[191] S. R. H. Jones and Ville (1996), 911; Winius and Vink (1991), 78–9.

4.2.1   Contemporary complaints

For one thing, contemporaries complained. In dry, objective reports and in impassioned petitions, they stated their views that alien merchant guilds enforced barriers to entry, fixed prices and imposed supply restrictions. This not only damaged other people in society – the primary concern of these contemporary grievances – but also imposed efficiency costs on the wider economy, in terms of foregone exchange, production, and consumption.

Contemporaries had no doubt at all that alien merchant guilds imposed barriers to entry. Citizens of other medieval Italian cities complained that Venetian merchant guilds abroad never admitted them to associate membership or let them share the exclusive Venetian commercial privileges.[192] Merchants from smaller German towns lamented that they were excluded from the Hanse because of opposition by merchants from the big Wendish cities who feared their competition.[193] Merchants from Dutch towns complained that their applications for Hanse membership were delayed for years because existing Hanse members feared Dutch entrepreneurship.[194] The merchants of Narva complained they were excluded from the Hanse so the merchants of Reval could maintain their town's monopolistic position as the place where western merchants assembled to travel to Novgorod.[195] Hans Steinchen, a Riga citizen of German ethnicity who was in other ways wholly entitled to be a member of the 'Große Gilde' (a mixed guild of German long-distance merchants), complained that his membership application was repeatedly rejected on grounds of 'hatred' of his family.[196]

Even within hanses, members complained that the constituent merchant guilds erected barriers against each other. In the mid-fourteenth century the Regensburg 'table' and the Nürnberg 'table' struggled for domination of the Fondaco dei Tedeschi, with Regensburg sending large sums of money to the Venetian government in an attempt to establish dominance, and both parties appealing against each other to the authorities. As Heyd points out, 'one cannot help seeing the extent to which that domination [over the Fondaco] brought with it real advantages, which could justify such a stubborn struggle'.[197] In the fifteenth century, merchants from York, Hull, Beverley, Scarborough and other northern English ports complained of the unaffordable admission fees

---

[192] Lopez (1987), 351.   [193] Dollinger (1970), 117.   [194] *Ibid.*, 89, 122–3.
[195] *Ibid.*, 127, 336.   [196] Brück (1999), 115–16.
[197] Heyd (1874), 208–9 (quotation from 209); Simonsfeld (1887), 46–8, 85–8; J. W. Hoffmann (1932), 248.

imposed by the London governors of the Merchant Adventurers.[198] In the fourteenth century, merchants from other Hanseatic towns accused the Cologne merchant guild of excluding them from the Hanse's privileges in London.[199] Prussian merchants complained that Lübeck merchants tried to exclude them from the Hanse privileges in Novgorod.[200] All the other Hanse merchants complained that the Wendish towns excluded them from the Hanse monopoly over the Norwegian trade.[201] The non-Livonian Hanse merchants complained that Reval, Riga and Dorpat exploited conflicts with the czar after 1494 to monopolize trade between Russia and northwest Germany, at the expense of other Hanse members.[202]

Contemporaries also complained about the ability of alien merchant guilds to expel them or exclude them from monopoly profits. In 1385 the Dortmund merchant Christian Kelmer complained that the London Kontor of the German Hanse had ejected him, ostensibly because he had paid a minor customs charge (amounting to 3 s. $1\frac{1}{2}$ d.) which allegedly weakened the Hanse's tax privileges, but in actuality because of fellow merchants' envy of his business success.[203] The merchants of Bremen complained of being excluded from the Hanse's monopoly privileges through group expulsions in 1285 and 1427.[204] The merchants of Hamburg complained in 1367 about being threatened with expulsion for refusing to participate in Hanse embargoes of particular cities.[205] These protests suggest strongly that exclusion from the monopoly privileges of one's alien merchant guild had real effects: in other words, the monopoly was effective.

Price-fixing, supply controls and other secretive machinations by alien merchant guilds also figure in the complaints of contemporaries. Some of the earliest can be observed in the Mediterranean trade. In the later tenth century, for instance, Italian travellers complained that they could not export silk garments from Constantinople because the privileges of the Amalfitan and Venetian merchant colonies made them the monopoly suppliers of these wares to Italian markets.[206] In 1062, the abbot of Montecassino had to journey specially to Amalfi to buy silk garments because the privileges of Amalfitan merchant guilds in Byzantium and North Africa gave them a near-monopoly over silk imports to Italy.[207] In 1277, the Italian merchants in Nîmes were permitted to form a corporative body only on condition they did not 'conduct secretive machinations

---

[198] Sutton (2002), 37.   [199] Dollinger (1970), 40.   [200] *Ibid.*, 91, 125, 231.
[201] *Ibid.*, 298.   [202] *Ibid.*, 312.   [203] *Ibid.*, 409, document 23.   [204] *Ibid.*, 119.
[205] *Ibid.*, 70.   [206] Citarella (1967), 301 with n. 15; Lopez (1945), 37–8, 41.
[207] Citarella (1967), 301–2 with n. 16.

and illicit associations among themselves' – an indication that contemporaries thought an alien merchant guild was quite likely to do this.[208] In 1306–7, Patriarch Athanasium I accused the Genoese merchant colony in Constantinople of holding the city in a vice by controlling its grain provisioning.[209] In 1487 and 1491, a Venetian merchant engaged in the English trade complained that he had been 'kept off the market by unfair practice', when the Venetian merchant fleet signed a collective merchandising contract agreeing to sell jointly in London and not to compete internally.[210] In 1621, merchants from Dubrovnik (Ragusa) trading to Venice complained that the Venetian merchant colony in Split was enjoying a monopoly because the Venetian Senate had excluded Dubrovnik merchants from the export trade between Venice and their home city.[211]

The same complaints about price-fixing and supply controls by alien merchant guilds can be observed in the northern European trade as soon as it began to expand. In 1280, accusations of cartellistic behaviour surrounded the Spanish and German merchant guilds as they removed themselves from Bruges to Aardenburg, with both the Aardenburg and the Bruges town councils issuing rules prohibiting illicit association, specifically forbidding foreign merchants from 'forming combinations' in the food and provisioning trades.[212] According to Häpke, 'the formation of cartels among the merchants had preceded this and had driven prices for consumption goods up high'.[213]

When the compulsory English wool staple in the Low Countries was established in 1313, merchants from Brabant and Italy complained bitterly that it was a tactic to exclude them from the English wool trade in order to enable the Staplers to dominate without competition.[214] In 1320 a group of foreign (mainly Italian) merchants complained that the 'mayor' of the English Staplers was 'vexing them illegally'.[215] In 1327, wool growers in the East Riding of Yorkshire complained that the Staplers were forming 'rings' (cartels) to keep down purchase prices.[216] In 1332, Nicholas Picheford of Bridgnorth complained that a shipment of his wool had been arrested by forty-two Staplers who objected to his exporting it to Brabant in violation of their privileges.[217] In 1363, the House of Commons complained that the Company was fixing wool export prices, and petitioned that wool might be sold freely by non-members of the Company, without having to observe the fixed Company prices.[218] In

---

[208] Germain (1861), 124, 280–1; Goldschmidt (1891), 196 n. 177 (quotation).
[209] Laiou-Thomadakis (1980–1), 188 with n. 49.   [210] Lane (1944), 193 n. 34.
[211] Carter (1971), 386–7.   [212] Höhlbaum (1876), 297 n. 1.
[213] Häpke (1908), 261–2.   [214] Power (1941), 94.
[215] Lloyd (1977), 101, 111.   [216] Power (1941), 94–5.
[217] Lloyd (1977), 12–10.   [218] Power (1941), 89.

1382, the merchants of fifteen English counties complained to Parliament that the Stapler privileges were impoverishing growers and traders of coarse English wool, favouring Stapler merchants trading in finer wool which could sustain higher overhead costs.[219] In 1394, the 'commons' of the counties of Hampshire, Somerset, Dorset and Berkshire again complained that the privileges of the Company discriminated against growers and traders of coarse wool.[220] In 1429–43, smaller English exporters were joined by representatives of the towns of the Low Countries protesting against the Partition Ordinance whereby the Company agreed a concerted price in selling wool in Bruges, facilitating control of the trade by a small group of wealthy Staplers.[221] All participants in the medieval English wool trade except the Staplers themselves thus believed that the privileges enjoyed by the Company of the Staple had negative economic effects.

The commercial privileges of the German Hanse likewise attracted vociferous complaints throughout medieval Europe. Some of the complaints came from customers, as in 1309 when Londoners accused the German Hanse of fixing high prices for the Baltic wax of which it was the monopoly supplier.[222] Likewise, in 1377 the new English king Richard II was presented with a petition accusing the Hanse of being 'the architects behind the rising prices of Baltic goods' in England.[223] Other complaints came from suppliers, as in fourteenth-century Flanders when the Hanse bought up the cloth output of entire towns and then arranged to 'fix the prices of these cloths, under the surveillance of a representative of the Kontor at Bruges'.[224] Outside merchants complained about Hanse privileges, as in 1481 when the Amsterdam merchants in Bergen accused the Hanse Kontor of limiting their trade,[225] or in 1484 when the Amsterdamers complained that the Hanse merchants had been attacking and hindering their trade even though 'all good merchants are obliged to love and further one another, and never to hinder or do violence against each other'.[226] In the fourteenth and fifteenth centuries, merchants from the Dutch Hanse towns of Deventer, Kampen and Zwolle complained that they were treated unfairly by the Lübeck-dominated Bergen Kontor, which constantly sought to block their trade, disadvantage them commercially, penalize them for violations of regulations of which they were unaware and debar them from doing business 'like other Hanse towns'.[227] Individual Hanse merchants complained about Hanse regulations

[219] Dodd (2002), 98.   [220] Ibid., 101.   [221] Power (1941), 90; Lloyd (1977), 265–6.
[222] Dollinger (1970), 245.   [223] Pedersen (2006), 164–5.
[224] Dollinger (1970), 248–9 (quotation from 249); cloth made up about 75 per cent of Hanseatic exports from Flanders.
[225] Wubs-Mrozewicz (2005), 220.   [226] Ibid.
[227] Henn (2005), 235–42 (quotation 242).

obliging them to travel in convoy and observe collective sailing dates, which prevented them from competing with their fellows.[228] In the fifteenth century, many Hanse merchants voted with their feet, forsaking the coercive regulations of the Kontor in Bruges for the more liberal regimes in Antwerp and Bergen-op-Zoom; the Hanse had to compel its members to go on trading in Bruges.[229] The regulations of the Hanse Kontor in London also attracted complaints from Hanse merchants outside London, especially those in Boston who traded mainly to the Norwegian port of Bergen and complained constantly about regulations imposed by the London Kontor – suggesting that these were a binding constraint.[230]

The merchant associations that survived and proliferated into the early modern period also attracted complaints about their monopolistic activities. In the sixteenth century, Spanish American colonists constantly complained about scarcity of necessities caused by the Seville consulado and the 'deliberate restriction by the merchants of the consulado for the purpose of maintaining prices'.[231] The governors of such colonies occasionally went so far as to turn a blind eye to illegal English interlopers who brought the colonists the wares they needed.[232] In 1705 Ambrosio Daubenton, a member of the Spanish 'junta concerning the re-establishment of commerce', advocated somewhat freer trade to the Indies by means of single ships, on the grounds that the monopolistic convoy system of the consulados had harmed commerce by delays, high costs, inflexibility and failure to send ships to particular destinations, 'forcing the inhabitants to illicit modes of supply'.[233] Eighteenth-century Cubans described the Royal Havana Trading Company, which monopolized trade between Spain and Cuba from 1740 to 1765, as a 'detestable monopoly which enriched, at most, four people to the detriment of the rest of the colony'.[234]

The English privileged companies attracted similar complaints. The English Muscovy Company (Russia Company) used its monopoly so blatantly to manipulate the supply and price of cordage from Russia that English Members of Parliament complained in 1604 that 'to sell their ware dear they [the Russia Company merchants] have contracted with the buyer not to bring any more of that commodity within three

---

[228] Dollinger (1970), 147.

[229] Maréchal (1951), 31, 35; on the extraordinarily liberal treatment of alien merchants in Antwerp, which dates back to 1315, see Häpke (1908), 259.

[230] Burckhardt (2005), 75.   [231] Hussey (1929), 5–6.

[232] Pérotin-Dumon (1991), 208.   [233] Hussey (1929), 21.

[234] Quoted in Paquette (2007), 283–4.

years'.[235] The English Levant Company (Turkey Company) consistently sought to inflate its members' profits by keeping the market, in the words of one famous contemporary, 'both for the goods which they export, and for those which they import, as much understocked as they can'.[236] Eighteenth-century English Members of Parliament complained that the Hudson's Bay Company limited the supply of furs on the market in London, calling for the Company to open its prices to greater competition.[237] Indian fur-trappers in the region around Hudson Bay in Canada complained that they were threatened with confiscation and violence if they refused to accept prices dictated by the Company or sought better prices illegally from non-Company interlopers.[238] English colonists complained that the Bermuda Company exploited its monopoly by keeping them under-supplied, and Governors of Bermuda tacitly permitted illegal Dutch interlopers to bring in the foodstuffs and clothing essential for keeping the colony afloat.[239]

The Dutch East India Company (VOC) was the object of widespread complaints by those injured by its monopoly. Contemporaries described how the VOC succeeded in keeping clove prices high through its deliberate extirpation of 'unauthorized' spice trees in the Spice Islands.[240] On VOC orders, all the clove plantations of northern Maluku and Huamoal in Indonesia were uprooted and the archipelago was patrolled to guard against unauthorized planting.[241] This strategy meant that by 1669 the VOC had acquired 'one of the most effective monopolies in history'.[242] In 1718–19 the VOC destroyed 4,500,000 pounds of cloves and 1,500,000 pounds of nutmeg in order to limit supplies.[243] Contemporaries were also well aware of how the VOC kept the Dutch colony of the Spice Islands (the Moluccan Islands of Indonesia) under-supplied to keep prices high, 'not just for the preferred varieties of rice and cotton cloth, but even more for countless other articles'.[244] In 1694, there were complaints from the population of Ceylon, too, that the VOC's monopoly had led to an acute shortage of rice.[245] In 1703 spice planters in Surinam petitioned for the abolition of the VOC, complaining about the low supply and high prices of the slaves whose importation it monopolized.[246]

[235] Quoted in S. R. H. Jones and Ville (1996), 911 n. 47.
[236] A. Smith (1776), Book 5, ch. 1, part 3, section a, para. 10.
[237] S. R. H. Jones and Ville (1996), 911–12.
[238] Carlos and Nicholas (1990), 867–8.   [239] Pérotin-Dumon (1991), 222.
[240] Steensgaard (1990), 121 (quotation); S. R. H. Jones and Ville (1996), 911.
[241] Tracy (1991), 8.   [242] Steensgaard (1990), 121.
[243] Ibid., 108 n. 12; Glamann (1958), 109.   [244] Tracy (1991), 7.
[245] Winius and Vink (1991), 79.   [246] S. R. H. Jones and Ville (1996), 911.

Contemporaries thus had no doubt that alien merchant guilds, hanses, consulados and privileged companies enforced their legal monopolies in practice. Members of these bodies themselves, different factions within them, traders they excluded, members of rival merchant guilds, public officials and customers all lamented the baneful economic impact of merchant guild monopolies. These contemporary reports can hardly be dismissed as referring to a few exceptional cases, since they emanate from many different societies and time periods, and include the most prominent examples adduced by efficiency approaches to merchant guilds – the Venetian merchant guilds in the Mediterranean, the German Hanse, the Spanish consulados, the English Merchant Adventurers, the Dutch East India Company. Attempts to defend alien merchant guilds as efficient institutions on the grounds that they did not enforce their monopolies in practice must explain why contemporaries so universally regarded these monopolies as exercising real, and negative, economic effects.

4.2.2   Lobbying

A second important source of evidence on the practical impact of guild monopolies is the political jostling they evoked. Alien merchant guilds invested time and money in official representations, gifts to powerful people and favourable loans to the state – all in explicit exchange for maintenance of their own privileges and restraints on outsiders. This vigorous lobbying suggests that merchant guilds regarded their privileges as enforceable.

The willingness of alien merchant guilds to invest resources in pressing rulers to grant and confirm monopoly rights can be observed throughout medieval and early modern Europe, as we shall see in detail in Chapter 5 – the eleventh-century Venetian merchant guilds' costly lobbying of the Byzantine emperors in Constantinople,[247] the thirteenth-century German Hanse's expensive persuasion of Prince Constantine over its Gotland monopoly,[248] the fourteenth-century Staplers' petitions to the English king to confirm their monopoly over wool exports,[249] and the fifteenth-century Fondaco dei Tedeschi's persistent pressure on the government of Venice.[250]

Guild lobbying campaigns involved not only substantial incidental expenses but also gifts and payments to rulers and officials – from German merchant guilds to the Danish crown in 1080,[251] from the Venetian merchant guild in Constantinople to the Byzantine imperial treasury in

---

[247] Madden (2002), 24; Frankopan (2004), 138.   [248] Dollinger (1970), 26.
[249] Dodd (2002), 97.   [250] Choroškevič (1996), 78.   [251] E. Hoffman (1980), 30–1.

1092, [252] from the Pisan and Genoese merchant guilds in Constantinople to the emperor in 1111 and 1155,[253] from the twelfth-century Hanse to the rulers of Novgorod,[254] from the fourteenth-century Venetian merchant guilds in Alexandria and Damascus to the Mamluk authorities,[255] from the Hanse in Skåne to the Danish crown in 1360,[256] and from Dutch and English merchant associations to the Spanish crown in the seventeenth and eighteenth centuries.[257]

Another guild lobbying strategy, discussed in detail in Chapter 5, was to offer rulers preferential loans.[258] The Venetian merchant guild in Constantinople, for example, made huge loans to the Byzantine emperor in return for extraordinary trading privileges.[259] The German, Florentine, Venetian and Catalan merchant colonies in medieval London made substantial loans to English monarchs to get monopolies over the wool trade.[260] The Florentine merchant guild in medieval Naples made large loans to the ruler to secure monopolies in the grain trade.[261] The Burgos consulado lobbied the Spanish crown in 1616 to 'slow down foreigners' trade' by compelling foreign merchants to move 120 kilometres inland to Burgos and cease operations in Spanish ports.[262] In eighteenth-century Bologna, the silk merchants' and hemp merchants' guilds regarded their monopolies as sufficiently valuable to lobby the city government continually to sustain them.[263] In 1750, the Stockholm merchant guild lobbied the Swedish crown for regulations enabling it to monopolize salt imports.[264]

The merchant consulados with monopolies over the Spanish American trade lobbied vigorously to defend their exclusive entitlements and attack those of others. In 1550, for instance, when the nobleman Ávaro de Bazán got permission to trade with the Spanish Indies in a new type of heavy galleon, the Seville merchant consulado lobbied the crown to rescind his licence.[265] In 1687, the Cádiz consulado lobbied energetically against a proposal to open trade with Puerto Rico and Hispaniola to *all* the king of Spain's vassals, insisting that inhabitants of Spanish Flanders had always been 'foreigners' as far as the Indies trade was concerned.[266] In 1707, the Cádiz consulado lobbied vociferously against a concession granted to a nobleman to send six frigates a year to the Indies, in contravention

---

[252] Runciman (1987), 146–7.   [253] *Ibid.*
[254] Choroškevic (1996), 70–1; Dollinger (1970), 100.
[255] Ashtor (1983), 206–7, 215, 249–52, 401–2.   [256] Dollinger (1970), 67.
[257] Schnurmann (2003a), 192; K. Weber (2004), 105 n. 72.   [258] Kohn (2003a), 17–18.
[259] Runciman (1987), 146.
[260] Dollinger (1970), 56–8; E. B. Fryde (1959), 2; Holmes (1960–1), 207 n. 2.
[261] Abulafia (1990), 135–6.   [262] Grafe (2001), 24.   [263] Farolfi (1998), 312.
[264] Müller (1998), 133.   [265] Pike (1965), 447.   [266] Hussey (1929), 15–18.

of its own monopoly.[267] The consulados of Cádiz, Mexico and Lima lobbied strenuously against initiatives to liberalize trade in 1765[268] and to abolish their monopolies altogether in 1778[269] – a strong indication that they regarded their monopolies as enforceable.

The privileged English companies also invested resources in lobbying to defend their monopolies in the early modern intercontinental trade. In 1730, for instance, the East India Company lobbied against opening up the trade to India, on the grounds that such competition would, 'by overstocking the market... [sink] their price so low that no profit could be made by them'.[270] The Hudson's Bay Company's exclusive rights, too, 'were regarded as a valuable privilege by shareholders who spent considerable sums defending their trading monopoly in Parliament, court, and the Bay'.[271]

As we shall see in Chapter 5, such examples can be replicated for every medieval and early modern European economy. Alien merchant guilds, hanses, consulados and privileged companies all invested time and money in lobbying campaigns, made direct gifts and payments to rulers, and provided preferential state loans, in return for political support in securing, extending and enforcing their monopolies. This willingness to spend resources suggests that guilds thought their monopolies were valuable – and thus had a real economic impact.

4.2.3   Inter-guild conflict

Alien merchant guilds also invested in conflict over their monopolies, another indication of their value. Rivalry over commercial monopolies sparked frequent disputes between alien and local merchant guilds – between the Venetian merchant guild in Constantinople and indigenous Greek merchant guilds in the 1180s,[272] between the guilds of Italian merchants in Constantinople and the Byzantine merchant guilds in the later thirteenth century,[273] between German merchant guilds and local Danish ones in Roskilde in 1157,[274] between the Hanse and local merchant guilds in English towns in the late thirteenth century,[275] and between the Venetian merchant guild in Alexandria and the indigenous Karīmi merchant association in 1327.[276]

---

[267] *Ibid.*, 24.   [268] Woodward (2005), 635–6.   [269] *Ibid.*, 636–7.

[270] A. Smith (1776), Book 5, ch. 1, part 3, section a, para. 26.

[271] S. R. H. Jones and Ville (1996), 909.   [272] Runciman (1987), 148.

[273] Madden (2002), 24.   [274] Schütt (1980), 109.

[275] Postan (1973), 240; Lloyd (1991), 22, 30.

[276] Northrup (1998), 285; Ashtor (1983), 52–3.

Commercial monopolies also triggered struggles between different *alien* guilds. Such conflict was rife in most Mediterranean trading centres from the very beginning of the medieval Commercial Revolution – among the various Italian merchant guilds in Constantinople from the late eleventh century on,[277] between the Pisan and Genoese merchant guilds in Messina in 1129,[278] between the Genoese and Pisan merchant guilds in Acre in 1222–4 and 1256–7,[279] between the Tuscan and Genoese merchant guilds in Nîmes in 1282,[280] among the Pisan, Venetian and Genoese merchant guilds in Cairo in the late 1280s,[281] and between the Genoese and Venetian merchant colonies on the Black Sea in the fourteenth century.[282]

Such conflicts gave rise not just to minor scuffles but to pitched battles. In the spring of 1162, for instance, over a thousand members of the Pisan merchant colony in Constantinople attacked three hundred members of the Genoese merchant colony, capturing the Genoese *fondaco* and looting 30,000 bezants worth of merchandise.[283] In 1348, when the new Byzantine emperor rescinded the privileges of the Genoese merchant colony in Constantinople, the Genoese ravaged the warehouses and shipping of the Byzantine merchants who had been allowed to infringe on Genoese privileges. The outcome was total victory for the Genoese in 1349, enabling them to block merchants of other nations – specifically the Venetians and Byzantines – from infringing on the monopoly they claimed over trade in Tana, the Sea of Azov and the Crimea, which they continued to enforce with violence throughout the 1350s.[284]

Vigorous conflicts over monopoly privileges arose among alien merchant guilds in northern European trading centres – between German and Scandinavian merchant guilds in thirteenth- and fourteenth-century Novgorod,[285] between different factions of the English Staplers in Flanders in the 1320s,[286] between Hanseatic and Dutch merchant guilds in fifteenth-century Livonia,[287] between the merchant guilds of different Spanish cities in fifteenth-century Bruges,[288] and between the Spanish merchant guild in Bruges and a proposed branch in Antwerp in the fifteenth century.[289]

Such conflicts were not restricted to the Middle Ages but continued into the early modern period, wherever merchant guilds survived. In the sixteenth and seventeenth centuries, the customs privileges and

---

[277] Runciman (1987), 148.   [278] Abulafia (1978), 72.
[279] Abulafia (1986a), 530; Pryor (2000), 427–8, 435–6.   [280] Limor (1991), 40.
[281] Ashtor (1983), 14.   [282] *Ibid.*, 76.   [283] Slessarev (1969), 96.
[284] Laiou-Thomadakis (1980–1), 192–5.   [285] Angermann (1987), 62, 68, 74.
[286] Lloyd (1977), 119–21.   [287] Dollinger (1970), 300.
[288] R. S. Smith (1940), 68–9; Henn (1999), 137.   [289] Harreld (2004a), 57.

commercial monopolies enjoyed by the Ragusan (Dubrovnik) merchant colonies in the Ottoman Balkans evoked conflicts with rival Bosnian merchant colonies, giving rise in Belgrade to decades of struggle for control of the combined Ragusan–Bosnian merchant colony, in which each faction appealed to the Islamic authorities against its Christian rivals.[290] In the early seventeenth century, the alien merchant guilds in Constantinople, led by Venice, lobbied vigorously to block the grant of trading permits to the Dutch, indicating their strong belief that increased competition would reduce their own oligopoly profits.[291] The Armenian merchant colony's successful bid for the legal monopoly over exports of raw silk from Persia in 1619 gave rise to conflict with the English East India Company for the rest of the seventeenth century.[292]

The monopolies of privileged merchant companies also had real economic effects, judging by the costly conflict they evoked. In the 1570s, the English Merchant Adventurers protested that the exclusive monopoly and membership policies of the proposed new Spanish Company would harm its members, 'to the great hindrance of the navigation. . . and the great diminishing of her majesty's customs'.[293] Ten years later, the Adventurers objected that permitting a merchant to belong both to the Adventurers and to the Spanish Company would breed even more conflict: 'we shall have opinions, sects, divisions, brawls and suspicions amongst us as if it were to begin hell on earth'.[294] In the 1580s, legal monopolies over importing currants from different sources evoked clashes among the Merchant Adventurers, the Levant Company and the Venice Company.[295]

Merchant company privileges gave rise to similar inter-corporate conflicts in the Netherlands. After 1621, the various local chambers of the Dutch West India Company (WIC) 'acted to monopolize the pre-1621 trades of their local merchants: Zeeland claimed exclusive privileges on the Wild Coast of South America, the North Holland ports fought bitterly to keep the Venezuela salt trade under their control, and the Amsterdam chamber monopolized the New Netherlands enterprise'.[296]

The monopolies of different privileged companies also provoked violent struggles in eighteenth-century Portugal. In 1755, the monopoly granted by the government to the Companhia do Grão-Pará e Maranhão was sufficiently effective to attract the immediate opposition of the Mesa do Bem Comum dos Homens de Negócio, a merchant fraternity

---

[290] Molnár (2007), esp. 104–26.   [291] Dursteler (2006), 132.
[292] Aslanian (2004), 49–50.   [293] Croft (1973a), xii (quotation); Archer (1991), 48.
[294] Quoted in Croft (1973a), xv.   [295] Archer (1991), 48.
[296] De Vries and Van der Woude (1997), 399, 465.

established in Lisbon a generation earlier. This opposition was in turn regarded as sufficiently serious that the prime minister dissolved the merchant fraternity instantly and condemned its members to penal banishment. In turn, the small-scale merchants were so furious at being excluded by the new monopoly that opposition to the Company spurred a series of violent riots, assassination attempts and state executions.[297]

In Spain and Spanish America, consulado monopolies created incentives for constant conflict. Throughout much of the eighteenth century, the monopoly of the Cádiz consulado over trade between Spain and Spanish America was perceived as sufficiently effectual to evoke escalating attacks from the Mexico consulado.[298] Within Spanish America, the rival Mexico and Lima consulados 'jealously guarded their privileged monopolies and successfully opposed new consulados in America for two centuries, despite petitions for such institutions from other cities from the mid-seventeenth century forward'.[299] When the Bourbon crown granted a charter to a new consulado in Vera Cruz in 1795, the Mexico consulado complained bitterly and demanded its abolition.[300]

Conflict is costly in terms of time, money and foregone trade. Most people avoid disputes that do not promise significant benefits. The willingness of so many alien merchant guilds in so many trading centres at so many different periods to invest in attacking rival guilds' monopolies and defending their own suggests that they saw these monopolies as enforceable and profitable.

4.2.4 Systems of enforcement

Another way alien merchant guilds revealed their belief that their legal privileges had commercial value was by setting up enforcement mechanisms. They invested in systems to police their admission requirements, detect trade by outsiders, enforce supply quotas and price regulations, and penalize clandestine trade by their own members. We even have records of some alien merchant guilds extending their enforcement systems to branches of their guilds in other trading centres and investing in regular revisions of their internal regulations. Would they have engaged in these activities had they not believed their economic regulations to be valuable and enforceable?

Most alien merchant guilds set up systems to detect merchants from their home polity who failed to register with the guild or pay its fees – as in

---

[297] Maxwell (2001), 173–4.   [298] S. J. Stein and Stein (2000).
[299] Woodward (2005), 635.   [300] Paquette (2007), 271.

the cases of the Lucchese merchant guild in Bruges,[301] the Fondaco dei Tedeschi in Venice,[302] the Catalan merchant guild in Bruges[303] and the German Hanse branches in Novgorod, Bergen, Bruges and London.[304] The London Hanse Kontor went so far as to formulate explicitly in 1388, and again in 1460, the formal procedure which a Hanse merchant had to follow to be admitted to privileges at the London Kontor, and the precise criteria he had to fulfil to achieve such admission.[305]

The obverse of policing admissions requirements was penalizing non-members who tried to trade in contravention of the guild's monopoly. So Florentine merchant guilds in medieval France boycotted any Florentine innkeeper who sought to expand into merchant trading.[306] In 1109, Genoa used military threats to force the count of Toulouse to refuse to permit any merchants except for members of the Genoese merchant colony to use his town of Saint-Gilles-du-Gard for the Mediterranean trade.[307] After 1143, Genoa used threats of military reprisal to prohibit the trade of Montpellier merchants beyond the Roads of Genoa, preventing them from competing with Genoese merchant colonies in the Levant.[308] The Genoese merchant guild in fourteenth-century Caffa set up a system to confiscate the goods of outsiders trying to encroach on its monopoly over the Black Sea trade.[309] In 1376, the English Company of the Staple brought about the impeachment of Lord Latimer and Richard Lyons for granting licences permitting foreign merchants to export wool from England in violation of the Company's privileges.[310] In the fifteenth century, the English Merchant Adventurers employed salaried officials in both Antwerp and Germany to search for contraband goods traded by Englishmen who were not members of the Adventurers.[311] In the seventeenth and eighteenth centuries, the Royal African Company made 'explicit provisions to ensure the enforcement of its monopoly, including courts on the West African coast to deal with interlopers'.[312] The Portuguese government enforced the monopoly of the Companhia do Grão-Pará e Maranhão by expelling from Brazil all traders acting as commission agents for foreign merchants in 1755,[313] and deploying the navy to make huge seizures of contraband from non-Company merchants as late as 1806.[314]

---

[301] R. De Roover (1948a), 18.   [302] Choroškevic (1996), 84–6.
[303] Gilliodts-van Severen (1901–2), 79.   [304] Dollinger (1970), 89–90.
[305] Burckhardt (2005), 74.   [306] Szabó (1983), 85.   [307] Reyerson (1994), 363.
[308] *Ibid.*   [309] Abulafia (1986b), 205.   [310] Dodd (2002), 97.
[311] Sutton (2002), 34–5; Willan (1959), 40–1.
[312] S. R. H. Jones and Ville (1996), 910 n. 42 (quotation); Davies (1957), 98–9, 106, 121, 126–9.
[313] Maxwell (2001), 173.   [314] Arruda (2000), 871.

Alien merchant guilds also set up systems to ensure that member merchants complied with internal guild rules. Supply quotas were crucial to profiting from legal monopoly privileges, so guilds unsurprisingly placed considerable emphasis on enforcing them. In the thirteenth century, German Hanse branch offices enforced supply restrictions in both Novgorod[315] and Bergen.[316] In the mid-fourteenth century, the Genoese merchant colony on Chios set up monitoring systems to enforce its monopoly of the mastic trade.[317] In the fifteenth century, the English Merchant Adventurers set up enforcement systems to police its export quotas to the Low Countries and Germany.[318] From 1416 on, the German Hanse branch in Bergen penalized violation of its stockfish staple using confiscation and expulsion, on the grounds that a Hanseatic merchant who violated the staple quota would be 'no longer worthy of the privileges of a merchant of the German Hanse'.[319] In 1456 the Hanse Kontor in Bruges shut down an illegal 'Hanseatic factory' in Nantes which violated its controls over supplying Russian furs to western Europe.[320]

Alien merchant guilds also set up systems to enforce their price regulations, again unsurprisingly given the importance of such rules for successful monopolies. In the fourteenth century, Venetian and Genoese merchant guilds in the Levant penalized members who paid spice suppliers above the guild-mandated monopsony price.[321] In 1343, members of the English Company of the Staple agreed 'to keep the wool at a high price' in Bruges.[322] In 1487, members of the Venetian merchant community in London agreed 'to avoid competition in the sale of soap in London' and to purchase gall-nuts jointly in Venice and refrain from competing internally in selling them in London.[323] In another such contract in 1506, members of the Venetian merchant community in Valencia agreed to refrain from bidding competitively against each other:

Joint action was ... stimulated by the desire for monopoly or for a favorable bargaining position. Merchants generally were on the lookout for ways of making agreements to effect some temporary monopoly or near monopoly. Groups that had learned to act together as a galley company or as a *maona* seeking cargo could the more easily act together to prevent competition.[324]

The participants in these agreements did not necessarily consist of the entire Venetian merchant guilds in London or Valencia, but they did

---

[315] Dollinger (1970), 48.   [316] *Ibid.*, 49.   [317] Goldschmidt (1891), 295–6.
[318] Kohn (2003a), 19, referring to Ramsey (1994), and Ball (1977).
[319] Quoted in Wubs-Mrozewicz (2005), 209 n. 15.   [320] Dollinger (1970), 254.
[321] Ashtor (1983), 415.   [322] Quoted in Power (1941), 89.
[323] Lane (1944), 192–3.   [324] *Ibid.*, 192.

include all the Venetian merchants involved in a particular galley fleet sailing, which, as Lane points out, could result in a 'temporary monopoly or near monopoly'.[325]

One of the most important mechanisms set up by alien merchant guilds to enforce their monopolies was to require all members to trade in public locations where compliance with quotas and prices could be collectively monitored. In the thirteenth and fourteenth centuries, Catalan merchant colonies in overseas trading locations such as Tunisia ensured compliance with regulations on volume, price and taxation by requiring members to conduct all transactions at the *fondaco*, where the colony's secretary recorded goods entering and leaving.[326] In the fourteenth and fifteenth centuries, to ensure compliance with Hanse regulations, the Bergen Kontor forbade commercial business on board ship or on the gangway, while the Novgorod Kontor forbade anyone to do business on his own or in the presence of only one other Hanse merchant.[327] Only in Bruges did German Hanse merchants live scattered in hostels all over the city instead of residing in a closed complex, so the Hanse aldermen in Bruges appointed one or two merchants in each hostel to report any violations of the Hanse statutes and privileges, keeping their identities secret so that they would also watch over each other.[328]

But merchant guilds also set up a myriad of other enforcement systems to ensure compliance with their monopoly privileges. In the thirteenth and fourteenth centuries, Italian merchant guilds in Alexandria penalized members who applied for permanent resident status to avoid guild price and quantity regulations.[329] Medieval Venetian merchant guilds in the eastern Mediterranean set up a system of fines to penalize any member using Anconitan shipping.[330] At the same period, Venetian and Genoese merchant guilds in the Levant penalized members who employed middlemen counter to guild regulations.[331] In 1320, the 'mayor' of the English Staple Company systematically monitored Customs registers to catch illegal exports of English wool, taking evidence on oath and fining violators.[332] In 1365 the Hanse Kontor in Bergen set up a system of penalties to be imposed on any member who violated 'the merchants' rules' (*des copmans wilkor*).[333] In 1395, the Genoese merchant guild in Bruges imposed banishment on any member violating the requirement

---

[325] *Ibid.*   [326] Hibbert (1949), 353.   [327] Burckhardt (2005), 63, 72.   [328] *Ibid.*, 71.
[329] Ashtor (1983), 400.   [330] *Ibid.*, 240.   [331] *Ibid.*, 415.   [332] Lloyd (1977), 111.
[333] Burckhardt (2005), 62. The term *wilkor* (modern *Willküren*) is used in Hanse internal regulations to refer to individual provisions on particular matters, in contrast to *Skra*, *Schra* or *Schrage*, which refer to more extensive collections of legal ordinances which covered the entire range of activities of Hanse merchants, whether in a particular trading centre or more generally; see Schlüter (1911), 1.

that galleys call at Bruges before sailing to England.[334] In the fourteenth and fifteenth centuries, the Hanse penalized members who formed commercial partnerships with outsiders,[335] transported wares of non-Hanse members[336] or illegally took foreign naturalization to circumvent Hanse regulations.[337] In the seventeenth and eighteenth centuries, the English East India Company set up monitoring systems to detect employees engaged in 'private trade' which violated the Company monopoly, erecting a schedule of sanctions including suspension, dismissal, prosecution and confiscation of wares.[338]

Different branches of the same alien merchant guild are known to have communicated with one another to ensure that all branches enforced penalties against members who violated guild regulations. In July 1378, for instance, Jean Interminelli offended so seriously against the rules of the Lucca merchant guild in Bruges that he was expelled. The Lucca consuls in Bruges then wrote to the Lucca merchant guilds in Paris and London to ensure that those branches also enforced the penalty and refused to receive Interminelli as a member.[339] The same thing happened in October 1382, when the Lucca merchant consuls in Bruges wrote to their counterparts in Paris and London to notify them of the fine of 125 florins imposed on two deviant members of the Bruges community, Francesco Panichi and Lazzaro Guinigi.[340] When one branch of an alien merchant guild was unable or unwilling to enforce penalties imposed by another, it regarded itself as obliged to justify its behaviour, as in 1378 when a Lucca merchant called Pietro di Buono was fined and expelled by the Lucca merchant guild in Bruges but absconded successfully to Paris. When the Lucca merchant guild in Paris failed, for unknown reasons, to maintain these penalties against Di Buono, it wrote a letter of self-exculpation to the Bruges branch, signed by 'Your brothers, the community of Lucchese living in Paris', reflecting the expectation that under normal circumstances it would have enforced the penalties imposed by its 'brother' guild in Bruges.[341]

Alien merchant guilds also expended resources keeping written records and revising their written regulations, something they would not have done had they not expected these regulations to be enforced. Perhaps the best documented practice is that of the German Hanse, which constantly issued edicts and revisions of its ordinances, at first for each Kontor separately and later for the Hanse as a whole. The view that these Hanse rules mattered is vividly illustrated by the fact that in 1370 it was discovered

---

[334] R. De Roover (1948a), 16. [335] Burckhardt (2005), 65, 71. [336] *Ibid.*, 63, 71.
[337] Dollinger (1970), 201. [338] Hejeebu (2005), 501–2. [339] Mirot (1927), 66.
[340] *Ibid.* [341] Quoted in *ibid.*

that the ordinance (*Schra*) of the Novgorod Kontor had been improperly emended, with several pages having been cut out, others written over, and supplementary notes added to the existing provisions; the Hanse central office immediately ordered that a new *Schra* be drawn up, with severe penalties for future illegitimate revisions.[342] Comparisons of the surviving ordinances for the four different Hanse Kontore show variations in regulations to govern conditions specific to each Kontor location, but also remarkable commonalities in those provisions relating to trading privileges, suggesting that Hanse ordinances were drawn up in the expectation that they would be enforced.[343]

Issuing regulations, monitoring compliance, penalizing violations and recording regulations are all costly. Organizations only incur such costs when rules are worth enforcing. Why would alien merchant guilds have set up elaborate systems of regulation, detection and punishment to enforce legal monopolies that were of no practical value? The fact that alien merchant guilds did incur these costs indicates that they regarded enforcement of their regulations as bringing real economic benefits.

4.2.5   Willingness to pay for licences and exemptions

A further test of whether merchant guild monopolies were effective in practice is whether people were willing to pay to get around them. If the price regulations, sales quotas or staple requirements of alien merchant guilds were not enforced, then no one should have been willing to pay for exemptions. Likewise, if merchant guild monopolies were unenforceable, no one should have been interested in obtaining a share of the profits they generated. What we observe is the opposite. Contemporaries eagerly purchased exemptions from guild monopolies and licences to share in their profits.

As early as 992, merchants of other origins – 'Amalfitans, Jews, Lombards of Bari, and others' – were incurring the costs and risks of illegally registering their goods as 'Venetian' so as to share the exclusive legal monopolies of the Venetian merchant guild in Constantinople.[344] In 1276, citizens of Mechelen who were not members of the cloth-merchants' guild paid a fee of 6 sous 4 deniers for 'rights of hanse' – essentially a guild permit to engage in trade beyond the Meuse and Escaut rivers.[345] In the fourteenth century, Venetian merchants eagerly paid for papers fraudulently stating them to hold Genoese citizenship so as to share in the monopoly privileges of Genoese merchant colonies in

---

[342] Burckhardt (2005), 76.   [343] *Ibid.*, esp. 76–7.
[344] Lopez (1945), 39 n. 2.   [345] Van Doorslaer (1907), 36.

'Romania' (Byzantine territories outside Constantinople).[346] In the fourteenth and fifteenth centuries, Greeks and Turks paid to acquire real or fraudulent Venetian papers so as to share in the exclusive monopolies enjoyed by the Venetian merchant guilds in Constantinople.[347] In fourteenth- and fifteenth-century Alexandria, Italian merchants found the price-fixing and sales quotas of their own merchant guilds so burdensome that they applied to Muslim rulers for permanent resident status so they could buy and sell competitively outside the guild framework.[348] In the sixteenth and seventeenth centuries, Bosnian merchants incurred costs and risks to label their goods fraudulently as 'Ragusan' so as to share in the privileges the merchant guilds of Ragusa (Dubrovnik) enjoyed from the Ottomans.[349]

One alien merchant guild which left particularly rich evidence of people's willingness to pay to circumvent (or share in) its monopoly was the English Company of the Staple. In the 1370s, non-members of the Company were willing to pay high fees to get licences exempting them from the Company's compulsory staple and its associated regulation of prices and quotas.[350] In the early 1380s, non-members made loans to the English crown on generous terms in return for licences to trade wool in circumvention of the Company's staple at Calais.[351] In 1435, a Hull merchant called Hamo Sutton, in association with two London merchants, loaned the English king 8,000 marks in return for a permit to sell wool in contravention of the privileges of the Company.[352] In 1468, Edward IV granted a licence to export wool in circumvention of the Company's privileges, to replace a previous grant worth £400 per annum, an indication of the high value placed on this legal exemption.[353] Creditors of Edward IV – including Stapler merchants themselves – accepted such exemptions in lieu of repayment of the royal debts.[354] The king, his family members and other great English personages sold such exemptions to Italian merchants to export wool directly to Italy via Southampton and the Straits of Gibraltar, bypassing the Company monopoly.[355] So valuable were these licences that they traded as a sort of parallel currency, purchased from their immediate recipients by merchants expecting to profit from circumventing the Company's monopoly while sharing in the high selling prices it created.[356]

From the sixteenth to the eighteenth century, the intercontinental trading monopoly of the Seville consulado (which shifted to the Cádiz

[346] Tai (1996), 127–8.   [347] Laiou-Thomadakis (1980–1), 212, 216 with n. 152.
[348] Ashtor (1983), 400.   [349] Molnár (2007), 109.
[350] Dodd (2002), 196; Lloyd (1977), 218–20; Power (1941), 89.
[351] Dodd (2002), 97.   [352] Lloyd (1977), 271.   [353] Power (1926), 21.
[354] Ibid.   [355] Ibid., 19–23.   [356] Ibid., 21–2.

consulado after 1680) was enforced so strictly that foreigners paid Spanish guild members to act as their *prestanombres* (front men), in order to participate in the Spanish American trade.[357] A firm set up by four Florentine merchants in 1532 obtained a licence to trade with the Indies in contravention of the monopoly of the Seville consulado, but when the consulado protested, the firm transferred its interests to a Sevillian who served as their *prestanombre*.[358] Other foreigners purchased 'concessions' from the Spanish crown permitting them to participate in the monopoly of the Seville or Cádiz consulado.[359] Still others married daughters of Spanish merchants or naturalized their children as Spaniards to acquire legal access to the Spanish American market.[360]

Similarly, English merchants were willing to buy special licences from the English East India Company to share in its monopoly and even pay the Company a consulage tax of 2 per cent of the value of their trade.[361] Likewise, Dutch merchants who were not members of the Dutch West India Company were willing to pay licence fees to participate legally in the Atlantic trade it monopolized.[362] People would not have been willing to spend resources to share or circumvent the monopolies of alien merchant guilds and privileged companies had these monopolies not been enforced in practice, making them valuable to both insiders and outsiders.

4.2.6   *Effects on prices and volume of trade*

The era of merchant guilds pre-dates most systematic statistical measurement. So we only have occasional snapshots of the effect of merchant guilds and privileged companies on prices and supplies. But when figures survive, they indicate that merchant guild monopolies could exert real effects on markets.

One relatively well-documented case is the German Hanse's monopoly over the Skåne fairs in what is now Sweden. In the thirteenth century, two fairs began to flourish from July to October–November each year at Skanör and Falsterbo on the south coast of Skåne, mainly focused around the trade in herring and other fish, much in demand in western Europe.[363] As long as Skåne was ruled by the Danish king, merchants from Flanders, Holland, England, Scandinavia and Germany visited the fairs in large numbers, not only purchasing herring, but selling their own cloth, wine, spices, drugs, furs, wax, wood, iron and copper.[364] The

---

[357] Woodward (2005), 635; J. Stein and Stein (2000); C. R. Phillips (1990), 90–1.
[358] Melis (1954).   [359] C. R. Phillips (1990), 95 n. 146.   [360] K. Weber (2002), 114.
[361] Hejeebu (2005), 503 n. 31.   [362] De Vries and Van der Woude (1997), 399, 465.
[363] Jahnke (1997).   [364] Jahnke (2000), 90–134.

German Hanse sought to exclude these western European competitors by threats and force, but without success. It was not until 1370 that the Hanse obtained political rights in Skåne and used them systematically to eject non-Hanse merchants. By 1400 English merchants were no longer frequenting the fairs; soon merchants from Friesia, Holland and Zeeland also ceased to visit; even the other North Sea merchants gradually withdrew. By the end of the fifteenth century, the Skåne fairs were being visited solely by members of the German Hanse and had become much smaller, no longer involving a wide range of wares or merchants from different destinations. They had become, essentially, herring fairs at which the only wares were fish, the only sellers were fisherman and the only purchasers were Hanse merchants. The Hanse's monopoly privileges in Skåne after 1370 visibly reduced the number of market participants, the range of wares and the overall volume of trade.[365]

Another documented example is provided by the Hanseatic and Dutch merchants in the Norwegian port of Bergen. In the early sixteenth century, 900–1,500 Hanseatic merchants resided in Bergen in winter and 2,000–3,000 in summer, compared to 56–66 Hollanders in summer and only 3 in winter – despite the growth of Dutch trade elsewhere in the North Sea. Wubs-Mrozewicz ascribes this to the fact that the Hanseatic privileges in Bergen meant that German merchants were legally permitted to reside there throughout the winter as well as to visit there as 'guest merchants' in the summer, whereas Dutch merchants were legally restricted even in summer, had winter residence limited in 1507 and were banned completely as winter residents after 1541.[366] According to the same study, the restriction of winter residence rights for Holland merchants in sixteenth-century Bergen was followed by the growth of Dutch trade with Trondheim, the formation of a Dutch merchant colony there, and an increasing tendency of the *nordfarere* (Norwegian traders and fisherman) to travel to Trondheim to trade with the competitive Dutch instead of to Bergen where they were obliged to trade solely with the monopolistic Hanse.[367] These findings suggest that the Hanse merchant monopoly in Bergen excluded outsiders and depressed the volume of trade.

The English Company of the Staple provides another example of a merchant guild whose impact can be analysed more systematically – in this case, through the English Customs registers. The compulsory English wool staple, first established in 1313, required all wool exporters to be members of the Company, to export English wool exclusively via a

---

[365] Irsigler (2002), 47–8; Jahnke (1997); Jahnke (2000), 90–134.
[366] Wubs-Mrozewicz (2005), 221–2.   [367] *Ibid.*, 228.

designated locality on the European continent and to submit to Company regulations governing prices and trade volumes.[368] As Power points out, the monopoly enjoyed by the Company was inversely related to growth in the wool trade:

> the free trade periods were the periods of greatest expansion; the trade rose rapidly from 1274 to 1313; it fell immediately the foreign staple was put on, and it rose again during the free trade period, 1328 to 1332. With the abolition of the foreign staple and the monopolies in 1353 it picked up again for twenty years under the home staples and export by aliens, but with the appearance of the Company of the Staple at Calais in 1363 it began to fall again and thereafter fell steadily.[369]

Power also argues that the creation of the monopolistic Company was associated with stagnation or even decline in the number of English merchants participating in the wool export trade, from about 400 before the Company was created in 1313, to only 300–400 Company members under Edward IV (r. 1461–83), most of them large and wealthy operators.[370]

Subsequent research has confirmed Power's findings, providing further details of the damage inflicted by the Company. Lloyd, Kermode and Dodd separately find that the privileges of the Company harmed English merchants and trading ports specializing in cheaper grades of wool.[371] The obligation to export to a compulsory location on the continent imposed disproportionate costs on producers and exporters of cheaper wool, especially in the north of England. For one thing, a lower-priced commodity was less able to bear the additional transaction costs and overheads involved in being transported to a particular location and being inspected for legality by the Staple officials.[372] Kermode calculated that in 1337, these transaction costs, together with 'the peculiar circumstances of the wool monopoly', caused the purchase price of wool in Yorkshire to be £3–£6 while its selling price in Flanders was over £11.[373] As pointed out in a fourteenth-century petition from merchants trading in coarse northern English wools, a sack of wool that sold for 4–5 marks incurred the same costs from the Staple as a sack that sold for 15–16 marks.[374] Moreover, low-grade northern English wool could often only compete in international markets when its exporters were free

---

[368] On the complicated history of the English wool staple in this period, see Lloyd (1977), 110–28; Power (1941), 86–103; Dodd (2002).
[369] Power (1941), 103.   [370] Power (1926), 19; Power (1941), 102–3.
[371] Dodd (2002), 94–5, 97, 101–2; Lloyd (1977), 126–8; Kermode (1998), 101.
[372] Dodd (2002), 94–5; Lloyd (1977), 126–7; Kermode (1998), 101; Power (1933), 71.
[373] Kermode (1998), 192.   [374] Dodd (2002), 94.

to exploit locational advantages making their wares cheaper than high-grade southern wool. But the compulsory staple made it illegal to seek out these locational advantages, forcing everyone to sell in the same location. The result was that, as Lloyd shows, wool exports from English towns specializing in lower grades of wool were crippled by the Stapler privileges.[375] The number of merchants participating in the English wool export trade contracted in the fifteenth century, he finds, as the 'delays and monopoly inherent in the new system' squeezed out small-scale traders and favoured an ever-narrower group of large-scale merchants, mainly from London.[376] The monopoly enjoyed by the Company of the Staple thus caused the wool export trade as a whole to contract and restricted participation to a smaller number of merchants.

Similar effects can be observed in reverse when merchant guilds and privileged companies lost their monopolies or stopped being able to enforce them: the number of market participants and the volume of trade both expanded. After *c.* 1440, when the Norwegian crown began to reduce the privileges of the German Hanse in Bergen, there was an influx of merchants from Holland, even though the surviving privileges of the Hanse merchants still prevented Dutch merchants from competing on equal terms.[377] In 1762, likewise, when the privileged Schwechat Company lost its monopoly, the textile trade in Upper Austria, the Waldviertel and southern Bohemia expanded hugely.[378] In 1778, when Spanish consulados lost their monopoly, legal trade expanded hugely in Central America, the Río de la Plata, Chile, Cuba and Venezuela.[379] In the early nineteenth century, when all surviving merchant consulados were abolished, Spanish America saw an immediate influx of previously excluded merchants from Germany and other countries.[380] When in 1808 the monopoly of privileged companies such as the Companhia do Grão-Pará e Maranhão over the trade between Portugal and Brazil was abolished, the proportion of manufactures in Portuguese exports to Brazil fell from 35.6 per cent in 1796–1806 to 21.6 per cent in 1816–22, and were replaced by lower-cost English manufactures carried by lower-cost English merchant shipping.[381] This was bad for high-cost Portuguese merchants and manufacturers but a boon for poor consumers and intermediate producers in Brazil. The loss of monopoly privileges by these various merchant guilds thus observably increased the number of market participants and the volume of trade.

---

[375] Lloyd (1977), 126–7, 136.   [376] *Ibid.*, 265–6.
[377] Wubs-Mrozewicz (2005), 218–19.   [378] Cerman (1993), 289.
[379] Woodward (2005), 635–7.   [380] K. Weber (2002), 114.
[381] Arruda (2000), 872–3.

4.2.7   Guild embargoes

Further evidence that alien merchant guilds were able to enforce their monopolies is provided by the sporadic embargoes they declared. Had these guilds not exercised market power, their embargoes would have been ineffective and neither they nor foreign rulers would have regarded them as a credible bargaining device. In practice, however, when alien merchant guilds imposed embargoes, trade often contracted and rulers bowed to pressure. This suggests that alien merchant guilds were in a position to enforce their monopolies at least on those routes, in those centres and over those markets in which they were major players. Although guild embargoes could be broken, and sometimes were, large merchant guilds could be such substantial players in certain markets that they were able to reap monopoly profits by limiting outgoing or incoming trade to those centres.[382]

The German Hanse, for instance, declared embargoes against various European trading centres at different times, limiting both *sales* of essential supplies (such as salt and grain) and *purchases* of key exports (such as Russian furs, Skåne herring and Flemish cloths). The Hanse's trade embargo against Novgorod in 1277 was intended to reduce western trade there to nil, and certainly limited it enough to put significant pressure on Russian and Lithuanian rulers in Livonia.[383] The Hanse imposed periodic embargoes on salt supplies to Pskov (Pleskau) which were effective enough to bring Russian rulers to heel in trade conflicts.[384] The joint embargo by the Hanse and Spanish merchant guilds against Bruges in 1280–2, during which both bodies decamped for two years to Aardenburg, reduced the volume of trade to Bruges to such dangerously low levels that the town granted sweeping concessions (including limits on local guild privileges) to entice the Hansards and Spaniards back.[385] Hanseatic embargoes of Bruges in 1307–9, 1351, and 1358–60 were also sufficiently effective that they resulted in Bruges making valuable concessions in order to induce the Hanse to return.[386] The Hanse's embargoes against Norway in 1284 and 1306 affected imports so seriously that famine broke out, the ruler capitulated and Hanseatic merchants secured wider trading privileges.[387] Skåne herring were always important enough that monopolizing them was a good way of exerting political pressure, as shown by the fact that the Danish king's confiscation of Lübeck merchants' goods and ships at the Skåne fair of 1201 was effective in forcing Lübeck to recognize

---

[382] Spruyt (1994), 127.   [383] Dollinger (1970), 48.   [384] Angermann (1987), 80.
[385] Dollinger (1970), 48.   [386] Paravicini (1992), 100–4.
[387] Riis (2005), 34; Dollinger (1970), 49.

Danish sovereignty.[388] Consequently, having the legal monopoly over Skåne herring became an extremely effective way for merchant guilds, in particular the Hanse, to exert pressure in later centuries. In 1392, for instance, the Hanseatic embargo of Skåne caused herring prices to rise all over central Europe, testifying to the Hanse's effective monopoly.[389] The Hanse's blockade against Swedish iron ore exports in the 1420s and 1430s is described as having been so effective that it led to war between the Swedish Crown and the Wendish Hanse towns from 1426 on.[390] The Hanse's threat of an embargo against the Flemish textile centre of Dendermonde in the 1430s prevented the town from seeking better prices by diversifying away from the Bruges staple to sell cloth in Brabant and Bergen-op-Zoom. The fact that the Hanse could compel the industrial producers of an entire town to continue to patronize the Bruges staple, despite offering poor prices and conditions, is clear evidence that it exercised monopsony power in the Flemish textile market.[391] As late as 1455, the Flemish crown's instructions to its ambassador to negotiate an end to the German Hanse's embargo of Bruges stated explicitly that 'the welfare of this country resides principally in two points, namely the merchantry and the drapery, which two points, with the absence and departure of the Easterlings [German Hanse merchants], are now asleep and undirected, to the great harm and disadvantage of the country'.[392]

The Hanse was by no means the only alien merchant guild to declare embargoes with economic effects real enough to put pressure on towns and rulers. In 1228, the Venetian merchant colonies in Greece and the Byzantine empire declared an embargo on trade with Epiros and Thessaloniki which, it is claimed, successfully compelled their belligerent ruler to sign a truce with the empire.[393] Similar embargoes were threatened by Flemish merchant guilds in England in 1261, exerting effective pressure on the English crown.[394] In 1280–2, as we have seen, the Spanish merchant guild in Bruges joined the German one in imposing an embargo which successfully put pressure on the government of Bruges and the count of Flanders.[395] On several occasions in the later thirteenth and early fourteenth centuries, the Venetians declared embargoes on trade with Egypt, and at least one of them – the embargo of 1323 – was so effective that in negotiations to end the embargo in 1345, the Sultan complained that not a single Venetian ship had visited his ports for twenty-three years.[396] In 1340, the Genoese merchant guild declared

[388] Christensen (1953), 244–5.
[389] Dollinger (1970), 80. [390] Olesen (1999), 216. [391] Stabel (1997), 156.
[392] Quoted in Henn (1999), 141. [393] See Bredenkamp (1996), 143–7.
[394] Moore (1985), 301. [395] Dollinger (1970), 48; Maréchal (1953), 12.
[396] Stöckly (1995), 133–4.

a *devetum* (embargo) against the city of Tabrīz in modern Iran, the most important centre of Italian commerce in continental Asia at that period. The embargo was so effective that in 1344, the ruler of Tabrīz promised to grant all demands if Genoa would relax the embargo.[397] In 1362, when Emperor John V unilaterally forbade the import of wine into Constantinople, the Venetian merchant colony threatened an embargo on Constantinople, Thessaloniki and the rest of the Byzantine empire, causing the emperor to back down.[398] In the fourteenth and fifteenth centuries, the Venetian merchant colony in Damascus periodically declared a boycott (*abatalatio*) against the ass and camel drivers who transported their wares to the port in Beirut, against Muslim and native Christian merchants, and against the sultan's officials.[399] In 1449–52, the English Company of the Staple declared a boycott of the Antwerp fairs, which is believed to have been a major factor influencing the dukes of Brabant to lift a ban on English cloth imports; the Staplers repeatedly gained wider privileges from the Antwerp city authorities by threatening to transfer their operations to Bergen-op-Zoom, Middelburg, Emden or Hamburg.[400] All of these alien merchant guilds, towns, territories and rulers evidently regarded an embargo by a major merchant guild as a credible threat, testifying to that guild's market power.

Where a particular merchant guild was the *sole* player in a particular market, as the German Hanse was in medieval Norway, it could affect the volume of trade enduringly.[401] Where it was a *large* player in a particular market – as the Hanse or the Spanish guild was in Bruges – it could affect the volume of trade sufficiently in the short term to extract significant commercial concessions. But this strategy was much more effective when more than one alien merchant guild acted in concert. Thus the 1280 embargo of Bruges was so effective because not only the German Hanse but also the Spanish merchant guilds there interdicted trade and moved their headquarters to Aardenburg.[402] A second embargo in 1307 was less successful because only the Hanse moved to Aardenburg while the other alien merchant guilds stayed put, the count of Flanders curtailed the rights of foreign merchants in Aardenburg, and Bruges was irreplaceable because it had become a meeting place for merchants from all over the world. Nevertheless, although the 1307 embargo was not perfect, the Hanse was able to influence the volume of trade to Bruges sufficiently to induce both the town government and the count of

---

[397] Briys and De ter Beerst (2006), 37; Di Cosmo (2005), 403; Lopez (1943), 181–4.
[398] Laiou-Thomadakis (1980–1), 216 with n. 150.
[399] Ashtor (1983), 400 with n. 241.   [400] Lloyd (1977), 272–3; Barnouw (1952), 104.
[401] Dollinger (1970), 49–50.   [402] W. Stein (1902), 123–30; Maréchal (1953), 12.

Flanders to grant it wider commercial privileges in 1309. Thus even in one of the major trading centres of medieval Europe, where there were at least a dozen different alien merchant guilds, the Hanse enjoyed sufficient market power to influence the volume of trade and extract commercial concessions.[403]

In more distant international trading centres, such as the Byzantine empire, the Genoese and Venetian merchant colonies enjoyed sufficient market power by virtue of their legal privileges and backing from their mother cities to influence the volume of trade. In 1306–7, the Genoese merchant colonies in Constantinople and Caffa were described by contemporaries as controlling the grain provisioning of Constantinople. By that date, Black Sea grain was important enough to Constantinople that the virtual monopoly of the Genoese merchant colony at Caffa over the Black Sea trade was a serious matter for the capital of the Byzantine empire.[404] In 1348, a Genoese trade embargo sparked partly by imperial reduction of the commercial privileges of the Genoese merchant guild at Pera caused scarcity and rising prices in Constantinople, even though by that time indigenous Greek merchants were also involved in supplying the capital.[405]

In the territory of the Golden Horde around the Black Sea, Italian merchant guilds also had sufficient market power to exert successful pressure on rulers. Between 1343 and 1347, the Genoese and Venetian merchant colonies agreed to embargo trade with the territory of the Golden Horde. Although the Venetians accused the Genoese of violations, the embargo nonetheless diminished the volume of trade sufficiently to force the ruler of the Golden Horde to grant trading concessions.[406] The effectiveness of the embargo was attested by the account of the Genoese merchant Tommaso Gentile who travelled to Hormuz on the Persian gulf in 1343, but could not use the Tabrīz route because of the embargo. When he fell ill and returned home the short (but illegal) way via Tabrīz he was prosecuted by the Genoese authorities and only escaped punishment by proving in court that he had passed through Tabrīz without merchandise.[407] In this period, the Black Sea was the pivot of international trade, intermediating between Europe and Central Asia, Persia, China and even India, and playing a major role in the long-distance interchange of silk, spices, pearls and precious stones from Asia as well as wheat, hides, furs, fish, caviar and slaves from its own catchment region.[408] The market power of the Genoese and Venetian merchant colonies on the Black Sea was

---

[403] Dollinger (1970), 50–1.   [404] Laiou-Thomadakis (1980–1), 188 with n. 49, 214.
[405] *Ibid.*, 192–4.   [406] Di Cosmo (2005), 415.   [407] Lopez (1943), 181–3.
[408] Di Cosmo (2005), 393, 397.

thus pivotal to the entirety of European trade, and gave the Genoese and Venetian merchant guilds great leverage in western trading centres. Such successful embargoes provide compelling evidence that in particular markets alien merchant guilds were able to enforce their monopolies (or at least exert significant oligopoly powers) in practice.

4.2.8   Variation in merchant guild monopolies

It might be argued that merchant guilds varied enormously across Europe. Surely not all of them necessarily sought to act as legal monopolists? Grafe and Gelderblom, for instance, argue that alien merchants trading abroad in medieval and early modern Europe can be classed ordinally along a continuum between perfect atomization (in which merchants delegated no control to a guild) and perfect corporative control (in which merchants delegated substantial control to a guild). In their proposed system, those alien merchants guilds that *were* established can be divided into three separate categories: guilds that merely negotiated with external bodies, guilds that negotiated externally and imposed internal economic rules, and guilds that did both those things and additionally controlled entry. Only the latter, Grafe and Gelderblom argue, can be viewed as monopolists or cartels.[409]

But the empirical findings cast doubt on the idea that the representation, internal regulation and entry restrictions of alien merchant guilds were separable, let alone that they were ordinally hierarchical in this way. For example, Grafe and Gelderblom categorize the German Hanse in Bruges in 1250 and in 1300 as an alien merchant guild which only negotiated with external bodies, but did not impose internal economic rules or control entry. But this ignores the implications of the two successful embargoes on Bruges in this period, in 1280–2 and 1307–9, imposed by the German merchants with the explicit aim of extorting better commercial privileges from the Flemish authorities.[410] The German merchant organization in Bruges must have been able to impose internal economic rules, since it evidently succeeded in ordering its members not to trade in Bruges during the embargo. The German merchant organization in Bruges must also have been able to regulate entry, since it evidently had no trouble in determining which German merchants were obliged to comply with the embargo, as well as which were entitled to enjoy the

---

[409] Grafe and Gelderblom (2010a), 487, 491–2.

[410] On this categorization of the German Hanse in Bruges at these points in time, see Grafe and Gelderblom (2010b), 1; on these German embargoes, see W. Stein (1902), 123–30; Paravicini (1992), 100–4.

new Hanse privileges once Bruges had capitulated to the pressure the embargo had so effectively exerted.

The same applies to the claim by Grafe and Gelderblom that the Castilian merchant guild in thirteenth- and early-fourteenth-century Bruges had political representation but no internal regulations or entry barriers. This assertion cannot be maintained, since the Spanish merchants also imposed an embargo on Bruges in 1280, decamping to Aardenburg until Bruges induced them to return by granting them wider privileges in 1282.[411] The Spanish merchants would not have been able to impose an effective embargo without enforcing economic rules (ordering all their merchants to comply with the embargo and to 'transfer the centre of their business dealings to Aardenburg') and circumscribing their own membership (defining which merchants had to comply with the embargo and who would enjoy the resulting privileges, which 'formed the basis of all those which the Spaniards obtained in the Low Countries thereafter').[412]

We even have evidence of some of the mechanisms by which the German and Spanish merchant groups in Bruges were able to negotiate externally, regulate their members' economic activities internally and demarcate their membership. As we saw in Chapter 3, the local merchant guilds in German and Spanish cities, of which the German and Spanish merchant colonies in Bruges were branches, imposed both internal economic regulations and entry restrictions.[413] Merchants from these cities trading at Bruges were already subject to these broader economic controls in the home polity. The home polity also supplied the diplomats who carried out the political representations on behalf of the merchants: the German merchants' privileges in Bruges in 1252–3 were negotiated by special envoys bearing 'a documentary power of attorney for this purpose from several cities of the Empire', while the Aardenburg privileges of 1280 giving rise to the German (and Spanish) merchants' embargo of Bruges was negotiated mainly by Lübeck which twice sent members of its town council to Flanders, supported by envoys from Dortmund and Soest, after consulting by letter with nine other German cities.[414] The German Hanseatic merchants' earliest petition for privileges in Bruges in 1252–3 envisaged the use of a common seal and the establishment of an enclosed German colony in which all members would reside and

---

[411] On this categorization of the Castilian merchant guild at these points in time, see Grafe and Gelderblom (2010b), 3–4; on this Spanish embargo, see W. Stein (1902), 128; Paravicini (1992), 100–4.

[412] Maréchal (1953), 12.

[413] Specifically on the local Spanish merchant guilds underlying the Spanish merchant groups in medieval Bruges, see Maréchal (1953), 13.

[414] See W. Stein (1902), 59 (quotation), 123–4.

from which they would all trade, a suggestive indication of their intention to impose internal rules and define their membership.[415] This petition is interpreted as being motivated by the German merchants' desire to prevent a contamination of their interests through excessively close contacts with the indigenous population.[416] The petition also envisaged the reception into the resulting community (*recipi in communitate*) of worthy persons, who would also enjoy the economic privileges of membership, such as freedom from the 'guest law' of Bruges.[417] Even though the Flemish authorities refused to grant the German merchants' requests for a closed compound, as discussed earlier in this chapter, the German Hanse organization in Bruges got around this lack of spatial circumvallation by setting up internal administrative systems to detect merchants from the home polity who failed to register with the organization, pay its fees and comply with its regulations.[418]

The outlines of the internal mechanisms enabling internal regulation and monitoring inside the German and Spanish merchant communities also emerge from the privileges granted by the count of Flanders to the German and Spanish merchants in 1280 on the occasion of their embargo of Bruges when they shifted economic operations to Aardenburg. This document referred repeatedly to the 'compagnons' and 'communes' of the merchants of Spain and Germany, implying a sense of membership in the groups receiving the privileges in question. The document guaranteed the two merchant *communes* the right to have four officials called *procureurs* (representatives, consuls) who would both defend their interests towards the outside and, together with four *échevins* (aldermen), judge their internal litigations. The text of this privilege indicates that the German and Spanish merchant groups moving from Bruges to Aardenburg in 1280 had the administrative mechanisms to impose internal rules and define which *compagnons* were members of the community that was going to enjoy these privileges, select these officials and be subject to this regulation of their internal conflicts.[419]

The evidence thus supports the view of Grafe and Gelderblom that alien merchant guilds engaged in multiple activities. But it casts doubt on the idea that these activities were separable, let alone that they can be classed into discrete ordinal categories. All three categories of guild activity – negotiations to get economic privileges, imposition of internal rules and demarcation of membership – in practice came as a complementary and mutually reinforcing package.

---

[415] *Ibid.*, 86–90.   [416] *Ibid.*, 89, 94.   [417] Quoted in *ibid.*, 90.
[418] Burckhardt (2005), 71; Dollinger (1970), 89–90.
[419] Höhlbaum (1876), 295–9, no. 862.

These empirical findings can be understood in a more general theoretical framework. An organization is unlikely to incur the costs of negotiating with external bodies unless it can, by imposing internal rules and restricting membership, prevent free-riding on these costs by defining who is entitled to enjoy the privileges that the negotiations obtain. Conversely, an organization is not likely to be able to negotiate effectively with external bodies unless it can impose internal rules and circumscribe its membership in order to mobilize finance and exert political pressure. An alien merchant guild would be effective in negotiating with rulers precisely in so far as it could impose internal rules and entry restrictions in such a way as to finance negotiations, enforce compliance with embargoes and prevent free-riding on the resulting privileges. For these reasons, no alien merchant guild would willingly permit a merchant to enjoy the economic privileges resulting from costly negotiations with rulers without establishing his membership of the guild and obliging him to comply with internal economic regulations. Outside entities such as rulers, too, had an interest in demarcating the precise membership of the body of merchants to which they were granting specific privileges, and from whom they could expect a tangible quid pro quo. Thus in the negotiations of the German merchants with the countess of Flanders over their first privilege in 1252–3,

the Flemish government . . . was not willing to be sufficed with reciprocal documents [from the Germans], some of which named as their issuer only 'the entirety of the merchants frequenting Gotland' or 'all towns of the Holy Roman Empire', i.e. communities which offered nothing tangible to a government concerned with a practical quid pro quo. Rather, it expected and demanded reciprocal documents from the individual towns whose merchants would participate in the Flemish privileges.[420]

Alien merchant guilds did vary across Europe, therefore. But this variation was in the *degree* to which a given merchant guild succeeded in effectively carrying out the entire package of complementary activities – negotiating with rulers, imposing internal rules, defining membership – not in *which* of those activities it attempted to practise. Some alien merchant guilds were relatively ineffective in doing all three things: they failed to negotiate very extensive privileges from rulers, they failed to enforce internal rules thoroughly and they found it difficult to exclude outsiders. These weak guilds tolerated a relatively extensive grey market of free-riders and interlopers. Other alien merchant guilds – such as those of the Venetians or the Hanseatics – were extremely effective in doing all three

---

[420] W. Stein (1902), 83.

things: they ruthlessly negotiated with rulers, they imposed strict internal rules and they were brutally intolerant of free-riders and interlopers. Alien merchant guilds varied, but in the degree to which they succeeded in negotiating, circumscribing and enforcing their monopolies, not in whether they tried to do all three of these things.

4.2.9   Empirical studies of alien merchant guilds

A wide array of direct evidence has consequently led most empirical studies to conclude that alien merchant guilds were often able to translate their legal monopolies into practice. Although these monopolies were seldom perfect, they were sufficiently effective to evoke bitter contemporary complaints, justify expensive guild lobbying campaigns, trigger violent struggles with other guilds, motivate elaborate enforcement systems, draw resources into purchasing exemptions and licences, make guild embargoes effective in pressuring rulers, and affect the number of market participants and the volume of trade. While a small number of recent, primarily theoretical works elect to ignore such empirical findings, the vast majority of scholars take them into account and conclude that the monopolies of alien merchant guilds were often enforced and hence exerted real effects on the pre-modern economy. This scholarship is not restricted, as sometimes claimed, to uncritical adherents of an outmoded ideological tradition based on eighteenth-century liberal guild critics such as Adam Smith.[421] Rather, it emanates from heterogeneous scholars covering the whole range of historiographical traditions and ideological approaches, dates from all eras of historical scholarship, and consists not only of over-arching syntheses but of detailed micro-studies of every region of pre-modern Europe, covering the period from the tenth to the late eighteenth century.

Italian merchant guilds, for instance, were able to act as effective monopolists in many periods and places in the medieval Mediterranean, according to the conclusions presented in studies spanning the last eighty years of scholarship.[422] The German Hanse, too, according to the last century of scholarship, managed to enforce its monopolies surprisingly thoroughly in many of its major spheres of commercial operations.[423]

---

[421] See, e.g., S. R. Epstein and Prak (2008), 1–2.

[422] Bloch (1930), 463; Krueger (1933), 387–8; Citarella (1967), 301; Ashtor (1983), 10; Lopez (1987), 351, 375; Spruyt (1994), 146; Northrup (1998), 285; Hunt and Murray (1999), 183; J. Day (2002), 808, 812; Kohn (2003a), 19; Briys and De ter Beerst (2006), 21, 47, 51, 53–4; Dursteler (2006), 3, 23–4, 78.

[423] Christensen (1953), 251; Dollinger (1970), 186; Postan (1987), 271; Angermann (1987), 62, 68, 74; Spruyt (1994), 134; Seifert (1995), 84–5; Irsigler (2002), 36, 46–50; Wubs-Mrozewicz (2005), 208–9, 218.

Even scholars convinced of the overall benefits of the German Hanse agree that it operated as a cartel: Selzer and Ewert's 2005 essay, for instance, argues that because the Hanse strengthened merchants' negotiating powers with rulers it benefited trade, 'despite cartellization'.[424] Iberian merchant guilds are also assessed by a wide array of modern scholars as having exercised monopolistic power in the Atlantic trade.[425] The English Company of the Staple, too, is regarded by the last half-century of scholarship as having exercised monopoly power over the trade in wool between England and the European continent during significant periods of the fourteenth and fifteenth centuries.[426] The privileged merchant companies of the early modern period are also widely adjudged, by historians writing in recent decades as well as in earlier ones, to have successfully enforced their monopoly rights – not perfectly, but enough to exert a real economic impact.[427]

Document-based empirical studies therefore almost universally conclude that alien merchant guilds, hanses, consulados and privileged companies possessed monopolies in law and enforced them in practice. Precisely because of this wide array of evidence, only some of which has been presented in this chapter, most empirical studies find that alien merchant guilds and privileged companies enforced their legal monopolies – perhaps not always perfectly, but certainly enough to damage the welfare of other social groups and inflict efficiency costs on the wider economy.

4.3   Conclusion

Why were alien merchant guilds so widespread in medieval European trade? Why did they survive in some sectors well into the early modern period? One possible answer is that they were efficient institutions that generated net economic benefits and encouraged the growth of trade. Most proponents of this view dismiss the idea that alien merchant guilds were monopolists, since this would imply that they inflicted economic harm, not just on other groups but on the economy at large.

This chapter has shown that alien merchant guilds universally enjoyed legal monopolies, claiming exclusive legal rights over certain lines of trade. The multiplicity of commercial privileges granted to alien

---

[424] Selzer and Ewert (2005), 29.
[425] C. R. Phillips (1990), 95 n. 146; Mauro (1990), 263; Arruda (2000), 868–9; Grafe (2001), 14; Kohn (2003a), 22 with n. 96; Schnurmann (2003), 192; K. Weber (2004), 105 n. 72; Paquette (2007), 270; Adelman (2007), 140.
[426] Power (1941), 89; Lloyd (1977), 143, 256; Dodd (2002), 94–5.
[427] Chaudhuri (1978), 134–5, 318–19; Mauro (1990), 285; Pérotin-Dumon (1991), 222; Steensgaard (1990), 121, 123; Pearson (1991), 88–9; Tracy (1991), 7; Müller (1998), 113; S. R. H. Jones and Ville (1996), 899, 911–12; Zakharov (2009), 2–3.

merchant guilds – one set from the home ruler and others from foreign rulers – could, if enforced, add up to impressive commercial clout in particular segments of the pre-modern trading arena.

What of the claim that even if the alien merchant guild itself enjoyed exclusive rights over a certain line of trade, this did not amount to a monopoly because the guild permitted entry? For this argument to be true, alien merchant guilds would have had to permit *free* entry. The evidence shows this claim to be false. No alien merchant guild permitted free entry. Alien merchant guilds were no more open to outsiders than the local merchant guilds of which they were foreign branches, and these, as Chapter 3 showed, imposed formidable barriers. Many alien merchant guilds, as this chapter has shown, imposed additional requirements restricting entry even more stringently than already achieved through local guild admission requirements. It is thus not the case that alien merchant guilds permitted free entry.

Alien merchant guilds, in fact, manifested all the forms of behaviour expected of a monopolist – claiming exclusive rights to engage in particular activities, imposing entry barriers, fixing selling prices, controlling supplies, setting buying prices and imposing costs on potential competitors. The fact that they universally obtained legal privileges to engage in precisely the forms of behaviour predicted of monopolists is in itself *indirect* evidence that they believed these legal privileges to be useful. But wherever documentary sources survive in sufficient detail, they provide additional *direct* evidence that alien merchant guilds enforced their monopolies sufficiently to exert real economic effects.

Contemporary reports, complaints and petitions testify to the belief of people at the time that alien merchant guilds reserved particular lines of trade for their own members, restricted entry, fixed selling and purchasing prices, limited supplies and imposed costs on competitors. Members of such guilds contributed money and time to lobbying rulers to confirm and extend their legal monopolies. Those excluded or harmed by guild monopolies engaged in bitter struggles against them, ranging from expensive lobbying to violent attacks. Alien merchant guilds spent resources on setting up systems of detection and punishment against violations of their exclusive rights. Conversely, outsiders spent resources on circumventing (or contracting into) the monopolies of alien merchant guilds, suggesting that these imposed binding constraints. Finally, alien merchant guilds periodically declared embargoes, in many cases exercising effective monopoly pressure, as shown by the commercial contraction brought about by the embargo and the capitulation of the foreign ruler.

Legal rules are seldom enforced perfectly, and alien merchant guilds' monopolies were indeed sometimes evaded. Guild members themselves sought to free-ride on their guild's collective monopoly by undercutting guild prices, exceeding quotas, overpaying suppliers or violating other rules, hoping to steal a march on their fellows. Non-members sought to encroach on the activities merchant guilds claimed as their exclusive entitlements. But these violations of guilds' privileges took places in the informal sector where transactions were illegal, risky and high cost. Infringements did not mean that guild monopolies lacked any economic impact. Rather it meant that part of these guilds' economic impact was to prevent competition altogether and another part was to push competing traders into the black market. As with local merchant guilds, so too with alien ones, imperfect enforcement of guild monopolies at best created an informal sector of illegal trade where costs and risks were higher. Even imperfectly enforced monopolies can impose real economic effects.[428]

But if merchant guilds enforced monopolies that harmed trade, why *did* they exist in so many economies for such long periods? Surely such a widespread and long-lasting institution must have existed for a reason? Is it not probable that merchant guilds were efficient solutions to economic problems, and that is why we find them in so many different economies?

Merchant guilds certainly existed for a reason, as we shall see. But this reason was not that they were efficient. The next chapter puts forward a more coherent and empirically grounded explanation for why merchant guilds existed – not because they efficiently increased the size of the economic pie, but because they ensured larger slices for powerful elites.

---

[428] On these features of economic informality, see Batini et al. (2010); Todaro (1989), 270–1; ILO (1989); Ogilvie (2007b), 671–4.

5   Merchant guilds and rulers

> If you come to a place where the king or some other chief who is
> in authority has his officials, seek to win their friendship; and if they
> demand any necessary fees on the ruler's behalf, be prompt to render
> all such payments, lest by holding too tightly to little things you lose the
> greater.
>
> ('The Activities and Habits of a Merchant', *The King's Mirror*,
> Norway, *c.* 1250)[1]

Why did merchant guilds exist for such a long time in so many different
economies? Some argue that they existed because they were efficient,
solving economic problems better than any available alternative, creating
net benefits. Yet as Chapters 3 and 4 showed, merchant guilds imposed
significant costs on the economy. The testimony and behaviour of contemporaries suggests that exclusive guild privileges harmed efficiency:
they reduced the overall volume of exchange, stifling the production and
consumption that depended on it.

How, then, can we explain why merchant guilds existed so widely
for so long? The answer lies in the fact that institutions affect not just
efficiency but also *distribution*. An institution that keeps the economic pie
small but distributes large slices to powerful groups can be sustained for
centuries by its powerful beneficiaries. Merchant guilds had two powerful
beneficiaries – the merchants who belonged to them, and the political
authorities who granted their privileges.

Merchants, as we saw in Chapters 3 and 4, used their guilds to reap
monopoly profits. They secured from rulers exclusive rights to engage
in trade, limit entry, fix prices, control supplies, depress input costs and
legally trammel competitors. Merchant guilds increased the profits their
members could extract from trading. This gave guilded merchants a
strong incentive to keep their guilds in being.

Rulers also used guilds to reap benefits. Guild monopolies reduced
the volume of exchange and thus the total trade that rulers could tax.

---

[1] Larson (1917), 83.

But merchant guilds more than compensated the political authorities (although not the rest of the economy) for this loss by giving rulers cash payments, favourable loans, tax-collection services, military support and political backing. Merchant guilds, as this chapter will show, increased the revenues rulers could extract from their subjects. This gave rulers a strong incentive to keep guilds in being.

Merchant guilds were not an efficient institution that increased the size of the aggregate economic pie. But they were an institution that enabled merchants and rulers to collaborate effectively in extracting larger slices of the pie for themselves.

Existing literature portrays the guild–ruler relationship in a surprisingly benign light. The most widely held view is that merchant guilds benefited the economy by persuading rulers to reduce taxes. The Byzantine emperor's grant of tax-free trading privileges to the Venetian merchant colony in Constantinople in 1082 is described by Frankopan as 'intended and bound to stimulate trade'.[2] The famous merchant guilds on the Saône and Loire Rivers in medieval France were formed, according to Mauro, when merchant shippers 'banded together to better protect themselves against abusive tolls'.[3] Medieval Flemish merchant guilds, in the account of Lambert and Stabel, were 'institutions whose primary goal was to negotiate fiscal and juridical arrangements with the lord of the city'.[4] Tax exemptions negotiated by medieval merchant guilds, according to Harreld, facilitated trade by reducing merchants' costs: 'it is with these more than any other privilege that the effectiveness of the guilds to decrease costs is evident'.[5] Merchant guilds solved the fundamental problems of exchange, according to Gelderblom and Grafe, partly through negotiating tax rebates with rulers, 'thus maximizing their members' income from commercial and financial transactions'.[6] A more elaborate, but still benign, picture of the guild–ruler relationship is advanced by Greif, Milgrom and Weingast, who argue that merchant guilds made rulers guarantee commercial security, an idea explored in detail in Chapter 6.[7] In all these interpretations, merchant guilds enabled rulers to commit themselves to permitting the efficient level of trade, thereby benefiting the entire economy.

But these accounts ignore important aspects of the relationship between guilds and rulers. If these portrayals were accurate, rulers should have granted merchant guilds simple trading permits with uniform tax

---

[2] Frankopan (2004), 138, 152.   [3] Mauro (1990), 263.
[4] Lambert and Stabel (2005), 1.
[5] Harreld (2004b), 10, 14–15 (quotation); see also Harreld (2004a), 41.
[6] Gelderblom and Grafe (2004), 1.   [7] Greif, Milgrom and Weingast (1994).

reductions. What happened was more complex – in revealing ways. First, a ruler did not just grant a merchant guild a straightforward permit for its members to do business, ensuring the efficient level of trade, but rather granted it an *exclusive* privilege for its members to trade in particular wares, transaction types, routes or destinations, which reduced trade below the efficient level by permitting that guild to act as a monopolist. Second, a ruler did not grant a uniform tax reduction to *all* merchant guilds, but rather discriminated among different groups of merchants by granting them *differential* tax reductions, enhancing the profits of the most favoured guilds commensurately with the flow of benefits which those guilds could offer in return. Third, benefits typically flowed in *both directions* between guild and ruler. The ruler granted an exclusive trading privilege and a specific tax reduction to a merchant guild, while the guild gave the ruler cash payments, favourable loans, fiscal cooperation, military assistance or political support. This pattern is not consistent with a benign efficiency theory that guild–ruler negotiations resulted in the efficient level of trade. It is, however, consistent with a distributional view, according to which merchant guilds benefited guilded merchants and rulers by enabling both parties to collaborate in extracting more resources from the rest of the economy.

This chapter shows how this relationship between merchant guilds and rulers worked, and how it explains the existence and survival of the merchant guild as an institution. Merchant guilds, we shall see, did not just lobby rulers to grant trading permits and tax reductions. Rather, each merchant guild negotiated a different bundle of trading privileges and tax cuts in exchange for delivering a different bundle of benefits to rulers. The differential trade monopolies and tax reductions that merchant guilds obtained from rulers gave them advantages over actual and potential competitors and enabled them to reap economic rents (monopoly profits). Guilds then delivered a share of these monopoly profits to the ruler.

As we shall see, rulers benefited from this arrangement in a variety of ways. Individual rulers were likely to discount the future more than guilds of merchants, so both parties could be made better off if rulers traded with merchants to get payments now even if it meant forfeiting revenues in future. Second, the ruler did not have to pay the costs of collecting the taxes he was relinquishing but rather received a lump sum from a guild which had incurred all the collection costs. Until some European states developed more sophisticated fiscal mechanisms in the early modern period, collecting trade taxes was often cheaper for merchants than for rulers, so both parties could be made better off through an exchange in which merchants collected contributions and transferred them to rulers in return for exclusive privileges. Third, rulers faced greater capital constraints than merchants because their coercive powers enabled them to default on debts, turning them into risky borrowers who had to pay high interest rates. So both parties could benefit through an exchange in which merchant guilds loaned capital to rulers in return for exclusive trading privileges. Fourth, often the only way for a ruler to obtain political support or military assistance was to grant economic privileges to the social groups that could supply them. As we shall see, merchants dominated one of the groups – the urban bourgeoisie – that could deliver political and military support to rulers. Finally, granting commercial monopolies did not cost the ruler anything (at least directly), so any guild payment in return appeared to be pure profit.

Guilded merchants could also benefit from this two-way exchange of favours with rulers. For one thing, the transaction costs of making lump-sum payments directly to rulers were often lower than those of perpetually paying trade taxes, especially via officials who imposed extra obstacles so as to extract additional perquisites for themselves. For another, because rulers did not lose anything (directly) by granting commercial monopolies, a merchant guild could pay less to the ruler than the value of the monopoly to its members. Because merchant guilds were in a position to discount the future less than rulers, both could be made better off through an exchange, in which merchants made payments to rulers now in exchange for a more-or-less lengthy future period in which they paid lower taxes and enjoyed commercial monopolies.

However, this collaborative relationship between merchant guilds and rulers had harmful wider effects. The economy at large was afflicted and its efficiency reduced because guilds' commercial monopolies reduced the volume of exchange and diminished gains from trade. Non-guilded traders suffered because they did not enjoy tax cuts, commercial monopolies or even the legal right to trade. This increased their costs, reduced their ability to compete and pushed them into the informal sector as black-market traders or predators on trade. Purchasers of traded goods suffered because guild monopolies increased the prices they had to pay. Producers who used traded goods as intermediate inputs were burdened with higher costs, and consumers who bought traded goods to eat or wear suffered from lower standards of living. Merchant guilds existed not because they maximized the size of the economic pie, therefore, but because they enabled powerful groups to distribute larger slices of that pie to themselves.[8]

---

[8] The discussion in this chapter builds on expositions of related arguments in Ogilvie (1996a), 30–7; Ogilvie (1996b), 285–96; Ogilvie (1997), 72–85, 431–46; Ogilvie (1999), 188–202; Ogilvie (2000b), 16–29; Dessì and Ogilvie (2003); Dessì and Ogilvie (2004); Ogilvie (2005); and Ogilvie (2007b), 654–5, 664, 670–1.

5.1   State privileges for merchant guilds

As we saw in Chapters 3 and 4, merchant guilds were not 'private-order' institutions set up informally by private agents without any involvement by the public authorities. Rather, guilds always had to be recognized by 'public-order' institutions – by rulers, bureaucracies and local governments. A pre-modern merchant could only trade if the political authorities let him do so: 'business in a principality without the purchased favor of the prince just could not be carried on at all'.[9] As soon as merchants formed guilds, the 'favor of the prince' was not restricted to a simple licence to trade, but rather consisted in an exclusive 'privilege' for guild members to trade in particular goods, transaction types, routes or destinations, and to exclude non-members from these activities. Even just the exclusive right to trade as an acknowledged merchant of a particular city or polity brought commercial advantages that attracted complaints, envy, conflict and willingness to pay for exemptions or shares – as we saw in Chapters 3 and 4. Not only did merchant guilds invariably obtain such privileges from rulers, but they implemented them in practice, leading them to return repeatedly to rulers for confirmation and enforcement.

Merchant guilds also bargained with rulers to have trade taxes reduced – although only for their own members. Almost the first act of any local merchant guild was to negotiate tax cuts from its ruler – as observed in twelfth-century Lübeck and Bremen,[10] thirteenth-century Dortmund[11] and Schleswig,[12] fourteenth-century Spanish cities,[13] and fifteenth-century English towns.[14] Alien merchant guilds, likewise, almost invariably began their existence by negotiating tax advantages with foreign rulers – as shown by eleventh-century Italian merchant guilds in Constantinople, the Levant and north Africa,[15] twelfth-century French merchant guilds in Flanders,[16] twelfth-century Italian merchant guilds in Sicilian ports,[17] thirteenth-century Italian merchant guilds in France[18] and the Crusader kingdoms,[19] fourteenth-century Genoese and Venetian

---

[9] R. L. Reynolds (1952), 364–5 (quotation); Dessì and Ogilvie (2003); Dessì and Ogilvie (2004), 26–7, 45–9. For a thoughtful consideration of the necessity to obtain privileges from rulers in order to trade, see also Greve (2001), 272.

[10] On Lübeck, Dollinger (1970), 22; on Bremen, Ehbrecht (1985), 426.

[11] Ehbrecht (1985), 425.   [12] E. Hoffman (1980), 49.

[13] Kohn (2003a), 12; referring to Mathers (1988); Woodward (2005), 631–4.

[14] Kohn (2003a), 12 with n. 52; referring to Masschaele (1997).

[15] Bernard (1972), 292–3; Madden (2002), 24; Frankopan (2004), 138.

[16] Laurent (1935b), 48.   [17] Abulafia (1978), 71–2; Abulafia (1986b), 198.

[18] Laurent (1935b), 118; Schulte (1900), 344–5; Alengry (1915), 75–6.

[19] Abulafia (1986a), 538–9.

merchant guilds in the kingdom of the Golden Horde,[20] or fifteenth-century English merchant guilds in Flanders.[21]

Such examples might appear to confirm the view that merchant guilds benefited the economy by negotiating to reduce fiscal burdens on trade. But the reductions in trade taxes that resulted from these negotiations were not uniform tax cuts on *all* trade, which might have given rise to an efficient volume of exchange – at least in principle, if trade taxes were (through some unclear mechanism) reduced to the 'optimal' level. Instead, tax reductions depended on guild membership, and were differentiated according to the compensatory flow of benefits which each merchant guild offered the ruler in return.[22] The German Hanse, indeed, explicitly demanded that the rulers of medieval Bruges *not* treat foreign merchants equally, but rather grant its own members the greatest privileges.[23]

Typically, tax exemptions, like other privileges rulers granted, varied from one merchant guild to another in the same polity. From the eleventh to the fourteenth century, for instance, the rulers of Constantinople granted tax reductions to the merchants of (in descending order of the value of the reductions) Venice, Genoa, Pisa, Catalonia, Narbonne, Ancona, Florence and Ragusa (Dubrovnik). By contrast, local Greek merchants, who had little to offer the emperor, had to pay full taxes.[24] Throughout the Levant, in fact, the most powerful alien merchant guilds, particularly those of Venice, Genoa and Pisa, enjoyed much larger tax exemptions than those of the 'minor nations' which could offer less fiscal and political support to rulers; 'unprivileged merchants' (i.e. those without their own merchant guild to negotiate privileges for them) paid the highest taxes of all.[25] The twelfth-century rulers of Utrecht let Norwegian merchants trade customs free, required Friesian and Saxon merchants to pay customs dues individually and charged Danish merchants a collective customs fee per ship.[26] The thirteenth-century kings of England granted privileges which reduced Hanse merchants' customs fees below those paid by other alien (and even local) merchant guilds.[27] In the late thirteenth and early fourteenth century, the English merchants in Bruges had to pay higher trade taxes than the Germans or the Spanish.[28] In the early fourteenth century, the ruler of Cyprus granted

---

[20] Ashtor (1983), 82; Di Cosmo (2005), 407.
[21] Sutton (2002), 30; Kohn (2003a), 12; Kermode (1998).
[22] On this differentiation in medieval and early modern Antwerp, see Harreld (2004a), 42, 58.
[23] Sprandel (1984), 22.   [24] Balard (2000), 829–30; Runciman (1987), 149.
[25] Abulafia (1988), 186–8; Abulafia (1995), 11–13; Abulafia (1986a), 535–6, 539; Ashtor (1983), 69.
[26] Hørby (1984), 46.   [27] R. De Roover (1965), 113.   [28] Häpke (1908), 66–7.

the Genoese and Venetian merchant guilds total exemption from trade taxes, and the merchant guilds of Pisa, Narbonne, Provence, Catalonia and Ancona a reduction to 2 per cent; merchants of most other nations had to pay full taxes.[29] In the mid-fourteenth century the Genoese and Venetian merchant guilds in Egypt enjoyed the privilege of paying only 10 per cent customs dues, whereas other foreign merchants had to pay 15 per cent.[30]

Differential taxes, indeed, were part of the way in which merchant guilds partitioned commerce into segments that made it easier for their members to monopolize. By obtaining tax privileges from rulers, merchant guilds created an uneven playing field, in which members of politically less powerful guilds traded at a disadvantage. The famous Chrysobull of 1082 granting the Venetian merchant guild tax exemptions in the Byzantine empire, for instance, meant that 'Venetian merchants could undercut their Italian and even Byzantine competitors, thus commanding an important share of Byzantium's commercial economy'.[31] In like manner, the Ragusa (Dubrovnik) merchant guilds in the Balkans in the mid-fifteenth century secured customs exemptions from the Ottoman authorities which enabled them to monopolize particular branches of trade by undercutting Bosnian competitors who had to pay full taxes.[32] Members of the English Staple Company paid wool tolls of 33 per cent in the fifteenth century, whereas non-Stapler exporters had to pay 44–70 per cent.[33]

Not only did rulers levy different taxes from different merchant guilds, but they typically levied *some* taxes from even the most powerful guilds. This was because rulers did not know the precise size of either the monopoly profits a particular merchant guild would be able to derive from any exclusive trading privileges, or the competitive advantage it would gain from its specific tax exemptions. Consequently, rulers preferred to retain the right to levy some taxes so they could vary them as foreign merchants' circumstances revealed themselves. This is well illustrated by the way in which the thirteenth-century king of Sicily adjusted the prices he charged foreign merchants for licences to export wheat. The initial price in early 1276 was set too high, discouraging purchases; by August, the ruler had extracted information by observing slow sales of licences and lowered the price by one-third.[34] Compelling guilded merchants to continue paying *some* trade taxes conveyed information to rulers about the value of the privileges they granted to each guild.

---

[29] Abulafia (1986b), 210.   [30] Ashtor (1983), 84.
[31] Madden (2002), 24 (quotation), 32; Laiou (2002), 751.
[32] Molnár (2007), 102–5.   [33] Barnouw (1952), 104.   [34] Abulafia (1987a), 60.

The differential tax cuts rulers granted to different groups of merchants cast doubt on the notion that the guild–ruler relationship consisted in a straightforward, benign bargain over tax cuts. They suggest instead that merchant guilds were engaged in rent-seeking, with each guild aiming to achieve a favourable position for itself at the expense of other guilds, so as to secure an artificial advantage for its members that would enable them to undercut rival merchants – not through economic competition, but through rent-seeking.

5.2   Cash transfers to rulers

This is borne out by evidence that each merchant guild offered a heterogeneous stream of benefits to the ruler to induce him to grant it a distinctive set of privileges. If guild–ruler relations had consisted in the simple negotiation of tax cuts, giving rise to the efficient level of trade, one would expect to observe rulers granting trade permits and tax reductions in the expectation of reaping benefits through the growth of trade, which they could then tax, albeit at a lower rate. Instead, the interaction between rulers and guilds was more complicated. Rulers did not *open up* trade in such a way that it could rise to the efficient level. Rather, they *segmented* trade by granting specific commercial 'privileges' to identifiable interest-groups in return for specific streams of payments and services. Relations between rulers and merchant guilds were governed, as Pearson puts it, by 'the age-old notion of an exchange, of a privilege being granted in return for a fiscal benefit to the state'.[35]

Individual merchants and firms had a long tradition of making payments to rulers for monopolies and other privileges, and the largest European merchant houses continued to do so throughout the medieval period. In 1252–4, for instance, the Tolomei and Bonsignori merchant firms of Siena made substantial loans to the ecclesiastical ruler of Volterra in exchange for exclusive control over the Montieri silver mines.[36] In the 1340s, consortia of English merchants made payments and favourable loans to the crown in exchange for shares in the monopoly over exporting English wool.[37] Later that decade, Tidemann Limberg formed consortia with other German merchants to lend money to the English crown in return for special trading privileges, but also made loans as an individual: 'In return for a loan of £3,000 to the Black Prince in 1347 he obtained the revenues of the Cornish zinc mines for three years and three

[35] Pearson (1991), 86 (quotation). See also Greve (2001), 272; Dessì and Ogilvie (2004), 38–41, 53–5.
[36] Bautier (1955), 107–8.   [37] Lloyd (1977), 198–201.

months, which gave him a monopoly in the export of this mineral.'[38] So merchants paying rulers for commercial monopolies was nothing new, and did not disappear in the course of the medieval period.

Merchant *guilds*, however, offered an organizational innovation that massively expanded the scale on which merchants could engage in such rent-seeking. By organizing the agglomeration of small contributions from individual merchants into significant sums, a merchant guild generated economies of scale in paying rulers to grant monopolies. Through their guilds, even smaller-scale traders now participated in the lucrative exchange whereby groups of merchants 'courted royal favor with gifts and loans and received numerous concessions and privileges'.[39]

Merchant guilds ensured that they were in a position to deliver benefits to rulers by collecting entry fees, annual dues, percentage taxes on trade and voluntary contributions from their members.[40] Local merchant guilds invariably levied such financial contributions – for example, the eleventh-century merchant guild of the Dutch town of Tiel,[41] the twelfth-century merchant guild of Flensburg,[42] the thirteenth-century salt merchants' guild in Laufen,[43] the fourteenth- and fifteenth-century merchant guilds of Catalonia.[44] The financial resources available to merchant guilds in some cases exceeded those of municipal governments, as in the medieval English town of Lynn, where 'the borough government's own fiscal resources were well below those of the Merchant Gild'.[45]

An alien merchant guild also typically levied financial contributions, on top of those its members paid to the local guild in the home city. Medieval Catalan merchant guilds abroad collected percentage dues on their members' trade not just in Catalonia, but in Tunis, Alexandria and Flanders.[46] Guild dues were onerous enough to create an incentive to avoid them, as shown by conflicts inside the Catalan merchant guild in medieval Bruges.[47] The Lucca merchant guild in Bruges collected substantial revenues from fines, compulsory offerings at masses in the guild church and an *ad valorem* tax on all purchases and sales made by members.[48] The Genoese merchant guild in Bruges levied a percentage tax on members' turnover, taxes for religious services and fines for

---

[38] Dollinger (1970), 171.   [39] Woodward (2005), 633.
[40] R. L. Reynolds (1952), 361; Gelderblom and Grafe (2004), 3.
[41] Volckart and Mangels (1999), 437–8 with n. 39; Dilcher (1984), 69.
[42] Schütt (1980), 112–21.   [43] Störmer (1985), 366–7.
[44] R. S. Smith (1940), 61–4; Woodward (2005), 632–3.
[45] Alsford (2003), 'History of medieval Lynn', www.trytel.com/~tristan/towns/lynn7.html, s.v. 'Economy'.
[46] R. S. Smith (1940), 61–4; Hibbert (1949), 356–8.
[47] Case of 25 September 1458, reproduced in Gilliodts-van Severen (1901–2), 79.
[48] R. De Roover (1948a), 19; Henn (1999), 135.

breaking guild rules.[49] Pisan merchant guilds in Sicily and Tunis levied taxes within the merchant compound and expropriated goods of merchants who died overseas.[50] Genoese merchant guilds in Alexandria and Damascus collected 1 per cent of the value of ordinary merchandise and 3 per cent on shipments of gold and silver, increasing the tax to 6 per cent or more in emergencies.[51] The Venetian merchant guild in Alexandria maintained a common fund to make payments to Mamluk rulers, sustaining it with regular imposts which rose from 1 per cent to 10 per cent during the fifteenth century – high enough to evoke constant attempts at evasion.[52] The English Merchant Adventurers imposed communal levies on all its members at its foreign trading marts.[53] The Portuguese merchant guild in fifteenth-century Antwerp could compel a member to open his business registers if the consuls suspected him of failing to pay the required guild levy on his turnover.[54] From its inception, the German Hanse levied fees from member merchants – Kontor fees, ad valorem taxes on turnover, rents on stalls and buildings in the Hanse compound, levies from affiliates of subordinate Kontore, fines for breaking Hanse rules, weight-based tolls on ships entering and leaving Hanseatic harbours, one-off military levies and many more.[55]

Financial levies from members enabled merchant guilds to offer rulers benefits in return for privileges. A first type of benefit was the direct cash transfer. *Local* merchant guilds habitually made cash transfers to their own rulers and governments in return for commercial favours – as in tenth-century Constantinople,[56] eleventh-century Pavia,[57] twelfth-century Flensburg,[58] thirteenth-century Catalonia,[59] thirteenth- to fifteenth-century England[60] and medieval Spain.[61] Local merchant guilds made cash transfers not only when they first got privileges from their ruler, but at intervals thereafter – annually, or when the ruler reconfirmed the privileges, or both.[62]

Alien merchant guilds also made cash transfers to foreign rulers in return for privileges.[63] In eleventh-century Denmark, alien merchant guilds paid King Knut the Holy for the right to trade on an equal footing

---

[49] Henn (1999), 135.   [50] Abulafia (1987a), 55.   [51] Ashtor (1983), 228, 230, 335.
[52] *Ibid.*, 251, 401–2, 415.   [53] Sutton (2002), 41.   [54] Goris (1925), 51–2.
[55] Burckhardt (2005), 62, 65; Choroškevic (1996), 71–2; Spruyt (1994), 127; Dollinger (1970), 99–100, 104–5, 300.
[56] Racine (1985), 139; Freshfield (1938), 17; Dagron (2002), 408.
[57] Racine (1985), 135–6.   [58] Schütt (1980), 112–21.   [59] Woodward (2005), 631–4.
[60] Lloyd (1977), 120; Gross (1890), I: 7, 58; Kohn (2003a), 44.
[61] R. S. Smith (1940), 48, 64–5.
[62] For examples, see Harreld (2004a), 42–3; Pryor (2000), 427–8; R. S. Smith (1940), 64–5, 85; Woodward (2005), 633–5.
[63] Kohn (2003a), 17–18.

with Danish merchants.[64] In eleventh- and twelfth-century Constantinople, Venetian, Pisan and Genoese merchant guilds delivered arbitrary payments to the emperor – enough, in Postan's assessment, to compensate the imperial treasury for any customs reductions they received.[65] In 1295, the merchants of Lombardy offered the count of Flanders money in return for permission to establish guild headquarters in Ghent and trade throughout his territories.[66] In medieval Alexandria and Damascus, Venetian merchant guilds made cash transfers to the Mamluk authorities and agreed to purchase state pepper and sugar stocks annually at above-market prices.[67] In 1324–5, the Lucca merchant guild in Paris transferred lump sums to the French king for his war in Gascony.[68] In the 1370s, the Florentine merchant guild in London made cash gifts to courtiers and officials for export licences and staple exemptions.[69] In fourteenth- and fifteenth-century Catalonia and Aragon, Italian merchant guilds made annual gifts of silk, cloth-of-gold and cash to the crown in return for trading privileges.[70] In the 1440s, the Amsterdam merchants promised 5,000 Rhenish florins to the king of Norway in return for trading privileges.[71] The German Hanse and its precursors made high payments for its commercial privileges to rulers throughout medieval Europe – to the rulers of Novgorod annually from the late twelfth century on;[72] to the English crown from the twelfth century on;[73] to the city government of London annually from the thirteenth century on;[74] and to the Danish king for privileges in Skåne from the fourteenth century on.[75]

Throughout medieval Europe, therefore, it was the norm for merchant guilds to purchase commercial privileges with cash payments, whether directly through open payments to princes or indirectly as bribes to officials. But this was only one of several ways in which merchant guilds shared their monopoly profits with the political authorities which made them possible.

5.3   Assistance in taxing trade

A second way merchant guilds induced rulers to grant them privileges was indirectly, through facilitating tax collection. Trade taxes were an important component of rulers' revenues, and became more so as the

---

[64] E. Hoffman (1980), 30–1.   [65] Runciman (1987), 147.
[66] Bourquelot (1865), I: 186.   [67] Ashtor (1983), 206–7, 215, 249–52, 401–2.
[68] Mirot (1927), 65.   [69] Holmes (1960–1), 201.
[70] Congdon (2003), 218, 228.   [71] Wubs-Mrozewicz (2005), 210 with n. 26.
[72] Choroškevic (1996), 70–1; Dollinger (1970), 100.
[73] Lloyd (1991), 22–4; Dollinger (1970), 39; Palais (1959), 865; Postan (1987), 298.
[74] Dollinger (1970), 40.   [75] Ibid., 67.

medieval period advanced.[76] Rulers had a long tradition of employing individual merchants to collect trade taxes because their superior information and skills made them effective in doing so – from the Greek merchants the Byzantine emperors entrusted with collecting tolls from Bulgarian merchants in the ninth century[77] to the fourteenth-century merchant Boninus de Meldeo of Novara who collected royal customs dues from his fellow merchants in Montpellier.[78]

But merchant guilds could be even more effective than individual merchants in helping rulers collect trade taxes because they possessed collective information about their members' trading activities, wielded collective sanctions against tax evaders and represented a unified body on which rulers could put pressure to deliver taxes reliably.

Local merchant guilds, in particular, frequently assisted rulers in collecting taxes. This benefited both parties since, as Spruyt points out, 'both monarchy and mercantile groups preferred regularized taxation which also allowed for urban negotiation'.[79] In medieval France, for instance, 'by giving the burghers a modest say in the taxation process, the king was assured that shirking would be less than when taxes were raised solely through duress'.[80] For these reasons, medieval rulers often subcontracted the collection of trade taxes to local merchant guilds.[81] The 1200 Schleswig law code, for instance, ordered the St Knud's merchant guild to collect the *moldskod* tax on the second day of its annual assembly.[82] Medieval Spanish and Catalan merchant guilds levied trade taxes and paid them directly to the crown.[83] In medieval England, different merchant guilds and merchant consortia collected the wool subsidy, 'the single most important element in the fiscal machinery of the state'.[84] The Karīmī merchant association in thirteenth- and fourteenth-century Alexandria collected customs revenues and transferred them directly to the ruler.[85]

One of the most widespread mechanisms through which local merchant guilds facilitated tax collection was through 'staple' regulations.[86] As we saw in Chapter 3, the institution of the staple, which existed in Europe from the twelfth century on, consisted of two components – the staple privileges, and a corporate group of merchants who enjoyed and

---

[76] For a survey of the variety and origin of these various taxes, see Bernard (1972), 313; Dessi and Ogilvie (2004), 19–20, 40–1, 55–7.

[77] Scholz (2001), 94.   [78] Reyerson (1985), 47.   [79] Spruyt (1994), 88.

[80] *Ibid.*, 106.   [81] Bernard (1972), 327.   [82] Schütt (1985), 270.

[83] Woodward (2005), 632–4; R. S. Smith (1940), 61–4, 86.

[84] E. B. Fryde (1959), 2–8; Postan (1987), 293; Ormrod (2000), 292 (quotation).

[85] Ashtor (1983), 73–4, 271–83.

[86] On the origins of the staple, see Kuske (1939); Kohn (2003a), 16.

helped enforce them. The staple privileges designated a fixed place (usually a town) through which all trade in particular wares over a particular territory was obliged to pass. The staple merchants were endowed with the exclusive right to regulate trade in those wares through that place. The most common pattern was for staple privileges to entitle a *local* merchant guild to compel foreign merchants travelling within a particular distance of the town to unload their wares in municipal warehouses for a specified period, during which local guilds had exclusive rights to buy the goods at privileged prices, or to take over their onward transport.

But an alien merchant guild could *also* enjoy staple privileges entitling it to compel all trade in particular commodities to pass through a particular location where its members monopolized the onward trade. The German Hanse, for instance, had staples in various locations on the Baltic and North Sea for the fish trade, and a staple at Bruges for Russian commodities and Flemish cloth. Likewise, the English Company of the Staple had a compulsory staple in English wool exports at a succession of continental European locations, where trade in English wool was largely monopolized by Company members.

A staple not only generated monopoly profits for the body of merchants that enjoyed the staple privileges. It also reduced costs of tax collection for rulers. A local staple forcing foreign merchants to unload goods in local warehouses and have them inspected greatly simplified the collection of trade taxes.[87] The local merchant guild was often required to collect an excise tax on all goods at the staple and deliver the revenues to the ruler.[88] Rulers also often profited by selling foreign merchants exemptions from the local staple.[89] The medieval English wool staple, for instance, simultaneously delivered monopoly profits to the Company of the Staple and fiscal benefits to the English crown: 'The king wanted a company of merchants to whom he could give a monopoly in the export of wool, so as to tax monopoly profits by means of a heavy export duty and raise loans from merchants on the security of the duty.'[90] The crown did not care which locality was designated for the wool staple – continental or English – so long as it involved a corporate body of merchants capable of extracting monopoly rents from which they could be required to render taxes and state loans.[91] The king regarded the 'local knowledge and contacts' of merchants from the staple towns as essential

---

[87] Kuske (1939), 38–45; Kohn (2003a), 16.

[88] Thus in Cologne, members of the local brokers' guild took an official oath obliging them to collect the 1 per cent excise tax on the value of goods deposited at the staple as they were inspecting and fixing prices for them; see Kuske (1939), 41.

[89] For examples, see *ibid.*, 37.   [90] Power (1941), 88.   [91] *Ibid.*, 92.

to the success of the staple, first for generating monopoly rents and then for taxing them.[92]

A similar fiscal purpose was served by 'hosting laws', obliging every foreign merchant to find a local 'host' – usually a member of the local merchant guild – to sponsor him during his stay. The local host was typically entitled to pre-empt a fixed share of the value of the visitor's merchandise and exclusively broker his trade with locals. Such privileges gave the local host an incentive to become fully informed about the visiting merchant's goods and legally obliged him to report that information to the local authorities. In medieval London, this fiscal role was formally recognized by granting the privileged local merchantry a share of the taxes:

the profits of scavage [a toll levied on foreign merchants] were divided equally between the sheriff of London and the hosts . . . The hosts were either merchants themselves or normally involved in trade on their own account or through agents. As was the case elsewhere, hosts probably exercised some right of pre-emption on the foreigners' goods and actively traded on their own and the foreigners' behalf. Profits from scavage and pre-emption helped to incentivize hosts to assist royal officials in controlling the activities and behaviour of foreign merchants.[93]

Alien merchant guilds also facilitated the collection of trade taxes. The fact that a visiting trader was legally obliged to join the relevant alien merchant guild (if one existed) indirectly helped rulers identify foreign merchants and thus tax them. But the alien merchant guild's own administrative structure often directly assisted foreign rulers in collecting trade taxes. The Genoese and Venetian merchant colonies on the Black Sea in the thirteenth and fourteenth centuries were used by the rulers of the Golden Horde as their main mechanism for extracting taxes from western merchants, and the colonies themselves developed elaborate internal regulatory structures to administer these tributes, including licences for each visiting merchant.[94] The Golden Horde evidently regarded tax gathering as the most important function of the Italian merchant colonies, threatening their members and imprisoning their consuls when taxes fell into arrears.[95] Relations between Italian merchant guilds and rulers in the eastern Mediterranean show the same pattern. The Venetian merchant guilds in fourteenth- and fifteenth-century Egypt and Syria, for instance, levied *cottimo* taxes from their members that could rise higher than 10 per cent – 'payments extorted by the Moslem authorities but collected by the European consuls'.[96]

---

[92] Kermode (1998), 162. [93] Middleton (2005), 337.
[94] Di Cosmo (2005), 391, 395–7, 399–400, 407–8, 411, 415, 418; Doumerc (1987), 6.
[95] Doumerc (1987), 9. [96] Ashtor (1983), 402–3.

The role of alien merchant guilds in helping rulers collect taxes from merchants was not restricted to Muslim or nomadic states, however, but was also widespread in the medieval west. The Fondaco dei Tedeschi, for instance, served Venetian fiscal purposes from the early thirteenth century onwards by drawing up itemized lists of all goods and money brought in by every German merchant, which then provided the basis for import and export taxes due to the Venetian state. The Fondaco oversaw each merchant's subsequent transactions, with two witnesses, to ensure that the merchant did not make clandestine sales that would cheat the merchant Fondaco or the Venetian government of its due.[97] The Fondaco was estimated in 1497 to contribute 100 ducats daily in taxes to the government of Venice, prompting its description by the Signoria as 'the best member of this city'.[98]

In north-west and northern Europe as well, alien merchant guilds explicitly agreed to help rulers collect taxes in return for commercial privileges. In 1303, for instance, alien merchant guilds in England agreed to deliver higher customs dues on exports of wool and hides in exchange for expanded trading privileges.[99] In 1311, the French crown ordered the 'captain' of the Italian merchant guild at the Champagne fairs to instruct all Italian merchants visiting France concerning the taxes to be rendered to the royal fisc.[100] In 1340–3, the English crown granted the Hanse the right to collect the entire revenues from the English customs in exchange for loans.[101] In fourteenth- and fifteenth-century Bergen, the Hanseatic merchant 'courtyards' were held responsible for collecting and delivering the customs dues owed by their merchants.[102] In the mid-fifteenth century the Norwegian crown granted trading privileges to Amsterdam merchants explicitly in return for the promise that they would collect taxes on Dutch trade to Bergen.[103]

The commercial expertise and superior information available to merchants, and the capacity of their guilds to mobilize it for fiscal purposes, thus enabled merchant guilds to render part of the stream of benefits they wished to offer rulers through facilitating tax collection. This is not to say that merchant guilds were the *only* source of fiscal assistance for rulers.[104] Rather, they were a convenient and attractive component of an array of interdependent institutional arrangements by which pre-modern rulers

---

[97] J. W. Hoffmann (1932), 248, 250 with n. 19; Heyd (1874), 199–200, 211–13.
[98] Heyd (1874), 217–18 (quotation 218); J. Day (2002), 811.
[99] Dollinger (1970), 55–6.   [100] Goldschmidt (1891), 198–9 with n. 189.
[101] E. B. Fryde (1959), 2–8.   [102] Burckhardt (2005), 75.
[103] Wubs-Mrozewicz (2005), 210–11.
[104] This misunderstanding regrettably leads astray the discussion in Stabel (2004); and Lambert and Stabel (2005), 16–19.

organized public finances. The widespread facilitation of tax collection by merchant guilds declined in importance, at least in the more fiscally advanced European states, as rulers developed more generalized bureaucratic and fiscal systems, especially after *c.* 1500. However, as shown by the example of the Spanish consulados, the particularistic fiscal system, whereby corporate intermediaries such as guilds assisted in tax gathering, survived in some European polities into the later eighteenth century.

5.4   State loans

A third way merchant guilds paid rulers for privileges was by making them loans on favourable terms. Medieval rulers were always seeking ways of borrowing to finance military campaigns, court display, building projects, conspicuous consumption and rewards to allies.[105] Rulers obtained loans from a variety of sources – nobles, Jews, towns – but above all from merchants. Indeed, in their demand for loans from merchants, medieval rulers 'were importunate and often could not be denied'.[106]

Individual merchants and firms had always made loans to rulers in exchange for commercial privileges, and the largest of them continued to do so throughout the medieval period.[107] The great medieval merchant houses, in fact, 'constantly used loans to public authorities as a trump card to obtain commercial favours'.[108] Merchant firms included commercial privileges as part of the pay-off in most loans they made to rulers:

the loans proper and the interest paid were in themselves only part of any deal. There were many wide avenues to profit opened to [merchant] houses high in a prince's favour – pre-emption rights, exemptions, business with courtiers and native merchants, commissions to purchase abroad on the prince's account, protection in even more remote states for goods and agents, and still others . . . [W]hen a [merchant] house got to a certain critical size, it *had* to help out princes or lose gains already made.[109]

What Hunt has termed the medieval Italian 'super-companies' (big merchant firms) made huge loans to European rulers, not so much in the expectation of profits from interest on the loans themselves, but in quasi-explicit exchange for legal privileges over particular branches of commerce: 'few of the important companies were prepared to undertake royal lending on its own merits; there are no known examples of

---

[105] Bisson (1984), 80–3, 88, 120, 130, 138, 141–2; Botticini (2000), 166, 179–83; E. B. Fryde (1959), 2–8; Dessi and Ogilvie (2004), 57–60.
[106] Bernard (1972), 326 (quotation); Spufford (2000), 195–6.
[107] Bernard (1972), 326.   [108] Lopez (1987), 359.   [109] R. L. Reynolds (1952), 365.

large-scale continuous financing of monarchs unaccompanied by important commercial privileges'.[110]

But among individual merchants and firms, only the largest were in a position to make the size of loans rulers demanded. Even wealthy merchants could find themselves fatally destabilized by extending credit to rulers because of the favourable terms they were required to offer and because rulers' coercive powers made it easy to default on repayment. Thus, for instance, the Florentine merchant houses of the Bardi and the Peruzzi were required to extend huge loans to King Edward III of England in exchange for commercial privileges. But in the 1340s the English king defaulted, bankrupting the two Florentine firms.[111] Likewise in 1480 Lorenzo il Magnifico withdrew his interest from the Medici Company in Bruges because its representative Tommaso Portinari had granted disastrously generous loans to the duke of Burgundy.[112]

Merchant guilds offered a solution to this problem by making it possible for smaller-scale merchants to combine to get a share of a legal monopoly from the ruler by contributing a share of a favourable state loan. This massively expanded the potential scale on which favours could be exchanged between rulers and merchants. Merchants used guilds to generate economies of scale in bribing rulers to grant monopoly rents, thereby enjoying advantages over individual merchants and firms who, as we have seen, could be bankrupted by the scale of rulers' demands and their incentive to default.

Local merchant guilds very commonly provided credit to rulers – the twelfth-century Cologne merchant guild to its ruler the archbishop,[113] the medieval Spanish and Catalan merchant *consulados* to their princes,[114] the thirteenth- and fourteenth-century Karīmī merchant association in Alexandria to the sultan of Cairo and the king of Yemen,[115] the Florentine merchant guilds to the Florentine Signoria,[116] the fourteenth- and fifteenth-century Company of the Staple to the English crown.[117]

Alien merchant guilds also frequently made foreign rulers loans on preferential terms.[118] This pattern can be observed throughout medieval Europe, from Byzantium to Italy and from England to Flanders and Germany. The origin of Venice's extraordinary trading privileges in the Byzantine empire was a huge military loan from Venice to Emperor Alexius I in 1082, in return for which the emperor granted Venetian

---

[110] Hunt (1994), 64.   [111] Van Houtte (1966), 39.
[112] *Ibid.*   [113] Planitz (1940), 73.
[114] Woodward (2005), 631–3; R. S. Smith (1940), 37, 48, 64–5, 85.
[115] Ashtor (1983), 73–4, 271–83; Abulafia (1987b), 440–1.
[116] Becker (1960a), 40, 44 with n. 23.   [117] Postan (1987), 292–3.
[118] Kohn (2003a), 17–18.

merchant colonies freedom of trade without interference from customs officials in most Byzantine ports, while all other merchants had to pay 10 per cent duties.[119]

Even rich and fiscally sophisticated western European states sometimes gave privileges to alien merchant guilds in return for loans. Throughout its fourteenth-century wars, the Venetian government granted foreign merchants wider trading privileges in exchange for assistance with war finances.[120] In 1312–13, Venice granted the Florentine merchant guild permission to go on trading in the city if it provided financial services to the state at below market rates.[121] In 1380–2, in return for loans to finance the War of Chioggia, the Venetian state showered alien merchant guilds with privileges including relaxation of ceilings on foreign participation in maritime trade, reductions in discriminatory taxation, greater ease in obtaining Venetian citizenship and permits to buy local real estate.[122] Other Italian city-states did the same, as in the 1470s when the ruler of Naples borrowed heavily from Florentine merchants, in return granting the Florentine merchant guild tax reductions, monopolies and grain export licences.[123]

Medieval English rulers also frequently granted alien merchant guilds trading privileges in exchange for favourable loans. From 1299 on, the German Hanse in England were 'acting as credit bankers, lending . . . considerable sums to the crown'.[124] In 1327 Hanse loans helped Edward III to the throne and then aided his French wars. In return, English monarchs granted the Hanse wool-exporting privileges, tax cuts and rights to collect customs dues from other merchants.[125] Fifteenth-century English rulers extracted loans from Florentine, Genoese, Venetian and Catalan merchant guilds in London in exchange for confirming their existing commercial privileges, refraining from persecuting or expelling them, and exempting them from export restrictions.[126]

Reliance on alien merchant guilds for state loans was understandably more important in fiscally less highly developed regions of Europe. In Lithuania, for instance, the prince's sole source of credit was the Hanse; when a loan was refused through an administrative misunderstanding in 1400, the Lithuanian ruler rescinded many of the Hanse's commercial privileges.[127] In the late fifteenth century, the ruler of Naples relied on loans from the Florentine merchant guild to help him quell his rebellious nobles, in return granting the Florentines significant tax reductions

---

[119] Runciman (1987), 146.   [120] Kedar (1976), 54–5.   [121] Mueller (1997), 258–9.
[122] *Ibid.*, 266–7.   [123] Abulafia (1990), 135–6.   [124] Dollinger (1970), 57.
[125] *Ibid.*, 56–8; E. B. Fryde (1959), 2.   [126] Holmes (1960–1), 207.
[127] Jenks (1982), 320–1.

and commercial monopolies.[128] But even Bruges, which had one of the most sophisticated fiscal systems in Europe, occasionally turned to alien merchant guilds for loans, as in 1379, 1411 and 1438 when the municipal government requested (or required) loans from nearly all the alien merchant guilds in the city.[129] Throughout medieval Europe, therefore, an important way merchant guilds shared their monopoly rents with the rulers whose favour made those rents possible was through advancing credit on favourable terms.

5.5   Military and naval assistance

The flow of benefits from merchant guilds to rulers in return for commercial privileges sometimes extended beyond the purely financial to the military and political spheres. *Local* merchant guilds are frequently observed facilitating rulers' military and naval activities – as with the eleventh-century St Omer merchant guild which maintained town walls, gates and fortifications;[130] the medieval Spanish merchant guilds whose privileges were routinely enlarged in return for assisting the crown in foreign military adventures;[131] the Catalonian consulados who provided merchant ships for the prince's 1229 invasion of Mallorca;[132] the consulados of Valencia, Barcelona and Mallorca which supported the Crown of Aragon's 1400–1 campaign against Sardinia in return for ejections of alien merchants;[133] or the English Staple Company which paid the wages of the Calais garrison in 1446 in return for additional commercial privileges from the crown.[134]

Alien merchant guilds also provided rulers with military and naval support – or, more frequently, ensured that their home polities did so – in exchange for commercial privileges. Venetian merchant colonies in the Byzantine empire owed their special commercial advantages partly to 'the valiant aid that Venice rendered at Durazzo against the Normans' (in the wording of the 1082 Chrysobull); they obtained even wider privileges because they served Byzantine rulers' military strategy against the Turks.[135] Genoese merchant colonies also got commercial privileges in the twelfth and thirteenth centuries by offering naval and military support to the Greek emperors.[136] Genoese, Pisan, Venetian,

---

[128] Abulafia (1990), 135–6.
[129] Lambert and Stabel (2005), 18–19; Stabel (1999), 35.
[130] Dilcher (1984), 70; Kohn (2003a), 4; Nicholas (1997a), 133.
[131] R. S. Smith (1940), 48, 64–5.   [132] Woodward (2005), 633.
[133] Congdon (2003), 224–5.   [134] Postan (1987), 293.
[135] Madden (2002), 23–4, 27 (quotation); Frankopan (2004), 149.
[136] Abulafia (1986b), 204; Runciman (1987), 149; Kohn (2003a), 18.

Catalan, Provençal and Anconitan merchant colonies got monopolies, tax breaks, customs exemptions, trading compounds and other commercial privileges in the ports of Palestine and Syria from the eleventh to the thirteenth centuries in return for naval and military assistance to the Crusader authorities.[137] Italian merchant colonies even provided military assistance to non-Christian rulers in return for commercial privileges: armaments to Egyptian rulers in the twelfth and thirteenth centuries,[138] military commodities such as timber and iron to the Mamluks in the early fourteenth century,[139] troops to the Khan of the Golden Horde in 1380.[140]

One might ascribe this exchange of military assistance for guild privileges to the peculiar circumstances of the eastern Mediterranean, were it not for the fact that it can also be observed in western Europe. Genoese merchant guilds obtained commercial privileges from local rulers in Hyeres, Fossis, Fréjus, Antibes and Marseilles by promising military aid against Saracen attacks in the 1130s.[141] Genoese and Pisan merchant guilds got trading privileges in Montpellier by providing military aid to Guilhem VI against rebels in 1141–3.[142] Genoese merchant colonies got a commercial monopoly in return for military aid to the count of Toulouse in the 1170s.[143] Venetian merchant guilds got privileges to go on trading in Aragonese and Catalan cities in return for military alliances in 1398, while other alien merchant nations were expelled.[144] The German Hanse got commercial privileges in England in return for support for the Lancastrian party during the Wars of the Roses.[145]

The Baltic shows the same pattern. The Gotland Community (the precursor institution to the German Hanse) provided military support to 'crusading' expeditions into Livonia in return for privileges and bases for trade into Russia from the late twelfth century on.[146] In 1201 the Gotland Community obtained commercial privileges in Riga in return for equipment and transport provided to the Baltic Crusade that led to the town's foundation.[147] In 1226–7, the Gotland Community and the German merchant colony in Riga received further privileges and booty in return for military and logistical assistance with the Crusade against

---

[137] Lopez (1987), 346; R. De Roover (1965), 60; Queller and Day (1976), 721; Kohn (2003a), 18; Abulafia (1986a), 535–6, 543; Abulafia (1995), 13, 18; Abulafia (1997), 54–5; Liu (1925), ch. II, section II.
[138] Abulafia (1995), 16–17; Queller and Day (1976), 730–1.
[139] Northrup (1998), 285; Ashtor (1983), 52–4.   [140] Di Cosmo (2005), 401.
[141] Krueger (1933), 378.   [142] Reyerson (1994), 362.   [143] *Ibid.*, 364.
[144] Congdon (2003), 221.   [145] Dollinger (1970), 307.
[146] Munzinger (2006), 174–7, 184–5; Johansen (1940), 9.
[147] Dollinger (1970), 28; Munzinger (2006), 177–8; Stoob (1995), 106.

Ösel.[148] In the 1340s, the Hanse got trading privileges in Norway in return for providing military support to King Magnus.[149] In 1469–70, the Dutch and German merchant colonies in Bergen obtained commercial privileges by providing the Norwegian king with support against Sweden.[150] Throughout the medieval period, the German Hanse secured and maintained its Russian trading privileges partly by supplying military materials to Russian rulers.[151]

5.6   Political support

Merchant guilds also offered benefits to rulers in the political sphere. A ruler could gain two political advantages from merchant guilds. First, merchant support could help secure the political agreement needed to increase taxes. Second, merchant backing could provide a countervailing force against the nobility. The mercantile strata could mobilize and deliver such political support more readily through guilds, which reduced the costs of organizing agreement among individual merchants and between merchants and rulers.

During the medieval period, European rulers increasingly sought to diversify sources of political support across different social groups. The nobility was indisputably the most important source of support for princes, but this was a two-edged sword. Rulers' plans for fiscal expansion were often hindered by the nobility, which preferred peasants to pay exactions to nobles themselves.[152] But by the twelfth century at latest, the bourgeoisie in general and merchants in particular had become an important additional source of political support for many European rulers.[153] In medieval France, for instance, 'there were benefits for the bourgeois to side with the French king and support his policies against the nobility and church'.[154] Medieval Spanish monarchs used cities such as Barcelona, in particular its merchant consulado, 'as a counterpoise to the feudal nobility'. In return for backing the crown against the nobles, 'Catalan merchants were granted privileges throughout the new conquests, and royal ambassadors secured franchises for them far beyond the frontiers of the realm'.[155]

The bourgeois political support which medieval rulers sought was often most effectively delivered through merchant guilds, which dominated the governments of most important medieval towns. In Catalonian and

---

[148] Munzinger (2006), 183; Dollinger (1970), 28.   [149] Daenell (1905), 27.
[150] Wubs-Mrozewicz (2005), 211.   [151] Angermann (1987), 86.
[152] Bisson (1984), 86, 137; Dessì and Ogilvie (2004), 60–1.
[153] On this development, see Spruyt (1994), esp. 86–108   [154] *Ibid.*, 86.
[155] Lopez (1987), 342.

Aragonese towns from the thirteenth century on, the consulados allied closely with the municipal administrations and played important roles in the political structure.[156] The same was true in Italy, where in cities such as Florence and Siena political decision-making was dominated by the various guilds of merchants.[157] Although Venice and Genoa did not have local merchant guilds, they established alien merchant guilds overseas, and each government was driven by the corporative interests of the city's merchants.[158] Merchant guilds also dominated political decision-making in German towns, where the offices of mayors and town councillors were often reserved for merchant guild members.[159] Medieval Flanders showed similarly close relations between merchant guilds and town governments, with town councils dominated by guild members and strongly influenced by their interests, an arrangement vigorously supported by the counts of Flanders.[160]

A similar pattern can be observed in France, where the same men often held the positions of city aldermen and foremen of the merchant guild.[161] Many medieval English towns likewise show close relationships between the local merchant guild and the municipal government, giving rise to an inevitable identity of interests.[162]

Because merchant guilds so often dominated urban political organs, they were in an excellent position to decide whether to provide bourgeois political support to princes. They did so in a variety of arenas – as a countervailing force to the nobility at home but also in a whole range of situations on the foreign stage.

At a surprisingly early period in the Middle Ages, merchant guilds became valuable political allies for rulers against the nobility. Many German towns allied with rulers against their own noble or ecclesiastical overlords as early as the eleventh century, alliances that also benefited the German kings in controlling over-mighty vassals.[163] The rulers of twelfth- and thirteenth-century Flanders also granted wide privileges to the towns and the merchant guilds that dominated them, in return for financial assistance against recalcitrant nobles.[164] In medieval France, too,

---

[156] Woodward (2005), 633–5.
[157] Lopez (1987), 335; Staley (1906); Blomquist (1971), 471–4; Becker (1960b), 430 with n. 45; Becker (1962), 366–7; Bowsky (1962), 370–1, 374.
[158] Dursteler (2006); Katele (1988); Tai (1996); Van Doosselaere (2009); S. A. Epstein (1996).
[159] Link and Kapfenberger (2005), 167–8; Brück (1999), 120; Nitzsch (1892), 33, 47.
[160] Nicholas (1997a), 222; Häpke (1908), 53, 58, 187–9; Nitzsch (1892), 38.
[161] Nicholas (1997a), 222.
[162] Alsford (2003), ch. 2, s.v. 'The mercantile interest', www.users.trytel.com/~tristan/towns/mc2_pt4.html.
[163] Spruyt (1994), 114.   [164] Blockmans (2000), 414.

monarchical power expanded partly through political support from towns, often dominated by merchant guilds; this was particularly important during the baronial rebellions of the thirteenth and fourteenth centuries.[165] Thirteenth- and fourteenth-century Catalan rulers saw the Barcelona consulado as a source of revenue, making it possible to avoid political concessions to the nobility.[166] In all these cases, urban oligarchies and merchant guilds (often indistinguishable from one another) gained institutional powers as part of a wider process during which princes sought to move away from exclusive political dependence on the nobility.[167]

The political support provided to rulers by merchant guilds and the towns they dominated extended to the international stage. The Venetian and Genoese merchant guilds in Sicily supported the Sicilian ruler against Emperor Lothar in the 1120s and 1130s, receiving commercial privileges denied to the Pisan merchant guild which supported the emperor.[168] Conversely, in 1162 the emperor promised privileges to Pisan merchant guilds in Sicily in return for support in overthrowing the upstart kingdom of Sicily.[169] The Pope granted trading privileges to Anconitan merchant guilds in the kingdoms of Sicily and Jerusalem in 1245 in an attempt to win support in his struggle against the Hohenstaufen emperor.[170] Charles V of France granted commercial privileges in France to the German Hanse in the fourteenth century 'in the hope of gaining new allies against the English'.[171] Contenders for the Danish crown in 1438 offered commercial privileges to the German Hanse in return for political support for their claims.[172]

The fact that local merchant guilds dominated most important medieval towns and their alien branches exerted leverage back home turned both types of guild into attractive political partners for rulers. Merchant guilds' influential position in urban politics enabled them to deliver political support to rulers at crucial junctures in exchange for monopolies and other privileges.

5.7   The decline of merchant guilds

This account explains the guild–ruler relationship better than views focusing solely on merchant guilds as advocates of mercantile interests against extortionate rulers. The guild–ruler relationship was less

---

[165] Spruyt (1994), 105, 107.   [166] Abulafia (2000b), 660.
[167] Stephenson (1933), esp. 150.   [168] Abulafia (1978), 72.   [169] *Ibid.*, 72–3.
[170] Abulafia (1986a), 531 (quotation), 532.   [171] Dollinger (1970), 253.
[172] *Ibid.*, 297.

oppositional than symbiotic: each party aided the other in extracting resources from the economy. Merchant guilds were willing and able to mobilize direct payments, favourable loans, fiscal compliance, political support and even military aid for rulers in return for commercial privileges whose profits they used partly to finance more favours from rulers. This gave rise to the 'particularistic' or 'corporative' institutional system which was characteristic of medieval European governance and trade.

This analysis of the guild–ruler relationship also provides a better explanation than existing accounts for the gradual weakening of merchant guilds in some European societies after *c.* 1500. From the later fifteenth century on, as we saw in Chapter 2, both local and foreign merchants in a number of Flemish, Dutch and English towns increasingly began to operate outside the guild framework. A new type of merchant trading emerged in these economies, dominated by 'individual entrepreneurs who did not belong to any formal kind of associations'.[173]

Merchants in the Low Countries began to move their operations from Bruges, still dominated by powerful alien merchant guilds, to Antwerp and then Amsterdam, where merchant guilds were weak or non-existent. Antwerp was increasingly characterized by an institutional framework within which individual merchants could trade outside guild restrictions.[174] Amsterdam prohibited alien merchant guilds and did not grant privileges to a single, over-arching local merchant guild, although some guild privileges survived over particular aspects of trade, especially retailing.[175] The Northern Netherlands declared independence from the Habsburgs in 1581, and the new Dutch Republic largely refused to grant privileges to corporative groups of merchants, whether indigenous or foreign.[176]

In English towns, as well, merchant guilds gradually lost their special economic privileges after *c.* 1500, even in cases where they still formally stayed in existence. In provincial trading towns such as Ipswich, powerful local merchant guilds metamorphosed into purely cultural and social associations by the later fifteenth century.[177] Even in London, the powerful livery companies gradually ceased to be able to enforce their economic privileges in the course of the sixteenth century, shifting towards sociability, cultural display and business networking.[178] Membership in alien

---

[173] Gelderblom and Grafe (2004), 1.

[174] Harreld (2004b), 3, 7; see also Harreld (2004a), 5–6.

[175] Gelderblom (2005a), 32–5; De Vries and Van der Woude (1997), 407–8.

[176] Gelderblom (2005a), 38–9.

[177] Alsford (2003), 'History of medieval Ipswich', www.trytel.com/~tristan/towns/ipswic13.html, s.v. 'Economy'.

[178] Kellett (1958).

merchant guilds became unnecessary or irrelevant for foreign merchants trading in London or other English towns, with the abolition of Hanseatic privileges and the disappearance of the Italian merchant colonies by the mid-sixteenth century.[179]

In the Low Countries and England, the one exception to the move away from the particularistic segmentation of commerce in the interests of special corporate groups after *c.* 1500 was, as we have seen, the privileged merchant companies in the trade to certain overseas destinations. These Dutch and English privileged companies dominated important transcontinental trade routes, harmed efficiency by stifling exchange and damaged the welfare of interloping merchants, consumers and suppliers on these routes. But most pre-modern trade, as we shall see in Chapter 6, consisted of local, regional and at most trans-European trade which had long been monopolized by traditional merchant guilds. This trade, at least in its English and Dutch manifestations, now passed into the hands of individual competitive traders and was removed from the grasp of privileged corporate groups.[180]

In the vast majority of European states, by contrast, the emerging 'absolutist' states of the sixteenth century satisfied their growing demand for revenues by continuing to grant economic privileges to corporate interest-groups, among them merchant guilds.[181] Traditional merchant guilds survived and new proto-industrial merchant associations emerged, nurtured by absolutist rulers who craved their cash transfers, their favourable loans, their fiscal collaboration and their political support.

Cash transfers from merchant guilds to political groups remained widespread in many parts of early modern Europe. In France, for instance, the proto-industrial merchant guild of Clermont-de-Lodève made payments to political figures, both locally and in Paris, in return for assistance in maintaining its monopoly privileges over the Languedocian textile export trade.[182] In Spain, the crown granted and reconfirmed the monopoly of the Seville *consulado* over trade with Spanish America during the sixteenth and seventeenth centuries in return for so-called *donativos* (money donations).[183] In the German Wupper Valley (south of the Ruhr region), the powerful merchant association of the Wuppertaler Garnnahrung had the right to collect substantial fines from anyone who encroached on its privileges over the textile trade from the sixteenth

---

[179] Lloyd (1982), 209.
[180] On the hostility towards European trade monopolies by the English House of Commons in debates of 1601 and 1604, see Archer (1991), 48.
[181] Lindberg (2007), 2–3, 15–19; Lindberg (2009), 606–7; Ogilvie (1992), 429–34; Ogilvie (1999), 199–202.
[182] J. K. J. Thomson (1982), 12.   [183] Woodward (2005), 634; Hussey (1929), 5.

to the later eighteenth century, and transferred a share of its profits to the ruler in return for state enforcement.[184] In the German territory of Württemberg, the Calwer Zeughandlungskompagnie paid the state officials responsible for administering and enforcing its monopoly over worsted exporting between 1650 and 1797 annual perquisites which 'seldom failed to bury the independence of the bureaucrats', and systematically paid *honoraria* to princely officials and councillors for political support.[185] In eighteenth-century Aachen, the Feine Gewandtschaft (woollen-cloth merchants' guild) obtained special commercial privileges, including the legal right to stifle the guild of their suppliers, the woollen weavers, through 'greasing the palms of important court officials'.[186]

Merchant guilds also continued to assist many early modern absolutist rulers in tax collection, in return for economic privileges. In German-speaking central Europe, traditional merchant guilds continued to enjoy the privilege of the compulsory 'staple' whereby trade had to pass through particular locations where local guilds exercised purchasing prerogatives and helped rulers take their fiscal cut; many central European staple privileges were not abolished until 1815.[187] In Spain and its overseas empire, too, merchant consulados continued to play a major role in tax collection into the late eighteenth or even the early nineteenth century.[188]

Besides their *direct* involvement in tax collection, merchant guilds also provided *indirect* fiscal assistance to many early modern rulers through monitoring trade in order to protect their members' monopolies, thereby assisting the state in the eradication of contraband. This advantage was explicitly recognized by the political authorities, as in 1785 when one Spanish intendant advocated the establishment of a new merchant consulado in Caracas on the grounds that merchants always 'know what contraband is being carried out, who introduces it, of what goods it consists, as well as the actors, the accomplices, and the participants'. A merchant consulado, he argued, 'would reduce the need to fret over this prospect and would guard most vigilantly against clandestine trade. Not even the officials of the Royal Treasury are as interested in the extinction of contraband as these merchants are.'[189]

In many European polities, merchant guilds and associations also continued to provide rulers with favourable loans. One of the major concerns of the Seville merchant consulado which enjoyed a legal monopoly over the Spanish trade with the Indies from 1543 onwards was 'assembling funds to provide large loans to the Crown as well as outright donations

---

[184] Kisch (1972), 314.   [185] Troeltsch (1897), 85.   [186] Kisch (1964), 528.
[187] Kuske (1939), 46.   [188] Woodward (2005), 633, 636–8; Paquette (2007), 271, 296.
[189] Quoted in Paquette (2007), 272–3.

(*donativos*) in times of war or other crisis'.[190] In seventeenth-century Sweden, associations of copper merchants were granted monopolies over the copper export trade by the crown in the 1660s in return for helping to finance the Bremen War.[191] In 1736, the Württemberg state extended the export monopoly of the Calwer Zeughandlungskompagnie on the grounds that the association 'was a substantial national treasure', as shown 'especially on the occasion of the recent French invasion threat and the military taxes proposed to be raised, when it became apparent that no just opportunity should be lost to extend the Company a helping hand in all just matters as much as possible'.[192] In eighteenth-century Spanish America, 'the consulados of Seville, Mexico, and Lima lent and donated millions of pesos to the crown' to help finance ineluctably increasing military costs.[193] So onerous were rulers' financial demands from consulados that in Spanish America 'some merchants resisted consulado efforts to register all merchants, realizing that registration made them more vulnerable to forced loan levies, special taxes, and government regulation . . . marginal merchants especially often preferred anonymity'.[194]

Some early modern rulers even continued to derive military support by granting commercial privileges to merchant guilds. In 1603, when the czar cancelled the 450-year-old trading privileges of the German Hanse, Lübeck alone was permitted to maintain merchant colonies in four Russian trading centres, partly because the czar hoped thereby to gain Lübeck's support in his struggle with Sweden.[195] Well into the eighteenth century the Cádiz consulado provided most of the Spanish coast-guard ships that patrolled the Caribbean; the Lima consulado maintained a major fleet in the Pacific; and several Spanish American consulados maintained privateers for the state.[196] Spanish Bourbon attempts to break down the privileges of consulados after 1780 were muted by 'the requirements of revenue and imperial defence', which softened 'regalist hostility toward corporate privilege and permitted alliances based on mutual interest to develop'.[197]

Many of the supposedly 'absolutist' states of Europe, therefore, were actually 'corporatist' states, heavily dependent on a particularized institutional system based on a symbiosis between governments and special interest-groups such as guilds.[198] Such absolutist–corporatist rulers continued to grant legal advantages over trade to merchant guilds and

---

[190] Woodward (2005), 634.   [191] Müller (1998), 101.
[192] Quoted in Troeltsch (1897), 84 n. 2.   [193] Woodward (2005), 636.
[194] *Ibid.*, 637.   [195] Angermann (1979), 230 n. 11.
[196] Woodward (2005), 633, 636, 638.   [197] Paquette (2007), 267.
[198] For a detailed discussion of the corporatist institutions on which 'absolutism' often relied, see Ogilvie (1999).

privileged companies because they continued to depend on the cash payments, favourable loans, fiscal assistance, monitoring of illegal trade and military support these merchant groups delivered to the state.[199]

The period after *c.* 1500, therefore, saw a widening divergence across Europe in the relationship between the political authorities and merchant guilds. In societies such as the Low Countries and England, the political authorities gradually ceased to grant and enforce merchant guilds' privileges, while more absolutist European states continued to do so. The reasons for this shift are still a matter of lively investigation and seem set to provide fruitful avenues for research for some time to come. Ongoing investigations into the institutional innovations which took place in the Low Countries and England during the sixteenth century suggest that a complex of factors created a self-sustaining equilibrium in which both rulers and merchants discovered they could do better for themselves by departing from the particularist path and beginning to use more generalized institutional mechanisms.

For one thing, a number of historians point to the existence, in the early modern Low Countries and England, of strong representative institutions which, from *c.* 1500 on, increasingly constrained how rulers could raise revenues and grant privileges to special interest-groups.[200] But since strong representative institutions can also entrench corporatism rather than restricting it, other historians point to a second distinctive characteristic of the Low Countries and England – a highly diversified urban system in which towns did not act in concert, but rather competed and limited each other's ability to secure privileges from the public authorities.[201] A

---

[199] For a rich discussion of fiscal strategies of different types of polity in medieval and early modern Europe, see Van Zanden and Prak (2006), 118–19; P. T. Hoffman and Norberg (1994), 299; Hopcroft (1999), 70–2, 76–84, 87.

[200] For a theoretical model of how a strong state may need to be constrained by strong representative institutions in order to prevent rent-seeking and improve resource allocation in developing economies, see Acemoglu (2010). The force of this argument is not vitiated by the fact that empirically that paper adopts as a stylized fact the mistaken view advanced in North and Weingast (1989), esp. 816, 819, that representative control over the English state was negligible before 1688. For a selection of the many counter-arguments showing this view to be mistaken, see Stasavage (2002), 164, 177; Clark (1996), 565–72, 587–8; Murrell (2009), 4–6, 30–34; Brewer (1989), 3–24; De Vries and Van der Woude (1997), 113–29; Priks (2005), 4–5. On how the English House of Commons opposed royal privileges for merchant companies trading to Europe in 1601 and 1604, see Croft (1973b), xxx–xxxii; Rabb (1964), 661–9; Archer (1991), 48.

[201] On the Low Countries, see 't Hart (1989), 680; De Vries and Van der Woude (1997), 113–29, 407–8; Harreld (2004b), 3, 7; Harreld (2004a), 5–6; Gelderblom (2005a), 32, 38; Van Zanden and Prak (2006), 124–35l; Van Bavel and Van Zanden (2004), 525–8; Lis and Soly (1996), 26–31. On the English urban system and constraints on corporative rent seeking in the fifteenth and sixteenth centuries, see Britnell (1991), esp. 31–3; Archer (1988); Nachbar (2005), 1342–65; W. H. Price (2006), 3–48; Murrell

further distinguishing characteristic of the Low Countries and England was the existence of broad social strata – including prosperous, articulate and politically influential individuals – who, although they were not merchants by occupation, were able and willing to participate in long-distance trade, and thus inclined to object to its being monopolized by members of exclusive merchant organizations.[202] A final strand of research emphasizes how rulers in the Low Countries and England freed themselves for crucial periods after *c.* 1500 from fiscal dependence on granting privileges to special interest-groups by developing alternative revenue sources, including confiscating property from the church by dissolving religious houses, making taxation socially more generalized and developing efficient markets for public borrowing.[203] To explain definitively why after *c.* 1500 the relationship between merchant guilds and the political authorities bifurcated in this way is a challenge for future research. What is not in dispute is that this bifurcation occurred, with political authorities in the Low Countries and England gradually ceasing to enforce privileges for merchant guilds and developing a more generalized institutional framework to mobilize public revenues and govern trade, while most other European states continued down the particularist path for much longer.

5.8   Conclusion

We can now return to the question with which this chapter began: why did merchant guilds exist for such a long time in so many different economies? The answer is not that they were economically efficient, in the sense that they maximized the size of the aggregate economic pie. Rather, merchant guilds were so widespread and long-lived because they offered a very effective way for two sets of powerful beneficiaries – rulers and guilded merchants – to redistribute larger slices of the pie to themselves, even at the cost of diminishing its overall size. Merchant guilds were institutions that enabled merchants and rulers to negotiate and manage a complex,

---

(2009), 8; Croft (1973b), xxxi–xxxii, xlv–xlvi; Rabb (1964), 663; Ashton (1967), 44–6, 55.

[202] On the existence of such social groups (and their strong representation among Members of Parliament opposing merchant monopolies) in sixteenth-century England, see Rabb (1964), 661–9; Ashton (1967), 42–54; Croft (1973b), xlv–xlvi; on the broad social strata able and willing to invest in long-distance trade in the sixteenth-century Low Countries, see De Vries and Van der Woude (1997), ch. 9; De Vries (1976), 116–23.

[203] On the Low Countries, see Fritschy (2003), esp. 80–1; Davids (2006); 't Hart (1989); 't Hart (1993). On the revolution in taxation in England in the 1530s and 1540s, see Schofield (1963); Elton (1975); Hoyle (1994).

two-way flow of benefits which neither party could have extracted from the pre-modern economy without the cooperation of the other.

Merchants liked merchant guilds because they reduced the per capita transaction costs of negotiating to get privileges from rulers. Such privileges were necessary to permit merchants to trade in the first place, and sometimes also secured them tax reductions. Above all, however, privileges from rulers gave guilded merchants the exclusive right to trade in particular wares, transaction types, routes and destinations – i.e. to act as a collective monopolist or cartel in specific branches of trade. A merchant guild provided an institutional mechanism whereby its members could legally restrict entry, fix prices, restrict supplies, depress input costs and increase the costs of competitors, as we saw in Chapters 3 and 4. This gave guilded merchants advantages over potential competitors and enabled them to reap monopoly profits – i.e. to extract a bigger slice of resources from the economy.

Rulers liked merchant guilds because guilds increased the ability of merchants to combine together to offer them cash transfers, facilitate tax gathering, make favourable loans, render military and naval assistance, and provide political alliances against domestic nobles and foreign foes. Rulers had several incentives to restrict trade by segmenting it into a series of closed monopolies for merchant guilds instead of increasing its volume at the cost of opening it to all comers. Rulers were individuals with limited life expectancies and often faced urgent political and military crises; guilds, by contrast, outlasted the lives of their members, and although an individual merchant business might go bankrupt, it was rare for the merchants of an entire city to go out of business. Consequently, rulers typically discounted the future more than merchant guilds, so both could be made better off through rulers trading with merchants so as to get benefits from their guilds *now* instead of having to wait to collect tax receipts from all traders in *future*. Moreover, since rulers typically faced higher risks than guilds of merchants, granting merchant guilds monopolies in return for fixed payments gave rulers certainty about what benefits they would receive rather than having to rely on generalized revenue streams from taxation and public borrowing whose price and availability, in the absence of effective fiscal mechanisms and a market for government debt, were uncertain. In the absence of effective bureaucracies, this type of fiscal bargain with guilds also saved rulers the costs of tax collection, since the merchant guild incurred all the costs of assembling the benefit from its members before transferring it to the ruler. Guilds also enabled merchants to commit themselves – and the towns whose governments they usually dominated – to providing rulers with political and military support which even the richest individual merchants or firms were not generally in a position to mobilize. Finally, the value of the benefits merchants were willing to offer for commercial privileges conveyed information to rulers about how good trading conditions were, and this in turn enabled rulers to tax trade in a more targeted way. For all these reasons, both merchants and rulers supported the existence of merchant guilds which made possible a two-way flow of benefits which neither party could obtain without the other.

The relationship between merchant guilds and rulers was thus more complicated – and less benign – than is usually recognized. Merchant guilds did not simply lobby rulers for tax cuts, thereby encouraging trade and benefiting the whole economy. Nor – as we shall see in the coming chapters – did merchant guilds substitute for unavailable state provision of commercial security, contract enforcement, information or price stabilization. Rather, merchant guilds enabled pre-modern rulers to transcend the limits on their ability to extract resources from their subjects. Without merchant guilds, medieval rulers were dependent on a primitive and poorly informed fiscal apparatus to levy trade taxes, a constrained and costly capital market to obtain loans and undeveloped representative institutions rendering them politically reliant on a single social group, the nobility. Merchant guilds enabled rulers to obtain lump-sum transfers in advance of tax receipts, to induce merchants to reveal information about trading conditions through their bids for privileges, to put pressure on merchants to make higher loans than would otherwise have been forthcoming, to benefit from merchants' knowledge and expertise in collecting taxes and to mobilize political support from the bourgeoisie. The price guilded merchants paid rulers for commercial and fiscal privileges was evidently low enough that they were happy to continue to strike this bargain. The price rulers paid for the benefits they obtained from merchant guilds in return for granting them privileges was simply a (to rulers largely imperceptible) diminution in trade taxes from the reduction in the volume of exchange resulting from merchant monopolies.

A much higher price, by contrast, was paid by the wider society. The economy as a whole suffered because the volume of exchange was reduced and gains from trade were lost. Those who wished to trade but could not gain admission to merchant guilds suffered because they were excluded from practising commerce legitimately. Merchants whose guilds were weaker suffered because traders with stronger guild organizations paid lower taxes and enjoyed more valuable monopolies. Consumers suffered because monopolistic merchants charged higher prices. The two-way flow of benefits between rulers and merchant guilds, although it enhanced the well-being of both rulers and guilded merchants, had a malign impact on the rest of the economy.

Nonetheless, one might still seek to claim that merchant guilds were beneficial in a broader perspective. Even though merchant guilds enabled merchants and rulers to extract more resources from trade, harming non-guild members and the wider economy, one might still argue that merchant guilds were efficient institutions. The pre-modern economy, one might argue, did not have the supporting institutions necessary to enable a well-functioning system of competitive markets. So the relevant comparison might not be between monopolistic guilds and competitive markets, but rather between monopolistic guilds that provided *some* support for market trade and a guildless economy with no trade at all. Or, as 'social capital' theorists would put it, merchant guilds might have used their monopolies to generate the social capital and the trust necessary for markets to work. Precisely the monopoly rents generated by merchant guilds, this argument would hold, provided incentives for guild members to commit themselves to beneficial forms of collective action that increased economic efficiency in other ways. This could have created benefits for the entire economy that were more than enough to compensate for the harm caused by merchant guilds in empowering merchants to act as monopolists and enabling rulers to extract more resources from the economy to spend on conspicuous display and warfare.

These arguments can be tested. But to do so, we have to investigate the particular types of market in which merchants and their guilds operated, assess the extent of the imperfections in such markets, scrutinize what merchant guilds did about them and explore the feasible institutional alternatives. We now undertake this project, starting with the provision of commercial security.

6   Commercial security

> If you practise commerce...keep your eyes wide open, night and day...And when someone comes to your place, open your eyes and look out; don't trust anyone, no matter who they are; pay attention to their hands!
>
> (Anonymous Genoese poet, late thirteenth century)[1]

Insecurity is a basic problem for all commerce. Pirates may attack ships, bandits hold up caravans, thieves break into storehouses. Enemy navies may board vessels, soldiers loot wagons, customs officers impound merchandise, rulers arrest traders or declare their goods forfeit. The merchant risks not only losing property but suffering bodily harm – imprisonment, injury, death. Such attacks increase costs, and if their probability is too high, merchants will refrain from trade, harming the wider economy.

Risk of attack creates a demand for institutional arrangements to improve commercial security. But security is a public good, which can make it difficult for private providers to supply in markets. For one thing, security is often 'non-excludable': once a police force, naval patrol or fortification is created to protect one merchant, it is hard to prevent others from enjoying it without charge. Second, it is frequently 'non-rival': providers often incur no higher costs by providing security to additional merchants. Consequently, the private benefits of providing security are often less than its social benefits, so it may be under-provided by private individuals transacting in markets. Either security is not provided at all, since potential providers cannot profit from doing so, or it is provided but in excludable forms to only a few paying customers, even though at zero additional cost it could benefit society more widely.

One possible solution to these public good problems is for a ruler to declare himself the monopoly supplier of legitimate coercion, using force to collect taxes that fund security for all. The problem is that anyone with a monopoly has an incentive to use it to benefit himself,

---

[1] Quoted in Lopez (1958), 502.

even if it harms the wider economy. Thus a ruler *can* use his monopoly of coercion to provide security to merchants, but why should he? He might benefit more by using his forces to do things that benefit himself (such as attacking rivals) rather than those that benefit others (such as defending merchants). Or he might use his forces to *attack* merchants, confiscating their merchandise or extorting ransoms. When a ruler elects not to spend resources on providing commercial security, or decides to profit by attacking traders himself, he increases the risk of doing business in his dominions. Potentially profitable exchange doesn't happen, gains from trade are lost, production and consumption are lower. If the ruler has a short time-horizon or imperfect information, he may prefer to use his monopoly of coercion for short-term profit even if it means reducing long-term economic growth.

Institutional arrangements can align the interests of a ruler more closely with those of the wider economy and encourage him to provide security as a public good. Efficient taxation and public borrowing can offer low-cost ways to tax and borrow from merchants, giving rulers incentives to foster trade by providing security. Parliaments, if they represent sufficiently broad socio-economic interests, can inform rulers about the demand for commercial security and even constrain their acts of confiscation. Finally, independent legal systems may circumscribe how rulers can deploy their monopoly of coercion. These institutions are all generalized: their rules and entitlements apply uniformly to everyone in society. In principle, at least, they constrain rulers' coercion not by counterposing the power of particularized interest-groups, but by conveying information, preferences and political repercussions to rulers anonymously from economic agents at large. Generalized institutional arrangements make it less likely that state coercive power will be hijacked by particular interest-groups.[2]

In theory, security problems might also be solved by particularized institutions – those whose rules and entitlements apply only to members of an identifiable group. The merchant guild is a prime example of such a particularized institution – as we saw in Chapters 3 and 4, it reflected the interests of a particular group of traders, to whom its rules and privileges exclusively applied. In principle, a well-organized, particularistic institution might be able to provide commercial security itself or press rulers to provide it. Some scholars argue that this is precisely why merchant guilds existed so widely and survived for so long. Either they provided their members with security as a *club* good, or they enabled their members

---

[2] On the distinction between generalized and particularized institutions, see Ogilvie (2005).

to organize collective threats which put pressure on rulers to provide security as a *public* good.[3]

The view that corporative merchant organizations were important for providing commercial security has been widely held for a long time. Merchant guilds themselves justified their own existence – and their demands for state privileges – partly in terms of mutual protection.[4] Later historians and economists elaborated these views into more general accounts of why merchant guilds existed. In 1892, for instance, the prominent medievalist Nitzsch argued that guilds of long-distance merchants were formed in eleventh- and twelfth-century towns to provide commercial security, thereby contributing to the growth of trade.[5] In 1969 the economist Hicks theorized that 'merchant communities' arose in medieval Europe to protect property against violence, something no other institution in 'traditional society' could do.[6] In 1990, Tracy argued that European merchants out-performed Asian ones because merchant guilds enabled Europeans to resist despotic confiscation more effectively than 'the religious or caste groups into which indigenous merchants of the great Asian entrepôts were organized'.[7]

These ideas were taken up in 1994 by Greif, Milgrom and Weingast, who formalized them into a theoretical model of the merchant guild as an efficient institution. They claimed to demonstrate that 'merchant guilds emerged during the late medieval period to allow rulers of trade centers to commit to the security of alien merchants', thereby 'laying an important institutional foundation for the growing trade of that period'. Their theoretical model showed that if foreign merchants belonged to an organization that could make credible collective threats against rulers, this organization – the merchant guild – could pressure rulers into committing themselves to refrain from attacking guild members and to provide these guilded merchants with adequate levels of security against outside aggressors. In particular, a merchant guild could threaten a trade embargo against a ruler who 'misbehaved', and could do so credibly because of its control over its own members. This threat could then induce the ruler to behave well by providing security. Having

---

[3] A *public* good is non-rival (consumption of the good by one person does not reduce the amount available for consumption by others) and non-excludable (it is impossible to exclude people from consuming the good); examples would be fresh air, a missile defence system, or general law and order. A *club* good is a type of public good that is non-rival (at least until the point at which congestion occurs) but excludable; examples include cinemas, cable television, private golf courses, security in gated communities and the services which religious groups (or merchant guilds) provide to their members.

[4] As illustrated in Schütt (1985), esp. 266–9; A. Smith (1776), Book 5, ch. 1, part 3, section a, para. 4.

[5] Nitzsch (1892), 83.   [6] Hicks (1969), 33–6.   [7] Tracy (1990a), 7.

demonstrated that the interaction between a merchant guild on the one hand and a ruler on the other could in theory give rise to this happy equilibrium, Greif, Milgrom and Weingast went on to claim that this is actually why the merchant guild arose and existed in medieval Europe – it was an efficient solution to the problem of providing commercial security. The fact that rulers as well as merchants favoured the establishment of merchant guilds, they contended, shows that guilds did not exercise harmful monopolies. The fact that merchant guilds proliferated at the same time as trade expanded, they claimed, shows that guilds were efficient institutions that benefited the entire economy. With the growth of the modern state at the end of the medieval period, they argued, merchant guilds were no longer needed to pressure rulers into providing security and therefore disappeared.[8]

In 1999, Volckart and Mangels proposed a slightly different economic theory of merchant guilds as an efficient solution to security problems.[9] Their article criticized Greif, Milgrom and Weingast for describing the 'younger' merchant guilds (of the twelfth to fifteenth centuries) as efficient while ignoring their cartellistic activities. Volckart and Mangels advocated focusing on the 'elder' merchant guilds (of the tenth and eleventh centuries) which in their view solved security problems efficiently without acting cartellistically. Tenth- and eleventh-century traders formed these 'elder' merchant guilds, Volckart and Mangels argue, in order to travel together and provide mutual protection against raiders. A subsidiary function was to provide contract enforcement by generating mercantile law, an idea we shall explore in Chapter 7. The 'elder' merchant guilds are supposed to have provided mutual security and legal contract enforcement as club goods, substituting for the public goods the undeveloped states of the period were incapable of supplying. The 'elder' merchant guilds thus benefited the wider economy, Volckart and Mangels argued, by encouraging 'the emergence of non-simultaneous transactions' in eleventh- and twelfth-century Europe.[10]

In 1988, Carlos and Nicholas put forward a third theory arguing that corporative merchant associations existed to provide commercial security. This theory focused on the privileged merchant companies active in Europe's trade with other continents from the sixteenth through the eighteenth centuries. The large volume of trade and 'frequent and recurring nature of transacting' which characterized such privileged companies, Carlos and Nicholas argued, enabled them to reap economies of scale in providing commercial security, through building forts in overseas

---

[8] Greif, Milgrom and Weingast (1994).   [9] Volckart and Mangels (1999), 437.
[10] Ibid., esp. 437–9, 442.

trading destinations and providing military defence against attacks. Consequently, they claimed, these companies should be regarded as economically efficient institutions.[11]

Three separate efficiency theories, therefore, have been elaborated by modern economists based on a claim sometimes made by merchant guilds themselves, that their monopolies were justified by their role in providing security. In some ways the three efficiency theories differ. They concentrate on different time periods – the 'elder' merchant guilds of the eleventh and twelfth centuries, the 'younger' merchant guilds of the thirteenth to fifteenth centuries, and the privileged merchant companies of the post-1500 period. They also focus on different security functions – providing security as a club good to substitute for incapable rulers, or alternatively imposing trade embargoes to extract security from capable rulers. But despite their differences, all three theories portray corporative merchant associations as efficient institutions for providing security in long-distance trade.

Implicit in these theories are three distinct claims. First, merchant guilds are supposed to have *existed* because they solved security problems in long-distance trade. Second, merchant guilds affected commercial security in ways that were *generally beneficial*, not just for their own members, but also for the wider society. And finally, the efficiency claims imply, no *alternative* institutions existed that were able and willing to provide commercial security as effectively as merchant guilds. Are these claims justified? Can the monopolies enjoyed by merchant guilds and privileged companies be justified in terms of countervailing security benefits, which no other institutions were capable of providing?

6.1   Did merchant guilds exist to solve problems in long-distance trade?

All three efficiency theories argue that merchant guilds were institutions that arose and existed to solve security problems in the *long-distance* trade carried out internationally, across borders between political units.[12] This emphasis is not surprising, since the risk that a ruler will fail to provide commercial security was much higher for international trade. This is not to say that there were no security problems in local and regional trade,

---

[11] Carlos and Nicholas (1988), 407 (quotation), 411–13.

[12] For explicit statements that these models relate to institutions supporting the development of long-distance trade crossing boundaries between political units, see Greif, Milgrom and Weingast (1994), 749; Volckart and Mangels (1999), 427–8; Carlos and Nicholas (1988), 400, 402–4, 407, 418.

but rather that they were easier to solve. For one thing, the geographical area over which the security had to be provided was limited, and hence lay within the capacities even of fairly primitive public authorities. For another, short-distance traders were typically taxable subjects of the ruler governing the region in which they did most of their business, so he had a clearer fiscal incentive to provide them with security. In international trade, by contrast, security problems were harder to solve, both because security had to be provided over much longer distances, and because international merchants were not the subjects of the rulers governing the routes they had to travel or the destination trading centre. Rulers therefore lacked clear fiscal incentives to provide long-distance traders with security. Consequently, although security problems were not completely absent in local and regional trade – especially in regions subject to fragmented political rule – they were much more serious in long-distance trade between different political units.

This raises a fundamental problem, however. Most pre-modern trade was local and regional rather than international. Most pre-modern merchants did not trade across international boundaries. And most merchant guilds were local organizations that obtained privileges from local rulers and did not form alien merchant guilds or hanses abroad.

Does it make sense, therefore, to explain the existence of an institution – the merchant guild – in terms of its efficiency in solving problems in a sector – international trade – in which most examples of that institution did not participate? Since this is a key point, it is worth examining the evidence that bears on it in greater detail.

6.1.1 Local and regional vs. international trade

Long-distance international trade is much more glamorous and copiously recorded than short-distance local and regional trade. This led the traditional historiography to over-estimate its size and importance. But since the 1970s at latest, economic historians have recognized that in the medieval and early modern periods only a tiny share of output was traded across international boundaries. For most of history, according to North, 'international trade has been a relatively small part of economic activity'.[13] Despite the growth in long-distance trade during the medieval and early modern period, on the eve of the Industrial Revolution international trade was, as Pearson points out, 'small in terms of the total economies' of the European nations.[14] As late as 1790, O'Brien

---

[13] North (1991), 23. [14] Pearson (1991), 94, 96.

estimates, only about 4 per cent of Europe's GNP was exported across international borders.[15] The share of *intercontinental* trade was even lower, at less than 2 per cent of total European GNP.[16] Tracy provides a similar estimate for major non-European economies: 'prior to 1800 no more than 5 percent of China's total domestic product was involved in trade with the "southern barbarians"'.[17] To put these figures in context, in 1960 international trade accounted for about 25 per cent of world GDP, rising by 2003 to about 50 per cent. For Europe, trade as a share of GDP was 45 per cent in 1990 and 67 per cent in 2003; for China, it was 15 per cent in 1980, 32 per cent in 1990 and 60 per cent in 2003; for low-income developing economies, it was 25 per cent in 1990 and 35 per cent in 2003.[18]

The relative unimportance of international trade in the pre-modern economy should not be surprising. For one thing, transport costs remained high until the late-eighteenth-century surge of road building and canal construction in western Europe: only goods with a high value-to-bulk ratio could be traded profitably over more than short distances.[19] For another, the monopolies and other protectionist privileges granted to merchant guilds (examined in Chapters 3 and 4) kept trade costs high, further constraining the volume of imports and exports. So although the attention of an older generation of scholarship was 'almost monopolised by the glamorous long-distance trade', economic historians now recognize that the overwhelming majority of pre-modern European commerce consisted of short-distance local and regional trade.[20] Local and regional trade was important not only for provisioning town dwellers and rural non-farmers, but also for ensuring supplies of industrial raw materials and bringing the products of rural industry onto the market.[21] Economic historians now ascribe much of the growth of the European medieval economy after about 1000 to short-distance exchange, either among villages or between towns and their rural regions, rather than to long-distance trade between nations or continents.

---

[15] P. K. O'Brien (1982).   [16] P. K. O'Brien (1990), 171.   [17] Tracy (1990a), 7.
[18] For China 1980 and World 1960, see Baumert, Herzog and Pershing (2004), 47–8. For 1990 and 2003, see World Bank (2005), Table 6.1 [www.devdata.worldbank.org/wdi2005/Section6.htm]. Figures on merchandise exports as a share of world GDP are even lower, at only 10.5 per cent in 1973 and 17.2 per cent in 1998; on this see Maddison (1995), 363 (Table F-5).
[19] Kriedte (1996), 102–5.   [20] Lopez (1987), 316–17, 333, 366 (quotation).
[21] Abulafia (1995), 2; Abulafia (1999), 25–6, 29–32, 34; Abulafia (1997), 50, 53, 57, 59, 61; Ashtor (1983), 8; Bernard (1972), 302–5; Blockmans (2000), 411–12; S. R. Epstein (1992), 243–5, 268–313; Prevenier (2000), 593; Spufford (2000), 155–7; Stabel (1997), 158–9; Theuerkauf (1996), 179, 189.

6.1.2   Local vs. long-distance merchants

The relative volume of long-distance and short-distance trade had implications for traders' institutional requirements. Only a minority of merchants expanded operations beyond their own immediate region and traded in alien polities. Most medieval European urban centres were hardly involved in long-distance trade. This was true even in the most prominent European trading regions – northern Italy, the Low Countries and southern Germany – and much more so in the rest of Europe.

Even for Italy, the earliest and most intense focus of international trade in medieval Europe, economic historians now recognize that

'international' trade and its associated activities... were predominant only in restricted circles in a small number of cities – above all Venice, Genoa, and Florence. Elsewhere small-scale short-range commerce and, above all, land-holding was more generally characteristic of the wealthier sections of the urban population.[22]

In some very large Italian cities such as Rome, merchants organized themselves into guilds but hardly participated in international trade.[23] Parma, too, was 'a thriving city' but played little role in long-distance trade.[24] The towns of Sicily, especially Messina, were favourably located on the route from northern Italy to the Levant, but only a minority of their merchants engaged in long-distance trade: the few Messinese merchants trading in the Levant had to seek associate membership in the colonies of the Pisans, other north Italians or Catalans.[25]

The Low Countries, too, were famous for their many urban centres attracting long-distance traders. Flemish merchants were active in the twelfth century in north Italian cities such as Genoa and at the Champagne fairs, but withdrew from the international arena after the Franco-Flemish wars of the early fourteenth century.[26] In some important Flemish cities such as Liège, guilded merchants exercised local economic influence but were never seriously involved in international trade.[27] From the fourteenth century on, Bruges was the 'undisputed fulcrum' of long-distance trade in north-west Europe.[28] But its own merchants were hardly active in international trade on their own account. Instead, they specialized in supplying intermediation services to visiting foreign merchants.[29]

---

[22] E. Coleman (1999), 388.   [23] Johanek (1999), 76–7.   [24] Lopez (1987), 368.
[25] Abulafia (1986b), 198, 201–2; Ashtor (1983), 31, 239–40.
[26] Doehaerd (1941), 212–17, 226–7; Laurent (1935b), 47–50.
[27] Prevenier (2000), 581–2.   [28] Ibid., 593.
[29] See Henn (1999), 131; Dollinger (1970), 41, 48, 65; Bahr (1911), 21–2; Daenell (1905), 15–16; Postan (1987), 274–5.

It was not until the fifteenth century that large numbers of merchants from the Low Countries themselves began to participate more actively in the international exchange that had long been focused on Bruges, Antwerp and Amsterdam:

> The competitive edge of these merchants lay in the marketing of local produce... Detailed knowledge of these products, personal relations with producers, and easy access to foreign buyers in France, Germany, England, and the Baltic area, allowed the indigenous merchants to compete with foreigners.[30]

A third major trading zone of medieval Europe lay in Germany – in the highly urbanized German south and later on the North Sea and the Baltic coasts. But most German towns and most German merchants were primarily involved in local and regional transactions. Across German-speaking central Europe as a whole, 'the economic influence of most individual towns and cities was limited to their immediate locality. Only a small number of towns succeeded in extending their influence to the whole of central Europe and beyond.'[31] Even in highly commercialized southern Germany, 'towns usually carried out some long-distance trade, but they lived mainly on production of fustian, cutlery and other products consumed chiefly in their agricultural districts'.[32] Further north, despite the rise of the German Hanse, there were many towns which 'never grew out of their inland position to any overseas significance... but saw a noticeable increase in their production, turnover and merchant links in various directions within the surrounding countryside'.[33]

Given these findings for the three most outward-oriented medieval trading zones, it should not be surprising that local trade predominated almost everywhere else in Europe. In England, despite a lively seagoing trade, many prosperous towns hardly engaged in long-distance commerce at all. The east-coast town of Colchester, for instance, had long been a trading centre, but in the medieval period only a handful of its citizens owned ships large enough to trade overseas.[34] In France, too, most towns 'did not generally participate in the long-distance trade of the Middle Ages', instead catering to regional markets; the French economy remained predominantly rural and agricultural.[35] In central and western France – the core of the kingdom – local trade was paramount.[36] The guilded merchants of Toulouse and Bordeaux engaged almost exclusively in local and regional trade.[37] Even Paris, the largest city in Europe, had

---

[30] Gelderblom (2005a), 25.   [31] Hlaváček (2000), 565.
[32] Lopez (1987), 368.   [33] Nitzsch (1892), 17.
[34] Alsford (2003), 'History of medieval Colchester', www.trytel.com/~tristan/towns/colchstr.html#economy, s.v. 'Economy'.
[35] Spruyt (1994), 64 (quotation); Bernard (1972), 302.   [36] Lopez (1987), 368.
[37] Bernard (1972), 299, 304–5; S. R. Epstein (2000), 27, 29.

a well-known guild of merchants, 'The Society of the "Marchands de l'Eau"', but its members engaged primarily in provisioning the inhabitants of the city itself.[38] Not until the fifteenth century was there was any notable French involvement in the Levant trade, in the form of the entrepreneurial Jacques Coeur from Bourges.[39] Only Provence and Languedoc, independent of France for much of the Middle Ages, developed cities such as Montpellier with significant international merchant groups.[40]

The Iberian peninsula shows the same pattern. In Castile, Portugal and Aragon, towns 'were usually centres of local exchange of low-grade industrial products for slightly below average agricultural staples'.[41] In all of Iberia, only in Catalonia were many merchants extensively involved in international trade.

In Scandinavian, Slavic and Byzantine Europe, too, towns and merchants were predominantly oriented to local and regional markets throughout the medieval period. The vast majority of medieval Swedish and Danish merchants engaged in short-distance trade.[42] In Slavic Europe, internal trade vastly dominated international trade and local products made up the overwhelming majority of economic exchange throughout the medieval period.[43] The Byzantine empire suffered much less than western Europe from the decline in trade in the centuries after the fall of Rome – so much so that they are held not to have experienced the Dark Ages – yet by the thirteenth century the guilded merchants of Byzantine provincial cities were trading mainly with the local hinterland, at most with the neighbouring region; they did not participate in long-distance trade.[44] The earliest surviving Byzantine merchants' accounts from the fourteenth century 'overwhelmingly or exclusively document domestic trade'.[45]

Even in the small minority of medieval European towns that were involved in international trade, only a subset of merchants were active abroad. The eleventh-century merchant guild of the Flemish city of St Omer, for instance, consisted mainly of local traders; it was only later that the St Omer merchant guild formed a hanse for those of its members with interests in long-distance trade.[46] The twelfth-century merchant guild of the German city of Stendal likewise mainly involved local merchants; the small circle of long-distance traders formed a separate *Seefahrergilde*

[38] Bernard (1972), 299, 304–5; Lopez (1987), 340; S. R. Epstein (2000), 27, 29.
[39] Goldschmidt (1891), 219: Coeur died in 1456.
[40] Reyerson (1985); Reyerson (1994); Reyerson (2002).   [41] Lopez (1987), 368.
[42] Daenell (1905), 23–35.   [43] Gieysztor (1987), 475–6, 502–3, 513–14.
[44] Johanek (1999), 72; Laiou (2000), 811–13; Laiou (2002), 739, 747–8.
[45] Scholz (2001), 104, quoting Schreiner (1991).   [46] Dilcher (1984), 70.

(sea-travellers' guild).[47] Even in the great Hanseatic centres, the large-scale merchants traded to many different foreign destinations, but the middle-rank merchants dealt with only one foreign country, the small-scale merchants traded overseas in modest wares such as herring in trifling shipments, while numerous tiny merchants focused on local trade and 'were not admitted into the associations of long-distance traders'.[48] This pattern continued into the early modern period in many European cities. In seventeenth-century Stockholm, for instance, about one-third of all burghers were merchants, but only a minority of merchants were members of the guild of the *grosshandlare* (those engaging in foreign trade): in 1644 there were only 32 *grosshandlare* in all of Stockholm, rising to 121 by 1669 – at most a third of the city's registered merchants.[49] Most medieval and early modern merchants mainly practised short-distance trade in the immediate region around their own home town.

6.1.3   Local merchant guilds vs. their alien branches

The institutional needs of medieval merchants, therefore, focused primarily on short-distance trade within the territory governed by their own ruler. Because most merchants only traded within the immediate region, most merchant guilds were also local ones, as we saw in Chapter 3.[50] Even when a local merchant guild did create offshoots abroad, as discussed in Chapter 4, it did so only some time after being established as a local association of the merchants in its home city. Throughout medieval Europe, alien merchant guilds were the offspring of local ones: 'the local merchant guild was the mother-guild for the external merchant guild... Everywhere, the beginning resided in the formation of a merchant guild at home.'[51]

The heavy dependence of alien merchant guilds on their local guild in the home city can be observed in the limitations on the authority they exercised, both over their own members and vis-à-vis alien rulers. Florentine merchant colonies abroad, for instance, had their consuls appointed by the Arte di Calimala, the dominant local merchant guild in Florence.[52] Barcelona's merchant colonies had their consuls appointed by the Consulate of the Sea in the home city.[53] Flemish merchant guilds in England were accompanied on trading expeditions by officers from their own local merchant guilds at home, 'who had absolute authority over

---

[47] Schulze (1985), 384–5.   [48] Dollinger (1970), 159–61 (quotation 161).
[49] Müller (1998), 51.
[50] Bernard (1972), 304; Ehrbrecht (1985), 430, 449; Schütt (1980), 411.
[51] Nitzsch (1892), 67, 83.   [52] Kohn (2003a), 8 n. 32; Henn (1999), 135–6.
[53] Ashtor (1983), 13; Kohn (2003a), 8 n. 32.

them'.[54] The alien merchant guild of the Castilians, set up in Bruges in 1428, was legally subordinate to the local merchant consulado in Burgos.[55] Likewise, Armenian merchant colonies in Europe throughout the seventeenth and eighteenth centuries were subject to the governing bodies of their merchant guild back 'home' in New Julfa (the Armenian quarter of the Persian city of Isfahan).[56]

At least hanses, it might be thought, were autonomous corporative organizations organized purely among long-distance merchants. But closer examination shows that all hanses were pre-dated by their constituent *local* merchant guilds. As we saw in Chapters 2 and 4, the German Hanse membership consisted of the merchants of a number of northern European (mainly German) towns, who had already formed local merchant guilds at home.[57] A member of the Merchant Adventurers of England, likewise, was first a member of his merchant guild or fraternity in the English town from which he came, and then of the Adventurers in the 'parties beyond the sea'.[58] Hanses, like alien merchant guilds, were not independent of the local merchant guilds that were their constituent building blocks.

The heavy dependence of hanses on the local merchant guilds that comprised them can be observed in their internal organization and negotiating authority. The prototype of the German Hanse was the twelfth-century Gotland Community at Visby on the island of Gotland. The Gotland Community was directed by four 'aldermen' (*olderlude*), of which only one was resident in the colony itself, while the other three were based in Lübeck, Soest and Dortmund, as the home cities of the most important sub-groups of members.[59] Once the German Hanse was formed, its four major Kontore in Bergen, Novgorod, Bruges and London never enjoyed complete autonomy from the local merchant guilds of the dominant factions, especially Lübeck. The German Hanse Kontor in Bergen had a membership consisting almost wholly of Lübeck merchants, for instance, which prevented that Kontor from ever enjoying real independence from the Lübeck town council, dominated by the local Lübeck merchant guild.[60] The Hanse Kontor in Novgorod had somewhat greater independence since although its membership was dominated by merchants from Lübeck, it also included merchants from four or five other German and Livonian towns.[61] However, as early as the twelfth century, members of the Novogorod Kontor derived their by-laws from the guilds

---

[54] Kohn (2003a), 8.   [55] C. R. Phillips (1983), 266–7.
[56] Aslanian (2004), 48, 82–5; Aslanian (2006), 393–8.
[57] See Daenell (1905), 6, 9, 19.   [58] Sutton (2002), 27, 33.
[59] Christensen (1953), 243–4.   [60] Dollinger (1970), 64, 101.   [61] *Ibid.*, 64.

of the individual home towns, paid annual dues that were sent back to their home guilds and continued to regard their home aldermen as the highest court of appeal.[62] In 1361, the Novgorod Kontor was definitively forbidden to promulgate any internal regulation without the consent of the five main towns of its merchants.[63] In 1392, a Hanseatic delegation led by a Lübeck merchant 'took advantage of its presence in Novgorod to demonstrate the authority of the Hanse over the Kontor. Without consulting a single member of the Kontor the delegation levied a tax on business transactions . . . and drew up a revised version of its statutes.'[64] The German Hanse Kontor in London had greater independence than those in Bergen or Novgorod, since its membership was more diverse, but threats to its privileges from English rulers ensured that by 1374 at latest its internal organization was also firmly subjected to the authority of its component towns.[65]

The German Hanse Kontor in Bruges initially had the greatest independence of all because its membership was drawn from the widest array of different towns, but even so it enjoyed limited negotiating power and was often overruled by legations from its constituent towns or from the Hanseatic Diet (consisting of delegates from the governments of those towns).[66] In 1356, for instance, the constituent towns of the Hanse became disturbed at the nature of the Bruges Kontor's relationship with the rulers of Flanders and sent a delegation which took over negotiations and intervened decisively in the affairs of the Kontor.[67] By issuing a detailed definition of the powers and competence of the Hanse aldermen at Bruges, the delegation established that the Kontor 'was now subordinate to the authority of the combined towns, and its decisions in future would be valid only if approved by the towns'.[68] In 1375, the Hanseatic Diet explicitly ordered the aldermen of the Bruges Kontor to take no independent decisions about declaring an embargo on Bruges but rather await the decision of the constituent towns.[69] In 1418, the aldermen of the Bruges Kontor had to obtain explicit permission from the Hanse central office in Lübeck before they could enter into negotiations with Scottish merchants in Bruges about arrangements 'serving the utility and well-being of the merchants'.[70] In 1428, likewise, the aldermen of the Bruges Kontor felt so little confidence in their authority to negotiate with Spanish envoys over commercial tensions that they wrote to Lübeck asking for new powers of attorney and new instructions, begging the central office to 'write to us all things clearly so that we can orient

---

[62] Choroškevic (1996), 71–2, 78, 86.   [63] Dollinger (1970), 64.   [64] *Ibid.*, 78.
[65] *Ibid.*, 64.   [66] Henn (1999), 142.   [67] Dollinger (1970), 63.   [68] *Ibid.*
[69] Henn (1999), 142.   [70] *Ibid.*, 140.

ourselves to them'.[71] The many smaller Hanse Kontore all over Europe may have begun with varying degrees of semi-autonomy but after *c.* 1350 they were brought under the control of the towns, which 'usually meant that they were controlled by the town whose merchants were present in the greatest number'.[72]

A similar pattern can be observed within the English Merchant Adventurers, which united guilded merchants from London and a number of English provincial towns.[73] By the fifteenth century, the London Mercers' Company had come to dominate the Adventurers both numerically and economically. The London Company financed the Adventurers' lobbying activities, and only later reclaimed expenses from the Adventurers as a whole.[74] So closely identified did the Merchant Adventurers become with the Mercers' Company that it became difficult to distinguish between 'the proceedings of the meetings of the mercers who were Adventurers' and 'the proceedings of the assemblies of the federation of London Adventurers'.[75] By 1464, the English king regarded the local London Mercers' Company as competent to speak for the English Merchant Adventurers, when he invited it to send representatives to negotiations to prolong the Anglo-Burgundian commercial treaty.[76]

Taken together, these findings cast doubt on the first assumption of efficiency theories – the idea that merchant guilds arose and existed because they were efficient solutions to problems of commercial security in international trade. Throughout pre-modern Europe, most trade was domestic rather than international. This primarily domestic orientation was reflected in the economic activities of pre-modern merchants, the vast majority of whom did not trade across international boundaries. This in turn affected merchants' institutional requirements. First and foremost they needed – and hence established – local guild organizations with commercial privileges from local rulers. Only a minority of these local guilds then formed branches abroad. Even then, these alien merchant guilds and hanses were closely controlled by their local guilds at home. Furthermore, as we shall see in the next section, important groups of foreign merchants traded for generations or even for centuries in international trading centres without forming guilds there. These findings cast serious doubt on the usefulness of theories explaining the institution of the merchant guild in terms of its efficiency at solving problems in a sector – international trade – in which most actual examples of that institution and most people who used it did not participate.

---

[71] *Ibid.*   [72] Dollinger (1970), 105.   [73] Sutton (2002), 31.
[74] *Ibid.*, 36.   [75] *Ibid.*, 38.   [76] *Ibid.*, 39.

Of course, it is still possible that having arisen and survived for other reasons – to extract monopoly profits for merchants and share these profits with rulers in return for enforcing the monopoly – merchant guilds might have had an *impact* on commercial security. If this impact was positive, it might have compensated for the malign effects of merchant guilds discussed in preceding chapters. So how did merchant guilds actually affect commercial security?

6.2   How did merchant guilds affect commercial security?

In theory, there are several ways in which merchant guilds might have affected security positively. They might have provided it as a club good to their members, as argued by Volckart and Mangels. They might have used embargo threats to pressure rulers into providing a secure trading environment, as modelled by Greif, Milgrom and Weingast. Or they might have provided security by building forts, organizing naval convoys and conducting military operations, as claimed by Carlos and Nicholas.

But while we are in the realm of theory, we should also reflect on the possibility that merchant guilds could reduce commercial security. Guild monopolies not only affected efficiency (they reduced it) but also altered distribution (they shifted resources from outsiders to guild members). And this could affect security – negatively. When a ruler granted exclusive privileges to a merchant guild, he made it illegal for non-members to trade. When non-members tried to trade anyway, the merchant guild typically tried to stop them – either by direct action or by appealing to rulers. Interlopers often responded in kind, attacking the guild that was preventing them from earning a living. This problem was particularly acute in international trading centres, where several merchant guilds – the local guild and one or more alien guilds – might be tussling over commercial privileges. The ruler gained by granting privileges to more than one merchant guild, since he then received benefits from all of them. But this gave rulers incentives to refrain from defining guilds' privileges absolutely clearly, in order to be able to grant overlapping privileges to two or more guilds simultaneously and then obtain further benefits when the different guilds asked to have their privileges clarified or confirmed. The fuzzy demarcations between the privileges of different merchant guilds – created either inadvertently or deliberately by rulers – created incentives for constant rivalry. The existence of merchant guilds thus inevitably encouraged conflict between different guilds, as well as between each guild and the inevitable interlopers. And conflict reduces commercial security. In theory, therefore, merchant guilds could either increase or decrease commercial security. Which effect predominated can only be determined empirically.

Three types of evidence are usually adduced to support the idea that merchant guilds enhanced security. First, merchant guilds often demanded security guarantees from rulers. Second, merchant guilds sometimes threatened rulers with trade embargoes unless they improved security. Third, merchant guilds sometimes organized naval convoys, built forts and engaged in military activities. Is this enough to establish that the net effect of merchant guilds on security was positive?

Let us begin with the first type of evidence – the grant of security guarantees. It is true that security guarantees were often included among the privileges alien merchant guilds secured from rulers. But *individual* long-distance traders also obtained security guarantees from rulers abroad, without forming guilds – at least where this was institutionally allowed.

The Champagne fairs, for instance, were the most important single locus of long-distance trade in western Europe between *c.* 1190 and *c.* 1300. The six fairs, held in four neighbouring towns of the sovereign county of Champagne, were in session sequentially throughout the year, thereby transcending periodic fairs by offering something approaching a permanent marketplace for international exchange. The fairs are continuously documented from 1114 on, were certainly hosting international trade by *c.* 1150, were being attended by Italian and Flemish merchants by the 1170s and were in full swing as international trading marts by the 1190s.[77] However, there is no evidence of the existence of alien merchant guilds at the fairs until 1245, from which year dates the first reference to a consul for any group of merchants (in this case the Sienese).[78] Consuls for another fifteen Italian cities whose merchants frequented the Champagne fairs were mentioned in the course of the second half of the thirteenth century.[79] The year 1245–6 also saw the first reference to a consul from Montpellier who may have been the first 'captain'

---

[77] Schönfelder (1988), 12–13, 19, 23; Bassermann (1911), 1, 2–7, 76; Verlinden (1965), 126–8, 130–2; Bautier (1952), 316–18. For evidence that the Champagne fairs were already being visited by Flemish merchants by 1137, see Bourquelot (1865), I: 192 with n. 1; and Laurent (1935b), 49, 84–5. For the argument that these fairs were already established as international trading centres for Italian merchants by 1180, see Face (1958), 428. According to Laurent (1935b), 44, Italian merchants can be found as early as 1074 at the 'fairs of France', which he argues are more likely to have been the fairs of Champagne than those of Lendit at St Denis near Paris.

[78] Bautier (1952), 126 with n. 1.

[79] Although Bautier (1970), 54, claims that 'prior to the mid-13th century . . . the Italians had installed a consulate for each of their trading colonies at the fairs', in actuality the only archival reference is to a document mentioning a Sienese consul in 1246; *ibid.*, 55, more accurately states that in the *second* half of the thirteenth century there are references to consuls for fifteen other Italian cities whose merchants traded at the fairs.

of a combined *universitas* (association) of Provençal merchants active later in the thirteenth century.[80] From 1258, there is a single reference to an organization of Aragonese merchants frequenting the fairs; and 1278 is the earliest reference to a *universitas* of Italian merchants at the fairs.[81] The substantial groups of Flemish merchants at the Champagne fairs never had consuls like the individual southern European cities or *universitas* like the Italians and the Provençals. The urban federation known as the 'Seventeen Towns', mentioned in a handful of documents relating to the Champagne fairs, is a shadowy body whose membership and activities are largely unknown but which appears to have been loosely organized, lacking either elections, jurisdiction or leadership at the fairs.[82] German merchants frequented the fairs in the second half of the thirteenth century, but as citizens of specific towns rather than members of German merchant guilds. The first specific corporative privileges to German Hanseatic merchants were those granted not to the Hanse but to 'persons of Lübeck' in 1294.[83] The merchants of the non-Hanseatic south German city of Konstanz did not form an alien guild at the Champagne fairs until 1289, when they established an association for ten years in the first instance, with the aim of 'abolishing the competition of the Konstanz sellers among one another and strengthening the reputation of the merchantry of Konstanz'.[84] The most detailed study of the nationalities of merchants frequenting the fairs lists merchants from many parts of France (until 1285 territorially separate from Champagne), a variety of different German towns and territories (both Hanseatic and non-Hanseatic), Savoy, Switzerland, Brabant, Hainaut, England and even Sweden – none of them with guilds.[85] Foreign merchants thus frequented the Champagne fairs from the 1170s onwards, generations before the first reference to merchant guilds in 1245, and there were substantial groups of merchants who never formed guilds at the fairs.

---

[80] Bourquelot (1865), I: 151, 154 n. 9, 174. Bautier (1970), 57, and Bautier (1953), 130–2, point out that Etienne Lobet was appointed as 'consul and captain' in 1246, but with no indication that he had jurisdiction over any merchants other than those of Montpellier; the first definitive indication of broader jurisdiction for the Montpellier consul dates from 1258; and the first list of other Provençal towns in the *universitas* dates from 1290.

[81] Bautier (1953), 130; Bautier (1970), 56.

[82] Although the literature often refers to this organization as the 'Hanse of the Seventeen Towns', the word 'Hanse' is a modern addition; see Bautier (1953), 129–30; Carolus-Barré (1965), 26–7; Laurent (1935a), 83–4, 89.

[83] See Bourquelot (1865), I: 199–201 (quotation 201); Schönfelder (1988), 21. The Lübeck privilege is reproduced in Dollinger (1970), 383–4.

[84] Schulte (1900), 163.   [85] Bourquelot (1865), I: 139–40, 196–204.

Merchant guilds were not necessary for the commercial success of the Champagne fairs because the counts of Champagne issued security guarantees to *all* merchants desirous of trading in their realms.[86] The famous *conduit des foires* ('safe-conduct of the fairs') guaranteed security on journeys to and from the Champagne fairs, and at the fairs themselves, for all merchants regardless of guild or community affiliation. By 1148–9, Count Thibaut II of Champagne was enforcing this safe-conduct sufficiently actively to threaten military measures against a French seigneur who had attacked a group of 'money changers' (i.e. merchants) on their way to the Champagne fairs, writing to the French regent in the following terms:

this is an insult to the king and to you, for me it is an injury and an affront; the king's highway was violated. I demand that you instantly order [the seigneur], who is under your hand, to render to the money changers without delay what has been taken from them. As for me, I will not let take place with impunity such an injury, which tends to nothing less than the ruin of my fairs.[87]

Shortly after 1200, the counts of Champagne managed to persuade rulers of neighbouring territories to enhance the security of all merchants visiting the Champagne fairs by adding their own safe-conducts: the king of France issued the desired guarantee in 1209, the duke of Burgundy in 1220, and the count of Boulogne in 1232.[88]

Security for merchants attending the Champagne fairs did not, therefore, rely on pressure from alien merchant guilds. In so far as merchant guilds existed at the fairs, they are only documented from 1245 onwards, generations after the fairs began to function as important centres of long-distance trade. Instead, security for long-distance merchants was provided by a princely ruler, who in turn negotiated further generalized guarantees from other rulers, in the interests of protecting 'his' fairs as a piece of property that delivered him a stream of revenues. In the categories established at the beginning of this chapter, the safe-conduct of the Champagne fairs was a generalized institutional guarantee issued by a political authority to *all* merchants, not a particularized privilege appertaining only to members of specific merchant guilds.

Similar patterns can be seen in other successful medieval trading centres. After the decline of the Champagne fairs (for reasons we shall discuss in the conclusion to this chapter), Bruges became the most important

---

[86] Laurent (1935b), 258–9.
[87] Bourquelot (1865), I: 323–8 (quotation 324–5); Bautier (1952), 318; Goldschmidt (1891), 229 n. 153.
[88] Bourquelot (1865), I: 174 with n. 2; Bassermann (1911), 4; Verlinden (1965), 128, 131.

locus of long-distance trade in north-west Europe. Greif has claimed that Italian trade with Flanders flourished only after merchants were allowed to form 'nations' (i.e. guilds) there.[89] But this claim is not factually correct. Large numbers of long-distance merchants traded in Bruges under security guarantees, but these were issued by the town government of Bruges and the princely government of Flanders to all merchants, not just to those who formed merchant guilds. Indeed, as Lambert and Stabel point out,

many foreign merchants did not organize their own nation [merchant guild] and relied totally on the Bruges authorities for their protection. Others chose only relatively late to establish proper guild structures, in a period when trade in Bruges was already past its peak.[90]

The significant groups of traders who never formed alien merchant guilds in Bruges included those from Pisa, Milan, Piacenza and Bologna, as well as Brittany, Gascony, Aquitaine and southern Germany.[91] Merchants from Piacenza, for instance, were trading in Bruges at latest from 1299 onwards, but never formed a merchant 'nation' in the city.[92] Merchants from the important south German trading city of Nürnberg are documented in Bruges at latest from 1300, but never formed an alien merchant guild there.[93] Merchants from Aquitaine conducted a quantitatively important trade with Bruges in wine and woollen cloth from the thirteenth century on, but also never formed an alien 'nation' in the city.[94]

Other important groups of foreign traders only formed alien merchant guilds in Bruges after having already traded there for generations. Merchants of the German Hanse were already trading in Bruges by 1212, nearly half a century before they obtained their first privileges in the city in 1252–3.[95] Scottish merchants were active in Bruges from the later twelfth century on, but did not obtain corporate privileges until 1359.[96] Genoese merchants were actively trading in Bruges from at least 1278 onwards, and began sending galleys to the city in 1309–12,[97] but only obtained collective privileges there in the mid-fourteenth century, only established a merchant consul and a *logia* (a house used for administration and display) in 1397–9, and only set up a separate building for

---

[89] Greif (2006a), 100.   [90] Lambert and Stabel (2005), 12.
[91] Henn (1999), 139; Lambert and Stabel (2005), 12, 22.
[92] Häpke (1908), 153; Lambert and Stabel (2005), 22.
[93] Häpke (1908), 118; Lambert and Stabel (2005), 22.
[94] Häpke (1908), 133–9; Lambert and Stabel (2005), 22.
[95] Paravicini (1992), 100, 102; Häpke (1908), 91.   [96] Henn (1999), 139.
[97] Häpke (1908), 156.

their consul in 1440, by which time Bruges was already in decline as a long-distance trading centre.[98] Florentine merchants were active in Bruges at latest from the 1280s, but are not recorded as establishing a formally constituted association until the 1420s.[99] Venetian merchants began sending galleys to Bruges in 1314, but it was eighteen years before they even sought the right to set up their own merchant guild there (in 1332), and forty-four years before they secured it (in 1358).[100] As at the Champagne fairs, so too in medieval Bruges, foreign merchants enjoyed sufficient commercial security to trade for generations without forming alien merchant guilds.

As Bruges in its turn declined, Antwerp became the most important western European trading centre. The success of Antwerp was also based on security guarantees which its municipal and princely governments issued to all merchants, not just members of formally constituted alien merchant guilds. As at the Champagne fairs and in Bruges, so too in Antwerp, important groups of foreign traders never formed (or joined) alien merchant guilds. The Italian merchant guilds in Antwerp represented only the most prominent merchants, while large numbers of smaller-scale Italian traders operated entirely outside the framework of alien merchant 'nations'.[101] South Germans were the most important and successful merchant group in Antwerp despite the fact that they did not secure 'the kinds of commercial privileges that the foreign merchant nations usually obtained'.[102] Likewise, French merchants traded for centuries in Antwerp but 'never organized themselves into nations'.[103]

One might wonder whether the willingness and ability of long-distance merchants to trade abroad without forming alien merchant guilds was an artefact of institutional precocity. After all, the Champagne fairs, Bruges and Antwerp were the dominant trading centres of north-west Europe in their time. Perhaps foreign merchants trading there did not have to worry so much about commercial risks? But long-distance merchants also voluntarily dispensed with forming (or joining) alien merchant guilds in more peripheral medieval trading centres.

In the medieval Levant, for instance, there were many trading centres in which western European merchants did not form guilds or keep consuls. In medieval Cairo, for instance, no European nation maintained

---

[98] Briys and De ter Beerst (2006), 21, 48, 67, 96.

[99] Mallett (1959), 156–8; Henn (1999), 135–6; Häpke (1908), 157.

[100] Briys and De ter Beerst (2006), 96; Henn (1999), 133–4; Häpke (1908), 159 states that a Venetian consulate was set up in 1332, but does not speak of a Venetian merchant guild.

[101] Blondé, Gelderblom and Stabel (2007), 166–7; Subacchi (1995), 78.

[102] Harreld (2004b), 13; Harreld (2004a), 58–9.   [103] Brunelle (2003), 290.

a merchant guild, even though European merchants traded in the city sufficiently often to keep a Venetian notary in business there.[104] Venetian, Genoese, Catalan, Florentine and French merchants traded in thirteenth- and fourteenth-century Damascus, but only the Venetians maintained a permanent organized colony, while the Genoese and Catalans only had a short-lived organization briefly around 1300, and the Florentines and French had no consul at all.[105] Even in Levantine centres that did have European merchant guilds, individual European traders often applied to the Muslim authorities for the status of permanent residents with individual commercial privileges, which they evidently found preferable to joining the appropriate alien merchant guild. So many merchants preferred this option that they were given the derogatory name of *fazolati* by the Italian merchant guilds, whose home cities took drastic measures against them on the grounds that their 'privileged status rendered unlawful competition with the other European merchants possible'.[106]

Another example is provided by French trading centres such as Rouen and Nantes, with large groups of Spanish merchants who traded vigorously from the medieval period onwards, without forming consulados until well into the early modern period.[107] In late medieval and early modern Rouen, for instance, the Spaniards were the most important foreign merchant group but did not set up a formal consulado in the city until 1556.[108] Even in such peripheral medieval trading centres, long-distance traders evidently did not view membership in an alien merchant guild as essential, or (in the case of the *fazolati*) even advantageous, for their commercial security.

Moreover, even when they *were* members of alien merchant guilds, traders continued to seek security guarantees as individuals. From the 1190s on, for instance, many Flemish and French merchants took care to obtain personal safe-conducts from the English monarch, since individual privileges offered greater safety than those granted to the Flemish or French merchant guilds in London.[109] In 1271, the Sicilian ruler Charles of Anjou granted the Lucca merchant firm of the Ricciardi a firm-specific safe-conduct for his territories, since the firms viewed security guarantees granted to the Lucchese merchant guild in Sicily as inadequate.[110] In 1401, the most important Tuscan merchants and firms, despite having their own merchant guilds in Catalonia and Aragon, purchased individual

---

[104] Ashtor (1983), 396 with n. 202.   [105] *Ibid.*, 396–7.   [106] *Ibid.*, 400.
[107] C. R. Phillips (1983), 269–70.
[108] Benedict (1981), 21–2; C. R. Phillips (1983), 270; W. D. Phillips (1986), 46.
[109] Lloyd (1977), 9, 14, 19.   [110] Del Punta (2004), 650–2.

protection orders from the Crown of Aragon permitting them to continue trading in safety, specifically to insure against attacks on the Tuscan merchant guilds by local merchant guilds in Valencia, Barcelona and Mallorca.[111] Having a merchant guild was thus neither necessary nor sufficient for ensuring one's commercial security in foreign lands. An individual merchant could and often had to purchase a safe-conduct *without* having a guild, and could and often had to do so even when he *did* have a guild.

What of the second type of evidence adduced in support of the view that merchant guilds had a positive effect on commercial security – the trade embargoes alien merchant guilds sometimes declared against rulers? Efficiency theorists interpret such embargoes as having been imposed primarily to put pressure on rulers to provide security. But when we examine the reasons merchant guilds gave for declaring embargoes, and the conditions they set for ending them, we find that they included a whole array of demands – not just security guarantees, but wider trading privileges for the guild (and narrower privileges for its competitors).

The German Hanse's embargoes of Bruges in 1280 and 1358 are two of the most famous merchant guild embargoes ever imposed, and Greif, Milgrom and Weingast rely heavily on these examples to support their model of the efficiency of merchant guilds in using embargoes to press rulers to ensure commercial security.[112] They portray the 1280 embargo as being undertaken mainly in retaliation for injuries to the persons and goods of Hanseatic merchants resulting from recent rioting, and support this portrayal by quoting from the German merchants' agreement to transfer their trade to Aardenburg: 'It is unfortunately only too well known that [German] merchants travelling in Flanders have been the objects of all kinds of maltreatment in the town of Bruges and have not been able to protect themselves from this.'[113] But this account is misleading. No document relating to the Hanse embargo of Bruges in 1280 makes any mention of violence or insecurity, whether arising from the rioting or from any other cause, as the reason for the embargo or a precondition for its relaxation. The word used is *iniurias*, which is a general term referring to any kind of maltreatment.[114] The only evidence available on the nature of this 'maltreatment' is contained in the privileges granted by the count of Flanders to the German merchants on their move to Aardenburg, whose central plank is a guarantee that they may enjoy there

---

[111] Congdon (2003), 226.   [112] Greif, Milgrom and Weingast (1994), 760–1.
[113] According to the translation in Dollinger (1970), 383; quoted in Greif, Milgrom and Weingast (1994), 759.
[114] See Verein für Lübeckische Geschichte (1843), 370–1, nos. 155–6.

'the right to buy, sell and trade all their merchandise freely and without discrimination both among themselves and with local citizens'.[115] This leads Stein, for instance, to conclude that the main 'maltreatment' which had caused the German merchants to declare the embargo against Bruges resided in that city's restrictive regulations forbidding foreign merchants to trade among themselves and with local citizens without employing the intermediation of a Bruges merchant.[116] Dollinger's account ascribes the 1280 riots to conflicts between German merchants and Bruges citizens over foreign merchant privileges and local intermediation.[117] It was the underlying struggle over commercial entitlements by different merchant guilds, not insecurity of property rights, that led to the 1280 Hanseatic embargo of Bruges.

Greif, Milgrom and Weingast also portray the 1358 Hanseatic embargo as being imposed 'mainly because Bruges was not ready to compensate the Germans for their damages in Flanders from the war between England and France'. They claim that the embargo was only relaxed when Bruges promised to provide better commercial security.[118] But this account, too, is misleading. The Hanse's grievances included not just violations of commercial safe-conduct arising from warfare between Flanders and England, but threats to its members' customs privileges, the levying of new duties on their business transactions, the monopolies practised by the local Bruges brokers' guild over many types of business and the extension of local Bruges guilds' staple privileges over salt and grain. The conditions the Hanse imposed for ending its 1358 embargo were not restricted to commercial security, but extended to tax exemptions, reductions in brokerage fees, permission to engage in retailing and extension of Hanse members' trading privileges beyond Bruges to other major Flemish towns such as Ghent and Ypres. Even with regard to security, the Hanse's demand was not that the city of Bruges or the count of Flanders provide better commercial security for merchants in general, but rather that the Hanse in particular should receive monetary compensation for ships already sunk through Anglo-Flemish naval action.[119]

The same is true of other medieval merchant guild embargoes. A guild embargo was typically directed at putting pressure on rulers not

---

[115] According to the translation in Dollinger (1970), 383; original in Verein für Lübeckische Geschichte (1843), 370–1, nos. 155–6. See also the wide variety of economic issues covered in the privilege granted by the count of Flanders to the Spanish and German merchants in Aardenburg, published in Höhlbaum (1876), 295–9, no. 862.

[116] See, e.g., the detailed analysis of the documents relating to this embargo in W. Stein (1902), 123–30.

[117] Dollinger (1970), 48.   [118] Greif, Milgrom and Weingast (1994), 760.

[119] Greve (2001), 272–3; Stützel (1998), esp. 28–61; Sprandel (1984), 21–2, 30; Dollinger (1970), 64–6; Bahr (1911), 21–2; Daenell (1905), 14–23.

to enhance *general security* for commerce, but rather to expand the *particular privileges* of members of that guild. The privileges named in a typical embargo related not just to security but to taxes, fees and the branches of trade and geographical locations in which the guild members were to be licensed to trade in that polity. Alien merchant guilds thus did use embargoes to secure a better bargain from rulers, but this bargain related to the entire framework of commercial privileges they sought from rulers, not specifically to security. This casts doubt on the idea that guild embargoes were primarily a means of ensuring commercial security.

What about the third type of evidence often deployed in support of the view that merchant guilds enhanced commercial security – convoys, forts and military action? Merchant guilds did sometimes organize convoys and build forts, which provided security to their members as a club good. But convoys could be – and were – also organized by ad hoc groups of merchants without the participation of merchant guilds, as in the cases of Flemish merchant caravans to the Champagne fairs in the thirteenth century or Genoese merchant convoys to the eastern Mediterranean in the fourteenth.[120] Convoys were also widely organized by town governments and rulers from early in the medieval Commercial Revolution. As early as the twelfth century, for instance, not just ad hoc groups of private merchants but also the government of Genoa provided convoys for its merchant ships in the trade with the eastern Mediterranean.[121] From the early thirteenth century on, English rulers organized convoys for merchant vessels exporting goods to the continent, especially in time of war with France.[122] From the early fourteenth century, the government of Venice organized and financed regular convoys for Venetian merchants in Flanders, Iberia, the eastern Mediterranean and the Black Sea.[123] It was also the Venetian government that built the fortifications to defend the headquarters of its merchant colonies in the Levant, such as the one at Tana on the Black Sea in the fourteenth century.[124] These findings from the medieval period cast doubt on the idea that the privileged companies could have been necessary for convoys and fort-building in the intercontinental trade of the early modern period. If both ad hoc groups of individual merchants and the governments of their cities and territories could organize convoys and provide fortifications in distant trading destinations as early as the twelfth century, then why could they not do so in the seventeenth or eighteenth?

[120] Laurent (1935b), 244–5; Dotson (1999), 167; González de Lara (2008), 263 n. 45.
[121] Byrne (1916), 131.   [122] Williams (1931), 274.
[123] Doumerc (1987), 6, 14–16; Lane (1963), esp. 189–91; Lopez (1987), 374; Stabel (1999), 32.
[124] Desroussilles (1979), 115–17; Doumerc (1987), 5–7, 14–15.

Serious weaknesses thus undermine much of the evidence adduced to support the idea that merchant guilds were the efficient institution to provide commercial security. Security guarantees were made by rulers to non-guilded merchants as well as guilded ones. In guild embargoes against alien trading centres, security was only one among many issues, and was often dominated by conflicts over other commercial privileges. And security-related goods such as convoys and forts were organized through institutional mechanisms other than merchant guilds, including ad hoc merchant groupings, cities and states. Merchant guilds were thus neither necessary nor sufficient for ensuring the security of medieval and early modern commerce.

By contrast, hard evidence exists to suggest that merchant guilds sometimes actually *damaged* commercial security. Merchant guilds, as we have seen, were not voluntary associations but coercive ones. Anyone who wanted to engage in particular trading activities was forced to belong to the relevant merchant guild; guilds sought to limit the number of participants by imposing entry barriers; and anyone who could not obtain admission to the guild was forced out of the trade. Nor did guild coercion stop at imposing compulsion on individual traders: it also extended to collective acts of aggression, since a guild was frequently empowered by its home ruler to exercise coercive force against rivals, sometimes even to engage in legal plunder and piracy.[125] A wide array of studies of medieval and early modern commercial insecurity have consequently come to the surprising conclusion that some of the insecurity that plagued pre-modern commerce arose from the coercive characteristics of merchant guilds themselves.[126] Since this evidence might at first sight appear counter-intuitive, and certainly runs against widely held views about the security-enhancing effects of merchant guilds, it is worth exploring in greater detail.

6.2.1   Merchants and pirates

Piracy might seem to be the classic example of exogenous commercial insecurity. Some piracy against merchant shipping clearly corresponds to this picture: it was pure predation by professional thieves. But detailed studies of medieval and early modern piracy have revealed that a

---

[125] North (1991), 25.
[126] See, e.g., Habib (1990), 398–9; Katele (1988), 865; North (1991), 25; Pérotin-Dumon (1991), 199–226; Postan (1987), 189–90. For an early recognition of these realities, see Barbour (1911), 534.

surprising amount of what was termed 'piracy' in pre-modern Europe was practised either by merchants themselves or by others on their behalf, and was cloaked in some form of legitimacy from those merchants' guilds or governments. Merchants shifted to piracy (or sub-contracted piracy to others) when they fell on hard times, were attacked by other groups of merchants or saw a chance of combating the privileges claimed by a rival merchant community. Many of those who attacked merchants were only defined as 'pirates' by their victims, and were legitimized as 'corsairs', 'privateers' or 'navies' by their own rulers.[127]

The fluid boundary between merchant and pirate was already recognized by contemporaries.[128] Around 1040, for instance, five shiploads of Arab pirates succeeded in taking the city of Demetrias on the eastern Greek coast, when they credibly claimed to be acting as merchants, declaring that 'we have come not to make war, but to trade, and to sell the captives and the loot we have collected...Let us trade.'[129] In the early thirteenth century, an English chronicler referred to the men of the Cinque Ports as *pirates regis* ('the king's pirates').[130] In 1317, the Genoese subject-city Savona established a special bureau, the *Officium Robarie*, to keep watch over the entire merchant community, 'since certain men assume the aspect of merchants and likewise honest men, with perverted spirit and the hope of deceiving, and take care to engage more in crafty piratical and evil deeds than decent and legitimate exchange'.[131] In 1395, Francesco Benini, an agent for the Prato merchant Francesco Marco di Datini, wrote in a letter that 'Everyone is turning corsair!' – 'Everyone' referring to the merchant world inhabited by himself and his correspondent.[132] In 1458, Benedict Cotrugli (or Kontrulic) of Dubrovnik wrote in his book, *On Commerce and the Perfect Merchant*, that 'When a Genoese is impoverished by some accident of adverse fortune, he becomes a pirate, and so do many Catalans.'[133] As late as the turn of the seventeenth century, contemporaries still saw merchants and pirates as two sides of the same coin, as when Sir Walter Raleigh observed around 1600, 'Did you ever know of any that were pirates for millions? They only that work for small things are pirates.'[134]

---

[127] Tai (1996), iii, 8–10, 12, 187–8; Tai (2003a); Tai (2003b), 260–1; Aloisio (2003), 193–4; Reyerson (2003).

[128] Tai (1996), 8–10, 12; Tai (2003b), 260–2.

[129] Quoted in Laiou (2002), 754 with n. 263.   [130] Murray (1935), 33.

[131] Quoted in Tai (1996), 427 with n. 22.   [132] Quoted in *ibid.*, 594 with n. 6.

[133] Quoted in Lopez (1987), 385; in a slightly different translation, Tai (1996), 641 with n. 110.

[134] Quoted in Barbour (1911), 534 n. 17.

Modern studies confirm the fluidity of the boundary between merchant and pirate. Thus Lopez observes, in matter-of-fact terms, that most medieval corsairs 'alternated privateering and ordinary trade'.[135] Likewise, Postan concludes that

> most of the piratical acts in medieval records were committed not by professional pirates practising their occupation in all seasons, but by merchants who turned pirate... They either were pressed into service by their princes or turned to privateering while trade was at a standstill, or were trying to recoup themselves for acts of piracy they or their compatriots had suffered at the enemy's hands.[136]

According to Tai's more recent study of medieval Mediterranean trade,

> Mercantile exchange was not so much piracy's antithesis in the medieval Mediterranean as its other face. By the mid-fourteenth century, the two sustained a complex and ambivalent relationship, neither invariably adversarial nor frankly cooperative, but one that could be best described as 'symbiotic' rather than 'parasitic'.[137]

This apparently paradoxical conclusion, that piracy against merchant shipping often emanated from other merchants, also emerges from many case studies. In medieval northern Germany, for instance, 'the merchant and the pirate were often so similar they could be mistaken for one another'.[138] In thirteenth- and fourteenth-century Malta, 'enterprising sea captains fell back on piracy to supplement lawful commerce in cotton and cloth',[139] and by the fifteenth century corsairing 'represented an economic opportunity that was frequently indistinguishable from ordinary commercial enterprise'.[140] In thirteenth- and fourteenth-century Catalonia, Genoa and Venice, merchants armed their ships for self-defence in normal trading ventures but also took for granted that they would use this coercive power to capture the ships of rival merchants en route: merchant contracts explicitly allowed for the possibility of switching from normal merchant trading to privateering and back in a single voyage.[141] In fifteenth-century English towns such as York, Beverley and Hull, 'it was not uncommon for some [merchants] to be accused of piracy one moment and to hold high civic office or a government appointment the next'.[142] In the early modern West Indies, likewise, 'It is probable that only a small portion of the violence committed... would square with the legal theory of piracy: generally speaking; the robbers were not *hostes humani generis*, but enemies of Spain; furthermore, the majority of them

---

[135] Lopez and Raymond (1955), 221.   [136] Postan (1987), 189–90.
[137] Tai (1996), 188.   [138] Nitzsch (1892), 83.
[139] McManamon (2003), 42.   [140] Aloisio (2003), 197.
[141] For illustrative examples, see Tai (1996), 104–7, 250–1, 530–3, 636.
[142] Kermode (1998), 193.

sailed under letters of marque or reprisal, which legally authorized them to seize Spanish ships and goods.'[143]

Such findings might be held merely to show that merchants themselves were responsible for many attacks on fellow merchants, but not that their guilds were complicit in these attacks. Perhaps the existence of merchant guilds at least acted to constrain such inter-merchant violence, even if inadequately? But recent analyses of commercial insecurity in medieval and early modern Europe suggest the contrary – namely, that one reason merchants so often attacked each other was that the existence of legally privileged guilds and communities of merchants created systematic incentives for them to do so.

The first way this worked was through a medieval legal practice known as a writ of reprisal (also called a letter of marque). This granted an injured party the legal licence to extract compensation not just individually from the person who had injured him, but collectively from all members of that attacker's 'community' – his state, town or guild of origin. The reprisal system, as Tai puts it, 'furnished justification for a quest for indemnity that could be as driven by aggression . . . as the act of piracy that had occasioned it'.[144] As we shall see in Chapter 7, individual merchants, merchant guilds and political authorities sought from the beginning of the medieval Commercial Revolution to restrict this practice of collective reprisal, both as a method of pursuing debts and as a method of obtaining redress for violence. But the existence of organized guilds or communities of merchants, in combination with the possibility of collective reprisals, continued into the late medieval and even the early modern period to tempt opportunists to fabricate claims against one merchant in order to obtain a legal entitlement to prey upon all other members of his guild or community. In combination, merchant guilds and the reprisal system licensed merchants to engage in retaliatory piracy.[145]

But violent attacks on merchants were even more profoundly endogenous to the whole system of privileged merchant guilds. This was because a non-trivial number of violent attacks on merchant shipping were *commissioned* by merchant guilds, either directly or via the town councils they

---

[143] Barbour (1911), 530.   [144] Tai (1996), 187.

[145] This argument is documented in detail for the merchants of medieval Genoa, Venice and the Crown of Aragon by Tai (1996), 9, 67–8, 140–1, 234–43; and Tai (2003b), 264. For detailed discussion of the medieval European reprisal system, see Chapter 7 below, as well as, among a vast literature, Barbour (1911), 530; Boerner and Ritschl (2005); Flórez (2003), 41, 48; Gelderblom (2005b), 32; Lopez (1987), 364; J. G. O'Brien (2002); Planitz (1919), 168–90; Van Houtte (1953), 179–80; Wach (1868), 48.

dominated, to defend their own commercial privileges and attack those of rivals.[146] This was a constant characteristic of the North Sea, Baltic and Russian trade from its inception. In 1188, for instance, the German merchant colony in Visby confiscated the goods of two Novgorod merchants with the aim of provoking Novgorod to eject all foreign merchants including the majority Scandinavian merchant colony in Visby, whose guild privileges in Novgorod the German Visby merchants resented.[147] In the 1360s and 1370s, the merchants of Novgorod itself sent out expeditions of merchant-pirates called *ushkuiniks* to raid settlements along the Middle Volga, with the aim partly of preserving their own guild's monopoly over their city's northern hinterland against rivals' incursions, and partly of forcing Volga towns to grant Novogorod merchants legal rights to trade.[148]

But it was not just on such distant trading frontiers as Russia that merchant guilds initiated violent attacks to further their corporate interests. It also happened in England, Germany and the Netherlands. In the 1390s, for instance, members of the Hull and Grimsby merchant obtained licences as privateers and 'seized the chance to take their commercial rivalry onto the high seas' by attacking Scottish, Danish, Dutch and, above all, Hanseatic merchants.[149] In the early fifteenth century, rivalry between Dutch and German merchant guilds in the Baltic 'led regularly to small military altercations, freebooting, and attacks on trading ships, for which both sides were responsible'.[150] In 1438–41 these ongoing skirmishes between merchant groups flared up into war between the Holland merchants and the six Wendish Hanse towns, in which twenty-two ships of neutral merchants were captured.[151]

The Mediterranean saw the same pattern of violent attacks organized by merchant guilds (or the city governments they dominated) against the commercial shipping of rivals. Genoese merchant guilds in the thirteenth- and fourteenth-century Mediterranean and Black Sea provided direct financial support to privateers, who were in any case themselves often members of the Genoese merchant nobility, and whom they regarded as serving the interests of Genoese merchant guilds against rival guilds of Venetian and Catalan merchants.[152] One of the most successful medieval Genoese merchants, Benedetto Zaccaria, alternated throughout his career between legitimate trade and predation on other

---

[146] Cheyette (1970), 47–8; Tai (1996), 71.

[147] For a detailed account, see Wase (2000).

[148] On the dual mercantile and piratical role of the *ushkuiniks*, see Martin (1975), 7–8, 14–18.

[149] Kermode (1998), 216–17.   [150] Sicking (1999), 42.

[151] *Ibid.*, 43–4.   [152] Tai (1996), 46–8.

merchants, often supported by Genoese merchant guilds abroad. In 1289, for instance, Zaccaria attacked several Egyptian galleys in Tripoli harbour, assisted by the consul of the Genoese merchant guild in the Crimea who convinced other Genoese merchants to invest 6,000 aspres in the venture and provide three galleys to assist in the attack.[153]

Venetian apologists claimed that such behaviour was typically Genoese, but medieval Venetian merchant communities often behaved similarly.[154] The Venetian Senate and Venetian merchant guilds abroad formally employed corsairs to assert the monopolies claimed by Venetian merchants by attacking shipping of rival merchant communities.[155] Katele shows that a central feature of the fourteenth-century disputes between Venetian and Genoese merchant guilds over commercial privileges in Mediterranean ports was a sharp rise in piracy, as both merchant cities and their merchant guilds abroad employed corsairs to attack rival merchant communities.[156] In similar manner, between the twelfth and fifteenth centuries the merchant guild of Savona instituted repeated campaigns of maritime theft against Genoese merchant shipping, to which the Genoese retaliated with accusations of 'piracy'.[157]

Catalonian and Castilian merchant guilds also protected the monopolies they claimed over particular routes and destinations by subsidizing privateers to prey on rival communities of merchants.[158] In 1331, the Barcelona consulado openly contracted with a group of privateers to prey on Genoese merchant shipping for a share of the loot.[159] In 1401, the Sicilian pirate Diego González Valderrama (better known as 'Barrasa') enjoyed so much support from the merchant community of Toulon where he had found a safe haven that when a Genoese fleet arrived to capture him, the Genoese merchant guild in Toulon entreated the Genoese admiral to abandon the project on the grounds that Barrasa's local allies would retaliate against them.[160] In 1402, Valencian ships, supported by the Valencian consulado and council, attacked Venetian merchant galleys returning from Flanders, as part of a long-running conflict between Valencian and Venetian merchant guilds over demarcations between the legal monopolies they claimed in various Adriatic ports.[161]

---

[153] Northrup (1998), 281; Briys and De ter Beerst (2006), 46–7 with n. 115; Bratianu (1927), 221.

[154] Katele (1986), e.g. 76–81, 146–84; Katele (1988), 867–89; Tai (1996), 62–3, 67–8, 130, 169, 177–8, 234.

[155] Katele (1986), 146–84; Tai (1996), 49–50, 160–1, 177–8.

[156] Katele (1986), 146–84; Katele (1988), esp. 865–7, 870–1, 878–80, 886; see also the discussion in Tai (2003a); and Tai (1996), 62–3, 67–8, 130, 177–8.

[157] Tai (2003a); Tai (1996), 490–3.   [158] Woodward (2005), 633, 636, 638.

[159] Tai (1996), 50, 192–3.   [160] Ibid., 593, 596.   [161] Congdon (2003), 228–9.

In some branches of European trade, as we saw in previous chapters, merchant guilds and privileged companies continued to enjoy legal monopolies well into the early modern period. These legal privileges perpetuated guild incentives to encourage – or themselves mount – violent attacks against rivals in defence of their monopoly profits. In the sixteenth and seventeenth centuries, for instance, Venetian and Spanish merchant guilds claimed exclusive rights over the eastern Mediterranean trade, seeking 'to bar North European competitors from their monopoly and treat them as pirates'.[162] In the sixteenth century a privileged company of Portuguese merchants 'treated the people of Malabar as pirates' in order to enforce its legal monopoly over the pepper trade.[163] In 1562, when the English privateer Hawkins encroached on the Spanish consulados' monopoly over trade to Hispaniola, the consulados declared that he could be legitimately attacked as a 'pirate'.[164] The Seville and later the Cádiz merchant consulados successfully called upon the Spanish fleet to attack English and Dutch merchants trading in the West Indies as 'pirates' on the grounds that they were infringing on the consulados' monopoly privileges.[165] In turn, privileged merchant companies from England orchestrated piracy against Spanish shipping in the Caribbean.[166] The monopolies of the Spanish consulados continued to evoke commercial insecurity in the Caribbean into the eighteenth century:

Spain began to organize a better resistance against companies of smugglers that had routinely cut into its colonial trade with impunity... In turn, those whose smuggling had been disturbed resisted with arms and resorted to 'forced exchange'. In imposing its interests by force, Spain induced the smugglers to return to piracy... Thus, ironically, the hegemonic nature of some merchant empires did much to keep piracy alive.[167]

Even when violent attacks on merchants were not explicitly committed in defence of the privileges of merchant guilds, they were still often endogenous to the whole pre-modern commercial system whereby trade was carved up into a mosaic of guild privileges. On the supply side, the legal monopolies of merchant guilds pushed outsiders who would otherwise have been able to trade legally into the black market. By defining non-members' trade as piracy or excluding them totally from legitimate commerce, merchant guilds left outsiders no alternative but to operate illegally. On the demand side, the monopoly privileges of merchant

---

[162] Pérotin-Dumon (1991), 213.   [163] Ibid., 199.   [164] Ibid., 208.
[165] Barbour (1911), 533–5.   [166] Ibid., 537–8.   [167] Pérotin-Dumon (1991), 226.

guilds kept supplies low and prices high, creating a demand for the services of privateers, freebooters, smugglers and other unlicensed traders. As Pérotin-Dumon points out for the early modern merchant companies, 'Contraband had to make up for the chronic undersupply and exorbitant prices imposed by chartered commercial companies and state-controlled trade circuits.'[168] This was acknowledged by contemporaries, as in 1619 when the English Bermuda Company sent only a single ship to the colony, leaving the colonists so short of goods that the governor was compelled to authorize trade with a Dutch freebooter who was willing to supply the freight services and basic imports – mainly food and clothing – which the monopolistic Company was unable or unwilling to supply.[169] But the freebooters and smugglers brought into existence by guild and company privileges had to operate illegally in the informal sector. They consequently conducted business and enforced contracts using informal – often violent – mechanisms, which increased insecurity for third parties as well as those directly involved.

Some scholars go so far as to argue that the reason we observe an upsurge in commercial insecurity in the early modern period, precisely when one would expect the growth of the state to have led to its decline, is that the European overseas 'discoveries' created a spate of new monopolies for European merchant guilds and privileged companies, which exported inter-merchant piracy overseas to every region in which such guilds and companies claimed exclusive privileges.[170] Piracy and commercial violence, according to these scholars, were generated by the cartellistic privileges granted to merchant associations and by efforts to enforce them: 'As long as monopolies went along with commercial wars, piracy simply fluctuated according to the degree of a state's authority at sea.'[171] Potentially legal traders were forced into piracy, not because they *preferred* to operate violently but because the legal monopolies granted to merchant guilds and privileged companies prevented outsiders from trading legally and peacefully. It was not until the monopolies of merchant guilds and privileged companies began to be weakened in the later eighteenth century that piracy and violent threats to commercial security began to decline, according to this view: 'In order fully to extinguish European piracy (and the American piracy that derived from it), it was thus necessary . . . to abandon commercial exclusivism in favor of free commerce.'[172]

---

[168] *Ibid.*, 222.   [169] *Ibid.*, 222–3.
[170] See, e.g., *ibid.*, 210, 222–3; Katele (1988), esp. 865–7, 870–1, 878–80, 886.
[171] Pérotin-Dumon (1991), 226.   [172] *Ibid.*, 222.

6.2.2   Violent conflicts between guilds

Merchant guilds did not just contribute *indirectly* to commercial insecurity, by employing pirates to attack rivals, defining non-member merchants as 'pirates' and pushing otherwise legal traders into the black
market. They also engaged directly in violent aggression against other
merchant guilds which they regarded as infringing on their privileges:
'the rivalry for trade was a rivalry among merchants and, in particular,
among merchant associations'.[173] Inter-guild conflicts were exacerbated
by the fact that merchant guilds' legal privileges seldom specified in
detail their members' precise commercial entitlements in all possible
contingencies. This left significant scope for subsequent disagreements.
Such conflicts between guilds were good business for rulers, however,
who therefore often deliberately left grey areas in the entitlements they
granted to guilds.

Even within the same polity, local merchant guilds created insecurity
by undertaking violent aggression to defend their monopolies against the
local merchant guilds of neighbouring towns. To give just one example
among many, in 1320 traders in the outport of Sluis saw the opportunity
of expanding their own trade rather than channelling wares through the
Bruges merchant-brokers in accordance with the latter's guild privileges.
The Bruges guild sought to prevent this infringement on its monopoly by
putting pressure on the Bruges town council, which resorted to violence,
ultimately razing Sluis to the ground. The Bruges guild then obtained
from the count of Flanders a staple privilege (which it jealously enforced)
legally requiring all merchandise entering the River Zwin to be traded
only in Bruges, through the intermediation of its members.[174] The fourteenth and fifteenth centuries also saw serious conflicts between large
Flemish cities such as Ypres and Ghent (spearheaded by their merchant
guilds) and smaller neighbouring towns over control of the regional textile
trade. These inter-city conflicts, driven by the desire of merchant guilds
to maintain their monopoly privileges over the surrounding regions, had
the incidental effect of increasing commercial insecurity in the whole
territory.[175]

Even more frequent were conflicts between local merchant guilds and
alien ones. One reason alien merchant guilds so consistently applied
to rulers for security guarantees was precisely because they expected
to be harassed by local merchant guilds which regarded themselves as
exclusively entitled to practise particular types of trade.[176] Many attacks

---

[173] Kohn (2003a), 9–10, 14 (quotation).   [174] Van Houtte (1966), 39–40.
[175] Stabel (1997), 144.   [176] Kohn (2003a), 15–16; Paravicini (1992), 112.

by mobs against foreign merchants were fomented by conflicts over legal privileges between local merchant guilds and alien ones.

Resentment of alien merchant guilds by local ones led to violent conflict in a number of Mediterranean trading centres from the eleventh century on. In 1082, as we have seen, the Byzantine emperor granted the first of a series of commercial privileges to the Venetian merchant guild in Constantinople. From the beginning, all parties recognized that these privileges would attract the enmity of local merchant guilds, and such conflict indeed materialized.[177] In 1171, Byzantine merchant guilds' endemic resentment against Italian competition boiled over into political pressure, triggering mass arrests of Venetian merchants in Constantinople.[178] A decade later, the privileges of the Italian merchant guilds in Constantinople enraged the indigenous Greeks to such an extent that in 1182 they overthrew the empress, massacred large numbers of Italian merchants and burnt the Italian merchants' compounds.[179] Similar motivations lay behind the violent attack by an Egyptian mob against the Venetian merchant guild in Alexandria in 1327, leading to several fatalities; the local merchant guild of the Karīmi, resentful of alien merchant privileges, was believed to have incited the attack.[180] In 1356–8, likewise, the Venetian merchant 'nations' in Catalan and Aragonese towns were attacked by local merchant guilds, enraged at their commercial privileges.[181]

Northern Europe shows the same pattern. Around 1157, German merchant guilds in the Danish city of Roskilde were attacked because of local merchant guilds' resentment of their trading privileges.[182] In 1284, Hanse merchants were attacked in Norway because local merchant guilds objected to their being allowed to trade there.[183] Conflict in Bruges between the German merchant guild and the local brokers' guild over trading privileges became so serious in the 1350s that, as we have seen, it helped trigger a Hanse embargo against the city.[184] From the late thirteenth century on, Hanse merchants were periodically attacked in London and other English towns because local merchant guilds viewed them as encroaching on their privileges.[185] In 1493, conflict over silk imports triggered an attack by a mob of five hundred Londoners, in which several German merchants were wounded and the Steelyard (Hanseatic compound) was set on fire.[186]

The Hanse was not only the victim but also the perpetrator of inter-guild attacks. In Bruges, for instance, whenever the privileges of the

---

[177] Frankopan (2004), 139.   [178] Madden (2002), 24.
[179] Runciman (1987), 148; Madden (2002), 24.   [180] Ashtor (1983), 52–3.
[181] Congdon (2003), 217.   [182] Schütt (1980), 109.   [183] Dollinger (1970), 49.
[184] *Ibid.*, 50, 62, 65; Bahr (1911), 21–2; Daenell (1905), 19–21.
[185] Postan (1973), 240; Lloyd (1991), 22, 30.   [186] Giuseppi (1895), 80.

north German merchants came under threat the Hanse either declared an embargo or 'resorted to violence'.[187] In Danzig (Gdańsk), English merchants were frequently attacked in the fourteenth century because of resentment by the local merchant guild, a Hanse member.[188] Many acts of piracy against English merchants in the North Sea and Baltic during the fourteenth century were carried out by Hanse merchants who regarded the English as encroaching on their legal monopoly.[189] Dutch merchants trading in the Baltic were violently attacked at intervals throughout the fifteenth century by German merchants seeking to prevent them from encroaching on Hanseatic trading privileges.[190]

Violent struggles among rival guilds of alien merchants also threatened commercial security. In Constantinople from the late eleventh century on,

Rivalry between the various Italian communities caused endless rioting in the city, damaging store-houses and interrupting trade. The rivalry extended to the seas. Each Italian city maintained a private fleet to prey on its neighbours' ships, and all would prey on Greek shipping.[191]

In 1162, a thousand members of the Pisan merchant colony in Constantinople attacked the three-hundred-strong Genoese merchant colony with the intention, according to a contemporary account, of 'despoiling and killing them'. This led to a two-day battle, in which the Pisans captured the Genoese merchant compound, killed one of its members, looted 30,000 bezants worth of Genoese goods and destroyed so much merchandise that the leading Genoese family of the Mallonus was ruined. This inter-guild struggle sparked warfare between Genoa and Pisa, which lasted until 1175, cost thousands of lives and caused inestimable damage to trade, including by third parties.[192] Similar inter-guild violence occurred in trading centres throughout the medieval Mediterranean – between the Pisan and the Genoese merchant guilds in Messina in 1129,[193] between the Pisan, Genoese and Anconitan merchant guilds in Acre in 1222–4,[194] between the Genoese and the Venetians in Acre in 1256–7,[195] between the Pisans, Venetians and Genoese in Cairo in the late 1280s,[196] and between the Genoese and all other merchant nations (especially the Venetians and Pisans) around the Black Sea throughout the thirteenth and fourteenth centuries.[197] Archaeological excavations in

---

[187] Paravicini (1992), 112.   [188] Postan (1973), 239, 251–2.
[189] *Ibid.*, 251–2.   [190] Dollinger (1970), 195.   [191] Runciman (1987), 148.
[192] Day (1988), 95; Slessarev (1969), 96–103 (quotation 96).
[193] Abulafia (1978), 72.   [194] Abulafia (1986a), 530; Pryor (2000), 427–8.
[195] Pryor (2000), 435–6.   [196] Ashtor (1983), 14.   [197] *Ibid.*, 76.

the Black Sea off the Crimea have discovered the remains of a heavily laden Pisan merchant vessel sunk in 1277 – by a Genoese ship.[198]

Conflicts between rival alien merchant guilds also generated commercial insecurity in Provence, Flanders and the Baltic. In 1281, for instance, the consuls of the Genoese merchant guild in Nîmes were imprisoned by the town authorities, which they ascribed to the machinations of the consuls of the merchant guilds of Florence, Piacenza and Siena in Nîmes; in reprisal, the Genoese authorities expelled the entire Florentine merchant guild from Genoa.[199] In fourteenth-century Bruges, the dozen or more different alien merchant guilds were constantly attacking one another, and in the mid-fifteenth century the city saw violent struggles among the merchant guilds of different Spanish cities.[200] Medieval Livonia saw repeated violent clashes between the German Hanse and Dutch merchant guilds, culminating in the Dutch seizure of a dozen Hanseatic salt vessels in 1438.[201] In all these cases, the privileges claimed by rival alien merchant guilds fomented, rather than moderated, commercial insecurity.

Rivalry between different merchant guilds over commercial entitlements could even lead to open warfare between their home polities, as we have seen, creating general commercial insecurity which spilled over onto third parties. According to late-eleventh-century Egyptian sources, for instance, Count Roger of Sicily mounted a military expedition to North Africa in order to protect the exclusive privileges of Sicilian merchant guilds by 'preventing the Italian city-states from obtaining trading concessions there'.[202] After 1182, the Italian city-states devastated the coasts of the Byzantine empire, hugely increasing commercial insecurity, in order to restore the privileges of their merchant guilds in Constantinople.[203] Throughout the medieval period, the German Hanseatic cities repeatedly resorted to war, sometimes to defend Hanse merchants' shipping against piracy, more often to put pressure on alien rulers to grant or renew its merchants' privileges against encroachments from rival merchant guilds.[204] In 1419 rivalry between Spanish and German merchant guilds in the French trade led King John II of Castile to attack the Hanseatic trading fleet off La Rochelle, capturing forty vessels and sinking their cargoes. This triggered a war between Spain and the Hanseatic League, which for twenty years increased commercial insecurity for merchants of both sides as well as numerous third parties and only ended

---

[198] See www.archaeology.kiev.ua/underwater/zelenko5.htm.
[199] See the documents relating to this conflict in Berti (1857), 167–72.
[200] R. S. Smith (1940), 68–9.   [201] Dollinger (1970), 300.
[202] McManamon (2003), 36.   [203] Runciman (1987), 148.
[204] Dollinger (1970), e.g. 51–5, 67–72, 111.

when the German Hanse agreed to cease competing with the Spaniards in various French and Spanish ports.[205] In the early sixteenth century, the German Hanse deliberately increased commercial insecurity for Dutch merchants by attacking them violently and pressing Denmark to close the Sound to Dutch ships, thereby excluding them from trade with the Baltic and north-east Europe.[206] Even such an enthusiast for the Hanse as its major historian, Dollinger, acknowledges that 'Hanseatic military action was essentially a war of piracy.'[207]

The monopolies of the privileged merchant companies also gave rise to violent conflicts that increased commercial insecurity. The privileged companies of Portuguese, Dutch and English merchants in Asia and the Americas used force to get advantages in trade, and 'sold protection from their own violence'.[208] The greatest financial success ever enjoyed by the Dutch West India Company in its entire history – and the only substantial dividend it ever paid – was not through peaceful trading but through violent aggression against the Seville merchant consulado, when in 1628 it captured the entire Spanish silver fleet.[209] In the seventeenth century, the monopoly claimed by the Hudson's Bay Company over the fur trade led to repeated clashes between the French and English in eastern Canada, decreasing security, increasing transaction costs and reducing trade: 'Shipping and insurance costs rose, while in some years, the company was unable to send even one ship to Hudson's Bay.'[210] In the seventeenth and eighteenth centuries, the rival privileges of the English East India Company and Armenian merchant colonies in India repeatedly gave rise to violent conflict: 'Numerous cases of outright English piracy against Armenian vessels in the Indian Ocean suggest that when the competition was too much to bear, the English did not hesitate to resort to extra-judicial means to hinder Armenian gains.'[211]

The violence fostered by the privileges of early modern merchant companies is perhaps most vividly illustrated by the Dutch East India Company (VOC). From the beginning, the VOC was legally empowered by the Dutch state to build forts and maintain armies,[212] and a large proportion of its employees consisted of soldiers.[213] In 1621, when the inhabitants of the Spice Islands rebelled against the VOC monopoly over the spice trade, the Company's governor general 'did not shirk from killing or expelling the entire native population of the clove-producing Banda

[205] Henn (1999), 140; Dollinger (1970), 257–8.
[206] De Vries and Van der Woude (1997), 352–3.
[207] Dollinger (1970), 111.   [208] Pearson (1991), 111.
[209] De Vries and Van der Woude (1997), 399.
[210] Rich (1957), 20: xx; Carlos and Nicholas (1990), 860 (quotation).
[211] Aslanian (2004), 51.   [212] De Vries and Van der Woude (1997), 385.
[213] Lucassen (2004), 15 (Table 1), 17, 22–4, 27.

islands and establishing plantations run by Dutchmen (the perkeniers) and worked by slaves'.[214] Early modern European merchant companies in Asia

did best where they were able to use their naval power to good advantage. Certainly it was by naked force that the Dutch gained control of the highly localized trade in fine spices, and they threatened to monopolize the pepper trade after their successful raid on the free port of Macassar on Sulawesi (1663) and their capture of Chochin on the Malabar Coast (1665).[215]

The VOC used violence to defend the legal monopoly it claimed, 'restricting English access to the spice trade by force of arms and using a combination of military might and commercial chicanery to exercise control over the production of cloves, nutmeg, and cinnamon in Ceylon, Java, and the Moluccas'.[216] When the VOC was denied direct access to China in 1624, it ravaged Chinese coastal shipping until it extorted the right to establish a trading post.[217]

This pattern, whereby the chartered merchant companies maintained their own privileges by increasing the commercial insecurity of others, was described by Adam Smith in 1776:

With the right of possessing forts and garrisons in distant and barbarous countries is necessarily connected the right of making peace and war in those countries. The joint stock companies which have had the one right have constantly exercised the other, and have frequently had it expressly conferred upon them. How unjustly, how capriciously, how cruelly they have commonly exercised it, is too well known from recent experience.[218]

Or, as Habib summarized it in 1990, the effect of the great European privileged companies in Asia was not to enhance commercial efficiency but rather to increase the insecurity of all traders – Indian or European – who were not members of those companies. The great commercial contribution of the European chartered companies to Asian trade, he concludes, was 'a matter of men-of-war and gun and shot, to which arithmetic and brokerage could provide no answer'.[219]

What can we conclude about the role of merchant guilds and privileged companies in commercial security? In theory, as we have seen, merchant guilds could have either increased or decreased security. Which effect predominated can only be decided by the evidence. When we examine such evidence, we find that in practice the security-enhancing activities of merchant guilds were minor. Convoys and forts were organized by

---

[214] De Vries and Van der Woude (1997), 386.   [215] Tracy (1990a), 10.
[216] S. R. H. Jones and Ville (1996), 911.
[217] De Vries and Van der Woude (1997), 387.
[218] A. Smith (1776), Book 5, ch. 1, part 3, section a, para. 29.
[219] Habib (1990), 398–9.

other institutional mechanisms than merchant guilds, including ad hoc groupings of individual merchants, city governments and states. Rulers made security guarantees to non-guilded merchants as well as guilded ones. And commercial embargoes were undertaken to secure an entire panoply of trading privileges, not just security guarantees. In so far as merchant guilds did enhance security, they did so almost exclusively for their own membership, which was limited in number and kind, as shown by the entry barriers examined in Chapters 3 and 4.

Merchant guilds' security-*reducing* activities, by contrast, were substantial. With the aim of extending their own privileges and reducing those of rivals, merchant guilds inflicted significant damage on members of other guilds, on unguilded traders forcibly excluded by guild privileges and on the vast mass of innocent bystanders caught up in guild-inspired riots, piracy and warfare. It thus seems likely that the net effect of merchant guilds was to reduce, not enhance, the security of pre-modern trade.

This evidence also illustrates a final key point. In so far as merchant guilds were able to take action to increase security for their members, they could only do so by virtue of support from their own home rulers, who intervened diplomatically and militarily to defend their merchants' guilds abroad and support their negotiations with alien rulers. But this implies that alternative institutions did exist which were able and willing to provide commercial security to merchants trading abroad – and thus that the theory of the merchant guild as the efficient solution to problems of commercial security contains an internal contradiction. The depth of this contradiction is explored in the remainder of this chapter.

6.3   Were there no feasible alternatives?

The view that merchant guilds were efficient institutions because they solved the problem of commercial security assumes (in fact, implies) that alternative institutions were unavailable. The most influential theory of this type, for instance, claims that alien merchant guilds were essential because 'in the age prior to the emergence of the nation-state, alien merchants could expect little military or political aid from their countrymen'.[220] Is this assumption accurate?

6.3.1   State support for merchant guilds

Quite the contrary. Not only alien merchants, but also their guilds in foreign trading centres, depended heavily on their home governments

---

[220] Greif, Milgrom and Weingast (1994), 747.

which provided them with constant political and military support. This casts serious doubt on the idea that pre-modern states were unable or unwilling to involve themselves in providing commercial security.

Alien merchant colonies only got recognition and privileges from political authorities abroad by virtue of their recognition by their own authorities at home. Italian merchant colonies in the Levant and northern Africa, for instance, secured commercial privileges from those rulers solely by virtue of the fact that their members were 'privileged merchants . . . in their home cities' and could rely on support from their own governments.[221] In 1087, Genoese and Pisan merchants were permitted to form colonies with trading privileges in Mahdia only because their home cities sent a fleet of three hundred ships to threaten its Arab ruler.[222] In 1250–64, the Barcelona merchant guilds in Tunis and Alexandria obtained privileges from the Muslim authorities only thanks to the recognition they enjoyed from their own ruler, King James I of Catalonia.[223] In 1257, the rulers of Acre confirmed the trade privileges of the Anconitan merchant guild only on condition that the government of their home town seal the agreement.[224] In the 1380s, the Catalan merchant guilds in Alexandria and Damascus secured privileges from the Mamluk rulers only because of recognition and support from their own ruler at home in Catalonia.[225]

In northern Europe, too, home rulers also played a key role in supporting their merchants' guilds abroad. From 1161 to around 1250, the authority enjoyed in foreign trading centres by the Gotland Community (the precursor to the German Hanse) 'rested in the last resort on the support given to it by the towns, especially Lübeck, where most of the merchants started their journeys, and Visby, the principal centre of their trade'.[226] In medieval England, members of Norwegian merchant guilds enjoyed their privileges by virtue of the recognition they enjoyed from the king of Norway.[227] In medieval Bruges, the charters granted to Italian merchant guilds 'were usually the result of lengthy negotiations in which official envoys of the Italian republics often played a conspicuous part'.[228] Throughout medieval Europe, an alien merchant guild could only be established 'with the tacit approval of the territorial prince and with the consent of the prince of the merchants' land'.[229]

Alien merchant guilds not only relied on political *recognition* by their home government to gain privileges abroad, but remained heavily

---

[221] Bernard (1972), 293.   [222] Krueger (1933), 377–8.
[223] Abulafia (2000b), 660–1.
[224] Abulafia (1986a), 530, 537–8; Abulafia (1997), 54–5.
[225] Ashtor (1983), 149.   [226] Dollinger (1970), 43.   [227] Blom (1984), 25.
[228] R. De Roover (1948a), 16.   [229] Mauro (1990), 262.

dependent on its practical *support*. Anglo-Saxon merchants in tenth-
and eleventh-century Lombardy, for instance, relied on intervention by
English kings to resolve conflicts and secure privileges from Lombard
rulers.[230] Medieval Danish merchants relied primarily on legal recognition from their own rulers, not their own corporate organizations, to
prevent foreign rulers from attacking them.[231] German merchant guilds
in twelfth- and thirteenth-century Danish towns relied on privileges from
the German emperor to sustain them against attacks from Danish merchant guilds and Danish rulers.[232] Italian merchant guilds in the twelfth-
century eastern Mediterranean enjoyed security because of treaties
concluded between their home governments and alien rulers – and threats
of violent reprisals from their home navies if they were mistreated.[233] The
Genoese merchant guild in Ceuta obtained fair treatment from that city's
ruler in 1231 by virtue of diplomatic and military support from the government of Genoa.[234] The Sicilian merchant colony in Armenia secured
trading privileges in 1331 as a direct reward to the Sicilian king for a
military alliance.[235] When the Lucchese merchant Betto Schiatta had
merchandise arrested at Tournai in 1383 to repay a debt in Bruges, it
was the town council of Lucca, not the Lucchese merchant guilds in Paris
or in Bruges, which intervened on his behalf.[236] When central European
merchants encountered problems from Venetian customs collectors in
1361 and 1418, it was Habsburg rulers, not the Fondaco dei Tedeschi
(German merchant guild in Venice), which negotiated on their behalf.[237]
The Spanish merchant guild in Bruges had its conflicts with the Hanse
Kontor resolved in 1428 not by its own consuls but by envoys of the king
of Spain.[238]

Venetian merchant colonies are often adduced as exemplars of alien
merchant guilds efficiently bargaining for security from foreign rulers to
compensate for the lack of political support from home rulers.[239] Yet
Venetian merchant guilds abroad enjoyed particularly consistent support
from their home government, which drove hard bargains to secure and
defend their privileges.[240] In 1122, for instance, when Emperor John
II Komnenos tried to limit the commercial privileges of Venetian merchant colonies in the Byzantine empire, a Venetian fleet attacked Corfu,
pillaged Byzantine territory on its further travels towards Palestine and

---

[230] Middleton (2005), 325.   [231] Hørby (1984), 49–50.
[232] E. Hoffmann (1980), 45, 47.   [233] Kohn (2003a), 11; R. De Roover (1971).
[234] Kohn (2003a), 13; R. L. Reynolds (1945), 12.   [235] Abulafia (1986b), 211.
[236] Mirot (1927), 80.   [237] Heyd (1874), 199–200, 202.   [238] Henn (1999), 140.
[239] See, e.g., Greif, Milgrom and Weingast (1994), 756.
[240] Lane (1973), ch. 10; Mazzaoui (1981), 35, 38.

repeated the treatment again on its return voyage, forcing the emperor to confirm and expand the privileges of Venetian merchant colonies.[241] In 1333, 1369 and 1380, ambassadors from Venice, not guild consuls, negotiated privileges from the Khan of the Golden Horde permitting Venetian merchants to form and maintain a colony at Tana on the Black Sea.[242] Throughout the medieval period Venetian merchant colonies in Egypt relied on government ambassadors, not guild consuls, to negotiate with the sultan, on the grounds that 'the intervention of the consuls did not carry enough weight' or 'the question seemed to be too important to be dealt with by a consul'.[243] In 1480, the Egyptian sultan imprisoned the entire Venetian merchant colony in its *fondaco* for three days and nights, and then held its members hostage in the customs house until they agreed to pay the price he dictated for pepper, only refraining from even worse treatment because he 'knew from experience that he could not outrage Venice without facing severe military reprisals'.[244] In the 1480s and 1490s, it was the Venetian Senate, not the guild consul, which defended the interests of the Venetian merchant guild in London by threatening a total withdrawal of Venetian galleys if England negotiated a wool staple with Pisa.[245]

Home polities exercised a striking degree of control and surveillance over alien merchant colonies. In 1224, the Italian city of Ancona was formally held responsible for controlling the actions of its alien merchant guilds as far away as Acre.[246] From the 1260s on, organized Catalan merchant consulates were established in North African ports, where they developed 'under royal aegis, indeed by the direct action of the crown': consular fees were fixed by royal envoys, and consuls themselves were appointed not by merchants but by royal authority.[247] Medieval Venetian merchant guilds in the Levant 'were closely watched, and their local authorities strictly supervised by the government of the Serenissima'.[248] Even the Venetian merchant colony on the Black Sea, which enjoyed unusual autonomy because of its difficult geopolitical position, was governed by a consul and *admiratus* selected by the Venetian Senate; only the subordinate council was elected by merchants on the spot.[249] The merchant colonies of Ragusa (Dubrovnik) in the Ottoman Balkans in the later fifteenth century also remained 'under the jurisdiction of the

---

[241] Laiou (2001), 160.
[242] Di Cosmo (2005), 396–7, 404, 407, 411–12; Doumerc (1987), 8.
[243] Ashtor (1983), 74, 122.   [244] Lopez (1987), 388.   [245] Mallett (1962), 261–3.
[246] Abulafia (1986a), 530, 537–8; Abulafia (1997), 54–5.   [247] Hibbert (1949), 356–8.
[248] Ashtor (1983), 68–9, 78, 411 (quotation); Di Cosmo (2005), 416–17.
[249] Doumerc (1987), 6, 8.

central government [of Ragusa] which exercised strict control over their existence'.[250]

The control of the home polity over alien merchant guilds also prevailed in medieval northern Europe. The guild of Cologne merchants in twelfth-century London was 'administered and supervised from home'.[251] In medieval Bruges, alien merchant guilds did not autonomously govern their members, but merely extended the jurisdiction of their home towns: 'For the Italians, the consul was the official representative of the home government and his orders had to be obeyed.'[252] The Florentine merchant 'nation' did not even let the resident merchants in Bruges elect the consul, who was instead appointed by the dominant political interests in Florence in consultation with the heads of the Arte di Calimala.[253] All judicial decisions imposed by the consuls of the Lucca merchant guild in Bruges had to be officially notified to the government of Lucca.[254] The only alien merchant nation in Bruges that formulated its own rules and regulations was the German Hanse, whose members drafted their own Kontorordnung (counting-house ordinance) in 1347, but in 1356 representatives of the Hanse towns travelled to Bruges 'to formally codify the new rules'.[255]

Autonomy from the home polity was enjoyed only by a few alien merchant guilds, only to a limited degree, and always subject to restrictions. The Hanse Kontor in Novgorod initially enjoyed the right autonomously to regulate its members through the *Steven* (general assembly of all merchants of the colony), but in the mid-fourteenth century decision-making was taken over by the Hanseatic Diet in Lübeck.[256] Genoese merchant colonies in the Levant were more independent than those of other trading nations, but even they relied on support from the home city and paid it taxes.[257] The Genoese merchant guild in Damascus was by 1400 supervised by the *Officium Alexandriae*, a supervisory body based at home in Genoa.[258] In so far as Genoese merchant guilds abroad did enjoy greater independence from the home city than did other alien merchant guilds, this is regarded as having given rise to unpredictable and conflictual behaviour which reduced members' security and contributed to commercial decline.[259]

Far from state weakness creating a security void into which merchant guilds moved as the only efficient solution, medieval rulers were willing and able to defend their merchants' security abroad. In the late

---

[250] Molnár (2007), 77–8.   [251] Nitzsch (1892), 67.   [252] R. De Roover (1948), 18.
[253] *Ibid.*, 19.   [254] Mirot (1927), 66.   [255] Gelderblom (2005a), 14.
[256] Angermann (1987), 66.   [257] Krueger (1933), 379.   [258] Ashtor (1983), 228.
[259] *Ibid.*, 83, 411, 485; Di Cosmo (2005), 416–17.

eleventh century Count Roger of Sicily mounted a military expedition to defend Sicilian merchants in North Africa against aggression.[260] In the late twelfth century, when Italian merchants were attacked in Constantinople, their mother cities sent naval expeditions to attack the Byzantine coast and demand compensation.[261] In the early thirteenth century, when Ceuta confiscated Genoese merchants' goods, the Genoese fleet attacked the port.[262] In the later thirteenth century, when Barcelona merchants were endangered in Tunis and Alexandria, King James I of Catalonia threatened military reprisal.[263] In the fifteenth century when Spanish merchants suffered threats from the German Hanse in French waters, King John II of Castile went to war against the Hanseatic League.[264] In the seventeenth century, when the English Hudson's Bay Company attacked French merchants in Canada, the French crown sent a military expedition: 'In the twelve years, 1686–97, the French attacked Moose, Rupert and Albany Rivers, New Severn, and York Fort three times; only once, at York in 1690, did they fail.' The English state in turn 'sent two expeditions to the Bottom of the Bay and one against York Fort; only that of 1688 failed'.[265] Throughout the entire period when merchant guilds and privileged companies dominated long-distance trade, therefore, rulers and states were willing, able and institutionally sophisticated enough to intervene in defence of their merchants' security abroad.

But surely hanses, at least, were autonomous corporative organizations organized purely among long-distance merchants? Hanses were certainly ambiguous organizations, sharing some features of a merchant guild and some characteristics of a federation of towns – at least in the case of the German Hanse in the later Middle Ages. But hanses, too, derived their power and legitimacy from the privileges and recognition their constituent *local* merchant guilds enjoyed from their *local* rulers. Thus German merchants trading through Hanse offices in medieval Oslo and Tönsberg enjoyed privileges from the Norwegian ruler by virtue of their membership in their local merchant guilds of Rostock and Wismar, whose governments had granted them legal recognition.[266] All agreements reached by the German Hanse with alien rulers 'were negotiated and ratified with the Hanseatic diet, but enforcement depended on the further ratification of the individual town councils'.[267] This was not surprising: 'When foreign states attempted to restrict their privileges, the German merchants needed the support of the towns, who

---

[260] McManamon (2003), 36.   [261] Runciman (1987), 148.
[262] Kohn (2003a), 13; R. L. Reynolds (1945), 12.   [263] Abulafia (2000b), 660–1.
[264] Dollinger (1970), 257–8.   [265] Rich (1957), 20: xx.   [266] Blom (1984), 20.
[267] Spruyt (1994), 168.

alone could protect them efficiently.'[268] Violence and confiscation against hanse members in international trading centres were kept in check, therefore, not by the *informal* and *corporative* threat of reprisal from the individual hanse branch, but rather by the *formal* and *political* threat of reprisal from the city governments that backed it.

Hanse branches in alien polities continued to depend heavily on political support from the rulers of the towns in which their constituent local guilds were located. The German Hanse 'was based ultimately on the councils of the individual member towns, which, especially in the case of the larger towns, played a decisive role'.[269] In the twelfth century, German merchants trading from the Hanse compound in Novgorod appealed back to their home towns – above all, Lübeck – for support in conflicts with Russian rulers.[270] In the 1350s, when conflict flared up with Flanders over German commercial privileges in Bruges, many Hanse towns 'were perturbed to see the Kontor taking the initiative in negotiations with Flanders, without mandate and at the risk of dragging the towns unwillingly into international conflicts'.[271] Serious pressure only began to be exerted on Flemish rulers to sustain Hanse privileges 'when the domestic cities themselves took in hand the representation of their merchants' interests'.[272]

Other hanses depended even more heavily on political support from members' home towns and territories. The joint merchant colonies of the Mediterranean 'minor nations' enjoyed privileges from rulers in the medieval Levant by virtue of diplomatic negotiations undertaken by their home rulers.[273] The Merchant Adventurers of England relied on support from the mayor of London and the king of England to enforce its regulations abroad.[274] When it declared a 'restraint of trading' against the Low Countries in 1485, it did so only after lobbying the king of England for support, and was able to force its members to comply with the embargo only by enlisting support from the mayor and aldermen of London.[275] This reflected a deeper and long-lasting recognition that the Adventurers could only enforce its interests against outsiders and its own members with political support:

many adventurers felt in need of some civic authorization within the city of London for their existing methods of transacting the business of a 'branch' of the full company beyond the seas: it was now plain there were things they could not do when members were recalcitrant. The obvious solution was to apply to

---

[268] Dollinger (1970), 64.   [269] *Ibid.*, 97.
[270] Choroškevic (1996), 71–2, 78, 86.   [271] Dollinger (1970), 63.
[272] Daenell (1905), 19–20 (quotation); Dollinger (1970), 63.
[273] Abulafia (1988), 184–5.   [274] Sutton (2002), 34–5.   [275] *Ibid.*, 41.

the mayor, the ultimate authority above the companies of London, who could summon their wardens together in emergencies, settle disputes or endorse their letters, as the highest citizen authority, when they were writing to a great lord or a city abroad.[276]

This practice was no new development of the fifteenth century, but reached much further back in time: 'there was a long history of co-operation between the Guildhall and the adventurers... over letters to the Low Countries'.[277]

So dependent were hanses on political support from their members' home governments that their policies were often rendered nugatory if town governments disagreed. Within the German Hanse, individual towns often reneged on contributions to military actions and entered into individual treaties with non-Hanseatic rulers.[278] The English Merchant Adventurers came to be dominated by the interests of London, giving rise to internal factional conflicts with other English towns which could only be resolved by royal intervention.[279] Conversely, hanse members rejoiced in effective military intervention as long as their home governments agreed. In the course of the German Hanse's existence, its merchants (or their legal monopolies) were protected by wars waged by its component cities (and its one territorial member, the Teutonic Order) against Denmark, Norway, England, Holland, France, Castile and Russia.[280]

The historical evidence thus refutes the third fundamental assumption underlying the view that merchant guilds were the efficient solution to providing commercial security – that alternative institutions were lacking. As early as the eleventh century European political authorities were willing and able to involve themselves in issues of commercial security affecting their merchants trading abroad. Indeed, merchant guilds themselves were only effective in international trading centres by virtue of systematic support from their home rulers.

6.3.2 Public-order institutions and commercial security

Commercial security did gradually improve in certain locations and periods during the course of the medieval Commercial Revolution. But this was not through corporative institutions such as guilds. Rather, it was through piecemeal institutional developments – particularly in representative institutions and public finance – which aligned the incentives

---

[276] *Ibid.*, 42. [277] *Ibid.*, 42 n. 67 (with examples). [278] Spruyt (1994), 164.
[279] Sutton (2002), 37.
[280] De Vries and Van der Woude (1997), 352–3; Dollinger (1970), 51–5, 67–72, 111.

of rulers not merely with the interests of particularized corporations of merchants but with those of the commercial economy as a whole. As we have seen, relationships between rulers and merchants were complex. Rulers could be merchants' foes as much as their friends: a ruler without a monopoly of legitimate coercion might see no benefit to himself in trying to protect merchants; a ruler who did have a monopoly of coercion might use it not to provide commercial security but to prey upon merchants himself. Moreover, as we saw in Chapter 5, even when rulers were merchants' friends, there were two ways this relationship could go – the particularized path whereby rulers granted commercial security as a favour to a privileged guild of merchants; or the generalized path whereby a ruler provided commercial security to all those engaged in exchange, regardless of whether they belonged to a merchant guild. Long-distance exchange was *possible* when rulers provided particularized security to merchant guilds, and this finding has provided encouragement to the efficiency theories. But some medieval rulers provided generalized security to all merchants, and this truly galvanized long-distance trade. A vivid illustration is provided by the Champagne fairs, where international trade flourished under generalized safe-conducts guaranteed by the counts of Champagne to all foreign merchants regardless of guild affiliation but collapsed within fifteen years of coming under the particularized regime of the kings of France, as we shall see shortly.

Medieval rulers had relatively good incentives to incur the costs of protecting their own local merchants because – as we saw in Chapter 5 – they could ordinarily recoup more than these costs by borrowing from and taxing them. Not only were medieval rulers able and willing to provide diplomatic and military support for their own merchants in alien trading centres, but they were also able and willing to provide military and organizational support for their merchants en route. By the twelfth century at latest, as we saw in Section 2, Italian city-states were organizing, financing and administering convoys to protect their merchants' shipping.[281] The most important and regular convoys in medieval Mediterranean trade, indeed, 'were subventioned and supervised by the governments of Genoa and Venice'.[282] Counter to the claims of efficiency theories, therefore, municipal and state institutions were sufficiently sophisticated and well-motivated during the medieval Commercial Revolution to provide security for their own merchant citizens trading abroad.

Rulers also began, early in the medieval Commercial Revolution, to be capable of providing security to *foreign* merchants – as long as they had

[281] Byrne (1916–17), 131; Tai (1996), 66 with n. 151; Lane (1963), esp. 189–91.
[282] Lopez (1987), 374.

incentives to do so. Such incentives increased as it became institutionally more possible to tax and borrow from foreign merchants as well as local ones. In the early medieval period, rulers had already begun to offer security guarantees to individual foreign merchants in return for taxes. From the late sixth century onwards, for instance, large-scale trading settlements developed along the coasts of England, Scandinavia and other parts of northern Europe:

> These ports, now commonly called *wics* (or *emporia*) were markets and centres for international exchange on the frontiers of kingdoms . . . Written sources . . . indicate that *wics* were located at places under the influence or control of kings and other rulers. *Wics* were actively involved in international trade and clearly on a scale implying much more than the provision of small luxuries for elites.[283]

Thus as early as *c.* 600, rulers were creating secure spaces for international trade to take place, not so much to provide an essential public good for the benefit of their subjects, but because 'controlling the activities of local and foreign merchants in the interests of collecting tolls, maintaining law and order, and gaining privileged access to imported goods was a central concern of medieval rulers'.[284]

By the tenth century, the larger-scale lords of western Europe had managed to eject the smaller-scale producers of coercion such as Viking raiding parties and were also bringing under control the small-scale robber barons – both groups that had limited early medieval rulers' ability to guarantee safe-conduct to foreign merchants outside small spheres such as the *wics* or *emporia*. This enabled later medieval rulers to offer more effective protection to foreign merchants, as shown by the issuing of many safe-conducts in the course of the eleventh century. These safe-conducts were sometimes specific to particular merchant guilds, but were also often granted impartially to *all* merchants visiting the fairs or towns of a particular ruler. An early eleventh-century chronicle, for instance, describes how the count of Flanders guaranteed safe-conduct to all merchants visiting the fair of Thorout. When a pack of knights nonetheless robbed a merchant on his way to the fair, the count captured the knights, imprisoned them, resisted pleas by their families to spare them and ultimately hanged them personally in a demonstrative display, ensuring that other potential small-scale producers of coercion would henceforth be deterred from robbing merchants travelling to his fairs – where, needless to relate, they paid taxes to the count.[285] The count of Champagne behaved in the same way in the twelfth century, as

---

[283] Middleton (2005), 313.   [284] *Ibid.*, 315.   [285] Nelson (1996), 38–9.

we have seen, issuing safe-conducts to all merchants visiting the Champagne fairs and threatening military measures against smaller-scale lords in surrounding territories who attacked traders travelling to or from the fairs – where the taxes they paid made him both wealthy and politically secure.[286] Foreign merchants visiting fairs abroad regarded the lord of the fair as the source of commercial security, as shown in 1127 when Lombard merchants attending the Ypres fair under the safe-conduct of the count of Flanders immediately departed for Italy when news reached the fair that the count had been murdered at Bruges.[287] By the eleventh century at latest, therefore, it was possible for a ruler to provide commercial security to foreign merchants, and at least some rulers were clearly motivated to do so.

Central and local political authorities – which were identical in important trading centres such as the north Italian city-states – also reached agreements with one another to provide commercial security against third-party threats. In 1169, for instance, it was not the Genoese merchant guild in Constantinople but the government of the Commune of Genoa that negotiated a commercial treaty with the Byzantine Emperor Manuel I, who guaranteed the restoration of any Genoese goods seized after shipwreck: 'My majesty will give satisfaction and restore these goods.'[288] Likewise, in 1238, when the Byzantine emperor began to threaten the security of Genoese and Venetian merchants trading in his territories, it was not the consuls of the Genoese and Venetian merchant guilds in Constantinople who took action, but the political authorities of the city-states themselves: the two city governments signed a treaty agreeing to intervene against pirates throughout the Mediterranean, with Venice taking responsibility for maritime order in the entire Aegean Sea, Genoa in the western basin of the Mediterranean, and joint surveillance by both states in the eastern part.[289]

Such developments make it clear that public-order institutions provided by the political authorities, not private-order institutions provided by merchants, were central to the provision of commercial security in the medieval Commercial Revolution. Where rulers developed more sophisticated mechanisms for taxing and borrowing from foreign merchants, they began to enjoy the same incentives to protect them as to protect local traders: the desire to keep the revenues flowing. In some cases rulers developed generalized institutional mechanisms for taxing and borrowing from *all* foreign merchants, while in others they favoured particularized institutional mechanisms for taxing and borrowing from specific

[286] Bautier (1952), 318.   [287] Laurent (1935b), 46.
[288] Quoted in Laiou (2001), 182.   [289] Balard (1966), 481.

merchant guilds. Where rulers failed to do one or the other, they responded to financial emergencies by expropriating foreign merchants and the merchants departed, guilds or no guilds. Both patterns – the generalized and the particularized – are observable, and there was no inevitable or teleological development over time.

A good illustration of these alternatives, which were available to European rulers from the earliest years of the medieval Commercial Revolution, is provided by the Champagne fairs. As we have seen, from the early twelfth century on the counts of Champagne carefully fostered the rise of this nearly permanent international market in their territory by guaranteeing security to all merchants, irrespective of guild or community affiliation. They succeeded spectacularly, as the Champagne fairs became the most important international trading node in western Europe. As we have seen, they achieved this without the involvement of merchant guilds, which did not establish themselves at the fairs before 1245 and never remotely encompassed all merchants there. Partly because the four Champagne fair-towns themselves lacked important communities of long-distance traders and did not develop powerful merchant guilds, the counts eschewed granting particularized privileges in their territories to merchant guilds in return for cash and loans, instead adopting the longer-term strategy of granting generalized privileges to all traders. The rich revenues from the success of the fairs then freed the counts from the necessity (or temptation) to grant privileges to local or alien merchant guilds.[290]

But in 1274, the last count of Champagne died without a male heir, and in 1285, Champagne and its fairs were annexed by King Philip IV of France, ambitious to centralize the French monarchy and expand its military and fiscal capacities. The tactics he used – war with Flanders, despoiling and excluding Flemish merchants, arresting and taxing Italian merchants, and barring exports of raw wool and undyed cloth – all affected security at the Champagne fairs within fifteen years of their coming under French governance.[291] The two most important groups of merchants that had made the Champagne fairs the pivot of European trade since the twelfth century were the Flemings who brought raw wool, textiles, hides and northern European raw materials, and the Italians, who brought spices and other Mediterranean and Levantine luxuries. In 1277, before Champagne became part of France, the French king had arrested all 'Lombard' (north Italian) merchants trading in France and

---

[290] See Chapin (1937) on how the revenues from the fairs enabled the counts of Champagne to avoid granting privileges to local merchants in the four fair-towns.
[291] Laurent (1935b), 116–18.

only released them after extorting heavy tax payments. By 1291, when the French king repeated this tactic, Champagne was part of France so the Italian merchants trading at the Champagne fairs were directly affected. The French authorities only freed Italian merchants and permitted them to continue trading in France (including Champagne) when they agreed to pay large sums as a sort of ransom to the royal exchequer.[292] Over the following years – in 1292, 1295, 1297, 1303 and 1311 – Italian merchants were repeatedly obliged to make substantial payments to the French crown as the price of being allowed to continue trading in French territory.[293] In response to protectionist lobbying by French textile guilds, the French crown also prohibited merchants from exporting raw wool and unfinished cloth from France between 1303 and 1315, and again between 1316 and 1360. These export restrictions helped to strangle the textile-oriented Champagne fairs by blocking those fairs' core merchandising activities – the transit trade in English wool and Flemish cloth via France.[294]

The French crown's tactics towards Flemish merchants, the other pivotal group at the Champagne fairs, were even more brutal. On 2 January 1297, at the opening of the Lagny fair (the first in the annual Champagne fair cycle), French royal officials arrested all Flemish merchants, confiscated their merchandise and sold it to profit the royal exchequer. Although Flemish merchants understandably stayed away from the later Champagne fairs of 1297, the French crown confiscated all the wares they had contracted to buy at those fairs, all letters of credit payable to them, and even the halls and hostels they owned in the fair-towns.[295] The losses of the Flemish town of Ypres as a result of these tactics was estimated at over 26,000 livres in that year alone.[296] Flemish merchants who were unable to make promised payments at the fairs because their goods had been confiscated were then penalized with a 'fair-ban', prohibiting them from visiting the fairs until they paid their debts.[297] Repeated resurgences of Franco-Flemish military conflicts, and the associated economic warfare against Flemish merchants by the French crown, deterred Flemish merchants from visiting the Champagne fairs into the early decades of the fourteenth century, and by 1315 the frontier between Flemish Flanders and French Flanders greatly hindered access to the Champagne fairs by Flemish merchants.[298] The French crown sought to replace the resulting lack of Flemish textiles at the fairs by granting special privileges to rival groups of Brabant merchants supplying similar

[292] *Ibid.*, 118.   [293] Strayer (1969), 115–17; Laurent (1935b), 119–20.
[294] Bourquelot (1865), I: 213–14.   [295] Laurent (1935b), 121–2.
[296] *Ibid.*, 122–3.   [297] *Ibid.*, 123.   [298] *Ibid.*, 123–6, 150.

merchandise, on condition that they did not act as illegal front men for Flemish merchants.[299]

But this was insufficient to reverse the decline of the Champagne fairs, from which the two largest and most important groups of merchants – the Flemings and the Italians – were now either altogether excluded or confronted with ever-increasing costs and risks. After *c.* 1300, Flemish and Italian merchants began to shift their mutual trade to Flemish cities, using the overland route through the Holy Roman empire or, after 1309, the maritime route, as Genoese and Venetian merchants started sending regular galley fleets through the Straits of Gibraltar and up the Atlantic coast to Bruges.[300] At the Champagne fairs, the move from generalized provision of security to all merchants under the counts of Champagne, to particularized provision of security to favoured 'nations' of merchants in return for exactions under the king of France, took place despite the existence of foreign merchant guilds and in the teeth of their protests.[301]

Bruges, by offering generalized commercial security to all merchants, replaced Champagne after *c.* 1300 as the new fulcrum of western European long-distance trade. Within Flanders, the gradual development of representative institutions, a tax-gathering bureaucracy and sophisticated financial instruments had begun to enable rulers to get more revenues out of foreign merchants through taxing and borrowing from them than through expropriating them. The gradual development of capital markets, in which rulers could borrow not only from their own local merchants but from foreign ones as well, created an incentive to provide protection to long-distance merchants as potential lenders. Bruges resembled the Champagne fair-towns in lacking significant guilds of indigenous long-distance merchants capable of lobbying for restrictions on foreign merchants. The local Bruges brokers' guild was powerful but usually could be satisfied with privileges over intermediation. Alien merchant guilds did exist in Bruges but, as we have seen, many foreign merchants traded there without guild privileges and other merchants only organized guilds generations after starting to trade in the city. Although the alien merchant guilds in Bruges did provide some fiscal support to the city government and the ruler, guild contributions were not central to the

---

[299] *Ibid.*, 135–8, 261.

[300] For persuasive arguments that the development of the sea route from Italy to Flanders was a response to, rather than a cause of, the decline of the Champagne fairs resulting from the economic warfare of the French crown against Flanders, see Laurent (1935b), 142–5. Munro (2001), 12, 20–1, concurs with this view but ascribes the decline of the fairs more broadly to the general resurgence of European warfare between the 1290s and the 1340s.

[301] On the vain attempts of Italian merchants in France to organize themselves into corporative organizations to resist French royal exactions, see Laurent (1935b), esp. 117–26.

tax system and guild loans were not central to public borrowing. Bruges became such a successful replacement for Champagne in so far as it provided an environment offering generalized security to all merchants rather than particularized security only to favoured merchant guilds.

Bruges also provides an excellent illustration of a second important institutional development that enhanced the security of international trade during the medieval Commercial Revolution – the growing sophistication of *local* government, particularly in towns. Many of the most vibrant international trading centres in medieval Europe were city-states in which the 'ruler' and the 'local government' were identical. In others, the local government was located much closer to where security problems actually arose for foreign merchants. Local levels of government, especially in cities, were in a position to recognize quite early in the medieval Commercial Revolution that they could benefit by guaranteeing the security of foreign merchants, and then taxing them or borrowing from them. Institutional developments aligning the interests of town governments with foreign as well as local merchants were a key component in enhancing the security of international trade, and emerged very early on. Again, this could take two forms – the particularized grant of security to specific merchant guilds in return for monetary or political support; or the generalized provision of security to all merchants, regardless of guild affiliation, in the interests of being able to tax trade in general. The generalized route required the development of representative institutions, fiscal systems and public finance, aligning governments' incentives with those of the wider commercial economy rather than merely those of specific interest-groups. As the fiscal benefits of the presence of international traders became more clearly recognized, particularly in the fiscally sophisticated urban centres of the Low Countries, cities such as Bruges sought deliberately to attract foreign merchants not so much by offering them guild-specific security privileges, but by guaranteeing them generalized protection, including against the aggressive practices of local guilds, and even protection from the obligation to form alien merchant guilds of their own.[302]

In Flanders more widely, there were relatively few important groups of long-distance merchants after the Flemings withdrew from the Champagne fairs around 1300. One result was that Flemish cities depended heavily on visiting foreign merchants and were willing to provide generalized guarantees of security. In 1380, for instance, when Count Ludwig of Flanders removed his protection from all foreigners and ordered them to

---

[302] Gelderblom (2005a), 26–8 with nn. 154–5; Coornaert (1961), II: 23–7; Harreld (2004a), 5–6.

leave the country, the town governments of Ghent, Ypres and Bruges persuaded many foreign merchants to remain by issuing formal promises to
protect them and to respect their privileges.[303] Antwerp, which replaced
Bruges as the fulcrum of north-west European trade in the fifteenth
century, did so by offering generalized security to all merchants and
not requiring them to form alien merchant guilds. Amsterdam, which
in turn replaced Antwerp in the sixteenth century, did not even permit
the formation of local or alien merchant guilds, and provided commercial security undifferentiatedly to individual merchants regardless of their
place of origin – just as the counts of Champagne had done in the twelfth
and most of the thirteenth century.

Even in the north Italian city-states, with significant groups of their
own long-distance traders, the medieval period saw local governments
gradually taking steps to guarantee security to foreign merchants. In
1296, for instance, Genoa established a special tribunal called the *Officium Robarie* to receive complaints by foreigners against acts of piracy
committed by Genoese citizens outside the territory of the commune.
Although some foreigners were dissatisfied with the judgements of this
tribunal, others – including Venetians, traditionally enemies of Genoa –
obtained significant redress.[304] The court functioned sufficiently neu-
trally to attract the objections of a French archbishop of Persia in 1328,
who regarded it as preventing religiously justified attacks by Christians
against Muslim shipping.[305] Furthermore, when the operations of the
tribunal were temporarily suspended in 1331–5 during the war between
Genoa and Catalonia, the Venetians immediately expressed consterna-
tion, an indication of the effectiveness of the bureau in the preceding
period.[306] Although responsibility for adjudicating cases of piracy later
moved into the remit of the doge's office, whose judgements were influenced by political considerations, nonetheless the establishment of the
Officium Robarie was an important judicial innovation indicating the
readiness of the city-state to provide security to foreign merchants, even
ones subject to Genoese writs of reprisal.[307]

The claim that merchant guilds were the efficient solution for providing commercial security is based on the theoretical assumption that there
was no alternative – that rulers and governments were unable and unwilling to provide security for long-distance traders. The evidence does not

---

[303] Henn (1999), 141 n. 119.
[304] On some cases in which the tribunal did not satisfy foreign merchants, see Kedar
(1985); Catoni (1974). On the redress provided to a number of Venetian and Sicilian
merchants, see Tai (1996), 430–1.
[305] Lopez (1958), 509; Mas-Latrie (1892), esp. 267–9; Tai (1996), 427.
[306] Tai (1996), 431–2.   [307] See *ibid.*, 449–50, 489–90, 494–5, 556.

bear out this assumption. Alternative institutions were available. Territorial rulers and town governments were able to provide security guarantees both to their own long-distance merchants and to foreign traders, and can be observed doing so from the beginning of the medieval Commercial Revolution. Admittedly, they followed two distinct strategies in doing this. One was the particularized strategy, whereby rulers issued security guarantees to specific merchant guilds in return for favours. The other, however, was a generalized strategy whereby a ruler guaranteed security to all traders, regardless of their ability to gain membership in guilds.

Both strategies involved the provision of security by public-order institutions such as princely or urban governments, not by corporative organizations such as guilds. Thus even the particularized component of medieval commercial security, the one that involved merchant guilds, fundamentally relied on the capacity and willingness of public-order institutions to provide the actual security. Moreover, from the very beginning of the medieval Commercial Revolution, there was always a nontrivial component of commercial security that was generalized – that was provided to all merchants independent of their guild affiliation or any intervention on the part of any merchant guild. The problem with the particularized strategy, whereby a ruler provided security differentially to merchant guilds depending on the benefits he thought he could extract from them, was that it could go badly wrong from the point of view of the economy at large, if the ruler decided that his short-term ends were better served by granting unusually good security to some merchant guilds while expropriating others. This is what happened when the Champagne fairs came under the regime of the kings of France, who were powerful enough to be able to shift from a generalized to a particularized security strategy and faced sufficiently serious military and fiscal crises that they found it hard to resist the temptation to do so.

In most European polities, the generalized and particularized strategies coexisted for centuries. Medieval rulers observably shifted back and forth between the two strategies according to changing circumstances. It was not until around 1500 that the changes discussed in Chapter 5 tipped rulers in a few European polities definitively away from particularized to generalized solutions, both to their own fiscal problems and to the provision of security for long-distance trade.

6.4   Conclusion

Commercial security was undeniably a problem for long-distance trade in medieval and early modern Europe. But this chapter has shown that merchant guilds were not the solution to this problem. Efficiency theories focus exclusively on the ways in which merchant guilds could, in theory, have enhanced commercial security by providing it as a club good or pressing rulers to provide it as a public good. But security infrastructure such as convoys, fortifications and military defence was organized by other institutional mechanisms, rulers issued security guarantees to non-guilded merchants, and guild embargoes were undertaken as a negotiating strategy in pursuit of general commercial privileges, not primarily to get security guarantees. In so far as merchant guilds did enhance security, they did so exclusively for their own members, not for the economy in general. The enhancements to security which merchant guilds might have generated in theory turn out to have been minor in practice.

Moreover, merchant guilds also harmed commercial security. They pressed their city governments to attack the trade of rival merchants, they employed corsairs to do so and they even directly organized predatory expeditions. Merchant guild monopolies kept supplies low and prices high, creating a demand for the services of unlicensed traders who, because guilds pushed them into the black market, often used violence to enforce contracts or engaged in piracy when excluded from legal trade. Merchant guilds also directly attacked outside traders as interlopers against their privileges. Merchant guild privileges created the incentive for rival guilds to attack each other, creating general commercial insecurity. Rivalry between different merchant guilds sometimes provoked open warfare between their home polities, creating commercial insecurity which spilled over onto third parties. The empirical findings thus suggest that merchant guilds enhanced security in relatively minor ways but reduced it in major ones. In so far as they *increased* security, they did so only for their own members. In so far as they *reduced* security, they did so for the economy at large.

Merchant guilds can only have been an efficient institution for ensuring commercial security if alternative institutions were not available. This assumption underlies all the theoretical models which purport to demonstrate that merchant guilds were efficient. But it is not borne out by the facts. From the beginning of the medieval Commercial Revolution, alternative institutional mechanisms existed which were capable of providing commercial security. Both princely states and local urban governments can be observed providing generalized security to all merchants, at least in some times and places, from the early Commercial Revolution onwards. It is thus inaccurate to claim that prior to the emergence of the modern nation-state, rulers were *unable* to provide commercial security to long-distance merchants. It is true to say that medieval (and early modern) rulers were not always *motivated* to do so. Rulers generally only incurred the costs of providing commercial security if they perceived some benefit to themselves, whether fiscal or political.

There were two main institutional pathways whereby the interests of rulers could be more closely aligned with those of long-distance merchants – the particularized path of providing security to privileged merchant guilds in return for favours; and the generalized path of providing security to all traders in the expectation of being able to tax an expanding trade. Both alternatives were feasible from the beginning of the medieval Commercial Revolution. Nor was there an inevitable progression from particularized to generalized security-provision in the course of the medieval period, as shown by the shift in the opposite direction at the Champagne fairs in the late thirteenth century. Rather, the political economy of different European societies caused their rulers to choose different options in providing security to merchants – neglecting the whole issue, preying on merchants themselves, granting particularized security to merchant guilds and granting generalized security to traders at large. Each polity chose a different combination of these strategies.

However, as we saw in Chapter 5, after c. 1500 certain European polities – beginning with the Low Countries and England – developed representative institutions, tax-gathering bureaucracies, public finance and inter-urban competition to the point where the political authorities more consistently chose to provide commercial security generally to all traders than particularistically in return for favours from merchant guilds. At no point during the medieval Commercial Revolution did merchant guilds *themselves* constitute the efficient institution for providing commercial security. Security was always provided publicly rather than corporatively to an overwhelming degree. The key change was not from private-order security to state security, but from particularized state security to generalized state security. Long-distance trade appears to have expanded more successfully in those periods and locations where the public authorities provided security in a generalized way to the whole economy rather than in a particularized way to privileged merchant guilds.

But this development was neither rapid, nor uniform, nor inevitable. International trading centres such as the Champagne fairs, which provided generalized security in one era, could revert to a more particularized provision of security under a later ruler. Rulers of European polities where representative institutions were weak or dominated by a single merchant oligarchy often preferred to solve fiscal and political challenges by providing particularized security to merchant guilds rather than generalized security to all long-distance traders. The corporatist–absolutist European polities of the post-1500 era, as discussed in Chapter 5, continued to grant particularistic guarantees of security to merchant guilds well into the early modern period. Although this strategy provided a stream of benefits to rulers and guilded merchants, it reduced the generalized security that could have encouraged trade to grow faster. It was only in a few European polities that generalized provision of commercial security gradually became the dominant form after *c.* 1500, and remained that way, resulting in the gradual decline of merchant guilds. The evidence on how security was provided for long-distance traders during the medieval Commercial Revolution thus provides no support for the view that the monopoly rents generated by merchant guilds were a price worth paying in return for positive externalities in the sphere of security.

7 Contract enforcement

> One must take good account of the types of people one deals with, or to
> whom one entrusts one's goods, for no man is trustworthy with money.
> (Advice to merchants by an anonymous Florentine, mid-fourteenth
> century)[1]

> A good merchant does not show his talents by selling good products,
> which everyone can do, but precisely by succeeding in getting rid of
> merchandise of poor quality.
> (Francesco Bartolomaei, Sienese merchant in Candia (Crete), to Pignol
> Zucchello, Pisan merchant in Venice, mid-fourteenth century)[2]

When we trade, we transfer property rights to another person. To do this,
we make a contract. Unless it is a spot trade – i.e. good and payment are
exchanged simultaneously – reneging is possible. The seller may take the
payment and not give the good, or the buyer take the good and not pay.
So contracts need to be enforced. If they are not, people will not trade,
even though exchange could profit both them and the wider economy.

Contract-enforcement problems exist everywhere, but are particularly
acute in trade across long distances or political frontiers. To solve them,
merchants use institutions – formal and informal – to reduce the probability that their trading partners will renege on agreements. Merchant
guilds are supposed to have been such institutions. Indeed, some scholars argue that the merchant guild was the *efficient* international contract-
enforcement institution – that it provided enforcement unavailable from
other sources.

That merchant guilds *existed* because they were efficient institutions
to enforce contracts in international trade can be rejected on the same
grounds as the idea, examined in Chapter 6, that they existed to ensure
security in such trade. Most merchants and most merchant guilds were
local. Local merchant guilds both pre-dated and vastly outnumbered
alien merchant guilds, which were in any case just foreign branches of
local guilds. Merchant guilds cannot have existed to enforce contracts

---

[1] Quoted in Molho (1969), 54.　　[2] Quoted in Romano (1960), 396.

in international trade, therefore, because most merchants and most merchant guilds were not involved in such trade. But although merchant guilds must have existed for other reasons – which Chapter 5 discussed – they might still incidentally have benefited the economy by helping traders enforce contracts.

Merchant guilds are supposed to have ensured contract enforcement in three ways – guild jurisdictions, peer pressure and collective reprisals. Guild jurisdictions operated formally: merchant guilds established their own tribunals which, it is argued, worked better than public law-courts. Peer pressure operated informally, through the social capital of closely knit, multi-stranded ties among guild members: when a merchant defaulted on a contract, his fellows penalized him for bringing discredit on the guild. Collective reprisals operated quasi-formally: the entire community of a defaulting merchant was penalized for his actions, creating an incentive for guilds to use informal peer pressure against members who broke contracts.

Guild jurisdictions, peer pressure and collective reprisals certainly existed, as we shall see. But how important were they, and how effective? Did pre-modern European societies lack other means of enforcing trade contracts, making merchant guilds the efficient institutions for doing so? Did merchant guilds' contract-enforcing activities create benefits for the economy that compensated for the harm caused by their monopolies?

7.1   Guild jurisdictions

A first way merchant guilds are thought to have improved contract enforcement was through guild courts. Local merchant guilds often established internal tribunals, and alien merchant guilds often secured privileges entitling them to operate consular courts with jurisdiction over guild members – and sometimes all expatriates – in international trading centres. Merchants attending trade fairs often came under the jurisdiction of 'fair-courts', some managed by merchant guilds, though many by municipal magistrates or the fair authorities.

7.1.1   Advantages theoretically offered by guild courts

Guild courts had greater commercial expertise than public courts, it is claimed, because they were manned by professional merchants better able to judge business matters than judges appointed by princes, nobles, clergy or even towns. Nitzsch, for instance, claims that the rise of merchant guilds in the twelfth century secured long-distance traders 'more appropriate treatment with greater business acumen than the local communities and their courts were willing or able to provide'.[3] Milgrom, North and Weingast contend that merchant courts at trade fairs developed a body of commercial law called the *lex mercatoria* ('law merchant' or 'merchant law') which offered more expert judgements than public legal systems.[4] Benson argues that

Merchant court judges were always merchants chosen from the relevant merchant community (fair or market). It was widely recognized that lawyers were not suitable judges in commercial matters... [They] lacked knowledge of commercial custom and practice... [and] tended to be preoccupied with strict rules that involved formalities which often hindered commerce.[5]

Guild courts, it is argued, also benefited from superior information. Guild adjudicators were already acquainted with the disputants through shared guild membership. So they could mobilize information within the social network of the guild to provide high-quality contract enforcement. Merchant courts at trade fairs, according to Milgrom, North and Weingast, extended the reach of private reputation mechanisms by conveying information on past behaviour between traders who otherwise had no way to get information about one another.[6]

Guild judges also shared the values of litigants, it is claimed, providing 'sympathetic courts to hear commercial disputes' and helping merchants circumvent the 'legalism and obstruction' of the public legal system.[7] According to this view, the non-commercial social origins of judges in princely, municipal, seigneurial or ecclesiastical courts made them unsympathetic to merchants, which led them to impose procedural obstacles or issue punitive judgements in commercial disputes. Judges in guild courts, by contrast, were themselves merchants who would render better judgements because of professional empathy with litigants.

Finally, guild courts are supposed to have offered culturally specific legal services, enabling foreign merchants to enforce contracts according to the laws and customs of their homeland.[8] As late as the eighteenth century, some scholars argue, international traders needed to solve disputes 'without having recourse to the justice of places where their manners and customs, as well as their real interests, were ignored'.[9] Guild courts are also supposed to have reduced foreign merchants' transaction costs by conducting proceedings in the disputants' native tongue, whereas local courts used the local language.[10] Finally, it is claimed, guild courts freed

---

[3] Nitzsch (1892), 9.   [4] Milgrom, North and Weingast (1990).
[5] Benson (1989), 650.   [6] Milgrom, North and Weingast (1990).
[7] Woodward (2005), 633.   [8] Grafe and Gelderblom (2010a), 485.
[9] Mézin (2006), 37.   [10] Gelderblom (2005b), 13, 15.

long-distance merchants from inappropriate or unjust intervention by foreign rulers.

7.1.2   How universal were merchant guild courts?

Does the historical evidence support these theories? Guild courts certainly existed in medieval and early modern Europe. Some – though not all – local merchant guilds established their own courts, a few of which even survived into the early modern period, as in the case of the consulado courts of Barcelona, Burgos and Bilbao.[11] Some – though not all – alien merchant guilds also set up consular courts in international trading centres.[12] And some – though not all – periodic trade fairs also had special fair-courts: although not all fair-courts were operated by merchants, some were, and others took advice from merchant experts.[13]

But many merchant guilds did *not* have their own courts, which casts doubt on the idea that guild tribunals were the efficient solution to commercial contract enforcement. Certainly, many *local* merchant guilds did not enjoy their own jurisdictions, or obtained them only in the late medieval or early modern period – as with the Burgos and Bilbao consulados which only got judicial privileges after 1469,[14] or the Toulouse and Paris merchant guilds which existed for centuries before they got their own courts in 1549 and 1563 respectively.[15] Nor did merchants trading abroad always have their own guild courts. Indeed, as Chapter 6 discussed, international merchants did not always even have guilds: many long-distance merchants traded without guilds in twelfth- and thirteenth-century Champagne, in fourteenth- and fifteenth-century Bruges and Antwerp, in the medieval Levant and in medieval France. These long-distance traders could not have relied on guild jurisdictions because they had no guilds. Yet they evidently managed to enforce their contracts, which means that other institutions were available and effective.

Even when merchants did form guilds abroad, they did not always obtain autonomous jurisdictions. In Venice from 1228 on, German merchants traded from their community hostel (the Fondaco dei Tedeschi) and possessed their own merchant consuls, but never had an autonomous jurisdiction: even private conflicts among German merchants were decided by Venetian magistrates.[16] In medieval Antwerp, although some

---

[11] Woodward (2005), 633–4; Kagan (1981), 221.

[12] Chaudhuri (1991), 436; Tai (1996), 121 with n. 146; Gelderblom (2005b), 13–15, 48 n. 83; R. De Roover (1948a), 18; W. D. Phillips (1986), 34; Burckhardt (2005), 75; Nicholas (1979), 24; Molnár (2007), 77.

[13] Moore (1985), 95–105, 297–302; Milgrom, North and Weingast (1990).

[14] Woodward (2005), 633–4.   [15] *Ibid.*, 632.   [16] Simonsfeld (1887), 37.

Italian merchants did form guilds, these had little power to regulate their commercial affairs.[17] Merchants from Venice, Lucca, the Netherlands and Scandinavia never sought permission to operate their own courts in Antwerp.[18] The Castilian merchant guild applied for a consular court in Antwerp in 1551 but its petition was rejected.[19] Amsterdam absolutely refused to permit any merchant guild courts, in 1413 ordering disputes between foreigners to be resolved by the municipal court, which was empowered to apply maritime law in conflicts involving seaborne trade.[20]

In the medieval Levant, as we have seen, not all western European merchants had guilds. Those alien merchant guilds that existed often obtained the right to judge civil conflicts among their members, but matters that were more serious or involved outsiders had to come before the Muslim authorities.[21] In Northern Africa, European merchant guilds obtained recognition of the principle that 'litigation between two men belonging to different nations was brought before a tribunal of the defendant's nation'. But in the Levant, cases between Italian merchants and Muslims had to be brought before Muslim courts even when the Italian was the defendant, with the only concession being that religiously mixed cases were judged by secular rather than Islamic judges.[22]

Many alien merchant guilds that got their own jurisdictions only did so in the late medieval period, long after state and municipal courts were offering reliable contract enforcement (as we shall see shortly). Venetian merchants were trading in Thessaloniki from the 1180s on, but not until the 1270s did they have a Venetian consul with (possible) jurisdictional powers.[23] German Hanseatic merchants began trading in Bruges around 1200, 'protected only by the common law'.[24] They obtained their first guild privileges in 1252–3, but were explicitly denied a guild jurisdiction until 1359.[25] In fact, Bruges permitted no foreign merchant guild jurisdictions until 1330, when the Aragonese merchants obtained a tribunal, which also had jurisdiction over Castilians until they got an independent jurisdiction in 1443.[26] A Venetian merchant 'nation' sought commercial privileges in Bruges in 1332, and secured them in 1358, but these did not yet include its own jurisdiction.[27] Florentine merchants were active in Bruges at latest from the 1280s, but it was the 1420s before they set up

---

[17] Harreld (2004b), 21.   [18] Harreld (2004a), 58–9; Goris (1925), 70–80.
[19] Goris (1925), 59, 63–6.   [20] Gelderblom (2005b), 18, 50 nn. 119–21.
[21] Constable (2003), 116, 136, 153, 210, 226–7, 327.
[22] Ashtor (1983), 412–13 (quotation 412).   [23] D. Jacoby (2003), 92, 98.
[24] Paravicini (1992), 100 (quotation), 102.
[25] Gelderblom (2005b), 13; Paravicini (1992), 100, 102.
[26] Gelderblom (2005b), 48 n. 83.   [27] Henn (1999), 133–4.

a formal association whose consuls had civil jurisdiction over members.[28] The Lucca merchant guild in Bruges did not get its own jurisdiction until quite a late date, and even then the evidence is ambiguous.[29] Scottish merchants were active in Bruges from the later twelfth century, but did not obtain a guild jurisdiction until 1407.[30] Portuguese merchants had commercial links to Flanders from the twelfth century, and were among the largest foreign merchant groups in Bruges in the 1360s, but obtained their own guild jurisdiction only in 1411.[31]

Many international trade fairs also flourished without guild courts. Some argue that the Champagne fairs, for instance, relied on consular merchant courts. Greif, for instance, claims that 'the authorities at the fairs . . . relinquished legal rights over the merchants once they were there. An individual was subject to the laws of his community – represented by a consul – not the laws of the locality in which a fair was held.'[32] But these claims are not supported by the evidence. Merchants from a wide array of different European cities and territories were frequenting the Champagne fairs by the 1180s at latest, and for the next sixty years all visiting merchants were subject to the public legal system – princely, municipal and ecclesiastical – prevailing at the fairs. It was not until 1245 that the count of Champagne issued a charter exempting Roman, Tuscan, Lombard and Provençal merchants from interference by his lower officials but replacing it with his own direct jurisdiction; he did not relinquish legal rights over them.[33] Around the same time, particular groups of Italian and Provençal merchants frequenting the fairs began to appoint consuls, some of whom gradually developed jurisdictional powers. The first reference to any foreign merchant consul at the Champagne fairs was for the Sienese in 1246.[34] Consuls for another fifteen Italian cities at the Champagne fairs were mentioned in the course of the second half of the thirteenth century.[35] From 1278 dates the first reference to a *universitas* (joint association) of Italian merchants at the fairs.[36] The year 1246 also saw the first reference to a consul from Montpellier, who initially had jurisdiction only over merchants from that city. A document of 1258 indicates that the Montpellier consul was extending his jurisdiction to merchants from other Provençal towns trading at the Champagne fairs,

---

[28] Mallett (1959), 156–8; Henn (1999), 135–6.
[29] R. De Roover (1948a), 18.   [30] Henn (1999), 139.
[31] J. M. Murray (2004), 96–7; Gelderblom (2005b), 48 n. 83.
[32] Greif (2006b), 227.   [33] Bourquelot (1865), I: 174.   [34] Bautier (1953), 126.
[35] *Ibid.* claims that 'already prior to the mid-13th century . . . the Italians had installed a consulate for each of their trading colonies at the fairs', but on p. 127 n. 3 more accurately states that fifteen other Italian cities record consuls in the *second* half of the thirteenth century.
[36] Bautier (1953), 130.

and one from 1290 provides a list of Provençal towns whose members formed a *universitas* under a *capitaneus* (captain) who exercised jurisdiction over them.[37] From 1258, there is also a lone reference to an organization of Aragonese merchants frequenting the fairs, although no evidence that it exercised jurisdiction.[38] But these merchant jurisdictions only applied to conflicts within that particular community of merchants, so they could not serve the requirements of trade between merchants of different communities. Moreover, they did not exempt their members from the public legal system in the form of the count's jurisdiction.

Merchants from other European territories – including important groups such as the Flemish – did not have consular organizations at the Champagne fairs, as we saw in Chapter 6.[39] The Flemish urban federation known as the 'Seventeen Towns', mentioned in a handful of documents relating to the Champagne fairs, is a shadowy organization whose membership and activities are largely unknown but scholars agree that it did not have any autonomous jurisdiction at the fairs.[40] German merchants frequented the fairs in the second half of the thirteenth century, but were not recognized as a community until 1294, and even then with no jurisdiction.[41] The most detailed study of the nationalities frequenting the fairs lists merchants from many parts of France (until 1285 territorially distinct from Champagne), Flanders, Brabant, Hainaut, Germany, Savoy, Switzerland, England, Scotland and even Sweden – none of them with consuls or community jurisdictions.[42]

Contract enforcement among all foreign merchants frequenting the Champagne fairs between *c*. 1180 and 1245, and among merchants of different communities even after that date, was provided by the public legal system – the princely courts of the counts of Champagne, the ecclesiastical courts of local religious houses and the municipal courts of the fair-towns.[43] By the 1220s, contract enforcement was being buttressed by the princely fair-wardens, who had hitherto exercised a primarily regulatory role but now began to hear broader merchant complaints,

[37] Bourquelot (1865), I: 151, 154 n. 9, 174; Bautier (1953), 132.
[38] Bautier (1953), 130.   [39] *Ibid.*, 128.
[40] Laurent (1935a), 86–95; Bautier (1953), 128–30; Carolus-Barré (1965), 26–7.
[41] Bourquelot (1865), I: 199–201; Schönfelder (1988), 21.
[42] Bourquelot (1865), I: 139–40, 145, 155–9, 168, 196–204, II: 24–5, 211–29.
[43] Alengry (1915), 48, 66, 68, 108, 110, 113–14, 116–17; Arbois de Jubainville (1859), 4–30; Arbois de Jubainville and Pigeotte (1859–66), III: 155–70, 235–6, 367, VI: 104; Bassermann (1911), 3–5, 26–9, 57–8; Bautier (1953), 118–20, 122–4; Berti (1857), 256–7; Bourquelot (1839–40), I: 117–19, 210, 409, II: 20 n. 1, 24–5, 210, 409, 416; Bourquelot (1865), I: 137, 151, 154, 164–5, 174, 182ff., II: 19–20, 24–5, 196; Boutaric (1867), I: 252, II: 440, 551; Chapin (1937), 126–30; Davidsohn (1896–1901), 8–9; Goldschmidt (1891), 229–30, 233; Verlinden (1965), 128, 131–2.

witness business deals, enforce mercantile contracts, collect fines,
imprison debtors and punish fraud.[44] From *c.* 1260 to *c.*
1320, the fair-wardens' court was an important tribunal, employing not just the
wardens themselves, but their lieutenants, clerks and as many as 140
sergeants to implement its decisions – all as employees of the prince.[45]
The Champagne fairs flourished, therefore, by virtue of contract enforcement provided by princely, ecclesiastical and municipal courts, supplemented in its final phase by a dedicated fair-court operated by princely
officials. There is no evidence of merchant judges operating in any of
these public tribunals. Long-distance trade among foreign merchants at
the Champagne fairs cannot have relied on guild courts, which did not
exist there until 1245, were not universal even after that date and could
not judge conflicts involving outsiders in any case.

Similar findings emerge for the fairs of Skåne (Scania), at which merchants from many northern European lands traded for herring between
c. 1200 and *c.* 1500. The thirteenth-century Skåne fairs were governed
by the so-called *Scanoerlogh* ('Scania Law') or *môtbôk*, a law code issued
by the Danish kings covering peacekeeping, market regulation, licensing
of fishermen and merchants, and justice over assault, homicide, fraud
and misappropriation of funds, with power to fine, imprison and execute. Merchant guild courts only gradually supplanted the royal Scania
Law and even the Hanse merchants did not obtain general privileges of
jurisdiction at the fairs until 1352.[46]

Other early trade fairs had no fair-courts at all, relying instead on
the local justice system. At the Bruges fairs starting in the twelfth century, commercial conflicts between visiting merchants were referred to
the local municipal court.[47] Likewise, the fairs of Bergen-op-Zoom
and Antwerp had no autonomous fair-courts; visiting merchants were
referred to special sittings of the local justices.[48] Fairs were established in
the northern Netherlands – especially Holland and Zeeland – from the
early thirteenth century on, but with no sign of special fair-courts: conflicts involving visitors to the fairs were resolved by the ordinary municipal tribunals, sometimes in special sittings or using swift procedures to
accommodate the needs of travelling merchants.[49]

The fact that merchant courts were not universal, and that from *c.* 1100
at latest princely, municipal and ecclesiastical tribunals were offering
contract enforcement good enough to attract long-distance merchants,

---

[44] Verlinden (1965), 131.   [45] *Ibid.*, 127.   [46] Christensen (1953), 246, 258–61.
[47] Van Houtte (1953), 201–2; Gelderblom (2005b), 12.
[48] See 'Deuxième keure de Bruges, 25 May 1281', in Gilliodts-van Severen (1874–5),
I: 249.
[49] Feenstra (1953), 220 n. 3, 230–1.

provides further evidence that independent merchant jurisdictions did
not offer a calibre of contract enforcement unavailable from other institutions. It might be argued that merchant guild courts were essential
in places lacking good legal institutions – but these apparently did not
include important trading centres such as Champagne, Skåne, Bergen-
op-Zoom, Bruges and Antwerp. That is, the most successful international
trading centres of the medieval Commercial Revolution were ones that
did not rely on merchant tribunals, but rather on law-courts provided by
the public authorities, either specifically to visiting merchants or more
generally to all economic agents in that locality.

7.1.3   Were guild courts independent?

How autonomous were merchant guild courts? Some scholars portray
them as autonomous, private-order institutions operating independently
of government. Milgrom, North and Weingast, for instance, claim that
fair-courts operated 'without the benefit of state enforcement of contracts', since public courts of the time were unable to 'seize the property
of individuals who resisted paying judgments, or put them into jail'.[50]
Benson claims that in order to 'steer clear of unnecessary litigation,
delays, and other disruptions of commerce', merchant guild courts forbade appeals to public courts.[51] A closer look at the evidence shows that
this picture is inaccurate. Merchant courts – whether operated by local
merchant guilds, alien merchant guilds or merchant consuls at fairs – were
established through licences granted by the public authorities, often on
public initiative, and sometimes even manned by public officials.

Local merchant guild courts enjoyed jurisdiction only in so far as it was
granted by the public authorities. Thus as early as 1020, the merchant
guild of Tiel was judging conflicts among its members because 'this is
permitted and established by an imperial charter'.[52] In 1254, the Reading
merchant guild acknowledged that its right to exercise jurisdiction in the
guildhall was subject to oversight by the abbot of Reading as the local
representative of the crown.[53] In Barcelona, the merchant consulado
took on jurisdiction over local merchant conflicts in 1257 only by virtue
of powers entrusted to it by the public authorities.[54]

The consular courts of alien merchant guilds and hanses also depended
on grants of jurisdiction by the public authorities, both those in the

---

[50] Milgrom, North and Weingast (1990), 20–1.
[51] Benson (2002), 130; also Benson (1989), 650.   [52] Pertz (1925), IV: 118.
[53] Florilegium Urbanum, in Alsford (2003), www.trytel.com/~tristan/towns/florilegium/
government/gvpoli19.html.
[54] Woodward (2005), 633.

mother city and those in foreign trading centres. In medieval Barcelona, it was the town council that 'appointed consuls in the foreign ports with which Barcelona traded who could govern, judge, and punish all the subjects of the Crown of Aragon who resided in those ports', retaining ultimate decision-making power even after devolving many functions to the merchant consulado in 1257.[55] The colony of Catalan merchants in Constantinople appointed a consul in 1281 from among their number, but had to get the approval of King Peter III of Aragon to do so.[56] The consuls with jurisdiction over Venetian merchants in Thessaloniki from the 1270s on were elected by the Venetian government; when the consul fell ill and returned to Venice in 1289, the Venetian merchant community in Thessaloniki was empowered to elect a consul from among their number 'as an emergency measure', but only until the home government could appoint a new consul in the normal way.[57] In medieval Bruges, any judgements or penalties decided upon by the consuls of the Lucca merchant guild had to be officially notified to the government of Lucca.[58] The Scottish consular court in Bruges was presided over by a judge who was not even a member of the Scottish merchant community, but rather a high official of the city of Bruges.[59]

At fairs, too, merchant courts typically operated through grants of jurisdiction from the municipal, seigneurial, ecclesiastical or princely authorities operating the fair. At the Champagne fairs, as already discussed, the fair-courts were operated by princely officials, not merchants; consuls and 'captains' exercised jurisdiction over Italian and Provençal merchants, but were appointed by authority of their home governments and only enjoyed jurisdiction over their members at the fairs by virtue of privileges issued by the counts of Champagne.[60] The thirteenth-century fair of St Ives, the earliest and best documented in England, had a fair-court, but its officials were appointed by the fair authorities (the abbot of Ramsey), supported in turn by a royal grant of jurisdiction; the abbey of Ramsey routinely summoned litigants, conducted prosecutions, distrained defendants, seized goods, collected damages, assessed fines and incarcerated lawbreakers.[61] The Skåne herring fairs, as we have seen, operated for their first century or so under a princely fair-court, after which the German Hanse got general rights of jurisdiction in 1352, but only through privileges from the Danish crown.[62] Merchant courts typically operated only by virtue of subordinate jurisdiction granted by the public authorities.

[55] *Ibid.*   [56] D. Jacoby (2003), 117.   [57] *Ibid.*, 98–9 (quotation 98), 100 n. 97.
[58] Mirot (1927), 66.   [59] Gelderblom (2005b), 48 n. 83; Henn (1999), 139.
[60] Bourquelot (1865), I: 151–6, 170–5.   [61] Sachs (2006), 699–703, 726–7.
[62] Christensen (1953), 261.

Merchant courts were also subordinated in the sense that they envisaged appeals to public courts. At the Champagne fairs, the consuls appointed by some individual Italian and Provençal towns had a limited jurisdiction: they could impose penalties only up to a certain sum, their decisions had to be confirmed by the princely fair-wardens and litigants could appeal against consular judgements to the municipal jurisdiction back home.[63] The captains of the two *universitas* formed by the Provençal and Italian merchants were granted jurisdiction over their members by the counts of Champagne from *c.* 1278 on, but implementation of consular judgements at the fairs themselves was the remit of the princely fair-wardens and required the support of those consuls' town governments back home.[64] At the St Ives fair between 1270 and 1324, litigants appealed beyond the fair-court to the royal courts in London.[65] The Italian merchant consuls in Nîmes enjoyed rights of jurisdiction after 1277, but only via privileges granted by the French king which reserved rights of intervention by the municipal court of Nîmes and the royal justice system.[66] In Catalonia, merchant consulados enjoyed jurisdiction after 1286 but only by virtue of royal privileges reserving civil appeals and all criminal cases for the royal courts.[67] In the Venetian merchant colony at Tana on the Black Sea, jurisdiction over commercial disputes was exercised in 1333 jointly by the consul and the local Mongol governor.[68] In medieval Bruges, the alien consular courts of Lucca, Spain and Portugal explicitly provided for appeals to the municipal courts of Bruges: the charter of the Lucca merchant guild, for instance, stated explicitly that the consul 'had disciplinary power over the Lucchese, but only in so far as his measures did not violate the sovereign rights of the count of Flanders nor conflict with the decisions of the *Loya di Bruggia*, that is, the municipal government'.[69]

The revealed preference of individual merchants casts doubt on the idea that guild courts provided better contract enforcement than the public justice system. Not only did many foreign merchants neither seek nor obtain guild jurisdictions, but even when merchants did use their guild courts, it was often because they were forced to do so. The 1397 maritime statute of Ancona, for instance, threatened a fine of 50 pounds against any Anconitan merchant bringing a dispute to an outside tribunal.[70] The

[63] Bassermann (1911), 4–6; Goldschmidt (1891), 196 with n. 177; Bourquelot (1865), I: 168, II: 258–72.

[64] Bassermann (1911), 4–6, 56–7; Goldschmidt (1891), 200 with nn. 192–3.

[65] Sachs (2006), 699–703, 726–7.   [66] Germain (1861), 124.

[67] Kadens (2004), 53.   [68] Di Cosmo (2005), 411.

[69] R. De Roover (1948a), 18 (quotation); Gilliodts-van Severen (1874–5), II:117.

[70] Liu (1925), ch. 1, section III.

statutes of the Florentine merchant guild in medieval London obliged all Florentines in England to resolve their disputes before the consular court, on pain of being heavily fined.[71] The Venetian merchant guild and the Hanse Kontor in Bruges had to compel their members to bring cases to their consular courts by threatening boycott or expulsion for any member who litigated in the Bruges municipal courts.[72] In the fifteenth century, Ragusa (Dubrovnik) forbade members of its merchant guilds in Balkan trading centres from taking disputes to the Turkish *kadi* instead of settling them in front of the consular courts, but many Ragusan merchants in Belgrade violated the rules by appealing to the *kadi* or the sultan.[73]

Merchants who had access to guild courts thus chose to take their commercial conflicts to other jurisdictions – even when it was prohibited. It might be argued that this was only a later development, or only in centres with precociously developed public courts. But the evidence indicates otherwise. Merchants voluntarily went to public jurisdictions from the earliest surviving records (which date from *c.* 1200), and in centres as far afield as Champagne, Flanders, France, Scandinavia, Germany, England, Spain, Tunisia and Egypt.

In North African and Levantine trading centres, western European merchants who had guild consuls are frequently observed using public courts operated by the Muslim authorities instead. In 1263, for instance, the Catalan merchant consul operated a consular court in Tunis, but enough Catalans found this tribunal unattractive that King James sent a plenipotentiary to investigate Catalan merchants who were avoiding the consular jurisdiction.[74] In Levantine trading centres in the fourteenth and fifteenth centuries, according to Ashtor,

frequently the [European] merchants applied to the Moslems instead of submitting their claims to the consul. In litigation between people of different trading nations, this was almost usual, although it was a generally accepted moral principle that the claimant should apply to the defendant's consul. Sometimes one even sued a compatriot before the Moslem authorities.[75]

In 1405, for instance, a Montpellier merchant indebted to a Genoese merchant was threatened with denunciation before a Muslim court, despite his protests that 'a European should not do this to another, but should apply to the latter's consul'.[76]

---

[71] *Ibid.*   [72] See, e.g., the 1350 case recounted in Paravicini (1992), 108.
[73] Molnár (2007), 93–4, 100.   [74] Hibbert (1949), 358.   [75] Ashtor (1983), 415.
[76] *Ibid.*, 415 n. 385.

In north-west Europe, too, merchants also often voluntarily chose public courts over guild consuls. In 1339, a member of the Lucchese merchant guild in Paris sought repayment of a 500-livre debt from another Lucchese merchant not through the Lucchese consular court in Paris but through a French state tribunal, the *Parlement de Paris*. When the competence of the French court was disputed, it was not the Lucchese guild consul in Paris but the town council of Lucca that claimed jurisdiction.[77] At the Skåne fairs, German merchants can be observed deliberately avoiding their own Hanseatic tribunals after 1352, preferring the older fair-courts operated by the Danish crown which they viewed as 'less severe'.[78]

Bruges became a major centre of long-distance trade after *c.* 1300, with many alien merchant guilds in the fourteenth and fifteenth centuries. Yet foreign merchants with their own consular courts often voted with their feet and preferred municipal jurisdictions. In twenty-seven years of surviving records for the Lucca consular court in Bruges between 1377 and 1404, the Rapondi firm, one of the most important Lucchese houses in Bruges, was involved in only six commercial cases before the guild court: 'In all other cases the disputes were solved before the normal juridical institution of the city of Bruges, the bench of aldermen that carried out the prerogatives of a Law Merchant under the protection of the regional prince, the count of Flanders.'[79] Smaller Lucchese merchant houses in Bruges also brought very few disputes before the consular court, using other mechanisms to solve most of their contract-enforcement problems.[80]

German merchants behaved similarly, despite the Hanseatic prohibition on appeals outside the Kontor jurisdiction. In 1350, the Cologne merchant Tideman Bloumeroot litigated against fellow merchants in the local Bruges court in violation of Hanse regulations, resulting in his being deprived of guild privileges and formally ostracized by all Hanse merchants – evidence for the strength of his motivation to seek justice outside his guild jurisdiction.[81] In 1420, two Hanseatic merchants seeking to retrieve distrained merchandise from a third appealed to Flemish law in violation of Hanseatic regulations; only after lengthy negotiations did the parties consent to bring the case before the Hanse Kontor in Bruges.[82] Even within Hanseatic territory, some German merchants preferred princely law to Hanse tribunals, as in the 1430s when Egghard Westranse of Danzig refused to appear before a Hanse arbitration panel in

---

[77] Mirot (1927), 80.   [78] Christensen (1953), 261.
[79] Lambert and Stabel (2005), 6.   [80] *Ibid.*   [81] R. De Roover (1948a), 172.
[82] Brück (1999), 118.

Greifswald, appealing to his home town of Danzig (Gdańsk), the Grand Master of the Teutonic Order and, ultimately, Emperor Friedrich III.[83]

Why might merchants have preferred public courts to merchant tribunals? Few cases give sufficient detail to answer this question. But the cases that do survive suggest two main motives – a demand for better enforcement and a desire for impartial judgements. Some merchants used public rather than guild courts because their commercial conflicts were too complicated for guild consuls to resolve or, if they could resolve them, to enforce their decisions. This motivation emerges from merchants' use of princely courts at medieval Spanish trade fairs. Merchants not only from other parts of Iberia but also from many foreign lands attended annual fairs at Medina del Campo, Medina del Rioseco, Villalón and other Spanish cities, where they preferred royal courts to merchant tribunals, which they regarded as incapable of providing adequate contract enforcement: 'only the king's courts could successfully monitor them'.[84] The scale of transactions undertaken by medieval Spanish merchants increasingly became such that the jurisdiction of guild courts 'was much too limited in competence and scope' to deal with the conflicts to which they gave rise.[85]

A second reason merchants might prefer public to guild courts was the desire for impartiality. One's fellow merchants may have been more highly informed about one's commercial conflicts, but they were also less able – and perhaps less willing – to judge them impartially. The arbitrary biases shown by merchant guild courts are evoked in one of the earliest surviving texts about them, Alpert of Metz's account of the Tiel merchant guild in 1020: 'They are hard men, unaccustomed to discipline, who judge suits not according to law but according to inclination.'[86] The same concern was echoed by an anonymous Florentine merchant in the mid-fourteenth century, advising a merchant pursuing a lawsuit to be aware that 'judgments rode on favors rather than reason and rectitude'.[87] Egghard Westranse refused to settle his case before a guild tribunal in the 1430s, as we saw, and one reason was undoubtedly his suspicion that a Hanse arbitration panel would favour heavy-hitting Hanse members like Lübeck and Wismar over a merchant from the much less influential town of Danzig (Gdańsk).[88] In sixteenth-century Bilbao, likewise, English merchants explicitly refused to have their own consular court on the grounds that 'a consul would only be a vehicle of a few important merchants to monopolize the trade'.[89]

---

[83] Wernicke (1999), 197–8; Selzer (2003), 86.   [84] Kagan (1981), 221.   [85] *Ibid.*
[86] Pertz (1925), IV: 118.   [87] Kuehn (2006), 1058–9 with n. 3.
[88] Wernicke (1999), 197–8.   [89] Grafe (2001), 23.

Merchants also feared that guild court judges would be drawn from factions unsympathetic to their interests, as in fourteenth-century Bergen, where Lübeck tried to pass a rule that no one could have jurisdiction over merchants – i.e. be an alderman of the Kontor – who was not a citizen of a Hanse town in which Lübeck law prevailed. This provision legally excluded merchants from the Zuiderzee (Dutch) Hanse towns, already facing hostility from Lübeck merchants as competitors to the Wendish near-monopoly of the Bergen trade. Consequently in 1397, the three Zuiderzee Hanse towns (Deventer, Zutphen and Harderwijk) agreed to elect a Deventer citizen as their alderman in Bergen, who would have power to resolve conflicts among the Zuiderzee merchants and ensure that their interests were represented.[90] Similar concerns about the difficulty of obtaining neutral judgement from a guild court may lie behind the decision of two Venetian-Greek merchants in mid-sixteenth-century London involved in conflict over a shipment of currants to elect ultimately to have their conflict judged neither by their consular court in London nor by a civil court for foreigners in Venice but rather by an arbitration panel consisting of two English wholesale merchants.[91]

Whatever their precise motivations, medieval merchants thus often voluntarily resorted to public courts in preference to their own guild tribunals. Sometimes they did not bother to establish merchant guilds at all, in other cases they were uninterested in (or incapable of) getting jurisdiction for these guilds, and in still others they had access to their own guild courts and yet voted with their feet by appealing to the public legal system. Guild courts, for whatever reason, did not provide contract enforcement of the quantity or quality required by medieval long-distance merchants. This was what rendered guild courts dependent – in most cases from their inception – on the public authorities. Guild courts did not offer contract enforcement unavailable from public institutions, but rather depended heavily on the public legal system for the relatively minor degree of contract enforcement that they did provide.

7.1.4   Did guild courts use a special 'merchant law'?

A final claim often made for guild courts is that they generated a private-order 'merchant law' – the so-called *lex mercatoria*. An older historiography claimed that *lex mercatoria* was generated by merchant guilds from the eleventh century onwards, as a coherent body of commercial legal rules separate from – and superior to – the Roman law or common law

---

[90] Henn (2005), 235, 238.   [91] Fusaro (2002), 14–15 with nn. 56–7.

of public legal systems.[92] *Lex mercatoria* is supposed to have been created autonomously by merchants – particularly by merchant guilds – on the basis of the unwritten customs of businessmen rather than the written statutes of lords, princes or states. This set of contracting rules, the story continues, reduced transaction costs because it was universally accepted by all merchants everywhere, thereby increasing the potential for impersonal, long-distance exchange. The fact that it was generated by the merchants themselves, the argument goes, meant that the *lex mercatoria* embodied greater business expertise than public law codes. This vision of medieval 'merchant law' has often been mobilized for political purposes over the centuries, most recently to support the view that private-order legal arrangements should be used to regulate cross-border transactions and the internet.[93]

Closer empirical investigation finds little support for the view that *lex mercatoria* existed in pre-modern Europe as a systematic commercial code autonomously generated by communities of merchants. In fact, there is no evidence that medieval Europe had any universally accepted merchant law.[94] *Lex mercatoria* was mentioned surprisingly rarely in medieval legal practice, even in consular courts and fair-courts.[95] When it was mentioned, it typically referred not to an encompassing body of *contracting* rules but rather to a restricted set of *procedural* rules for swift settlement of disputes and adequate standards of proof in private contracts.[96] Even then, these procedural rules emanated not from 'an accepted body of mercantile procedural rules' or from 'mercantile customary law', but rather from 'the common customary law of the realm . . . with some addition from the common elements in the procedure of local courts'.[97] Unsurprisingly, given that 'merchant law' was derived from customary law, local ordinances and national statutes, it varied from one locality to

[92] Milgrom, North and Weingast (1990), 4–6; Benson (1989), 646–51; Berman (1983), 333–51; Trakman (1983), 7–8, 10–11, 13 16, 20–1, 24, 26–7, 30; Mitchell (1904), 11, 13, 16, 72.

[93] On the nineteenth- and twentieth-century revival of enthusiasm for an autonomous merchant law and attempts to mobilize medieval evidence to support it, see Basile et al. (1998), 162–78. For an example of how this view of merchant law is used to advocate 'stateless legal systems', see Benson (1989), 658–61; Benson (2002). On the distinction between private-order and public-order institutions and their respective strengths and weaknesses, see Katz (2000). For a lucid discussion of the historical evidence, see Sachs (2006).

[94] On this, see Baker (1979), esp. 298–300, 321–2; Baker (1986); Basile et al. (1998), 128–30, 179–88; Donahue (2005), 74–8; Gelderblom (2005b), 20, 24; Sachs (2006); Volckart and Mangels (1999).

[95] See, e.g., Sachs (2006), 730, 755–61.

[96] Baker (1979), 300–1; Baker (1986), 386; Moore (1985), 168.

[97] Donahue (2004), 30 (quotation); Baker (1979), 322.

the next. The 'merchant law' occasionally mentioned at the fair-court of St Ives, for instance, was not universal, even to England: 'rather, there only existed a diversity of local practices, a diversity which has since been reified by scholars into a single – and fictional – "Law Merchant"'.[98] Even the by-laws of the German Hanse were solely procedural in nature and differed significantly across the four main Hanse branch offices in London, Bruges, Bergen and Novgorod.[99]

Another source of commercial law sometimes referred to in medieval merchant conflicts was the maritime law or 'sea law' (*ius maritimum*). But this, too, simply laid down *procedural* rules governing shipping conflicts, and varied from one part of Europe to another.[100] In southern Europe, maritime law was based on the Rhodian Sea Law (probably dating from the early Middle Ages),[101] a maritime law code published in Ravenna and Amalfi in 1010[102] and the fifteenth-century *Llibre del Consolat de mar* of Barcelona.[103] The maritime law collected in these works did contain some common elements but varied considerably from one collection to another even within the same maritime area. In much of north-western Europe, the maritime law was based on a code called the *rôles d'Oléron*, probably dating from the period 1204–24, was initially devised to govern the wine trade between south-west France and northern Europe, and was later copied by neighbouring trading centres.[104] But not until the fourteenth century did the Ordinances of Visby emerge as one major version of the *rôles d'Oléron*, and even then they were not formally codified until 1407.[105] Even within the north-west European trading area around the North Sea and Baltic, maritime law varied from centre to centre, with Bruges adopting the Damme version while Amsterdam adopted the Visby version.[106]

These different versions of *maritime* law, although they varied greatly, were at least recorded in written collections. The *merchant* law, by contrast, does not exist in any general collection from the medieval or early modern period. If a coherent body of merchant law existed at all, it must have been customary and oral. But that means it is all but impossible to establish its existence.[107] The absence of merchant law from contemporary written collections and legal manuals raises the question of how significant or widely used it can have been, given that other bodies of law did appear in written form at the same period.

[98] Sachs (2006), 695.   [99] Dollinger (1964), 125–32.
[100] Gelderblom (2005b), 20–1; Volckart and Mangels (1999), 435–6; Hunt and Murray (1999), 96.
[101] Donahue (2005), 75.   [102] Woodward (2005), 631.   [103] *Ibid.*, 633.
[104] Shephard (2005).   [105] Woodward (2005), 632.
[106] Gelderblom (2005b), 21; Woodward (2005), 632.   [107] Donahue (2005), 74–5.

The *contractual* rules applied in merchant courts were those of the surrounding public law system and therefore varied from one locality to another. On the European continent, these usually consisted of some combination of the general contractual principles of Roman Law, statutes issued by the prince or other central authorities and community custom. The maritime law code proclaimed in Ravenna and Amalfi in 1010, for instance, was based on Roman Law and on the seventh-century Rhodian Sea Law.[108] In medieval England, the contractual rules applied in merchant courts, including those occasionally referred to using the term *lex mercatoria*, were largely identical to those applied by borough, communal and seigneurial courts.[109] Even those medieval contemporaries most enthusiastic in claiming that *lex mercatoria* was autonomous and widely valid admitted explicitly that 'The common law . . . is the mother of mercantile law.'[110] Around 1240, the municipal authorities in Bristol ordered that 'in disputes between merchants and merchants, or merchants and sailors, or sailors and sailors, whether they are burgesses or foreigners, "right shall be done according to the laws and customs of the town"'.[111] The voluminous surviving records of the St Ives fair-court from the period 1270–1324 contain only eleven references to *lex mercatoria*, in contrast to the much more frequent references to the regulations of the local seigneurial authority (the abbot of Ramsey), royal statutes and the dictates of local custom.[112] Public authorities, not merchant courts, were responsible for gradually creating a comprehensive code of rules governing merchant contracts, based on existing law in the public legal system.

7.1.5 What can we conclude about merchant guild jurisdictions?

The historical evidence thus provides little support for the theory that merchant guild tribunals offered better contract enforcement than public law-courts. This should not be surprising, when we reflect on why special law-courts existed in pre-modern Europe. Merchants were only one among many groups that sought special legal treatment acknowledging their special corporate privileges – their exemption from the ordinary operation of the law. No one has claimed that the legal privileges granted to nobles, priests, university students or salt-miners (to name just a few of the groups with privileges to resort to special law-courts) enhanced economic efficiency. If anything, such privileges enabled these groups to maintain socio-economic demarcations and seek benefits for themselves

---

[108] Woodward (2005), 631. [109] Henry (1926), 9; Basile et al. (1998), esp. 23–34.
[110] *Lex Mercatoria* (c. 1280), ch. 9; quoted according to Basile et al. (1998), 27.
[111] Quoted in Basile et al. (1998), 42. [112] Sachs (2006), 731.

at the expense of outsiders – i.e. to serve redistributive ends rather than efficiency. It is therefore not surprising that merchant guild courts offered no better commercial contract enforcement than public law-courts.

7.2   Peer pressure

Peer pressure is a second way merchant guilds are supposed to have helped enforce contracts. Merchant guilds were closely knit networks whose members were linked in multi-stranded ties combining commerce, kinship, marriage, religion and sociability. Some claim that guilds used this social capital to put pressure on members not to break contracts. If one guild member reneged on a business agreement, information would pass rapidly through the guild and other members would impose social sanctions on him for harming their collective reputation. North, for instance, argues that contract enforcement in medieval trade 'had its beginnings in the development of internal codes of conduct in fraternal orders of guild merchants; those who did not live up to them were threatened with ostracism'.[113] Benson claims that 'the threat of ostracism by the merchant community at large' was a widespread means of contract enforcement among medieval merchants – 'if anything more effective than physical coercion'.[114] Grafe and Gelderblom argue that at least after 1300, 'peer pressure was certainly an important instrument to discipline relatives and friends'.[115]

Scholars point to two distinct variants of peer pressure in merchant guilds – one affecting contracts between members of the same guild, the other governing deals with outsiders. The first variant is widely observed in most economies – a closed network of traders reduces risks by transacting only with a trusted circle and then imposing informal penalties if someone reneges. This mechanism is widely observed in nearly every trading society, whether or not it has merchant guilds – closed networks can be based on kinship, ethnicity, religion and many other criteria.[116] Intra-network peer pressure offers clear advantages for trade: swift information transmission, multi-stranded relationships and collective sanctions mean that network members who harm each other face a high probability of being detected and punished, deterring them from doing so. But it also imposes disadvantages: limiting trade to partners from a closely defined circle of trusted individuals linked by pre-existing ties reduces exchange with people from different regions, occupations, ethnicities and social strata. Economic theory suggests that gains from trade are likely to be larger the more dissimilar the transaction partners.

[113] North (1991), 30.   [114] Benson (2002), 129–30 (quotation); Benson (1998), 649.
[115] Grafe and Gelderblom (2010a), 482.   [116] Mathias (1995).

If the only way to enforce contracts is to limit exchange to a circle well acquainted for other reasons, this will seriously reduce gains from trade.

The second form of peer pressure – that directed at enforcing contracts with outsiders – is supposed to have characterized the High Middle Ages (c. 1000–c. 1300) during the heyday of collective 'reprisals'. Network members who broke contracts with outsiders brought collective penalties on the whole network, which therefore used peer pressure to discipline them. This form of peer pressure did not suffer from the disadvantage of limiting trade to members of the same network. But it depended on a functioning reprisal system, which had a number of disadvantages in its own right, as we shall see in the next section.

Do we have much evidence that merchant guilds effectively exercised peer pressure against members who defaulted on contracts? Some guild ordinances did threaten ostracism for members who violated guild rules. In 1240, for instance, the Flemish merchant guild in England ('Those Men of Ypres and Douai Who Go to England') ordered that

If any man of Ypres or Douai shall go against those decisions . . . for the common good, regarding fines or anything else, that man shall be excluded from selling, lodging, eating, or depositing his wool or cloth in ships with the rest of the merchants . . . And if anyone violates this ostracism, he shall be fined 5s.[117]

But hard evidence of ostracism being used to make guild members fulfil *private contracts*, as opposed to obeying *guild rules*, is hard to find. The surviving court rolls of the fair of St Ives between 1270 and 1324, studied by Sachs, contain no evidence that the merchant community used ostracism against cheats or defaulting debtors: 'given that some defendants appear repeatedly in the rolls, one infers that they lived to trade again'.[118] In 1291, for instance, a London merchant cheated a German merchant at the fair of Lynn, and then fled from town to town without being impeded by any sort of merchant ostracism. The contract was ultimately enforced not through peer pressure, boycotts or any other guild action, but rather by the debtor's arrest and imprisonment by royal officials in London.[119] Gelderblom likewise finds little evidence that alien merchant guilds in Bruges or Antwerp used peer pressure against members who defaulted on contracts; the few observed cases are ones in which peer pressure failed, resulting in formal litigation.[120] According to Ashtor, Venetian merchant guilds in the Levant also failed to exercise effective peer pressure, as in 1376 when the Venetian merchant guild in Damascus made no move to ostracize several Venetian traders (including the guild

[117] Quoted from translation in Moore (1985), 298; for original, see Häpke (1908), 54 n. 1.
[118] Sachs (2006), 706.   [119] *Ibid.*, 711–12 n. 80.   [120] Gelderblom (2005b), 7.

consul himself) who had failed to pay for merchandise purchased from Muslims; guild action was limited to feebly petitioning the Mamluk authorities to forbid Muslims to sell goods to Venetians on credit, in order to remove the temptation to default.[121]

There may have been cases in which merchant guilds used peer pressure to compel members to fulfil their contracts, but which are unrecorded because successful peer pressure left no written traces. But those cases that are recorded – in England, Flanders and the Mediterranean – contain intriguing hints of the limits to the peer pressure that could be exercised by even the most powerful merchant guilds in their heyday in the High Middle Ages.

In theory, merchant guilds had the necessary characteristics – closure and multi-stranded relationships – to deploy peer pressure against members who broke contracts. In so far as peer pressure was used only against merchants who cheated other members of the same guild, it would have had little impact on international trade since it would not have applied to transactions between strangers where gains from trade are typically greatest. In so far as peer pressure was used against guild members who cheated outsiders, it was interdependent with a functioning reprisal system, discussed in the next section. Empirically, we have little evidence that merchant guilds did exercise successful peer pressure. This may be because informal pressure is under-recorded or it may be because there was little of it to record. We cannot therefore offer a reliable assessment of the economic impact of peer pressure by merchant guilds. Theoretically, peer pressure seems more likely to have been effective where guild membership was limited, the international trading centre was small and monopoly rents provided through guild membership were high, giving the guild more power to deprive defaulting members of corporate benefits. Surviving records suggest, however, that even the most powerful merchant guilds – such as those of the Venetians – could exercise very little effective peer pressure against members who chose to default on contracts.

7.3   Collective reprisals

Collective reprisals (sometimes termed 'joint liability' or 'community responsibility')[122] are a third way merchant guilds improved commercial

---

[121] Ashtor (1983), 123.

[122] The most frequently used term in medieval Europe was 'reprisals' (French *représailles*, German *Repressalien*, Italian *rappresaglie*, Latin *pignioratio*). Modern legal historians generally adopt the same terminology although some refer to the concept as 'joint liability'. A few modern economists use the term 'community responsibility'.

contract enforcement, according to some scholars. Reprisals involved penalizing an entire community if one member committed an offence. Community punishments were used as an instrument of internal social control and external diplomatic pressure in many polities, not just in western Europe but also in Russia, China and Mongolia, from antiquity well into the modern period.[123] Depending on the interests of those inflicting the reprisal, the 'community' that was held collectively responsible could be defined in a wide variety of ways – a kinship group, village, town, guild, ethnic group, religious sect, political party, nationality or 'justiciables' (persons subject to a particular jurisdiction). Collective reprisals were used not just for violations of commercial contracts, but to punish a variety of actions included treaty violations, breaches of the peace, piracy, revolt, tax evasion, illegal migration, religious deviance, theft, murder and many other alleged offences.[124] Collective reprisals were thus a recognized form of penalty in most pre-modern societies – albeit, as we shall see, one which most European societies sought to limit, circumscribe or abolish.

Recently, however, Greif has placed collective reprisals (under the cosier name of the 'community responsibility system') at the centre of a theory about how merchant guilds benefited the medieval Commercial Revolution. According to this theory, the practice of imposing collective reprisals on guilds or communities of foreign merchants was the institution responsible for the emergence of long-distance impersonal trade in Europe in the eleventh century and its expansion until the late thirteenth century, at which point it was replaced by contract-enforcement institutions based on individual legal liability.[125] Greif constructed a theoretical model showing that an equilibrium exists in which collective reprisals could enable strangers to commit themselves credibly to a contract because both parties would know that their respective guilds or communities would be punished for any default. This could theoretically motivate merchant communities to exercise internal sanctions against members who broke contracts, which in turn could theoretically deter members from contract-breaking.[126] Other scholars have extended this theoretical analysis to financial transactions, concluding that the mutual threat of collective reprisals could have enabled medieval merchant guilds to improve contract enforcement in credit relationships as well as the merchandise trade.[127]

---

[123] Dewey and Kleimola (1970); Dewey and Kleimola (1984); and Dewey (1988).
[124] Dewey and Kleimola (1970); Dewey and Kleimola (1984); and Dewey (1988).
[125] See Greif (1997); Greif (2002a); Greif (2004); Greif (2006b).
[126] Greif (2002a), 168–72, 175–82.   [127] Boerner and Ritschl (2005).

This theoretical model has been used to draw far-reaching lessons for modern developing economies. Greif, for instance, claims that the medieval reprisal system shows that 'the modern European state's involvement in contract enforcement was not a precondition to impersonal exchange'. Instead of having to build formal legal structures, he argues, the community responsibility system shows that economies can develop through 'reputation-based' institutions.[128] Other scholars have taken up this argument, using the supposed success of collective reprisals in medieval trade to advocate systems of informal contract enforcement in modern less-developed economies or on the internet.[129]

7.3.1   Were reprisals informal?

Community responsibility, according to this view, offered a solution to contract-enforcement problems which was on the one hand efficient and impersonal, but on the other hand informal and collective. Its efficiency resided in the support it provided to impersonal exchange in the absence of public institutions capable of doing so.[130] Its impersonality resided in its enabling people to trade without having personal ries: 'a trader's decision to transact [was] independent of his partner's reputation'.[131] Its informality resided in the fact that 'all relevant incentives – to individual traders and their communities – were provided endogenously'.[132] And its collective nature resided in the fact that legal liability was imposed on communities of merchants, not individually identifiable traders.[133]

The evidence, however, does not support this portrayal. The reprisal system was not a self-enforcing institution arising autonomously within merchant 'communities' but rather, as contemporary legal treatises and law codes stated explicitly, a formal component of the public legal system. In medieval Italian city-states, for instance, imposition of collective reprisals for debts required the creditor to provide evidence that he had applied for public justice from his debtor's home jurisdiction, had been refused, had asked his own home jurisdiction for diplomatic intervention, and that these steps had also failed. The complaining creditor was then summoned to appear by the *podestà* (chief magistrate) who required him

---

[128] Greif (2002a), 201–2; Greif (2006b), esp. 232–4.

[129] See note 128; Greif (2002b), 1999–2000, 2006, 2019. On implications for modern LDCs, see Bardhan (1996), 3; on implications for modern internet transactions, see Ba (2001), 328. See also the popularity of the Greif model in the literature on 'spontaneous order' or 'private-order institutions', e.g., McMillan and Woodruff (2000), 2444, 2456–7; Bernstein (2001), 1763. For criticisms of over-optimistic assessments of private-order institutions in developing economies, see Katz (2000).

[130] Greif (2002a), 190.   [131] Greif (2006b), 221.   [132] Greif (2002a), 200.

[133] Greif (2006b), 222.

formally to present his demand for restitution. Only if this demand was not met could an act of collective reprisal against his debtor's compatriots be declared, and even then a formally defined series of steps had to be followed before it could be implemented. Most Italian cities kept public registers recording the formal writs of reprisal that had been issued and listing the objects taken into pledge as a consequence of such reprisals.[134]

Likewise, in the German imperial law code by 1231 at latest, collective reprisals were fully embedded into the formal legal system. The injured party was required to provide evidence, either in writing or orally on oath from at least two witnesses, that the contract existed, that the accused party had defaulted on it and that an attempt had already been made to enforce the contract in a public law-court to which the accused was currently subject. After this evidence was presented, the injured party was required to notify the public law-court in his own home town, which would then undertake formal legal procedures to institute collective reprisals against those subject to the legal system that had refused redress.[135]

The most famous of all medieval collective reprisals, the 'fair-bans' sometimes imposed at the Champagne fairs for non-payment of fair-debts, were also not informal. For one thing, as we saw in section 7.1, the Champagne fair-wardens' court which declared the fair-ban was a princely jurisdiction. Second, imposing the fair-ban involved a lengthy series of formal legal steps. The fair-wardens first had to send a summons to the magistrates of the legal system under which the absconding debtor was currently located, demanding that he and his property be delivered to answer for his debts. If this was refused, a new letter had to be sent, repeating the demand. Only after three written demands had been sent could the wardens threaten a collective fair-ban. The demand, explicitly stating the possibility of a collective fair-ban, had to be formally issued by the princely fair-court and formally presented to the legal system to which the debtor was currently subject. Only after all these formalities had been observed could the fair-ban be officially declared. Even then, the debtor's legal authorities could still deal with the ban by complying with the demand, reporting to the princely fair-court or appealing to a royal tribunal.[136]

Similar formality attended collective reprisals for mercantile debts in England and Flanders. At the St Ives fair in the thirteenth and fourteenth

---

[134] Wach (1868), 49; J. G. O'Brien (2002), 26–8; Fortunati (2005), 148–9; Tai (1996), 141–4.

[135] Planitz (1919), 177–9; Wach (1868), 49–50.

[136] Bassermann (1911), 43–4; Goldschmidt (1891), 231–3; Bourquelot (1865), I: 177ff., 220ff., 293ff.

centuries, a creditor was required first to pursue a debt in the courts of the debtor's own home town or polity. Only when this had failed could he apply for a collective reprisal against the debtor's compatriots. Even then, a collective reprisal was formulated as a punishment not against a community of merchants but against a legal system that had failed to render justice.[137] This was a legal norm in medieval Europe, as shown by a 1311 letter from the king of England to the count of Flanders pointing out 'it has hitherto been observed between the king's and [the count's] ancestors that no arrest of bodies or goods was made for debts or trespasses until the lord of the persons, for whom amends of the trespass or payment of the debt were sought, had been properly requested and had failed to do justice'.[138]

The basic principle in European law codes was that collective liability related not to *the accused party's offence abroad* but rather to the *failure of his home court* to provide legal remedy. That is, the collective responsibility of all members of a merchant community derived from their legal subordination to a particular formal jurisdiction, not from their membership in the same merchant guild.[139] This is nicely illustrated by an example from the Champagne fairs. In September 1299, the Champagne fair-wardens wrote to the lord mayor of London requesting that he arrest the person and goods of a Florentine merchant for a debt of 1,600 livres tournois which had been contracted at the Champagne fairs with a Prato merchant. The lord mayor wrote back in March 1300 stating that he had heard the Florentine merchant's account and come to the conclusion that no debt was owed. In May 1300 the fair-wardens wrote again, threatening a fair-ban, not against Florence as the 'community' of which this merchant was indisputably a member, but rather against London, as the justice system to which he was currently subject and which had refused to render legal remedy for a debt incurred at the fairs.[140]

A second basic principle of medieval European law governing collective reprisals was that they could only be granted by the sovereign power, were subject to the control of public courts and were formally circumscribed.[141] Community- or guild-based reprisals were only one among many possible formal sanctions, and were regarded as a measure of last resort which should (it was usually argued) be formally regulated and carefully monitored by the public authorities. Reprisals did not *substitute* for public-order legal provision, but rather *depended* on it. They

---

[137] For English examples, see Sachs (2006), 710 n. 76.
[138] Quoted in Lloyd (1977), 104–5.
[139] On Germany, see Planitz (1919), 183. On Italy, see Wach (1868), 47–9; Cheyette (1970), 60.
[140] Huvelin (1897), 430–1; Bassermann (1911), 46.   [141] Mas-Latrie (1866), 566–7.

were not an informal enforcement mechanism generated autonomously within guilds of merchants, but rather a component of the public legal system, a means for the magnification and projection of sovereign justice abroad through formal diplomatic threats.

7.3.2   Were reprisals based on collective legal responsibility?

What of the argument that reprisals for unpaid merchant debts were based on a distinctively pre-modern idea of legal liability as collective rather than individual? Greif goes so far as to argue that under the 'community responsibility system' individual debtors were not identified in detail: the practice of using surnames was still so rare, he claims, that the only way a merchant could be described was according to his community of origin.[142] In this view, collective reprisals were only abandoned in the final years of the thirteenth century when the legal system made a transition to the idea of individual liability: 'during the late thirteenth century the [community responsibility system] was gradually replaced by a system based on individual legal responsibility'.[143]

The evidence shows that this portrayal is inaccurate. This emerges clearly from the earliest recorded example of a collective reprisal imposed for unpaid debts at the Champagne fairs, a letter of 1263 from the fair-wardens to the bishop and consuls of the town of Cahors. In this letter, Thibault d'Acenay and Etienne du Plessy, wardens of the Champagne fairs, state that a fair-ban had recently been pronounced against the Cahorsins on account of the unpaid debts of Pierre and Etienne de Salvetat, citizens of Cahors. They remind the bishop and consuls of Cahors of a long series of formal steps they had taken to draw the attention of the Cahors authorities to the default before they had implemented the ban. Finally, they declare that after having arrested certain merchants of Cahors and seized their merchandise at the fairs, they had consented to release them out of pure benevolence and on the merchants' promise to appear with their effects at the first summons; but they warn that henceforth the fair-ban against merchants of Cahors will be implemented in its full rigour.[144] The same procedure of individually naming the merchants responsible for unpaid mercantile debts is followed in another early collective reprisal at the Champagne fairs. In 1279, the fair-wardens wrote a series of letters to the authorities in Florence, describing how Lapo Rustichi of Florence, factor and associate of Bartolo and Grifo Bencivenni and their firms, had absconded from the fair of Lagny with certain moneys owed to various Piacenzan merchants. The fair-wardens requested

---

[142] Greif (2002a), 174.   [143] *Ibid.*, 170.   [144] Bourquelot (1865), I: 159–160, II: 150.

first the Florentine merchant guild and then, when that guild disclaimed responsibility, the podestà and Capitano of the government of Florence, to render justice by requiring Lapo Rustichi to provide restitution and expenses, on pain of collective reprisals in the form of a fair-ban against all Florentine merchants.[145]

These examples are not unique, but are echoed in collective reprisals threatened or imposed for mercantile debts throughout medieval Europe. Procedures for pursuing unpaid debts, even when collective reprisals were envisaged, began by naming a particular merchant, complete with details of his prename, surname, the merchant firm for which he was acting and the town to whose justice system he was subject or where his property was currently located. It is thus not the case that the only thing that was known about a merchant and that mattered legally was his community affiliation.[146] The procedure involved demanding that the legal jurisdiction to which the debtor was currently subject obtain repayment and expenses from that individual. Only if this jurisdiction failed to render justice would a collective reprisal be imposed. Thus the reprisal system did not involve a substitution of collective for individual legal responsibility. Rather, individual legal responsibility came first, and collective legal responsibility was only invoked to render individual legal responsibility effectual. The community reprisal system did not represent a collective alternative to individual responsibility but was rather embedded – as a measure of last resort – in a system based on individual legal liability.[147] Whatever its merits, therefore, the medieval reprisal system was neither informal nor collective, but rather was deeply rooted in a formal legal system based on individual legal responsibility.

7.3.3   Did merchant guilds support collective reprisals?

But how efficient was the system of collective reprisals in practice? Some modern scholars see reprisals as efficient, but medieval merchants viewed them in a rather different light. A writ of reprisal granted a complainant the legal right to extract compensation from compatriots of the accused in what was effectively an act of licensed retaliation against innocent third parties.[148] Medieval merchants themselves showed a clear recognition of the destructive effects of reprisals – their tendency to provoke endless quarrels, wild acts of confiscation, violence against foreigners and a

---

[145] For the original documents, see Berti (1857), 247, no. XIV; 251 no. XV; 254, no. XVI. On this case, see also Bourquelot (1865), I: 180 with n. 2; Bassermann (1911), 44; Bautier (1952), 321.

[146] Counter to what is claimed in Greif (2002a), 170–1, 174, 182, 190–1, 200–1.

[147] Planitz (1919), 168–90.   [148] Tai (1996), 9; Tai (2003b), 264.

spiral of mutual retaliation. Many of the earliest documentary sources in medieval Europe reflecting the views of merchants themselves mention the reprisal system as a threat to traders, an obstacle to trade and a harmful legal practice that should at least be severely regulated and preferably be wholly abolished. Contemporaries actively sought to replace reprisals with superior institutional arrangements which, while not enforcing contracts perfectly, at least limited the notorious and hated spiral of violent retaliation.[149]

The twelfth century is the earliest period from which documents survive recording collective reprisals being used to penalize non-payment of long-distance trading debts. Yet already at this time, merchants were recorded demanding the suspension of collective responsibility before they would trade in a particular territory abroad.[150] In 1191/2, for instance, when Scandinavian and German merchants from Visby negotiated the Treaty of Jaroslav with the rulers of Novgorod, enabling them to set up an alien merchant colony in Novgorod, one provision of the treaty explicitly forbade either side to confiscate wares in reprisal for violations of commercial contracts, as had happened between them as recently as 1188.[151] At around the same time, in 1193, the merchants of Ypres demanded that the king of France guarantee that an Ypres merchant could not be arrested or his goods seized in reprisal for debts contracted by anyone other than himself or those for whom he had formally entered into guarantorship; this even included debts of his overlord, the count of Flanders.[152] In 1192–3, after Pisan and Genoese pirates captured a Venetian ship carrying Byzantine merchants and imperial ambassadors, seizing their goods and killing them, the Byzantine Emperor Isaac II imposed reprisals on Genoese and Pisan merchants in Constantinople, whereupon the Commune of Genoa promised to pursue the corsairs but also demanded 'that the Commune not be made to suffer for the actions of individuals'. The positive response of the emperor in releasing the confiscated Genoese goods is interpreted by Laiou as indicating that the principle that collective reprisals should not be exercised against innocent parties was emerging in the eastern Mediterranean at latest by the 1190s.[153] The counts of Champagne attracted foreign merchants to the Champagne fairs from the 1180s on partly by guaranteeing freedom from collective reprisals, except for the fair-bans that might be imposed by the fair-wardens themselves.[154] Even for fair-debts, merchant guilds at the Champagne fairs engaged in separate negotiations to gain exemptions

[149] Planitz (1919), 168–90.   [150] *Ibid.*   [151] Wase (2000), 16 with n. 26.
[152] Laurent (1935b), 99, 259–60.   [153] Laiou (2001), 159.
[154] Goldschmidt (1891), 34ff., 115ff., 228–9.

from collective reprisals for their members, as in the 1290s when the 'captain' of the Italian merchant *universitas* at the Champagne fairs negotiated an exemption from a fair-ban declared against Lucca for the debts of a single Lucca merchant firm.[155] Elsewhere in north-west Europe, merchants also demanded suspension of collective reprisals before they would trade abroad, as in 1253, when German merchants successfully demanded that the rulers of Flanders, Holland and other territories guarantee them security against reprisals before they would trade in those realms.[156] At around the same time, merchants from Ghent, Bruges, Ypres, Douai, St Omer and Lübeck successfully demanded that Henry III of England declare that a merchant would be held legally responsible only for debts for which he was the principal or a pledge, as a precondition for their coming to trade in England.[157]

Not only did merchants put pressure on foreign rulers to suspend reprisals before they would trade abroad, but they also put pressure on their own rulers to abolish the practice. The north Italian city-states were in the forefront of the revival of long-distance trade in Europe after the Dark Ages, and their governments were also the earliest to limit collective reprisals for mercantile debts. According to the detailed study by Del Vecchio and Casanova of the Italian usages governing collective reprisals, the first treaty between Italian polities agreeing mutually to restrict the use of collective reprisals was signed between Naples and the prince of Benevento in 836.[158] But it was in the tenth and eleventh centuries that regulations restricting collective reprisals for debts proliferated in Italian city charters and annals.[159] During the twelfth and thirteenth centuries, Italian cities and polities signed a whole series of treaties prohibiting the use of collective reprisals against each other's citizens.[160] As early as 1213, a Bolognese document explicitly stated the principle of individual responsibility for debts in the famous phrase *cui dabitur ab illo requiratur*, literally 'to whom it will be given, from him it will be required' – i.e. debts will only be demanded from a principal debtor and not from his fellow citizens.[161] This dictum subsequently began to appear in nearly all trade treaties and agreements among Italian cities.[162] In 1216, Bologna signed a treaty with Florence providing that reprisals should not be exercised in future except against the goods and person of the debtor himself.[163] From the early thirteenth century on, all Sienese governments tried to

[155] Laurent (1935b), 298.
[156] Planitz (1919), 173–4; Gilliodts-van Severen (1901–2), I: 44; Häpke (1908), 109–10.
[157] Ashley (1888), 105.   [158] Del Vecchio and Casanova (1894), 62–3.
[159] Wach (1868), 47–9; Cassandro (1938), 7–12.
[160] Del Vecchio and Casanova (1894), 68 71.   [161] Bowsky (1981), 240.
[162] Schevill (1909), 119 n. 1.   [163] Mas-Latrie (1866), 572.

restrict reprisals or eliminate them altogether,[164] and in 1250, the podestà issued a *charta bannorum* with a clause promising that the government would compel citizens of Siena to pay their debts to any foreign creditor, explicitly 'so that he will not molest other Sienese for that debt'.[165] The success of Venice in increasing trade with areas such as the Mamluk dominions from 1250 on is explicitly ascribed to the fact that 'they abstained from acts of retaliation'.[166] The crown of Aragon governed a number of successful long-distance trading cities, and here too the ruler began in the early thirteenth century to limit collective reprisals for commercial contract enforcement, requiring Aragonese merchants to bring their debt demands formally to foreign courts and request diplomatic intervention from the crown of Aragon before even broaching the possibility of collective reprisals.[167]

The same developments can be seen in north-west Europe. Flanders was another important epicentre of north-west European commerce and there, too, rulers early began to suspend or curtail collective reprisals for commercial debts, precisely in order to remove an obstacle to long-distance trade.[168] In 1178, Flanders signed a treaty with Cologne outlawing collective reprisals for debt.[169] In 1252, Countess Margaret of Flanders drew up privileges for all foreign merchants visiting the fairs of Flanders, which included the explicit provision that they would be exempt from reprisals: 'Imprisonment for debt existed only for the principal debtor or his guarantor.'[170]

In France, as well, by the twelfth century trading cities were signing treaties restricting the use of reprisals and devising substitutes such as 'establishing a flat rate tax on goods moving in and out of the ports involved to pay those who otherwise would have demanded reprisals'.[171] In 1193, as we have seen, the French King Philip Augustus guaranteed to the merchants of Ypres that in future they could not be arrested 'either for the debts of their fellow citizens or for those of the count of Flanders, unless they had become sureties'.[172] In a series of treaties beginning in 1228, France and England created a committee of reconciliation, an international jurisdiction to decide issues relating to mercantile debts and damages before they could give rise to collective reprisals.[173]

Even in German-speaking central Europe, which was by no means in the forefront of the medieval Commercial Revolution, rulers began

---

[164] Bowsky (1981), 235.   [165] *Ibid.*   [166] Ashtor (1983), 252.
[167] Mas-Latrie (1866), 548.   [168] Planitz (1919), 96–7, 168–90.
[169] Goldschmidt (1891), 122 n. 91.
[170] Verlinden (1965), 135 (quotation); Stein (1902), 55, 98.
[171] Cheyette (1970), 55–6.   [172] Quoted in Mitchell (1904), 122.
[173] Mas-Latrie (1866), 571.

quite early to suspend or limit collective reprisals for mercantile debts. According to Planitz, by the twelfth century,

The documentary sources make the fundamental assumption that reprisal arrests are not permitted. Only the true debtor, not his fellow citizens, can be arrested in the town. The towns certified this among one another as early as the twelfth century in numerous treaties . . . But at almost the same period identical treaties were reached with foreign territorial princes.[174]

In 1173, for instance, Emperor Frederik I Barbarossa issued a privilege to Flemish merchants according to which they were not to be subject to collective reprisals for debt while trading in Germany.[175] In 1178, Cologne signed treaties with both Verdun and Flanders, mutually outlawing collective reprisals.[176] Subsequently, Cologne signed treaties with Soest, Liège, Deventer and Nürnberg, all promising not to use collective reprisals to pursue debts against each other's citizens.[177] Between 1159 and 1285, Cologne also signed treaties with Nijmegen, Ghent, Siegburg, the count of Berg and the king of England, in which both parties promised to abolish collective reprisals against each other's citizens.[178] Strasbourg signed a treaty with Speyer in 1227 outlawing collective reprisals for debts.[179] In 1249, the city-state of Fribourg im Üechtland (in what is now Switzerland), which traded actively in textiles throughout central Europe, issued a law code decreeing that no citizen of the town was to pursue debts using collective reprisals, even against foreign merchants.[180]

These examples show definitively that merchants and merchant guilds themselves disliked collective reprisals strongly and demanded their suspension or abolition. They were already doing so in the twelfth and thirteenth centuries, long before the putative watershed of the 1280s when individual legal liability is supposed to have superseded collective responsibility for merchant debt.[181] Medieval merchants had a clear view that collective reprisals deterred trade, increased risks, harmed innocent third parties and provoked spirals of mutual retaliation. Guilds of merchants therefore did the exact opposite of seeking to shore up the 'community responsibility system' as a valued mechanism for efficiently enforcing commercial contracts in the absence of formal institutions. Rather, from the very beginning of the medieval Commercial Revolution, merchant

[174] Planitz (1919), 171.   [175] Boerner and Ritschl (2002), 206.
[176] Goldschmidt (1891), I: 121–2 n. 91.
[177] E. B. Fryde and M. M. Fryde (1965), 529.
[178] Volckart and Mangels (1999), 445; Kuske (1978), 2–19.   [179] Planitz (1919), 173.
[180] Volckart and Mangels (1999), 445 n. 48.
[181] For this chronology, see Greif (2002a), 199–200.

guilds put pressure on the public authorities, both in their own home polities and abroad, to limit what they openly regarded as a dangerous and abusive practice that deterred long-distance traders from venturing abroad.

7.3.4   Were reprisals efficient?

These findings already suggest that collective reprisals were not an efficient institution. Merchants clearly recognized the disadvantages of collective reprisals as a mechanism for enforcing mercantile contracts as early as the twelfth century and put pressure on both local and foreign rulers to curtail or abolish the practice.

One reason collective reprisals had uncertain benefits is that the type of commercial debt they made it possible to pursue was not, as we have seen, impersonal. The community responsibility system is portrayed as facilitating impersonal exchange between merchants of different communities who did not know one another and, indeed, did not *need* to know any details of each other's identity other than their community affiliation – something that is supposed to have been particularly important because many merchants did not even use surnames.[182] But as we have seen, the reprisal system was far from impersonal. For reprisals to function, a merchant had to be identified personally as a member of a particular guild or community against whom collective punishment could be directed. As we saw, actual procedures of collective reprisal always identified the individual debtor, providing details of prename, surname, which firm he was affiliated with and the town he came from. The fair-bans issued by the Champagne fair-wardens also often recorded the property owned by a particular merchant debtor in his home community, the fact that he had recently been observed frequenting that or other locations, and his known debts and claims on other merchants.[183] This suggests strongly that mercantile contracts were concluded between merchants who knew a considerable amount of individual detail about each other, precisely in order to facilitate chasing up any debts later. In order to get a debtor's guild to put pressure on him to repay his debt, the more information one knew about him as an individual, the better. Any long-distance exchange which the collective reprisal system encouraged cannot have been impersonal in the sense of being anonymous.[184] This is one reason why collective reprisals offered uncertain benefits – at least, no more certain benefits than were offered by the formal legal system of which it was a part.

[182] *Ibid.*, 169.   [183] Laurent (1935b), 286, 288, 300–1, 303–4.
[184] Boerner and Ritschl (2002), 208.

A second reason the benefits of collective reprisals were uncertain is that for the defrauded creditor, collective reprisals against a debtor's compatriots was a last-resort, high-cost solution fraught with delay and risk. Those debtor merchants desperate enough to renege on their debts to foreign merchants were often also desperate enough to ignore the pressure of their own compatriots or guild fellows.[185] A creditor merchant had a low expectation of recouping a loss via collective reprisal, since the process was costly and involved long debates and delays.[186] As Bassermann has shown, the process of imposing a collective fair-ban against compatriots of a defaulting debtor at the Champagne fairs was costly, lengthy and uncertain.[187] In 1295, for instance, a Florentine merchant failed to pay his debts at one of the Champagne fairs: the fair-wardens wrote their first letter to his community in Florence in 1296, were still threatening (though not yet imposing) a fair-ban in 1298, but received no cooperation from the Florentine municipal court; in the meantime the creditor had had to wait for three years, pay the costs of the fair-court and forego interest payments on the debt.[188] The same delay and uncertainty characterized many collective reprisals imposed by town courts. Bowsky shows that a collective reprisal granted by Siena in 1350 against the subjects of the Counts Ubaldini in retaliation for losses suffered by a group of Sienese merchants yielded a risibly small sum in recompense – nothing remotely approaching the amount of the damages to the Sienese merchants – and took five years to collect.[189]

If the benefits of collective reprisal were frequently doubtful, the costs were altogether too certain. Reprisals harmed entire communities of law-abiding merchants who were unable to control the odd loose cannon among their members, thereby increasing the risks of trade for any merchant and deterring some from trading at all.[190] For the average merchant, the reprisal system meant that when he arrived in a foreign trading centre he might be arrested because of some unpaid debt by a fellow citizen of which he was completely unaware.[191] Consequently, medieval merchants deliberately avoided trading centres that had made themselves notorious for exercising reprisals or, as we have seen, demanded suspension of community responsibility before they agreed to trade in a particular location.[192] If a merchant did decide to trade abroad, he typically took out formal insurance against the risk of reprisal, and for

---

[185] Cunningham (1910), 302–3.   [186] Bassermann (1911), 45–6.   [187] *Ibid.*, 44–50.
[188] *Ibid.*, 45–6.   [189] Bowsky (1981), 234–5.   [190] Cunningham (1910), 302–3.
[191] Lopez (1987), 364.
[192] Cunningham (1910), 302–3; Planitz (1919), 97, 171; Bautier (1952), 321; Van Houtte (1953), 179–80.

good reason.[193] As soon as a court abroad declared a verdict of collective reprisal, all members of that alien merchant community would collect all the debts and goods they could get their hands on and flee precipitately.[194] This not only caused them costs because they inevitably had to leave some goods and debts behind, it also created an incentive for *all* long-distance traders to keep their assets fungible, refrain from long-term deals and avoid bulky wares.

Above all, as contemporaries recognized, collective reprisals gave rise to spirals of violent retaliation between different merchant guilds and communities: 'murder, fire and war were often the outcome of this unedifying game of tit-for-tat'.[195] As soon as one polity declared reprisals against the citizens of another, the latter's polity had an incentive to declare reprisals against the first, even if there was no debt to be pursued, if only to motivate the cessation of the reprisal.[196] The spirals of fruitless retaliation to which reprisals between English and Flemish merchants in the 1190s gave rise rendered trade insecure between the two countries well into the thirteenth century, except when individual merchants obtained special safe-conducts or princes signed treaties.[197] At the thirteenth-century St Ives fair, Sachs finds that reprisals 'were accompanied by a torrent of litigation, with repeated disagreements as to which merchants were members of which communities, as well as hasty (and potentially arbitrary) seizures of goods'.[198] In 1265, when Flemish goods were arrested in a collective reprisal for a grievance of a burgess of Lynn, it led to a long series of tit-for-tat retaliations, ultimately resulting in the near disappearance of Flemish merchants from England and their replacement by Italians.[199] In the Mediterranean, too, collective reprisals led to spirals of retaliation, as in 1392 when Thessaloniki imprisoned Venetian merchants not for unpaid debts, but simply in reprisal for action taken by the Venetian authorities in Negroponte against Thessalonian merchants the preceding year.[200]

These spirals of reprisal inflicted costs not just on the communities of creditor and debtor merchants, but often on innocent third parties.[201] If a Genoese merchant whose Valencian creditor had failed to pay a debt was granted a writ of reprisal, for instance, he was entitled to use his merchant ship to prey on Valencian shipping until he had captured enough goods to cover the unpaid debt. As we saw in Chapter 6, merchant voyages frequently combined actual commerce with attacks

[193] F. E. De Roover (1945), 188; Constable (1994), 211.
[194] Cheyette (1970), 55–6; Bowsky (1981), 234.   [195] Wach (1868), 48.
[196] Schevill (1909), 118–19; Bowsky (1981), 234.   [197] Lloyd (1977), 9–23, 28–39.
[198] Sachs (2006), 709.   [199] Lloyd (1977), 9–23, 28–39.   [200] D. Jacoby (2003), 107.
[201] R. De Roover (1965), 45–6.

on other merchants, often legitimized by a writ of reprisal. In practice, this meant that innocent merchants travelling on the same ship as Valencian merchants could find themselves subjected to violence or confiscation by a Genoese creditor under the cloak of the 'collective responsibility system'. As Tai has shown, this type of legitimation lay behind many cases of 'piracy' against merchant shipping in the medieval Mediterranean.[202]

Why, then, did collective reprisals against entire guilds or communities of merchants arise and survive for so long in so many medieval economies? It was not because individual legal responsibility was as yet unknown. Nor, as we shall see, was it because contract enforcement through public law-courts was unavailable. That is, it was not because collective reprisals were efficient. Rather, it was because important subgroups of merchants and rulers saw collective reprisals as a source of personal profit. Merchants could benefit from collective reprisals against rivals, either because a writ of reprisal could exclude competitors at crucial junctures or because it gave one a licence to plunder rivals legally.[203] This was explicitly recognized by contemporaries such as the Genoese legal scholar Bartolomeo Bosco who wrote c. 1400 that reprisals 'are too often utilized for theft and undertakings of evil by all the citizens of Italy'.[204] Rulers could also benefit from collective reprisals because merchants were willing to pay – either directly or indirectly – for licences to prey legitimately on other merchants. If the ruler himself implemented the collective reprisal, he could often directly confiscate merchant wares for his own coffers. In 1195, for instance, the English merchant Nicholas Morel offered King Richard of England £60 to distrain the goods of Flemish merchants trading in England in reprisal for £343 he claimed to have lost in Flanders at the hands of men of Ghent. The English king accepted the £60 and welcomed the legitimacy Morel's complaint gave him to engage in widespread confiscations, but found it more profitable to sell the confiscated wares of Flemish merchants himself. Uninvolved merchants suffered, the insecurity of trade was increased and Morel as the supposed victim received nothing.[205] Similar motives appear to have actuated King Martin of Aragon in 1400 to grant a writ of collective reprisal against the Knights Hospitaller – the hope of replenishing royal coffers with a share of the property seized in reprisals from the wealthy order.[206]

---

[202] Tai (2003a); Tai (1996).
[203] For specific examples, see Barbour (1911), 530; Tai (1996), 586.
[204] Quoted in Tai (2003b), 271 with n. 34, 279 with n. 66; also Tai (1996), 514 with n. 12.
[205] Lloyd (1977), 9.   [206] Tai (1996), 569–73.

Collective reprisals were thus never an *efficient* institutional instrument to enforce long-distance trading contracts – or at least there is no evidence that they were. However, they were an effective *redistributional* instrument which was attractive to powerful groups. This explains why attempts to restrict collective reprisal started long before the late thirteenth century, but the actual practice of collective reprisal can be observed at intervals for centuries after that date. In the twelfth and thirteenth centuries, those European trading centres flourished where collective reprisals against the compatriots of defaulting merchant debtors were either suspended altogether or else were carefully circumscribed. In the fourteenth and fifteenth centuries, this became the case for more trading centres, but there were still places and periods when collective reprisals were rife. Where they were, it was not because formal, legal contract enforcement was lacking but because rulers or merchants themselves found the profits of legitimized predation too enticing to resist. The fact that long-distance merchants demanded the suspension of collective reprisals from the very beginning of the medieval Commercial Revolution suggests that alternative institutions were already available for enforcing contracts, and that it was the emergence of these institutions that enabled trade to grow.

7.4   Alternative contract-enforcement mechanisms

There is thus no evidence that merchant guilds played a major role in enforcing long-distance trading contracts in medieval Europe – whether through guild courts, informal peer pressure or collective reprisals. But they might still have been the efficient institution if the choice was between spotty contract enforcement through guilds and no enforcement at all because alternative institutions were unavailable. This is the picture painted by advocates of 'private ordering', who claim that medieval businessmen had to generate their own informal, self-enforcing arrangements because European societies of that era lacked alternative institutions to do the job.[207]

But is this bleak picture of the medieval European institutional landscape accurate? The evidence suggests the opposite. From the eleventh century at latest, a whole range of informal, quasi-formal and formal mechanisms existed in European economies, and were voluntarily used by long-distance merchants to enforce contracts in different situations. These mechanisms included transacting within trusted circles, using

---

[207] Milgrom, North and Weingast (1990), 20–1; Benson (2002), 130; Benson (1989), 650; Greif (2002a), 201–2; Greif (2006b), esp. 232–4.

contractual instruments, recording transactions in writing for future reference, negotiating out-of-court settlements before arbitration panels and litigating in public law-courts. All these mechanisms coexisted in an interconnected system of institutions – the family, the legal system, the urban community, the church, the state – within which guilds were only one component, and often a fairly minor one at that. This is not to say that any of these institutional mechanisms were perfect – far from it. But merchants' own behaviour reveals that in most situations these other contract-enforcement institutions were preferred by those for whom the enforcement of long-distance trading contracts was most crucial.

7.4.1   Transacting with a trusted circle

A first component of this system was the practice of transacting within a trusted circle which imposed informal peer pressure on those who defaulted on contracts. We have already touched on this practice, since a merchant guild is one possible example of such a network. But trusted trading circles could consist of family members, fellow citizens, co-religionists, speakers of the same language, members of the same cultural group or prior acquaintances – any group with closure (clearly defined membership) and multiplex ties (relationships in various spheres of activity). In theory, transacting within a trusted circle can improve contract enforcement in several ways. First, before merchants enter into a contract, network membership increases their *information* about one another, enabling them to select trustworthy partners. Second, when opportunism becomes tempting, network membership may cause parties to expect *non-material benefits* from complying with ethical norms of behaviour towards network members. Finally, if a contract is broken, network membership enables merchants to put pressure on one another via shared social ties in *multiplex relationships*. The theoretical disadvantage of networks, as we saw, are that they facilitate contract enforcement only among a narrow group of similar individuals. Potentially profitable exchanges with outsiders cannot be enforced and may thus be avoided, with the loss of gains from trade.

If merchants continue to favour trade with close circles of kin and friends, it suggests that other contract-enforcement mechanisms are not wholly efficient. This is exactly what occurred in pre-modern Europe. The pattern of doing business within a trusted circle of trading partners survived throughout the Middle Ages and well into the early modern period. The medieval Italian merchant houses, according to De Roover, often favoured business relationships within the extended family.[208] Likewise, the business ledgers of the fourteenth-century Hanseatic merchant Hildebrand Veckinchusen show him selecting friends and relatives as business associates, precisely in order to apply personal pressure in case of default.[209] The great merchants of eighteenth-century Stockholm, who were collectively termed the 'Skeppsbron Nobility', also carried out much of their business among relatives because of higher levels of trust within families than with outsiders.[210]

These examples suggest that it is inappropriate to portray merchant guilds as having offered enforcement mechanisms more efficient than available alternatives – even than this most primitive option, the pattern of doing business with a trusted circle. The medieval Italian merchant houses belonged to merchant guilds, Veckinchusen belonged to the German Hanse and the Skeppsbron Nobility belonged to the Stockholm merchant guild. Their transaction partners also belonged to merchant guilds. In principle, therefore, all these merchants could have relied on guild jurisdictions, informal peer pressure among guild members and collective reprisals against entire merchant guilds to enforce their contracts. The fact that medieval and early modern merchants continued to favour transactions with relatives, friends and members of their own social circles suggests that merchant guilds did not offer an efficient general alternative to the 'trusted circle' mechanism. Indeed, given the relatively minor role we have seen merchant guilds playing in contract enforcement, it seems likely that transacting with a trusted circle remained more important in enforcement than guilds were, despite the lost gains from potentially profitable exchanges with outsiders.

7.4.2   Contractual instruments: pledges, guarantors, cessions of credit

But medieval merchants did trade with outsiders, which raises the question of how they enforced exchanges. Contractual instruments offered one early and widely used mechanism. From the tenth century at latest, European, Muslim and Jewish merchants trading around the Mediterranean used contractual instruments called 'pledges' or 'guarantorships', where one party designated a piece of property or another individual as security that he would fulfil his bargain.

Medieval correspondence and notarial acts reveal long-distance merchants commonly promising – or even depositing – property or merchandise to guarantee compliance with contracts. In the tenth and

---

[208] R. De Roover (1948a), 21, 31–5.
[209] Lesnikov (1973); Schweichel (2001), 350–1; J. Gies and F. Gies (1972), ch. 16.
[210] Hasselberg, Müller and Stenlås (1997), 14–15.

eleventh centuries, Scandinavian and German merchants trading in the
Baltic deposited items of property to guarantee that they would fulfil
their bargains.[211] The notarial contracts of Venetian merchants in the
eleventh and early twelfth centuries similarly record the use of material pledges.[212] Merchants trading at the Champagne fairs in the twelfth
century pledged their property to guarantee fulfilment of long-distance
trading contracts.[213] In the thirteenth century, material pledges supporting commercial contracts were observed among long-distance spice
and silk merchants in Montpellier,[214] and among Cologne wine merchants at English fairs.[215] Around 1300, we see them used by Genoese
merchants trading alum to Bruges[216] and by Cypriot merchants trading cotton to Venice.[217] In eleventh-century Venice and in thirteenth-
century Montpellier, debtor merchants went so far as to promise double
indemnity if they delayed or defaulted on payment.[218] Merchants thus
pledged property as surety on long-distance trading contracts from the
eleventh to the fourteenth century, and as far afield as Italy, Provence,
Champagne, Flanders, England, Scandinavia and Germany. The fact
that the practice was voluntarily chosen by so many merchants over such
a long period and over such long distances suggests that they found it
worked well. The only disadvantage, of course, was that it limited a merchant's trade to the value of the goods he could nominate as a material
pledge.

An alternative, which did not suffer from the same limitation, was to
name a personal pledge – appointing a third party to stand surety for a
debt. This mechanism was also widely deployed by medieval merchants.
In early medieval Danish towns, for instance, any man with property
worth at least 3 marks was allowed to pledge surety to support a fellow
merchant.[219] In 1229, personal pledges were being used by Italian merchants trading in Smolensk.[220] In medieval Montpellier, a long-distance
merchant often named a *fidejussor* (literally 'oath-swearer') who undertook joint responsibility for a particular debt and offered his own person
and possessions as surety for repayment.[221]

The 'guest law' so widespread among long-distance merchants
throughout medieval Europe was also based on the concept of the personal pledge, since it required each foreign merchant to obtain a local

---

[211] Müller-Boysen (1990), 124–5.   [212] González de Lara (2008), 258 n. 30.
[213] W. J. Jones (1979), 12.   [214] Reyerson (1985), 41.   [215] Sachs (2006), 687.
[216] Briys and De ter Beerst (2006), 76–8.   [217] Coureas (2002), 3.
[218] Reyerson (1985), 41; González de Lara (2008), 275; Briys and De ter Beerst (2006),
78.
[219] Jacobsen (1993), 541.   [220] Dewey and Kleimola (1970), 341–2.
[221] Reyerson (1985), 41.

'host' to stand surety for his local liabilities.[222] This guest system was widely used from the tenth to the fifteenth century in most European economies, including Germany, the Low Countries and Italian city-states.[223] Medieval Bruges and Amsterdam had an entire system of hostellers and brokers who not only provided accommodation for foreign merchants but officially vouched for their sales and stood surety for their debts.[224] In medieval Florence, the local host was only held liable for a foreign merchant's debts up to the value of any goods and money the guest had deposited with him.[225] But in Amsterdam and Bruges, hosts had almost unlimited liability for their guest merchants' debts, in principle pledging their 'own life and property'.[226] So effective was this system of personal guarantors that Bruges hostellers and brokers developed additional institutional mechanisms to diversify risks: increasing their numbers of guest merchants, reducing guests' overdraft limits, fostering long-term relationships with particular guests and obtaining their own personal guarantors to bail them out in turn if a guest merchant defaulted.[227] This contract-enforcement mechanism was not only widespread, therefore, but was taken seriously by its participants, testifying to its commercial importance.

The 'cession of credit', which made a third party responsible for enforcing a contract, offered a further instrument through which medieval merchants guaranteed contracts. A 'cession of credit' was a formal mechanism by which an international merchant transferred his rights as creditor to a third party. Documents recording cessions of credit survive in large numbers for many medieval trading centres. In thirteenth-century Montpellier, Reyerson finds that a long-distance spice or silk merchant would transfer his claim against another merchant to a third party for various reasons – sometimes to obtain payment earlier than the term of the debt, but sometimes because 'the new creditor might have greater facility for the collection of the debt'; in particular, 'when foreign merchants were involved as debtors, a Montpellier creditor might cede or sell a credit to a foreign colleague of the same locality as that of the debtors'.[228] Similar acts of cession of credit have also been observed for other Mediterranean cities such as twelfth- and thirteenth-century Genoa[229] and Toulouse.[230] These contractual instruments survive in sufficient numbers to suggest

[222] On the guest system, see Peyer (1983).
[223] On Germany, see Schultze (1908); Süberkrüb (1951); and Peyer (1982). On the Low Countries, see Greve (2001), esp. 285–9, and Greve (2007). On Florence, see Szabó (1983), esp. 78–91.
[224] Greve (2001), esp. 285–9, and Greve (2007).   [225] Szabó (1983), 87.
[226] Gelderblom (2005b), 31 (quotation), 56 n. 222.   [227] Greve (2001), 281–4.
[228] Reyerson (1985), 104.   [229] Doehaerd (1941), 115–16.   [230] Wolff (1954), 378.

that they, too, were viewed as effective enforcement devices from early in the medieval Commercial Revolution.

7.4.3   Written records

Enforcing contracts requires proving what parties have agreed to and what they actually deliver. Such information can be gathered through personal observation by the parties themselves, observation by others who report orally, or written records. The transition from a legal system reliant on oral testimony (*ars dictaminis*) to one based on written evidence (*ars notaria*) increased enforceability of commercial contracts in several ways. Written evidence extended the time over which contracts could be enforced, since a particular agreement was no longer restricted to the lifespan of individual witnesses. It also extended the geographical range of contract enforcement, since it was no longer restricted to locations where witnesses could be present in person to give evidence. Written evidence reduced costs, as well, since assembling, transporting and presenting written records was almost always cheaper than doing the same thing with human beings.[231] Even those who regard the 'community responsibility system' as efficient admit that once contracts were recorded in writing, and written records became acceptable as evidence, the arguments for collective reprisals against entire merchant communities weakened, since the records made clear who was individually liable to do what.[232]

In the *early* medieval period, the favoured – and in many cases, the sole – form of proof in commercial litigation involved physical rather than written evidence. Physical evidence included bodily ordeal, presentation of tally sticks and oral testimony given under oath. Bodily ordeal as a method of proof in mercantile contracts disappeared quite early in the medieval Commercial Revolution: even in commercially less advanced regions of Europe, such as German-speaking central Europe, it was explicitly ruled out for merchant contracts by the twelfth century.[233] But most medieval law-courts long continued to accept the wooden tally stick with transactions carved into it and split between the transacting partners.[234] In eastern central Europe, the tally stick was still used into the seventeenth century.[235] Oral testimony delivered under oath was by far the most widely favoured form of physical testimony, and

---

[231] For a thoughtful consideration of these issues, see Lydon (2009), 647–52, 656–7.
[232] Greif (1992), 99–100.   [233] Munzinger (2006), 167.
[234] Hunt and Murray (1999), 66–7; Moore (1985), 117.
[235] For an example of it in use in seventeenth-century Bohemia, see Statní Okresní Archiv Děčín, Historická Sbírka Frýdlant, Karton 77, Amtsprotokolle 1611–16, fol. 25r, 5 May 1612.

long-distance merchants continued to rely on it throughout the medieval period; indeed, it is still used to this day in business litigation.[236]

But contemporaries – including merchants – regarded these physical forms of proof as costly and unsatisfactory. The anonymous English author of a thirteenth-century treatise on commercial litigation, for instance, described both oral testimony and tally sticks as 'hard and very tedious, and a kind of burden and continuous obstacle'.[237] Most merchants preferred written testimony because it reduced the cost of contracts, extended their time span and widened their geographical range. As a result, the more commercially advanced regions of Europe, especially Italy, saw the growth of commercial record-keeping from the tenth century on. Although initially commercial records were kept mainly by merchants for their own information (as we shall see in Chapter 9), they also began to be drawn up by notaries and local authorities, and gradually came to be accepted as legal evidence separate from the oral testimony of the individuals who wrote or witnessed them. By the later twelfth century, the use of written records as legal evidence in mercantile disputes was spreading to other advanced commercial regions such as the Low Countries.[238] By c. 1200, even in an economy such as Norway's, not renowned for its commercial precocity, an educational handbook could take it for granted that a merchant should be literate, numerate and well acquainted with the written law.[239]

Merchants' own business records were a basic form of written proof which both European and Muslim merchants used to enforce contracts from the beginning of the medieval Commercial Revolution. From the tenth century on, the so-called 'Maghribi traders' (more correctly termed 'Geniza merchants', Jews who traded as a minority in the predominantly Muslim societies of Northern Africa and the Near East) were recording their long-distance trade in a range of written documents, including slips of paper, bills of lading, marketing accounts, lists of expenses, correspondence, daily notebooks of accounts and main ledgers into which transactions were copied from daybooks. The Geniza merchants regarded it as a matter of course to keep such accounts, to request copies from those they did business with, to provide such copies when requested and to collate their accounts with those of their business associates elsewhere.[240] They also deliberately stored, copied and certified such correspondence to ensure contract enforcement, as shown by the behaviour of the

---

[236] Gelderblom (2005b), 25, 30, 55 nn. 207–13; Cauchies and Schepper (1997), 241.
[237] Basile et al. (1998), 14. The treatise is the *Lex Mercatoria*, probably written in the 1280s.
[238] Gelderblom (2005b), 25; Cauchies and Schepper (1997), 241–3.
[239] Larson (1917), chs. 3–4.   [240] Gil (2003), 282–6; Lydon (2009), 652.

eleventh-century merchant Joseph b. Jacob b. Yahbōy from Qayrawān who not only kept letters written by his deceased partner recording the receipt and sale of merchandise, but 'took the trouble of certifying all of the letters in court and preparing three copies of them' so as to prove his claims.[241]

The precise legal status of written evidence in mercantile conflicts in medieval Muslim societies is still debated. On the one hand, Gil has argued that the Geniza merchants used their records as proof in eleventh-century Jewish and Muslim law-courts: 'These various statements of accounts were deemed legally valid, as were the letters'.[242] But other scholars have argued that Muslim law limited the legal weight of written evidence in ways that significantly circumscribed contract enforcement in medieval Islamic economies compared to Christian Europe, in particular by requiring written records to be supported by oral testimony.[243] However this may have been, it seems unlikely that the Geniza merchants would have spent money on preparing multiple copies of commercial correspondence and having them certified in court if these documents did not at least enhance their ability to prove commercial contracts.

By the time of the Champagne fairs, and thus by the twelfth century at latest, European merchants were also keeping written records – correspondence, bonds, receipts, contracts, ledgers and daybooks – and one reason they did so was to provide evidence in litigation against transaction partners who broke contracts.[244] Fair-courts in England and Champagne appear to have been some of the earliest legal tribunals that admitted merchants' own informal records as legal proof.[245] But in the thirteenth century we observe municipal courts in trading cities, such as Venice and Genoa, letting merchants support their claims using business records such as ledgers and shipping documents, and by the fourteenth century we find the same practice in German cities.[246] The twelfth century also saw the appearance of the chirograph – two identical texts on a single sheet of paper, cut in two along an irregular line through some letters, with one copy given to each party to the contract, which could be matched up later when the contract was fulfilled or disputed. Mediterranean merchants started abandoning the chirograph after the twelfth century in favour of the notarial deed, as we shall see shortly. But German merchants continued to use it into the fourteenth century, by which time they were depositing copies of chirographs in town halls where

[241] Gil (2003), 280.   [242] Ibid., 288.   [243] Lydon (2009), 654–8.
[244] R. De Roover (1948a), 12–13; Bec (1967), 1215.   [245] Gelderblom (2005b), 25.
[246] Lopez and Raymond (1955), 212, 229–30.

they formed part of the growing system of contract registration by local authorities (discussed shortly).[247]

Along with use of written evidence came a need for certification and deposit services. These were provided by various institutional mechanisms – in southern parts of Europe primarily by the notarial system, in northern parts mainly by municipal offices. This was because long-distance commerce expanded earlier in Mediterranean Europe, and merchants required methods for officially certifying and depositing documents before local governments were able or willing to provide such services. Official notaries of the state and church had existed since Roman antiquity and survived through the Dark Ages, so documents drawn up, certified and stored by notaries were already recognized as legal evidence under Roman law. This existing tradition laid the basis for lay notaries to emerge in Italian cities by the eleventh century. Both the notarial tradition and the Roman Law's recognition of documentary evidence were lacking under the customary legal traditions of northern Europe; also, merchants' demand for certification and depositing of documentary evidence arose later, at the point at which municipal administrations had become sufficiently sophisticated to provide those services.

Under the notarial system, a contract was registered in front of the notary, a licensed professional who made written copies for both parties and wrote a copy into his 'protocols'. In a typical notarial debt recognition, a merchant formally declared in person to a notary that he owed his creditor a specific sum of money, that he had received specific merchandise from the creditor for it, that he promised to pay according to particular terms, and often that he provided particular security for the debt and submitted himself to the judgement of particular jurisdictions in case he did not pay.[248] Notaries also wrote up contracts to cover more complicated commercial arrangements, including business partnerships (discussed in the next chapter) and real estate transactions.[249] They prepared full credit-sales contracts, too, in which a seller promised to sell certain merchandise, a buyer promised to buy it, and both parties agreed on the amount of payment, the circumstances under which it was to be made and how the delivery was to take place.[250] In the long-distance trading cities of Italy, Iberia and Provence, and increasingly throughout the Mediterranean trading world, the written records of contracts kept by notaries in their formal protocols were admitted as evidence in courts of law.[251]

---

247 Dollinger (1970), 156.
248 Reyerson (1985), 41–3; Doehaerd (1941), 106–8, 116–19.
249 Gelderblom (2005b), 25; Doehaerd (1941), 106–41.   250 Reyerson (1985), 42–3.
251 Gelderblom (2005b), 25.

A related institutional mechanism, observed among Genoese traders in the thirteenth century, was the *scriba* system. A *scriba* was an official accountant or bookkeeper appointed by a merchant to travel on board ship for a particular trading venture, during which he was responsible for recording all the financial operations in a register called the *cartularium navis*. These included all movements of assets and liabilities, expenses for the journey, wares sold and cash collected from customers. Genoese law adopted this practice, already widespread among merchants, and appointed a public *scriba* to use the same bookkeeping techniques for transactions within Genoa's public finances. The registers of a *scriba* could be used by a judge to enforce a contract or resolve a commercial dispute which was brought to court. The *scriba* system was already being used in financial litigation in Genoa as early as 1259 and reference to the *scriba*'s registers as a way of resolving later disputes was incorporated into commercial contracts by Genoese merchants as early as 1298.[252]

As municipal governments in southern European cities became more sophisticated, they transformed notaries into official document keepers, for instance by only admitting documents as legal proof when written up by a notary. In some cases, this function appears to have been taken on even by innkeepers, as in thirteenth-century Verona where the legality of a contract was guaranteed by an innkeeper's registering a transaction concluded in his tavern in return for a small fee from the contracting parties.[253] But more typically the profession of notary became a specialized occupation, often with its own guild organization.[254] The earliest surviving notarial acts for Genoa date from the years 1155–64, in the cartulary of Giovanni Scriba.[255]

The importance of the notarial system is shown by the large numbers of notaries operating in most Italian trading cities. A 1288 description of Milan noted specially that, 'The notaries are more than 1500, among whom there are a great many who are excellent in drawing contracts.'[256] By the mid-thirteenth century Genoa had about 200 notaries, and by *c.* 1298 500–1,000, one for every 100–200 inhabitants. Notaries from other parts of Italy, Provence, France, Switzerland and Germany settled in Genoa in order to serve its substantial communities of foreign merchants.[257] By *c.* 1300 Pisa had nearly 300 notaries.[258] In 1245, a

---

[252] Briys and De ter Beerst (2006), 57, 60, 68–70, 79, 88–9.
[253] Szabó (1983), 82.   [254] Doehaerd (1941), 103–6; Mitchell (1904), 109–10.
[255] F. E. De Roover (1940), 41–2.   [256] Lopez and Raymond (1955), 65.
[257] Doehaerd (1941), 105–6; Briys and De ter Beerst (2006), 40, 68; Mitchell (1904), 108.
[258] Mitchell (1904), 108.

single Marseilles notary drew up more than 1,000 commercial documents, and on one day of that year he drew up nearly 60.[259]

The notarial system thus arose very early in the Commercial Revolution in southern Europe, and provided certification services long before public municipal institutions did so. It was only in the fourteenth century that the legal obligation to certify commercial documents with notaries began gradually to die out in many parts of Mediterranean Europe, and not until the sixteenth century that business correspondence began to enjoy an autonomous legal validity as evidence in courts of law.[260]

In northern Europe, long-distance commerce developed somewhat later, coinciding with the period when local governments were becoming sophisticated enough to provide merchants with record-keeping, certification and document-deposit services. The notarial system gradually spread from southern Europe to the more important northern European trading cities, such as Bruges and Antwerp, to serve the needs of Italian and Iberian merchants accustomed to using notaries. A small community of Italian notaries set up business in Bruges, as did a community of Portuguese notaries in Antwerp.[261] So essential were notaries to a long-distance merchant's business that one sanction imposed on violators of the rules of the Portuguese merchant guild in early sixteenth-century Antwerp was exclusion from the services of Portuguese notaries in the city.[262] Although in northern Europe the indigenous notary lacked the independent role he assumed in southern Europe, other quasi-public intermediaries such as money changers and brokers kept similar records of the contracts they negotiated, and their records began increasingly to be accepted as legal proof in courts of law.[263]

But northern European local authorities did not typically require documents to have been drawn up by professional notaries in order to be admissible as legal proof.[264] Instead, the protocols and registers of local municipal authorities themselves largely performed the role that notarial registers performed in the south. In northern France, Germany and the Low Countries, local magistrates were responsible for keeping formal protocols officially recording commercial contracts, real estate transfers, debts and guarantees, and these formal protocols were used as legal proof in commercial litigation.[265] In Flanders by the eleventh century, aldermen's courts were issuing simple written contracts stating the indebtedness of one person to another, and in Holland the same

---

[259] *Ibid.*   [260] Trivellato (2007), 84.
[261] Gelderblom (2005b), 25; Lopez and Raymond (1955), 279.
[262] Goris (1925), 52–3.
[263] Greve (2000), 43–4; Ehrenberg (1995), 441–4; Frensdorff (1901), 302–10.
[264] Gelderblom (2005b), 29, 55 n. 204.   [265] *Ibid.*, 25–6.

documents emerged in the second half of the thirteenth century.[266] In German-speaking central Europe by the 1270s at latest, town governments were sufficiently involved in contract enforcement that they had begun to keep registers in which merchants could record debts and contracts with a municipal certificate of authenticity. The first recorded German municipal contract register was the Hamburg *Schuldbuch* ('Book of Debts') whose surviving volumes begin in 1270, followed by the Lübeck *Niederstadtbuch* ('Lower Town Book') in 1277. Similar debt and contract registers survive in Riga from 1286, Stralsund from 1288 and Lüneburg from 1290.[267] Thus by 1270, German and Baltic town governments had institutionalized the practice whereby they registered, authenticated and enforced merchant contracts.[268] In southern Europe, too, local governments became more sophisticated in the thirteenth century, and Italian cities began maintaining public registries listing individual cases of defaulted debts and towns that refused legal protection to creditors.[269]

Medieval European merchants thus had at their disposal, and actively used, a range of mechanisms to minimize the probability that contracts would be disputed – transacting with kin and friends, using contractual instruments such as pledges and cessions of credit, and keeping written records which were officially certified and deposited with notaries or municipal offices. These institutional mechanisms were much more observable in limiting contract-breaking than merchant guilds were. This does not mean that these mechanisms were perfect – merchants still sometimes violated their contracts. Nor were these mechanisms efficient, in the sense of dominating all others. But they did play a more observable role than merchant guilds in the menu of available institutions for reducing the probability that contracts would be disputed. And they were eagerly and voluntarily used by merchants themselves, to a much greater extent than guilds were employed for that purpose.

7.4.4   Arbitration

But conflicts over long-distance trading contracts did still occur. What happened then? Did long-distance merchants then have to use guild tribunals, peer pressure or collective guild reprisals, because there were no alternative mechanisms for pursuing debtors? The evidence shows not. When contracts *did* come under dispute, medieval merchants used an array of institutional mechanisms – ones in which merchant guilds also played little role.

---

[266] Dijkman (2007), 12–13.   [267] Dollinger (1970), 164.   [268] *Ibid.*, 156.
[269] Wach (1868), 48.

One important mechanism was arbitration, by which merchants tried to solve contractual disputes without litigation. Medieval merchants preferred to avoid the pecuniary and time costs of formal legal proceedings, which could consume a large share of the yield expected from enforcing a broken contract. Involvement in formal litigation also sent a signal to potential transaction partners that one might have undesirable characteristics, such as a tendency towards conflict or a shaky business. Well into the early modern period, merchants can be observed deliberately avoiding legal proceedings in the interests of preserving their reputations, even when it meant writing off commercial debts.[270] For all these reasons, arbitration offered an attractive alternative to formal litigation, in pre-modern trade just as in the modern business world.[271]

There were two kinds of arbiters in medieval and early modern trade – the first nominated by the disputing parties (often a fellow merchant), the second appointed by a public law-court (as a sort of lay judge).[272] Just as in modern business arbitration, a pre-modern arbitration panel was required to apply a particular code of rules – usually those prevailing in the legal system in that locality, although in disputes exclusively involving foreign merchants panels might be permitted to use the commercial laws of the merchants' homeland.[273] The arbitration panel typically heard witness statements, consulted written records and conducted one or more oral hearings of the disputants before issuing a ruling. The arbitration system was interdependent with other contract enforcement institutions, particularly the notarial system and the local legal system, since in general the decisions of arbiters had to be registered with a notary, confirmed by local magistrates or both.[274]

Arbitration was used to enforce contracts from the very beginning of the medieval Commercial Revolution. In the eleventh century, it was already widespread in many European legal systems, and it was certainly being used in merchant contract enforcement by the early thirteenth century.[275] In thirteenth-century Genoa, for instance, the Commune appointed arbiters to settle commercial disputes between merchants.[276] In Marseilles in 1230, a dispute between two merchants over a contract to ship skins to the Levant was solved by arbitration, in which both

[270] J. M. Price (1991), 296; Gelderblom (2003), 634; Gelderblom (2005b), 5.
[271] Volckart and Mangels (1999), 432–3.
[272] Lambert and Stabel (2005), 14; Goris (1925), 67.
[273] Gelderblom (2005b), 9–10, 47.
[274] Lambert and Stabel (2005), 14; Gelderblom (2005b), 9–10, 48 n. 72.
[275] Basile et al. (1998), 41; Powell (1983), 53; Powell (1984); Sachs (2006); Cheyette (1970); White (1978).
[276] Briys and De ter Beerst (2006), 8, 40, 69; S. A. Epstein (1996), 70.

parties agreed to submit the dispute to two 'freely chosen' judges without taking it to court.[277] In 1287, two long-distance merchants sued a third in the fair-court of St Ives, and instead of litigating, asked for a day in which to negotiate a settlement under the arbitration of a fourth party; the abbey officials operating the fair-court agreed, conditional on the defendant's paying a fine to the court, a practice widespread in English local courts of the period.[278] In 1282, the privileges granted to English merchants in Flanders included provision for an arbitration process to resolve commercial conflicts.[279] Contract enforcement at the Champagne fairs also involved the appointment of arbitration panels by the fair-wardens, as in 1311 when numerous Italian and French creditors used such a panel to enforce a contract against a merchant of Malines (Mechelen).[280] So widespread was the practice of arbitration that some three-quarters of lawsuits involving Spanish merchants in fifteenth-century Bruges were ultimately resolved by the use of arbiters.[281]

Merchant guild officers sometimes acted as arbiters, but so did many other knowledgeable merchants. In 1311, for instance, in a debt conflict between Italian, French and Flemish merchants at the Champagne fairs, the arbitration panel consisted of a Genoese merchant and a burgher of one of the fair-towns, both designated simply by name, not as guild officials; the Champagne burgher could not have been a merchant guild officer, as he was a local.[282] In medieval Bruges, although the consuls of alien merchant guilds were sometimes invited to act as arbiters in cases involving foreign merchants, they did not monopolize these positions, and many other long-resident merchants were also appointed as arbiters. The key characteristic for a man to be acceptable as an arbiter was not whether he held office in a merchant guild but how long he had been resident in Bruges and how neutral he was towards the two parties to the conflict.[283]

Arbitration was not just a primitive contract-enforcement institution of the Middle Ages, but continued to be employed well into the early modern period and in sophisticated trading centres such as Amsterdam. It was used not only to enforce straightforward commercial contracts, but to resolve complex matters such as the bankruptcy of entire merchant firms.[284] In a dispute over non-fulfilment of a freight contract in 1596 between a Dutch merchant resident in Castile and a Dutch shipmaster in Amsterdam, for instance, it was an arbitration panel that issued

---

[277] Cave and Coulson (1936), 157–8.   [278] Sachs (2006), 721.
[279] Häpke (1908), 66.   [280] Laurent (1935b), 293–4.
[281] Gilliodts-van Severen (1901–2), 35.   [282] Laurent (1935b), 293–4.
[283] Lambert and Stabel (2005), 14.
[284] Gelderblom (2005b), 10, with examples on 47 n. 60.

the complicated judgement, which involved 'the payment of tolls, fines and damages, the lifting of the seizure of goods and the freeing of a hostage in Seville, the return of business papers, and finally the pledging of sureties'.[285] Likewise, in mid-sixteenth-century London a complicated conflict between two Venetian-Greek merchants over a shipment of currants was ultimately resolved by both parties agreeing to an arbitration judgement from a panel consisting of two English merchants.[286] Julfa-Armenian merchant colonies in seventeenth- and eighteenth-century trading centres such as Amsterdam, Paris, Livorno, Venice, Madras and Hyderabad operated a type of arbitration panel called a *Jumiat*, manned by foreign merchants if not enough Julfan merchants were available to make up a quorum.[287] Arbitration was thus effective enough to be voluntarily chosen as a contract-enforcement mechanism by merchants from the eleventh century until well into the seventeenth – and indeed is widely used in international trade to this day.

Merchant guilds themselves often preferred to resort to an arbitration panel, instead of invoking their own guild tribunals. The Spanish merchant guild in medieval Bruges, for instance, can be observed using arbitration rather than its own consular court to resolve commercial disputes.[288] A wide-ranging conflict in 1452 between the Castilian and the Biscayan merchants trading in Bruges about who would formally represent them in the city was ultimately resolved through referring to an arbitration panel.[289]

Arbitration is sometimes portrayed as a private-order institutional arrangement,[290] but in fact it was interdependent with the public legal system. Local governments and central authorities approved of arbitration and supported it institutionally. Arbiters were often appointed by local courts and were expected to use the rules and customs of the public legal system, as we have seen – sometimes the local one, although sometimes the one accepted by foreign merchants if foreigners were the sole disputants. The decisions of arbiters were endowed with the force of law and were enforced by local and central authorities. In Genoa by 1157 at latest, the commune was appointing official arbiters, who served for a term of two years and took an oath to dispense justice fairly.[291] A 1225 treaty between Florence and St Gimignano provided that commercial disputes between their respective citizens should be settled within twenty

---

[285] *Ibid.*, 11–12 (quotation 12), 47 n. 71.   [286] Fusaro (2002), 14–15 with nn. 56–7.
[287] Aslanian (2006), 398–9.   [288] Gelderblom (2005b), 14.
[289] See the published case in Gilliodts-van Severen (1901–2), 50–2.
[290] Benson (1989), 653; Benson (1992), 8–10, 20–5.
[291] S. A. Epstein (1996), 67, 69–70.

days 'by judgment, arbitration, sentence, or friendly agreement'.[292] In the medieval Low Countries, local law-courts often ordered disputants to submit to arbitration rather than continuing with a formal lawsuit.[293] In most trading centres in medieval Europe, the ruling of an arbitration panel was customarily confirmed by local magistrates.[294] The 1225 treaty between Florence and St Gimignano provided that any judgement reached through arbitration would be enforced by the 'the Podestà or Rector of the territory or land from which the accused comes'.[295] In 1311, when an arbitration panel decided a dispute between various international merchants over a debt incurred at the Champagne fairs, the decision of the arbiters was explicitly endorsed (and enforced) by the princely fair-wardens.[296] In 1359, the count of Flanders granted the English merchant guild in Bruges a charter giving it internal jurisdiction over its own members, but providing for conflicts between English and Flemish merchants to be decided by an arbitration court consisting of two Englishmen and two 'good citizens of Bruges'.[297] Arbitration was thus a widely used method by which medieval merchants could enforce contracts legally without incurring the expenses and delays of formal litigation.

7.4.5   Litigation

If all these other mechanisms failed, a medieval merchant could sue his defaulting debtor in a court of law. This possibility is dismissed in a number of accounts of how merchants enforced long-distance trading contracts during the medieval Commercial Revolution. Milgrom, North and Weingast, for instance, claim that the Champagne fairs operated without public courts able to penalize defaulting debtors through physical sanctions or seizure of goods. The revival of trade in medieval Europe took place, they argue, 'without the benefit of state enforcement of contracts', so merchants had to evolve 'their own private code of laws' and use private-order sanctions such as ostracism and exclusion.[298] Greif, too, describes medieval Europe as failing to provide adequate state enforcement for commercial contracts, and claims that in the thirteenth century 'English law precluded . . . punishing a borrower who defaulted

---

[292] Cave and Coulson (1936), 212–15, quoted according to the text modernized by Jerome S. Arkenburg at www.fordham.edu/halsall/source/1225florence-gig.html.

[293] Gelderblom (2005b), 11, 47 n. 67.   [294] Ibid., 10.

[295] Cave and Coulson (1936), 212–15, quoted according to the text modernized by Jerome S. Arkenburg at www.fordham.edu/halsall/source/1225florence-gig.html.

[296] Laurent (1935b), 294 with n. 1.   [297] Henn (1999), 138.

[298] Milgrom, North and Weingast (1990), 2.

with imprisonment'; as a result, merchants developed the 'community responsibility system' to impose collective reprisals on the communities of defaulting debtors.[299] Nivet claims that in Europe as late as the sixteenth century, 'courts specialized in commercial disputes were less significant than internal voluntary mechanisms designed by the contractors themselves, like internal codes of conduct in merchant guilds'.[300] According to this widely held view, the revival of European long-distance trade after the eleventh century was based on private-order, self-enforcing institutions – 'law merchants', 'community responsibility' and merchant guilds. This was because contract enforcement in public law-courts was impossible: the state was weak, the church uninterested and towns unwilling to provide impartial judgements to foreigners. How accurate is this portrayal?

7.4.5.1 State courts Closer examination of the evidence suggests that although public law-courts were by no means perfect in medieval Europe, they did offer contract enforcement which long-distance merchants voluntarily utilized from the eleventh century at latest. Public provision of commercial contract enforcement was taken for granted in the Mediterranean from the early centuries of the medieval Commercial Revolution. When the First Crusade conquered Palestine and established the kingdom of Jerusalem in 1099, for example, the Crusader authorities set up the so-called *Assises de Jérusalem*, which consisted of a Commercial Court (for civil and commercial disputes, with two Christian and four Syrian jurors) and a *Cour des Bourgeois* (for criminal matters) – despite the presence of Italian merchant colonies that could have provided private-order enforcement.[301] In Italy itself, early treaties between city-states envisaged the municipal resolution of commercial conflicts that failed to yield to arbitration, as in the 1225 treaty between Florence and St Gimignano mentioned earlier.[302] In the spice and silk trades of thirteenth-century Montpellier, notarial recognitions of debts often stated that the debtor merchant submitted himself to the jurisdiction of the king of France's specialized commercial courts.[303]

In north-west Europe, too, counter to the claims of Milgrom, North and Weingast, the public legal system provided contract enforcement to long-distance merchants. At the Champagne fairs from the 1180s onwards, conflicts involving foreign merchants were resolved directly by the counts of Champagne as the sovereign,[304] his *châtelain* (jurisdictional

---

[299] Greif (2002a), 195.   [300] Nivet (2004), 8.
[301] Liu (1925), ch. II, section II.   [302] Cave and Coulson (1936), 212–15.
[303] Reyerson (1985), 41, 100–3.   [304] Alengry (1915), 110.

deputy),[305] and the princely *bailli* or *prévôt* who maintained a 'lodge' at each fair.[306] This public legal provision was enhanced by the appointment of princely fair-wardens who first appear in 1174,[307] were witnessing merchant contracts by 1225,[308] and were dispensing justice to foreign merchants alongside the princely *baillis* by 1252,[309] although not until after c. 1260 did their contract-enforcement role surpass that of ecclesiastical courts (discussed shortly).[310] Foreign merchants frequenting the Champagne fairs could also appeal against decisions of these princely courts to higher ones – the *Jours de Troyes* and, after 1285, the *Parlement de Paris*.[311] In medieval Flanders, Brabant and Holland, likewise, princely courts provided contract-enforcement services, indeed becoming so popular among merchants that it proved necessary to limit their accessibility, restricting them to cases involving damages above a certain value.[312] In German-speaking central Europe, as well, by the twelfth century written norms of commercial conduct were prevalent and third-party adjudication of mercantile disputes was commonplace.[313] A series of commercial treaties between German and Russian trading centres from 1189 onwards explicitly stated their shared legal norms concerning legal protection by the political authorities of persons and goods active in long-distance trade.[314] In England, too, the crown made the state legal system available for enforcing mercantile contracts. As early as the reign of King John (1199–1216), the crown provided that the machinery of the exchequer could be used by merchants to pursue commercial debts.[315] English common law courts were hearing conflicts involving foreign merchants from 1260 at latest, despite the simultaneous existence of so-called Piepowder Courts, to adjudicate mercantile disputes at fairs and markets.[316] In 1283 (with the Statute of Merchants) and 1285 (with its re-enactment), the English crown issued a series of measures, with foreign merchants specifically in mind, to ease pursuit of commercial debts with a rapid legal process.[317]

Wherever European merchants traded during the medieval Commercial Revolution, therefore, state enforcement was available and

---

[305] Bautier (1953), 122–3.

[306] Arbois de Jubainville (1859), 22; Bourquelot (1865), II: 20 n. 1; Arbois de Jubainville and Pigeotte (1859–66), III: 235; Bourquelot (1839–40), II: 409, 416; Boutaric (1867), II: 551 (no. 7394).

[307] Arbois de Jubainville and Pigeotte (1859–66), III: 235–6, 367; Bautier (1953), 118.

[308] Bautier (1953), 118–19.   [309] Bourquelot (1839–40), II: 409.

[310] Bautier (1953), 119, 122–3.   [311] Bassermann (1911), 3; Alengry (1915), 116–17.

[312] Gelderblom (2005b), 16–17.   [313] Munzinger (2006), 167.

[314] Goetz (1916), 14–72, 230–97; Munzinger (2006), 167.   [315] Miller (1965), 311–12.

[316] Baker (1979), 302–6; Gelderblom (2005b), 49 n. 105; Basile et al. (1998), 32–3.

[317] Ashley (1888), 104–5; Miller (1965), 312.

long-distance merchants voluntarily used it to enforce contracts. This does not mean that state legal systems provided perfect enforcement. In some cases, princes were unable to enforce contracts satisfactorily because territorial fragmentation limited their coercive reach. In others, princes were swayed by pecuniary or political pressure – from their own merchants, foreign merchants or foreign princes – to issue less than impartial judgements. But the fact that long-distance traders demanded mercantile conflict resolution from the state and voluntarily chose to use public law-courts – even when guild courts existed – suggests that rulers provided a quality of commercial contract enforcement superior to many alternatives.

7.4.5.2 Ecclesiastical courts Public alternatives to state courts did exist, however, and this was arguably another strength of the institutional framework available to medieval European merchants, since jurisdictional competition could create incentives for all courts to provide impartial judgements. The medieval church offered a second set of law-courts – ones with, in principle, a universal competence – to which long-distance merchants could bring commercial conflicts. Some of the earliest records of the medieval Commercial Revolution – those dating from the twelfth century – show the church operating canon law-courts which were also used for commercial contract enforcement.

From the twelfth century on, long-distance merchants attending the Champagne fairs had their commercial contracts drawn up in front of ecclesiastical authorities, litigated against defaulting debtors before ecclesiastical courts and appealed to papal tribunals to ensure payment from reluctant debtors. Before 1260, ecclesiastical tribunals were more important than the fair-wardens' courts in witnessing and enforcing trading contracts at the Champagne Fairs.[318] The international importance of ecclesiastical jurisdictions was explicitly recognized in letters from the Champagne fair-wardens pursuing defaulting debtors, addressed 'to all justices, as much of the church as secular ones, who see these present letters'.[319] At the fairs of St Ives, likewise, surviving plea rolls for 1270–1324 show that long-distance merchants 'did not create their own legal order out of their own needs and views', but rather relied primarily on the jurisdiction of the local abbey (as the fair authority).[320]

---

[318] Arbois de Jubainville (1859), III: 166, 169, 235; Goldschmidt (1891), 229–30, 233; Bassermann (1911), 4–5; Bourquelot (1865), I: 182ff., II: 24–5; Bautier (1952), 318–20; Bassermann (1911), 4–5; Verlinden (1965), 128, 132.
[319] See, e.g., Berti (1857), e.g. 256–7 (quotation 256), no. XVII.
[320] Sachs (2006), 693–4 (quotation 694), 727–8.

In medieval Provence, too, defaulting debtors were frequently brought before ecclesiastical tribunals which imposed penalties ranging from fines to excommunication.[321]

Again, this is not to claim that ecclesiastical courts offered perfect commercial contract enforcement. But they were evidently in a position to compete with other tribunals for jurisdiction over commercial conflicts, as shown by the fact that merchants frequenting the Champagne fairs voluntarily took their disputes to ecclesiastical courts, long before guild jurisdictions even existed at the fairs. This should not be surprising. In principle, at least, the medieval church exercised a jurisdiction which transcended territorial and linguistic frontiers, was recognized by temporal authorities throughout Christendom and disposed of enviable moral suasion and a far-flung network of personnel. Ecclesiastical jurisdictions were thus in a position to compete effectively with other tribunals in judging temporal as well as spiritual disputes – and one important set of temporal disputes it judged were commercial conflicts among long-distance merchants.

7.4.5.3 Municipal courts   Municipal law-courts provided a further public alternative to guild jurisdictions.[322] Municipal law-courts suffered from the disadvantage that important trading cities often had their own bodies of merchants with the incentive and capacity to influence local magistrates. The existence of these poor incentives has led recent scholarship to dismiss medieval city courts as incapable of supporting long-distance trade because foreign merchants could not trust them to provide impartial justice. Some scholars argue that although municipal courts can be observed resolving commercial conflicts, they were actually simply acting in the interests of local merchants, and this is why foreign merchants needed merchant guilds to ensure impartial contract enforcement, whether directly through guild jurisdictions or indirectly through the reprisal system.[323] It is true that local courts in some medieval European towns sometimes discriminated against foreign merchants. Volckart and Mangels, for instance, argue that in the twelfth and thirteenth centuries, local courts in Germany and eastern Europe favoured local merchants over foreigners.[324]

But municipal law-courts also had advantages. Urban magistrates were knowledgeable about commercial practices in general and local business

---

[321] Wolff (1954), 375; Malausséna (1969), 229.
[322] Pirenne (1925), 170, 175–6, 189–212.
[323] Greif (1997), 8; Greif (2004), 129; Van Houtte (1961), 276.
[324] Volckart and Mangels (1999), 44.

conditions in particular. If poor incentives to behave impartially towards foreigners could be overcome, local courts were in a position to provide high-quality contract enforcement to long-distance traders. Various solutions to these poor incentives existed. One was inter-urban competition. If foreign merchants could not get impartial justice in one city, and if there were enough other cities nearby, long-distance trade would move to cities that offered more impartial contract enforcement. A second pressure towards impartiality was the competition among jurisdictions we have just been discussing. If local municipal courts would not enforce contracts fairly, foreign merchants would register their contracts with (and pay court fees to) princely or ecclesiastical jurisdictions, taking lucrative business away from dysfunctional municipal tribunals. A third solution was deliberate action. Those in charge of municipal governments recognized that foreign merchants would not trade in their city without assurances of impartial contract enforcement, so cities had an incentive to enter into binding commitments to provide all litigating parties with fair justice.

One way municipal governments did this was by reaching agreements with other cities. Thus from the twelfth century at latest we observe treaties between Italian city-states, in which they agreed which court should have jurisdiction over mercantile disputes (usually the debtor's municipal court), as well as promising impartial justice to each other's citizens.[325] In 1200, a treaty between the count of Holland and the duke of Brabant agreed that a creditor in one of their territories was only to be permitted to seize the property of a debtor in the other if application to the debtor's local court was rejected, a provision believed to be inserted upon pressure from Brabant merchants.[326]

A second approach was for major trading cities to establish tribunals explicitly guaranteeing impartial justice to foreign merchants. Pisa, for instance, set up a court called the 'Judges for Foreigners' that offered enforcement of claims by foreigners against citizens of the town, which was used by successfully by Venetian merchants from 1176 at latest.[327] In 1296, Genoa followed this pattern by establishing 'a special tribunal to hear claims against its own citizens'.[328]

A third way a trading city could signal its intention of providing good mercantile justice was by standardizing and writing down its law code, explicitly incorporating provisions governing commercial conflicts, and then in practice adjudicating disputes between merchants fairly. As early as the twelfth century, the magistrates of Italian, Spanish, German,

---

[325] Boerner and Ritschl (2002), 208.   [326] Dijkman (2007), 11.
[327] Robbert (1983), 382.   [328] Lopez (1987), 364.

Dutch, Flemish and English cities can be observed pursuing this strategy, which must have enjoyed some success since otherwise foreign merchants would not have brought their litigation to these municipal courts.[329] Unsurprisingly, some of the earliest evidence of municipal courts judging merchant disputes comes from the Italian and Provençal cities which spearheaded the Commercial Revolution in the medieval Mediterranean. By c. 1150 at latest, Italian city-states began to write down their law codes and establish courts willing to adjudicate between merchants.[330] Genoa, for instance, developed permanent courts in the twelfth century, with law codes governing commercial contract enforcement.[331] Surviving thirteenth-century copies of the Genoese law code show that it punished contract-breaking severely: a notary who falsified a document was to lose his hand; a false witness was to be publicly beaten and lose his nose;[332] a merchant who behaved opportunistically towards creditors or partners was to be incarcerated in the Malapaga prison.[333] In Montpellier by the thirteenth century, merchants were bringing their commercial disputes before the court of the *bayle* of the king of Mallorca, in practice controlled by the Montpellier town council.[334] After presenting a debtor for non-payment before the local court, a merchant creditor could seize the debtor bodily, imprison him in chains with bread and water, and (after a designated period) sell his property.[335]

Other early examples come from the Champagne fairs, where trade between long-distance merchants was supported by municipal jurisdictions, both in the fair-towns and in the home cities of foreign merchants. The four Champagne fair-towns of Troyes, Provins, Lagny and Bar-sur-Aube operated mayoral courts at which foreign merchants trading at the Champagne fairs in the early thirteenth century had their commercial contracts drawn up and certified, so as to be able to use these municipal jurisdictions in case of default, a practice that pre-dated their using the princely fair-wardens for this purpose.[336] Municipal jurisdictions outside Champagne also contributed to enforcing fair-contracts, since foreign

---

[329] Baker (1986), 349–51; Basile et al. (1998), 69–70 and passim, 114; Dijkman (2007), 10–13; Gelderblom (2005b), 20–4; Nörr (1987), 196; Volckart and Mangels (1999), 443.

[330] Ascheri (2000), esp. 141.

[331] *Ibid.*, 144; Briys and De ter Beerst (2006), 68–70; S. A. Epstein (1996), 68–70; Vitale (1955).

[332] S. A. Epstein (1994), 317–18 with n. 13.   [333] Briys and De ter Beerst (2006), 70.

[334] Reyerson (1985), 95–6, 100.   [335] *Ibid.*, 95–6.

[336] Arbois de Jubainville and Pigeotte (1859–66), VI: 104; Bourquelot (1839–40), I: 210, II: 409, 416; Bourquelot (1865), I: 210, II: 19–20, 196; Bautier (1952), 318–19; Arbois de Jubainville (1859), 18–30; Chapin (1937), 126–33; Davidsohn (1896–1901), 30.

merchants brought disputes to the courts of their own and their debtors' home cities.[337]

In the early twelfth century the great Flemish cities had also developed municipal jurisdictions which enforced commercial contracts, not just for local merchants but for foreign ones too. In Bruges, for instance, a local court was established around 1100 which took responsibility for judging commercial conflicts, including those of foreign merchants visiting the Bruges fairs or residing in the city itself.[338] The charter granted by the count of Flanders to Bruges around 1190 promised that foreign merchants were to have their disputes adjudicated by the town aldermen.[339] Indeed, Bruges developed into the most important international trading centre in north-west Europe by the mid-fourteenth century without offering any alternative jurisdiction other than its local municipal court, apart from a maritime court in Damme which dealt with conflicts between sailors, shipmasters and Flemish merchants.[340] The earliest Hanse privileges in Bruges explicitly provided for access to municipal and princely courts, indicating the German merchants' desire to use such tribunals.[341] This was not surprising, given that by the twelfth century written norms of commercial conduct and third-party adjudication of mercantile disputes were commonplace in the larger German trading cities.[342]

The same early development of municipal jurisdictions serving the needs of foreign merchants can be seen in other cities in the Low Countries. When Spanish and German merchants obtained guild privileges in Aardenburg in 1280, commercial conflicts were judged jointly by the *procureurs* of the guild and the local justices of Aardenburg.[343] In the permanent markets of Antwerp and Amsterdam and at the fairs of Flanders and Brabant from 1330 at latest, 'local courts were the principal third party enforcer in commercial conflicts'.[344] In medieval Antwerp, too, local courts operated by the aldermen issued certificates to foreign merchants concerning ownership, wares, terms of debts and customary business practices, thereby enabling long-distance traders to resolve disputes or avoid them altogether.[345] Amsterdam never permitted guild

---

[337] Bourquelot (1865), I: 137; Carolus-Barré (1965), 26–7; Berti (1857), 247–50; Bassermann (1911), 57–8.

[338] Stabel (1999), 35–6; Gelderblom (2005a), 10 with n. 50; W. Stein (1902), 96 with n. 1; 'Deuxième keure de Bruges, 25 May 1281', article 23, in Gilliodts-van Severen (1874–5), I: 248–9; 'Des citations en justice contre des bourgeois, des absent et des étrangers, 9 Dec 1396', in *ibid.*, I: 441–8; 'Les affaires de commerce peuvent être portées devant la chambre échevinale (14 May 1481)', in *ibid.*, II: 114–16.

[339] Gilliodts-van Severen (1901–2), 16.   [340] Gelderblom (2005b), 80, 48 n. 80.

[341] Jenks (2005), 40.   [342] Munzinger (2006), 167.   [343] Henn (1999), 136.

[344] Gelderblom (2005b), 38 (quotation); Harreld (2004b), 18–19.

[345] Harreld (2004b), 19.

courts, as we have seen, instead requiring foreign merchants to resolve conflicts before the local municipal courts, whose capacity was expanded by creating subsidiary, specialized tribunals for bankruptcies, insurance, exchange and maritime conflicts as the caseload increased.[346]

England, too, saw a proliferation of local courts offering contract-enforcement services to foreign as well as indigenous merchants. Local courts operating under jurisdictions granted by the crown exercised coercive power – including fines and imprisonment – in debt cases between visiting merchants from 1270 at latest.[347] This involvement of local courts in resolving merchant conflicts was reflected in the legislation concerning trade with foreign merchants promulgated by King Edward I in 1285 which devolved enforcement to local authorities, in practice the towns, while reserving the crown's right to intervene when required.[348] Contemporary legal manuals took for granted that local courts would hear mercantile cases, and medieval English legal formularies provided sample mercantile judgements for the guidance of local judges.[349]

How effective were municipal courts in providing the impartial contract enforcement necessary for long-distance trade? The strongest evidence for their effectiveness was that foreign merchants chose to use them. At the Champagne fairs from the 1180s onwards, as we have seen, foreign merchants used local courts in the fair-towns to draw up their commercial contracts.[350] They also brought commercial disputes before the municipal courts of their own and their debtors' home cities. In 1230, for instance, a conflict over a debt allegedly incurred by merchants of Cambrai with merchants of Bologna at the Provins fair in Champagne in 1213 was resolved before the local court of the archbishop of Cambrai, advised by municipal councillors attesting to the authenticity of the seal on the debt contract; several 'wise men' of the 'Seventeen Towns' (a loosely organized Flemish merchant hanse) were alleged to have witnessed the original contract but were not involved in its enforcement.[351] In 1292 a group of Florentine merchants demanded payment of a debt incurred at the Champagne fairs by a Venetian merchant the preceding year, but did so through mobilizing their own municipal jurisdiction in Florence to put pressure on the Venetian municipal court.[352] In 1294, the Flemish merchants frequenting the fairs of France (which by then included the fairs of Champagne) secured the right to bring commercial disputes arising out of their trade at the fairs before their own municipal

---

[346] Gelderblom (2005b), 18–19.   [347] Sachs (2006), 702–5.
[348] Basile et al. (1998), 42, 69–70, 114; Baker (1986), 349–51.
[349] Maitland and Baildon (1891), 20, 40–1; Sachs (2006), 727, 740.
[350] Bourquelot (1865), II: 19–20; Bautier (1952), 318–19.
[351] Carolus-Barré (1965), 26–7.   [352] Bassermann (1911), 58.

jurisdictions back in Flanders.[353] All these merchants chose municipal jurisdictions to enforce long-distance trading conflicts despite the fact that they could have used guild courts or community reprisals. Revealed preference suggests that they regarded municipal jurisdictions as an effective way of enforcing long-distance trading contracts.

Bruges shows a similar pattern, whereby from the beginning of long-distance trade in the city, foreign merchants used the municipal courts to resolve commercial disputes with an array of different transaction partners, including local Bruges merchants, other members of the same alien merchant guild and foreign merchants from other countries.[354] Even where foreign merchants had guild jurisdictions – which, as we saw earlier, were not universal in medieval Bruges – these typically envisaged appeals to local municipal courts.[355] The Bruges town magistrates established a court called the Vierschaar to provide impartial third-party enforcement in conflicts between merchants, and a study of the important Lucchese merchant firm of the Rapondi brothers shows that they preferred this to the consular court operated by the Lucca merchant guild because the urban institution 'could also judge quarrels with non-Lucchese and . . . had more means at its disposal to enforce its decisions'.[356] Merchants from Lucca, Spain and Portugal also appealed to the local justices of Bruges against the decisions of their own merchant guilds.[357] The Venetian and German merchant guilds, unlike the other alien merchant guilds in Bruges, outlawed appeals to the municipal courts of Bruges, mainly because of pressure from their powerful mother cities. But their own members, as we have seen, demonstrated their preference for the Bruges courts by attempting to take contracts for enforcement before it, risking guild sanctions.[358]

The revealed preferences of merchants themselves thus cast doubt on the idea that public law-courts could not enforce long-distance trading contracts, making merchant guilds the efficient institutional basis for the medieval Commercial Revolution. Princely, ecclesiastical and municipal law-courts offered contract-enforcement services to foreign merchants from the twelfth century on, and are observed doing so actively in

---

[353] Bourquelot (1865), I: 137.

[354] R. De Roover (1948a), 18; Gelderblom (2005a), 3, 6–16; 'Les affaires de commerce peuvent être portées devant la chambre échevinale (14 May 1481)', in Gilliodts-van Severen (1874–5), II: 117; Gilliodts-van Severen (1901–2), 62–3.

[355] R. De Roover (1948a), 18; Gelderblom (2005a), 14.

[356] Lambert and Stabel (2005), 8.

[357] R. De Roover (1948a), 18; Gelderblom (2005b), 14; 'Les affaires de commerce peuvent être portées devant la chambre échevinale (14 May 1481)', in Gilliodts-van Severen (1874–5), II: 117.

[358] For examples, see Paravicini (1992), 108; Stabel (1999), 36.

every location in which long-distance trade expanded. Public law-courts were by no means perfect. They suffered from territorial fragmentation, jurisdictional conflicts, communication problems and potential corruption through pressure exerted by powerful merchants and their guilds. But the jurisdictional fragmentation of medieval Europe – the coexistence of state, ecclesiastical, municipal and seigneurial lawgiving side by side in the same geographical region – also had benefits. It permitted trade to migrate to a more impartial *jurisdiction* without necessarily being forced to forsake an advantageous trading *location*. Long-distance merchants observably took up these opportunities, shopping around among multiple jurisdictions to enforce commercial contracts. Guild tribunals certainly formed part of this patchwork of multiple jurisdictions, and collective reprisals which could affect entire merchant communities certainly played a role in the public legal system. But even where guild tribunals and community reprisals were available, long-distance traders can be observed voluntarily choosing to use other contract-enforcement mechanisms. This suggests that merchant guilds played a relatively minor role in commercial contract enforcement.

7.5   Conclusion

What are the wider implications of these findings? Long-distance trade gradually accelerated in Europe after about 1050, in what is known as the medieval Commercial Revolution. International merchants traded across large distances, with strangers from different polities, with long gaps between purchase and payment. How did they enforce these challenging contracts? How did merchants from different polities deter each other from reneging on agreements, or pursue foreigners who did default? More generally, how do people in developing economies make the transition from trading only with people they already know and can control through pre-existing social ties, but with whom they are so similar that gains from trade are low, to trading with strangers whom they do not know and cannot easily control but with whom gains from trade are high?

This chapter has shown that medieval Europe, both before and during the medieval Commercial Revolution, had an array of institutions offering different types of contract enforcement to merchants: families, personal networks, guilds, guarantorships, written records, arbitration panels, state law-courts, ecclesiastical tribunals and municipal jurisdictions. These institutions fall into two main analytical categories. On the one hand were particularized institutions offering services to specific groups of people: families offered contract enforcement only to family members, ethnic and religious groups only to adherents of that ethnicity or religion, merchant guilds only to members of that guild. On the other hand were generalized institutions offering services to all. At least in principle, anyone was supposed to be allowed to enter into guarantorship, register his contracts in writing before a notary or urban office, bring his disputes before an arbitration panel, or litigate in a court operated by a prince, church or city.

All of these institutions coexisted in medieval Europe, and long-distance merchants made use of them all. There was thus no single efficient institution for enforcing long-distance trading contracts, but rather an array of different institutional mechanisms which offered different advantages for different types of contract, for different contracting parties, in different locations and in different economic circumstances. Nonetheless, the balance between these different contract-enforcement mechanisms varied across different time periods and different trading locations. Which institutions were new or more widely preferred after c. 1050, compared to before?

Particularized institutions providing economic services to identifiable groups of traders long pre-dated 1050. The family, the ethnic group, the network of friends are some of the most ancient of economic institutions. As we have seen, they continued to be important throughout the medieval Commercial Revolution, and still played a role in long-distance trade in many parts of Europe well into the early modern period. This was nothing new.

The merchant guild was a second type of particularized institution providing economic services to an identifiable group of traders, and some have argued that it was the key institution enabling long-distance trade during the medieval Commercial Revolution. Indeed, as we have seen, some go so far as to claim that private-order merchant organizations came into being precisely because they offered an efficient solution to the contract-enforcement problem in long-distance trade – through their autonomous guild courts, internal peer pressure or 'community responsibility system' involving collective reprisals against the entire guild of a defaulting debtor.

Yet merchant guilds were not a new institution. As we saw in Chapter 2, collegia and fraternities of local merchants existed in ancient times, left indications of their presence throughout the early medieval period and were present in the earliest surviving records even of non-dynamic towns in which few or no merchants engaged in long-distance trade. Guilds and hanses of alien merchants were merely the foreign branches or offshoots of local merchant guilds which had their roots in the stagnant pools of local privilege and monopoly all over Europe. Corporative groups of merchants seeking monopoly profits for their own members were, as we saw in Chapters 3 and 4, nothing new in the High Middle Ages. And in so far as they generated benefits, they explicitly reserved them for their own members.

This is not surprising behaviour in a particularized institution providing services to an identifiable group. But it does cast doubt on the extent to which merchant guilds can have been the institutional innovation that revolutionized long-distance trade after *c.* 1050. Further doubt is cast on this notion by the findings presented in this chapter, which show that merchant guilds played a relatively minor role in enforcing international trading contracts during the medieval Commercial Revolution.

For one thing, there is little sign that autonomous guild jurisdictions were important in enforcing international trading contracts. The courts established by merchant guilds were far from autonomous, as they were typically established under licence from the public authorities and envisaged appeals to the public legal system in all but the most straightforward disputes. Many merchant guilds neither sought nor obtained independent jurisdictions, and many guilded merchants preferred public courts to guild courts which they viewed as unable to resolve complex issues, impotent to enforce compliance or skewed to the interests of richer merchants or rival guild factions. The claim that merchant guild courts generated an autonomous 'merchant law' also turns out to be unfounded: guild courts used the rules prevailing in public legal systems, and commercial law emerged primarily through piecemeal developments in public law-courts.

The second way merchant guilds might have improved contract enforcement was through peer pressure – mobilizing their social capital of shared norms and information to impose sanctions on offending members. Sanctions against guild members who cheated outsiders could in theory have improved enforcement in long-distance trade, especially in combination with threats of collective reprisal against the entire guild of a defaulting merchant. But there is almost no evidence that merchant guilds did exercise effective peer pressure to enforce commercial contracts. Surviving records suggest the contrary – that even the most powerful merchant guilds were severely limited in the effectiveness of the pressure they could exert against members who chose to default on their agreements. Instead, in order to protect themselves from collective reprisals, merchant guilds petitioned the public authorities to impose formal rules restricting the possibility of default by their own members.

The third way merchant guilds might have improved contract enforcement is through the 'community responsibility system' of collective reprisals against an entire merchant guild if one member defaulted. But even in theory, the reprisal system cannot be regarded as unambiguously efficient, since although it offered a possible benefit to creditors and a possible deterrent to debtors, it harmed entire communities of long-distance merchants and increased the risks of trade for innocent third parties. The empirical findings confirm that these serious disadvantages of reprisals were widely recognized by contemporaries, who sought to limit or abolish the reprisal system as soon as trade began to expand. When collective reprisals were invoked, they were fully embedded in the public legal system as a final stage in a series of formal steps based on consulting written records, mobilizing sureties, invoking arbitration panels and litigating in public law-courts. Collective reprisals against the communities of offenders were an ancient practice reaching back into antiquity. What was new in the medieval Commercial Revolution was the gradual and uneven attempt to circumscribe them within formal, public legal proceedings.

As this suggests, the new and dynamic component of the institutional system during the medieval Commercial Revolution was represented by our second category of contract-enforcement mechanisms – generalized institutions offering services to all economic agents, not just members of particular families, networks or guilds. Contractual instruments such as guarantees and cessions of credit were institutional innovations devised by business and legal professionals in the great trading cities. The notarial system of registering contracts in writing, depositing and storing them, and ultimately certifying them before arbitration panels or in courts of law was another institutional innovation devised in Mediterranean trading cities at the beginning of the Commercial Revolution. Princes and churches had operated notarial systems before, but lay notaries providing services to private individuals were new in the eleventh century. A little later, the development of municipal offices offering analogous registration, depository and certification services for long-distance trading contracts in northern European cities was another institutional innovation which had not been present in the early medieval period. Arbitration panels manned by arbiters appointed not exclusively from among merchant guild officials, but from a broader circle of experienced lay judges and neutral merchants, whose decisions were recognized and enforced by public law-courts, constituted a further institutional innovation observable from the early years of the Commercial Revolution. Finally, if all these mechanisms failed, public law-courts operated by princes, feudal lords, religious institutions and local municipalities competed to provide justice to international merchants in every locality and time period in which long-distance trade expanded after c. 1050. Long-distance commerce grew in those places and time periods in which generalized institutions began to offer acceptable contract enforcement to long-distance merchants.

This is not to say that these generalized institutions emerged evenly or offered perfect contract enforcement. As previous chapters discussed, rulers and governments in principle provided institutional mechanisms offering services to all economic agents – or at least to a larger subset of economic agents than did families and guilds. But rulers and governments could also be corrupted by particularized institutions, such as clans and guilds, into providing services that benefited only certain small groups – indeed, into enforcing the particularistic privileges of clans and guilds even more effectively than they could themselves. This accounts for the dual role of rulers and governments in the medieval Commercial Revolution. When rulers generated generalized institutional mechanisms providing services to all economic agents, long-distance trade flourished; when they yielded to the temptation to supply particularized contract enforcement serving the interests of specific groups, trade stagnated or collapsed. The same was true of city governments: when they acted in the interests of the city as a whole, trade flourished; when they were captured by special interest-groups (such as merchant guilds), trade stagnated.

Fortunately, with contract-enforcement services there was a certain amount of competition among different providers, and much of this competition was quite peaceful. As we have seen, long-distance merchants could and did choose among the contract-enforcement services provided by princes, feudal lords, religious institutions and local municipalities from the earliest years of the medieval Commercial Revolution. In many parts of Europe, these institutions and jurisdictions coexisted in the same polity, so long-distance merchants did not need to leave the locality altogether in order to obtain better contract enforcement; often, they could just quietly migrate to more impartial jurisdictions within the same locality. This provided an incentive for different jurisdictions to compete for merchants' business by rendering impartial judgements. No jurisdiction was perfect, especially in the long term, as shown by the rise and decline of different trading centres such as Champagne, Bruges and Antwerp. But the fact that merchants voluntarily used public jurisdictions suggests that such jurisdictions were at least partly successful in providing contract enforcement sufficient to sustain long-distance trade. In so far as they were successful in doing so, it was these generalized institutions, not particularized institutions such as guilds, that offered the innovations necessary to enforce long-distance trading contracts during the medieval Commercial Revolution.

8   Principal-agent problems

Many frauds are committed by travelling partners concerning the goods
in a societas or commenda.

(Genoese law code, 1316)[1]

I curse fortune when I think of the day on which I got involved with
him, not believing that he would be dishonest.

(Gherardino Strozzi writing to Matteo Strozzi concerning a dishonest
business associate, Modena, 1426)[2]

Do not give money or a consignment [of goods] to an inexperienced
man. Even if you know for certain that he is a man of good reputation
[akhtibar], ascertain the truth by questioning several people. Only then
give him money or credit with a bill [tamasuk] and with witnesses. But
[make sure] to write down all your transactions several times.

(Armenian merchant training manual, 1680s)[3]

Any merchant trading beyond the scale that can be handled by a single
individual has to use other people – agents – to do business on his behalf.
This is particularly important in long-distance trade, which can be more
efficiently conducted if one trader stays home to manage the local end
of the business, while his partners or agents trade abroad, enabling the
business to trade simultaneously in multiple locations and diversify its
activities.[4]

But once a merchant gets someone else to trade on his behalf, he
confronts the principal-agent problem. An agent entrusted with a merchant's capital or wares has an incentive to pursue his own interests at
the expense of his principal. If the probability of misconduct by agents is
too high, principals will not employ them. Potentially profitable business
will not be transacted because the merchant cannot oversee it personally,
and gains from trade will be lost.

This creates a demand for institutional mechanisms to align agents'
behaviour with their principals' interests. In pre-modern trade, it is

---

[1] Quoted in S. A. Epstein (1996), 70, 336 n. 39.   [2] Quoted in Bec (1967), 1211.
[3] Quoted in Aslanian (2006), 392.   [4] R. De Roover (1948a), 29–30.

sometimes argued, these mechanisms were provided by merchant guilds and, later, by privileged merchant companies. Such corporative associations are supposed to have solved agency problems better than individual traders or firms because of two special advantages – their social capital and their monopoly position.

A social capital of shared norms, information and collective action was generated within merchant guilds and privileged companies, it is claimed, by closed membership and multiplex internal relationships. These features solved principal-agent problems, it is held, by establishing agreed norms about agent behaviour, transmitting information swiftly about misconduct and facilitating collective penalties against bad agents. If one merchant was cheated by an agent, the argument goes, other merchants in his guild would learn about it and refuse to employ that agent.

Merchant guilds and privileged companies are also believed to have solved principal-agent problems in a second way. Their legal monopolies gave them size, scale and vertical integration, it is argued, turning them into hierarchical organizations that could solve agency problems efficiently by treating agents as employees. Internal contracts within the merchant organization provided efficient monitoring and remuneration, aligning agents' behaviour with their principals' interests. If an agent nonetheless behaved opportunistically, the monopoly position of the merchant guild or privileged company ensured that he would not find another employer.

In their simplest version, these are efficiency theories claiming that merchant guilds and privileged companies *existed* because they were the most efficient solution to principal-agent problems in pre-modern trade. In more complex variants, such theories argue that although merchant guilds and companies *existed* for other reasons (e.g. because they secured monopoly profits for their members), they compensated for any harm their monopolies inflicted on the economy by providing efficient ways of solving principal-agent problems.

This chapter begins by investigating whether merchant guilds and privileged companies solved principal-agent problems using social capital. Did closure and multiplex relationships within a network of principals generate norms, information and sanctions that efficiently controlled the behaviour of agents? We then examine whether guild and company monopolies helped solve agency problems. Did monopolistic merchant organizations contract more efficiently with agents than competitive traders were able to do? Finally, since the claim that merchant guilds and privileged companies were the efficient solution to agency problems implies that alternatives were lacking, we examine the other institutions used by medieval and early modern merchants to manage relations with agents.

8.1   Social capital and agency problems

Social capital is one way merchant guilds – as social networks – are thought to have solved agency problems. According to this view, any agent who violated norms of honest behaviour towards a member of a merchant network would be readily detected by other members, information about his conduct would be transmitted swiftly within the network and collective sanctions would be easily organized against him. This is the same argument sometimes advanced concerning enforcement of contracts between merchants, as we saw in Chapter 7 – not surprisingly, since the dividing line between agency relationships and other agreements between merchants was not always clear-cut.

A number of scholars postulate that merchant guilds might have solved principal-agent problems by virtue of their closely knit relationships and internal information-transmission mechanisms. De Roover, for instance, speculates as follows:

If a member of the Lucchese colony in Bruges misbehaved and neglected his business . . . it is likely that his principals or his partners in Lucca would soon be informed either directly or indirectly and would thus be able to remedy the situation, before it was too late. On the other hand, the Lucchese in Bruges, because of their frequent contacts with the mother city, would surely find out if their interests in Italy or elsewhere were neglected.[5]

Ewert and Selzer paint a similar picture of the German Hanse in the Baltic:

cooperation between . . . business partners was enforced by reputation and . . . guaranteed by cultural agreement and trust . . . Celebrating sociability and circulat[ing] information on other members' reputation clearly had the function of strengthen[ing] mutual relationships in order to make cheating within the network more difficult . . . All partners operated within the same set of norms . . . Information on the reputation of possible trading partners could be gathered during social events. As a consequence of the mechanisms of cultural agreement and trust, in most cases merchants were assured that their distant trading partners executed the actions that were necessary for gaining the best interest of both the parties involved.[6]

Link and Kapfenberger argue that the Artushof, a Hanse merchant fraternity in Danzig (Gdańsk), efficiently reduced transaction costs because

---

[5] *Ibid.*, 20.
[6] Ewert and Selzer (2005), 20–1 (quotation); Selzer and Ewert (2005), 24–9.

it enabled Hanse merchants to discover information about the trust-worthiness of third parties with whom they might in future do business.[7] Gelderblom views early modern Dutch merchant guilds as efficient orga-nizations because 'close-knit communities made it easier to monitor agents'.[8] According to Grafe, too, 'it was one of the main purposes of the early modern mercantile bodies like the *Consulados* (Spanish merchant guilds) to limit opportunistic behaviour between principals and agents'.[9]

A completely opposite view of medieval European merchant guilds is advanced by Greif, who argues that they did *not* engage in collective pun-ishment of fraudulent agents. Greif compares the eleventh-century Jewish 'Geniza merchants' (whom he terms the 'Maghribi traders' although they did not all come from or trade in the Maghreb) with the merchants of twelfth-century Genoa. Greif describes the Maghribi traders as a closed 'coalition' with strong 'collectivist' norms of behaviour. Any agent who cheated a Maghribi merchant is supposed to have had his misconduct swiftly revealed to all other members of the Maghribi network, who then mobilized 'collectivist' cultural norms and refused to employ him ever again. Knowing this would happen is supposed to have deterred agents from cheating. According to Greif, Genoese merchant guilds did *not* behave in this way. Instead, the Italians had 'individualistic' cultural norms that led them to develop an impersonal system of public law which individual merchants could use to prosecute fraudulent agents.[10] Greif does not explain what it was about Genoese merchant guilds that pre-vented them from operating in the same way as the Maghribi traders, except for the 'individualistic' norms which, he claims, had character-ized European cultures since antiquity, in contrast with the 'collectivist' norms of Judaic and Islamic cultures.[11]

A number of scholars therefore believe that medieval European mer-chant guilds benefited long-distance trade by solving agency problems through their social capital of collective information and sanctions. But an opposing view holds that European merchant guilds were too individ-ualistic to behave in this way and that such mechanisms were reserved to merchant 'coalitions' imbued with collectivist Judaic and Islamic norms. What light does the evidence shed on these different views?

Merchant guilds are unlikely to have *existed* because they were the effi-cient solution to agency problems, for the same reason they are unlikely to have existed to provide commercial security or contract enforcement.

---

[7] Link and Kapfenberger (2005), 165.   [8] Gelderblom (2005a), 14.
[9] Grafe (2001), 10.   [10] Greif (1989); Greif (2006a), ch. 9.
[11] On the theoretical and empirical problems with Greif's portrayal of the Maghribi traders and the contrasts he draws with European merchants, see Edwards and Ogilvie (2009).

Principal-agent problems were a much less serious problem in local or regional trade, where merchants and agents typically worked in close proximity, so principals could oversee agents personally, arrange personal meetings with agents more easily and collect local information about their behaviour at lower cost. The truly challenging agency problems arose in long-distance trade where agents were based far away from principals, personal meetings were rare or impossible, and information transmission was costly and slow. As we have seen, however, most European merchant guilds (like most merchants) were local and thus cannot have existed to solve a problem that was not very acute in local trade.

Nonetheless, merchant guilds, while *existing* for other reasons, might still *incidentally* have brought benefits by offering efficient institutional mechanisms for solving principal-agent problems. Unfortunately, little evidence exists to support the idea that the social capital of merchant guilds ameliorated agency problems. The only concrete examples are provided by Ewert and Selzer, who suggest that information about fraudulent agents may sometimes have been conveyed at Hanseatic institutions of sociability, such as the Artusbruderschaft (a merchant drinking fraternity) in Danzig (Gdańsk) or the Zirkelgesellschaft (a society of long-distance merchants) in Lübeck. Certainly, merchants who had violated Hanse regulations – e.g. by breaking Hanseatic embargoes or litigating before non-Hanseatic courts – were occasionally excluded from participation in the sociability at these merchant fraternities.[12] And on one occasion in the sixteenth century, a merchant affixed a defamatory letter about a fraudulent trading partner on the gate of the Danzig Artushof.[13] Although this indicates that the Hanse and its associated fraternities did possess internal mechanisms that could be, and occasionally were, used to spread the word about unsatisfactory agents, posting a notice on the Artushof door was commonly used for a variety of other purposes that had nothing to do with agency problems. The Artushof drinking fraternity was simply an efficient way of spreading news among Hanse merchants and to the urban elite more broadly, and was used by town councils as well as the Hanseatic Diet for that purpose.[14] All the example of the Artushof shows is that merchants could sometimes use their guilds to transmit information about unsatisfactory agents; it does not tell use how common this was, how effective or what the alternatives were.

Solving agency problems through social capital within a merchant guild also has economic disadvantages. To be effective in detecting and

---

[12] Ewert and Selzer (2005), 11–13; Selzer (2003), 83–4, 96–7; Selzer and Ewert (2001), 152; Selzer and Ewert (2005), 25.
[13] Selzer (2003), 84–5 with n. 61.   [14] *Ibid.*

punishing deviant agents, a merchant guild had to be a non-anonymous closed network with multiplex internal relationships. For a merchant network to solve agency problems through internal social capital, its members would have to refrain from entering into agency relationships with outsiders, against whom social sanctions could not be exercised. But closure imposes costs by excluding commercial ties outside the network. Members of the network would limit their agency relationships, forming links only with other network members, even when profitable relationships could be concluded with outsiders. In so far as any guild of merchants did enforce network closure to diminish agency problems, its members would limit their business.

Spruyt argues that the German Hanse suffered from precisely this problem: 'To guarantee that agents in the field are not cheating and to have access to help overseas, individuals rely on group associations and social mechanisms to overcome short-run, self-interested behavior.' But this could only be achieved by enforcing network closure, which the Hanse did through imposing restrictions on marriage with non-Hanseatics, on non-Hanseatics acquiring citizenship in Hanse towns and on business ventures with non-Hanseatics.[15] Even Ewert and Selzer, despite believing that the Hanse was efficient given the circumstances prevailing in the early modern Baltic trade, admit that it limited commercial associations with non-Hanse-members: 'it was extremely difficult, if not impossible, for merchants from outside who operated in a different style, to enter this structure and to become a part of it'.[16] They also speculate that this may be one reason why Hanseatic merchants had so much more difficulty than south German firms in expanding into the Venetian or the intercontinental trade.[17] Ewert and Selzer also acknowledge that the Hanse's 'network' solution to principal-agent problems blocked the development of hierarchical firms, financial institutions and commercial venture capital. They conclude that 'this lack of financial backing later on turned out to be a great disadvantage of the network structure'.[18] If their characterization is accurate, the Hanse might have used its social capital to mitigate principal-agent problems but only at the cost of restricting trade with outsiders, blocking more sophisticated forms of enterprise and limiting access to external capital.

How likely is it that the social capital of merchant guilds played an important role in solving principal-agent problems? European

---

[15] Spruyt (1994), 241–2.
[16] Selzer and Ewert (2001), 156–7; Ewert and Selzer (2005), 2, 9, 15–18 (quotation 17).
[17] Selzer and Ewert (2001), 156.
[18] Ewert and Selzer (2005), 21 (quotation); Selzer and Ewert (2005), 26–7.

merchants, as we saw in Chapter 6, did not always form guilds and hanses in distant trading centres. The four Champagne fair-towns, for instance, constituted an almost permanent market for international exchange from the 1180s onwards, yet the first alien merchant guilds appeared there only in 1245. Foreign merchants from many parts of Europe traded in Champagne without ever forming guilds at the fairs, a strong indication that they solved their agency problems in other ways. After the decline of the Champagne fairs around 1300, Bruges became the undisputed fulcrum of international trade in north-west Europe, with large numbers of long-distance merchants trading there from many lands. But as we saw in Chapter 6, many of these foreigners never formed alien merchant guilds in Bruges, or did so only quite late in the medieval period when Bruges had begun to decline.[19] Such unguilded merchants traded successfully in Bruges, and must therefore have been certain of making a profit despite not being able to solve their agency problems by mobilizing social capital within a guild or hanse. These findings suggests that the theoretical benefits of merchant guilds as solutions to agency problems were not important in practice – perhaps precisely because of the lost gains from trade involved in limiting one's agency relationships to members of the same social network.

8.2   Monopoly as a solution to agency problems

Merchant guilds are also supposed to have solved agency problems in a second way – through the large scale and vertical integration created by their monopoly position. As we saw in Chapters 3 and 4, a merchant guild, hanse or privileged company always enjoyed legal advantages giving it exclusive trading rights over particular transactions, wares, routes or destinations. Some scholars claim that these monopoly rights enabled a merchant guild or privileged company to operate on a large scale and integrate vertically, enabling it to solve agency problems through internal contracting – essentially by treating its agents like employees. Its monopoly gave it both the scale to cover the fixed costs of internal contracting and the market domination to deny future employment to any agent who misbehaved. Postan, for instance, argues that medieval merchant guilds enjoyed legal privileges that made them 'able to regulate the scale and the methods of individual enterprise and to lay down rigid rules . . . for relations with agents, and for the latter's residence and conduct'.[20] Dollinger claims that the German Hanse exercised strong centralized control over shipmasters and foreign agents, so much so that

---

[19] Lambert and Stabel (2005), 22.   [20] Postan (1987), 270.

agents often did not dare to over-ride instructions from Hanse head office.[21] Carlos and Nicholas elaborate this argument for the early modern privileged companies whose market domination, they argue, made it possible to economize on negotiating optimal employment contracts, in which salaries, pre-employment bonds and profit shares aligned agents' incentives with company interests. Market domination, the story continues, also helped the privileged companies reap economies of scale in collecting information on agents' activities and in creating a corporate ethos to deter opportunism.[22] The monopolistic companies, according to Carlos and Nicholas, dominated early modern long-distance trade 'not because a private market did not exist, but because operating by managerial fiat inside the hierarchical firm was less costly than using the market'.[23]

But there are a number of theoretical problems with this whole edifice of arguments. For one thing, it is not clear why large scale should generate the claimed benefits. If paying a wage and operating by managerial fiat was a good way of dealing with agency problems, why could a wage not also have been used by individual merchants and trading firms, operating competitively within a fragmented market? Very small businesses have managers and pay wages to employees in most economies – and, as we shall see in a later section of this chapter, medieval European merchant firms did sometimes provide compensation to their agents and factors in the form of wages. In any case, a wage is not self-evidently the best way of dealing with agency issues – certainly not if it is a fixed wage – and that is why medieval firms also used other forms of compensation to motive their agents abroad.

Some of these problems are addressed by Hejeebu for the English East India Company (EIC). She finds no evidence to support Carlos and Nicholas's idea that salaries and pre-employment bonds helped solve agency problems within the EIC. Nor does she claim that a monopolistic merchant company was more efficient than private traders. However, she does argue that the EIC devised employment contracts 'that kept employee malfeasance within tolerable bounds'.[24] This she ascribes to the EIC's policy – unique among early modern chartered companies – of permitting employees to enjoy a share of the EIC's monopoly rents by letting them trade legally on their own accounts *within* Asia. This ought, at least in theory, to have given them incentives to be loyal agents in the EIC's trade *between* Asia and Europe, since dismissal would deprive them of their private share in the company monopoly: 'Private trade gave them

---

[21] Dollinger (1970), 185.   [22] Carlos and Nicholas (1990).
[23] Carlos and Nicholas (1988), 404.   [24] Hejeebu (2005), 500.

a reason to join and, more importantly, to stay with the company and obey its orders.'[25] Hejeebu contrasts the EIC with the Dutch East India Company (VOC), which barred its agents from participating privately in either its intra-Asian trade or its Asian-European trade, deprived them of incentives to act loyally so as to retain a share of monopoly rents and consequently suffered from rampant clandestine trade by its own agents. The VOC, in her view, illustrates how the monopolistic position of a privileged company could actually worsen agency problems unless combined with carefully designed internal contracts.[26]

These comparisons draw attention to some of the theoretical reasons monopolistic market domination might exacerbate agency problems rather than solving them. For one thing, large organizations typically experience *diseconomies* as well as economies of scale. A large, hierarchical organization will face high costs of information, enforcement and employee motivation because of the multiple layers of monitoring and management required by its scale of operations. These supervisory diseconomies of scale can only be overcome by sophisticated internal control mechanisms. The fact that managerial shirking and cheating continued to be a serious problem even in long-lived organizations such as the Dutch East India Company and the Hudson's Bay Company – as we shall see – suggests that such diseconomies could be significant.[27]

A second disadvantage of a large, hierarchical organization is inflexibility caused by centralization. To control agency problems, large merchant associations such as the German Hanse and the early modern privileged companies established centralized mechanisms for setting policy and making decisions at head office. But this inevitably reduced the flexibility with which agents in distant trading locations could respond to changing business opportunities. Fluctuations in supply and demand inherent in international trading gave rise to unforeseen situations that could not be dealt with through policies and precedents established at the central office, however efficient those policies might have seemed in the circumstances of their original formulation. The sort of precedent-based internal bureaucratic systems instituted, in different ways, by the Hanse and the early modern privileged companies to ensure that agents always responded by the rule instead of being tempted to shirk or cheat could give rise to inflexible and inappropriate responses by agents who hesitated to deviate from the rule book for fear of penalties.

---

[25] *Ibid.*, 496–7, 502–6, 510 (quotation), 519.
[26] De Vries and Van der Woude (1997), 451; Hejeebu (2005), 517–19.
[27] Carlos and Nicholas (1996), 921 with n. 32; Rich (1942), 101.

Finally, if there were an efficiency advantage to large scale because large organizations can better solve agency problems through internal contracting, then international trade would be a natural monopoly.[28] If that were the case, then the competitive advantages of guilds, hanses and privileged companies would have created monopolies by driving out higher-cost competitors. That is, the monopolies of merchant guilds or privileged companies would not have required lobbying or legal restrictions in order to exist. Since, as we saw in Chapters 3 and 4, a merchant guild, hanse or privileged company typically acquired and sustained its monopoly position through constant lobbying for legal privileges and constant struggles against interlopers, it is highly unlikely that international trade really was a natural monopoly. Any putative advantages a large-scale merchant guild or privileged company might have enjoyed in contracting with agents cannot have been of much actual commercial importance, or the guild would have been able to sustain its monopoly without state support or coercion.

In theory, therefore, the monopolies enjoyed by pre-modern merchant guilds and privileged companies *might* have given them sufficient scale and market domination to create effective instruments for mitigating agency problems. But monopoly, scale and vertical integration also have theoretical disadvantages – supervisory diseconomies of scale and inflexibility in decision-making which can increase costs and reduce competitiveness. Smaller, competitive firms with fewer layers of supervision and management could economize on information, enforcement and decision-making in ways not open to large, monopolistic merchant guilds. Economic theory, therefore, points out advantages and disadvantages to both forms of organization. We need to examine the evidence to find out which predominated in practice.

The evidence adduced in support of the view that monopolistic merchant guilds and companies solved agency problems is not all that one would desire. It consists almost exclusively of formal rules and contracts, with little evidence of practical implementation. Postan and Dollinger refer to charters and ordinances, which show that medieval merchant guilds and hanses formulated regulations to try to control agency problems. But these scholars do not provide evidence of how – if at all – these rules were enforced. Greater detail is provided by Carlos and Nicholas

---

[28] A natural monopoly is a situation where because of economies of scale there cannot be more than one efficient provider of a good because a single provider always has lower costs. Monopolies also exist for other reasons – because of sole access to some resource or technology (geographical or technological monopolies); or because of the use of institutional means to eliminate competition, such as the methods used by merchant guilds discussed in Chapters 3 and 4 (legal or institutional monopolies).

on the Hudson's Bay Company and Hejeebu on the English East India Company. But closer examination shows that their arguments consist in identifying employment contracts and internal monitoring mechanisms that ought, in theory, to have mitigated agency problems. Carlos and Nicholas show that the Hudson's Bay Company set up a formal contract structure for employment which 'should have' helped to limit opportunistic behaviour by employees. They show that the Hudson's Bay Company also established internal monitoring systems which 'should have' reduced private trade by managers (the main form of agent opportunism). Likewise, they provide evidence that the Company created an internal corporate ethos that 'should have' made private trade less likely to occur.[29] They base their claims on evidence that the Company pursued strategies for solving principal-agent problems. Since they do not have direct evidence of the success of these strategies, they very properly couch their conclusions in the form of speculations that these strategies 'should have' reduced agent opportunism. Their study does not assess the effectiveness of these strategies in practice. It does not evaluate the costs of these strategies compared to their benefits. And it does not compare the success of the monopolistic companies in addressing agency problems with that of private, unincorporated, unchartered merchants.

When we turn to detailed studies of how agency relationships actually worked, we find that the rules were not enforced and may not even have been up to the challenge to begin with. The German Hanse is well known for setting up elaborate bureaucratic mechanisms to control agents and to ensure that they complied with the policy of the Hanse central office in Lübeck. But actual Hanse trading activities show that these bureaucratic mechanisms were often implemented inflexibly and inefficiently. In 1399, for instance, when new regulations governing letters of exchange were issued by the count of Flanders, the Hanse managed its Bruges agents with spectacular inefficiency. The Hanse central office in Lübeck delayed its response for ten weeks longer than the head offices of private Italian and Catalonian merchant firms, leaving Hanse agents in Bruges unable to take action during the most serious phase of the crisis. When the Hanse central office in Lübeck did finally respond, it completely misunderstood the actual situation on the ground in Bruges, imposing an unnecessary prohibition on all credit operations by Hanseatic agents, which damaged Hanse trade throughout Europe.[30] The costs of centralized decision-making manifested themselves in a different way in 1485, when the Hanse's Danzig fleet sailed to the French port of Bourgneuf to load salt, but found none for sale. The Hanse agents in

---

[29] Carlos and Nicholas (1990), 874–5.   [30] See the analysis in Jenks (1982), 309–15.

Bourgneuf and the skippers of the Hanse fleet were so terrified of punishment by their principals at central office that they did not dare 'to take it upon themselves in these unforeseen circumstances to override their freighters' instructions and load up with other merchandise in order to make some profit for their journey'. So the entire fleet returned home with empty holds.[31] Such cases illustrate how the elaborate bureaucratic system for controlling agents from head office, which the Hanse could afford because of its size and monopoly status, made agency relationships inefficient.

Similarly disappointing findings emerge from studies of the actual trading activities – as opposed to the bureaucratic systems – of privileged merchant companies. Carlos and Nicholas provide evidence of the bureaucratic systems set up by chartered companies such as the Hudson's Bay Company to control their agents. But as Jones and Ville point out, evidence on business outcomes suggests that 'there was a large discrepancy between what the systems were designed to achieve and what happened in practice'.[32] Information was not collected or analysed carefully enough to monitor agents' behaviour effectively, and 'efficient utilization of information was further impeded by the mingling of company operations with the private ventures of shareholders and company servants, a situation that increased the level of confusion and the scope for opportunistic behavior'.[33] The above-market salaries which putatively deterred company agents from behaving opportunistically turn out to have been 'no larger on average than those earned elsewhere and did not contain a premium to compensate for private trade forgone'.[34] The oaths and bonds which the privileged companies required of their managers do not appear to have been effective: bonds were seldom confiscated from disloyal agents despite 'repeated instances of private trading and gross inefficiency'.[35] Finally, the 'company culture' which is supposed to have deterred agents from opportunistic behaviour is hard to measure or compare with the culture of the smaller-scale, monopoly-breaking interlopers with which the company was competing. Jones and Ville argue that one must look behind the piously encouraging homilies contained in company correspondence with agents and instead try to assess the implications of other aspects of agents' working environment, 'in which censorship, searches, and harsh discipline were the norm, and where servants were offered incentives to spy on each other'.[36] Certainly the Company's bureaucratic systems did not eradicate opportunistic behaviour by agents. Carlos and Nicholas themselves calculate that despite the bureaucratic

[31] Dollinger (1970), 185.   [32] S. R. H. Jones and Ville (1996), 900–1.
[33] *Ibid.*, 901.   [34] *Ibid.*, 904.   [35] *Ibid.*   [36] *Ibid.*, 907.

systems, 'agency, monitoring, and inefficiency accounted for about 25 percent of total revenue for the Hudson's Bay Company', while Jones and Ville arrive at the higher estimate of 32–5 per cent.[37] In the assessment of the great Company historian Rich, 'the business of private trade was a perpetual worry to the [Hudson's Bay] Company, as it always was to the East India Company'.[38]

Other privileged merchant companies solved agency problems even less successfully than the Hudson's Bay Company. One prime example is the Royal African Company, which was established in 1660 with a legal monopoly over the slave trade between England and the American colonies in the Caribbean, yet spectacularly failed to keep afloat as a business.[39] According to Galenson, a major reason for its failure was its inability to develop effective mechanisms to monitor agents. Its ship captains systematically took advantage of the company; the agents who sold the slaves in the West Indies were a continual problem; and the agents manning its African forts manifested both incompetence and dishonesty.[40] According to Davies, as well, 'too much had to be left to the discretion of employees abroad who for the most part followed their own concerns to the detriment of the company's'.[41] In 1691, for instance, the Company complained that 'our factors and some of the chiefs manage private trade which is the way to encourage interlopers and ruin our stock by bearing the charge without having the advantage'.[42] Carlos contends that the Royal Africa Company failed simply because high mortality rates made it difficult to introduce efficient employment contracts along the lines of the Hudson's Bay Company.[43] But high African mortality did not have the same effect on the African Company's competitors which, as North points out, 'were able to overcome the problems of agency . . . that all firms faced, and still fare better than the company protected by the Crown' – despite the fact that these interlopers not only lacked a legal monopoly but suffered from the costs and risks of operating in the black market.[44]

Likewise, most studies of the English East India Company (EIC) are equivocal about its success in solving agency problems. Chaudhuri, for instance, concludes that the EIC 'was never able to solve satisfactorily the difficult task of controlling officials in Asia and extracting compliance to its orders . . . the problem of exercising effective control remained endemic'.[45] Watson argues that the EIC was unable to exercise effective

[37] Carlos and Nicholas (1996), 921 with n. 32.   [38] Rich (1942), 101.
[39] North (1991), 34.   [40] Galenson (1986), 15–16, 25–7, 148–50.
[41] Davies (1957), 165.   [42] Quoted in *ibid.*, 255.   [43] Carlos (1991), 150.
[44] North (1991), 35.   [45] Chaudhuri (1978), 40, 118, 208.

control from London over the activities of its agents in India.[46] Hejeebu describes how, in 1731–2, the EIC found itself paying excessively high prices for raw silk because its own employees were securing supplies for their own private trade and letting the Company, according to its own complaint, 'have but very little and that little at excessive high prices, gradually rising upon us year after year'.[47] That same year, the EIC's directors accused members of the Company's Calcutta Council of selling their own goods at inflated prices to the Company.[48] The extent of the EIC's agency problem is illustrated by the finding that 13.2 per cent of those employed by the EIC in Bengal in the first half of the eighteenth century were dismissed or suspended – although it is unclear whether this was high or low compared to other privileged companies or merchant firms.[49] One explanatory factor, as with the Royal African Company, may be that mortality in India was so high that EIC employees had limited time-horizons, seeking their own profit in the short term because they did not have a high probability of continuing to be employed by the Company in future.[50] However, the illegal interlopers who competed with the EIC faced the same mortality rate and the same agency problems, but still fared better than the monopolistic, legally protected Company.

The Dutch East India Company (VOC) was even less effective in solving its principal-agent problems. Glamann recounts how the VOC accused its Bengali agents in 1710 of fraudulently reserving the most profitable selection of textiles for their own side-dealing.[51] According to Prakash, VOC employees were notorious for trading clandestinely in opium, raw silk and silk textiles on the Bengal–Batavia route, a form of agent opportunism the Company never managed to curb.[52] De Vries and Van der Woude conclude that the VOC 'suffered from both corruption and inadequate performance of duties on a scale that exceeded that of its competitors . . . private trading at the expense of the Company's well being . . . proliferated, giving rise to demoralization and a deterioration of the Company's performance'.[53] The problem of corruption was not merely a matter of low-level employees with little influence over Company performance. Rather, doubts about the quality and faithfulness of VOC personnel went 'right to the top', encompassing the officers and high officials themselves.[54]

---

[46] Watson (1980), 74, 161–4.   [47] Hejeebu (2005), 507–8.   [48] *Ibid.*, 513.
[49] *Ibid.*, 514.   [50] Marshall (1976), 217; Hejeebu (2005), 508–10.
[51] Glamann (1958), 147.   [52] Prakash (1985), 83–9.
[53] De Vries and Van der Woude (1997), 450–1.   [54] *Ibid.*, 452.

Most studies of the privileged companies which focus on their actual trading activities rather than their bureaucratic systems therefore come to pessimistic conclusions about their ability to control shirking and fraud by agents in distant trading centres. In his survey of the privileged companies as a whole, Coornaert concludes that

For the most part the bonds between these agents and their companies were exceedingly tenuous; distances were often immense, and everywhere the companies' representatives of all ranks were empowered to carry on trade for their private accounts and were often, in effect, the most dangerous rivals of their own companies.[55]

Jones and Ville conclude their more recent survey in similarly sober terms:

Attempts were made to align the interests of companies and individuals by granting servants trading and other privileges, but our review of the evidence strongly suggests that, in spite of a variety of monitoring and incentive systems, technological constraints and opportunistic behavior by company servants resulted in the excessive dissipation of monopoly rents.[56]

The success of private, unincorporated, unchartered traders casts the most striking doubt on the notion that merchant guilds and privileged companies were the efficient solution to principal-agent problems. At the medieval Champagne fairs, as we have seen, foreign merchants from many lands traded successfully without forming alien merchant guilds. In medieval Bruges, too, many alien merchants traded successfully without guild privileges. Italian merchant firms, operating with fewer monopoly privileges and on a much smaller scale, managed their agents in Bruges more effectively than the gigantic German Hanse with its militarily enforced monopoly over trade with northern and eastern Europe.

The early modern intercontinental trade was the same, with small-scale, unincorporated traders often outcompeting the privileged companies, despite lack of monopoly privileges or even outright illegal status. As Chaudhuri has pointed out, 'The East India companies did not set the general institutional norm of long-distance trade in the seventeenth and eighteenth centuries, which was firmly based on private partnerships and individual family-owned business houses both in Asia and Europe.'[57] Price concurs that 'the joint-stock chartered company did not have an unbroken record of success in all fields'.[58] The English trade to North and South America, for instance, was carried out after 1624 almost wholly by private, unincorporated, unchartered merchants

---

[55] Coornaert (1967), 262.   [56] S. R. H. Jones and Ville (1996), 908.
[57] Chaudhuri (1991), 440.   [58] Price (1991), 277.

from the British and Spanish Caribbean colonies, except for the brief and unsuccessful monopoly secured by the English South Sea Company between 1711 and 1739.[59] The slave trade with Africa also saw the chartered Royal African Company outcompeted by interloping private traders who enjoyed neither the monopoly privileges nor the economies of scale of the Company.[60] The trade between France and its empire in the early modern period was characterized by a plethora of private traders who competed remarkably successfully with the privileged French companies despite having no monopolies, operating illegally and being so small that they could not have enjoyed any economies of scale in solving agency problems.[61] Some of these successful independent traders were the very interlopers who, as we saw in Chapter 6, were defined as 'pirates' and subjected to violent attacks by merchant guilds and privileged companies.

It cannot be argued that independent merchants were simply free-riding on solutions to the principal-agent problem devised by merchant guilds and privileged companies, since such solutions could by their nature only be enjoyed by guild and company members – they did not have spillover benefits for the wider economy.[62] Thus the independent merchants must have been certain of making a profit despite not being able to solve agency problems via guild or company mechanisms. This suggests that even if monopolies had given merchant guilds and privileged companies economies of scale in controlling agents, these scale economies cannot have been very important in practice since they did not confer a decisive competitive advantage against non-guilded interlopers. Principal-agent problems were rife in pre-modern trade, but monopolistic merchant guilds and companies did not offer the solution.

8.3   Alternative institutions for solving agency problems

Integral to the claim that the merchant guild or privileged company was the efficient solution to principal-agent problems is the assumption that alternative institutions were lacking. But is this true? A close look at the evidence reveals a wide array of institutional mechanisms by which medieval and early modern merchants managed their agents. These included employing kin and friends, using contractual instruments such as partnerships, keeping written records of agency agreements and undertaking formal litigation against fraudulent agents. All these mechanisms existed simultaneously within an interconnected system of institutions for dealing with agency problems. Merchant guilds were only

[59] *Ibid.*   [60] Galenson (1986), 15–16, 25–7, 148–50; North (1991), 35.
[61] Ames (1996).   [62] Counter to the claims in Carlos and Nicholas (1996), 918.

one component of this interlinked system and, as we have seen, not a particularly important one.

8.3.1   Family firms

A first indication that merchant guilds were not the efficient solution to principal-agent problems is that merchants continued to use family and kinship networks to bind agents to principals. Probably the earliest form of commercial association was the family-oriented partnership.[63] This form of enterprise was (and is) highly attractive precisely because family ties within the partnership 'provided some assurance to the principal that the orders and directions of the principal were safely carried out'.[64]

The merchant guild did not substitute for the solution to principal-agent problems offered by family partnerships, since these continued to be favoured by merchants who were members of guilds and privileged companies. The Piacenzan merchant firms that were so successful at the Champagne fairs in the thirteenth century, for instance, were closely linked by blood relationships among approximately twenty families, both within and between individual firms.[65] The phenomenally successful medieval Florentine trading house of the Medici consisted of a 'loose combination of quasi-independent partnerships', in each of which

the members of the Medici family... were the senior partners and controlled the major part of the capital, even when the name of Medici did not appear in the style of the partnership... the Medici family controlled the conduct of the business of each subsidiary.[66]

The Medici family used this form of enterprise despite being members of the Florentine merchant guild at home and its alien merchant guilds abroad. The highly successful long-distance merchants of Venice, likewise, formed family firms – particularly *fraterne*, partnerships between adult brothers – to do business in international trading destinations, even though they were all members of Venetian merchant guilds abroad.[67] Merchants of the German Hanse are well known to have organized much of their business around family relationships, acted as unpaid agents for family members and employed fictive kinship ties such as godparenthood to bind non-related business associates more closely to their interests.[68] The Hanse merchant Hildebrand Veckinchusen, for instance, based his

---

[63] Reyerson (1985), 35–9; Renouard (1949), 152–216.   [64] North (1991), 28.
[65] Bautier (1987), 187.   [66] R. De Roover (1948a), 34.
[67] See, e.g., Lane (1944), 178–85.
[68] Selzer and Ewert (2001), 139, 145–6; Selzer and Ewert (2005), 24–5.

trade out of Bruges on associations with brothers, cousins, a father-in-law, nephews and other relatives in London, Lübeck, Danzig, Riga, Reval and Dorpat.[69] Hanseatic merchants' use of relatives as agents is repeatedly confirmed by prosopographical micro-studies for specific trading centres such as Riga, Reval, Lübeck and Bruges.[70]

Family partnerships as a way of organizing agency relationships survived well into the early modern period. Thus, for instance, the Van der Molen commission house in sixteenth-century Antwerp consisted of four brothers in partnership; many of its employees were cousins or longstanding family friends; and its most important agency relationships were among the brothers themselves, with the youngest brother Daniel as the Venice agent.[71] The same was true in the early modern privileged companies. Hejeebu, for instance, argues that 'insider hiring' may have been one of the mechanisms by which the English East India Company solved principal-agent problems: 'bonds of friendship and kinship between Directors and servants were commonplace'.[72] The Armenian merchants who were one of the East India Company's greatest rivals in the India trade also used the family firm as their basic organizational unit even though they also formed alien merchant guilds.[73] That merchants who were members of guilds and privileged companies continued to employ kin as agents suggests that guilds and companies did not offer the efficient solution to agency problems for most pre-modern traders.

8.3.2   Legal forms of enterprise

Of course, relying solely on family and friends as agents limited the scope of the resources (information, expertise, finance) that could be mobilized by agency relationships. This constraint could only be loosened by developing mechanisms for extending discretionary authority to persons who were not relatives of the principal. One way was to develop more sophisticated accounting and auditing methods, as well as 'more elaborate procedures for monitoring the behavior of agents'.[74] From the earliest origins of trade, therefore, merchants strove to clarify and formalize the legal relationship between principals and agents. They did so by developing a whole array of 'forms of enterprise' – different ways of

---

[69] Irsigler (1985b); Stark (1984), 141; Stark (1993), esp. 193–4; Selzer and Ewert (2001), 145–6.

[70] Brück (1999), 117; Militzer (1997), 113–15; Asmussen (1999), 149–67; Selzer and Ewert (2001), 155–8.

[71] Edler (1938), 94–7.   [72] Hejeebu (2005), 506.   [73] Aslanian (2004), 58.

[74] North (1991), 28.

organizing associations among merchants for borrowing capital, pooling labour and spreading risk.[75]

The origins of legal forms of commercial enterprise are, literally, lost in antiquity. Both the terms used to refer to them (*commenda, societas, collegiantia*) and the legal structure for enforcing them are thought to derive from the ancient Roman empire,[76] although some scholars argue that the medieval European forms of enterprise were also strongly influenced by Islamic commercial practice.[77] In the western Mediterranean, Roman law had handed down from antiquity several different types of contractual arrangement for borrowing and pooling capital which were used between both kin and non-kin.[78] New forms of commercial association began to emerge in the Byzantine and Islamic legal systems in the seventh and eighth centuries.[79] By the eighth century, Islamic law had developed the *qîrad*, which is regarded as being 'the earliest example of a commercial arrangement identical with the later commenda, and containing all its essential features'.[80]

The new forms of commercial association that emerged in Islamic law by the seventh or eighth centuries can be observed in Venetian and southern Italian law by the ninth century.[81] The earliest surviving sources documenting actual commercial activities by European Mediterranean merchants date only from the eleventh century, but already contain references to these forms of commercial association, as illustrated by a *commenda* contract dating from 1072.[82] By the twelfth century, when sources become somewhat more plentiful, Italian (especially Genoese) merchants were already using quite sophisticated forms of enterprise in order to trade simultaneously in multiple locations. These included associations outside the family group and agency relationships granting full power of attorney to non-relatives. These contractual forms were also sophisticated enough to circumscribe legally the activities permitted to the agent, as shown by Genoese contracts from 1191 onwards in which principals prohibited factors in Constantinople from undertaking projects in Romania (the wider Byzantine empire outside the capital).[83] The cartularies of Genoese notaries in the twelfth and thirteenth centuries contain such a large number of careful legal designations of agency relationships that, according to Doehaerd, 'no contractual agreement exists that does not make allusion to the possible substitution of an agent for the main parties'.[84] By the 1180s at latest, agency relationships can

[75] R. De Roover (1948a), 12–13; North (1991), 29.   [76] Reyerson (1985), 9–10.
[77] Lieber (1968), 240.   [78] Lopez (1987), 313.
[79] Reyerson (1985), 9–10; Lieber (1968), 240; Gil (2003), 274, 278.
[80] Udovitch (1962), 207.   [81] Reyerson (1985), 9–10; Lieber (1968), 240.
[82] See note 81.   [83] Balard (1966), 469, 471–2.   [84] Doehaerd (1941), 111.

be observed among Italian merchants – even small-scale traders – at the Champagne fairs.[85] These new forms of enterprise spread from Italy throughout western Mediterranean Europe during the twelfth century, and to northern European centres, especially in Flanders, in the course of the thirteenth.[86]

Very early in the medieval Commercial Revolution, therefore, merchants developed an array of forms of enterprise precisely to solve agency problems, and exploited these contractual forms flexibly to suit particular circumstances. The *rogadia* contract, for instance, enabled one merchant to promise to transport and trade the goods of another, without compensation but, it is thought, in return for the expectation that the favour would be returned in future.[87] The *colonna* contract enabled merchants travelling in the same ship to agree to divide the risks and profits of a common venture in predetermined shares.[88] The *commenda* contract was a short-term agreement enabling a sedentary partner to provide all the capital and receive the major profit share in a venture, while the travelling partner or agent provided all the labour in return for a smaller profit share or even just a fixed retainer. Because third-party liability was limited to the amount of the investment, the *commenda* contract did not require much mutual trust between principal and agent.[89] The classic *commenda* was bilateral, with just one sedentary partner and one travelling partner or agent, but there were also multilateral *commenda* partnerships, between more than one sedentary partner or more than one travelling agent.[90] The *societas* contract enabled both the sedentary and the travelling partner to provide both capital and labour to the venture – i.e. both could act as principals and both could act as agents.[91] The *compagnia* contract enabled a large number of merchants to form an association in which all of them agreed to supply both capital and labour, alternating the 'principal' and the 'agent' roles, enduring for many years, and involving unlimited liability of each partner towards third parties for the debts of the whole enterprise.[92] There were also a number of mixed forms of enterprise which allocated risks and profits differently among variable numbers of sedentary 'principals' and travelling 'agents', and which lasted for periods measured in numbers of voyages or

[85] Face (1958), 430–3; R. De Roover (1948a), 312.
[86] Reyerson (1985), 9–10; Lieber (1968a), 240; R. De Roover (1948), 12–13; Doehaerd (1941), 172.
[87] Lopez (1987), 313–14, 364.   [88] *Ibid.*
[89] Doehaerd (1941), 119–26; Lopez (1987), 313–14, 364.
[90] Reyerson (1985), 10, 14–18, 33.
[91] Doehaerd (1941), 126–7; Reyerson (1985), 10, 16, 25–6.
[92] Lopez (1987), 313, 364.

numbers of months or years, in ways that could be flexibly adjusted to suit the financial strength, commercial expertise and personal preferences of the contracting parties.[93] In the course of the medieval period, *rogadia* and *colonna* contracts gradually died out while *commenda* contracts (for sea trade) and *compagnia* contracts (for land trade) became the norm.[94] At the same time, new forms of enterprise began to emerge. The only thing that was not yet possible was to combine indeterminate duration and limited liability. For that sort of investment, one needed to buy shares in a public loan floated by a big urban commune, or invest in real estate.[95]

In northern Europe, the merchants of the German Hanse also developed various legal forms of enterprise to manage relations between principals and agents. One was the *Wedderleeginge* (also called *Widerlegung*, *kumpanie* or *vera societas*), in which the principal (*Kapitalnehmer*) provided the capital while the agent (*Kapitalführer*) used it to trade independently under his own name, and the profits were shared between the two.[96] Another was the so-called *Sendegutgeschäft*, in which a principal (*Sendegutabsender*) gave or sent wares to an agent (*Sendegutempfänger*) to sell for him, with the principal bearing all risk and profit himself.[97] Hanseatic merchants also practised what has been called 'long-distance trading partnership based on reciprocity' (*Fernhandelgesellschaft auf Gegenseitigkeit*), whereby two merchants in different locations sent each other wares to sell in the name of the sending partner, rewarded only by being able to call on reciprocal services from the partner in future.[98]

In all of the southern European forms of association, and to a lesser extent also in the Hanseatic forms, the sedentary or investing partner tended to become a 'principal' and the travelling or labour-providing partner tended to become his 'agent' or quasi-employee. From this situation, it was a short step to adopting new forms of agency relationship, whereby a sedentary merchant (or group of merchants) set up a 'trading house' or 'firm' (often governed by some legal form of enterprise), which then established *branches* in commercially strategic locations. The main trading house would then man each branch with agents, who might be equal partners in the firm enjoying a share of the profits, employees paid a

[93] Reyerson (1985), 16–18, 25.   [94] Lopez (1987), 313–14.
[95] *Ibid.*, 365.   [96] Cordes (1999), 67–71; Selzer and Ewert (2001), 140–1.
[97] Cordes (1999), 67–71; Selzer and Ewert (2001), 141.
[98] Mickwitz (1937); Selzer and Ewert (2001), 141–2. This arrangement was similar to the *ṣuḥba* ('formal friendship') used by the 'Maghribi traders' or 'Geniza merchants'; see the discussion in Goldberg (2005); Goldberg (2008), 11, 14–17, 51 n. 86, 53 nn. 116–18.

fixed salary or hybrid agents receiving a combination of salary and profit share.[99]

This legal arrangement for managing principal-agent relationships spread rapidly as medieval trade expanded. By the twelfth century Genoese merchants were employing agents to handle their business at the Champagne fairs, and in the thirteenth they began setting up large-scale firms with permanent representation abroad through partners and agents.[100] In the secret ledgers of the Bardi and Peruzzi trading houses of medieval Florence, each factor was recorded with a curriculum vitae noting his starting wages, his successive raises and the fines he incurred for professional mistakes.[101] The Castracani business in Lucca, while remaining mainly a family firm, had by 1284 metamorphosed from a small, locally oriented partnership into 'an enlarged organization, including outsiders as partners, with at least one agent stationed abroad'.[102] By the fifteenth century, the house of Medici can be observed carefully laying down, in the articles of association for its Bruges branch, precisely how the junior partner was supposed to behave in all matters touching upon the business.[103] A very few examples of such hierarchical firms can also be observed among German Hanseatic merchants, but before the sixteenth century such forms of enterprise were much commoner among Italian, Spanish and south German merchants.[104] This type of principal-agent arrangement was also used by the privileged early modern companies, whose legal form of enterprise was a sort of hybrid between a merchant guild and a firm: the privileged company shared with the merchant guild its exclusionary character and monopoly privileges, as we saw in Chapter 4, but shared with the modern firm institutional mechanisms enabling a large number of investors to engage in risky activities and monitor each other and their agents.[105]

If anything, merchant guilds were an obstacle to the development of these new ways of controlling agents through legal forms of enterprise. Genoese merchant guilds in the Levant tried to prohibit Genoese merchants from forming partnerships with non-Genoese traders, and Venetian merchant consuls in the Levant tried to prevent Venetian merchants from entering into business associations with Muslim partners.[106] But

[99] Reyerson (1985), 36; Renouard (1949), 152–216.
[100] Face (1958), 427ff.; Blomquist (1971), 471–3.   [101] Bec (1967), 1218.
[102] Blomquist (1971), 471.
[103] R. De Roover (1948a), 37–8; R. De Roover (1948b), 342–3.
[104] Stromer (1976), 208–10; Selzer and Ewert (2001), 136–8, 145 n. 50.
[105] North (1991), 29, regards the early modern regulated and chartered companies as descendants of the medieval *commenda* (a voluntary commercial association), ignoring the monopolistic features causing them to resemble medieval merchant guilds.
[106] Ashtor (1983), 410.

principal-agent relationships and partnerships between merchants of different nations were so attractive that Italian merchants risked penalties to go on forming them, and it was a common practice for Genoese to act as factors of Venetians, merchants of both cities to form business associations with one another, and western European merchants to go into partnership with Muslims.[107] The German Hanse also forbade members to form commercial partnerships with outsiders, and – unfortunately for north German merchants – was much more successful in enforcing these regulations than Italian merchant guilds in the Levant.[108]

Still another widespread arrangement enabling pre-modern merchants to manage distant agents was the 'correspondent relationship'. Instead of setting up an agency agreement with a partner or employee, a merchant formed a tie with a correspondent, also called a factor or a commissionaire, who was formally an independent merchant trading on his own account, and 'alone responsible at law for his actions, even when acting as a factor on commission for another'.[109] The correspondent would agree to execute almost any business task on behalf of his principal – ranging from buying and selling wares to handling bills of exchange to arranging insurance. In return, the correspondent charged the principal a fixed percentage, usually between 2 and 5 per cent depending on the location.[110]

Correspondent relationships were common from the medieval period into the nineteenth century, and coexisted alongside merchant guilds and privileged companies.[111] In the mid-fourteenth century, for instance, the Prato merchant Francesco di Marco Datini managed a geographically dispersed trade throughout Europe by means of correspondent relationships in numerous cities.[112] So important were correspondent relationships still in the early modern period that Jacques Savary's influential merchant manual of 1675 went so far as to declare that 'nothing preserves commerce as much as commissioners and correspondents'.[113] The correspondent relationship was widespread in the early modern intercontinental trade, and helped interloping merchants compete successfully (if illegally) with the monopolistic chartered companies:

> For students of transaction costs, the interesting thing about the merchant correspondent system is its low cost and flexibility. There were considerable overhead costs in maintaining an employee in a foreign port . . . But a merchant could have correspondents all over Europe and in many colonies without overhead and need pay commission only when he used a correspondent.[114]

---

[107] Constable (2003), 117, 131–2; Ashtor (1983), 411.   [108] Burckhardt (2005), 65, 71.
[109] Price (1991), 279.   [110] *Ibid.*   [111] R. De Roover (1948a), 29–30.
[112] Padgett and McLean (2006), 1474–5.   [113] Savary (1675), Book 2, ch. 55, p. 143.
[114] Price (1991), 279.

Of course, agency problems arose between principals and their correspondents, just as they arose between sedentary and travelling partners in the *commenda*, and between employers and employees in the great medieval trading houses. To some extent, in correspondent relationships as in other forms of contract, principals chose agents who were family members, fellow religionists or members of the same ethnic group. However, it is clear that 'such bonds were not absolutely necessary': many merchants could not or did not choose their correspondents from their extended family, religious group or ethnic network, and yet managed to trade profitably.[115]

Remarkably, the correspondent relationship was a very successful alternative to the employee relationship, despite its potential for agency problems. Small, unincorporated firms without employees used correspondent relationships to trade on the same routes and in the same wares as the great privileged companies with their employee contracts. Moreover, they were very competitive in doing so, judging by the anxiety of the privileged companies to exclude them, often by law or force. Indeed, a number of smaller-scale British and French private merchants trading to the New World experimented with trading through employees but 'increasingly realized that resident factors could trade more efficiently', because having employees led to high overheads 'and often did not significantly reduce the agency problem'.[116] A further important advantage was that employees were generally less skilled and experienced in commercial matters, whereas correspondents were themselves fully fledged merchants. There were straightforward sorts of transaction (such as the simple bilateral sugar and tobacco trades) that could be handled by employees, such as ship captains or supercargoes, who were not themselves experienced merchants, but more complex dealings 'required merchant correspondents'.[117]

8.3.3   Written record-keeping

With all these different contractual forms – commercial partnerships, merchant houses with employees and correspondent relationships – an important further ingredient in monitoring and managing agents was maintenance of written records. We have already seen in Chapter 7 how from the beginning of the medieval Commercial Revolution merchants began to keep written records of their business activities – correspondence, bonds, receipts, contracts, ledgers, daybooks. Record-keeping not only enabled merchants to enforce contracts, but also enhanced their

[115] *Ibid.*, 279–80.   [116] *Ibid.*, 280.   [117] *Ibid.*, 283.

ability to monitor agents, especially those entrusted with complicated business in distant locations. Venetian merchant factors in fourteenth- and fifteenth-century Levantine trading centres were legally obliged to maintain a *recordatio* in which they wrote down the orders of the merchant who employed them, and were sued in court if they neglected or violated these orders.[118] According to one study, not just in the medieval period but also long after 1500, 'letters remained the main instruments for a merchant to exert control over his agents overseas'.[119]

Official registration of business agreements by notaries and local authorities enhanced the legal effectiveness of written records, as we saw in Chapter 7. It also played an important role in helping merchants manage agents. In thirteenth-century Montpellier, for instance, the sedentary partner (principal) and travelling partner (agent) in a *commenda* partnership typically signed a contract in front of a notary in advance of the venture. On the travelling agent's return from the venture, he was legally obliged to settle accounts with his principal according to the provisions laid down in the contract, receiving a formal acquittal in front of the notary. In some ventures to Muslim lands, the Crusader states and the Byzantine empire, these acquittals were recorded up to a year after the establishment of the original contract, demonstrating their effectiveness in enforcing principal-agent relationships over long distances and considerable time lapses.[120]

Local municipal authorities also increasingly offered official registration of agreements between principals and agents. This was especially important in northern European trading centres such as Bruges and London, where the notarial system was largely lacking, except among expatriate Italian merchant communities. But municipal record-keeping, as we saw in Chapter 7, also became increasingly important in Mediterranean Europe in the course of the medieval period.

8.3.4   Public law-courts

Finally, as Chapter 7 discussed, law-courts operated by the public authorities offered formal enforcement of agreements from an early date. Formal arbitration and litigation in courts of law were used not just to enforce contracts with other merchants, but also to manage relationships with agents and factors. Among twelfth-century Genoese merchants, for instance, merchants can be observed suing defaulting agents in municipal courts.[121] In thirteenth-century Montpellier, if the travelling

---

[118] Ashtor (1983), 403.   [119] Trivellato (2007), 83.
[120] Reyerson (1985), 15 with nn. 30–1.   [121] Greif (2006a), ch. 9.

agent in a *commenda* contract failed to settle accounts properly after the voyage was over, the sedentary principal would report the agent to the municipal court to enforce restitution.[122] In the early fourteenth century, the Peruzzi firm successfully sued its dishonest Bruges and London factor Silimanno Botteri in the commercial court of the city of Florence.[123] In 1310–11, when a dishonest London agent could account for only £77 out of £110 he had been sent by the Hull merchant John Box, he was prosecuted in the public legal system and incarcerated in the Fleet prison.[124] In fourteenth- and fifteenth-century Venice, merchants sued their disobedient or fraudulent Levantine agents in the *Giudici di petiziòn*, a municipal tribunal whose records contain 'countless acts of such litigations'.[125] In fourteenth- and fifteenth-century Lübeck, German Hanseatic merchants used the municipal court to prosecute fraudulent partners and agents.[126] The market-based contractual instruments devised to manage agency relationships during the medieval Commercial Revolution were thus supported by the institutions of the public legal system.

8.4   Conclusion

What broader implications emerge from these findings? The medieval Commercial Revolution saw a huge growth in international trade. Long-distance merchants needed agents so they could trade simultaneously in multiple locations. But how could they ensure that agents acted according to their interests? In developing economies more widely, how can merchants minimize the risks of employing agents, enabling them to expand their businesses beyond the reach of personal observation and local information transmission?

Medieval and early modern Europe, as this chapter has shown, possessed an array of institutional mechanisms offering different ways of controlling agents – kinship networks, merchant guilds, legal forms of enterprise, written documents, notarial systems, municipal contract registration and public law-courts. Many of these mechanisms were the same ones that we observed in Chapter 7 being used by merchants to enforce contracts with other merchants, since an agency relationship is often simply a form of contract, albeit one with special characteristics.

Some of the mechanisms were provided by particularized institutions, solving agency problems for specific groups of people – members of the same family, merchants of the same guild, hanse or privileged company.

---

[122] Reyerson (1985), 15 with nn. 30–1.   [123] R. De Roover (1948a), 33.
[124] Kermode (1998), 209.   [125] Ashtor (1983), 403.   [126] Ebel (1957), 84.

Others were provided by generalized institutions such as the market or the legal system, solving agency problems for anyone – in principle, any economic agent could set up a legal form of enterprise with someone else, record his agency agreements in writing before a notary or a municipal office, and seek sanctions against a defaulting agent in a public court of law.

Particularized institutions such as the family, kinship network or merchant guild, as we have seen, long pre-dated the medieval Commercial Revolution and the early modern expansion of intercontinental trade. This casts doubt on the extent to which merchant guilds or privileged companies can have been the institutional innovation which made it possible to solve the challenging agency problems posed by the expansion of long-distance trade. Further doubt is cast by the findings in this chapter.

For one thing, there are quite serious doubts about the idea that social capital inside merchant guilds can have solved agency problems in long-distance trade. In theory, merchant guilds – as social networks – might have offered swift transmission of information about a fraudulent agent and effective collective sanctions against him by all network members. But theory also suggests costs arising from the very characteristics that enabled merchant networks to address agency problems – network closure and multi-stranded relationships. If closure and multiplex ties are the main way a merchant controls agency problems, this will deter him from employing outside agents against whom he cannot use these instruments, and that will reduce his gains from trade. In so far as merchant guilds such as the German Hanse limited commercial associations between members and outsiders, they would have deprived their members of profitable exchange and constrained the growth of their businesses. Empirically, as we have seen, there is little direct evidence about whether closed networks of European merchants brought members corresponding benefits by mitigating agency problems. Even if these benefits existed, doubt is cast on their economic significance by the success of competitors who never joined such merchant networks but evidently solved agency problems without resorting to this kind of social capital.

A second way merchant guilds and privileged companies are supposed to have solved agency problems was by exploiting their monopoly position so as to reap economies of scale through internal contracting with agents as employees. But economic theory suggests that large, vertically integrated organizations also suffer from *diseconomies* of scale. Multiple layers of monitoring can increase costs of information, enforcement and employee motivation, and centralized policy setting can lead to inflexibility. Furthermore, if large-scale operations enjoyed cost advantages over other organizational forms, monopoly would emerge 'naturally' as the outcome of competitive success and would not need legal restrictions to sustain it. The existence of legal restrictions implies that large-scale organization was more costly and that monopoly could only be sustained by institutional privileges.

Some monopolistic merchant guilds – particularly the German Hanse and the early modern privileged companies – did set up elaborate bureaucratic systems to regulate agents' behaviour. But analysis of actual business activities reveals that they often enforced these systems quite ineffectively. Centralized decision-making, as shown by some spectacular failures, led to supervisory diseconomies of scale. The success of small-scale private traders and illegal interlopers in competing with merchant guilds and privileged companies suggests that any advantages the latter's legal monopolies created in mitigating agency problems were commercially unimportant.

There was, however, a new and dynamic component of the institutional system during the medieval Commercial Revolution and the early modern emergence of intercontinental trade. This was the growth, as we saw in Chapter 7, of generalized institutions which offered solutions to agency problems which were available to all economic agents, whether or not they were members of merchant guilds or privileged companies. From the tenth century onwards, European merchants began to use a whole range of formal legal instruments – partnerships, associations, employment contracts and correspondent relationships – enabling principals and agents to enter into legal agreements about precisely how each party was supposed to behave. These formal agreements between principals and agents were increasingly recorded in writing, both within merchant businesses and by outside parties such as notaries. Such 'market' mechanisms were made more effective by 'state' institutions, such as the legal recognition of contractual instruments, the official registration of agency contracts with municipal offices and the punishment of fraudulent agents in public law-courts.

Pre-modern merchants thus had at their disposal a whole array of institutions offering different types of solution to the principal-agent problem, which could be adapted to the precise requirements of a given venture or trading context. These institutions existed simultaneously in an interdependent system, within which merchant guilds were only one component, and often a fairly minor one at that. The true institutional innovations that enabled better – if by no means perfect – solutions to the principal-agent problem and hence encouraged the growth of trade in premodern Europe were not entrenched, corporative social networks such as merchant guilds. Rather, as has already become clear in earlier chapters, the Commercial Revolution was made possible by the emergence of increasingly impersonal market instruments and impartial public institutions that were available to all – not just to members of merchant guilds and privileged companies.

9   Information

> If you wish to be counted a wise man . . . you ought never to let a day pass without learning something that will profit you. Be not like those who think it beneath their dignity to hear or learn from others such things even as might avail them much if they knew them. For a man must regard it as great an honor to learn as to teach, if he wishes to be considered thoroughly informed.
>
> ('The Activities and Habits of a Merchant', *The King's Mirror*, Norway, *c.* 1250)[1]

Trade requires information. Buyers and sellers need to know the attributes of goods. Merchants with contracts need to know whether other parties are complying. Principals need to know what agents are doing. Traders in general want to transform *uncertainty* about the future into *risk* – to move from being unable to ascertain the probability of a particular event to being able to predict and thus prepare for it.[2] To plan business dealings, merchants need to know about price movements, supply chains, demand conditions, political developments, military events, geographical obstacles, weather patterns, commercial techniques, foreign languages and alien customs.[3]

The medieval and early modern trading world brought new information requirements. Trade routes – particularly as international trade expanded – were uncertain. Maps were imperfect. Transportation techniques were stretched to the limit. Communication lines were longer. Existing merchandise varied in quality. Novel goods were being discovered. Prices fluctuated wildly. Currencies differed across space and time. New methods of transferring and exchanging money were being invented. Weights and measures were still not standardized in Europe, let alone overseas. Mortality was high. Personal rule by monarchs vulnerable to demographic accidents could change regimes from one day to the next.

---

[1] Quoted in Larson (1917), 84.   [2] North (1991), 28–9.
[3] *Ibid.*, 24; Denzel (2001), 73.

For all these reasons, pre-modern merchants were constantly desperate for up-to-date information.[4]

But information is scarce and expensive, so much so that it is a key determinant of what economists call transaction costs – costs incurred in making economic exchanges. One reason trade grows is that people work out ways of reducing transaction costs, including costs of information. More seriously still, information (like security) is what economists call a public good, with two peculiar characteristics making it complicated to buy and sell in markets. First, it is non-excludable: once an item of information has been sold to one consumer, it is hard to prevent it from being communicated without charge to others. Second, information is non-rival: the producer of a piece of information incurs no higher costs if he provides it to extra consumers. These features mean that the *private* benefits of collecting and diffusing information may be less than the *social* benefits. So information may be under-provided by private individuals transacting in markets. Either information may not be collected at all, since potential collectors cannot profit from their own efforts. Or it may be collected but – in order that private collectors of information can profit – diffused only to a few paying customers, even though at zero additional cost it could benefit society more widely.[5]

Because markets have these problems dealing with public goods, other institutions might in principle be more efficient at providing information. In pre-modern trade, merchant guilds are sometimes claimed to have been those institutions. According to De Roover, for instance, the main purpose of alien merchant guilds in medieval Bruges was 'to facilitate the exchange of information on business failures, wars, market conditions, exchange rates, and similar topics of interest to practical merchants and financiers'.[6] Kohn argues that merchant guilds provided 'the merchant at home with information about the trading possibilities that his agent faced in the distant market'.[7] Lambert and Stabel describe the consul of an alien merchant guild in an international trading centre as 'a crucial figure in distributing market information'.[8] According to Mazzaoui, the *mercanzia* (merchant guild) of a medieval Italian city provided its members with 'a continuous flow of information on supplies of raw materials, prices, transport and general market conditions, both foreign and domestic'.[9] Harreld argues that merchant guilds

---

[4] Spruyt (1994), 122; Ashtor (1983), 69–70; Denzel (2001), 73.
[5] Stigler (1968), esp. 171–90; North (1981), esp. 33–44.   [6] R. De Roover (1948a), 20.
[7] Kohn (2003a), 28.   [8] Lambert and Stabel (2005), 13.
[9] Mazzaoui (1981), 121.

developed during the Middle Ages to 'decrease the costs involved in obtaining information'.[10]

Why might merchant guilds have been efficient institutions for providing commercial information? First, their monopolies are supposed to have given them the size, vertical integration and market domination to reap scale economies in *collecting* information and to internalize the externalities (spillover benefits) involved in its characteristics as a public good. Second, guilds' social capital of dense, multiplex internal relationships is held to have lowered the cost of *disseminating* information: the existence of strong, reduplicated connections among members is supposed to have created 'bandwidth', ensuring a reliable flow of data to everyone in a network.[11]

This chapter begins by examining the theoretical arguments for how merchant guilds might have affected commercial information – both positively and, as we shall see, negatively. It then confronts these theoretical arguments with evidence on how merchant guilds actually dealt with information. Finally, since any claim that merchant guilds were efficient assumes that alternative institutions were lacking, we explore the other institutions pre-modern merchants used to collect and transmit commercial information.

9.1   Theoretical effects of merchant guilds on information provision

A first way merchant guilds are supposed to have solved information problems was through their monopolies. The monopolies enjoyed by merchant guilds and privileged companies, it is claimed, created the scale and vertical integration necessary to reduce the costs of asymmetric information in recurrent transactions. Monopolies also gave merchant guilds the scale to engage in integrated planning, processing information faster and more appropriately than smaller-scale competitive traders. Finally, by being legal monopolists and thus dominating the markets in particular transaction types, routes and destinations, merchant guilds and privileged companies are believed to have internalized the positive externalities created by the 'public good' features of information.[12]

---

[10] Harreld (2004a), 41 (quotation), 45, 58; however, the examples he provides (p. 46) of information transmission by merchants in medieval and early modern Antwerp were undertaken by city institutions or individual merchant firms.

[11] Burt (2005), 165.

[12] For arguments to this effect, see Van Tielhof (2002), 144; W. D. Smith (1984), 990–5; Grafe (2001), 10; Link and Kapfenberger (2005), 165; Steensgaard (1973), 22–59; Das Gupta (1979), 11–12; Carlos and Nicholas (1988), 407.

A second way merchant guilds are supposed to have improved information provision was through social capital. As Coleman pointed out,

An important form of social capital is the potential for information that inheres in social relations . . . One means by which information can be acquired is to use social relations that are maintained for other purposes . . . [A] person who is not deeply interested in current events but who is interested in being informed about important developments can save the time required to read a newspaper if he can get the information he wants from a friend who pays attention to such matters.[13]

Coleman's seminal discussion of social capital and information gave rise to the 'bandwidth hypothesis', which postulates that the greater the closure of a social network and the more multiplex the links among its members, the denser will be its internal interrelationships and the more efficient its internal flow of information. That is, closure and multi-stranded relationships expand the bandwidth of channels through which information can flow.[14] According to this view, guilds offered merchants a network of contacts that enabled them to communicate information efficiently.

But while in the realm of theory, we should also consider ways merchant guilds might have diminished or restricted commercial information. For one thing, the very monopolies putatively helping guilds collect information also entitled them to reserve it for their own members. Outsiders were not supposed to be operating in that branch of commerce anyway and thus has no right to obtain information about it.

Second, a monopolist will tend to do business less efficiently than a competitive producer. It lacks the 'stick' incentive, in the sense that if a monopolist fails to minimize costs, it will not lose business to a competitor who does. It may also lack the 'carrot' incentive to maximize profits since, as Hicks famously observed, 'The best of all monopoly profits is a quiet life.'[15] Thus a monopolistic merchant guild or privileged company had less incentive than a competitive individual trader to minimize costs of information provision, collect the optimal quantity of information and analyse information efficiently, since it would not lose business to more efficient competitors.

Third, size leads to information slippage. If a merchant guild or privileged company was large enough to reap economies of scale in collecting information and internalizing its public good characteristics, it was also large enough to have to employ agents. But, as we saw in Chapter 7, agency relationships have costs – and one is the potential for information

[13] J. S. Coleman (1990), 310.   [14] Burt (2001).   [15] Hicks (1935), 8.

slippage. Unless a merchant guild or privileged company set up very effective management mechanisms, its agents would find themselves free to shirk in processing information and to exploit corporate information in their own interests.

Fourth, as we saw in Chapter 7, size creates supervisory diseconomies of scale. If a merchant guild or privileged company was large enough to reap scale economies, it was large enough to suffer from costs in transmitting information through multiple management layers. Within a large organization, the level where decisions are taken is often not the one where information is available. This creates the risk of inappropriate responses to unexpected events.[16]

Social networks also suffer from 'echo effects' or 'information cascades' – convergence in beliefs for reasons unrelated to their accuracy. Experiments in social psychology suggest that information obtained through personal contacts is not as reliable as information obtained through direct experience. This is because in personal contacts it is polite to share those of our facts consistent with the perceived dispositions of our interlocutors. But people fail to compensate for this tendency and regard information transmitted through personal contacts with more certainty than it deserves. The biased sample of facts shared in contacts within a social network becomes 'information'. A closed network creates a system of repeated transmissions of the same piece of information through multi-stranded interactions among network members. Repetition amplifies people's opinions – both positively and negatively. Favourable opinion is amplified into trust and doubt into distrust. The collective sanctions sometimes applied within social networks further intensify members' incentives not to deviate from network norms with regard to what information they assess and transmit. As a result, a closed network may generate 'information' for its members which consists excessively of amplified predispositions.[17] Such 'ignorant certainty', amplified within a social network, can reduce the quality of business decisions.

Finally, economic theory suggests that if important scale economies existed in the collection of commercial information, then international trade would be a natural monopoly. Monopolistic information collectors would emerge naturally. Precisely this is claimed by some theorists of guilds, who argue that the 'thin markets' of pre-modern Europe created natural monopolies, especially in goods and services reliant on expert information.[18] But this is not what happened with merchant guilds.

---

[16] Stigler (1942), 133–8; Robinson (1932), 43–4, 108–16.

[17] Burt (2001), 29–30.

[18] For this argument as applied to guilds of craftsmen, see S. R. Epstein (2004), 36.

Instead, as we saw in Chapters 3 and 4, merchant guilds and privileged companies constantly had to use political pressure and even force to maintain and defend their monopolies against smaller-scale interlopers who were evidently quite able to collect and process the information necessary to compete in those markets. This implies that international trade – 'thin markets' or not – was not a natural monopoly, and thus that the postulated scale economies in information collection either did not exist or were economically unimportant.

9.2   Evidence on merchant guilds and information

In theory, therefore, merchant guilds could have affected information either positively or negatively. The only way to assess the relative importance of these countervailing effects is to examine how merchant guilds and privileged companies managed information in practice.

9.2.1   Economies of scale

The first way merchant guilds are postulated to have improved information provision is through economies of scale. Size and market dominance, it is argued, meant that a merchant guild or privileged company could economize in setting up bureaucratic systems to collect information cheaply on behalf of all its members and internalize the positive externalities created by the fact that information is a public good. Van Tielhof, for instance, claims that reports from consuls of Dutch merchant communities in foreign locations provided Dutch merchants in general with 'a wealth of business information'.[19] Grafe argues that merchant guilds in Spain and Spanish America 'built up a vertically integrated structure as a means to internalise information costs'.[20] Link and Kapfenberger argue that the German Hanse reduced transaction costs because 'a newcomer in trade could make contacts in the Kontor, collect information and get assistance, which . . . saved immense search costs, e.g. for reliable trading partners'.[21] Steensgaard claims that the monopolistic size of the privileged European companies enabled them to reap scale economies in collecting and processing information, outcompeting the individual Asian traders whose small scale meant they worked on faulty information and could not plan their business well.[22] Carlos and Nicholas contend that

[19] Van Tielhof (2002), 144 (quotation); W. D. Smith (1984), 990–5.
[20] Grafe (2001), 10.   [21] Link and Kapfenberger (2005), 165.
[22] Steensgaard (1973), 22–59; for similar views of pre-colonial Indian traders, see Das Gupta (1979), 11–12.

the monopolistic companies far surpassed individual traders competing in an open market: 'it was the efficient processing of information . . . that gave the early trading companies their advantage over the market'.[23]

These studies suffer from certain weaknesses. First, they focus mainly on the internal bureaucratic systems merchant guilds and privileged companies set up, without providing evidence on how this information actually helped merchants trade. Even some scholars sympathetic to the view that merchant communities were important for providing commercial information acknowledge, like Kallioinen, that 'the benefits of community in reducing information or negotiation costs are . . . difficult to demonstrate'.[24] Second, almost all the evidence such studies do provide dates from the early modern period – after around 1500. But as we saw in Chapter 5, this was the period when merchant guilds gradually began to decline in one European economy after another, without harming the growth of their trade (indeed, rather the contrary). Third, if these claims about the information efficiencies of monopoly are true, there should be evidence of merchant guilds emerging as natural monopolies due to competitive success, driving out individual, non-guilded traders who could not exploit such economies of scale in information collection.

The evidence shows the precise opposite. Individual, unincorporated merchants operating competitively and on a small scale were able not only to stay in business but to mount a serious competitive threat to the large-scale, monopolistic guilds and companies, as we have seen. This was true even in the often literally uncharted waters of the early modern intercontinental trade. After 1595, for instance, unincorporated Dutch merchants organized a series of expeditions to Asia to encroach on the Portuguese monopoly over the pepper trade, even though three of the expeditions were so poorly informed that they sought a north-east passage to Asia through the Arctic. Despite their lack of information and initial setbacks, by 1600 these individual expeditions were so successful that they were evoking anti-competitive action on the part of both Portuguese and English merchant guilds and privileged companies.[25] It required state action and a legal monopoly in 1602 to bring about the merger of these successful but unincorporated Dutch merchants into the gigantic Dutch East India Company (VOC). Neither the VOC nor any of the other great regulated or chartered companies emerged as natural monopolies – they emerged as *legal* monopolies based on state privileges and they survived not because of their commercial advantages but

---

[23] Carlos and Nicholas (1988), 407.   [24] Kallioinen (1998), 6 with n. 18.
[25] De Vries and Van der Woude (1997), 384.

through constant military coercion to exclude private interlopers and compel suppliers and customers to do business with them.

It might be argued that the small-scale, non-guilded interlopers were simply free-riding on information costs incurred by the merchant guilds and privileged companies.[26] But the evidence suggests otherwise. On certain routes – such as those within Europe and to its 'near abroad' in the Near East, Africa and even India – there was no need to grant a monopoly to encourage information collection, since information had been available since the medieval period and private merchants had been eagerly travelling there for generations. On other routes, including the transatlantic trade and the North American fur-trading destinations, private merchants created their own information flows, as we shall see shortly.[27] Such evidence casts doubt on the argument that merchant guilds were efficient because they could reap economies of scale in information collection. Had such economies of scale existed, small-scale, unincorporated competitors could not have been so serious and ubiquitous a threat to the big merchant guilds and privileged companies.

9.2.2   Network bandwidth

The second way merchant guilds might, in theory, have improved information provision was through closely knit, multi-stranded internal relationships which increased network 'bandwidth' – a multiplicity of reduplicated channels for ensuring the diffusion of data to everyone in a network.[28] Mauro, for instance, argues that medieval European merchant guilds facilitated the diffusion of commercial news and information about innovative trade techniques in this way.[29] According to Gelderblom and Grafe, 'the personal relations that evolved between the members of a guild could be used to collect and disseminate information about market conditions and the creditworthiness of business partners'.[30] Spruyt claims that medieval merchant guilds – particularly the German Hanse – 'acted as information centers regarding alien business practices' and 'facilitate[d] the exchange of information between merchants'.[31] Dollinger vividly describes the social networking that might in theory have facilitated this information flow:

---

[26] As claimed by Carlos and Nicholas (1996), 918.

[27] For examples of successful interloping by private traders on the Atlantic route, despite the legal monopoly of the Seville consulado, see Woodward (2005), 634, 637–8.

[28] Burt (2005), 165.   [29] Mauro (1990), 285.

[30] Gelderblom and Grafe (2004), 1.   [31] Spruyt (1994), 121, 123.

Outside the office the merchant spent his time within the framework of the trade associations, similar in spirit and organisation to the trade guilds. Almost every day he would go to the headquarters of his association, where in the common-room (*Schüttung*) he would meet his fellows, sit in his usual place, talk about public and private matters, gather information, take part in the drinking, banqueting and, on occasion, the welcoming of foreign guests, and the voting in the general assemblies which elected aldermen and jurors.[32]

Selzer argues that a major function of the Hanseatic drinking societies known as Artusbruderschaften, at which long-distance merchants congregated and other high-status individuals were admitted as guests, was to enable merchants to transmit and receive commercially relevant information.[33] Well into the early modern period, according to Holbach, members of the German Hanse, 'because of their broadly extended relationships, possessed contacts with the leading locations, were informed about potentially successful techniques, and were financially in a position to invest in production. Only they had an overview over demand and possessed access to the markets.'[34]

Similar arguments are advanced for other early modern merchant guilds. The seventeenth- and eighteenth-century London livery companies offered little obvious benefit to international merchants 'in strictly business terms', according to Gauci, but nonetheless played an essential role in providing information:

The challenges of overseas trade, particularly to far-distant lands, would simply have overwhelmed traders who lacked the support of trading associations and government-backed organisations... the increasing competitiveness of international commerce demanded ever more of the resourcefulness of the individual, and ineluctably forced him to rely on greater associations, and ultimately the state itself.[35]

Aslanian argues that the New Julfa colony of Armenian merchants in the Persian city of Isfahan, together with its branch colonies in overseas trading centres, were essential in transmitting commercial information across the Armenian diaspora.[36]

What is striking about these studies is that they focus mainly on *inputs* – the fact that merchant guilds met frequently and fostered contacts among their members. But what about information outputs and their impact on commercial outcomes? Contemporaries already recognized this weakness in the argument for merchant networking. According to the anonymous author of 'More Advice for Remedying the Decay of Trade' in 1675, there was a widely held view,

[32] Dollinger (1970), 181.   [33] Selzer (2003), 77–95.   [34] Holbach (2001), 369.
[35] Gauci (2002), 129.   [36] Aslanian (2006), 400.

that some men's business lies abroad, and cannot be so well managed at home, and these meetings or societies are advantageous to them. As first, merchants, by these clubs or meetings, have intelligence of ships going out, and coming in; and also of the rates and prices of commodities, and meet with customers by accident, which possibly might never make enquiry at their houses or warehouses. The like excuses all men of business and trade pretend.

The author, however, is quite unpersuaded:

To this I answer: that indulging this custom hath made it seemingly necessary; but yet there is no absolute necessity for it . . . For, by these idle meetings, they lose not only what they spend, but what might be improved by the [sic] overseeing their goods, and examining their accounts . . . From this negligence and loss of time come many more inconveniencies, that heap on poverty, and entail it upon themselves and generations.[37]

At least one contemporary commentator thus believed merchant guilds provided sociable luxuries, not informational necessities.

More substantive doubt is cast on the bandwidth argument by the fact that merchants who were not members of alien merchant guilds traded successfully wherever this was legal. At the Champagne fairs, as we have seen, the first alien merchant guilds only appeared in 1245, even though the fairs had been operating as important international trading centres since the 1180s. Even after 1245, many visiting merchants, including important groups such as the Flemings, never formed guilds at the fairs. After the decline of the fairs, the centre of international trade in north-west Europe shifted to Bruges where again important groups of foreign merchants traded without establishing guilds, or did so only in the late medieval period. In the medieval Mediterranean, as we saw in Chapter 4, non-guilded interlopers constituted a serious competitive threat, which merchant guilds could only keep under control through legal coercion and violent attack. In the early modern intercontinental trade, the privileged companies faced constant competition from outsiders, again evoking coercive intervention by the companies. The ability of unguilded merchants to trade successfully suggests that guilds' bandwidth effects cannot have been of great economic importance.

9.2.3   Censorship

A merchant guild or privileged company had an incentive to prevent outsiders from gaining access to information about the wares or routes over which it claimed exclusive rights. Of course, any businessman has an

---

[37] R. T., 'More advice for remedying the decay of trade, 1675', in Thirsk and Cooper (1972), 98–9.

incentive to be secretive about details of his business. But merchant guilds and privileged companies had the legal entitlements and political clout to restrict access to commercial information. According to Blanchard, medieval merchant guilds 'consistently tried to maintain market imperfections, restricting the incomer's movements and limiting his access to information'.[38] The thirteenth-century Italian merchant colonies in Bruges studied by De Roover jealously protected information and sought to prevent it from being communicated to outsiders:

> The clerical staff of each fondaco or agency in Bruges was composed exclusively of Italians . . . Only porters and other minor employees were presumably chosen from local residents . . . Business information was a closely guarded secret, probably more so in the Middle Ages than it is today. . . . By keeping the foreigners out, the Italians succeeded for a long time in maintaining their control over foreign trade, but they could not entirely prevent outsiders from learning and copying their methods.[39]

The medieval Hanse forbade its members to communicate information about Russia to non-Hansards, prohibited translations between Russian and western European languages, and fined members of its Bergen Kontor who revealed Hanseatic 'secrets' to outsiders.[40] The desire to prevent rivals from sharing its commercial information led the Hanse to exclude merchants from other places – Nürnberg, Holland, England – from its drinking societies in Thorn and Danzig (Gdańsk) in the 1440s, 1470s and 1490s.[41]

The surviving merchant guilds and new privileged companies of the early modern period, according to McCusker and Gravesteijn, continued these restrictive practices:

> Businessmen in the mercantile centers of early modern Europe tended both to be jealous of their rights and privileges and well organized to protect and extend them. Moreover they either controlled city government or exercised a strong voice in it . . . An obvious concern of local government was the administration of the local market, be it the fair or the bourse or exchange. Information about that market was valuable, coveted, potentially disruptive, and therefore subject to strict control.[42]

In 1579, the English Merchant Adventurers objected to the proposal that a merchant might be simultaneously a member both of the Adventurers and of the new Spanish Company, mainly on the grounds that such joint members would reveal to outsiders 'the secrets of the commodities and reckonings of our company'. Although Croft interprets these 'secrets'

---

[38] Blanchard (2004), 179.   [39] R. De Roover (1948a), 21.
[40] Reitemeier (2002); Burckhardt (2005), 66.   [41] Selzer (2003), 82.
[42] McCusker and Gravesteijn (1991), 29.

which the Company was so worried about as referring to 'some form of price fixing', they may also have related to commercial information that would have enabled outsiders to encroach on the company monopoly.[43] The Portuguese merchant company which enjoyed a royal monopoly over trade to Brazil banned release of information about the route, so outside traders had to obtain it illegally through bribery and theft.[44] Spanish consulados banned dissemination of information about the West African trade over which they claimed a legal monopoly, so English privateers had to obtain the censored navigation details illegally.[45] The Dutch East India Company also restricted commercially valuable information in order to protect monopoly profits:

> Somewhat apart from the general interchange of information in Amsterdam was a more privileged level among members of the city's merchant elite, frequently involving elite-dominated institutions such as [the Dutch East India Company] . . . Information about the imminence of war or peace in Europe obtained through the government, or about the size of pepper cargoes coming from Asia acquired from the [Company], tended to circulate first among the heads of the major commercial houses. Although leakage into the information exchange as a whole tended to be quite rapid, first access gave the bigger businessmen a decided advantage.[46]

The existence of merchant guilds and privileged companies gave businessmen better tools for amplifying individual efforts to restrict commercial information, and their monopoly privileges intensified their incentives to do so to protect their rents.

9.2.4   Inefficiency

Merchant guilds' internal administrative systems, as we have seen, are often emphasized in claims about their efficiency in providing information. However, what matters for trade is not administrative inputs, but business outcomes. For information to be useful, it must be collected early, transmitted swiftly and analysed appropriately. But monopolists can stay in business without processing information efficiently, and evidence on merchant guilds suggests this was quite often the outcome, however impressive the administrative inputs.

The medieval German Hanse provides instructive examples of the slippage between bureaucratic systems and commercial outcomes. As we saw in an earlier chapter, in 1399–1400 the duke of Burgundy and the magistracy of Bruges changed the regulations governing letters of

---

[43] Croft (1973a), xv.   [44] Pérotin-Dumon (1991), 206.   [45] Ibid., 208.
[46] W. D. Smith (1984), 995. See also De Vries and Van der Woude (1997), 430.

exchange, greatly increasing the costs of trading on credit in the city. The appropriate response would have been to convey information to all merchants doing business with Bruges as swiftly as possible about when the new regulations were to come into effect so merchants could refrain from sending letters of exchange to Bruges, and subsequently to convey information swiftly about the regulations' repeal so that merchants could return to credit-based business which was, in normal times, more profitable. But the German Hanse collected, transmitted and analysed information about the new rules with spectacular inefficiency. While private Italian and Catalonian firms in Bruges established their strategy within six weeks of the new regulations' being published, the Hanse did not respond until ten weeks after that – a total delay of four months.[47] Even then, the Hanse responded inappropriately, banning credit transactions by all Hanse merchants throughout Europe, which caused commercial losses and diplomatic difficulties. The private Italian and Catalonian merchant houses, by contrast, merely recommended that their foreign correspondents refrain from sending letters of exchange to Bruges for the duration of the regulations, but still act as remittents there.[48]

A second illustration is provided by the Hanse's response in 1410 to a 17 per cent devaluation of the Flemish groten. Duke John the Bold decided on this devaluation on 17 August 1409, but kept the decision secret. Nevertheless, by 23 December 1409 the Bruges office of the Datini, a private merchant firm from the Italian city of Prato, was writing to warn its correspondents in Barcelona of the impending devaluation. The Hanse Kontor in Bruges, by contrast, did not obtain information about the devaluation (let alone convey it to Hanse merchants elsewhere in Europe) until the new groten actually began to be minted, at the beginning of April 1410 – more than three months after the private Italian firm. As Jenks points out,

In a business world in which a head start of a day or even several hours was decisive for profit and loss, the Hanse's informational backwardness was catastrophic. Because the Hanse got to know about events too late, it was repeatedly surprised by new developments. The informational backwardness of the Hanse intensified its vulnerability.[49]

These problems with information processing cannot be ascribed to slow communications, as Samsonowicz has demonstrated impressively fast transmission between various Hanse offices in the early to mid fifteenth century.[50] Rather, the problem resided in slow collection and

[47] Jenks (1982), 315.   [48] See the analysis in *ibid.*, 309–15.   [49] *Ibid.*, 318.
[50] Samsonowicz (1999), esp. 212.

inefficient processing. The backwardness of the Hanse in collecting and processing information, in comparison to private merchant firms, supports the view that its guild monopoly encouraged inefficiency – Hicks's 'quiet life' – rather than creating scale economies or bandwidth.[51]

The merchant guilds and privileged companies of the early modern period also set up internal administrative systems to collect and convey information. But, like the Hanse, they did not always analyse it very effectively. Thus, for instance, both the Seville consulado that enjoyed a legal monopoly over the Spanish trade with America and the consulados in Mexico and Lima that enjoyed similar monopolies in the vice-regal capitals generated voluminous reports and manuals containing detailed commercial information. Yet the consulados were noticeably inefficient in making use of it in actual business dealings: 'delays, high transport costs, taxes, complicated credit terms, inefficiency, and corruption characterized the mercantilist system of the Seville merchants'.[52]

The Royal African Company, with its legal monopoly over the slave trade between England and the Caribbean, also set up administrative systems requiring frequent written reports from its agents in Africa. But according to Davies, although the reports arrived, the managers at head office made little attempt to digest the information they contained.[53] The Company spectacularly failed to keep itself afloat, and one major reason was its failure to process information well enough to monitor agents or to respond to market conditions.[54] Illegal competitors, despite being forced by the Company to operate in the black market, processed information and did business more effectively than the state-protected Company.[55]

The Dutch East India Company (VOC) also set up elaborate systems requiring its overseas agents to report massive volumes of information. But according to Furber, 'There is no doubt that hundreds of pages sent home were never even read. Anyone working among the company's records at the Dutch National Archives is likely to open a volume to find thousands of grains of sand used to blot the ink lying undisturbed between its pages.'[56] It is therefore not surprising that the VOC was less effective in obtaining information about gem and spice supplies in India than were the local Bania traders, who did not form any monopolistic associations. According to one seventeenth-century observer, the VOC 'had no agents at Golconda to warn them of the quantities of goods being sent thence to

[51] Jenks (1982), 326.   [52] Woodward (2005), 636.   [53] Davies (1957), 111.
[54] Galenson (1986), 15–16, 25–7, 148–50.   [55] North (1991), 35.
[56] Furber (1976), 191.

Agra, so that they could be forewarned like the Indian merchants, who received the requisite intelligence from their agencies'. As Habib points out, this is 'an interesting inversion of the picture . . . of the well-informed European companies and ignorant, rumor-fed Asian peddlers'.[57]

The Hudson's Bay Company (HBC) is adduced as the prime example of a privileged merchant company that flourished for centuries partly because of its efficiency in collecting and processing information. The HBC did institute elaborate information-processing systems, which might in principle have given it advantages over small-scale merchants competing in an open market. But closer examination casts doubt on how well its systems functioned in practice. Jones and Ville, for instance, find that

> information was often slow to be processed, books were sometimes years out of date . . . In spite of a plethora of committees, extensive reporting systems, and a mass of paperwork, specific orders were not always met, freight rates were not invariably the most advantageous, goods might be both overpriced and deficient in quantity and quality, and warehouses were sometimes swollen with unsaleable stock.[58]

This picture is borne out by the work of Fender, who points out that in the territory and on the routes legally monopolized by the HBC

> others did discover the necessary geographic and cultural information, as shown by their success in challenging the HBC's control of the northwest trade. This is evidence that the Company could not monopolize information. Further, the HBC was a follower to the northwest, not a leader.[59]

It is therefore not surprising that throughout its history the HBC had to use state privileges and violent coercion to maintain its monopoly against private interlopers, despite their lack of scale, bandwidth or even simple legality. Such evidence casts doubt on any claim that merchant guilds or privileged companies enjoyed a natural monopoly in information collection.

9.2.5   Internal agency relations

Merchant guilds and privileged companies also suffered from a cost that can arise out of size, scale and monopoly power – poor relationships with their own agents. Such agents were supposed to incur the costs of collecting and processing information on behalf of the guild or company, but what ensured that they would do so conscientiously? Why resist the

---

[57] Habib (1990), 390 (quotation), 390–1 (quotation).
[58] S. R. H. Jones and Ville (1996), 901.   [59] Fender (2004), 26.

incentive to benefit by shirking, or by profiting from the information personally?

As we saw in Chapter 8, there is no evidence that large, monopolistic merchant guilds and privileged companies had better solutions to principal-agent problems than small-scale, competitive traders and firms. Partly, it appears, this was because small-scale traders were better at guaranteeing agents personal benefits from managing information efficiently. Thus the Datini firm's correspondents in Bruges, the Orlandini firm, knew that they would profit by conveying information about changes in Flemish policy swiftly to the Datini, who would reciprocate with information from their correspondents elsewhere that would be useful to the Orlandini. By contrast, officials of the Hanse Kontor in Bruges would not profit personally by communicating information quickly to Lübeck. Nor did anyone at the Hanse central office in Lübeck profit personally by processing new information quickly, or lose personally by making slow or inappropriate decisions. Employees in the privileged companies also lacked personal motives to provide more than formulaic and limited reports to their principals. Agent reports for the Royal African Company and the Dutch East India Company, for example, focused primarily on the type of trade goods required and the state of the market in imported products, and even in those limited spheres 'information was often incomplete'.[60]

More crucially still, agents of the privileged companies feared sharing superior information with head office if it inhibited their ability to engage in private trade on their own account. Most of the privileged companies suffered from insider dealing by managers and employees who exploited corporate information illegitimately for their own profit. The Dutch East India Company was frequently given 'misinformation' by overseas agents, who exploited the ignorance of head office about the uncertainties of trade in Asia to collude fraudulently with local traders.[61] Even at home in the Netherlands, the monopolistic Company's unique information about the European pepper market was 'regularly exploited by its directors and their friends for private business – often to the detriment of the Company as an institution'.[62] Company insiders would not have been able to derive such private profits if, as is sometimes averred, Company information was freely available as a positive externality to the entire trading world.[63]

---

[60] On the Datini and the Hanse, see Jenks (1982), 309–15, 318, 326; on the Royal African Company and the Dutch East India Company, see S. R. H. Jones and Ville (1996), 906 (quotation).
[61] *Ibid.*   [62] W. D. Smith (1984), 998.
[63] As argued, for instance, in *ibid.*, 997–1000.

9.2.6   Centralized information processing

Centralization was another problem for merchant guilds and privileged companies. As Chapter 8 discussed, large organizations typically solve the agency problems arising from multiple management levels by centralizing decision-making. But this solution causes new problems, because information quality is higher at the local level. Centralizing decisions when information is decentralized generates inappropriate responses. Smaller organizations can afford to decentralize decision-making because they have fewer levels of management and thus fewer stages at which principal-agent problems can distort decisions.

Even the largest merchant firms in medieval Europe were still quite small and hence could afford to decentralize decision-making, especially when they operated performance-based career monitoring and profit sharing of the sort discussed in Chapter 8. In the early fourteenth century the third-largest merchant house in Florence, that of the Acciaiuoli, employed only 41 factors across Europe, rising to 53 in 1341. In 1371–2 only two of the 89 merchant houses in Lucca employed more than 10 factors, and the largest Lucchese merchant house employed only 19 persons in all. The Alberti Company of Florence, with a payroll of fewer than 20 men in the early fourteenth century, was larger than average for the period. The great Florentine merchant house of the Medici, even at its zenith, employed fewer than 50 factors and fewer than a dozen branch managers throughout Europe.[64] According to De Roover, moreover, much of the success of the Medici firm derived from its decentralized decision-making: 'Because of the slowness of mediaeval communications, the branch managers had to be given a free hand within the limits of the policy which was outlined in their instructions.'[65] Merchant firms also monitored their factors' and employees' performance in secret ledgers, as we saw in Chapter 8, rewarding and punishing them for business decisions. This reduced the potential for supervisory diseconomies of scale and excessive centralization within firms.[66]

Merchant hanses and privileged companies were typically much larger than individual merchant houses, and in combination with their monopoly privileges this encouraged centralization. The German Hanse, for instance, had to transmit information from each local Kontor (branch office) to its head office in Lübeck, transform information into policy in Lübeck and send instructions back to each Kontor, which in turn

---

[64] R. De Roover (1948a), 39–40; R. De Roover (1958), 27.
[65] R. De Roover (1948a), 38.
[66] Within such small groups, personal relationships may have also enhanced sentiments of mutual loyalty.

conveyed them to individual Hanse members. This could have disastrous business effects, as Jenks points out: 'where the Bruges Hanse Kontor called for dirigiste, planned-economy measures in order to forbid the merchant from doing things that might cause him losses, the Italian and Catalonian merchants simply agreed among one another without any intervention by their government on strategies which can be termed market-oriented ones'.[67]

Excessive centralization was also a problem for the Dutch East India Company (VOC). At home in the Netherlands the VOC was rigidly divided into six chambers, in Asia its Batavia headquarters strictly controlled all activities, and organizational mechanisms were seldom revised because the VOC charter came up for renewal only at long intervals.[68] The English East India Company (EIC) surpassed the VOC in sales in the course of the eighteenth century, while never adopting the VOC's mechanisms for information collection or processing. Instead, it obtained information through brokers and exchanges (including those in Amsterdam) – information mechanisms available to ordinary non-EIC merchants, discussed later in this chapter.[69] The VOC's administrative mechanisms for collecting and processing information, however admirable in theory, appear not to have been very useful in practice.

The Hudson's Bay Company (HBC) also instituted elaborate information-processing systems that led to highly centralized business decisions. As Mackay has shown, the HBC head office in London could take as long as two years to provide operational decisions in response to information sent in from North American outposts.[70] Furthermore, 'not all company servants understood the significance of what lay before them or had the capacity or freedom to respond appropriately'.[71]

Of course, as these examples show, shirking by agents and excessively centralized decision-making were most serious for the larger merchant guilds and privileged companies. Many merchant guilds were smaller and more loosely organized than the Hanse or the VOC. This naturally reduced their capacity to employ agents and organize internal hierarchies. But it also reduced their size, scale and ability to internalize information externalities. To the extent that a merchant guild or privileged company was small enough not to have to employ agents and organize multiple layers of decision-making, it would surely also have been too small to generate those informational benefits theoretically deriving from economies of scale and the internalization of externalities.

---

[67] See the analysis in Jenks (1982), 309–15 (quotation 315).   [68] Neal (1990), 221–2.
[69] W. D. Smith (1984), 1003 n. 59.   [70] Mackay (1937), 134.
[71] S. R. H. Jones and Ville (1996), 901.

9.2.7   Information cascades

What can we say about the possibility that merchant guilds conveyed high-quality information because of social capital and bandwidth – multiple, reduplicated channels of communication among members? In principle, repeated transmissions of the same information within a closed social network can generate benefits such as rapid responses to new business realities and swift identification of misconduct. But networks, as already discussed, also suffer from problems in processing information accurately. In a network, 'information' can consist of the statement of a single individual, inevitably guided by his or her own interests, and then amplified by repeated transmission through the multiple, reduplicated channels of the network. Theories about merchant networks usually assume that the opinion on which a network converges is accurate – but why should it be?

The German Hanse provides a vivid example of these two principles at work. As we have seen, some scholars argue that the Hanse was an efficient institution for solving information problems because it transmitted news about business conditions and merchants' reputations at social gatherings. This information circulation within the Hanse network, it is claimed, led to stable, long-term partnerships, which in turn ensured that 'information about market conditions at distant places where their goods and products were sold by their trading partners had not necessarily to be gathered by the sending merchants themselves'.[72]

But was the information conveyed by personal contacts within the Hanse accurate, as opposed to confirming pre-existing opinion? Even some scholars who are enthusiastic about this strong network structure acknowledge that its repeated confirmation of collectively held opinion led Hanseatic merchants to be unusually closed towards associations with non-members, new forms of enterprise and use of external finance. By the fifteenth century at latest, Ewert and Selzer admit, closure towards outside information was contributing to Hanseatic stagnation.[73] As Jenks has shown, it was the Italian merchants, obtaining their information through hierarchical firms, correspondent relationships and sophisticated financial instruments, who obtained and processed commercial information more accurately.[74]

Closed networks, in short, do not necessarily transmit accurate information. Rather, they transmit opinion, perception and gossip, and this

---

[72] Ewert and Selzer (2005), 15 (quotation); Selzer and Ewert (2005), 25–6.
[73] Ewert and Selzer (2005), 16 21.   [74] Jenks (1982), 314–15.

can give rise to 'scapegoating, groupthink, and distorted reputations defined by polarized trust and distrust'.[75] In how many cases when a merchant network converged on a view was it merely an inaccurate collective prejudice? Clearly it sometimes was, as illustrated by the information conveyed at Artushof drinking societies in Hanseatic trading centres.[76] In 1431, for instance, a certain John Knight appeared in Danzig (Gdańsk), equipped with letters of recommendation from Bristol merchants describing him as a nobleman who wanted to travel in Prussia and meet members of its elite. Knight was welcomed with a brilliant reception at the Artushof, and exploited the contacts he made there for commercial purposes, buying up wares on credit. However, it turned out that he was not a nobleman but rather a confidence trickster who disappeared with wares for which he had not paid, leaving his new trading partners out of pocket.[77] The information cascade that enabled John Knight to transmit false information about himself, to his own profit but at the expense of his trading partners, was amplified by recommendations from the Bristol merchant guild and amplified again by Danzig merchant drinking fraternity.

Such examples suggest that pre-modern merchant networks suffered from the problem Burt points out for networks in the present day, in which 'network closure does not facilitate trust so much as it amplifies predispositions, creating a structural arthritis in which people cannot learn what they do not already know'.[78] The pressure social networks exert on members to share information and converge on shared judgements may not, in fact, be economically efficient or socially just. Innocent parties may be pilloried because of baseless gossip or private envy, while unreliable parties may be eulogized because of baseless praise or private error. Repeated echoing of the same prejudice may lead to conservatism and groupthink.

Medieval people recognized this themselves, as with the anonymous Florentine merchant who wrote in his advice manual around 1350 that, 'It is a very grave error to base one's commercial activities on mere opinion, and not on reason.'[79] It may also have been what William Petty had in mind when he wrote in 1676 that trade was 'most vigorously carried on in every state and government by . . . such as profess Opinions different from that are publickly established'.[80]

---

[75] Burt (2001), 29.   [76] Selzer (2003), 77–95; Link and Kapfenberger (2005), 165.
[77] See the summary in Selzer (2003), 81.   [78] Burt (2001), 29–30.
[79] Translated in Molho (1969), 57.
[80] Petty (1690), 25–6; quoted in Habib (1990), 384. Petty wrote this passage c. 1676, but the work was not published until 1690.

9.3   Other institutions for collecting and transmitting information

The idea that merchant guilds and privileged companies existed for so long in so many different pre-modern economies because they were efficient institutions for processing information is based on the assumption that alternative institutions were lacking – that there were no other mechanisms by which merchants could collect, analyse and disseminate the information they needed to trade over long distances. Was this true?

As will become clear, this assumption is already untenable for the early stages of the medieval Commercial Revolution and becomes ever less justified for its later phases. The information that fuelled the medieval expansion of long-distance trade was not generated by the entrenched privileges of particularistic, closed-access institutions such as merchant guilds. Rather, it was encouraged by the growth of generalized, open-access institutions – both market and state.

Pre-modern merchants, as we shall see, disposed of an array of institutional mechanisms for obtaining, disseminating and processing commercial information. These included locational clusters, middlemen, correspondence, publications, legal forms of enterprise and public offices. This interlinked institutional system was not perfect, as shown by the ceaseless efforts of merchants throughout medieval and early modern Europe to improve their information systems. But the evidence makes clear that medieval merchants voluntarily used and invested in these other institutional mechanisms, even when they had guilds and privileged companies at their disposal. This is consistent with the relatively minor role we have seen merchant guilds playing in information provision in practice.

9.3.1   Locational clustering

A first way pre-modern merchants collected information was through institutions that facilitated locational clustering – cities, fairs, marketplaces, business streets, 'bourses' and exchanges. As the economic theory of industrial organization suggests, clustering enables people to get information simply by observing each other's actions:

The information people possess is reflected in the decisions they make. Other people's decisions are often easier to observe than the information they acquire. It follows that imitation of behaviour is often an effective substitute for other ways of obtaining information.[81]

---

[81] Casson (1997), 149.

Simply doing business in spatial proximity to one another enabled merchants to observe each other's decisions, which itself conveyed information in dense and preprocessed form. The importance of collecting information by observing other merchants was explicitly recognized in one of the earliest educational guides for merchants, *The King's Mirror*, written in Norway around the year 1250, in which the young merchant is told, 'When you are in a market town ... observe carefully how those who are reputed the best and most prominent merchants conduct their business. ... see what other good merchants are employed with, or whether any new wares have come to the borough which you ought to buy.'[82] These precepts appear to have been eminently practicable, because much medieval business was conducted in the public arena. Epstein's analysis of medieval Genoese notarial acts, for instance, found that about four-fifths of all business contracts were concluded in public, typically being read out loud to participants and witnesses in busy city squares.[83]

But locations where merchants met to trade, and thus to learn and reveal information inadvertently through their actions, were also places where they obtained and exchanged information deliberately, through personal contacts. Indeed, the contacts facilitated through locational clustering had an advantage over those fostered by merchant guilds: they took place within a wider, more pluralistic and inclusive network that was more open to new persons and new items of information. This made it less likely (although not impossible) for 'echo effects' to arise, in which the entire network of merchants converged on the same opinion regardless of whether it was true or false.

One way merchants obtained information through clustering was simply by trading in urban centres. Rulers had long sought to centralize long-distance trade in specific towns so that they themselves could collect fiscally relevant information. Thus as early as 823, Lothar I forbade merchants in Frankish Italy from trading outside officially recognized ports (*portura legitima*), in order to enable royal toll-collectors to collect better information on the volume of trade so as to maximize the tax take.[84] However, the locational clustering that produced fiscally relevant information for rulers also produced commercially relevant information for merchants, and thus caused traders to congregate not just in any urban centre, or even in the ones favoured by rulers, but in cities where they could be sure of the presence of a large number of other merchants as both sellers and buyers. In the medieval period, Venice and Bruges

---

[82] Larson (1917), 80.   [83] S. A. Epstein (1994), 320–4.
[84] Middleton (2005), 320–1.

were prime examples of such cities, ones where merchants knew they could collect accurate information that had been vetted by innumerable other traders.

Pre-modern traders themselves recognized the importance of specific cities in centralizing information provision, as in 1617 when an English merchant in Amsterdam wrote to his brother in London describing Amsterdam as 'a great Staple of News'.[85] Revealed preference suggests that contemporaries also realized that the information available in such recognized locations, by virtue of the fact that a large variety of different traders congregated there with highly variegated sources of knowledge, was superior to the information that could be collected by merchant guilds whose sources were limited and homogeneous. Thus, for instance, 'when the directors of the English East India Company wanted quick and reliable information about what was going on in their *own* factories in Asia, they consulted their correspondent in Amsterdam'.[86]

A limited degree of path dependency appears to have operated, whereby particular cities remained dominant information centres for some time after they ceased to be dominant trading centres. But over the longer term those cities that functioned as information clearinghouses for merchants gradually changed, so that after the fifteenth century Venice and Bruges were replaced by Antwerp, then Amsterdam and subsequently London.[87]

Clustering operated not just through the centralization of trade in particular urban centres – occasionally by fiscal or staple regulations, more frequently through spontaneous decisions by merchants themselves – but also through the development of particular places of assembly for merchants *within* cities.[88] Early in the medieval Commercial Revolution, merchants in each north Italian city clustered in particular streets or church squares, not just to do business but to obtain information.[89] It was the same in north-west European cities where, according to Blanchard, 'Within an area only a little larger than a small village within each of the great commercial emporia, like London, or Antwerp, everyone knew everyone else's business not only within the "city" but also from within each of those settlements which were embedded within its commercial hinterland.'[90] As late as the seventeenth century a majority of actual exchanges of information, according to Smith, took place

---

[85] Quoted in Lesger (2006), 214.   [86] W. D. Smith (1984), 987 n. 7.
[87] *Ibid.*, 987.   [88] Blanchard (2004), 177.
[89] Blomquist (1971), 463–4; Braudel (1979), II: 78–92; III: 106; Bullard et al. (2004), 115; Mueller (1996); Mueller (1997).
[90] Blanchard (2004), 177.

through 'face-to-face encounters among businessmen and interchange of short-distance correspondence within Amsterdam'.[91]

Hostels, inns and taverns also operated as quasi-formal information clearing-houses. Innkeepers often acted as brokers, formally witnessed negotiations and contracts, supplied storage space for wares and operated their inns as the beginning and end points for transporting merchandise.[92] The commercial quarter of medieval Bruges contained more than one hundred hostels, each accommodating between ten and twenty merchants.[93] Merchants from specific foreign regions would congregate in specific inns: thus, for instance, the Hanseatic merchants in Bruges patronized inns run by Germans, while the Florentine merchants in France used ones kept by Florentines.[94] Not only did merchants sleep, eat and drink at the hostel, but they also stored their merchandise, met other merchants, bought and sold wares, and changed currency. This multiplicity of functions facilitated the transmission of commercial information. According to Gelderblom, 'The continual presence of merchants and their goods turned these hostels into market places in their own right where goods were easily inspected, valued, and sold.'[95]

By the sixteenth century, the hostel appears to have become less important, at least in Amsterdam, suggesting that its informational services had been superseded by other institutions.[96] But other early modern cities continued to see merchants congregating in particular places of public refreshment, partly to collect information. In seventeenth-century Milan, for instance, long-distance trade continued to centre around inns, in which foreign merchants lodged for months at a time, warehoused their goods, met other foreign merchants and used the innkeepers as witnesses and sponsors.[97] Likewise, in seventeenth- and eighteenth-century London, coffee houses were established which were patronized by different groups of merchants.[98]

Medieval trading cities saw entire streets or squares develop into commercial clusters, initially coalescing around important hostels, merchant houses or guild headquarters, but later sustained by path dependency. Because these streets were where existing merchants gathered to exchange information, they were also where newcomers went to obtain

[91] W. D. Smith (1984), 995.

[92] Greve (2001), 265–7; Hunt (1994), 99; Kowaleski (1995), 143–4; Kümin (1999), 163–4; Muldrew (1998), 40; Reyerson (2002), 166–75.

[93] Greve (2000), 38–9, 41–2; Greve (2001), 259–60 with n. 5; Gelderblom (2005a), 15; Van Houtte (1983), esp. 178, 181; Murray (2000), 12–13.

[94] Greve (1994), 102–3; Greve (2001), 85; Reyerson (2002), 167–74.

[95] Gelderblom (2005a), 15–16.   [96] Ibid., 36.

[97] D'Amico (2001), 718–19.   [98] Gauci (2002), 129.

information. In Venice, for instance, the Rialto was famous for being the street where merchants met to exchange information, not least because values from all sectors of the European financial market were quoted there every day.[99] In Lucca by the twelfth century, the money changers and bankers set up their tables and stalls in the court of the Cathedral of San Martino.[100] In medieval Antwerp, it was the Wolstraat and the Hofstraat where English merchants and the purchasers of their wool and cloth met to conduct business.[101] In London, it was the steps of St Paul's, where information was picked up and at the end of each business day conveyed beyond the 'node' to the rest of the European trading world via correspondent relationships (to be discussed shortly).[102]

Exchanges or bourses were set up in many European trading centres during the medieval period, often on the basis of pre-existing hostels and trading streets. The famous exchange in Bruges, which gave its name to the word 'bourse', came into being in the plaza in front of an inn owned by the wealthy Van der Buerse family, who operated it as a merchant hostel from the late thirteenth century on. The importance of the Buerse hostel attracted the Venetian merchant guild to establish its headquarters in the adjoining house in 1397, the Genoese merchant guild to build its headquarters on the other side in 1399 and the Florentine merchants to move in next to the Venetians in 1420. The city authorities posted a bailiff at the entrance to the square formed by this cluster of houses at a bend in the road, to increase security. That in turn created an additional incentive for merchants to use the space to meet, strike deals, agree prices and relay information. A German traveller remarked in 1495 that in Bourse Square 'Spaniards, Italians, English, Germans, Easterlings, and all other nations gathered'.[103] But the Buerse hostel pre-dated the merchant guilds that were eventually attracted to the location because it had already been an information clearing-point for generations.

Similar exchanges arose in other pre-modern European trading centres. In early sixteenth-century Antwerp, the merchant Antoine van Bombergen obtained most of his information by visiting the bourse in person, sometimes to do business 'but more often simply to gather commercial and financial market intelligence'.[104] In fifteenth- and sixteenth-century Amsterdam, before the opening of the Amsterdam Bourse as

[99] Braudel (1979), II: 78–92; III: 106; Bullard et al. (2004), 115; Mueller (1996); Mueller (1997).
[100] Blomquist (1971), 463–4.   [101] Harreld (2004a), 51.
[102] Blanchard (2004), 177.
[103] R. De Roover (1948a), 17; Gelderblom (2005a), 16 with n. 80 (quotation); Ingersoll (2005); Stabel (1999), 36.
[104] Blanchard (2004), 175.

a separate building in 1611, merchants met first on a particular street (the Warmoesstraat) in the neighbourhood of the port, later on a particular bridge (the Nieuwe Brug) and, if the weather was bad, in nearby churches. The fact that neighbours complained about the noise and the inappropriateness of doing business in church indicates that merchants were already using these places for information exchange before they became institutionalized.[105]

These clusters were quasi-formal institutions, since merchants drew up regulations governing how business should be conducted in these locations, long before the building of any formal Bourse. Moreover, merchants' gathering places rapidly became incorporated into public commercial regulations. At the bourse in sixteenth-century Antwerp, for instance, a merchant was expected to appear every day, and 'unexplained absence was considered proof of insolvency'.[106] Indeed, the bourse or exchange was so central to merchants' information provision that in the view of one early modern English author, there was 'no absolute necessity' for membership in merchant guilds and privileged companies, 'for the Exchange is appointed for the merchant's intelligence'.[107]

9.3.2   Brokers and notaries

A second set of institutional mechanisms for conveying information was provided by systems of intermediaries. These included the notarial system and the brokerage system, both of which enabled merchants to obtain information about wares, suppliers, buyers and trading practices in places with which they were not familiar. In southern Europe, as we saw in Chapter 7, notaries were omnipresent, operating in the great Italian cities from the twelfth century onwards and soon becoming widespread in most Mediterranean trading centres.[108] They spread to some parts of northern Europe in the thirteenth century, as Italian merchants introduced the notarial system to cities such as Bruges.[109] In the sixteenth century the States of Holland (a parliamentary body) permitted a large number of notaries to practise in the city of Amsterdam so as to satisfy demand from foreign merchants trading there.[110] As we saw in Chapters 7 and 8, the notarial system played a central role in recording merchant agreements, thereby facilitating contract enforcement and mitigating principal-agent problems. But notaries also served a second function: their offices became

---

[105] Van Tielhof (2002), 146–7.   [106] Gelderblom (2005b), 45.
[107] R. T., 'More advice', in Thirsk and Cooper (1972), 97–8.
[108] Stabel (1997), 143; Reyerson (2002), 147–54.
[109] Stabel (1997), 143; J. M. Murray (1983).   [110] Gelderblom (2005a), 36.

clearing-houses for information. Because they recorded debt and insurance contracts, they were well informed about potential trading ventures for merchants with capital to invest, sources of financing for those in search of funding for trading ventures, and the risks and conditions surrounding particular voyages.[111]

Alongside the notarial system, the brokerage system provided a parallel set of mechanisms for merchants to obtain commercial information. In medieval Montpellier, merchants used specialized brokers to obtain information about supplies of goods and potential trading partners.[112] In medieval Bruges, foreign merchants used brokers to find suppliers and purchasers and to represent them while they were out of town.[113] In medieval London, the information-conveying activities of brokers were so widely recognized that the Commons complained in 1422 that 'Several aliens, under the name of brokers, do . . . inform merchants alien of the privity of the realm, and of all the ways and means by which they may enhance the price of their merchandise and abate the price of the merchandise of the realm.'[114] In Antwerp from c. 1540 onwards, and in Amsterdam from 1585 onwards, brokers not only enhanced commercial information as a by-product of their ordinary operations, but also provided it more formally by supplying the prices for the lists of current prices that were published weekly.[115] By the mid-seventeenth century at latest, Amsterdam had a large number of specialized information brokers who collected information by 'bribing government officials, maintaining contacts in all of the institutions involved in information handling, and collating gossip'.[116]

Guilded merchants and even privileged companies themselves used these brokers, suggesting that they did not regard their own guild or company mechanisms as having a particular advantage in gathering or processing information. It was from specialized information brokers, for instance, that the English East India Company 'regularly purchased the secret schedules and ladings of VOC ships before their arrival from Asia'.[117] Thus even information censored by monopolistic merchant guilds could be laid bare through the market institution of brokerage.

These intermediation systems did not offer perfect information provision to long-distance traders. Indeed, as we saw in Chapter 3, many local merchant guilds obtained legal privileges which gave their own members the exclusive right to act as brokers for foreign merchants. In so far as

---

[111] Kedar (1977).   [112] Reyerson (2002), 176–9.
[113] Greve (2001).   [114] Quoted in Giuseppi (1895), 83.
[115] Gelderblom and Jonker (2005), 194, 202; Van Tielhof (2002), 149–52; McCusker and Gravesteijn (1991), esp. chs. 1–2.
[116] W. D. Smith (1984), 996.   [117] Ibid.

local merchant guilds regulated local brokerage, they could limit access by foreign merchants to both business information and opportunities, as shown by the protests of foreign traders against abuses by brokers in some international trading centres. Where the brokers constituted a separate guild that did not itself engage in long-distance trade (as in medieval Bruges), were mainly regulated by the government (as in Venice), or actually included foreigners among their number (as in London), the informational services they provided were more open – as shown by the protests of London merchants in 1422. Systems of commercial intermediation and the informational services they provided appear to have worked best where they were independent of merchant guilds rather than controlled by them.

9.3.3   Merchant correspondence

A third institution for conveying commercial information was provided by correspondence, both informally through letters written for specific business purposes and formally through the 'correspondent relationship', whereby merchants in different trading centres contracted to provide each other with regular news. Individual merchants and merchant firms had strong incentives to obtain commercial information, and invested substantial resources in doing so.

A first form this investment took was in human capital, providing merchants themselves with the education needed to collect and process information more effectively. Parallel to the Commercial Revolution – and arguably interdependent with it – a significant expansion of commercial education occurred.[118] By c. 1250, the Norwegian handbook *The King's Mirror* took literacy and numeracy for granted when it instructed the young merchant:

whenever you have an hour to spare you should give thought to your studies, especially to the law books; for it is clear that those who gain knowledge from books have keener wits than others, since those who are the most learned have the best proofs for their knowledge... I regard no man perfect in knowledge unless he has thoroughly learned and mastered the customs of the place where he is sojourning. And if you wish to become perfect in knowledge, you must learn all the languages, first of all Latin and French, for these idioms are most widely used; and yet, do not neglect your native tongue or speech... Learn also how to mark the movements of the ocean and to discern how its turmoil ebbs and swells; for that is knowledge which all must possess who wish to trade abroad. Learn arithmetic thoroughly, for merchants have great need of that.[119]

---

[118] Ashtor (1983), 381–2.   [119] Larson (1917), 81–3.

Such counsel was reiterated in the advice written by an anonymous mid-fourteenth-century Italian merchant on how to succeed in business:

> You should not postpone tending to your correspondence. Paper is cheap, and often brings in good profit... One must know how to keep books and records; to write and answer letters, which is not a small thing, particularly that of knowing how to dictate letters... It is a most useful thing to know how to keep records properly; and this is among the principal lessons a merchant can learn.[120]

By the time Benedict Kontrulic of Dubrovnik was writing his 1458 book *On Commerce and the Perfect Merchant*, this had become a stereotype: 'When you see a merchant to whom the pen is a burden, you may say that he is not a merchant.'[121]

Rising literacy rates have been observed among Italian merchants from the eleventh century, among north German merchants from the thirteenth century and in the German south by the mid-fourteenth century.[122] By 1395, it was possible for the Prato merchant Francesco Datini to write, 'Since this morning, Stoldo and I have done nothing but read, except for prayers and lunch, and we still have enough to read to last us two days.'[123] This increasing literacy was used for keeping business accounts (already discussed in Chapter 7) and reading merchant handbooks (discussed in the next section), but perhaps its major use was to communicate information through personal correspondence.[124]

Indeed, personal correspondence was one of the very earliest uses to which merchant literacy was put, and is one reason we know about it. The importance of correspondence for conveying commercial information is shown by the quasi-formal expectations and etiquette governing merchant letters. A medieval merchant writing to another merchant in a distant trading centre was expected not just to discuss their mutual business dealings but also, as a matter of mandatory courtesy, to include information about the wider commercial environment: sales successes, market opportunities, prices of major commodities, exchange rates, commercially relevant political events, news of personalities and occurrences in merchant circles.[125] Merchant correspondence also functioned as a grapevine or early warning system about the presence of predators in particular locations, descriptions of their ships and even their precise identities, since (as we saw in Chapter 6) pirates and corsairs were often former merchants, and vice versa.[126] A merchant who did not receive

---

[120] Translated by Molho (1969), 55, 57.
[121] Quoted in Lopez (1969), 35 (1573 edition).   [122] Denzel (2001), 74.
[123] Quoted in Hyde (1979), 115.   [124] *Ibid.*, 113–16.
[125] R. De Roover (1948a), 29–30, 34–5, 55; Ashtor (1983), 379–80.
[126] Tai (1996), 542–3; for an example from the Datini letters, see *ibid.*, 589–90.

letters lost status because he was presumed to be under-informed, as shown by the famous passage in which the Hanse merchant family Veckinchusen agreed that they would send letters from Bruges assid-uously to their agent in Venice, 'so that he would always have letters via every courier, like other people' – i.e. so that he would never go away empty-handed when letters were distributed and thus be viewed as poorly informed.[127] By the sixteenth century at latest, standard formats existed for business letters to ensure that relevant commercial information was always included.[128]

The sheer volume of private merchant correspondence is impressive. In 1260, a Sienese merchant firm instructed its factor in France to send it a report from each Champagne fair, i.e. at least six times a year.[129] From 1265 dates a surviving letter which the Champagne representative of a Sienese merchant house wrote to the firm's central office from the St John's Fair in Troyes, reporting on wares, prices, precious metals and exchange rates.[130] An even more detailed report from the Champagne factors of a Sienese firm survives from 1279, recording not only debts and credits at the current fair, but also debts owed from previous years and the state of the firm's wares in storehouses in Champagne, with quan-tities and prices of goods.[131] Probably the richest surviving merchant archive, that of the Prato merchant Francesco Datini, contains 125,549 commercial letters covering the 27 years 1384 to 1411, representing 267 places of origin, with 2,383 letters sent from Bruges alone.[132] The Hanseatic merchant Hildebrand Veckinchusen left some 540 surviving business letters during his period of operations in the fifteenth century.[133] The Antwerp family firm, Pieter van der Molen and Brothers, sent more than 1,150 letters in the six years between 1538 and 1544, at an average of nearly 200 letters annually for a medium-sized family firm consist-ing of four brothers; the letters (mainly in Italian, but also in Flemish and French) were addressed to correspondents in Genoa, Brescia, Man-tua, Ferrara, Venice, Bologna, Ancona, Rome, Messina, Palermo, Lon-don, Lyons and Cadiz.[134] The Medina de Campo merchant Simon Ruiz took receipt of more than 50,000 letters between 1558 and 1598.[135] Even in the seventeenth and eighteenth centuries, by which time the Amsterdam Exchange was fully functional as the acknowledged infor-mation clearing-house for European commerce, 'The correspondence of

[127] Quoted in Selzer (2003), 83 with n. 54.
[128] W. D. Smith (1984), 992; Denzel (2001), 75; Schweichel (2001), 342–3.
[129] Bautier (1955), 113–15.   [130] Schaube (1897), 252ff.
[131] Bautier (1955), 113–15.   [132] Hyde (1979), 114; Denzel (2001), 85.
[133] Stieda (1921).   [134] Edler (1938), 80–2.
[135] Lapeyre (1955); Vázquez de Prada (1960).

individual Amsterdam merchants and their houses with businessmen in other cities . . . probably constituted the largest input into the Amsterdam exchange.'[136]

The quasi-formal etiquette governing ordinary merchant correspondence shaded over into the correspondent relationship, in which individual merchants in different cities agreed to keep each other informed on all matters concerning their respective markets.[137] At the end of each business day, the information which a merchant or factor had collected personally was processed, summarized and despatched by letter to his correspondents in distant European trading centres.[138] As the representative of a Florentine merchant in Venice wrote to the factor of a merchant in Pisa in 1383, 'I shall keep you posted on news from [Venice and] Alexandria and you do the same for all news from Pisa and Genoa; write regarding any change and write often; it can only be advantageous.'[139] Around 1450, Leon Battista Alberti described how a member of the exiled Florentine merchant house of the Alberti 'kept the ear of the Duke of Milan by supplying him with the news of the world as he heard it from the branches of his family's businesses, from "Our Alberti of England, Flanders, Spain, France, Catalonia, Rhodes, Syria, Barbary and of all those places where they still today maintain and direct trade . . . "'[140] As late as the 1540s, the forwarding of letters to grease the wheels of correspondent relationships was a major component of the responsibilities of foreign agents of the Antwerp firm of the Van der Molen.[141] The importance of correspondence to the profitability of merchant factors was emphasized in Gerard Malynes's influential 1622 book on merchant law, where he wrote that 'a Factor is created by Merchant Letters'.[142]

Correspondent relationships were highly effective. The Italian and Catalonian merchant firms in Bruges, as we have seen, relayed information about commercial changes swiftly and effectively to their correspondents all over southern Europe.[143] Even small-scale merchants in Antwerp, according to Blanchard, operated on the basis of 'excellent market intelligence' by visiting the Bourse at home and maintaining correspondent ties all over Europe.[144] The effectiveness of correspondent relationships is shown by the routine use of merchants as spies.[145] In 1349, for instance, it was Genoese merchants who informed the royal governor of Mallorca

---

[136] W. D. Smith (1984), 990; for a nearly identical assessment, see Van Tielhof (2002), 144.
[137] R. De Roover (1948a), 29–30.   [138] Blanchard (2004), 177.
[139] Quoted in Mueller (1997), 268.   [140] Holmes (1960–1), 194.
[141] Edler (1938), 92, 130.   [142] Malynes (1622), 111.
[143] See Jenks (1982), 314–15.   [144] Blanchard (2004), 176.
[145] Mattingley (1954), esp. 254–5.

of an impending *coup d'état* by the exiled King James III.[146] In sixteenth-century England, 'when spy-masters, like Walsingham, wanted information of clandestine military movements in the Low Countries, he utilised the service of [the merchant] Thomas Gresham who through his commercial agents was in a position to gather such intelligence'.[147] In sixteenth-century Hungary, Serbian and Greek merchants were 'the general informers, footholds, couriers or misinformers of the Ottoman and Habsburg intelligence services'.[148]

Courier and postal services supplemented correspondent relationships. Trade at the thirteenth-century Champagne fairs, one of the earliest international trading centres of the medieval Commercial Revolution, was supported by couriers operating a fast and regular service between the fairs and the major Mediterranean trading cities.[149] One regular courier service between Italy and the Champagne fairs was organized by the main merchant guild of Florence – the Arte di Calimala – and members of that guild could use this service on a subscription basis. But at the same time, private merchant houses and the town authorities maintained their own courier services, the clearest possible indication that the merchant guilds were neither necessary nor sufficient for information transmission.[150] Because timing was so crucial for commercial profits, merchants could not rely on guild couriers whose timing was decided by guild interests; they had to send the information to their business associates when it was freshest and that meant employing private couriers.[151]

After *c.* 1350, public authorities began to provide (or license) regular postal services. By the later fourteenth century, Italian trading cities such as Venice and Lucca were 'very well connected by overland posts', although overseas correspondence was still mainly conveyed by private courier.[152] At the same period, the Italian and other European trading nations had their own mail services conveying news swiftly to and from the Levant in a type of small, fast ship called a *grippo*.[153] By the early sixteenth century many cities in the Low Countries were included in a network of regular postal services which increasingly reached foreign cities as well.[154] The Van der Molen merchant letters from Antwerp in the 1540s show couriers of the ordinary post departing to Italy approximately every three weeks.[155] Letters to Antwerp from Genoa sent overland took 12–15 days, from Rome and Venice 14–16 days (exceptionally 12), from Ancona via Florence 17–23 days and from Ancona via Venice

---

[146] Tai (1996), 129.   [147] Blanchard (2004), 177.   [148] Gecsényi (2007), 66.
[149] Schaube (1897); Face (1958), 434–5; Huvelin (1898).   [150] Face (1958), 434–6.
[151] *Ibid.*, 436.   [152] Hyde (1979), 115.   [153] Ashtor (1983), 380.
[154] Van Tielhof (2002), 156–61.   [155] Edler (1938), 128–9.

21–4 days.[156] These public postal services came into being chiefly to serve the needs of merchants.[157]

The correspondence of pre-modern merchants was a sort of hybrid between private letters, inter-office memoranda and informal newsletters. Supported by correspondent relationships, courier services and postal systems, it offered a quasi-formal and very effective set of mechanisms for systematically conveying not only information specific to the business relationship of the writer and the recipient, but also news of political events, wars, epidemics, famines, trade routes, navigation and contractual partners.[158] Merchant guilds played a quite peripheral role in this system as occasional organizers of courier services, alongside individual merchants, firms, towns and the state.

9.3.4   Newsletters, price lists and handbooks

Even more formal and impersonal news channels also existed, through which information was provided collectively although often still paid for individually. From the twelfth century on, as we have seen, merchants were exchanging commercial correspondence, in which an important (indeed, often mandatory) component of each letter was a price list. The earliest merchant correspondence that survives from Italian trading cities and the Champagne fairs includes lists of current prices of important wares.[159] By the fourteenth century, Italian merchant houses were arranging for their local agents in all the major commercial centres of western Europe and the Mediterranean to organize systematically the collection and reporting of local price data back to the firm's head office.[160] These price lists followed a standardized format which included a range of specified commodities, was carefully complied with by agents, and was reproduced when handwritten price lists gave way to printed ones after the invention of the printing press.[161] Exchange rates were disseminated in the same way as merchandise prices. Although the earliest surviving copies date only from c. 1550, these almost certainly derived from the handwritten lists of earlier centuries.[162] By the 1260s at latest, we know that Italian agents at the Champagne fairs were reporting current exchange rates to their firms' head offices.[163]

---

[156] Ibid., 130–1.   [157] W. D. Smith (1984), 990–1.   [158] Denzel (2001), 75–6.
[159] W. D. Smith (1984), 992; Denzel (2001), 75; Schaube (1897), 252ff.
[160] R. De Roover (1948a), 29–30, 34–5, 55; McCusker and Gravesteijn (1991), 22.
[161] McCusker and Gravesteijn (1991), 22–3.   [162] Ibid., 23–4.
[163] Schaube (1897), 252ff.

The later phases of the medieval Commercial Revolution saw the rise of commercial newsletters. The first one we know of began in Venice in the early fifteenth century.[164] The south German merchant firm of the Fugger produced an in-house newsletter disseminated from its Augsburg headquarters across Europe to its own agents and factors, but also to favoured clients – i.e. it collected and disseminated information at a price.[165] Entrepreneurs in Antwerp and Amsterdam published weekly newspapers called *tijdingen* and sold them by subscription.[166] In sixteenth-century Venice, between the booths of the money changers and goldsmiths on the Rialto lay a commercial news bureau which made money by collecting political and commercial news, copying it and selling it to customers.[167] By the seventeenth century, most European trading centres had weekly or even daily broadsheets, journals and newsletters.[168] Although printing reduced the costs of producing both price lists and newsletters, it did not create them: both had existed in handwritten form for centuries.[169]

Lists of prices and exchange rates shaded over into merchant 'notebooks' and commercial manuals.[170] By the 1270s, we possess surviving merchant manuals by anonymous authors in Tuscany and Venice.[171] The earliest extant manual is the *Memoria de tucte le mercantie*, compiled by a Pisan merchant or notary in 1278,[172] and by 1340 Francesco Balducci Pegolotti had published his famous *Pratica della Mercatura*.[173] The earliest surviving German merchant 'notebook' is thought to be Ulman Strohmeir's *Püchel von meim geslecht und von abenteur*, begun in 1360, which was simultaneously a personal chronicle and a notebook of customs privileges, weights, merchant usages, prices and currencies.[174] Merchant manuals in English, French and Dutch survive in larger numbers from the later fifteenth century, with the spread of printing and the shift in the commercial centre of gravity towards north-west Europe.[175]

Merchant manuals fell into two main categories – *Zibaldoni* (commonplace books or notebooks, usually privately circulated within a particular merchant family or firm) and *Manuali* (standard texts or manuals,

---

[164] Bücher (1922), 242–3; Small (1982), 53.
[165] Klarwill (1923); Klarwill (1924); Klarwill (1926).
[166] Limberger (2001); Van Tielhof (2002).   [167] Bücher (1922), 243.
[168] Small (1982), 64.   [169] McCusker and Gravesteijn (1991), 26.
[170] Denzel (2001), 76–82; Lopez (1969), 35–6.
[171] Denzel (2001), 78; Hyde (1979), 114; Dotson (2003), 204–5; Spufford (1991), esp. 105.
[172] For a detailed dicussion of this manual, see Lopez (1969).
[173] Pegolotti (1936), originally published 1340.
[174] Denzel (2001), 80; Hegel (1862).   [175] Denzel (2001), 81.

circulated more widely and including a broader range of information).[176]
A typical example of either category would address the merchant of a
certain time period, region or specialization, providing information on
currencies, weights, measures, freight charges, brokerage fees, customs
tolls and regulations, warehousing prescriptions and payment systems,
and other commercial usages in each major trading centre.[177] Such handbooks also often contained descriptions of the characteristics each different type of merchandise should have,[178] the institutions of exchange
such as the great international trading fairs in Champagne, Geneva
and Lyon,[179] and, from the fourteenth century, the usages, charges and
exchange rates of the expanding cashless payment system.[180] Such manuals were also incorporated into the commercial curriculum, and by the
fifteenth century, compiling a business notebook or copying a pre-existing
manual was a standard component of a young merchant's education, indicating the central role ascribed to collection, processing and transmission
of information by individual traders.[181]

The role played by merchant guilds in this was, if anything, negative.
Publishing a merchant handbook or manual was regarded as a violation
of the censorship of guild 'mysteries' vis-à-vis non-members, discussed
in section 9.2.3. As late as 1558, when the German merchant Lorenz
Meder published his merchant manual, he clearly acknowledged in the
preface that he was breaking the taboo against 'making public strictly
protected merchant secrets'.[182] In 1595–6, when Jan van Linschoten,
a former employee of the Portuguese merchant guild, published travel
journals providing information on sailing routes, winds, ports and the
Portuguese empire in Asia, they were regarded as constituting an 'invi-
tation to interlope'.[183] If anything, therefore, the role of merchant guilds
was to restrict rather than improve the flow of commercial information –
at least to anyone outside their own exclusive membership.

9.3.5   Individual merchants and firms

Individual merchants also collected commercial information for their
own purposes, without needing merchant guilds to do it for them. This
pattern was so common that members of diplomatic and religious 'spying'
missions would disguise themselves as merchants since it was assumed
that traders would have innocent reasons for collecting information in

[176] Spufford (1991), esp. 103–4, 113; Denzel (2001), 78–9; Lopez (1969), 35, 38–9.
[177] Denzel (2001), 78; Lopez (1969), 36, 38–40; Ashtor (1983), 381.
[178] Reyerson (1982), 71 n. 12; Lopez (1969), 36, 38–9.   [179] Denzel (2001), 78.
[180] Ibid.   [181] Spufford (1991), 110.   [182] Denzel (2001), 81–2.
[183] De Vries and Van der Woude (1997), 383.

enemy territory. A vivid example comes from the 1230s, when four Dominican friars travelled from Hungary into the Volga–Ural region to search for fellow Magyars in order to convert them to Christianity, as well as to collect information about the Mongol threat on the southern Russian steppe. The only one who experienced any success in this endeavour was 'one priest called Otto, who travelled disguised as a merchant' and who returned to Hungary after a three-year journey to explain the route to others.[184] A second mission, sometime before 1235, involved Dominican friars again travelling with merchants in disguise.[185] This was long before the existence of guilds or communities of western merchants in Mongol Asia, which did not arise before the 1260s, even though there were many individual western merchants present throughout the Mongol empire as early as the 1230s.[186] The formation of European merchant guilds in Greater Hungary and Mongolia came *after* the collection of information through expeditions of individual merchants.

Not just individual merchants, but the merchant firm as a legal form of enterprise facilitated information transmission. From the very beginning of the medieval Commercial Revolution, as we saw in Chapter 8, merchants formed firms using a variety of legal forms of enterprise. In the eleventh century, Italian merchants were operating in firms containing both family members and non-relatives. The twelfth-century expansion of trade saw a proliferation in Italian cities of merchant houses that were both vertically and horizontally integrated. The medieval merchant firm typically consisted of managing directors (some located in the home city, some in distant trading centres), middle-rank employees (agents, factors, etc.), and apprentices (young men who did chores in return for training, although their employment took place through voluntary individual contracts rather than guild apprenticeships). These merchant firms also instituted a range of internal information-processing mechanisms – accounting techniques, formal internal contracting and correspondence between head office and branch offices in international trading centres.[187] By the thirteenth century at latest, it was a fundamental expectation in Italian merchant firms that a core responsibility of its representatives abroad was to communicate commercially relevant news to all firm members as swiftly as possible. This emerges from a passage in the statutes of Piacenza, first approved in 1321, but dating from much earlier (some have argued from before 1250), according to which any representative of a merchant firm who did not take steps to communicate commercial information by letter to all (or at least a majority) of

---

[184] Guzman (1996), 56–8 (quotation 56).   [185] *Ibid.*, 57–8.
[186] *Ibid.*, 65–7.   [187] R. De Roover (1948a), 11, 21–2; Gelderblom (2005a), 15.

associates of the firm as fast as possible was to be fined 100 soldi. If, before he imparted the information, he used it for business on his own account, the other associates were to have a claim to the profit as if the speculation had been undertaken on the account of the firm.[188]

Legal forms of enterprise, and the legal norms governing the behaviour of firm members towards one another, enabled individual merchants to establish organizations which had sufficient scale to process information efficiently, without any necessity for the legal monopolies of merchant guilds or privileged companies. This was evidently already the case as early as the thirteenth century, as shown by the example of early Genoese merchant enterprises into 'Romania' (territories of the Byzantine empire outside Constantinople), from which Genoa had been largely excluded before the mid-thirteenth century because of conflict with Venice. The Genoese possessed a consul for its merchant guild in Constantinople as early as 1238, but in 1254 it was not this consul or the Genoese merchant guild as a whole, but rather a partnership of six individual merchants who contracted to hire a ship to travel into Romania. They knew so little about their destination that their contract included the unusual provision that they would hire an expert pilot if they could find one and have a man land from their ship at Skyros in the Aegean to collect information before pursuing their voyage further to Negropont, Salonica or Constantinople.[189] Even medieval merchants moving into commercial territories so unknown to them that they had to hire local pilots and provide for information collection en route thus operated through merchant firms, not alien merchant guilds. This procedure was evidently successful, since despite the lack of information and high risks expected by this partnership when it made its first venture in 1254, three years later one of its members can be observed selling wax from Romania to a merchant from Piacenza.[190]

The same pattern can be observed when European merchants began expanding their commerce to other continents after c. 1500. Counter to claims that the Dutch and English East India Companies were efficient institutions because they could solve information problems in ways impossible for competitive traders, Barendse points out that 'the VOC and the other East India companies were simply using a pre-existing network which had gradually been perfected by Asian merchants and missionaries from the sixteenth century onwards'.[191] Individual firms had their own corps of messengers who carried commercial information in the intercontinental trade. So well did these firm-specific information

---

[188] Schaube (1897), 250.   [189] Balard (1966), 486–7.   [190] *Ibid.*, 487.
[191] Barendse (1988), 26.

systems function that the English and Dutch East India Companies made use of the Armenian firms' courier systems or hired away the Armenians' own messengers to carry information between India and Europe.[192]

This casts doubt on the claim that merchant guilds and privileged companies were the efficient organizations for collecting and transmitting commercial information when merchants expanded into unknown regions, whether into Mongolia and Romania in the thirteenth century or into India in the seventeenth.[193] Indeed, as we have seen, private firms could be more effective in obtaining, conveying, interpreting and acting upon commercial information than ponderous merchant guilds and privileged companies.[194]

9.3.6 Public information

Public bodies also gradually developed mechanisms that helped collect and transmit commercial information in the course of the medieval period. In the thirteenth century, as already mentioned, the governments of north Italian city-states were already operating official courier services to convey letters to their representatives abroad, often carrying private merchant correspondence at the same time. As northern European trade expanded, the same pattern was followed by city governments there, as in the case of Lübeck, whose Marstallamt was by the later fifteenth century employing thirty messengers who regularly conveyed correspondence to destinations including Pomerania, Danzig (Gdańsk) and Bruges.[195] On one trip from Lübeck eastwards in August 1462 just a single messenger of the Lübeck town council was carrying more than one hundred letters.[196] The importance of municipal messenger services for conveying commercial information throughout the Baltic region is pointed out by Kallioinen on the basis of Finnish findings:

> It was not until the rise of towns in the Baltic that there was continuous information about the relative prices and the underlying supply and demand conditions for the whole Baltic area... [Towns] provided generalized knowledge of prices for an international market, reducing the costly search by individuals for market information.[197]

It is particularly interesting that town governments should have started to provide courier services that were used to convey commercial

---

[192] Aslanian (2004), 65–6; Aslanian (2006), 391.
[193] As argued in Carlos and Nicholas (1988), 407, 411; see also W. D. Smith (1984), 993–5.
[194] Jenks (1982), 309–15, 318.   [195] Neumann (1977), 130, 134.
[196] *Ibid.*, 131.   [197] Kallioinen (1998), 6 with n. 18.

information, given that nearly every major trading city also had a merchant guild that could have been doing so. This suggests that the more generalized institutional mechanisms of local government may have had advantages over the particularized institution of the merchant guild, perhaps precisely because it provided services that could be used by anyone rather than only by guild members.

Intelligence gathering had always been a concern of the political authorities, and inevitably it was also used for commercial purposes. Reyerson, for instance, reconstructs the sources of commercial information available to merchants in twelfth- and thirteenth-century Montpellier, which included a number of public sources generated by the royal or municipal government: royal orders, town chronicles, public messengers, judicial announcements of criers and heralds at pre-designated times and places, and the posting of public notices around the town.[198] As foreign trade was gradually recognized as an important basis for foreign policy, state intelligence networks began systematically to collect information abroad that was directly relevant to trade – as in the case of the *dispacci* and *relazioni* sent home by Venetian ambassadors from the thirteenth century on.[199] As Kohn points out, the government officials who accompanied the Venetian fleet abroad and were stationed in Venice's overseas colonies 'provided regular and reliable information on trading conditions'.[200] By the second half of the fifteenth century, European capital cities were linked by a stable network of ambassadors, who conveyed not only their own observations but also extracts from merchant letters from outside Europe, which they checked with colleagues in other capitals.[201]

By the early modern period, municipal governments were commonly providing publicly available commercial information, especially in more highly developed trading zones such as the Netherlands:

much of the state's information-gathering capacity was organized to provide business information. In the seventeenth century the Dutch organized their consuls (the senior members of the Dutch merchant communities in foreign towns) into a quasi-diplomatic information-gathering system . . . the Dutch consul in Cadiz was responsible for summarizing intelligence about the annual American trading fleet and estimating the demand for imported goods that would be generated by the fleet's preparation.

This information was archived by the town government and then 'made available to the leading Amsterdam merchants, from whom it would

---

[198] Reyerson (2002), 145–8.   [199] Queller (1973), esp. 176, 178, 183–6.
[200] Kohn (2003a), 28.   [201] Infelise (2007), 34–5.

rapidly pass to the rest of the business community'.[202] The fact that the consuls of the Dutch merchant communities in foreign trading centres were not autonomously engaging in information gathering before the seventeenth century, and needed to be organized by the government to do so, suggests that the information-gathering functions of alien merchant guilds were minor. It was not until municipal governments put pressure on the consuls of merchant communities to collect and transmit information that they bothered to exploit their ability to do so. This finding is consistent with those from other sources, discussed in section 2, indicating that merchant guilds played at most a peripheral role in improving the availability of commercial information.

9.4   Conclusion

In the medieval Commercial Revolution, beginning after *c.* 1050, European merchants expanded their long-distance trade into unfamiliar regions of Europe and adjacent parts of Africa and the Near East. In the early modern Commercial Revolution after *c.* 1500, Europeans began trying to trade with continents of whose very existence they had not previously known. During both these periods, unfamiliar trading environments created a particularly acute demand for information. How did European merchants meet these challenges? Did their guilds play a major role?

Because pre-modern merchants evidently did obtain commercial information somehow, and because they also often formed guilds (in the medieval period) and privileged companies (in the early modern period), it is sometimes argued that the two phenomena were effect and cause. Moreover, theory suggests that the size, vertical integration, monopolistic market power and social capital of merchant guilds might have solved the problem that information is a public good.

But theory alone is not enough. To find out whether merchant guilds helped solve the information challenges posed by expanding trade into new environments, we need empirical findings. The evidence surviving from pre-modern trade is imperfect. Statistical data are largely lacking, and qualitative information is scattered and may suffer from sample selection bias since different institutions leave documentary traces in different ways and to differing extents. It will probably never be possible to carry out a systematic comparison of the quantitative importance of the performance of different information-providing institutions in medieval and early modern trade. On the other hand, there is no reason to think that

[202] W. D. Smith (1984), 994.

merchant guilds and privileged companies would not have left at least as many documentary traces as the 'atomized' individuals – merchants, notaries, brokers, hostellers, factors, agents and correspondents – with which they are so favourably compared. So what does the surviving evidence suggest about the importance of merchant guilds and privileged companies for solving information problems?

First, did their size and legal monopolies enable merchant guilds and privileged companies to reap economies of scale and internalize information externalities? The short answer is no. The medieval German Hanse and the early modern privileged companies did set up administrative systems to process information. But most of the evidence about these systems dates from after 1500, which suggests that these mechanisms cannot have been important in the medieval Commercial Revolution. Even for the period after 1500, the evidence relates almost exclusively to administrative inputs. Shifting the focus to business *outcomes* casts serious doubt on the importance of the administrative systems of the big guilds and companies, since unincorporated interlopers successfully traded on the same routes.

It might be argued that these non-guilded individual traders were just free-riding on guild or company information systems. But this cannot be true, either. The medieval German Hanse explicitly excluded outsiders from access to information about the Baltic and Russian trade. The privileged companies often followed, not preceded, non-company merchants on the intercontinental routes. Had economies of scale in commercial information existed, international trade would have been a natural monopoly, individual merchants would not have pioneered international trade routes as they did, and merchant guilds would not have needed legal privileges to stave off the competition they posed.

But perhaps merchant guilds minimized information costs through social capital? Merchant guilds and privileged companies did maintain common rooms, convene general assemblies, hold drinking sessions and organize banquets. There are even a few examples of commercially relevant information being discussed at such social occasions, despite the doubts expressed by more ascetic contemporaries who advised merchants to stay home and attend to their accounts.

But again we know more about inputs than outcomes. Members of merchant guilds certainly participated in sociability and probably even conveyed information while doing so. But we have no evidence about whether or how such information was used in business. The jury remains out on the issue of whether guild sociability conveyed commercial information that would not have been obtainable by other means. Again, focusing on outcomes casts doubt on the importance of guild social capital, since merchants who were not members of merchant guilds traded successfully at the thirteenth-century Champagne fairs, in fourteenth-century Bruges and in the fifteenth-century Baltic. This suggests that guild social capital was of no great importance in supplying commercial information.

Though merchant guilds and privileged companies left little evidence of influencing business outcomes through their information systems, it might still be argued that they played an important role that for some reason did not leave documentary traces. This argument would be particularly persuasive if it could be demonstrated that no *other* institutional mechanisms left documentary traces of solving informational problems, either. But as we have seen, this was not so. During both the medieval Commercial Revolution of the eleventh to fourteenth centuries and the early modern Commercial Revolution of the sixteenth and seventeenth centuries, merchants devised a rich array of mechanisms for collecting and processing commercial information which left surprisingly copious documentary traces. These mechanisms coexisted with merchant guilds and privileged companies without depending on them more than peripherally.

Periodic fairs, marketplaces, cities and other locational clusters, with their dense populations of sellers and buyers, constituted institutions for collecting and conveying information tacitly, as merchants observed other traders. From the beginning of surviving records concerning the medieval Commercial Revolution, in the twelfth and thirteenth centuries, merchants traded preferentially in specific locations. They attended fairs and periodic markets, some of which became almost permanent, as in the case of the Champagne fair cycle which operated throughout the year. Merchants also flocked to trade in cities such as Venice, Genoa and Bruges, where they could expect numerous other merchants to congregate because of locational or regulatory advantages. At these fairs and in these cities merchants stayed in specific hostels and gathered in specific streets and squares, where they knew they would meet other merchants. Notarial and brokerage systems emerged in the early Commercial Revolution not only to record and enforce contracts, but to collect and transmit the information that made contracts possible. Merchant literacy, merchant correspondence and quasi-formal correspondent relationships conveyed the information gathered in locational clusters to networks of contacts across Europe and beyond. Individual traders and merchant firms operated courier services to convey this correspondence more quickly. From the early years of the Commercial Revolution, merchants also began to experiment with legal forms of enterprise, whereby agents abroad were legally obliged to convey information to partners in the home office or to other branches.

In the fourteenth and fifteenth centuries, further information-transmission mechanisms arose. The locational clusters of fairs, cities, hostels, and merchant streets or squares were enhanced by the establishment of more formal bourses. Behavioural rules were codified and locational clusters were advertised in merchant handbooks. Merchants prepared handwritten newsletters, price lists and business manuals – ways of collecting and disseminating information whose existence probably pre-dated the oldest surviving examples of these publications in the fourteenth century. The private courier systems of individual merchant houses began to be supported logistically by the development of public courier systems by town governments and princes. Notarial and brokerage systems began to be more formally regulated. Innovations from southern Europe were introduced into north-west Europe and vice versa. Legal forms of enterprise began to be integrated horizontally with foreign branches and vertically with agents and factors specifically instructed to collect and convey information to managers and owners.

A further series of institutional mechanisms for conveying commercial information were developed after c. 1500. The invention of printing accelerated (and reduced the costs of) reproducing and diffusing newsletters, price lists and business manuals. The growing sophistication of municipal and princely government in the sixteenth century gave rise to public postal systems. In the early seventeenth century, quasi-formal bourses were replaced or enhanced by the foundation of formal exchanges, governed by standard codes of conduct. The growth of the early modern state gave rise to diplomatic systems, in which foreign consuls were expected to convey information from their postings abroad, including commercial information relevant to long-distance merchants from the home country. On the other hand, evidence of information flow from merchants to governments testifies to the fact that the centuries-old information-collection mechanisms of individual merchants still often remained unsurpassed.

These institutional mechanisms used by merchants during the medieval and early modern Commercial Revolutions were generated through interplay between the private decisions of individual merchants and public systems provided by towns and princes. In aggregate, the individual decisions of merchants generated locational clusters, notarial and brokerage systems, correspondent relationships and courier systems, price lists and business handbooks, and sophisticated forms of partnership. But these decisions taken individually through voluntary market transactions were only possible because of public institutions such as legal infrastructure at fairs and urban markets; legal recognition of partnerships, firms, notaries and brokers; and ultimately the development of exchanges, postal systems, official registers and diplomatic information services.

These methods of collecting and conveying commercial information shared an additional key feature: they consisted of *generalized* institutional mechanisms providing services on a relatively open-access basis. Anyone could visit the fairs of Champagne, trade in Bruges, frequent the Rialto, write or receive a letter, subscribe to a town courier service, employ a correspondent or factor, enter into a partnership obliging agents to send information home frequently, employ a notary or broker, or buy a merchant manual. This distinguished these mechanisms from merchant guilds and privileged companies, which operated *particularized* institutional mechanisms that collected and transmitted information only to certain groups – essentially their own memberships. Because generalized informational services were susceptible to being used by a much wider array of economic agents than particularized ones, the breadth, volume and density of information they transmitted was higher, and this permitted its accuracy to be checked more fully. The particularized informational services offered by merchant guilds and privileged companies could only be used by guild and company members, giving rise to a relatively narrow and sparse flow of information whose accuracy could only be checked through internal sources. This may have been the reason that generalized institutional mechanisms for conveying commercial information predominated, at least in so far as can be judged from traces left in documentary records.

But perhaps one might argue that merchant guilds and privileged companies, even though they left relatively little evidence of conveying commercially relevant information in ways crucial to economic outcomes, nonetheless played a pioneer role, even if only for a short period? Perhaps merchant guilds were essential for information services at the very beginning of the medieval Commercial Revolution in the twelfth or thirteenth centuries, when international trade was just picking up after the Dark Ages, even if they were soon surpassed by other information mechanisms? Perhaps the privileged companies played an essential role in collecting information at the very beginning of the early modern Commercial Revolution in the sixteenth century, when European merchants were first trying to trade to new continents, even if they were then surpassed by other mechanisms? It might be argued that traditional alien merchant guilds declined at the end of the fifteenth century because alternative informational mechanisms had finally become good enough that merchants could dispense with them, but that the privileged companies existed well into the early modern period because alternative mechanisms could still not deal with the informational challenges of trading to other continents. Alternatively, one might argue that merchant guilds and privileged companies were essential for information transmission (albeit in a fairly minor way) because they facilitated the functioning of these other information-transmission mechanisms. Perhaps one might make the case that trade fairs, hostels, merchant correspondence, courier systems and brokerage systems could not have functioned without merchant guilds?

But closer examination of the evidence refutes these arguments. The basic institutional mechanisms for collecting and conveying commercial information were available from the very beginning of the medieval Commercial Revolution, in the eleventh and twelfth centuries – locational clustering in fairs, cities, hostels, streets and squares; the notarial and brokerage systems; merchant literacy and merchant correspondence; private courier systems; legal forms of enterprise involving the obligation that travelling agents would report regularly to sedentary principals. Although alien merchant guilds and hanses were *also* widespread from the beginning of the medieval Commercial Revolution, there were locations such as the Champagne fairs and the city of Bruges where they were not universal and where lively international trade was nonetheless carried out by non-guilded merchants using these other information-transmission mechanisms. Thus, as we have seen, merchant guilds did not arise at the Champagne fairs until 1245 (and never became universal there), but Flemish and Italian merchants were trading there from the 1180s at latest, getting their information through locational clustering, merchant correspondence, private courier systems and legal forms of enterprise involving correspondent obligations. When Bruges became the fulcrum of international trade in north-west Europe after *c.* 1300, not all foreign merchants trading there formed guilds, yet they traded successfully on the basis of locational clustering in the town itself, in its hostels and squares, through its notarial and brokerage system, through private correspondence and couriers, and through multi-branched merchant firms and partnerships.

Conversely, almost all the evidence adduced in support of the idea that merchant guilds were essential for information transmission during the medieval Commercial Revolution actually dates from quite late in the Middle Ages. The evidence on the internal information-transmission mechanisms of the Hanse, for instance, mostly dates from the later fifteenth or even the sixteenth century – the period at which traditional merchant guilds and hanses were in decline in north-west Europe, the Hanse itself was being increasingly outcompeted by individual merchants from the Netherlands and England, and town governments and princely states were providing information services such as postal systems and consular systems. The evidence thus cannot support the view that the Hanse was in some way a pioneer, even in the slightly backward chronology of long-distance trade in the Baltic.

Other evidence shows that merchant guilds occasionally undertook information-transmission activities that private individuals and town governments were already engaged in, as in the case of the Florentine merchant guild's courier system in the fourteenth century. Merchant guilds were neither pioneers nor essential facilitators of this information-transmission mechanism, as shown by the fact that private merchant firms and city governments were already operating courier systems over the same routes before this date and continued to do so afterwards. The evidence on medieval trade thus does not support the view that merchant guilds were either pioneers or facilitators of the information-transmission mechanisms operated by other institutions.

But what of the early modern Commercial Revolution? Perhaps the reason the privileged companies emerged and existed for so long in this branch of trade was precisely because the information-transmission mechanisms developed for long-distance trade within Europe could not deal with the challenges posted by much longer-distance trade between Europe and other continents?

Here, too, a closer look at the evidence provides no support for this argument. For one thing, if privileged companies were the efficient institution for dealing with the informational challenges of intercontinental trade, there should be evidence that they emerged as natural monopolies, driving out 'atomized' traders who would have had higher costs due to their lack of scale, of monopolistic market dominance and of social capital. But, as we have seen, precisely the opposite was the case. Individual merchants tackled the intercontinental trade before the foundation of the privileged companies and continued to operate throughout their existence, obtaining and transmitting commercial information through locational clustering, correspondence, merchant handbooks and legal forms of enterprise – information mechanisms which the privileged companies had played no role in creating. The privileged companies themselves did not emerge as natural monopolies but rather lobbied for state charters granting them legal monopolies, which they then found themselves compelled to defend constantly against individual interlopers whom they regarded as a serious competitive threat. Nor did the 'atomized' individual merchants merely free-ride on information collected by the privileged companies. On the routes and in the overseas territories legally monopolized by privileged companies, non-company merchants did discover the necessary cultural and geographical information. Indeed, sometimes, as on the routes to Africa and North America, the non-privileged merchants were the pioneers and the privileged companies were the followers. The evidence on the early modern Commercial Revolution, therefore, provides little support for the view that privileged merchant companies were the institutional pioneers or facilitators of commercial information-transmission.

Finally, the evidence in this chapter reveals some broader implications of the particularized information transmission of merchant guilds. We saw how some merchant guilds and privileged companies censored the release of information to outsiders so as to protect their members' monopoly profits. The legal monopolies enjoyed by the German Hanse and the early modern privileged companies often reduced incentives to use information efficiently. Large merchant guilds and privileged companies suffered from shirking and insider dealing by both employees and managers, reducing the quantity and quality of information available to the membership at large, let alone to the wider economy. The German Hanse and many privileged companies suffered from excessive centralization of decision-making leading to inappropriate responses to rapidly changing commercial conditions. Finally, the Hanse at least suffered from 'information cascades', whereby its members converged in beliefs about business conditions and merchant reputations, regardless of whether these beliefs were accurate. It is thus unsurprising that the information-transmitting activities of merchant guilds and privileged companies to their own members are outweighed in the documentary record by those of more generalized institutional mechanisms offering information services to anyone – not just to members of privileged merchant organizations.

> If the calends of January fall on a Sunday . . . grain will be neither cheap nor expensive. If they fall on a Monday . . . there will be plenty of grain. If they fall on a Tuesday . . . grain will be dear.
>
> (Anonymous Pisan author of earliest surviving Italian merchant manual, 1278)[1]

> For just as water will naturally flow into valleys, so goods will be attracted to places where they are most required.
>
> (Venetian merchant Marino Sanudo, 1306)[2]

> In truth, the traffic and conservation of money are very difficult and in the hands of fortune; rare are they who know how to manage it amid all the contrary tempests, exiles and catastrophes.
>
> (Florentine merchant Giovanni Rucellai, 1473)[3]

A basic problem for trade is uncertainty. If economic prospects are too uncertain, people will refrain from doing business. This is bad not just for them but for the entire economy, since it limits exchange and the gains from trade. Price volatility is one major source of uncertainty. Unexpected fluctuations in prices can wipe out a merchant's profits or even his entire business.

One strategy for reducing such uncertainty is to gather information about prices and the factors that might affect them.[4] To obtain information, as we saw in Chapter 9, medieval and early modern merchants used a whole array of institutional mechanisms.

But an even better strategy, some have argued, was for merchants to use institutions to influence prices directly. Merchant guilds and privileged companies, it is claimed, enabled merchants to stabilize prices, reducing uncertainty for themselves and the whole economy. Lopez, for instance, describes the merchant guilds of medieval Constantinople, Florence,

---

[1] Quoted in Lopez (1969), 41.
[2] Sanudo (1306), ch. 1; quoted in Tyerman (1982), 60 with n. 24.
[3] Rucellai (1960), 8; quoted in Bec (1967), 1211.
[4] See the discussion in R. De Roover (1948a), 76–8, 354.

Ypres and London as being actuated by underlying principles of 'stability, control, and sharing of business opportunity'.[5] Dollinger holds that the Hanse, by restraining competition among north German merchants, helped to prevent 'disastrous price fluctuations on the home markets'.[6] Gelderblom and Grafe believe that European merchant guilds benefited trade because they enabled a merchant 'to protect his trade against price fluctuations',[7] and argue that 'by concentrating trade on the premises of foreign merchants, they facilitated the matching of supply and demand'.[8] Harreld describes the merchant guild as 'an engine of stability', since 'cooperation allowed competitors to institute a certain amount of stability in the marketplace, thereby decreasing the costs of doing business'.[9] Schechter argues that indigenous and alien merchant guilds in early modern Istanbul were a force for economic stability, 'shielding city inhabitants against a variety of economic upheavals'.[10] Steensgaard believes that the great European chartered companies stimulated trade by putting an end to competition among 'atomized' Asian traders which had led to 'violent gluts and scarcities in different markets, great price fluctuations and therefore an enormous wastage of economic effort'.[11] Carlos and Nicholas argue that the Hudson's Bay Company fostered intercontinental trade by stabilizing the prices of Canadian furs.[12]

The idea that merchant guilds and privileged companies benefited the economy by stabilizing prices is widely held in the literature, therefore, and must be considered carefully. However, this hypothesis is less straightforward to investigate than those discussed in earlier chapters. Relatively clear-cut economic arguments have been advanced for merchant guilds' efficiency in improving commercial security, contract enforcement, principal-agent relations and information provision, so they can be readily subjected to theoretical analysis and empirical investigation. By contrast, the idea that merchant guilds stabilized prices, though widely stated, is seldom given extensive exposition. The discussion in this chapter is therefore perforce less rigorous than in preceding ones.

Perhaps the most serious difficulty is created by the assumptions on which claims about price volatility are implicitly based: first, that an institutional intervention that stabilizes prices is inherently beneficial; and second, that regulation by a monopolistic supplier is the best way to

---

[5] Lopez (1945), 18.   [6] Dollinger (1970), 147.
[7] Gelderblom and Grafe (2004), 1.   [8] Grafe and Gelderblom (2010a), 483.
[9] Harreld (2004b), 1–2.   [10] Schechter (2005), 261, 271, 273 (quotation).
[11] See the summary in Habib (1990), 397 (quotation), referring to Steensgaard (1973), esp. 22–59.
[12] Carlos and Nicholas (1990), 868.

achieve price stability. More careful consideration reveals problems with both assumptions.

Economic volatility – often expressed as price volatility – is widely regarded as harmful for economic growth and human well-being. Income volatility, it is argued, reduces people's investment in physical and human capital. Producers who are unable to protect themselves against risk respond to volatility in their incomes by diversifying their income-generating activities towards alternatives with lower average risks (even though these have lower average returns), and by reducing their overall levels of investment.[13] Consumers who are poor and imperfectly protected against risk because they lack access to credit and insurance markets find it difficult to smooth expenditures when afflicted by income shocks, resulting in lower consumption of food, health and education, which in turn reduces welfare for individuals and human capital accumulation in the whole economy.[14] For these reasons, at a given average *level* of prices, lower volatility is preferable.

But this does not imply that institutional intervention to stabilize prices would necessarily improve growth and welfare. In any economy – medieval or modern, developing or developed, poor or rich – knowledge of the facts relevant for making economic decisions is dispersed among many different people. Prices condense and communicate this diffuse information about supply and demand, thereby coordinating the separate actions of scattered economic agents. If prices are institutionally 'stabilized' at values that do not reflect underlying economic conditions, an inefficient resource allocation will result. If economic conditions change, prices must change – if they do not do so, then prices will not carry out their key function of coordinating economic decisions.

Thus in a developing economy in which producers and consumers are imperfectly protected from risk and hence cannot smooth production and consumption between years of high prices and years of low ones, the appropriate policy intervention is not to damp down price volatility. Volatile prices are merely conveying information about economic conditions that are making supplies volatile. Rather, the appropriate policy intervention is to address directly either the underlying conditions making prices unstable, or the factors preventing poor producers and consumers from protecting themselves against risk, or both. Studies of price volatility in Europe and the Near East between the medieval period and the early twentieth centuries, for instance, find that price volatility reflected real

[13] Fafchamps (2003); Dercon (2004).
[14] H. G. Jacoby and Skoufias (1997); Jensen (2000); Persson (1999), 21, 31–39; Söderberg (2004), 8.

economic factors. These included weather, transport costs, urbanization, political centralization, security for traders and travellers, access of peasants to marketplaces, currency stability, standardization of weights and measures, tariffs and other trade barriers, means of enforcing contracts and disputes, and market integration.[15] In medieval and early modern economies volatile prices were conveying information about changes in all these variables. Consumers, producers, merchants and policymakers needed to know this information in order to adjust their actions appropriately to changing circumstances. Policy intervention to dampen price volatility that was registering real changes in supply and demand would have denied information to consumers who needed to know it to guide their consumption and savings decisions; to peasants who needed to adjust their labour inputs, crop choices and investments; to merchants who needed to know when to bring in sufficient grain supplies from other regions; and to policymakers who needed to prepare grain stores and welfare funds. Even for the poor, therefore, institutional intervention to reduce price volatility will not in itself improve welfare: intervention must address not the volatility per se, but its underlying sources in the real economy.

There are only two circumstances in which there may be a case for intervention to stabilize prices. First, if there is reason to believe that 'noise' or variation around the price trend is deterring people from adjusting their behaviour to the true price signal, then it may be desirable to 'stabilize' prices in the sense of dampening noisy fluctuations. To maintain this argument for pre-modern Europe, it would be necessary to demonstrate that price fluctuations reflected noise rather than true information signals and that merchant guilds had the capacity and the desire to make prices convey a more accurate signal. Doubt is cast on the first proposition by the plethora of studies of price volatility in medieval and early modern Europe that find that price fluctuations typically reflected changes in real economic factors.[16] The second proposition – that merchant guilds and privileged companies were able to determine 'true' prices by filtering out the 'noise', and were willing to set prices at that true level to benefit the whole economy, will be discussed shortly.

The second circumstance in which a case might be made for price stabilization is if commodities are perishable and cannot be stored. Even

---

[15] On medieval Europe and the Near East, see Söderberg (2004), 7–15, 17; on medieval and early modern Sweden, see Söderberg (2007), 130–1, 135, 141, 147–9; on early modern France and Europe more generally, see Persson (1999), xv, 1, 17–18, 65–6, 90, 92–3, 107; on the wider trading world between the eighteenth and the early twentieth century, see Jacks, O'Rourke and Williamson (2009), 8, 15–19.

[16] See note 15.

for such goods, however, the unambiguous conclusion of the classic survey by Newbery and Stiglitz is 'to question seriously the desirability of price stabilization schemes, both from the point of view of the producer and of the consumer'.[17] In any case, arguments for institutional intervention to stabilize prices of perishable commodities would not apply to the activities of pre-modern long-distance merchants, who hardly traded in perishable goods because transportation methods were too slow. The main medieval food grains were not 'perishable' in this sense as they could be, and were, stored from year to year.

Institutional intervention to stabilize prices is not, therefore, inherently beneficial. Only if traded goods are perishable or prices reflect noise rather than information might institutional intervention to stabilize prices benefit the economy. Otherwise, it is important for prices to fluctuate so they can convey signals to economic agents about changing supply and demand and help ensure that resources are allocated appropriately. An economy needs institutions that improve the *accuracy* of prices, not their *stability*, and that address the underlying causes of economic volatility more directly than by tinkering with prices.

Even if it could be established that pre-modern price fluctuations reflected 'noise' rather than accurate information, it is not clear that a monopolistic merchant guild would be the best way to obtain a more accurate price signal. True, merchant guilds and privileged companies are supposed to have had features that enabled them to stabilize prices. Some argue that merchant guilds used their legal monopolies to set prices directly or regulate them indirectly by controlling supplies. Others point out that merchant guilds prevented their members from engaging in risky forms of entrepreneurship that might have caused prices to fluctuate unpredictably. Finally, some claim that merchant guilds and privileged companies possessed superior information, which enabled their members to plan controlled business responses rather than engaging in ill-informed speculative ventures – although, as we saw in Chapter 9, there is little evidence to support this argument.

But merchant guilds and privileged companies also had characteristics that could reduce the accuracy of price signals, diminishing prices' capacity to convey information and coordinate economic activity. For one thing, a monopolistic market structure with artificially fixed prices provides inaccurate signals to producers and consumers, thereby preventing them from adjusting their behaviour to what is actually happening in the economy. Second, legal monopolies prevent supply streams from becoming more diversified, and this increases the vulnerability of prices

[17] Newbery and Stiglitz (1981), 23.

to shocks. Third, in so far as a merchant guild or privileged company stabilized prices but at a high level so as to ensure its own monopoly profits, this inflicted a deadweight loss on the economy and reduced consumer welfare.

This chapter begins by examining the arguments advanced in the literature according to which merchant guilds and privileged companies stabilized prices through monopolies, restraints on risky competition, and information provision. It moves on to the ways in which merchant guilds and privileged companies reduced the accuracy of prices – by diminishing their information content, preventing diversification of supply and imposing prices higher than those that reflected true supply and demand conditions. It then investigates the role of alternative institutions – in particular, permanent markets – in gradually increasing the stability of prices in the course of the medieval and early modern periods. The chapter concludes by drawing the implications of these findings for price formation in pre-modern European trade.

10.1   Merchant monopolies and entrepôts

The main way in which merchant guilds and privileged companies are supposed to have stabilized prices was through their monopolies. The most influential version of this argument claims that price stability increased in Europe after about 1500 because of the emergence of a phenomenon called the 'staple market' – a central urban 'entrepôt' monopolized by a cohesive group of merchants. This idea was first advanced in 1931 by the Dutch historian Van der Kooy, who claimed that failures of transportation, communication and production in the medieval economy caused enormous volatility in supplies and prices. For sustained economic growth, he contended, what was needed was a *stapelmarkt* – a single, general world entrepôt to concentrate supply and demand in one place and control price formation. In his view, the stabilizing force was that a key group of merchants in a single location would buy up stocks of crucial goods and keep them in their own warehouses until the prices were 'right'. These buffer stocks ironed out inequalities of supply and demand, he argued, ensuring that prices moved stably rather than fluctuating wildly. According to Van der Kooy, the role of this single, global entrepôt was performed by Amsterdam from about 1500 on.[18]

---

[18] For early statements of this view, see Van der Kooy (1931); Barbour (1963); Klein (1965); Van der Kooy (1970); Klein (1982). For more recent deployments of this concept, see Israel (1989), 13–16; Müller (1998), 20; Jacks (2004), 308–9. For trenchant criticisms, see De Vries and Van der Woude (1997), 690–3; Lesger (2006), 197–205.

In the 1960s this argument was taken up by Klein, who argued that Van der Kooy's model needed an additional element – merchant monopolies. The only reason merchants in the single world entrepôt would have been willing to invest in warehousing the buffer stocks that stabilized world prices, according to Klein, was that they were able to engage in monopolistic practices. Competition increased risks, he argued, and higher risks reduced merchants' incentives to incur the cost of warehousing buffer stocks. Only if a merchant was able to monopolize supply could he be certain that the costs he incurred by warehousing buffer stocks would pay off.[19] Monopolies – whether by large-scale individual traders or by merchant guilds – reduced price fluctuations, he claimed, creating more predictable trading conditions, increasing exchange and encouraging economic growth. In Amsterdam after c. 1500, Klein argued, specific groups of merchants monopolized key sectors, regulated the flow of commodities from one region to another, dampened price fluctuations and thereby reduced transaction costs within the entire European trading system.[20]

A variant of this argument was subsequently applied by other scholars to the Dutch East India Company and the Hudson's Bay Company. According to one interpretation of Dutch history, the sixteenth century had seen ruinous competition among a large number of small merchant firms trading in Asia, leading to price volatility and merchant bankruptcies. The only way to stabilize prices and ensure the survival of the early modern Dutch trade to the East Indies, this story continues, was to set up a single, monopolistic company. Accordingly, in 1602, the Dutch East India Company was established and subsequently ensured that prices ceased to fluctuate and trade expanded in a stable and sustained way.[21] Applying similar arguments, Carlos and Nicholas argued that the monopoly prices which the Hudson's Bay Company set for beaver furs and for the trade goods they gave the Indians in return were beneficial because 'these fixed price standards . . . satisfied the Indians' demand for certainty of the prices that they would receive for the skins'.[22] This in turn ensured that the Indians brought a predictable volume of furs to the Company posts, ensuring continuous supply and stable selling prices for furs in Europe.

The Van der Kooy–Klein view that central 'entrepôts' worked symbiotically with merchant monopolies to stabilize prices has been applied to

---

[19] Doubt is cast on this idea by evidence from modern markets where storage is important, which does not support the view that monopoly power is necessary; see Newbery and Stiglitz (1981).

[20] Klein (1965), esp. 478; Klein (1982).

[21] Israel (1989), 16–17; Müller (1998), 21 n. 14.   [22] Carlos and Nicholas (1990), 868.

a wide variety of European economies, including the Low Countries,[23] Scandinavia,[24] Italy[25] and England.[26] It is adopted, whether consciously or unconsciously, by a large number of economic historians writing about merchant guilds and privileged companies. But is it borne out by the evidence?

Studies of normal trading practices in early modern Europe cast doubt on Klein's argument that merchant monopolies were responsible for stabilizing prices. For one thing, Amsterdam's merchant monopolies are supposed to have arisen from the concentration of warehousing capacity, enabling the city's merchants to control the flow of commodities among European regions and stabilize the prices at which goods were sold. But warehousing capacity is not an exogenous variable: it arises because of decisions to invest in physical and circulating capital. Amsterdam confronted many rival trading centres in the late medieval and early modern period, and there was nothing to prevent such rivals from increasing investment in their own warehousing capacity, building up their own facilities and breaking Amsterdam's monopoly.[27] In a recent detailed assessment of the Van der Kooy–Klein theory, Lesger concludes that

the stapling of goods in physical markets was not an indispensable element of international trade. No evidence has been found to suggest that Amsterdam or the [Dutch] Republic in fact operated as a magazine or warehouse for Europe (to say nothing of the rest of the world).[28]

That is, there was no such thing as a 'staple market' along the lines postulated by Van der Kooy and Klein.

Another objection relates to the empirical basis of Klein's original argument which, as Veluwenkamp points out, was almost exclusively reliant on a single example, that of the brothers Elias and Pieter Trip, large-scale merchants who enjoyed a commanding position in certain branches of seventeenth-century commerce, notably the Dutch trade in copper and tar.[29] But the Trippen were exceptional. By the early modern period, most sectors of Dutch commerce were not ones in which merchants – whether as individuals or as guilds – were able to dictate prices. In his analysis of the Neufville merchant firm in early modern Amsterdam, for instance, Veluwenkamp found that there were very few goods whose prices Amsterdam merchants were able to influence. This was because most goods traded in the city – linen, hemp, flax, woollen

[23] As discussed in W. D. Smith (1984), 986–7; Lesger (2006), esp. 197–205.
[24] Müller (1998), 20–1; Hasselberg, Müller and Stenlås (1997), 13; Müller (2001), 7–8.
[25] Caligaris (1998), 62.   [26] Carlos and Nicholas (1990), 868.
[27] W. D. Smith (1984), 987 n. 5.   [28] Lesger (2006), 250.   [29] Klein (1965).

cloth, grain, wine, salt and iron – could be (and were) imported from numerous different sources and by many competing merchants. Arguably the only important goods of which this was not true were copper and tar. This meant that monopolistic price setting by merchants was the exception rather than the rule in early modern Amsterdam, and hence cannot have been the source of its remarkable price stability.[30]

Similar findings emerge for a number of other early modern trades. Müller, for instance, finds that the early modern Swedish iron trade functioned efficiently, with low price differences between different locations. This was because there was a large number of traders in the iron sector, overseas markets could be supplied from a variety of sources other than Sweden, the number of production units even in Sweden itself was large and Swedish rulers never granted monopolistic merchant guilds privileges over iron along the lines of those they granted over copper and tar. Thus even *without* monopolistic practices by privileged merchant guilds, the Swedish iron trade worked well and prices were fairly stable – or at least not damagingly volatile.[31]

Such examples cast doubt on the argument that the growing price stability which Van der Kooy and Klein identified in north-west Europe after about 1500 was caused by monopolies – whether by individual merchants or by merchant guilds. Veluwenkamp, for instance, found that Amsterdam's merchants were successful not because they enjoyed monopolies, but because they created networks of useful contacts and satisfied customers.[32] Furthermore, Amsterdam was the European city that was probably the most antagonistic towards merchant guilds, refusing to grant privileges to colonies of alien merchants and compelling all traders to submit to municipal jurisdictions. It thus seems unlikely that in early modern Amsterdam, merchant guilds were *capable* of affecting prices significantly. Precisely because Amsterdam was so open and pluralistic, it was difficult for any individual trading organization to have a large impact on prices there. It seems more likely that prices in entrepôts such as Amsterdam were so stable because the confluence of many diverse sources of supply and demand in a single urban centre created a thick market in which prices adjusted smoothly rather than being destabilized by shocks to specific large players. It was precisely the *competitive* nature of trade in the great urban entrepôts of the early modern period – and thus, if anything, their increasing reluctance to grant privileges to merchant guilds – that caused their prices to become increasingly stable. This was made possible by the changes discussed in Chapter 5 which made it

---

[30] Veluwenkamp (1981), 21–30, 130–2.   [31] Müller (1998), 90–1; Müller (2005), 74.
[32] Veluwenkamp (1981), 21–30, 130–2.

politically more feasible, at least in some European societies, to diminish the privileges of merchant guilds after about 1500.

10.2   Preventing risky behaviour

A second way in which merchant guilds are supposed to have stabilized prices was by forbidding their members to engage in risky entrepreneurial activities. Merchants varied in their taste for risk. A risk-preferring merchant might undertake highly speculative ventures which could result in either startling success (reducing prices for customers but harming other members of his guild) or startling failure (increasing prices to customers and putatively harming the public). Some scholars claim that merchant guilds benefited the pre-modern economy by imposing rules prohibiting their members from engaging in forms of entrepreneurship that led to such volatility. Guild regulations, it is argued, prevented the decisions of a few risk-preferring merchants from destabilizing prices and inflicting negative externalities on the wider merchant community.

Even from a purely theoretical standpoint, it is not clear that this argument holds water. An individual merchant, even one who engages in highly speculative ventures, is unlikely to be able to affect prices unless he operates on a very large scale. An entire merchant guild or privileged company might often be a large actor in particular markets and able to influence prices and supplies, as we saw in Chapters 3 and 4. But it would surely be unusual for an individual merchant to be a large enough actor that his success or failure would affect prices. It is thus unclear that the assumption underlying this argument is justified.

The argument also encounters empirical problems. The major example adduced in support of this view is the German Hanse, which in the late medieval period restrained speculative ventures by prohibiting its members from undertaking trading voyages outside the framework of Hanse convoys. From c. 1350 onwards, the Hanse imposed rules such as requiring its members to join a group of at least ten other ships and restricting them to three specified sailing dates each year. According to Dollinger, these regulations were intended partly to ensure safety from piratical attacks, but were also motivated by the belief that voyaging alone made it possible for an individual merchant to be highly successful, which was thought to cause catastrophic price fluctuations.[33]

The fact that these regulations were compulsory, and were opposed by many of the Hanse's own merchants, casts doubt on the idea that travelling in convoy led to an efficient level of safety. This impression is

[33] Dollinger (1970), 147.

intensified by the fact that protests came particularly from ship captains, who are likely to have been more highly informed about navigational risks than the Hanse central office. Individual merchants not only voiced complaints, alluding to risks of collision in convoy, losses caused by having to sail from a particular rendezvous and long delays waiting for other ships. Individuals also took action, separating themselves from the official Hanse convoys despite threats of fines or exclusion from Hanseatic privileges.[34] Evidently both merchants and ship captains regarded the risks of undertaking independent trading ventures as being worth the returns.[35]

In fact, the major aim of the regulations, as Dollinger points out, was 'ensuring equal opportunity for all merchants, both as buyers and sellers. Travelling alone ensured high profits for some to the detriment of others.'[36] But it is not clear that prohibiting behaviour that might reduce *inequality in profits* would necessarily have reduced *fluctuations in prices*. If a disaster overtook the Hanse convoy, then prices would fluctuate hugely on the market because the entire source of supply would be lost. The existence of independent voyages by non-convoy merchants would actually moderate price volatility by providing alternative sources of supply. Holding other factors constant, diversification of entrepreneurial behaviour was likely to generate multiple sources of commodities, reducing the likelihood of large shocks to supply and prices. By prohibiting individual decision-making about risks, a merchant guild like the Hanse actually increased, not decreased, the probability of large price fluctuations.

The Dutch East India Company (VOC) is a second example of a privileged merchant company that is supposed to have stabilized prices by reining in individual entrepreneurial risks. After about 1670 the VOC succeeded in excluding all rivals in the lucrative trade in 'fine spices' (cloves, nutmeg and mace) from the Spice Islands (Macassar and the Moluccas), establishing 'one of the most effective monopolies in history'.[37] It achieved this, as we saw in Chapter 4, by extirpating unauthorized spice trees, mounting military raids against rival traders and deliberately keeping the European market under-supplied. This stabilized European spice prices and generated high profits for the VOC.

This 'stabilization' policy, however, had two long-term effects that were not generally beneficial. The first was the impact on consumers. The VOC kept prices stable, but it also kept them *high*, so much so

---

[34] *Ibid.*, 147–8.

[35] The same was true of the convoys organized by the Venetian state: privately owned ships voyaged independently, incurring higher risks but increasing the flexibility (and thus the stability) of merchant trading; on this, see Stabel (1999), 34.

[36] Dollinger (1970), 147.   [37] Steensgaard (1990), 121.

that some historians have concluded that the level of prices imposed by the VOC 'prevented an increase in European spice consumption'. That is, European consumers were less well off as a result of VOC price stabilization. The second effect was the impact on the VOC's own long-term commercial success:

> there can be hardly any doubt that the spice monopoly diminished the ability of the VOC to maneuver in a changing world. Large investments were sunk into the eastern archipelago, and the whole structure of the company trade in Asia as well as Europe was tied to a constant flow of spices. It was a safe source of income but had little potential for development, whereas the European rivals . . . promoted a trade in new commodities with a much larger potential market: textiles, tea, and coffee.[38]

The Hudson's Bay Company (HBC) is a third example of a privileged merchant company that is supposed to have stabilized prices by prohibiting excessively entrepreneurial behaviour by individual traders. The HBC, Carlos and Nicholas argue, created wider economic benefits by fixing the prices it paid to indigenous people for furs. The indigenous fur-trappers desired such fixed prices, it is claimed, because they had a strong aversion to risk. Fixed prices are also supposed to have helped the HBC to control opportunistic behaviour by its own distant managers, thereby solving its internal agency problems.[39]

However, it is not clear that this attempt at price stabilization actually benefited either the HBC or its suppliers. This was a trading world in which war, inflation and the normal fluctuations of supply and demand meant that prices were constantly changing to reflect new information. Denying distant managers discretion in setting prices was bad for business because it prevented them from negotiating the prices the market would bear.[40] Furthermore, other evidence indicates that indigenous fur-suppliers did not seek stable prices at all costs, but rather shopped around among different Canadian trading posts to obtain the best price: 'the Indians knew the official prices for furs and what was received at other posts'.[41] At least the indigenous fur-suppliers, and possibly the HBC as well, would therefore have been better off negotiating prices that reflected true economic conditions rather than having to trade at a fixed price imposed through monopolistic fiat by HBC head office.

The examples of the German Hanse, the Dutch East India Company and the Hudson's Bay Company thus do not support the view that merchant guilds and privileged companies, by preventing individual entrepreneurial decisions, improved the operation of the price

---

[38] *Ibid.*, 123.   [39] Carlos and Nicholas (1990), 867–8.
[40] *Ibid.*, 867.   [41] *Ibid.*, 868.

mechanism. On the contrary: in so far as merchant guilds and privileged companies were able to prevent individual knowledge from contributing to price formation, they probably increased the 'noise' of price signals in pre-modern trade.

10.3 Ensuring accurate information

A third way merchant guilds and privileged companies are supposed to have stabilized prices was through information advantages. A major weakness of Asian compared to European merchants in the seventeenth century, according to Steensgaard, was that the Asian traders were competitive, small-scale and dispersed, which meant that they often operated on faulty information and could not plan controlled commercial responses. Steensgaard argues that this led to violent fluctuations in supply in different markets, enormous volatility in prices and consequent waste of economic effort. The European chartered companies, by contrast, possessed superior information and were able to rectify this price volatility and its deleterious consequences for the whole economy.[42] Steensgaard's view is shared by Das Gupta, who describes indigenous merchants in eighteenth-century India as being 'atomized men' with imperfect information, leading them to make commercial decisions that generated volatility in supplies and prices.[43]

This argument is untenable even on purely theoretical grounds. It would only hold if all trade was in non-storable commodities. Even when a merchant does not have perfect information, if goods can be stored then prices will adjust smoothly without violent fluctuations.[44] As already observed, pre-modern long-distance merchants seldom traded in perishable commodities because of the length of time it took to move goods using available transportation technology. But it is only if goods cannot be stored that prices are likely to fluctuate in the way postulated by Steensgaard and Das Gupta, even if individual merchants are operating on poor information.

There are also a number of empirical problems with the argument that the privileged merchant companies stabilized prices through informational advantages. As Chapter 9 showed, merchant guilds and privileged companies do not seem to have been especially efficient at collecting, processing or diffusing information; in some notable cases they were *less* efficient than the outsiders they sought to exclude. Counter to Steensgaard's assumption that indigenous traders in India were mostly small-scale

[42] Steensgaard (1973), esp. 22–59.   [43] Das Gupta (1979), 11–12.
[44] Newbery and Stiglitz (1981).

peddlers, many of them actually conducted substantial businesses, employing correspondents and commission agents who kept them informed about supply and demand in distant markets and using sophisticated credit and brokerage systems which helped them dampen price fluctuations. Some studies even suggest that competitive Indian merchants were more highly informed about supplies and prices in distant markets than the privileged European merchant companies operating in the same time and place.[45] Wherever Indian merchants were not excluded through the legal monopolies imposed by the privileged European companies, they obtained relevant information, operated rational business strategies and avoided debilitating price fluctuations. According to Habib,

The fact that the Red Sea, not the Cape of Good Hope, remained the main conduit for India's external trade in the seventeenth century shows that the 'atomized' commerce was by no means less efficient than the trade of the Dutch and English companies (using the Cape of Good Hope route) wherever there were possibilities of free and open competition... Could it be that the European triumph over Indian (and Asian) merchants was not, then, one of size and techniques, of companies over peddlers, of joint-stock over atomized capital, of seamen over landsmen? Might it not have been more a matter of men-of-war and gut and shot, to which arithmetic and brokerage could provide no answer...?[46]

The evidence thus does not support the view that monopolistic merchant guilds and privileged companies were better than individual traders at processing information relevant to prices. The chief advantages of the privileged guilds and companies were their state monopolies and the military coercion at their disposal. Since coercion and conflict tend to destabilize prices, it seems likely that the net effect of such merchant privileges on prices was detrimental.

10.4   Is price-setting by a single supplier desirable?

What, then, *were* the institutional foundations of pre-modern price formation? Three assumptions underlie the view that merchant guilds and privileged companies were good for prices. First, it is assumed that price stability is inherently desirable. Second, it is assumed that prices will be more stable when they are set by a single supplier than when they emerge through competition among numerous different suppliers. Finally, it is assumed that the existence of a single dominant supplier will not have any further, deleterious effects on prices.

---

[45] For a lucid exposition, see Habib (1990), esp. 396–9.   [46] *Ibid.*, 398–9.

Is price stability inherently desirable? We have already touched on the reasons this may not be so, and it is worthwhile exploring these more deeply. The role of prices in any economy – medieval or modern – is to convey information. Knowledge of the facts relevant for making economic decisions is dispersed among many decision-makers, most of them not in communication with one another. But the information they possess is reflected in their economic decisions – producing, consuming and exchanging – and these in turn affect prices. Prices thus incorporate all the information known to economic agents in a very concise and economical form and convey it to other agents without the need for deliberate action. The information contained in competitive prices ensures that producers and consumers respond appropriately and allocate resources according to their scarcity and relative value in different activities.[47] Prices thus coordinate the separate actions of different economic agents. If prices are artificially fixed at levels that reflect factors other than supply and demand – e.g. at levels that suit the interests of rulers or guilded merchants – an inefficient resource allocation will result. If economic conditions change, prices must change – if they do not do so, then prices will not carry out their key function of coordinating economic decisions. Price stability is thus not inherently desirable. Indeed, artificially imposed price stability is inherently undesirable.

Second, will prices set by a single supplier be more stable than those arising through market transactions among a large number of suppliers and customers? The short answer is no. Monopoly prices *may* be stable, if it is in the interest and capacity of the monopolist to keep them stable. But a monopolist may also have incentives to change prices suddenly, or may be forced to do so by an outside shock, which is likely to have a disproportionate effect because there is only a single source of supply. Economic theory contains no general result stating that a monopolistic supplier will offer more stable prices than an array of individual competing suppliers.[48] So even if price stability were inherently desirable, there is no reason to believe that a single, monopolistic supplier such as a merchant guild would create such stability.

Third, what other effects on prices might be exerted by the existence of a single, dominant supplier? In a perfectly competitive market, firms

---

[47] The exception to this proposition is if there are important externalities or other market failures, in which case prices may not accurately reflect supply and demand. But even if serious externalities or other market failures exist, it is very hard to calculate and impose 'better' prices, even for a sophisticated modern regulatory regime, as shown by the difficulties of devising systems of road-pricing or carbon-trading.

[48] For a discussion of these distributional issues in the context of agricultural price stabilization in modern developing economies, see Newbery and Stiglitz (1981).

are 'price takers'. Since a customer can buy a good from one supplier as easily as another, any supplier of that good on the market faces a horizontal demand curve at the equilibrium price. If a supplier tries to sell that good above the equilibrium price, customers will simply buy it elsewhere and that supplier will lose all their business. A monopolistic supplier, by contrast, faces a downward-sloping demand curve because of the lack of competition. Although he will lose some business by raising prices, he will not lose it all, and under normal market conditions it will be profitable for him to sell at a higher-than-competitive price. So the existence of a single, dominant supplier, whether an individual merchant, a government bureaucrat or a merchant guild, will have the harmful effect of raising prices above the competitive level.

This is borne out by empirical findings from medieval and early modern economies. An early example comes from the eleventh-century Byzantine empire. In the second half of the eleventh century, people brought their grain in carts to the city of Rhaidestos, the trade outlet for goods from Thrace and Macedonia for supplying consumers in Constantinople. In marketplaces in Rhaidestos, these individual producers sold their grain unrestrictedly to both individuals and middlemen. But in the 1170s, Nikephoritzes, principal adviser to Emperor Michael VII, replaced this small-scale, heterogeneous market, characterized by a large number of buyers and sellers, with an oligopolistic arrangement. Nikephoritzes used his power as a senior minister of state to set up a so-called *foundax* (grain-exchange) outside the town centre, to which suppliers were legally forced to bring their grain, pay him a high fee for a selling licence, deliver taxes to the state and sell the grain to a small group of *sitonai* (rich wholesale merchants) who were now 'the only ones who had the right to buy' and who in turn resold the grain at three to four times the purchase price.[49] In the words of a contemporary commentator,

And so, the *foundax* growing, the earlier prosperity of the city fell into a state of inexorable injustice, and the price of corn went from 18 *modii* per coin to 1 *modios*... those from the countryside and the neighbors of Rodosto were prevented from selling their personal crops in their own houses. Their measures of grain were taken away, and a single *foundax* was lord and master over all measures of grain... if someone was denounced for selling at home grain from his own harvest, he was treated as a murderer or a thief or some other stranger, and his property was confiscated and seized by the man who presides over the *foundax*. A hundred military aids, representing every sort of evil man, attended the *foundacarius* and obeyed his orders, and attacked the pitiful merchants and farmers from all sides with many vexations.[50]

[49] Laiou (2002), 742–3.
[50] Account by Michael Attaliates (*c.* 1080), quoted in Constable (2003), 151–2.

Some modern historians have claimed that this monopolistic grain-exchange was justified because it enabled the authorities to control the market price of grain and to prevent speculation by limiting the role of private middlemen.[51] Contemporaries such as Michael Attaliates and John Skylitzes writing in the 1080s were more sceptical, interpreting the imposition of the monopolistic grain-exchange as a tactic used by Nikephoritzes to enrich himself by limiting market access in return for 60 pounds of gold annually.[52] All commentators agreed that the replacement of a competitive grain market in which a large number of small-scale sellers and buyers participated by an oligopolistic grain-exchange restricted to a small circle of rich wholesalers resulted in a spectacular rise in the grain price in Constantinople – whether or not this price was 'stabilized'.[53] The oligopolistic grain-exchange was discontinued after the accession of a new emperor in 1079.

The same effect, whereby imposition of a legal monopoly 'stabilized' prices but at a higher level, can be observed when a particular merchant guild acted as the single, dominant supplier of a certain good. Fourteenth-century Antwerp, for instance, suffered from 50 per cent higher grain prices than Ghent because of the grain staple enjoyed by the Ghent merchant guild upstream on the Scheldt River. As a consequence, Antwerp eagerly welcomed the advent of an alternative supply stream from German merchants to break the monopoly of the Ghent staple merchants.[54] Likewise, the accounts of the Teutonic Order show a considerable drop in prices in Prussia in the last third of the fourteenth century, resulting from the diminution in the ability of the German Hanse to monopolize trade between Prussia and western Europe. English and Dutch ships appeared in increasing numbers in the Baltic, causing freight charges and prices to fall.[55]

Some would argue that this is a good example of how competition *destabilizes* prices. When these merchant guild monopolies were broken, prices declined abruptly. But was this a bad thing? Admittedly, the decline in grain prices in fourteenth-century Antwerp reduced the monopoly profits of the Ghent merchants. But it increased the profits of German merchants, reduced the costs of Antwerp's craftsmen and merchants and, perhaps most importantly, increased the welfare of Antwerp's consumers, especially the poor, in whose budgets food purchases played a larger role. Likewise, it is certainly true that the price decline in

---

[51] See the interpretation advanced in Dagron (2002), 453.
[52] For a detailed account of the Rhaidestos monopoly, but with diametrically opposed interpretations, see Laiou (2002), 742–3; and Dagron (2002), 453.
[53] Laiou (2002), 743; Dagron (2002), 453; Constable (2003), 151–2.
[54] Nicholas (1997b), 41; Harreld (2004a), 50.   [55] Dollinger (1970), 216.

late-fourteenth-century Prussia reduced the monopoly profits of Hanseatic merchants. But it increased the profits of English and Dutch merchants, and brought cloth and other goods to Prussian consumers at lower prices, increasing overall economic welfare. When military insecurity deterred outside merchants from visiting Prussia after *c.* 1410, and high Hanseatic prices were restored, even the Hanseatic merchants did not benefit: 'Customers refused to buy at the higher prices and business stagnated for several years.'[56] This is as clear an illustration as possible that when a merchant guild or privileged company *was* able to regulate prices by defending its legal position as sole supplier, the effects were harmful to customers and not even necessarily beneficial to guild members.

Further evidence is provided by the seventeenth-century European copper trade which – unlike most other branches of European commerce by that era – was still partially monopolized by merchant guilds and privileged companies. In the first half of the seventeenth century, a limited number of European copper suppliers existed, dominated by Sweden. Within Sweden, over 90 per cent of all copper was supplied by a single mine in the town of Falun.[57] This situation enabled the Swedish crown to grant a series of legal monopolies over copper exporting to a series of merchant syndicates between 1619 and 1638. These syndicates did manage to keep prices higher than the competitive level – and in that sense stabilized them. But the combination of high monopoly prices and the Spanish government's abandonment of copper currency in 1626 led to a disastrous fall in demand for copper, and the monopolistic syndicate of Swedish copper merchants collapsed.[58]

Better success attended the syndicate of copper merchants that was granted monopoly privileges by the Swedish crown in the 1660s. This syndicate was so successful in imposing monopoly prices in European markets that it attracted criticism from Swedish government officials for making excessive profits.[59] However, the response of European markets was not to value the benefits of price stabilization beneficently conferred upon them by these merchant monopolies, but rather urgently to seek outside sources of supply. In the 1670s, Dutch merchants hugely increased their imports of copper from Norway and Japan, causing copper prices in the key Amsterdam market to fall.[60] Swedish copper exports suffered, along with the monopolistic Swedish copper merchant syndicate, so in this limited sense the downward fluctuation in prices was bad for trade. But the downward fluctuation in prices benefited producers

---

[56] *Ibid.*, 216–17.   [57] Müller (1998), 99–100.   [58] *Ibid.*, 100.
[59] *Ibid.*, 100–1.   [60] *Ibid.*, 107.

of copper in Norway and Japan, buyers of copper on the Amsterdam market, and all the customers they supplied. It seems unlikely that anyone other than the Swedish copper monopolists and the Swedish crown would have preferred the stable, above-market copper prices of the 1660s to the plunging, competitive copper prices of the 1670s.

Findings such as these for medieval Byzantium, medieval Flanders, medieval Prussia and early modern Sweden cast doubt on the assumption that even when merchant guilds or privileged companies did stabilize prices, such stability was inherently beneficial. The prices imposed by the Constantinople *sitonai*, the Ghent merchant guild, the German Hanse or the Swedish copper syndicates may have been stable in these cases, but they were also artificially high. They benefited members of these merchant groups, and the rulers who granted them monopolies, but harmed consumers and other merchants and inflicted deadweight losses on the wider economy. When prices were 'destabilized' by the entry of competing traders, everyone except guild members benefited, exchange increased and the economy grew because of greater gains from trade. The 'destabilized' prices arising in the absence of monopolistic merchant guilds or privileged companies not only were lower, but also reflected underlying supply and demand instead of the legal powers of privileged merchants. These prices, precisely because they were allowed to fluctuate rather than being fixed by merchant guilds, conveyed more accurate information to economic agents, ensuring that resources were allocated more efficiently.

10.5   Competitive markets and stable prices

There is one circumstance in which price fluctuations might be harmful. As discussed at the beginning of this chapter, a price fluctuation might reflect 'noise' rather than accurate information about economic conditions, and hence lead people to allocate resources inefficiently. In these circumstances, institutional intervention to reduce price fluctuations might be beneficial. Is there evidence that price fluctuations in pre-modern trade did reflect 'noise' rather than accurate information? And is there evidence that a merchant guild monopoly rather than a competitive market structure was better at decreasing such 'noise'?

We have already seen that a monopolistic market structure has features likely to increase 'noise' in the price signal or to give rise to temporary supply shocks (and hence price fluctuations) that do not reflect underlying supply and demand. First, by fixing prices artificially, a monopolist muffles the information that prices convey to producers and consumers about underlying economic conditions, thereby preventing output and prices from adjusting to changing circumstances. Second, by legally restricting supply to a single source, a monopoly renders the economy more vulnerable to temporary shocks. A more diverse stream of suppliers will ensure that supplies, and thus prices, reflect the actual availability of goods.

These considerations can only be set aside by making the assumption that pre-modern economies were largely non-market-oriented, with the result that prices did not transmit accurate information. This is the assumption made by 'staple-market' theorists. Thus Van der Kooy and Klein assume that pre-modern Europe was characterized by economic dualism between a large traditional sector where prices did not convey information because most people did not participate in the market, and a small modern sector where prices were fixed by monopolistic merchants in dominant staple-markets.[61]

Perhaps it is understandable that early scholars such as Van der Kooy and Klein should have believed that market participation was non-existent outside the great urban entrepôts and that without deliberate intervention by monopolistic merchants prices would have fluctuated randomly and failed to convey accurate information. But the last half century of research has refuted the old-fashioned assumption that in pre-modern Europe economic agents outside great urban entrepôts and privileged merchant circles were unwilling or unable to participate in markets or respond to prices. Rather, it is now clear that as early as the medieval period, people from social circles extending far beyond those of the privileged urban merchants were involved in markets and thus that prices conveyed accurate information about supply and demand.[62]

These findings have far-reaching implications for theories about the need for deliberate price stabilization by monopolistic merchants. Without evidence of any fundamental economic dualism between a price-unresponsive traditional sector on the one hand and a modern urban entrepôt on the other, there is no reason to believe that the traditional sector generated any greater price volatility than the machinations of monopolistic merchants or their guilds. Rather, with agents throughout the economy willing and able to transact in markets, prices reflected the information known to large numbers of producers and consumers and hence did not need to be imposed deliberately by monopolists.

Of course, prices could adjust more smoothly in 'thicker' markets such as those of early modern Amsterdam. But the reason for this smooth

---

[61] De Vries and Van der Woude (1997), 690.
[62] On the Netherlands, see *ibid.*, 690–3; and De Vries (1974). On England, see R. M. Smith (1974); and Wrightson (1982). On eastern Europe see Ogilvie (2001), esp. 450; Dennison (2011).

adjustment was not that supply or demand was concentrated in a single hand which deliberately fixed prices. Rather, it was precisely that in 'thicker' markets a plurality of different suppliers and customers came together in the same place, compensating for fluctuations in each other's behaviour. The confluence of numerous suppliers and customers stabilized prices, since a shock to one source was more likely to be compensated for by another source. Van der Kooy and Klein were thus right to describe the urban entrepôt of early modern Amsterdam as having unusually transparent and thus particularly stable prices. But they were wrong to ascribe this stability to merchant monopolies, rather than competition among diverse traders. It was this diversified portfolio of uncoordinated supply and demand that increasingly stabilized prices in late medieval and early Europe – not the deliberate steering of purchases and sales by closed circles of monopolistic merchants.

A final example of price stability emanating from competitive trading rather than merchant monopolies is provided by European colonies overseas. In 1619, the English Bermuda Company, which enjoyed a legal monopoly over supplying trade goods to Bermuda, sent only a single ship to the colony. Within a month, the colonists were short of essential goods including food and clothing. Fortunately a Dutch freebooter was willing to supply the colonists with the basic imports which the monopolistic merchant company denied them.[63] The governor of Bermuda, Nathanial Butler, justified authorizing trade with this illegal competitor in terms of stability: 'ther is not a securer nor speedier waye to firm this plantation and to refine it from the miscarriages that maye betide it by accidental meanes than the discreet admittance and kind wellcome of such as shall warrantably passe in course this waye'. The Dutch freebooter was, in theory, not 'warrantable' (i.e. legal) in the eyes of the privileged merchant company and the English government. But in practice such monopoly-breaking was essential to the stability of the colony – indeed, to its very survival. This difference between theory and practice was pointed out by Butler in his letter: 'it is noe small advantage that a very mean conceit hath over the perfectest judgement in the world, when the one worcks upon the ground of experience, this other from a discourse of reasonable apprehension only'.[64] A theoretical 'discourse' underpinned the exclusive, cartellistic privileges of guild-like merchant companies. But 'experience' suggested that their monopolies had to be circumvented in order to create stability for vulnerable consumers and their communities.

---

[63] Pérotin-Dumon (1991), 222–3.   [64] Quoted in *ibid.*, 223.

10.6   Conclusion

What are the wider implications of these findings about pre-modern price formation? Medieval and early modern Europe did suffer from large price fluctuations, and contemporaries as well as modern economists deplored their impact.[65] Some scholars have gone further, claiming that merchant guilds and privileged companies offered an institutional solution to this problem.

Is it true that the legal monopolies enjoyed by merchant guilds and privileged companies enabled them to stabilize prices and supplies in centralized entrepôts? The short answer is no. The stable prices observed in early modern entrepôts such as Amsterdam did not arise because such cities favoured merchant monopolies. In fact, Amsterdam was less welcoming to merchant guilds and privileged companies than were other trading centres at the same period. Rather, Amsterdam enjoyed stable prices because – and to the extent that – it encouraged diverse streams of supply and demand to converge in a permanent market. This enabled prices to be negotiated continuously and reduced their vulnerability to exogenous shocks afflicting a single supplier.

What about the argument that guild and company regulations against risky behaviour prevented individual merchant ventures from achieving startling successes and failures which destabilized prices? Merchant guilds and privileged companies did sometimes seek to forbid their members from engaging in high-risk entrepreneurial activities. But although they justified these prohibitions in terms of preventing ruinous price fluctuations, in practice the motivation appears to have been to prevent internal competition that might weaken the guild monopoly. Nor is there any evidence that prohibiting risky entrepreneurial behaviour that might reduce *inequality in profits* would necessarily have reduced *fluctuations in prices*. Indeed, permitting diverse ventures by different merchants reduced the probability of a disastrous exogenous shock that would afflict all merchants equally, thereby causing an abrupt price fluctuation. Diversifying patterns of entrepreneurial behaviour did not destabilize prices but rather stabilized them.

What of the idea that merchant guilds and privileged companies enjoyed information advantages enabling them to engage in rational business planning rather than wild speculative ventures, thereby stabilizing supplies and prices? Chapter 9 found little evidence that merchant guilds and privileged companies actually did enjoy information advantages. Deeper empirical studies question whether the information

---

[65] For perceptive discussions, see R. De Roover (1948a), ch. 5; Persson (1999), 3–13.

available to 'atomistic', competitive Asian merchants was indeed, as originally argued, inferior to that collected by large, monopolistic European merchant companies. In so far as Asian merchants were unable to pursue a planned business strategy in long-distance trade it was not because their competitive behaviour reduced information and increased price volatility, but because they were legally and militarily prevented from participating in particular markets by the monopolistic European companies. The resulting violent struggles over access to markets, resulting from the state privileges claimed by European merchant companies, increased, rather than decreased, price fluctuations.

Those who argue that merchant guilds and privileged companies benefited the economy by dampening price volatility assume that price stabilization policies are inherently desirable. But prices convey information about underlying supply and demand, enabling economic agents to allocate resources efficiently. As long as prices convey accurate information, it is important that they be allowed to fluctuate, rather than being artificially fixed by merchant guilds or privileged companies. This theoretical insight is borne out by evidence on medieval and early modern commerce, which suggests that where competition broke open the monopolies of merchant guilds and privileged companies, the resulting price fluctuations conveyed accurate information and enabled markets to allocate resources more efficiently, in ways that benefited all economic agents – except, perhaps, for members of merchant guilds.

Modern research has refuted the old-fashioned assumption that the pre-modern European economy lacked markets, necessitating concerted action by monopolistic merchants in urban entrepôts to control supply and fix prices by fiat. We now know that pre-industrial people from social circles extending far beyond those of the privileged merchants were involved in markets and responsive to prices. The emerging entrepôts of early modern Europe did enjoy increasingly stable prices. But this was not because they fostered monopolistic merchant guilds and privileged companies which institutionally 'stabilized' these prices. Rather, it was because early modern entrepôts such as Amsterdam gradually broke down the privileges of closed groups of merchants and allowed competition to bring together diverse streams of supply and demand. The notion that merchant guilds and privileged companies benefited the pre-modern economy because they stabilized prices is therefore a chimera.

11 Institutions, social capital and economic development

Merchant guilds are one of the most widespread and long-lasting economic institutions in European history. Their roots reach back to Greek and Roman antiquity, there are persistent indications of their survival through the centuries after the collapse of the western Roman empire, and as soon as documentary sources become richer after *c.* 1000, they can be found in every European economy during the Middle Ages. Local merchant guilds were formed in most medieval European towns, and alien merchant guilds and hanses were formed by many traders operating abroad in foreign lands. Although traditional medieval-style merchant guilds weakened in the Low Countries and England after about 1500, they survived elsewhere into the early modern era, enduring in some societies – particularly in Italy, Iberia and Germany – well into the eighteenth century. In many parts of Europe between *c.* 1500 and *c.* 1800, guild-like merchant associations also formed in new sectors such as the proto-industrial trades. Spain exported its institutions to its overseas empire, and merchant consulados survived in many Spanish American economies until the nineteenth century. And between *c.* 1500 and *c.* 1800 every European state, including England and the Netherlands, formed privileged merchant companies which, for better or worse, became the standard-bearers of European globalization.

Any economic institution that exists so widely and survives for so long raises important questions. For one thing, merchant guilds were nearly (though not quite) omnipresent during the medieval Commercial Revolution of the eleventh to fifteenth centuries, as were privileged merchant companies during the early modern Commercial Revolution after *c.* 1500. Of course, just because merchant guilds and privileged companies were *present* during the growth of long-distance commerce does not necessarily mean they *caused* it. But a number of scholars have advanced just this argument. So scrutinizing the merchant guild as an institution is important for understanding economic growth and globalization between medieval and modern times.

Merchant guilds also play a central role in theories of institutions. Economists, historians, political scientists, sociologists and policy makers, in trying to explain institutions, have focused much attention on merchant guilds. Many describe them as efficient institutions which solved economic problems better than available alternatives and made the whole economy work better. Some portray them as beneficent products of distinctively European or Christian norms and values which fuelled European economic dynamism compared to non-European (especially Islamic) cultures. Merchant guilds have even been placed at the centre of a whole theoretical approach to explaining institutional change in terms of cultural beliefs. So understanding why merchant guilds existed and how they affected the economy has important implications for how we understand institutions more widely.

Merchant guilds are also the most widely discussed historical example of social capital. Social scientists concerned about what they see as the decline of 'trust' have turned to European history in search of the closely knit and multi-stranded social networks believed to foster it. Merchant guilds appear to fit these requirements. So one more reason to investigate merchant guilds is to illuminate the institutional sources of social capital – and its economic consequences.

These issues are intricately interconnected. The first of them – the role of merchant guilds in the medieval and early modern Commercial Revolutions – has been explored throughout this book. We can now draw out the implications of these findings for two broader questions. First, what light do merchant guilds shed on how we explain institutions more generally? And second, what implications do merchant guilds have for the role of social capital in economic development?

11.1   Merchant guilds and theories of institutions

As economists have come to recognize the central role of institutions in economic growth, they have also tried to explain them. Since institutions typically evolve over very long periods, economic models of institutional change frequently seek support in European history – and, surprisingly often, in the history of merchant guilds. So what we discover about merchant guilds has implications for how we explain institutions more broadly.

One influential school of thought, as we have seen, views merchant guilds as supporting an efficiency view of institutions. This is the idea that an institution exists because it solves economic problems better than available alternatives, thereby generating net benefits for the whole economy. Thus Greif, Milgrom and Weingast claim that medieval merchant guilds sustained 'the efficient level of trade' by guaranteeing security.[1] Ewert and Selzer argue that the German Hanse provided Baltic merchants with 'an efficacious as well as an efficient solution to their problems of information and coordination'.[2] Volckart and Mangels suggest that the 'elder' merchant guilds were efficient providers of security and contract enforcement in eleventh- and twelfth-century Europe.[3] Carlos, in separate papers with Nicholas and Kruse, contends that privileged merchant companies were the efficient solution to principal-agent problems and information asymmetries in the early modern intercontinental trade.[4]

Merchant guilds also hold centre stage in cultural theories of institutions. Greif and Aoki, for instance, regard institutions as self-enforcing systems of cultural rules and beliefs, in which the motivation provided by the beliefs of different cultures plays the decisive role.[5] Merchant guilds arose in medieval Italian trading cities such as Genoa, Greif argues, because of distinctively Christian, European beliefs. Oddly, he characterizes these cultural beliefs as 'individualistic', oblivious to the deep roots of European guilds in 'corporatist' values antithetical to the 'individualist' strand of European thought from the twelfth century on.[6] But according to Greif, the 'individualistic' beliefs of the Christian Europeans engendered merchant guilds, while the 'collectivist' values of the 'Maghribi traders' (Jews who had adopted Muslim culture) generated very different merchant organizations. Each culture, he argues, chose the merchant institution that could coexist efficiently with its own beliefs and norms. Fortunately for Europe, according to Greif, its cultural beliefs created the motivations necessary to form merchant guilds, which in turn proved to be economically efficient, leading to economic dominance by the Europeans and decline for the Maghribis and the wider Muslim world.[7] These

---

[1] Greif, Milgrom and Weingast (1994), 748, 752, 753, 766, 767, 768, 769 (on all of which the phrase appears).

[2] Ewert and Selzer (2005), 1 (quotation), 20–1.

[3] Volckart and Mangels (1999), 437–9, 442.

[4] Carlos and Nicholas (1988), 407; Carlos and Kruse (1996), 296, 312; Carlos and Nicholas (1996), 916, 919, 923; Carlos and Nicholas (1990), 854–5, 859.

[5] Greif (2006a), 'places motivation to follow rules – and consequently beliefs and norms – at the center of the analysis' of institutions (p. 39), and states that 'motivation provided by beliefs and norms . . . is the linchpin of institutions' (p. 45). Aoki (2001), 10, defines an institution as 'a self-sustaining system of shared beliefs about a salient way in which the game is repeatedly played'.

[6] For discussion of this antithesis, see, for instance, Wiarda (1997), 9, 15–19, 26, 28, 30–5, 54, 75, 80–3, 98, 128, 131, 133, 138, 145–6, 149; Sibalis (1988), 720–1; Fairchilds (1988), 688, 692; Pelling (2006).

[7] For references to the efficiency-fostering properties of the European merchant guild, see Greif (2006a), 58, 61–3, 71, 74, 79–80, 85–8, 93–4, 96, 98–9, 107, 110–14, 120–3, 247–8.

putative cultural roots of medieval merchant institutions are used to draw lessons for modern economic development: 'the Maghribis' institutions resemble those of contemporary developing countries, whereas the Genoese institutions resemble the developed West, suggesting that the individualistic system may have been more efficient in the long run'.[8]

Here we have two influential theories of institutions in which the European merchant guild is recruited to play a central role. One – the pure efficiency theory – claims that institutions exist because they are the efficient solution to economic problems. The other – the cultural efficiency theory – argues that institutions exist because they are compatible with particular cultural beliefs, but that the right cultural beliefs will give rise to institutions (such as merchant guilds) which are the efficient solution to economic problems.

But are these the only possible explanations for why merchant guilds – or institutions in general – exist? The findings of this book suggest otherwise. As we have seen, the historical evidence provides no support for the view that merchant guilds were the efficient institution for guaranteeing commercial security, ensuring contract enforcement, solving principal-agent problems, correcting failures in information markets or stabilizing prices. Not only is there no evidence that merchant guilds made a significant contribution to enhancing efficiency in any of these spheres, but there is clear evidence that alternative institutional arrangements existed and were voluntarily chosen by medieval and early modern merchants to deal with these problems. Merchant guilds cannot, therefore, have been efficient. Their prevalence in medieval and early modern Europe supports neither a 'pure efficiency' nor a 'cultural efficiency' account of institutions.

But what is the alternative? If merchant guilds were not efficient, why did they survive in so many economies for such long periods? The answer can be found, as we saw in Chapter 5, in the distributional services guilds offered to two powerful groups. Merchant guilds provided a mechanism whereby merchants and rulers could collaborate to extract more resources for themselves at the expense of the rest of the economy. Rulers gave merchant guilds leverage to extract monopoly profits from commerce through exclusive trading privileges, as we saw in Chapters 3 and 4. In return, as Chapter 5 discussed, merchant guilds gave rulers leverage to extract extra revenues from subjects through cash transfers, favourable loans, fiscal help, military assistance and political support. In short, rulers enabled guilded merchants to transcend the limits placed by economic competition on their ability to extract profit

---

[8] *Ibid.*, 300–1.

from trade, while merchant guilds enabled rulers to transcend the technical and political limits on their ability to extract resources from subjects. Merchant guilds existed in so many economies for such a long time not because they were efficient in solving commercial problems in ways that benefited everyone, but because they were effective in enabling influential social groups to transfer resources to their own members, at the expense of the wider economy.

What does this imply for our theories of economic institutions? Not only do these findings cast doubt on both efficiency and cultural efficiency theories, but they show the direction in which to seek an alternative – a conflict or distributional approach. Institutions, after all, affect not just the efficiency of an economy (the size of the total economic pie) but also how its resources are distributed (who gets how big a slice). Most people might well want the pie to be as big as possible – the assumption of the efficiency theorists. But they will typically disagree about how to share out the slices. They may also disagree about what kind of pie it should be, since different people place different weights on various measures of well-being – material consumption, leisure, longevity, reproduction, environmental amenities, social equality, political freedom, religious observance and so on. Since institutions affect not only the size of the pie (through influencing efficiency) but also the type of pie it is (through establishing who is entitled to allocate inputs) and the distribution of the slices (through apportioning the output), people typically disagree about which institutions are best. This causes conflict. Some people strive to maintain particular institutions, others merely cooperate, others quietly sabotage them and still others resist. Which institution (or set of institutions) results from this conflict will be affected not just by its efficiency but by its distributional implications for the most powerful social groups, which can use their existing endowments to coerce other groups into accepting their favoured institutional outcomes.[9]

In so far as we can draw implications from the European merchant guild for general theories of economic institutions, therefore, these point in one direction – conflicts over distribution strongly influence which institutions arise and survive. Any approach to institutions that ignores their distributional activities is inadequate in theory, incompatible with the facts and, if used to recommend policies, dangerous in practice.

But our findings on European merchant guilds have even broader implications. An institution typically does many things. Theories of

---

[9] For different distributional views of institutions, see Knight (1995), 107–10, 117–18; Acemoglu, Johnson and Robinson (2005), 389–95, 427–8; Ogilvie (2007b), 662–7.

efficiency or cultural efficiency generally focus on one single aspect of an institution in isolation, claiming that efficiency in that particular activity explains the institution's survival. But people typically use a given institution for many purposes. Most of the ways an institution is used will affect efficiency, whether positively or negatively. Moreover, its efficient and inefficient activities are generally not separable; an institution comes as a package. In general, an institution can only do the efficient things it does (if any) by virtue of the other things it does (which may turn out to be inefficient). So even if a certain institution did one thing that increased efficiency, we would have to weigh up the effects of *all* its activities before concluding that it was efficient in any general sense.

The dangers of ignoring institutions' multiple activities are vividly shown by accounts of merchant guilds that focus solely on those of their activities that are supposed to have made trade more efficient: providing security, enforcing contracts, controlling agents, gathering information, stabilizing prices. Leaving aside whether these guild activities actually took place – an idea this book has questioned – we must ask what *else* guilds did. As we have seen, merchant guilds engaged in a whole range of activities. They undertook rent-seeking, lobbied rulers for legal privileges to trade exclusively in certain wares and locations, excluded non-members from trade and restricted competition among members. They limited entry by making guild membership impossible for many – Jews, women, foreigners – and expensive for everyone else. They celebrated festivities, organized cultural spectacles and participated in common worship. They helped rulers collect taxes, made favourable state loans, organized and financed military expeditions, participated in local government and arbitrated in commercial disputes. They engaged in prolonged, costly and violent struggles against rival merchant guilds, craft guilds and individual interlopers. Although some of these activities may have been economically neutral, some of them – especially barriers to entry, limits on competition, and rent-seeking were inefficient, harming the wider economy.

It might be argued that merchant guilds varied enormously across Europe. Surely not all of them necessarily engaged in efficiency-reducing activities? But this raises two questions. First, were merchant guilds' efficiency-enhancing activities separable from their efficiency-reducing ones? Even efficiency theorists tacitly acknowledge that they were not. If a ruler failed to guarantee commercial security, for instance, a merchant guild could credibly threaten an embargo only if that guild exercised some market power in that ruler's polity. It could force its members to comply with such an embargo only by securing their loyalty with monopoly profits and penalizing those who sought to free-ride.[10] Like-wise, enforcing contracts through collective reprisals or solving agency problems through collective punishments required merchant guilds to regulate admission, motivate members with monopoly profits and penalize free-riders by excluding them from benefits. To coordinate members so as to negotiate credibly with rulers, or to 'stabilize' prices, a merchant guild had to enjoy the legal right to intervene in markets.

This raises a second question: why would merchant guilds refrain from seeking monopoly profits to which they were legally entitled and which would benefit their members? Once a merchant guild had legal rights to exercise market power, why should it refrain from using that power to redistribute resources in favour of its members, even if that reduced aggregate welfare in the economy at large?

A general lesson to emerge from analysis of the merchant guild is that a given institution will typically engage in a variety of activities, which all have to be assessed and may not be separable.[11] Efficiency in one sphere may only be generated at the cost of inefficiency in another.

A further lesson to emerge from investigating merchant guilds is that institutions can operate to exclude many people from their benefits – or even from entire spheres of economic activity. Merchant guilds were 'limited-access' institutions that coercively prevented the vast mass of the population from engaging in particular activities, in order to create monopoly profits for tiny, powerful elites. Limiting economic access affects not only distribution but efficiency. It reduces the volume of economic activity in the formal sector and creates incentives for the excluded to violate institutional rules by moving into the informal sector. Informal economic activity is better than none at all, but typically involves higher costs and risks than if the same agents could do the same things using formal institutions. So a key feature of any formal institution is the size and nature of the informal sector it creates.[12]

This is vividly illustrated by merchant guilds, which defined trading as an exclusive 'privilege', reserved it solely for members and excluded many applicants for admission. Even when guild restrictions were evaded, evasion was not without cost, as we saw in Chapters 3 and 4. Non-members of the guild who sought to trade illegally had to avoid official notice, work in the black market, forego legal protection for fear of being

---

[10] Greif (2006a), 100–5, for instance, describes merchant guilds' ability to put pressure on rulers as depending on their ability to motivate members through ensuring a stream of monopoly rents.

[11] Indeed, for the reasons discussed in Chapter 4, they are unlikely to separable in the type of schema proposed in Grafe and Gelderblom (2010a).

[12] Batini et al. (2010); Schneider (2006); ILO (1989); De Soto (1989).

prosecuted and constantly evade confiscation, fines, prison, violence and expulsion. Women, Jews, foreigners and other outsiders who illegally traded in wares, transaction types, routes or destinations reserved for guild members faced difficulties in enforcing contracts and risked sanctions if detected. Illegality was so costly that interlopers often tried to meet guild entry requirements, which were in turn fixed at prohibitive levels precisely to exclude applicants, limit membership and generate monopoly profits for insiders.

The informal sector does offer the excluded – often a majority in society – opportunities better than those they can obtain under formal, limited-access institutions. But these opportunities are still poor. The informal sector does have huge economic dynamism, compared to the costly rigidities imposed by limited-access institutions in the formal sector. But unless this dynamism breaks open formal-sector institutions – which non-guilded interlopers did not succeed in doing to merchant guilds until after 1500, and then only in some parts of Europe – economic growth emanating from the informal sector will be choked off by poor contract enforcement and property rights. In the informal sector, risks are high, information is poor, violence and theft are common, time horizons are short, workers are unprotected and investments in physical and human capital are limited.[13] Formal institutions that create large informal sectors thus impose inefficiencies on the whole economy. They may also block economic change. As Dasgupta points out, informal institutions in less developed economies may bring benefits, but their continued existence may also block the emergence of more productive social arrangements such as formal markets and impersonal states.[14]

The history of merchant guilds shows that any adequate theory of institutions must assess them in terms of the shadow they cast – the share of economic activity they push into the informal sector. Where formal institutions limit access – as merchant guilds did – they create large informal sectors because they turn entire social groups into potential lawbreakers. Efficiency models usually assume that institutions such as guilds generated benefits for insiders which spilled over as positive externalities for the rest of society – that guilds created the basis for later market economies. But what if it was the reverse? Closed-access institutions, to generate more enticing rents for insiders, had strong incentives to push economic activity into the informal sector, strangling economic growth.

---

[13] See Ogilvie (2007b), 671–4; Batini et al. (2010); Schneider (2006); ILO (1989); De Soto (1989).
[14] Dasgupta (2003), 310.

When merchant guilds acted in this way, their externalities for the rest of the economy were not positive, but negative.

The history of merchant guilds has one final implication for theories of economic institutions: we must take account of the wider institutional framework. Existing theories of economic institutions typically focus on one institution at a time, but institutions do not exist in isolation. In practice, they are held in place by an interconnected framework of other institutions. Typically, the institutions of a society have coexisted for centuries, continually working out a division of activities, supporting one another in all sorts of ways. These ways may not necessarily be efficient, but they are often self-sustaining.

This is vividly exemplified by European merchant guilds which, as this book has shown, can only be understood within the wider framework of pre-modern institutions. The claim that merchant guilds were the efficient institutions for providing security, enforcing contracts, solving agency problems, managing information or stabilizing prices implies there were no alternative institutions that could do these things so well. But as this book has shown, during the medieval and early modern Commercial Revolutions merchants solved all these problems using a rich array of institutional tools emanating from princes, urban governments, feudal lordships, religious bodies, legal systems, educational arrangements and markets – to name just a few.

This can be seen in the provision of commercial security which, as Chapter 6 discussed, was by the eleventh century being supplied in European societies by a whole array of interconnected institutional arrangements. To the extent that merchant guilds did not actually *reduce* commercial security through conflicts undertaken to defend their privileges, they played a minor role in this institutional system by providing security for their own members as a club good. It was *other* components of the institutional framework – particularly urban governments and princely states – that constituted the true innovation in the medieval Commercial Revolution. They began, in however gradual and piecemeal a way, to provide commercial security in a generalized way to a wide range of economic agents, rather than in a particularized way solely to members of privileged guilds. These developments were, if anything, resisted by merchant guilds, whose members wanted municipal and princely governments to provide security to members of the guild, but preferably deny it to outsiders. Although merchant guilds were able to put pressure on town governments and rulers, as we saw in Chapter 5, they did so as part of a bargain in which they reserved their bargaining counters for the favours they wanted most – commercial monopolies. Municipal and princely governments found that they could extract more favours if they granted different monopoly privileges to multiple merchant guilds, and provided commercial security to them all, so as to attract more traders to their territories. Some political authorities – the twelfth-century counts of Champagne, the fourteenth-century rulers of Bruges, the sixteenth-century rulers of Amsterdam and London – even calculated that they could benefit most by providing commercial security to all merchants, whether or not they were members of guilds, and then taxing them once they arrived. As we saw in Chapter 6, long-distance commerce flourished to the extent that the political authorities provided security as a public good to all rather than as a corporate privilege to members of closed merchant associations.

The same was true of contract enforcement, as we saw in Chapter 7. Not only did merchant guilds play an insignificant role in enforcing trading contracts, but from the earliest decades of the medieval Commercial Revolution merchants used a rich array of alternative mechanisms to deter and penalize contract-breaking. These included using legal instruments such as pledges and cessions of credit, registering contracts in writing, certifying agreements through notarial systems and urban offices, submitting to formal arbitration panels and litigating in public law-courts provided by towns, religious bodies, lords and princes. That is, pre-modern European societies had developed multiple institutions offering different types of informal, quasi-formal and formal enforcement to suit different types of commercial contract – an interdependent institutional system, within which merchant guilds were only one, quite minor component. It was other components of this system – particularly the new business instruments and the emerging public law-courts – that gradually began to offer contract enforcement to anyone, regardless of guild membership. If anything, merchant guilds resisted such changes, trying to compel their members to use guild courts and putting pressure on local judges to discriminate against foreigners. As we saw in Chapter 7, commerce expanded to the extent that some municipal and princely governments perceived a benefit in permitting public courts to overrule guild courts and providing contract enforcement that was impartial and accessible to all, even non-members of merchant guilds.

A similar pattern can be seen with principal-agent problems. As Chapter 8 showed, from the eleventh century on European merchants used a whole range of legal instruments – partnerships, firms, employment contracts and correspondent relationships – enabling principals and agents to enter into formal agreements about precisely how each party was supposed to behave. These legal agreements were increasingly recorded in writing, both inside merchant businesses and by outside parties such as notaries, brokers and hostellers. Such market institutions were made more effective by state-provided ones such as legal recognition of notarized documents, official registration of agency contracts with municipal offices and punishment of fraudulent agents in public law-courts. Pre-modern merchants thus had at their disposal an array of institutions offering different types of solution to the principal-agent problem, which could be adapted to their precise commercial requirements. These institutions existed simultaneously in an interdependent system, within which merchant guilds played quite a minor role. It was other components of this framework – contractual forms, new business methods, legal enforcement, official record-keeping – that constituted the true institutional innovations, offering services available to all, not just members of privileged guilds.

For collecting and transmitting information, likewise alternative institutions existed simultaneously with merchant guilds and were preferred by merchants. From the eleventh century on, as Chapter 9 showed, commercial information was provided through locational clusters, notarial and brokerage systems, informal merchant correspondence, formal correspondent relationships, courier services and legal forms of enterprise. As the medieval period passed, these were enhanced by newsletters, price lists, business manuals, multi-branch firms, bourses and exchanges. Public institutions – especially town governments and princely bureaucracies – provided legal support and official enforcement for these market arrangements. Again, these various institutional mechanisms coexisted in an interdependent system, within which merchant guilds were relatively unimportant. And again it was other components of this institutional system – literacy, correspondence, notaries, firms, bourses, public records – that offered the institutional innovations. If anything, merchant guilds resisted such changes, seeking to reserve commercial information for their own members rather than sharing it more widely, censoring information they regarded as part of their guild 'mysteries' and even trying to deny the services of brokers and notaries to those who could not demonstrate guild membership or who violated guild rules. For the most part, however, these institutional innovations were ones that could not be monopolized by closed merchant associations, but instead offered information services to all, regardless of guild affiliation.

The transparency and stability of prices, too, was supported by an interdependent framework of institutions during the medieval Commercial Revolution. As we saw in Chapter 10, integrated markets and political centralization kept price volatility relatively low in north-west Europe from the thirteenth century on, at least compared to the Mediterranean or the Near East.[15] Within this institutional structure, merchant guilds played a role that was, if anything, counter-productive, since by limiting the number of traders legally permitted to operate, they made supply chains more vulnerable to shocks. The trade barriers and market segmentation which merchant guilds encouraged and profited from may be one reason why price volatility in north-west Europe, though already relatively low in the thirteenth century, did not fall significantly before the sixteenth.[16] It was only after c. 1500, and in large urban entrepôts, such as Amsterdam, where merchant guilds were not permitted to operate, that price volatility began to subside. When it did decline, it was not because of merchant monopolies, but rather because long-distance trade was opened up to diverse streams of supply and demand, enabling prices to be negotiated continuously and reducing their vulnerability to shocks striking a single supplier. Such permanent markets were sustained and supported by public institutions which guaranteed property rights, enforced contracts and gradually drew back from enforcing the kind of monopolistic privileges that had previously prevented market integration.

These findings on the European merchant guild illustrate how wildly astray an analysis can go if it focuses on a single institution while ignoring the wider institutional framework. Claiming that one institution is efficient implies that there are no more adequate alternatives, a claim that cannot be sustained unless one analyses the whole framework of institutions available to people in that economy. Arguing that a particular institution is efficient also ignores the effect of institutions on each other – especially the understandable attempts of closed-access institutions to defend the privileges of their members against institutional innovations that threaten to open up trade to all comers.

The history of the European merchant guild also suggests that the *existence* of an institution can be explained only by placing it in the wider institutional framework. Merchant guilds were so widespread, as Chapter 5 showed, because they offered an effective way for two important groups in medieval society – guilded merchants and rulers – to collaborate to extract resources from the rest of society. Merchants valued the exclusive privileges their guilds enabled them to negotiate from rulers precisely because they inhabited a wider society in which other institutional developments – particularly the dynamism of markets and the emergence of generalized legal systems – were threatening to open commerce to wider social groups. The privileges they got from rulers helped guilded

---

[15] Söderberg (2004), 7–15, 17.   [16] *Ibid.*, 15, 17.

merchants to protect their monopoly profits against the competition arising from the growth of open-access institutions. Likewise, rulers valued
the benefits they received from guilded merchants precisely because they
inhabited a wider institutional framework in which they were seeking to
establish a monopoly of coercion vis-à-vis their own nobles and other
princes who might make claims to their domains and revenues. It was
the threats and opportunities created by this wider institutional framework of developing markets, legal systems and political coercion that
motivated both merchants and rulers to invest in maintaining merchant
guilds.

The general lesson is that interdependencies among institutions are
widespread. We cannot study one institution in isolation, but must analyse entire institutional frameworks. When we do, we may find that
there are inherent complementarities causing whole clusters of institutions to be mutually reinforcing. Some self-reinforcing institutional
frameworks may be efficient, but others may be inefficient. In modern
developing economies, for instance, retention of existing techniques and
institutions despite alternatives that are known to be more productive is
widely ascribed to *institutional interlinkages* among markets. Any innovation would disequilibrate an entire system of interlinked markets, and
so is rejected unless it provides substitutes for everything it threatens to
displace and compensation to the most powerful losers.[17] One reason
merchant guilds survived in certain European societies long after 1500
was that they were held in place by other institutions of those societies
which benefited from their continued existence, even in situations in
which many individual merchants might have preferred to dissolve guild
powers.

The European merchant guild thus has fundamental implications for
how we explain and analyse economic institutions. First, explaining institutions in terms of their pure economic efficiency or their cultural efficiency is inadequate – we must take account of how institutions influence distribution and motivate conflict. Second, we must investigate all
the activities of any institution and assess all its economic effects. Third,
we must examine how an institution limits access and pushes economic
activity into the informal sector. And finally, we must recognize that any
institution is embedded in a broader institutional framework that itself
requires economic analysis. These lessons from analysing the history of
the merchant guild may make our analyses of institutions more complicated, but they are indispensable for explaining how economies and
institutions actually behave and develop.

[17] See the discussion in Basu (1997), esp. 287–316.

11.2   Merchant guilds and social capital

Merchant guilds are not just widespread institutions of the pre-modern economy, interesting to economic historians and theorists. They are also a major historical example of social capital. As we saw in Chapter 1, merchant guilds are widely portrayed as having used their closely knit and multi-stranded internal relationships to generate the social capital and trust needed for economic development. So what implications do merchant guilds have for how we think about trust and social capital more generally?

Social capital is defined as a store of value that is generated when a group of people invests in fostering a body of relationships with each other – a social network such as a guild or other cohesive community.[18] The returns to social capital fall into four categories, each of which is believed to enhance trust in the wider society. Social networks foster shared *norms*, it is argued, creating expectations of trustworthiness which reduce the costs associated with violation of agreements. They improve *information* flow, it is claimed, fostering the trust necessary to solve market failures caused by incomplete or asymmetric information. Social networks are also held to generate the trust that facilitates group *sanctions* against deviations from the norms of the network. Finally, networks are supposed to create the trust that overcomes obstacles to *collective action* against outside threats.[19]

According to this view, all four forms of value associated with social capital – norm fostering, information flow, deviance sanctioning and collective action – have strong 'public good' characteristics. Individual investors in social capital enjoy only part of the benefits, so they may allocate too few resources to generating them.[20] To the extent that social capital is a public good, there is a case for public action to create, subsidize or privilege social networks, whether to substitute for states or markets or to make them work better.[21] Investing in social capital and social networks – rather than, for instance, effective states and efficient markets – is often recommended as a solution to economic problems, especially in developing economies. These policy implications make it particularly

---

[18] Scepticism has been expressed about the analogy with capital as it is ordinarily conceived by economists: see Arrow (2000), 4; Solow (2000), 7–8.

[19] J. S. Coleman (1989); Dasgupta (2003); Gambetta (1988a); Gambetta (1988b); Narayan and Pritchett (2000); R. D. Putnam, Leonardi and Nanetti (1993).

[20] J. S. Coleman (1989), S115–S119; Dasgupta (1988), 64.

[21] United Nations Development Program (1993), 8; World Bank (1994), i; Brett (1996), esp. 5–6.

important to look closely at networks and institutions – such as merchant guilds – that are supposed to foster social capital.

What kind of institution is best at creating social capital? Coleman, one of the earliest theorists focusing on this question, postulated that social capital is generated by networks possessing two key features: closure and multiplex relationships. 'Closure' means that network membership is clearly defined, so that members' actions can be easily monitored, norm-violating behaviour effectively punished and norm-compliant behaviour collectively rewarded. 'Multiplex relationships' refer to the fact that members of tightly knit networks typically engage in transactions with one another that encompass different spheres of activity – economic, social, political, religious. This generates multi-stranded ties giving members multiple means of sharing norms with, getting information about, punishing deviance in and urging collective action on one another.[22]

European merchant guilds confirm Coleman's insights about the importance of closure and multiplex relationships for generating social capital. Merchant guilds, as we saw in Chapters 3 and 4, carefully rationed membership. They were not wholly closed to new members, but they limited the quantity and selected the qualities of new entrants. Many members of the wider society had a high probability (or, if female, near certainty) of never being admitted to these networks and thus never enjoying the benefits of any social capital they generated. Merchant guilds also fostered multiplex relationships. Members were linked not just through shared occupation, as we saw in Chapter 1, but through multi-stranded ties extending into residential propinquity, leisure, sociability, worship, politics, charity, intermarriage and kinship. Merchant guilds thus confirm Coleman's insight that closure and multiplex relationships are strongly associated with generating social capital and trust – at least trust of a certain kind.

But not all forms of trust are the same – and this is one of the most important insights to emerge from scrutinizing merchant guilds. Trust takes different forms, which play fundamentally different economic roles. For one thing, there are two distinct kinds of trust in persons; a 'particularized' trust in persons of known attributes or affiliations, and a 'generalized' trust that applies even to complete strangers. Particularized trust depends on specific personal attributes or affiliations of your transaction partner. You are willing to enter into a transaction because you either know the other party personally or he is a member of a group whose other members you trust as a result of knowing their personal

[22] J. S. Coleman (1989), S104–S110.

attributes.[23] Generalized trust, by contrast, is a propensity to enter into transactions with all persons on an equal footing, even with strangers – people of whose characteristics or affiliations you are ignorant. It is this generalized trust in strangers which social scientists find particularly interesting, since it has wide social and economic benefits – indeed, is essential for sustained economic growth and development.[24] The unspoken assumption of the social capital literature is that a particularized trust in people who are members of your social network (e.g. your merchant guild) somehow encourages a generalized trust in people you do not know, and that this makes states and markets work better.[25] But European merchant guilds raise serious doubts about this assumption, as we shall see.

A second and even more crucial distinction is between two very different kinds of trust in institutions – a particularized trust in institutions with closure (institutions mainly trusted by their members), and a generalized trust in 'open-access' institutions (ones whose provisions apply to anyone). Particularized trust is a propensity to allow your transactions to be mediated by a particular institution because it can be trusted to enforce your *particular* rights and privileges. Thus, for instance, a medieval European merchant might allow his transactions to be mediated by his merchant guild because he trusted it to enforce his particular rights and entitlements as a guild member. Generalized trust, by contrast, is a propensity to allow your transactions to be mediated by an institution because it can be trusted to enforce *anyone*'s rights and privileges in an impartial way, regardless of personal attributes. Thus, for instance, an efficient market or a just state is supposed to mediate the transactions of any economic agent impartially, without regard to any personal characteristic appertaining to the individual (such as gender, ethnicity, religion, occupation or guild membership); the only consideration is the nature of the transaction in question (its property rights, legality and so on).

It is this generalized trust in institutions as being impartial, fair and accessible to all members of society which the social capital literature – and theories of economic development based on it – emphasize as a desirable, long-term outcome. But the immediate priorities of the social capital literature are guilds, associations, communities and

[23] For a description of this kind of trust in the context of the Italian mafia, see Gambetta (1988b), 165–6.

[24] On the centrality of generalized trust to the social capital literature, see Stolle and Hooghe (2003), 232–3; on the origins of generalized trust in persons who are strangers, see Seabright (2004).

[25] For cogent criticisms of the failure of social capital theory to substantiate this assumption, see Stolle and Hooghe (2003), 236–7.

clubs – institutions that generate a particularized trust, a perception that they are specifically accessible to certain groups, generating a propensity among their members to allow transactions to be mediated by these institutions because they can be trusted to enforce members' particular rights and privileges. The tacit assumption in much of the literature seems to be that encouraging a particularized trust in group-specific institutions such as guilds will somehow encourage generalized trust in impartial institutions such as markets and governments.[26]

But is it indeed true that particularized trust in other guild members and in the institution of one's merchant guild favoured the transition to generalized trust in strangers and in impartial institutions – the sort of trust which social scientists regard as important for economic development? Or was this transition – so crucial to the development of European economies between the Middle Ages and the Industrial Revolution – actually brought about by a quite different type of institution?

This book has found that merchant guilds fostered a particularized, not a generalized, trust in persons. Members of a merchant guild trusted each other and were willing to transact with each other because of the personal attributes associated with membership in that guild, and because the guild itself penalized deviations from corporate norms. As we saw in Chapters 3 and 4, merchant guilds defined certain wares, transactions, routes and destinations as being the exclusive privilege of guild members, and forbade members to transact with anyone who did not share in the appropriate guild entitlement. As Chapter 6 showed, merchant guilds fostered not only distrust of strangers but violence against them, by defining trade as the exclusive privileges of guild members and creating incentives to attack rival guilds and non-guilded interlopers. As we saw in Chapter 7, collective guild reprisals compelled guild members to trust one another in order to avoid outside condemnation and created an incentive to penalize any member who engaged in an activity that might attract such external attacks. Chapter 8 showed that in so far as merchant guilds solved agency problems through internal ostracism, as the German Hanse is supposed to have done, they discouraged agency relationships with outsiders. As Chapter 9 discussed, information relevant to branches of trade defined as the exclusive privileges of a given guild was entrusted only to other members of that guild, and denied to outsiders. Merchant guilds thus did not create a generalized trust in persons, encouraging transactions with strangers. If anything, they did the opposite. Merchant guilds blocked generalized trust by fostering a defensive mistrust between

---

[26] For evidence on modern economies, questioning whether social capital goes beyond fostering a particularized trust in associative institutions to generating a generalized trust in impartial (e.g. state) institutions, see Stolle and Hooghe (2003), 236–40.

guild members and anyone they suspected of threatening their special privileges.

Merchant guilds also fostered a particularized, not a generalized, trust in institutions. A merchant guild encouraged its members to trust the guild alone to negotiate on their behalf with rulers, to guarantee them exclusive trading privileges, to provide defence against outside attacks, to resolve commercial conflicts in guild courts, to collect and process commercial information and to 'stabilize' prices and supplies. Merchants who tried to negotiate independently with rulers could be ostracized or expelled by their guilds. Merchants who sought profits through market transactions that violated guild regulations on prices and quotas faced collective penalties. Merchants who took their conflicts to municipal or state courts were penalized by their guilds. Merchants who transacted independently in commercial information were regarded as betraying the 'mysteries' of the guild. And merchants who sought stability of prices and supply through open market transactions rather than observing the monopolistic regulations of their guilds were penalized for violating guild norms.

Merchant guilds thus did not create a generalized trust in institutions by encouraging traders to allow transactions to be mediated by institutions that impartially enforced *anyone*'s rights and privileges, regardless of personal attributes. Rather, they sought to maintain the corporative pattern, whereby one mediated one's transactions exclusively through a certain institution because it could be trusted to enforce the *particular* rights and privileges of the corporate group to which one belonged. In so far as merchant guilds are exemplars of the closely knit associative networks emphasized in the social capital literature, therefore, they do not support the view that such networks encourage the transition to generalized trust.

If anything, the evidence on merchant guilds suggests the reverse – that particularized trust is often a *substitute* for generalized trust. Associative institutions such as merchant guilds foster a particularized trust in persons of known attributes, and this can hinder the spread of the generalized trust in strangers which is essential for societies to adapt and economies to grow. Privileged, guild-like networks foster a particularized trust in institutions that enforce the rights of certain groups, and this can block the development of a generalized trust in impartial institutions that are open to all – even those lacking network-specific privileges.[27] In so far as merchant guilds did act, for instance, to ensure commercial

---

[27] On the role of reliable markets and impartial states in creating generalized, uniform trust to supplant the particularized, differential trust fostered by associative organizations such as mafias, see Gambetta (1988b), 167.

security, enforce contracts, solve agency problems, provide information or stabilize prices, they did so for their members but not for outsiders. This did not translate into a generalized trust in strangers or in impersonal, open-access institutions within the wider economy.

The findings of this book suggest, by contrast, that generalized trust was associated with the gradual emergence of impersonal markets and impartial states – often at the *expense* of special privileges enjoyed by institutions such as merchant guilds. A generalized trust in hitherto unknown transaction partners could arise when one knew that one's transactions would be mediated by an institutional framework that recognized property rights and contracts regardless of attributes of the contracting parties. Knowledge of the personal characteristics or group affiliations of transaction partners was unnecessary because one could be confident that impersonal markets were conveying reliable information and that where that information was faulty and a contract was violated, an impartial legal system would punish the offending party.

Thus, as we saw in Chapter 6, it was not the particularistic guarantees of protection to specific guilds of privileged merchants but piecemeal moves towards uniform guarantees of protection to all economic agents regardless of their ability to gain membership in guilds, which improved the security of trade in twelfth-century Champagne, fourteenth-century Bruges or sixteenth-century Amsterdam. As Chapter 7 showed, it was not the particularistic enforcement of contracts provided by merchant guilds to their members, but gradual development of business methods and impartial legal systems, which enforced long-distance trading contracts on a generalized basis for all economic agents. Chapter 8 suggested that it was not the particularistic ostracism of fraudulent agents by merchant guilds, but the gradual emergence of impersonal contractual forms and notarial registration, supported by impartial public law-enforcement and record-keeping available to all, which helped solve agency problems in long-distance trade. As Chapter 9 showed, commercial information was provided to long-distance traders not by particularized collection and diffusion through merchant guilds, but by generalized institutions such as correspondence, legal forms of enterprise, notarial and brokerage systems, bourses and exchanges, supported and legitimized by impartial legal systems. As we saw in Chapter 10, price volatility fell, not through the monopolistic fiat of particularized merchant guilds but through the emergence of markets and legal institutions accessible to any economic agent. Corporative institutions such as merchant guilds, with their social capital of particularized trust, played a minor and peripheral role in facilitating long-distance trade, compared to impersonal and impartial institutions which gradually widened the sphere of generalized trust that was independent of social capital.

The history of merchant guilds not only shows that particularized trust failed to nurture the generalized trust needed for economic growth. It also suggests that particularized trust fostered abusive practices. Closure and multiplex relationships enabled merchant guilds to sustain norms privileging a status quo that benefited insiders and discriminated against outsiders. Merchant guilds punished advantageous as well as harmful deviations from their norms and suppressed entrepreneurial behaviour that could have benefited the wider society. Information was conveyed to trusted insiders but denied to outsiders. Network membership became a trusted signal ensuring the long-term exclusion of productive economic agents such as women, Jews, migrants and the lower social strata, thereby sustaining economic discrimination. Collective action enabled guilds to seek monopoly profits and distort markets, harming outsiders and the wider society. Merchant guilds enabled their members to transcend the limits imposed by competition on their ability to extract profit from trade and enabled rulers to transcend the limits imposed by politics on their ability to extract resources from subjects. The particularized trust generated by merchant guilds enabled mercantile and political elites to redistribute resources to themselves, imposing costs on outsiders and damaging the economy as a whole. As this book has shown, the very features that enable social networks such as merchant guilds to generate particularized trust also enable them to act collusively against the common good.[28]

The final lesson from the history of the European merchant guild is at once the most important and most disquieting, especially for modern developing economies. Even an institution that generates trust, efficiency or other benefits in a given state of technology, costs and incomes, may cease to do so when constraints change. Precisely the particularized trust fostered by social capital may encourage conservatism. Thus the guild-dominated societies of Italy, Iberia and German-speaking central Europe were unable to adjust to the rapid institutional, commercial and demographic changes of the sixteenth century. They lost out to the market-oriented civic culture of the Low Countries and England with their increasingly impersonal markets and impartial states, which encouraged forms of generalized trust that favoured adaptation and growth. The weakening of the particularized trust generated by associative institutions such as merchant guilds created interstices in English and Dutch society

---

[28] As pointed out for modern developing economies by Dasgupta (2000), 367; and for pre-modern European economies by Ogilvie (2005).

within which people could experiment with generalized trust in strangers mediated by impersonal markets and impartial states. This cannot be regarded as an accident. To generate social capital and the particularized forms of trust it fosters, social networks need to have closure, information advantages, collective penalties and commitment devices. Once these are in place, it is hard to prevent them from being abused to resist changes that threaten existing benefits enjoyed by network members.

Even in medieval and early modern Europe, where constraints changed quite slowly, the particularized trust fostered by social networks could prove a long-term economic obstacle. Nowadays, constraints change immeasurably faster. In such a world, one must question whether poor economies can afford the inflexibility of entrenched social networks that foster particularized trust rather than impersonal, open-access institutions where trust must be more generalized. Institutions that generate social capital foster forms of trust that may bring some benefits in less developed economies. But the continued existence of such institutions may also prevent the rise of more productive social arrangements such as impersonal markets and states. It is precisely the strength of social networks – their favouring of trust in insiders and their fostering of internal commitment devices – that may be their greatest weakness, not merely for outsiders to the networks (although these are often the poorest in society), but also for the economy at large. For the particularized trust fostered by institutions such as merchant guilds, the lessons of history are bleak. But the history of merchant guilds also casts light on the alternatives – open-access institutions that generate the trust in strangers which, although less visible or emotionally sustaining than trust in neighbours, is a more secure foundation for economic adaptation and growth.

Bibliography

Abulafia, D. (1978). 'Pisan commercial colonies and consulates in twelfth-century Sicily', *English Historical Review*, **93**, 68–81.

— (1986a). 'The Anconitan privileges in the Kingdom of Jerusalem and the Levant trade of Ancona', in *I comuni italiani nel regno crociato die Gerusalemme*, ed. G. Airaldi and B. Z. Kedar, Genoa, 525–70.

— (1986b). 'The merchants of Messina: Levant trade and domestic economy', *Papers of the British School at Rome*, **54**, 196–212.

— (1987a). 'A Tyrrhenian triangle: Tuscany, Sicily, Tunis, 1276–1300', in *Studi di storia economica toscana nel Medioevo e nel Rinascimento in memoria die Federigo Melis*, ed. C. Violante, Pisa, 53–75.

— (1987b). 'Asia, Africa, and the trade of medieval Europe', in *The Cambridge Economic History of Europe, Vol. 3: Economic Organization and Policies in the Middle Ages*, ed. M. M. Postan and E. Miller, Cambridge, 402–73.

— (1988). 'The Levant trade of the minor cities in the thirteenth and fourteenth centuries: strengths and weaknesses', *Asian and African Studies*, **22**, 183–202.

— (1990). 'The crown and the economy under Ferrante I of Naples (1458–94)', in *City and Countryside in Late Medieval and Renaissance Italy: Essays Presented to Philip Jones*, ed. T. Dean and C. Wickham, London, 125–46.

— (1995). 'Trade and crusade, 1050–1250', in *Cross Cultural Convergences in the Crusader Period: Essays Presented to Aryeh Grabois on His Sixty-fifth Birthday*, ed. M. Goodich, S. Menache and S. Schein, New York, 1–20.

— (1997). 'East and west: comments on the commerce of the city of Ancona in the Middle Ages', in *Città e sistema adriatico alla fine del medioevo. Bilancio degli studi e prospettive di ricerca*, ed. M. P. Ghezzo, Padua, 49–66.

— (1999). 'Grain traffic out of the Apulian ports on behalf of Lorenzo de'Medici, 1486–7', in *Karissime Gotifride. Historical Essays Presented to Professor Godfrey Wettinger on His Seventieth Birthday*, ed. P. Xuereb, Malta, 25–36.

— (2000a). 'Introduction', in *The New Cambridge Medieval History, Vol. V: c. 1198–c. 1300*, ed. D. Abulafia, Cambridge, 1–10.

— (2000b). 'The rise of Aragon-Catalonia', *The New Cambridge Medieval History, Vol. V: c. 1198–c. 1300*, ed. D. Abulafia, Cambridge, 644–67.

Acemoglu, D. (2006). 'A simple model of inefficient institutions', *Scandinavian Journal of Economics*, **108**(4), 515–46.

— (2010). 'Institutions, factor prices and taxation: virtues of strong states?', *MIT Department of Economics Working Papers*, 10–02.

—, S. Johnson and J. A. Robinson (2005). 'Institutions as a fundamental cause of long-run growth', in *Handbook of Economic Growth*, ed. P. Aghion and S. Durlauf, Amsterdam / London, Vol. 1A, 385–472.

Adelman, J. (2007). *Sovereignty and Revolution in the Iberian Atlantic*, Princeton.

Alengry, C. (1915). *Les foires de Champagne: Etude d'histoire économique*, Paris.

Aloisio, M. A. (2003). 'The Maltese corso in the fifteenth century', *Medieval Encounters* 9(2–3), 193–203.

Alsford, S. (2003). *The Men Behind the Masque: Office-holding in East Anglian Boroughs, 1272–1460*, published online at www.trytel.com/~tristan/towns/ mcontent.html#menu.

Alston, R. (1998). 'Trade and the city in Roman Egypt', in *Trade, Traders, and the Ancient City*, ed. H. Parkins and C. Smith, London / New York, 168–202.

Ames, G. J. (1996). *Colbert, Mercantilism, and the French Quest for Asian Trade*, DeKalb, IL.

Angermann, N. (1974). 'Zum Handel der deutschen Kaufleute in Pleskau', in *Rußland und Deutschland*, ed. U. Liszkowski, Stuttgart, 73–82.

— (1979). 'Der Lübecker Hof in Pleskau', *Zeitschrift des Vereins für Lübeckische Geschichte und Altertumskunde*, **59**, 227–35.

— (1987). 'Die Hanse und Rußland', *Nordost-Archiv*, **20**, 57–92.

Aoki, M. (2001). *Toward a Comparative Institutional Analysis*, Cambridge, MA.

Arbois de Jubainville, M. H. de (1859). *Histoire de Bar-sur-Aube sous les comtes de Champagne*, Paris / Troyes / Bar-sur-Aube.

— and L. Pigeotte (1859–66). *Histoire des ducs et des comtes de Champagne*, 7 vols, Paris.

Archer, I. W. (1988). 'The London lobbies in the later sixteenth century', *Historical Journal*, **31**(1), 17–44.

— (1991). *The Pursuit of Stability: Social Relations in Elizabethan London*, Cambridge.

Arrow, K. J. (2000). 'Observations on social capital', in *Social Capital: A Multifaceted Perspective*, ed. P. Dasgupta and I. Serageldin, Washington DC, 3–5.

Arruda, J. J. d. A. (2000). 'Decadence or crisis in the Luso-Brazilian empire: a new model of colonization in the eighteenth century', *Hispanic American Historical Review*, **80**(4), 865–78.

Asch, J. (1961). *Rat und Bürgerschaft in Lübeck 1598–1669*, Lübeck.

Ascheri, M. (2000). 'Formes du droit dans l'Italie communale: les statuts', *Médiévales*, **19**(39), 137–52.

Ashley, W. J. (1888). *An Introduction to English Economic History and Theory, Vol. 1, Part 1: The Middle Ages*, London.

Ashton, R. (1967). 'The parliamentary agitation for free trade in the opening years of the reign of James I', *Past and Present*, **38**, 40–55.

Ashtor, E. (1983). *The Levant Trade in the Later Middle Ages*, Princeton.

Aslanian, S. (2004). 'Trade diaspora versus colonial state: Armenian merchants, the English East India Company, and the High Court of Admiralty in London, 1748–1752', *Diaspora*, **13**(1), 37–100.

— (2006). 'Social capital, "trust" and the role of networks in Julfan trade: informal and semi-formal institutions at work', *Journal of Global History*, **1**(3), 383–402.

Asmussen, G. (1999). *Hansekaufleute in Brügge. Teil 2: Die Lübecker Flandernfahrer in der zweiten Hälfte des 14. Jahrhunderts (1358–1408)*, Frankfurt am Main.

Attman, A. (1973). *The Russian and Polish Markets in International Trade 1500–1650*, Gothenburg.

Ausbüttel, F. M. (1982). *Untersuchungen zu den Vereinen im Westen des römischen Reiches*, Kallmünz.

Ba, S. (2001). 'Establishing online trust through a community responsibility system', *Decision Support Systems*, **31**(3), 323–36.

Bahr, K. (1911). *Handel und Verkehr der Deutschen Hanse in Flandern während des vierzehnten Jahrhunderts*, Leipzig.

Baker, J. H. (1979). 'The law merchant and the common law before 1700', *Cambridge Law Journal*, **38**, 295–322.

— (1986). 'The law merchant and the common law', in *The Legal Profession and the Common Law: Historical Essays*, ed. J. H. Baker. London, 341–86.

Balard, M. (1966). 'Les Génois en Romanie entre 1204 et 1261. Recherches dans les minutiers notariaux génois', *Mélanges d'archéologie et d'histoire*, **78**(2), 467–502.

— (2000). 'Latins in the Aegean and the Balkans in the fourteenth century', in *The New Cambridge Medieval History, Vol. VI: c. 1300–c. 1415*, ed. M. Jones, Cambridge, 825–38.

Ball, J. N. (1977). *Merchants and Merchandise: The Expansion of Trade in Europe, 1500–1630*, London.

Barbour, V. (1911). 'Privateers and pirates of the West Indies', *American Historical Review*, **16**(3), 523–66.

— (1963). *Capitalism in Amsterdam in the Seventeenth Century*, repr. of 1st edn 1950, Baltimore, MD.

Bardhan, P. (1996). 'The nature of institutional impediments to economic development', *Center for International and Development Economics Research Papers*, C96–066.

Barendse, R. (1988). 'The long road to Livorno: the overland messenger service of the Dutch East India Company in the seventeenth century', *Itinerario: International Journal on the History of European Expansion and Global Interaction*, **12**, 25–45.

Barnouw, A. J. (1952). 'Review of Oskar de Smedt, "De Engelse Natie te Antwerpen in de 16e eeuw (1496–1582)"', *American Historical Review*, **58**, 103–5.

Basile, M. E. et al., eds. (1998). *Lex Mercatoria and Legal Pluralism: A Late Thirteenth-century Treatise and Its Afterlife*, Cambridge.

Baskin, J. B. (1988). 'The development of corporate financial markets in Britain and the United States 1600–1914: overcoming asymmetric information', *Business History Review*, **62**(2), 199–237.

Bassermann, E. (1911). *Die Champagnermessen. Ein Beitrag zur Geschichte des Kredits*, Tübingen.

Basu, K. (1997). *Analytical Development Economics: The Less Developed Economy Revisited*, Cambridge, MA.

Bateson, M., ed. (1899). *Records of the Borough of Leicester*, London.

— (1902). 'A London municipal collection of the reign of John', *English Historical Review*, **17**, 480–511, 707–30, 1206–16.

Batini, N. et al. (2010). 'Informal labour and credit markets: a survey', *IMF Working Papers*, **10**/42.

Baumert, K. A., T. Herzog and J. Pershing (2004). *Navigating the Numbers: Greenhouse Gas Data and International Climate Policy*, Washington DC.

Bautier, R.-H. (1952). 'Les principales étapes du développement des foires de Champagne', *Comptes-rendus des séances de l'Académie des inscriptions et belles-lettres*, **96**(2), 314–26.

— (1953). 'Les foires de Champagne. Recherches sur une évolution historique', *Recueils de la Société Jean Bodin*, **5**, 97–147.

— (1955). 'Les Tolomei de Sienne aux foires de Champagne. D'après un compte-rendu de leurs opérations à la foire de mai de Provins en 1279', in *Recueil de travaux offerts à M. Clovis Brunel par ses amis, collègues et élèves*, ed. Société de l'École des chartes, Paris, Vol. I: 106–29.

— (1970). 'The fairs of Champagne', in *Essays in French Economic History*, ed. R. Cameron, Homewood, IL, 42–63.

— (1987). 'Les marchands et banquiers de Plaisance dans l'économie internationale du XIIe au XVe siècle', in *Il 'Registrum magnum' del comune di Piacenza: Atti del Convegno Internazionale di studio (Piacenza, 1985)*, Piacenza, 182–237.

Bec, C. (1967). 'Mentalité et vocabulaire des marchands florentins au début du XVe siècle', *Annales ESC* **22**(6), 1206–26.

Becker, M. B. (1960a). 'The Republican city state in Florence: an inquiry into its origin and survival (1280–1434)', *Speculum* **35**(1), 39–50.

— (1960b). 'Some aspects of oligarchical, dictatorial and popular signorie in Florence, 1282–1382', *Comparative Studies in Society and History* **2**(4), 421–39.

— (1962). 'Florentine Popular Government (1343–1348)', *Proceedings of the American Philosophical Society*, **106**(4), 360–82.

— (1966). 'Economic change and the emerging Florentine territorial state', *Studies in the Renaissance*, **13**, 7–39.

Benedict, P. (1981). *Rouen during the Wars of Religion*, Cambridge.

Benson, B. L. (1989). 'The spontaneous evolution of commercial law', *Southern Economic Journal*, **55**, 644–61.

— (1992). 'Customary law as a social contract: international commercial law', *Constitutional Political Economy*, **3**(1), 1–27.

— (1998). 'Law merchant', *The New Palgrave Dictionary of Economics and the Law*, ed. P. Newman, London.

— (2002). 'Justice without government: the merchant courts of medieval Europe and their modern counterparts', in *The Voluntary City: Choice, Community and Civil Society*, ed. D. Beito, P. Gordon and A. Tabarrok, Ann Arbor, MI, 127–50.

Berman, H. J. (1983). *Law and Revolution: The Formation of the Western Legal Tradition*, Cambridge, MA.

Bernard, J. (1972). 'Trade and finance in the Middle Ages 900–1500', in *The Fontana Economic History of Europe, Vol. 1: The Middle Ages*, ed. C. Cippola, London / Glasgow, 274–338.

Bernstein, L. (2001). 'Private commercial law in the cotton industry: value creation through rules, norms, and institutions', *Michigan Law Review*, **99**(7), 1724–90.

Berti, P. (1857). 'Documenti riguardanti il commercio dei Fiorentini in Francia nel secoli XIII e XIV, e specialmente il loro concorso alle fiere di Sciampagna', *Giornale storico degli archivi di Toscana*, 1, 163–95, 247–74.

Bigwood, G. (1906). 'Gand et la circulation des grains en Flandre du XIVe au XVIIIe siècle', *Vierteljahrsschrift für Sozial- und Wirtschaftsgeschichte*, 4, 397–460.

Bird, W. H. B. (1925). *The Black Book of Winchester*, Winchester.

Bisson, T. N. (1984). *Fiscal Accounts of Catalonia under the Early Count-Kings (1151–1213)*, Berkeley, CA.

Black, A. (1984). *Guilds and Civil Society in European Political Thought from the Twelfth Century to the Present*, Ithaca, NY.

Blanchard, I. (2004). 'Foreign merchants in early modern towns and international market intelligence systems', *Annual of Medieval Studies at CEU*, 10, 175–9.

Bloch, M. (1930). 'Review of G. I. Bratianu, "Recherches sur le commerce des Génois dans la mer Noire au XIIIe siècle"', *Annales d'histoire économique et sociale*, 2(7), 463–4.

Blockmans, W. (1993). 'Formale und informelle soziale Strukturen in und zwischen den großen flämischen Städten im Spätmittelalter', in *Einungen und Bruderschaften in der spätmittelalterlichen Stadt*, ed. P. Johanek, Cologne / Weimar / Vienna, 1–15.

— (2000). 'Flanders', in *The New Cambridge Medieval History, Vol. V: c. 1198–c. 1300*, ed. D. Abulafia, Cambridge, 405–18.

— and W. Prevenier (1999). *The Promised Lands: The Low Countries under Burgundian Rule, 1369–1530*, Philadelphia, PA.

Blom, G. A. (1984). 'Der Ursprung der Gilden in Norwegen und ihre Entwicklung in den Städten während des Mittelalters', in *Gilde und Korporation in den nordeuropäischen Städten des späten Mittelalters*, ed. K. Friedland, Cologne / Vienna, 5–28.

Blomquist, T. W. (1971). 'The Castracani family of thirteenth-century Lucca', *Speculum*, 46(3), 459–76.

Blondé, B., O. Gelderblom and P. Stabel (2007). 'Foreign merchant communities in Bruges, Antwerp and Amsterdam, c. 1350–1650', *Cultural Exchange in Early Modern Europe, Vol. 2: Cities and Cultural Exchange in Europe, 1400–1700*, ed. D. Calabi and S. T. Christensen, Cambridge, 154–74.

Boerner, L. and A. Ritschl (2002). 'Individual enforcement of collective liability in premodern Europe', *Journal of Institutional and Theoretical Economics*, 158, 205–13.

— and A. Ritschl (2005). 'Making financial markets: contract enforcement and the emergence of tradable assets in late medieval Europe', *Humboldt-University Berlin Economics Working Papers*.

Boldorf, M. (1999). 'Institutional barriers to economic development: the Silesian linen proto-industry (17th to 19th century)', *Institut für Volkswirtschaftslehre und Statistik, Universität Mannheim Working Papers*, 566–99.

— (2006). *Europäische Leinenregionen im Wandel. Institutionelle Weichenstellungen in Schlesien und Irland (1750–1850)*. Cologne / Weimar / Vienna.

Botticini, M. (2000). 'A tale of "benevolent" governments: private credit markets, public finance, and the role of Jewish lenders in medieval and renaissance Italy', *Journal of Economic History*, 60(1), 165–89.

Bottin, J. (1988). 'Structures et mutations d'un espace protoindustriel à la fin du XVIe siècle', *Annales ESC*, **43**(4), 975–95.

Bourdieu, P. (1986). 'The forms of capital', in *Handbook of Theory of Research for the Sociology of Education*, ed. J. E. Richardson, Westport, CT, 241–58.

Bourquelot, F. (1839–40). *Histoire de Provins*, 2 vols, Paris.

— (1865). *Études sur les foires de Champagne, sur la nature, l'étendue et les règles du commerce qui s'y faisait aux XIIe, XIIIe et XIVe siècles*, 2 vols, Paris.

Boutaric, E. P. (1867). *Actes du Parlement de Paris, Première série: de l'an 1254 à l'an 1328*, 2 vols, Paris.

Bowsky, W. M. (1962). 'The Buon Governo of Siena (1287–1355): a mediaeval Italian oligarchy', *Speculum*, **37**(3), 368–81.

— (1981). *A Medieval Italian Commune: Siena under the Nine, 1287–1355*, Berkeley / Los Angeles.

Brandt, A. v. (1956). 'Stadtgründung, Grundbesitz und Verfassungsanfänge in Lübeck', *Zeitschrift des Vereins für Lübeckische Geschichte und Altertumskunde*, **36**, 79–95.

Bratianu, G. I. (1927). *Actes des notaires génois de Péra et de Caffa*, Bucharest.

Braudel, F. (1979). *Civilisation matérielle, économie et capitalisme, XVe–XVIIIe siècle*, 3 vols, Paris.

Braun, R. (1978). 'Early industrialization and demographic change in the Canton of Zürich', in *Historical Studies of Changing Fertility*, ed. C. Tilly, Princeton, NJ, 289–334.

Bredenkamp, F. (1996). *The Byzantine Empire of Thessaloniki (1224–1242)*, Thessaloniki.

Brett, E. A. (1996). 'The participatory principle in development projects: the costs and benefits of cooperation', *Public Administration and Development*, **16**, 5–19.

Brewer, J. (1989). *The Sinews of Power: War, Money and the English State, 1688–1783*, London.

Britnell, R. H. (1991). 'The towns of England and Northern Italy in the early fourteenth century', *Economic History Review*, **44**(1), 21–35.

Briys, E. and D. J. De ter Beerst (2006). 'The Zaccaria deal: contract and options to fund a Genoese shipment of alum to Bruges in 1298', paper presented at the XIV International Economic History Congress, Helsinki, August 2006.

Brück, T. (1999). 'Bemerkungen zur Kaufmannschaft Rigas in der ersten Hälfte des 15. Jahrhunderts unter besonderer Berücksichtigung der Schwarzhäupter zwischen 1413 und 1424', in *'Kopet uns werk by tyden': Beiträge zur hansischen und preussischen Geschichte. Walter Stark zum 75. Geburtstag*, ed. N. Jörn, D. Kattinger and H. Wernicke, Schwerin, 113–30.

Bruijn, J. R. (1990). 'Productivity, profitability and costs of private and corporate Dutch shipping in the seventeenth and eighteenth centuries', in *The Rise of Merchant Empires: Long-distance Trade in the Early Modern World, 1350–1750*, ed. J. D. Tracy, Cambridge, 174–94.

Brulez, W. (1973). 'Bruges and Antwerp in the 15th and 16th centuries: an antithesis', *Acta Historiae Neerlandicae. Studies on the History of the Netherlands*, **6**, 1–26.

Brunelle, G. K. (2003). 'Migration and religious identity: the Portuguese of seventeenth-century Rouen', *Journal of Early Modern History*, 7(3–4), 283–311.

Bücher, K. (1922). *Die Entstehung der Volkswirtschaft*, Leipzig.

Bullard, M. M. et al. (2004). 'Where history and theory interact: Frederic C. Lane on the emergence of capitalism', *Speculum*, **88**, 88–119.

Bulst, N. (2002). 'Fremde in der Stadt. Zur Wahrnehmung und zum Umgang mit "den Anderen" im Spiegel der mittelalterlichen deutschen Stadtrechte', in *Kloster – Stadt – Region. Festschrift für Heinrich Rüthing*, Bielefeld, 46–64.

Burckhardt, M. (2005). 'Die Ordnungen der vier Hansekontore Bergen, Brügge, London und Novgorod', in *Das Hansische Kontor zu Bergen und die Lübecker Bergenfahrer: International Workshop Lübeck 2003*, ed. A. Grassmann, Lübeck, 58–77.

Burt, R. S. (2001). 'Bandwidth and echo: trust, information and gossip in social networks', in *Networks and Markets: Contributions from Economics and Sociology*, ed. A. Casella and J. E. Rauch, New York, 30–74.

— (2005). *Brokerage and Closure: An Introduction to Social Capital*, Oxford.

Byrne, E. H. (1916). 'Commercial contracts of the Genoese in the Syrian trade of the twelfth century', *Quarterly Journal of Economics*, **31**, 128–70.

Caligaris, G. (1998). 'Trade guilds, manufacturing and economic privilege in the kingdom of Sardinia during the eighteenth century', in *Guilds, Markets and Work Regulations in Italy: 16th–19th Centuries*, ed. A. Guenzi, P. Massa and F. P. Caselli, Aldershot, 56–81.

Carlos, A. M. (1991). 'Agent opportunism and the role of company culture: the Hudson's Bay and Royal African Companies compared', *Business and Economic History*, 2nd ser., **9**, 142–51.

— and J. B. Kruse (1996). 'The decline of the Royal African Company: fringe firms and the role of the charter', *Economic History Review*, **49**(2), 295–317.

— and S. Nicholas (1988). '"Giants of an earlier capitalism": the chartered trading companies as an analogue of the modern multinational', *Business History Review*, **26**(3), 398–419.

— and S. Nicholas (1990). 'Agency problems in early chartered companies: the case of the Hudson's Bay Company', *Journal of Economic History*, **50**(4), 853–75.

— and S. Nicholas (1996). 'Theory and history: seventeenth-century joint-stock chartered trading companies', *Journal of Economic History*, **56**(4), 916–24.

Carolus-Barré, L. (1965). 'Les XVII villes, une hanse vouée au grand commerce de la draperie', *Comptes-rendus des séances de l'Académie des inscriptions et belles-lettres*, **109**(1), 20–30.

Carter, F. W. (1971). 'The commerce of the Dubrovnik Republic, 1500–1700', *Economic History Review*, ns, **24**(3), 370–94.

Carus, A. W. and S. C. Ogilvie (2009). 'Turning qualitative into quantitative evidence: a well-used method made explicit', *Economic History Review*, **62**(4), 893–925.

Cassandro, G. I. (1938). *Le rappresaglie e il fallimento a Venezia nei secoli XIII–XVI: con documenti inediti*, Turin.

Casson, M. (1997). *Information and Organization: A New Perspective on the Theory of the Firm*, New York.

Catoni, G. (1974). 'La brutta avventura di un mercante senese nel 1309 a una questione di rappresaglia', *Archivio storico italiano*, **132**, 65–77.

Cauchies, J.-M. and H. d. Schepper (1997). 'Legal tools of the public power in the Netherlands, 1200–1600', in *Legislation and Justice*, ed. A. Padoa-Schioppa, Oxford, 229–68.

Cave, R. C. and H. H. Coulson (1936). *A Source Book for Medieval Economic History*, Milwaukee, WI.

Cerman, M. (1993). 'Proto-industrialization in an urban environment: Vienna, 1750–1857', *Continuity and Change*, **8**(2), 281–320.

Chapin, E. (1937). *Les villes de foires de Champagne des origines au début du XIVe siècle*, Paris.

Chaudhuri, K. N. (1978). *The Trading World of Asia and the English East India Company, 1600–1760*, Cambridge.

— (1991). 'Reflections on the organising principle of pre-modern trade', in *The Political Economy of Merchant Empires: State Power and World Trade, 1350–1750*, ed. J. D. Tracy, Cambridge, 421–42.

Cheyette, F. L. (1970). 'The sovereign and the pirates, 1332', *Speculum*, **45**(1), 40–68.

Choroškevic, A. L. (1996). 'Der deutsche Hof in Novgorod und die deutsche Herberge (Fondaco dei Tedeschi) in Venedig im 13./14. Jahrhundert. Eine vergleichende Vorstudie', in *Zwischen Lübeck und Novgorod. Wirtschaft, Politik und Kultur im Ostseeraum vom frühen Mittelalter bis ins 20. Jahrhundert. Norbert Angermann zum 60. Geburtstag*, ed. O. Pelc and G. Pickhan, Lüneburg, 67–87.

Christensen, A. E. (1953). 'La foire de Scanie', *Recueils de la Société Jean Bodin*, **5**, 241–66.

Citarella, A. O. (1967). 'The relations of Amalfi with the Arab world before the Crusades', *Speculum*, **42**(2), 299–312.

— (1968). 'Patterns in medieval trade: the commerce of Amalfi before the Crusades', *Journal of Economic History*, **28**(4), 531–55.

Clark, G. (1996). 'The political foundations of modern economic growth: England, 1540–1800', *Journal of Interdisciplinary History*, **26**(4), 563–88.

Coleman, E. (1999). 'The Italian communes: recent work and current trends', *Journal of Medieval History*, **25**, 373–97.

Coleman, J. S. (1989). 'Social capital in the creation of human capital', *American Journal of Sociology*, **94**, S95–S120.

— (1990). *Foundations of Social Theory*, Cambridge, MA.

Congdon, E. A. (2003). 'Venetian and Aragonese/Catalan relations: protectionist legislation in 1398–1404', *Medieval Encounters*, **9**(2–3), 214–35.

Constable, O. R. (1994). 'The problem of jettison in medieval Mediterranean maritime law', *Journal of Medieval History*, **20**(3), 207–20.

— (2003). *Housing the Stranger in the Mediterranean World: Lodging, Trade, and Travel in Late Antiquity and the Middle Ages*, Cambridge.

Coornaert, É. (1961). *Les Français et le commerce international à Anvers, fin du XVe–XVIe siècle*, 2 vols, Paris.

— (1967). 'European economic institutions and the New World: the chartered companies', in *The Economy of Expanding Europe in the Sixteenth and Seventeenth Centuries*, ed. E. E. Rich and C. H. Wilson, Cambridge, 223–75.

Cordes, A. (1999). 'Einheimische und gemeinrechtliche Elemente im hansischen Gesellschaftsrecht des 15.–17. Jahrhunderts. Eine Projektskizze', in *'Kopet uns werk by tyden': Beiträge zur hansischen und preussischen Geschichte. Walter Stark zum 75. Geburtstag*, ed. N. Jörn, D. Kattinger and H. Wernicke, Schwerin, 67–72.

Cotter, W. (1996). 'The collegia and Roman law', in *Voluntary Associations in the Graeco-Roman World*, ed. J. W. Kloppenborg and S. G. Wilson, London.

Coureas, N. (2002). 'Cyprus and Ragusa (Dubrovnik) 1280–1450', *Mediterranean Historical Review*, 17(2), 1–13.

Crafts, N. F. R. (1985). *British Economic Growth during the Industrial Revolution*, Oxford.

Croft, P. (1973a). 'Introduction: the first Spanish company, 1530–85', in *The Spanish Company*, ed. P. Croft, London, London Record Society, [www.british-history.ac.uk/report.aspx?compid=63964].

— (1973b). 'Introduction: the revival of the company, 1604–6', in *The Spanish Company*, ed. P. Croft, London, London Record Society, [www.british-history.ac.uk/report.aspx?compid=63965].

Cunningham, W. (1910). *The Growth of English Industry and Commerce during the Early and Middle Ages*, 5th edn, Cambridge.

Daenell, E. R. (1905). *Die Blütezeit der deutschen Hanse. Hansische Geschichte von der zweiten Hälfte des XIV. bis zum letzten Viertel des XV. Jahrhunderts*, Berlin.

Dagron, G. (2002). 'The urban economy, seventh to twelfth centuries', in *The Economic History of Byzantium: From the Seventh through the Fifteenth Century*, ed. A. E. Laiou, Washington DC, 393–461.

Daileader, P. (2000). *True Citizens: Violence, Memory, and Identity in the Medieval Community of Perpignan, 1162–1397*, Leiden.

Dam, K. W. (2006). 'Institutions, history and economic development', *John M. Olin Law & Economics Working Paper*, 2nd ser., 271.

D'Amico, S. (2001). 'Rebirth of a city: immigration and trade in Milan, 1630–59', *Sixteenth Century Journal*, 32.

Das Gupta, A. (1979). *Indian Merchants and the Decline of Surat, c. 1700–1750*, Wiesbaden.

Dasgupta, P. (1988). 'Trust as a commodity', in *Trust: Making and Breaking Cooperative Relations*, ed. D. Gambetta, Oxford, 49–72.

— (2000). 'Economic progress and the idea of social capital', in *Social Capital: A Multifaceted Perspective*, ed. P. Dasgupta and I. Serageldin, Washington, 325–424.

— (2003). 'Social capital and economic performance: analytics', in *Social Capital: A Reader*, ed. E. Ostrom and T. K. Ahn, Cheltenham, 309–42.

— and I. Serageldin, eds. (2000). *Social Capital: A Multifaceted Perspective*. Washington.

Davids, K. (2006). 'Monasteries, economies and states: the dissolution of monasteries in early modern Europe and T'ang China', paper presented at the Global Economic History Network (GEHN) Conference 10, Washington DC, 8–10 September 2006.

Davidsohn, R. (1896–1901). *Forschungen zur Geschichte von Florenz*, 3 vols, Berlin.

Davies, K. G. (1957). *The Royal African Company*, Oxford.

Day, G. W. (1988). *Genoa's Response to Byzantium, 1155–1204: Commercial Expansion and Factionalism in a Medieval City*, Urbana, IL.

Day, J. (2002). 'The Levant trade in the Middle Ages', in *The Economic History of Byzantium: From the Seventh through the Fifteenth Century*, ed. A. E. Laiou, Washington DC, 807–14.

De Roover, F. E. (1940). 'The business records of an early Genoese notary, 1190–1192', *Bulletin of the Business Historical Society*, **14**(3), 41–6.

— (1945). 'Early examples of marine insurance', *Journal of Economic History*, **5**(2), 172–200.

De Roover, R. (1948a). *Money, Banking and Credit in Mediaeval Bruges: Italian Merchant-bankers, Lombards and Money-changers: A Study in the Origins of Banking*, Cambridge, MA.

— (1948b). *The Medici Bank*, New York.

— (1958). 'The story of the Alberti Company of Florence, 1302–1348, as revealed in its account books', *Business History Review*, **32**(1), 14–59.

— (1963). *The Rise and Decline of the Medici Bank, 1397–1494*, Cambridge, MA.

— (1965). 'The organization of trade', in *The Cambridge Economic History of Europe, Vol. 3: Economic Organization and Policies in the Middle Ages*, ed. M. M. Postan, E. E. Rich and E. Miller, Cambridge, 42–156.

— (1971). 'Early banking before 1500 and the development of capitalism', *Revue internationale d'histoire de la banque*, 4, 1–16.

De Smedt, O. (1950–4). *De Engelse Natie te Antwerpen in de 16e eeuw (1496–1582)*, Antwerp.

De Soto, H. (1989). *The Other Path: The Invisible Revolution in the Third World*, New York.

De Vries, J. (1974). *The Dutch Rural Economy in the Golden Age, 1500–1700*, New Haven, CT.

— (1976). *The Economy of Europe in an Age of Crisis, 1600–1750*, Cambridge.

— and A. Van der Woude (1997). *The First Modern Economy: Success, Failure, and Perseverance of the Dutch Economy, 1500–1815*, Cambridge.

Del Punta, I. (2004). 'Principal Italian banking companies of the XIIIth and XIVth centuries: a comparison between the Ricciardi of Lucca and the Bardi, Peruzzi and Acciaiuoli of Florence', *Journal of European Economic History* **33**(3), 647–62.

Del Vecchio, A. and E. Casanova (1894). *Le rappresaglie nei comuni medievali e specialmente in Firenze*, Bologna.

Demonet, M. and G. Granasztói (1982). 'Une ville de Hongrie au milieu du XVIe siècle (analyse factorielle et modèle social)', *Annales ESC*, **37**(3), 523–51.

Dennison, T. K. (2011). *The Institutional Framework of Russian Serfdom*, Cambridge.

— and S. C. Ogilvie (2007). 'Serfdom and social capital in Bohemia and Russia', *Economic History Review*, **60**(3), 513–44.

Denzel, M. A. (2001). '"Wissensmanagement" und "Wissensnetzwerke" der Kaufleute. Aspekte kaufmännischer Kommunikation im späten Mittelalter', *Das Mittelalter*, **6**(1), 73–90.

Dercon, S. (2004). *Insurance Against Poverty*, Oxford.

Desroussilles, F. D. (1979). 'Vénitiens et Génois à Constantinople et en mer Noire en 1431', *Cahiers du monde russe et soviétique*, **20**(1), 111–22.

Dessì, R. and S. C. Ogilvie (2003). 'Social capital and collusion: the case of merchant guilds', *CESifo Working Papers*, 1037.

— and S. C. Ogilvie (2004). 'Social capital and collusion: the case of merchant guilds (long version)', *Cambridge Working Papers in Economics*, 0417.

Dewey, H. W. (1988). 'Russia's debt to the Mongols in suretyship and collective responsibility', *Comparative Studies in Society and History*, **30**(2), 249–70.

— and A. M. Kleimola (1970). 'Suretyship and collective responsibility in pre-Petrine Russia', *Jahrbücher für Geschichte Osteuropas*, **18**, 337–54.

— and A. M. Kleimola (1984). 'Russian collective consciousness: the Kievan roots', *Slavonic and East European Review*, **62**(2), 180–91.

Di Cosmo, N. (2005). 'Mongols and merchants on the Black Sea frontier in the thirteenth and fourteenth centuries: convergences and conflicts', in *Mongols, Turks, and Others: Eurasian Nomads and the Sedentary World*, ed. R. Amitai and M. Biran, Leiden / Boston, 391–424.

Dijkman, J. (2007). 'Debt litigation in medieval Holland, c. 1200 – c. 1350', Paper presented at the Global Economic History Network (GEHN) conference, Utrecht, 20–22 September 2007.

Dilcher, G. (1984). 'Personale und lokale Strukturen kaufmännischen Rechts als Vorformen genossenschaftlichen Stadtrechts', in *Gilde und Korporation in den nordeuropäischen Städten des späten Mittelalters*, ed. K. Friedland, Cologne / Vienna, 65–78.

— (1985). 'Die genossenschaftliche Struktur von Gilden und Zünften', in *Gilden und Zünfte. Kaufmännische und gewerbliche Genossenschaften im frühen und hohen Mittelalter*, ed. B. Schwineköper, Sigmaringen, 71–112.

Dodd, G. (2002). 'The Calais staple and the parliament of May 1382', *English Historical Review*, **117**(470), 94–103.

Doehaerd, R. (1941). *Les relations commerciales entre Gênes, la Belgique, et l'Outremont d'après les archives notariales génoises aux XIIIe et XIVe siècles*, Brussels / Rome.

Dollinger, P. (1964). *La Hanse: XIIe–XVIIe siècles*, Paris.

— (1970). *The German Hansa*, Stanford.

Donahue, C. (2004). 'Medieval and early modern lex mercatoria: an attempt at the probation diabolica', *Chicago Journal of International Law*, **5**(1), 21–38.

— (2005). 'Benvenuto Stracca's De Mercatura: was there a Lex mercatoria in sixteenth-century Italy?', in *From Lex Mercatoria to Commercial Law*, ed. V. Piergiovanni, Berlin, 69–120.

Dotson, J. E. (1999). 'Fleet operations in the first Genoese-Venetian war, 1264–1266', *Viator: Medieval and Renaissance Studies*, **30**, 165–80.

— (2003). 'Commercial law in fourteenth-century merchant manuals', *Medieval Encounters*, **9**(2–3), 204–13.

Doumerc, B. (1987). 'Les Vénitiens à La Tana (Azov) au XVe siècle', *Cahiers du monde russe et soviétique*, **28**(1), 5–19.

Dursteler, E. R. (2006). *Venetians in Constantinople: Nation, Identity, and Coexistence in the Early Modern Mediterranean*, Baltimore / London.

Ebel, W. (1957). *Lübisches Kaufmannsrecht vornehmlich nach Lübecker Ratsurteilen des 15./16. Jahrhunderts*, Göttingen.

Edler, F. (1938). 'The Van der Molen commission merchants of Antwerp: trade with Italy, 1538–44', *Medieval and Historiographical Essays in Honor of James Westfall Thompson*, ed. J. L. Cate and E. Anderson, Chicago, 78–145.

Edwards, J. S. S. and S. C. Ogilvie (2009). 'Contract enforcement, institutions and social capital: the Maghribi traders reappraised', *Cambridge Working Papers in Economics*, 0928.

Ehbrecht, W. (1985). 'Beiträge und Überlegungen zu Gilden im nordwestlichen Deutschland (vornehmlich im 13. Jahrhundert)', in *Gilden und Zünfte. Kaufmännische und gewerbliche Genossenschaften im frühen und hohen Mittelalter*, ed. B. Schwineköper, Sigmaringen, 413–50.

Ehrenberg, R. (1995). 'Makler, Hosteliers und Börse in Brügge vom 13. bis zum 16. Jahrhundert', *Zeitschrift für das gesamte Handelsrecht*, **3**, 403–68.

Elton, G. R. (1975). 'Taxation for war and peace in early Tudor England', in *War and Economic Development: Essays in Memory of David Joslin*, ed. J. M. Winter, Cambridge.

Ennen, E. (1979). *The Medieval Town*, Amsterdam.

Epstein, S. A. (1994). 'Secrecy and Genoese commercial practice', *Journal of Medieval History*, **20**(4), 313–25.

— (1996). *Genoa and the Genoese, 958–1528*, Chapel Hill, NC.

Epstein, S. R. (1992). *An Island for Itself: Economic Development and Social Change in Late Medieval Sicily*, Cambridge.

— (2000). *Freedom and Growth: The Rise of States and Markets in Europe, 1300–1750*, London.

— (2004). 'Craft guilds', in *Oxford Encyclopedia of Economic History*, ed. J. Mokyr, Oxford, 35–9.

— and M. Prak (2008). 'Introduction: guilds, innovation and the European economy, 1400–1800', in *Guilds, Innovation and the European Economy, 1400–1800*, ed. S. R. Epstein and M. Prak, London, 1–24.

Esch, A. (1992). 'Viele Loyalitäten, eine Identität. Italienische Kaufmannskolonien im spätmittelalterlichen Europa', *Historische Zeitschrift*, **254**, 581–608.

Ewert, U.-C. and S. Selzer (2005). 'The commercial networks of Hanseatic merchants: a "modern" organization of trade at work already during the late Middle Ages?', Paper presented at the Workshop on Mercantile Organization in Pre-Industrial Europe, Antwerp, 18–19 November.

Face, R. D. (1958). 'Techniques of business in the trade between the fairs of Champagne and the south of Europe in the twelfth and thirteenth centuries', *Economic History Review*, 2nd ser., **10**(3), 427–38.

Fafchamps, M. (2003). *Rural Poverty, Risk and Development*, Cheltenham, UK / Northampton, MA.

Fairchilds, C. (1988). 'Three views on the guilds', *French Historical Studies*, **15**(4), 688–92.

Farolfi, B. (1998). 'Brokers and brokerage in Bologna from the sixteenth to the nineteenth centuries', in *Guilds, Markets and Work Regulations in Italy, 16th–19th centuries*, ed. A. Guenzi, P. Massa and F. Piola Caselli, Aldershot, 306–22.

Federowicz, J. K. (1979). 'The history of the Elbing staple: an episode in the history of commercial monopolies', *Jahrbücher für Geschichte Osteuropas*, 27, 220–30.

Feenstra, R. (1953). 'Les foires aux Pays-Bas Septentrionaux', *Receuils de la Société Jean Bodin*, 5, 209–39.

Fehr, N.-H. v. d. and D. Harbord (2007). 'Coordination, Commitment and Enforcement: The Merchant Guild Revisited', *Munich Personal Repec Archive Working Paper*.

Fender, A. (2004). 'The Hudson's Bay Company's institutional adaptation to economic conditions', Paper presented at the Fifth European Social Science History Conference, Berlin, 24–27 March.

Flambard, J. M. (1987). 'Éléments pour une approche financière de la mort dans les classes populaires du Haut-Empire. Analyse du budget de quelques collèges funéraires de Rome et d'Italie', in *La mort, les morts et l'au delà dans le monde romain. Actes du colloque de Caen (20–22 novembre 1985)*, ed. F. Hinard, Caen, 209–44.

Flik, R. (1990). *Die Textilindustrie in Calw und in Heidenheim 1705–1870. Eine regional vergleichende Untersuchung zur Geschichte der Frühindustrialisierung und Industriepolitik in Württemberg*, Stuttgart.

Flórez, G. C. (2003). 'Vicissitudes of commercial trading: Castile and Flanders at the end of the fifteenth century (1474–94)', *Medieval History Journal*, 6(1), 33–53.

Fortunati, M. (2005). 'The fairs between *lex mercatoria* and *ius mercatorum*', in *From Lex Mercatoria to Commercial Law*, ed. V. Piergiovanni, Berlin, 143–64.

Francotte, H. (1900–1). *L'industrie dans la Grèce ancienne*, Brussels.

Frankopan, P. (2004). 'Byzantine trade privileges to Venice in the eleventh century: the chrysobull of 1092', *Journal of Medieval History*, 30, 135–60.

Frensdorff, F. (1901). 'Der Makler im Hansagebiete', in *Festgabe der Göttinger Juristenfakultät für Ferdinand Regelsberger zum 70. Geburtstag*, ed. Göttinger Juristenfakultät, Leipzig, 255–316.

Freshfield, E. H. (1938). *Roman Law in the Later Roman Empire: Byzantine Guilds, Professional and Commercial. Ordinances of Leo VI c. 895 from the Book of the Eparch*, Cambridge.

Freudenberger, H. (1966). 'Three mercantilist protofactories', *Business History Review*, 40(2), 167–89.

— (1979). 'Zur Linzer Wollzeugfabrik', in *Wirtschafts- und sozialhistorische Beiträge. Festschrift für Alfred Hoffmann zum 75. Geburtstag*, ed. H. Knittler, Vienna, 220–35.

Fritschy, W. (2003). 'A "financial revolution" reconsidered: public finance in Holland during the Dutch Revolt, 1568–1648', *Economic History Review*, 56(1), 57–89.

Frölich, K. (1972). 'Kaufmannsgilden und Stadtverfassung im Mittelalter', in *Die Stadt des Mittelalters, Vol. 2: Recht und Verfassung*, ed. C. Haase, Darmstadt, 11–54; originally published 1934.

Fryde, E. B. (1959). 'The English farmers of the Customs, 1343–51', *Transactions of the Royal Historical Society*, 5th ser. (9), 1–18.

— and M. M. Fryde (1965). 'Public credit, with special reference to north-western Europe', in *The Cambridge Economic History of Europe, Vol. 3:*

Economic Organization and Policies in the Middle Ages, ed. M. M. Postan, E. E. Rich and E. Miller, Cambridge, 430–553.

Fryde, N. (1985). 'Gilds in England before the Black Death', in *Gilden und Zünfte. Kaufmännische und gewerbliche Genossenschaften im frühen und hohen Mittelalter*, ed. B. Schwineköper, Sigmaringen: 215–30.

Fullana Ferré, G. d. E. et al. (1998). 'Foreign merchants in medieval Barcelona', Paper presented to the conference 'La ville en Europe', Paris, 23–29 April.

Furber, H. (1976). *Rival Empires of Trade in the Orient, 1600–1800*, Minneapolis, MN.

Fusaro, M. (2002). 'Coping with transition. Greek merchants and ship owners between Venice and England in the sixteenth century', paper presented at the XIII Economic History Congress, Buenos Aires, 22–26 July.

Galenson, D. W. (1986). *Traders, Planters, and Slaves: Market Behavior in Early English America*, Cambridge.

Gambetta, D. (1988a). 'Can we trust trust?', in *Trust: Making and Breaking Cooperative Relations*, ed. D. Gambetta, Oxford, 213–37.

— (1988b). 'Mafia: the price of distrust', in *Trust: Making and Breaking Cooperative Relations*, ed. D. Gambetta, Oxford, 159–75.

Gauci, P. (2002). 'Informality and influence: the overseas merchant and the livery companies, 1660–1702', in *Guilds, Society, and Economy in London, 1450–1800*, cd. I. A. Gadd and P. Wallis, London, 127–39.

Gayot, G. (1981). 'La longue insolence des tondeurs de draps dans la manufacture de Sedan au XVIIIème siècle', *Revue du Nord*, 63, 105–134.

Gecsényi, L. (2007). '"Turkish goods" and "Greek merchants" in the Kingdom of Hungary in the 16th and 17th centuries', *Acta Orientalia*, 60(1), 55–71.

Gelderblom, O. (2003). 'The governance of early modern trade: the case of Hans Thijs (1556–1611)', *Enterprise and Society*, 4(4), 606–39.

— (2005a). 'The decline of fairs and merchant guilds in the Low Countries, 1250–1650', *Economy and Society of the Low Countries Working Papers* 2005–1.

— (2005b). 'The resolution of commercial conflicts in Bruges, Antwerp, and Amsterdam, 1250–1650', *Economy and Society of the Low Countries Working Papers* 2005–2.

— and R. Grafe (2004). 'The costs and benefits of merchant guilds, 1300–1800: position paper', Paper presented at the Fifth European Social Science History Conference, Berlin, 24–27 March.

— and J. Jonker (2005). 'Amsterdam as the cradle of modern futures trading and options trading, 1550–1650', in *The Origins of Value: The Financial Innovations That Created Modern Capital Markets*, ed. W. N. Goetzmann and K. G. Rouwenhorst, Oxford, 189–206.

Germain, A. (1861). *Histoire du commerce de Montpellier*. Montpellier.

Gies, J. and F. Gies (1972). *Merchants and Moneymen: The Commercial Revolution, 1000–1500*, New York.

Gieysztor, A. (1987). 'Trade and industry in eastern Europe before 1200', in *The Cambridge Economic History of Europe, Vol. 3: Economic Organization and Policies in the Middle Ages*, ed. M. M. Postan and E. Miller, Cambridge, 474–524.

Gil, M. (2003). 'The Jewish merchants in the light of eleventh-century Geniza documents', *Journal of the Economic and Social History of the Orient*, **46**(3), 273–319.

Gilliodts-van Severen, L. (1874–5). *Coutumes des Pays et Comté de Flandre. Quartier de Bruges*, Brussels.

— (1901–2). *Cartulaire de l'ancien Consulat d'Espagne à Bruges. Recueil de documents concernant le commerce maritime et interieur, le droit des gens public et privé, et l'historie économique de la Flandre*, 2 vols, Bruges.

Giuseppi, M. S. (1895). 'Alien merchants in England in the fifteenth century', *Transactions of the Royal Historical Society*, ns, **9**, 75–98.

Glaeser, E. L., D. Laibson and B. Sacerdote (2002). 'An economic approach to social capital', *Economic Journal*, **112**(483), 437–58.

Glamann, K. (1958). *Dutch-Asiatic Trade, 1620–1740*, Copenhagen / The Hague.

Goetz, L. K. (1916). *Deutsch-russische Handelsverträge des Mittelalters*, Hamburg.

Goldberg, J. (2005). 'Geographies of Trade and Traders in the Eleventh-century Mediterranean: A Study Based on Documents from the Cairo Geniza', Columbia University Ph.D. dissertation.

— (2008). 'Merchants and merchant work in the eleventh century', Precirculated paper for the Social Norms Workshop, Princeton University, December.

Goldschmidt, L. (1891). *Universalgeschichte des Handelsrechts, Vol. 1: Geschichtlich-literärische Einleitung und die Grundlehren*, Stuttgart.

González de Lara, Y. (2008). 'The secret of Venetian success: a public-order, reputation-based institution', *European Review of Economic History*, **12**(3), 247–85.

Goris, J. A. (1925). *Étude sur les colonies marchandes méridionales (Portugais, Espagnols, Italiens) à Anvers de 1488 à 1567. Contribution à l'histoire des débuts du capitalisme moderne*, Louvain.

Götz, B. (1976). 'Über das Zunftwesen im Weinbau', *Der badische Winzer*, **2**, 17–18.

Grafe, R. (2001). 'Atlantic trade and regional specialisation in northern Spain 1550–1650: an integrated trade theory-institutional organisation approach', *Serie de Historia Económica e Instituciones Universidad Carlos III de Madrid Working Paper*, 01–65.

— and O. Gelderblom (2010a). 'The rise and fall of the merchant guilds: rethinking the comparative study of commercial institutions in pre-modern Europe', *Journal of Interdisciplinary History*, **40**(4), 477–511.

— and O. Gelderblom (2010b). 'Appendix to Gelderblom & Grafe, "The rise, persistence and decline of merchant guilds"', [www.history.northwestern.edu/people/docs/AppendixtoGelderblomandGrafe.pdf].

Grassmann, A., ed. (1988). *Lübeckische Geschichte*, Lübeck.

Green, L. (2000). 'Florence', in *The New Cambridge Medieval History, Vol. V: c. 1198–c. 1300*, ed. D. Abulafia, Cambridge: 479–96.

Greif, A. (1989). 'Reputation and coalitions in medieval trade: evidence on the Maghribi traders', *Journal of Economic History*, **49**(4), 857–82.

— (1992). 'Institutions and international trade: lessons from the Commercial Revolution', *American Economic Review Papers and Proceedings*, **82**(2), 128–33.

— (1997). 'On the social foundations and historical development of institutions that facilitate impersonal exchange: from the community responsibility system to individual legal responsibility in pre-modern Europe', *Stanford University Working Papers*, 97–016.

— (2002a). 'Institutions and impersonal exchange: from communal to individual responsibility', *Journal of Institutional and Theoretical Economics*, **158**(1): 168–204.

— (2002b). 'Economic history and game theory', in *Handbook of Game Theory with Economic Applications*, ed. R. J. Aumann and S. Hart, Amsterdam / New York, Vol. 3, 1989–2024.

— (2004). 'Impersonal exchange without impartial law: the community responsibility system', *Chicago Journal of International Law*, **5**(1), 109–38.

— (2006a). *Institutions and the Path to the Modern Economy: Lessons from Medieval Trade*, Cambridge.

— (2006b). 'History lessons: the birth of impersonal exchange: the community responsibility system and impartial justice', *Journal of Economic Perspectives*, **20**(2), 221–36.

— (2006c). 'Family structure, institutions, and growth: the origins and implications of western corporations', *American Economic Review Papers and Proceedings*, **96**(2), 308–12.

—, P. Milgrom and B. Weingast (1994). 'Coordination, commitment, and enforcement: the case of the merchant guild', *Journal of Political Economy*, **102**(4), 912–50.

Greve, A. (1994). 'Gast und Gastgeber: Hansekaufleute und Hosteliers in Brügge im 14. und 15. Jahrhundert', in *Norwegen und die Hanse. Wirtschaftliche und kulturelle Aspekte im europäischen Vergleich*, ed. V. Henn and A. Nedkvitne, Frankfurt am Main, 95–107.

— (2000). 'Brokerage and trade in medieval Bruges: regulation and reality', in *International Trade in the Low Countries 14th–16th centuries*, ed. P. Stabel, B. Blondé and A. Greve, Leuven / Apeldoorn, 37–44.

— (2001). 'Die Bedeutung der Brügger Hosteliers für hansische Kaufleute im 14. und 15. Jahrhundert', *Jaarboek voor middeleeuwse geschiedenis*, 4, 259–96.

— (2007). *Hansen, Hosteliers und Herbergen: Studien zum Aufenthalt hansischer Kaufleute in Brügge im 14. und 15. Jahrhundert*, Turnhout.

Grimm, C. M., H. Lee and K. G. Smith (2006). *Strategy as Action*, Oxford.

Gross, C. (1890). *The Gild Merchant: A Contribution to British Municipal History*, 2 vols, Oxford.

Grüll, G. (1974). 'The Poneggen hosiery enterprise, 1763–1818: a study of Austrian mercantilism', *Textile History*, 5, 38–79.

Guignet, P. (1979). 'Adaptations, mutations et survivances proto-industrielles dans le textile du Cambrésis et du Valenciennois du XVIIIe au debut du XXe siècle', *Revue du Nord*, 61, 27–59.

Gullickson, G. L. (1986). *Spinners and Weavers of Auffay. Rural Industry and the Sexual Division of Labor in a French Village, 1750–1850*, Cambridge.

Gutkas, K. (1983). 'Österreichs Städte zwischen Türkenkriegen und staatlichem Absolutismus', in *Städtewesen und Merkantilismus in Mitteleuropa*, ed. V. Press, Cologne, 82–110.

Guttkuhn, P. (1999). *Die Geschichte der Juden in Moisling und Lübeck von den Anfängen 1656 bis zur Emanzipation 1852*, Lübeck.

Guzman, G. G. (1996). 'European clerical envoys to the Mongols: reports of Western merchants in Eastern Europe and Central Asia, 1231–1255', *Journal of Medieval History*, **22**(1), 53–67.

Habib, I. (1990). 'Merchant communities in pre-colonial India', in *The Rise of Merchant Empires: Long-distance Trade in the Early Modern World, 1350–1750*, ed. J. D. Tracy, Cambridge, 371–99.

Häpke, R. (1908). *Brügges Entwicklung zum mittelalterlichen Weltmarkt*, Berlin.

Harreld, D. J. (2004a). *High Germans in the Low Countries: German Merchants and Commerce in Golden Age Antwerp*, Leiden.

— (2004b). 'Merchant and guild: the shift from privileged group to individual entrepreneur in sixteenth-century Antwerp', Paper delivered at the Fifth European Social Science History Conference, Berlin, 24–27 March.

Harris, R. (2000). *Industrializing English Law: Entrepreneurship and Business Organization, 1720–1844*, Cambridge.

Hasselberg, Y., L. Müller and N. Stenlås (1997). 'History from a network perspective', *CTS Working Paper*, 1997-01.

Heers, J. (1971). 'La mode et les marchés des draps de laine: Gênes et la Montagne à la fin du moyen âge', *Annales ESC*, **27**(5), 1093–117.

Hegel, K. V. (1862). 'Ulman Stromeier's "Püchel von meim geslecht und von abentewr" (1349 bis 1407)', *Die Chroniken der fränkischen Städte. Nürnberg*, ed. Bayerische Akademie der Wissenschaften, Leipzig, Vol. 1, 1–312.

Hejeebu, S. (2005). 'Contract enforcement in the English East India Company', *Journal of Economic History*, **65**(2), 496–523.

Helle, K. (2005). 'The emergence of the town of Bergen in the light of the latest research results', in *Das Hansische Kontor zu Bergen und die Lübecker Bergenfahrer: International Workshop Lübeck 2003*, ed. A. Grassmann, Lübeck, 12–27.

Henn, V. (1999). 'Der "dudesche kopman" zu Brügge und seine Beziehungen zu den "nationes" der übrigen Fremden im späten Mittelalter', in *'Kopet uns werk by tyden': Beiträge zur hansischen und preussischen Geschichte. Walter Stark zum 75. Geburtstag*, ed. N. Jörn, D. Kattinger and H. Wernicke, Schwerin, 131–42.

— (2005). 'Die Bergenfahrer und die süderseeischen Städte. Ein "Werkstattbericht"', in *Das Hansische Kontor zu Bergen und die Lübecker Bergenfahrer: International Workshop Lübeck 2003*, ed. A. Grassmann, Lübeck, 231–44.

Henneman, J. B. (1995). 'Bourgeoisie', in *Medieval France: An Encyclopedia*, ed. W. W. Kibler, London, 139.

Henry, R. L. (1926). *Contracts in the Local Courts of Medieval England*, New York.

Heyd, W. (1874). 'Das Haus der deutschen Kaufleute in Venedig', *Historische Zeitschrift*, **32**, 193–220.

Heymann, F. G. (1955). 'The role of the town in the Bohemia of the later Middle Ages', *Journal of World History / Cahiers d'histoire mondiale*, **2**, 326–46.

Hibbert, A. B. (1949). 'Catalan consulates in the thirteenth century', *Cambridge Historical Journal*, **9**, 352–8.

— (1963). 'The economic policies of towns', *The Cambridge Economic History of Europe, Vol. 3: Economic Organization and Policies in the Middle Ages*, ed. M. M. Postan, E. E. Rich and E. Miller, Cambridge, 157–229.

Hicks, J. R. (1935). 'Annual survey of economic theory: the theory of monopoly', *Econometrica*, **3**(1), 1–20.

— (1969). *A Theory of Economic History*, Oxford.

Hilton, R. H. (1984). 'Women traders in medieval England', *Women's Studies*, **11**, 139–55.

Hlaváček, I. (2000). 'The Luxemburgs and Rupert of the Palatinate, 1347–1410', in *The New Cambridge Medieval History, Vol. VI: c. 1300–c. 1415*, ed. M. Jones, Cambridge, 551–69.

Hoffman, E. (1980). 'Beiträge zur Geschichte der Stadt Schleswig und des westlichen Ostseeraums im 12. und 13. Jahrhundert', *Zeitschrift der Gesellschaft für Schleswig-Holsteinische Geschichte*, **105**, 27–76.

Hoffman, P. T. and K. Norberg (1994). 'Conclusion', in *Fiscal Crises, Liberty, and Representative Government, 1450–1789*, ed. P. T. Hoffman and K. Norberg, Stanford, 299–310.

Hoffmann, J. W. (1932). 'The Fondaco dei Tedeschi: the medium of Venetian-German trade', *Journal of Political Economy*, **40**(2), 244–52.

Hofmann, V. (1920). 'Beiträge zur neueren Wirtschaftsgeschichte. Die Wollenzeugfabrik zu Linz an der Donau', *Archiv für österreichische Geschichte*, **108**, 345–778.

Höhlbaum, K., ed. (1876). *Hansisches Urkundenbuch, Bd. 1: Urkunden von 975 bis 1300*, Halle an der Saale.

Holbach, R. (2001). 'Zum Austausch von Personen und Wissen im Handwerk des niederländischen und norddeutschen Raumes im Mittelalter und zu Beginn der Neuzeit.' '. . . *in guete freuntlichen nachbarlichen verwantnus und hantierung . . .*': *Wanderung von Personen, Verbreitung von Ideen, Austausch von Waren in den niederländischen und deutschen Küstenregionen vom 13.–18. Jahrhundert*, ed. D. E. H. d. Boer, G. Gleba and R. Holbach, Oldenburg, 361–82.

Holmes, G. A. (1960). 'Florentine merchants in England, 1346–1436', *Economic History Review*, 2nd ser., **13**, 193–208.

Hopcroft, R. L. (1999). 'Maintaining the balance of power: taxation and democracy in England and France, 1340–1688', *Sociological Perspectives*, **42**(1), 69–95.

Hørby, K. (1984). 'Königliche-dänische Kaufleute. Dänische Wanderkaufleute des frühen Mittelalters, ihre korporative Organisation und ihre Beziehungen zu dänischen Städten, Handelszentren und Märkten', in *Gilde und Korporation in den nordeuropäischen Städten des späten Mittelalters*, ed. K. Friedland, Cologne / Vienna, 41–50.

Hoyle, R. W. (1994). 'Parliament and taxation in sixteenth-century England', *English Historical Review*, **109**(434), 1174–96.

Hunt, E. S. (1994). *The Medieval Super-companies: A Study of the Peruzzi Company of Florence*, Cambridge.

— and J. M. Murray (1999). *A History of Business in Medieval Europe, 1200–1550*, Cambridge.

Hussey, R. D. (1929). 'Antecedents of the Spanish monopolistic overseas trading companies (1624–1728)', *Hispanic American Historical Review*, 9(1), 1–30.

Huvelin, P. (1897). *Essai historique sur le droit des foires et des marchés*, Paris.

— (1898). 'Les courriers des foires de Champagne', *Annales de droit commercial français, étranger et international*, 10, 376–92.

Hyde, J. K. (1979). 'Some uses of literacy in Venice and Florence in the thirteenth and fourteenth centuries', *Transactions of the Royal Historical Society*, 5th ser., 29, 109–28.

Infelise, M. (2007). 'From merchants' letters to handwritten political avvisi: notes on the origins of public information', in *Cultural Exchange in Early Modern Europe, Vol. 3: Correspondence, 1400–1700*, ed. F. Bethencourt and F. Egmond, Cambridge, 33–52.

ILO (International Labour Organization) (1989). 'The informal sector', in *Leading Issues in Economic Development*, ed. G. M. Meier, Oxford, 147–51.

Ingersoll, R. (2005). 'Medieval cities, Bruges and Florence', Rice University unpublished lecture [www.owlnet.rice.edu/~arch343/lecture9.html].

Irsigler, F. (1985a). 'Zur Problematik der Gilde- und Zunftterminologie', in *Gilden und Zünfte. Kaufmännische und gewerbliche Genossenschaften im frühen und hohen Mittelalter*, ed. B. Schwineköper, Sigmaringen, 53–70.

— (1985b). 'Der Alltag einer hansischen Kaufmannsfamilie im Spiegel der Veckinchusen-Briefe', *Hansische Geschichtsblätter*, 103, 75–100.

— (2002). 'Messehandel – Hansehandel', *Hansische Geschichtsblätter*, 120, 33–50.

Israel, J. I. (1989). *Dutch Primacy in World Trade, 1585–1740*, Oxford.

Jacks, D. S. (2004). 'Market integration in the North and Baltic seas, 1500–1800', *Journal of European Economic History*, 33(2), 285–330.

— , K. H. O'Rourke and J. G. Williamson (2009). 'Commodity price volatility and world market integration since 1700', *NBER Working Paper*, w14748.

Jacobsen, G. (1993). 'Review of Müller-Boysen, *Kaufmannsschutz und Handelsrecht im frühmittelalterlichen Nordeuropa*', *Speculum*, 68(2), 540–2.

Jacoby, D. (2003). 'Foreigners and the urban economy in Thessalonike, ca. 1150–ca. 1450', *Dumbarton Oaks Papers*, 57, 85–132.

Jacoby, H. G. and E. Skoufias (1997). 'Risk, financial markets, and human capital in a developing country', *Review of Economic Studies*, 64, 311–35.

Jahnke, C. (1997). '"Und ist der fisch- und Heringsfangh das erste beneficium . . . ". Städtische und freie Markt-Fischerei im mittelalterlichen Ostseeraum', *Zeitschrift der Gesellschaft für Schleswig-Holsteinische Geschichte*, 122, 289–321.

— (2000). *Das Silber des Meeres. Fang und Vertrieb von Ostseehering zwischen Norwegen und Italien (12.–16. Jahrhundert)*, Cologne / Weimar / Vienna.

— (2008). 'Handelsstrukturen im Ostseeraum im 12. und beginnenden 13. Jahrhundert: Ansätze einer Auswertung', *Hansische Geschichtsblätter*, 126, 145–85.

Jehel, G. (1978). 'Januensis ergo mercator ou le petit monde d'un homme d'affaires génois, le juge Guarnerius (1210–1221)', *Journal of Medieval History*, 4(3), 243–66.

Jenks, S. (1982). 'War die Hanse kreditfeindlich?', *Vierteljahrschrift für Sozial- und Wirtschaftsgeschichte*, 69, 305–38.

— (1996). 'Zum hansischen Gästerecht', *Hansische Geschichtsblätter*, 114, 3–60.

— (2005). 'Transaktionskostentheorie und die mittelalterliche Hanse', *Hansische Geschichtsblätter*, **123**, 31–42.

Jensen, R. (2000). 'Agricultural volatility and investments in children', *American Economic Review*, **90**, 399–404.

Johanek, P. (1999). 'Merchants, markets and towns', in *The New Cambridge Medieval History, Vol. 3*: c. *900*–c. *1024*, ed. T. Reuter, Cambridge, 64–94.

Johansen, P. (1940). 'Die Bedeutung der Hanse für Livland', *Hansische Geschichtsblätter*, 65/66, 1–55.

Johnson, C. H. (1982). 'De-industrialization: the case of the Languedoc woolens industry', in *VIII Congrès Internationale d'Histoire Economique, Budapest 16–22 août 1982, Section A2: La protoindustrialisation: Théorie et réalité, Rapports*, ed. P. Deyon and F. F. Mendels, Lille, Vol. I.

Jones, S. R. H. and S. P. Ville (1996). 'Efficient transactors or rent-seeking monopolist? The rationale for early chartered trading companies', *Journal of Economic History*, **56**(4), 898–916.

Jones, W. J. (1979). 'The foundations of English bankruptcy: statutes and commissions in the early modern period', *Transactions of the American Philosophical Society*, ns, **69**(3), 1–63.

Kadens, E. (2004). 'Order within law, variety within custom: the character of the medieval merchant law', *Chicago Journal of International Law*, **5**(1), 39–66.

Kagan, R. L. (1981). *Lawsuits and Litigants in Castile 1500–1700*, Chapel Hill, NC.

Kahl, H. D. (1978). 'Einige Beobachtungen zum Sprachgebrauch von *natio* im mittelalterlichen Latein mit Ausblicken auf das neuhochdeutsche Fremdwort Nation', in *Aspekte der Nationenbildung im Mittelalter: Ergebnisse der Marburger Rundgespräche 1972–1975*, ed. H. Beumann and W. Schröder, Sigmaringen, 63–108.

Kallioinen, M. (1998). 'Town council and the transaction costs in medieval foreign trade', *Finnish Economic History Association Yearbook*, [www.cc.jyu.fi/~pete/yearbook/TCOSTS.htm, consulted on 26 April 2004].

Karr, G. (1930). *Die Uracher Leinenweberei und die Leinwandhandlungskompagnie. Ein Beitrag zu Wirtschaftsgeschichte Alt-Württembergs*, Stuttgart.

Katele, I. B. (1986). 'Captains and corsairs: Venice and piracy, 1261–1381', University of Illinois at Urbana-Champaign Ph.D. dissertation.

— (1988). 'Piracy and the Venetian state: the dilemma of maritime defense in the fourteenth century', *Speculum*, **63**, 865–89.

Katz, E. D. (2000). 'Private order and public institutions: comments on McMillan and Woodruff's "Private order under dysfunctional public order"', *Michigan Law Review*, **98**(8), 2481–93.

Kedar, B. Z. (1976). *Merchants in Crisis: Genoese and Venetian Men of Affairs and the Fourteenth-century Depression*, New Haven, CT.

— (1977). 'The Genoese notaries of 1382: the anatomy of an urban occupational group', in *The Medieval City*, ed. H. A. Miskimin, D. Herlihy and A. L. Udovitch, New Haven / London, 73–94.

— (1985). 'L'Officium Robarie di Genova: un tentativo di coesistere con la violenza', *Archivio storico italiano*, **143**(525), 331–72.

Kellenbenz, H. (1958). *Sephardim an der unteren Elbe. Ihre wirtschaftliche und politische Bedeutung vom Ende des 16. bis zum Beginn des 18. Jahrhunderts,* Wiesbaden.

Kellett, J. R. (1958). 'The breakdown of guild and corporation control of the handicraft and retail trades in London', *Economic History Review,* ns, **10**(3), 381–94.

Kemble, J. M. (1876). *The Saxons in England: A History of the English Commonwealth till the Period of the Norman Conquest,* London.

Kermode, J. (1998). *Medieval Merchants: York, Beverley, and Hull in the Later Middle Ages,* Cambridge.

Kisch, H. (1964). 'The growth deterrents of a medieval heritage: the Aachen-area woollen trades before 1790', *Journal of Economic History,* 24, 518–37.

— (1972). 'From monopoly to laissez-faire: the early growth of the Wupper Valley textile trades', *Journal of European Economic History,* 1(2), 298–407.

Klarwill, V. v. (1923). *Fugger-Zeitungen. Ungedruckte Briefe an das Haus Fugger aus den Jahren 1568–1605,* Vienna.

— (1924). *The Fugger Newsletter, Being a Selection of Unpublished Letters from the Correspondents of the House of Fugger During the Years 1568–1605,* London.

— (1926). *The Fugger News-letters: Second Series, Being a Further Selection from the Fugger Papers,* London.

Klein, P. W. (1965). *De Trippen in de 17e Eeuw. Een studie over het Ondernemersgedrag op de Hollandse Stapelmarkt,* Assen.

— (1982). 'Dutch capitalism and the European world-economy', in *Dutch Capitalism and World Capitalism,* ed. M. Aymard, Cambridge, 75–92.

Knight, J. (1995). 'Models, interpretations, and theories: constructing explanations of institutional emergence and change', in *Explaining Social Institutions,* ed. J. Knight and I. Sened, Ann Arbor, MI, 95–119.

Kohn, M. (2003a). 'Merchant associations in pre-industrial Europe', *Dartmouth College Department of Economics Working Paper,* #03–11.

— (2003b). 'Organized markets in pre-industrial Europe', *Dartmouth College Department of Economics Working Paper,* #03–12.

Kotilaine, J. T. (2009). 'Russian merchant colonies in 17th-century Sweden', Paper presented at the XV World Economic History Congress, Utrecht, 3–7 August.

Kowaleski, M. (1995). *Local Markets and Regional Trade in Medieval Exeter,* Cambridge.

Kriedte, P. (1982). 'Die Stadt im Prozeß der europäischen Proto-Industrialisierung', *Die alte Stadt,* 9, 19–51.

— (1996). 'Trade', in *Germany: A New Social and Economic History, Vol. II: 1630–1800,* ed. S. Ogilvie, London, 100–33.

Krueger, H. C. (1933). 'Genoese trade with northwest Africa in the twelfth century', *Speculum,* 3, 377–95.

Kuehn, T. (2006). 'The Renaissance consilium as justice', *Renaissance Quarterly,* **59**(4), 1058–88.

Kümin, B. (1999). 'Useful to have, but impossible to govern: inns and taverns in early modern Bern and Vaud', *Journal of Early Modern History,* 3, 153–75.

Kuran, T. (2003). 'The Islamic commercial crisis: institutional roots of economic underdevelopment in the Middle East', *Journal of Economic History*, **63**(2), 414–46.

— (2004). 'Why the Middle East is economically underdeveloped: historical mechanisms of institutional stagnation', *Journal of Economic Perspectives*, **18**(3), 71–90.

Kuske, B. (1939). 'Der Kölner Stapel und seine Zusammenhänge als wirtschaftspolitisches Beispiel', *Jahrbuch des Kölnischen Geschichtsvereins*, **21**, 1–46.

—, ed. (1978). *Quellen zur Geschichte des Kölner Handels und Verkehrs im Mittelalter, Vol. I: 12. Jahrhundert bis 1448*, Berlin.

Laiou, A. E. (2000). 'The Byzantine empire in the fourteenth century', in *The New Cambridge Medieval History, Vol. VI: c. 1300–c. 1415*, ed. M. Jones, Cambridge, 795–824.

— (2001). 'Byzantine trade with Christians and Muslims and the Crusades', in *The Crusades from the Perspective of Byzantium and the Muslim World*, ed. A. E. Laiou and R. P. Mottahedeh, Washington DC, 157–96.

— (2002). 'Exchange and trade, seventh–twelfth centuries', in *The Economic History of Byzantium: From the Seventh through the Fifteenth Century*, ed. A. E. Laiou, Washington DC, 697–770.

Laiou-Thomadakis, A. E. (1980–1). 'The Byzantine economy in the Mediterranean trade system: thirteenth–fifteenth centuries', *Dumbarton Oaks Papers*, **34**, 177–222.

Lambert, B. and P. Stabel (2005). 'Squaring the circle: merchant firms, merchant guilds, urban infrastructure and political authority in late medieval Bruges', Paper presented at the Workshop on Mercantile Organization in Pre-Industrial Europe, Antwerp, 18–19 November.

Landman, J. H. (1998). 'The laws of community, Margery Kempe, and the "Canon's Yeoman's Tale"', *Journal of Medieval and Early Modern Studies*, **28**(2), 389–426.

Lane, F. C. (1944). 'Family partnerships and joint ventures in the Venetian Republic', *Journal of Economic History*, **4**(2), 178–96.

— (1963). 'Venetian merchant galleys, 1300–1334: private and communal operation', *Speculum*, **38**, 179–205.

— (1973). *Venice and History*, Baltimore, MD.

Lapeyre, H. (1955). *Une famille de marchands: les Ruiz*, Paris.

Larson, L. M., ed. (1917). *The King's Mirror (Speculum regale – Konungs skuggsjá), Translated from the Old Norwegian with Introduction and Notes*, New York / London / Oxford.

Laurent, H. (1935a). 'Nouvelles recherches sur la Hanse des XVII villes', *Le Moyen Âge*, 3rd ser., **6**(2), 81–94.

— (1935b). *Un grand commerce d'exportation au moyen âge: la draperie des Pays-Bas en France et dans les pays méditerranéens (XIIe–XVe siècles)*, Paris.

Lefebvre, E. (1997). 'A historical profile of Belgium: from urban to modern Belgian citizenship', *ZERP Discussion Paper 3*.

Leguay, J.-P. (2000). 'Urban life', *The New Cambridge Medieval History, Vol. VI: c. 1300–c. 1415*, ed. M. Jones, Cambridge, 102–25.

Lesger, C. M. (2006). *The Rise of the Amsterdam Market and Information Exchange: Merchants, Commercial Expansion and Change in the Spatial Economy of the Low Countries, c. 1550–1630*, Aldershot / Burlington.

Lesnikov, M. P. (1973). *Die Handelsbücher des Hansischen Kaufmannes Veckinchusen*, Berlin.

Lewis, A. R. and T. Runyan (1985). *European Naval and Maritime History, 300–1500*, Bloomington, IN.

Lewis, G. (1993). *The Advent of Modern Capitalism in France, 1770–1840: The Contribution of Pierre François Tubeuf*, Oxford.

Liebenam, W. (1890). *Zur Geschichte und Organisation des römischen Vereinswesens*, Leipzig.

Lieber, A. E. (1968). 'Eastern business practices and medieval European commerce', *Economic History Review*, 21, 230–43.

Limberger, M. (2001). 'No town in the world provides more advantages: economies of agglomeration and the golden age of Antwerp', in *Urban Achievement in Early Modern Europe: Golden Ages in Antwerp, Amsterdam and London*, ed. P. O'Brien et al., Cambridge, 39–69.

Limor, O. (1991). 'Missionary merchants: three medieval anti-Jewish works from Genoa', *Journal of Medieval History*, 17(1), 35–51.

Lin, N. (2001). *Social Capital: A Theory of Social Structure and Action*, Cambridge.

Lindberg, E. (2004). 'The revival of guilds: a preface to a study of institutions and trade in the Baltic area, c. 1650–1880', Paper delivered at the Fifth European Social Science History Conference, Berlin, 24–27 March.

— (2007). 'Mercantilism and urban inequalities in eighteenth-century Sweden', *Scandinavian Economic History Review*, 55(1), 1–19.

— (2008). 'The rise of Hamburg as a global marketplace in the seventeenth century: a comparative political economy perspective', *Comparative Studies in Society and History*, 50(3), 641–62.

— (2009). 'Club goods and inefficient institutions: why the important medieval trading cities of Danzig and Lübeck failed in the early modern period', *Economic History Review*, 62(3), 604–28.

Link, C. and D. Kapfenberger (2005). 'Transaktionskostentheorie und hansische Geschichte: Danzigs Seehandel im 15. Jahrhundert im Licht einer volkswirtschaftlichen Theorie', *Hansische Geschichtsblätter*, 123, 153–69.

Lis, C. and H. Soly (1996). 'Ambachtsgilden in vergelijkend perspectief: de Noordelijke en de Zuidelijke Nederlanden, 15de–18de eeuw', in *Werelden van verschil: ambachtsgilden in de Lage Landen*, ed. C. Lis and H. Soly, Brussels, 11–42.

Litchfield, R. B. (1969). 'Les investissements commerciaux des patriciens florentins au XVIIIe siècle', *Annales ESC*, 24(3), 685–721.

Liu, S. S. (1925). *Extraterritoriality: Its Rise and Its Decline*, New York.

Lloyd, T. H. (1977). *The English Wool Trade in the Middle Ages*, Cambridge.

— (1982). *Alien Merchants in England in the High Middle Ages*, Brighton.

— (1991). *England and the German Hanse, 1157–1611: A Study of Their Trade and Commercial Diplomacy*, Cambridge.

Lopez, R. S. (1943). 'European merchants in the medieval Indies: the evidence of commercial documents', *Journal of Economic History*, 3(2), 164–84.

— (1945). 'Silk industry in the Byzantine empire', *Speculum*, **20**(1), 1–42.

— (1958). 'Le marchand génois: un profil collectif', *Annales ESC*, **13**(3), 501–15.

— (1969). 'Stars and spices: the earliest Italian manual of commercial practice', *Explorations in Economic History*, **7**(1), 35–42.

— (1987). 'The trade of medieval Europe: the south', in *The Cambridge Economic History of Europe, Vol. 3: Economic Organization and Policies in the Middle Ages*, ed. M. M. Postan and E. Miller, Cambridge, 306–401.

— and I. W. Raymond (1955). *Medieval Trade in the Mediterranean World*, New York.

Lucassen, J. (2004). 'A multinational and its labor force: the Dutch East India Company, 1595–1795', *International Labor and Working-class History*, **66**, 12–39.

Lydon, G. (2009). 'A paper economy of faith without faith in paper: a reflection on Islamic institutional history', *Journal of Economic Behavior and Organization*, **71**, 647–59.

MacKay, D. (1937). *The Honourable Company: A History of the Hudson's Bay Company*, London / Toronto.

Madden, T. F. (2002). 'The chrysobull of Alexius I Comnenus to the Venetians: the date and the debate', *Journal of Medieval History*, **28**, 23–41.

Maddison, A. (1995). *Monitoring the World Economy 1820–1992*, Paris.

Maitland, F. W. and W. P. Baildon, eds. (1891). *The Court Baron: Being Precedents for Use in Seignorial and Other Local Courts*, London.

Malausséna, P.-L. (1969). *La vie en Provence orientale aux XIVe et XVe siècles. Un exemple: Grasse à travers les actes notariés*, Paris.

Mallett, M. E. (1959). 'The Sea Consuls of Florence in the fifteenth century', *Papers of the British School at Rome*, **27**, 156–68.

— (1962). 'Anglo-Florentine commercial relations, 1465–1491', *Economic History Review*, **15**(2), 250–65.

Malynes, G. d. (1622). *Consuetudo, vel lex mercatoria, or the Ancient Law*, London.

Maréchal, J. (1951). 'Le départ de Bruges des marchands étrangers (XVe et XVIe siècle)', *Annales de la Société d'Emulation de Bruges / Handelingen van het Genootschap voor Geschiedenis te Brugge (Emulatie)*, **88**, 16–74.

— (1953). 'La colonie espagnole de Bruges du XIVe au XVIe siècle', *Revue du nord*, **35**(137), 5–40.

Marsh, D. (2006). 'A fellowship on the fringes: the Gardeners' Company of London in the seventeenth century', in *Guilds and Association in Europe, 900–1900*, ed. I. A. Gadd and P. Wallis, London: 123–46.

Marshall, P. J. (1976). *East Indian Fortunes*, Oxford.

Martin, J. (1975). 'Les uškujniki de Novgorod: marchands ou pirates?', *Cahiers du monde russe et soviétique*, **16**(1), 5–18.

Mas-Latrie, L. d. (1892). 'L'officium robarie ou l'office de la piraterie à Gênes au Moyen Âge', *Bibliothèque de l'école des chartes*, **53**, 264–72.

Mas-Latrie, R. d. (1866). 'Du droit de marque ou droit de représailles au Moyen Âge [premier article]', *Bibliothèque de l'école des chartes*, **27**, 529–77.

Masschaele, J. (1997). *Peasants, Merchants, and Markets: Inland Trade in Medieval England, 1150–1350*, New York.

Mathers, C. J. (1988). 'Family partnerships and international trade in early modern Europe: merchants from Burgos in England and France, 1470–1570', *Business History Review*, **62**, 367–97.

Mathias, P. (1995). 'Strategies for reducing risk by entrepreneurs in the early modern period', in *Entrepreneurs and Entrepreneurship in Early Modern Times: Merchants and Industrialists within the Orbit of the Dutch Staple Market*, ed. C. Lesger and L. Noordegraaf, Den Haag, 5–24.

Mattingley, G. (1954). *Renaissance Diplomacy*, Boston.

Mauro, F. (1990). 'Merchant communities, 1350–1750', in *The Rise of Merchant Empires: Long-distance Trade in the Early Modern World, 1350–1750*, ed. J. D. Tracy, Cambridge, 255–86.

Maxwell, K. (2001). 'The spark: Pombal, the Amazon and the Jesuits', *Portuguese Studies*, **17**(1), 168–83.

Mayer, T. (1956). 'Die Anfänge von Lübeck. Die Entstehung und Auflösung eines Schlagwortes', *Westfälische Forschungen*, **9**, 244–54.

Mazzaoui, M. F. (1981). *The Italian Cotton Industry in the Later Middle Ages, 1100–1600*, Cambridge.

McCusker, J. J. and C. Gravesteijn (1991). *The Beginnings of Commercial and Financial Journalism: The Commodity Price Currents, Exchange Rate Currents, and Money Currents of Early Modern Europe*, Amsterdam.

McManamon, J. M. (2003). 'Maltese seafaring in mediaeval and post-mediaeval times', *Mediterranean Historical Review*, **18**(1), 32–58.

McMillan, J. and C. Woodruff (2000). 'Private order under dysfunctional public order', *Michigan Law Review*, **98**(8), 2421–58.

Medick, H. (1996). *Weben und Überleben in Laichingen 1650–1900. Untersuchungen zur Sozial-, Kultur- und Wirtschaftsgeschichte aus der Perspektive einer lokalen Gesellschaft im frühneuzeitlichen Württemberg*, Göttingen.

Meiggs, R. (1960). *Roman Ostia*, Oxford.

Melis, F. (1954). 'Il commercio transatlantico di una compagnia florentina stabilita a Siviglia a pochi anni dalle imprese di Cortes e Pizarro', in *Ferdinando el Católico y la cultura de su tiempo, V Congreso de Historia de la Corona de Aragón*, ed. A. Bóscolo et al., Zaragoza, Vol. III: 129–206.

Mézin, A. (2006). 'La fonction consulaire dans la France d'Ancien Régime: origine, principes, prérogatives', in *La fonction consulaire à l'époque moderne: l'affirmation d'une institution économique et politique, 1500–1700*, ed. J. Ulbert and G. Le Bouëdec, Rennes, 37–50.

Michaud-Quantin, P. (1970). *Universitas. Expressions du mouvement communautaire dans le Moyen-Age latin*, Paris.

Mickwitz, G. (1937). 'Neues zur Funktion der hansischen Handelsgesellschaften', *Hansische Geschichtsblätter*, **62**, 24–39.

Middleton, N. (2005). 'Early medieval port customs, tolls and controls on foreign trade', *Early Medieval Europe*, **13**(4), 313–58.

Milgrom, P. R., D. C. North and B. R. Weingast (1990). 'The role of institutions in the revival of trade: the medieval law merchant, private judges and the Champagne fairs', *Economics and Politics*, **2**, 1–23.

Militzer, K. (1997). 'Der Handel rheinischer Kaufleute in Reval bis zum 16. Jahrhundert', in *Reval. Handel und Wandel vom 13. bis zum 20. Jahrhundert*, ed. N. Angermann and W. Lenz, Lüneburg, 111–34.

Miller, E. (1965). 'Economic policies of governments II: France and England', in *The Cambridge Economic History of Europe, Vol. 3: Economic Organization and Policies in the Middle Ages*, ed. M. M. Postan, E. E. Rich and E. Miller, Cambridge, 290–339.

Mirot, L. (1927). 'Études lucquoises', *Bibliothèque de l'école des chartes*, **88**, 50–86.

Misāns, I. (2008). 'Deutsche und ihre Nachbarn in den Hansestädten des östlichen Ostseeraums', in *Kontinuitäten und Brüche: Zuwanderer und Alteingesessene von 500 bis 1500*, ed. K. Kaser et al., Klagenfurt, 465–74.

Mitchell, W. (1904). *Essay on the Early History of the Law Merchant*, New York.

Molho, A., ed. (1969). *Social and Economic Foundations of the Italian Renaissance*, New York.

Mollat, M. (1970). 'Le rôle international des marchands espagnoles dans les ports de l'Europe occidental à l'époque des Rois Catholiques', *Anuario de Historia Económica y Social*, **3**, 41–55.

Molnár, A. (2007). 'Struggle for the chapel of Belgrade (1612–1643). Trade and Catholic church in Ottoman Hungary', *Acta Orientalia*, **60**(1), 73–134.

Moodie, D. W. and J. C. Lehr (1981). 'Macro-historical geography and the great chartered companies: the case of the Hudson's Bay Company', *Canadian Geographer*, **25**(2), 267–71.

Moore, E. W. (1985). *The Fairs of Medieval England: An Introductory Study*, Toronto.

Mueller, R. C. (1996). 'Foreign investment in Venetian government bonds and the case of Paolo Guinigi, lord of Lucca, early 15th century', in *Cities of Finance*, ed. H. Diederiks and D. Reeder, Amsterdam, 69–90.

— (1997). *The Venetian Money Market: Banks, Panics, and the Public Debt, 1200–1500*, Baltimore, MD.

Muldrew, C. (1998). *The Economy of Obligation: The Culture of Credit and Social Relations in Early Modern England*, New York.

Müller, L. (1998). *The Merchant Houses of Stockholm, c. 1640–1800: A Comparative Study of Early-modern Entrepreneurial Behaviour*, Uppsala.

— (2001). 'Institutional change and entrepreneurial behaviour in Sweden 1600–1800', Paper presented at the 'Workshop on entrepreneurship and institutional context in a comparative perspective', Utrecht, 23 November.

— (2005). 'The Dutch entrepreneurial networks and Sweden in the Age of Greatness', in *Trade, Diplomacy and Cultural Exchange: Continuity and Change in the North Sea Area and the Baltic, c. 1350 – 1750*, ed. H. Brand, Hilversum, 59–74.

Müller-Boysen, C. (1990). *Kaufmannsschutz und Handelsrecht im frühmittelalterlichen Nordeuropa*, Neumünster.

Munro, J. H. (2001). 'The "new institutional economics" and the changing fortunes of fairs in medieval and early modern Europe: the textile trades, warfare, and transaction costs', *Vierteljahrschrift für Sozial- und Wirtschaftsgeschichte*, **88**(1), 1–47.

Munzinger, M. R. (2006). 'The profits of the Cross: merchant involvement in the Baltic Crusade (c. 1180–1230)', *Journal of Medieval History*, **32**(2), 163–85.

Murray, J. M. (1983). 'Notaries public in Flanders in the late Middle Ages', Northwestern University Ph.D. dissertation.

— (2000). 'Of nodes and networks: Bruges and the infrastructure of trade in fourteenth-century Europe', in *International Trade in the Low Countries 14th–16th centuries*, ed. P. Stabel, B. Blondé and A. Greve, Leuven / Apeldoorn, 1–14.

— (2004). *Bruges, Cradle of Capitalism, 1280–1390*, Cambridge.

Murray, K. M. E. (1935). *The Constitutional History of the Cinque Ports*, Manchester.

Murrell, P. (2009). 'Design and evolution in institutional development: the insignificance of the English Bill of Rights', *University of Maryland Department of Economics Working Paper*, 13 December.

Nachbar, T. B. (2005). 'Monopoly, mercantilism, and the politics of regulation', *Virginia Law Review*, **91**(6), 1313–79.

Narayan, D. and L. Pritchett (2000). 'Social capital: evidence and implications', in *Social Capital: A Multifaceted Perspective*, ed. P. Dasgupta and I. Serageldin, Washington DC, 269–95.

Neal, L. (1990). 'The Dutch and English East India Companies compared: evidence from the stock and foreign exchange markets', in *The Rise of Merchant Empires: Long-distance Trade in the Early Modern World, 1350–1750*, ed. J. D. Tracy, Cambridge, 195–223.

Nelson, L. H., ed. (1996). *Liber de restauratione Monasterii Sancti Martini Tornacensis: the restoration of the Monastery of Saint Martin of Tournai, by Herman of Tournai*, Washington DC.

Neumann, G. (1977). 'Vom Lübecker Botenwesen in 15. Jahrhundert', *Zeitschrift des Vereins für Lübeckische Geschichte und Altertumskunde*, **57**, 128–37.

Newbery, D. M. G. and J. E. Stiglitz (1981). *The Theory of Commodity Price Stabilization: A Study in the Economics of Risk*, Oxford.

Nicholas, D. (1979). 'The English trade at Bruges in the last years of Edward III', *Journal of Medieval History*, **5**, 23–61.

— (1997a). *The Growth of the Medieval City: From Late Antiquity to the Early Fourteenth Century*, London.

— (1997b). *The Later Medieval City, 1300–1500*, London / New York.

Nitzsch, K. W. (1892). 'Die niederdeutsche Kaufgilde', *Zeitschrift der Savigny-Stiftung für Rechtsgeschichte, germanistische Abteilung*, **13**, 1–95.

Nivet, J.-F. (2004). 'Corporate and public governances in transition: the limits of property rights and the significance of legal institutions', *European Journal of Comparative Economics*, **1**(2), 3–21.

Nörr, K. W. (1987). 'Procedure in mercantile matters: some comparative aspects', in *The Courts and the Development of Commercial Law*, ed. V. Piergiovanni, Berlin, 195–202.

North, D. C. (1981). *Structure and Change in Economic History*, New York / London.

— (1990). *Institutions, Institutional Change and Economic Performance*, Cambridge.

— (1991). 'Institutions, transaction costs, and the rise of merchant empires', in *The Political Economy of Merchant Empires: State Power and World Trade, 1350–1750*, ed. J. D. Tracy, Cambridge, 22–40.

— and R. P. Thomas (1971), 'The rise and fall of the manorial system: a theoretical model', *Journal of Economic History*, **31**(4), 777–803.

— and B. R. Weingast (1989). 'Constitutions and commitment: the evolution of institutions governing public choice in seventeenth-century England', *Journal of Economic History*, 49(4), 803–32.

Northrup, L. S. (1998). 'The Bahrī Mamlūk sultanate, 1250–1390', in *The Cambridge History of Egypt, Vol. I: Islamic Egypt, 640–1517*, ed. C. F. Petry, Cambridge, 242–89.

Nye, J. S. (2003). *Understanding International Conflicts: An Introduction to Theory and History*, New York / Harlow.

O'Brien, J. G. (2002). 'In defense of the mystical body: Giovanni da Legnano's theory of reprisals', *Roman Legal Tradition*, 1, 25–55.

O'Brien, P. K. (1982). 'European economic development: the contribution of the periphery', *Economic History Review*, 2nd ser., 35, 1–18.

— (1990). 'European industrialization: from the voyages of discovery to the Industrial Revolution', in *The European Discovery of the World and Its Economic Effects on Pre-industrial Society, 1500–1800*, ed. H. Pohl, Stuttgart, 154–77.

Ogilvie, S. C. (1992). 'Germany and the seventeenth-century crisis', *Historical Journal*, 35, 417–41.

— (1993). 'Proto-industrialization in Europe', *Continuity and Change*, 8, 159–79.

— (1996a). 'Social institutions and proto-industrialization', in *European Proto-industrialization*, ed. S. C. Ogilvie and M. Cerman, Cambridge, 23–37.

— (1996b). 'The beginnings of industrialization', in *Germany: A New Social and Economic History, Vol. II: 1630–1800*, ed. S. C. Ogilvie, London, 263–308.

— (1997). *State Corporatism and Proto-industry: The Württemberg Black Forest, 1580–1797*, Cambridge.

— (1999). 'The German state: a non-Prussian view', in *Rethinking Leviathan: The Eighteenth-century State in Britain and Germany*, ed. E. Hellmuth and J. Brewer, Oxford, 167–202.

— (2000a). 'The European economy in the eighteenth century', in *The Short Oxford History of Europe, Vol. XII: The Eighteenth Century: Europe 1688–1815*, ed. T. W. C. Blanning, Oxford, 91–130.

— (2000b). 'Social Capital, Social Networks, and History', Working paper, Faculty of Economics, University of Cambridge (12 June 2000) [www.econ. cam.ac.uk/faculty/ogilvie/social-capital-and-history.pdf].

— (2001). 'The economic world of the Bohemian serf: economic concepts, preferences and constraints on the estate of Friedland, 1583–1692', *Economic History Review*, 54, 430–53.

— (2003). *A Bitter Living: Women, Markets, and Social Capital in Early Modern Germany*, Oxford.

— (2004a). 'How does social capital affect women? Guilds and communities in early modern Germany', *American Historical Review*, 109(2), 325–59.

— (2004b). 'Women and labour markets in early modern Germany', *Jahrbuch für Wirtschaftsgeschichte*, 2, 25–60.

— (2004c). 'Guilds, efficiency and social capital: evidence from German proto-industry', *Economic History Review*, 57, 286–333.

— (2005). 'The use and abuse of trust: the deployment of social capital by early modern guilds', *Jahrbuch für Wirtschaftsgeschichte*, 1, 15–52.

— (2007a). 'Can we rehabilitate the guilds? A sceptical re-appraisal', *Cambridge Working Papers in Economics*, 0745.

— (2007b). '"Whatever is, is right"? Economic institutions in pre-industrial Europe', *Economic History Review*, **60**(4), 649–84.

— and M. Cerman (1996). 'The theories of proto-industrialization', in *European Proto-industrialization*, ed. S. C. Ogilvie and M. Cerman, Cambridge, 1–11.

Ogris, A. (2004). 'Die Linzer Wollzeugfabrik und die Orientalische Kompanie: Reaktionen in Kärnten (1725/26) auf eine Privilegierung', in *Stadtarchiv und Stadtgeschichte. Forschungen und Innovationen. Festschrift für Fritz Mayrhofer zur Vollendung seines 60. Lebensjahres*, ed. W. Schuster, M. Schimböck and A. Schweiger, Linz, 375–86.

Ojala, J. (1997). 'Approaching Europe: the merchant networks between Finland and Europe during the eighteenth and nineteenth centuries', *European Review of Economic History*, **1**(3), 323–52.

Olesen, J. E. (1999). 'Die preußischen Hansestädte in der nordischen Politik 1434–1450', in *'Kopet uns werk by tyden': Beiträge zur hansischen und preussischen Geschichte. Walter Stark zum 75. Geburtstag*, ed. N. Jörn, D. Kattinger and H. Wernicke, Schwerin, 215–22.

Origo, I. (1986). *The Merchant of Prato, Francesco di Marco Datini, 1335–1410*, Boston.

Ormrod, W. M. (2000). 'England: Edward II and Edward III', in *The New Cambridge Medieval History, Vol. VI: c. 1300–c. 1415*, ed. M. Jones, Cambridge, 273–96.

Oxford English Dictionary, OED Online, 2nd edn 1989, [www.dictionary.oed.com/entrance.dtl].

Pach, Z. P. (2007). 'Hungary and the Levantine trade in the 14th–17th centuries', *Acta Orientalia*, **60**(1), 9–31.

Padgett, J. F. and P. D. McLean (2006). 'Organizational invention and elite transformation: the birth of partnership systems in Renaissance Florence', *American Journal of Sociology*, **111**(5), 1463–1568.

Pakucs, M. (2003). '"Greek" merchants in the Saxon towns of Transylvania in the late Middle Ages', Paper presented at the Interdisciplinary Workshop on Segregation, Integration, and Assimilation in Medieval Towns, Central European University, Budapest, 20–22 February.

Palais, H. (1959). 'England's first attempt to break the commercial monopoly of the Hanseatic League, 1377–1380', *American Historical Review*, **64**(4), 852–65.

Paquette, G. B. (2007). 'State-civil society cooperation and conflict in the Spanish Empire: the intellectual and political activities of the ultramarine *Consulados* and economic societies, c. 1780–1810', *Journal of Latin American Studies*, **39**, 263–98.

Paravicini, W. (1992). 'Bruges and Germany', in *Bruges and Europe*, ed. V. Vermeersch, Antwerp, 99–128.

Pearson, M. N. (1991). 'Merchants and states', in *The Political Economy of Merchant Empires: State Power and World Trade, 1350–1750*, ed. J. D. Tracy, Cambridge, 41–116.

Pedersen, F. (2006). 'Trade and politics in the medieval Baltic: English merchants and England's relations to the Hanseatic League 1370–1437', in *Public Power in Europe: Studies in Historical Transformations*, ed. J. S. Amelang and S. Beer, Pisa, 161–80.

Pegolotti, F. B. (1936). *La Pratica della Mercatura*, repr. of 1st edn 1340, Cambridge, MA.

Pelling, M. (2006). 'Corporatism or individualism: parliament, the navy, and the splitting of the London Barber-Surgeons' Company in 1745', in *Guilds and Association in Europe, 900–1900*, ed. I. A. Gadd and P. Wallis, London, 57–82.

Pelus-Kaplan, M.-L. (2007). 'Merchants and immigrants in Hanseatic cities, c. 1500–1700', in *Cultural Exchange in Early Modern Europe, Vol. 2: Cities and Cultural Exchange in Europe, 1400–1700*, ed. D. Calabi and S. T. Christensen, Cambridge, 132–53.

Pérotin-Dumon, A. (1991). 'The pirate and the emperor: power and the law on the seas', in *The Political Economy of Merchant Empires: State Power and World Trade, 1350–1750*, ed. J. D. Tracy, Cambridge, 196–227.

Persson, K. G. (1999). *Grain Markets in Europe, 1500–1900: Integration and Deregulation*, Cambridge.

Pertz, G. H., ed. (1925). *Monumenta Germaniae Historica, Scriptorum Tomus IV*, Hanover.

Petty, W. (1690). *Political Arithmetick*, London.

Peyer, H. C. (1982). 'Gastfreundschaft und kommerzielle Gastlichkeit im Mittelalter', *Historische Zeitschrift*, **235**(2), 265–88.

— (1983). 'Einführung', in *Gastfreundschaft, Taverne und Gasthaus im Mittelalter*, ed. H. C. Peyer and E. Müller-Luckner, Munich / Vienna, vii–xiii.

Pfister, U. (1992). *Die Zürcher Fabriques: protoindustrielles Wachstum vom 16. zum 18. Jahrhundert*, Zürich.

Phillips, C. R. (1983). 'Spanish merchants and the wool trade in the sixteenth century', *Sixteenth Century Journal*, **14**(3), 259–82.

— (1990). 'The growth and composition of trade in the Iberian empires, 1450–1750', in *The Rise of Merchant Empires: Long-distance Trade in the Early Modern World, 1350–1750*, ed. J. D. Tracy, Cambridge, 34–101.

Phillips, W. D. (1986). 'Local integration and long-distance ties: the Castilian community in sixteenth-century Bruges', *Sixteenth Century Journal*, **17**(1), 33–49.

Pike, R. (1965). 'The Sevillian nobility and trade with the New World in the sixteenth century', *Business History Review*, **39**(4), 439–65.

Piola Caselli, F. (1998). 'The regulation of the Roman market in the seventeenth century', in *Guilds, Markets and Work Regulations in Italy, 16th–19th centuries*, ed. G. Alberto, M. Paola and C. Fausto Piola, Aldershot, 132–49.

Pirenne, H. (1925). *Medieval cities*, Princeton.

Planitz, H. (1919). 'Studien zur Geschichte des deutschen Arrestprozesses, II. Kapital: Der Fremdenarrest', *Zeitschrift der Savigny-Stiftung für Rechtsgeschichte, germanistische Abteilung*, **40**, 87–198.

— (1940). 'Kaufmannsgilde und städtische Eidgenossenschaft in niederfränkischen Städten im 11. und 12. Jahrhundert', *Zeitschrift der Savigny-Stiftung für Rechtsgeschichte, germanistische Abteilung*, **60**, 1–116.

Poni, C. (1982a). 'A proto-industrial city: Bologna sixteenth–eighteenth century', in *VIII Congrès Internationale d'Histoire Economique, Budapest 16–22 août 1982, Section A2: La protoindustrialisation: Théorie et réalité, Rapports*, ed. P. Deyon and F. F. Mendels, Lille., Vol. 1.

— (1982b). 'Maß gegen Maß: wie der Seidenfaden lang und dünn wurde', in *Klassen und Kultur. Sozialanthropologische Perspektiven in der Geschichtsschreibung*, ed. R. M. Berdahl et al., Frankfurt am Main, 21–53.

— (1985). 'Proto-industrialization, rural and urban', *Review (Fernand Braudel Center for the Study of Economies, Historical Systems and Civilizations)*, **9**, 305–14.

Postan, M. M. (1972). *The Medieval Economy and Society: Economic History of Britain, 1100–1500*, London.

— (1973). *Medieval Trade and Finance*, Cambridge.

— (1987). 'The trade of medieval Europe: the North', in *The Cambridge Economic History of Europe, Vol. 2: Trade and Industry in the Middle Ages*, ed. M. M. Postan and E. Miller, Cambridge, 168–305.

Powell, E. (1983). 'Arbitration and the law in England in the late Middle Ages', *Transactions of the Royal Historical Society*, 5th ser., **33**, 49–67.

— (1984). 'Settlement of disputes by arbitration in fifteenth-century England', *Law and History Review*, **2**(1), 21–43.

Power, E. (1926). 'The wool trade in the reign of Edward IV', *Cambridge Historical Journal*, **2**(1), 17–35.

— (1933). 'The wool trade in the fifteenth century', in *Studies in English Trade in the Fifteenth Century*, ed. E. Power and M. M. Postan, London.

— (1941). *The Wool Trade in English Medieval History*, Oxford.

Prakash, O. (1985). *The Dutch East India Company and the Economy of Bengal, 1630–1720*, Princeton.

Prevenier, W. (2000). 'The Low Countries, 1290–1415', in *The New Cambridge Medieval History, Vol. VI: c. 1300–c. 1415*, ed. M. Jones, Cambridge, 570–94.

Price, J. M. (1991). 'Transaction costs: a note on merchant credit and the organization of private trade', in *The Political Economy of Merchant Empires: State Power and World Trade, 1350–1750*, ed. J. D. Tracy, Cambridge, 276–97.

Price, W. H. (2006). *The English Patents of Monopoly*, repr. of 1st edn 1906, Cambridge, MA.

Priks, M. (2005). 'Optimal rent extraction in pre-industrial England and France: default risk and monitoring costs', *CESifo Working Papers*, 1464.

Pryor, J. H. (2000). 'The Maritime republics', in *The New Cambridge Medieval History, Vol. V: c. 1198–c. 1300*, ed. A. David, Cambridge, 419–46.

Putnam, R. D. (2000). *Bowling Alone: The Collapse and Revival of American Community*, New York.

—, R. Leonardi and R. Y. Nanetti (1993). *Making Democracy Work: Civic Traditions in Modern Italy*, Princeton.

Queller, D. E. (1973). 'The development of the ambassadorial *relazione*', in *Renaissance Venice*, ed. J. R. Hale, Totowa, NJ, 174–96.

— and G. W. Day (1976). 'Some arguments in defense of the Venetians on the Fourth Crusade', *American Historical Review*, **81**(4), 717–37.

Rabb, T. K. (1964). 'Sir Edwyn Sandys and the Parliament of 1604', *American Historical Review*, **69**(3), 646–70.

Rabinowitz, L. I. (1938a). 'The medieval Jewish counterpart of the gild merchant', *Economic History Review*, **8**, 180–5.

— (1938b). 'The Talmudic basis of the Herem Ha-Yishub', *Jewish Quarterly Review*, ns, **28**, 217–23.

Racine, P. (1985). 'Associations de marchands et associations de métiers en Italie de 600 à 1200', in *Gilden und Zünfte. Kaufmännische und gewerbliche Genossenschaften im frühen und hohen Mittelalter*, ed. B. Schwineköper, Sigmaringen, 127–50.

Raiser, M. (2001). 'Informal institutions, social capital and economic transition', in *Transition and Institutions: The Experience of Gradual and Late Reformers*, eds. G. A. Cornia and V. Popov, Oxford, 218–39.

Ramsey, P. (1994). 'Thomas Gresham: a sixteenth-century English entrepreneur?', in *Entrepreneurship and the Transformation of the Economy (10th–20th Centuries): Essays in Honor of Herman Van der Wee*, ed. P. Klep and E. v. Cauwenberghe, Leuven, 487–96.

Redlich, F. A. (1934). *Sitte und Brauch des livländischen Kaufmanns*, Riga.

Rei, C. (2007). 'The organisation of merchant empires: a case study of Portugal and England', Paper presented at the Economic History Society Annual Conference, Exeter, 30 March–1 April, draft of 14 March.

Reitemeier, A. (2002). 'Sprache, Dolmetscher und Sprachpolitik im Rußlandhandel während des Mittelalters', in *Novgorod. Markt und Kontor der Hanse*, ed. N. Angermann and K. Friedland, Cologne / Weimar / Vienna, 157–76.

Renouard, Y. (1949). *Les hommes d'affaires italiens du moyen âge*, Paris.

Reyerson, K. L. (1982). 'Commercial fraud in the Middle Ages: the case of the dissembling pepperer', *Journal of Modern History*, **8**, 63–74.

— (1985). *Business, Banking and Finance in Medieval Montpellier*, Toronto.

— (1994). 'Montpellier and Genoa: The dilemma of dominance', *Journal of Medieval History*, **20**(4), 359–72.

— (2000). 'Commerce and communications', in *The New Cambridge Medieval History, Vol. V: c. 1198–c. 1300*, ed. A. David, Cambridge, 50–70.

— (2002). *The Art of the Deal: Intermediaries of Trade in Medieval Montpellier*, Leiden / Boston.

— (2003). 'Commercial law and merchant disputes: Jacques Coeur and the law of Marque', *Medieval Encounters*, **9**(2–3), 244–55.

Reynolds, R. L. (1945). 'In search of a business class in thirteenth-century Genoa', *Journal of Economic History*, **5**, S1–S19.

— (1952). 'Origins of modern business enterprise: medieval Italy', *Journal of Economic History*, **12**, 350–65.

Reynolds, S. (1997). *Kingdoms and Communities in Western Europe, 900–1300*, Oxford.

Rich, E. E., ed. (1942). *Minutes of the Hudson's Bay Company, 1671–74*, London.

— ed. (1957). *The Hudson's Bay Copy Booke of Letters, Commissions, Instructions Outward (1688–1696)*, London.

Riemersma, J. C. (1950). 'Oceanic expansion: government influence on company organization in Holland and England (1550–1650)', *Journal of Economic History* **10**(Supplement), 31–9.

Riesenberg, P. (1992). *Citizenship in the Western Tradition*, Chapel Hill, NC.

Riis, T. (2005). 'Der Einfluß des hansischen Handels auf die Entwicklung der norwegischen Wirtschaft', in *Das Hansische Kontor zu Bergen und die Lübecker Bergenfahrer: International Workshop Lübeck 2003*, ed. A. Grassmann, Lübeck 28–40.

Robbert, L. B. (1983). 'Twelfth-century Italian prices: food and clothing in Pisa and Venice', *Social Science History*, 7(4), 381–403.

Robinson, E. A. G. (1932). *The Structure of Competitive Industry*, New York.

Romano, R. (1960). 'Marchands toscans et vénitiens au XIVe siècle', *Annales: économies, sociétés, civilisations*, 15(2), 392–7.

Rörig, F. (1922). *Der Markt von Lübeck. Topographisch-statistische Untersuchungen zur deutschen Sozial- und Wirtschaftsgeschichte*, Leipzig.

— (1928). *Hansische Beiträge zur deutschen Wirtschaftsgeschichte*, Breslau.

Rösch, G. (2000). 'The *Serrata* and Venetian society, 1286–1323', in *Venice Reconsidered: The History and Civilization of an Italian City-state, 1297–1797*, ed. J. Martin and D. Romana, Baltimore / London, 76–87.

Rothman, E.-N. (2006). 'Between Venice and Istanbul: trans-imperial subjects and cultural mediation in the early modern Mediterranean', University of Michigan Ph.D. dissertation.

Rowell, S. C. (2000). 'Baltic Europe', in *The New Cambridge Medieval History, Vol. VI: c. 1300–c. 1415*, ed. M. Jones, Cambridge, 699–734.

Rucellai, G. (1960). *Giovanni Rucellai ed il suo Zibaldone, Vol. 1: Il Zibaldone Quaresimale*, repr. of 1st edn 1473, ed. A. Perosa, Warburg Institute, London.

Runciman, S. (1987). 'Byzantine trade and industry', in *The Cambridge Economic History of Europe, Vol. 3: Economic Organization and Policies in the Middle Ages*, ed. M. M. Postan and E. Miller, Cambridge, 132–67.

Sachs, S. E. (2006). 'From St. Ives to cyberspace: the modern distortion of the medieval "Law Merchant"', *American University International Law Review*, 21(5), 685–812.

Salicrú i Lluch, R. (2001). 'The Catalano-Aragonese commercial presence in the sultanate of Granada during the reign of Alfonso the Magnanimous', *Journal of Medieval History*, 27(3), 289–312.

Samsonowicz, H. (1999). 'Time is money. Der Austausch von Informationen zwischen den Hansestädten im 15. Jahrhundert', in *'Kopet uns werk by tyden': Beiträge zur hansischen und preussischen Geschichte. Walter Stark zum 75 Geburtstag*, ed. N. Jörn, D. Kattinger and H. Wernicke, Schwerin, 211–13.

Sanudo, M. (1306). *Conditiones Terrae Sanctae*, Venice.

Sarnowsky, J. (1999). 'Das Thorner Patriziat und der Fernhandel', in *'Kopet uns werk by tyden': Beiträge zur hansischen und preussischen Geschichte. Walter Stark zum 75. Geburtstag*, ed. N. Jörn, D. Kattinger and H. Wernicke, Schwerin, 223–32.

— (2002). 'Märkte im mittelalterlichen Preußen', *Hansische Geschichtsblätter*, 120, 51–72.

Savary, J. (1675). *Le parfait négociant ou Instruction générale pour ce qui regarde le commerce des marchandises de France et des pays étrangers*, Paris.

Schaube, A. (1897). 'Ein italienischer Coursbericht von der Messe von Troyes aus dem 13. Jahrhundert', *Zeitschrift für Sozial- und Wirtschaftsgeschichte*, 5(3), 248–308.

Schechter, R. (2005). 'Market welfare in the early-modern Ottoman economy: a historiographic overview with many questions', *Journal of the Economic and Social History of the Orient*, **48**(2), 253–76.

Schevill, F. (1909). *Siena: The History of a Medieval Commune*, New York.

Schlüter, W. (1911). *Die Nowgoroder Schra in sieben Fassungen vom XIII. bis XVII. Jahrhundert*, Dorpat.

Schmitter, M. (2004). '"Virtuous Riches": The Bricolage of Cittadini Identities in Early-Sixteenth-Century Venice', *Renaissance Quarterly*, **57**(3), 908–69.

Schneider, F. (2006). 'Shadow economies and corruption all over the world: what do we really know?', *IZA Discussion Paper*, 2315.

Schnurmann, C. (2003). '"Wherever profit leads us, to every sea and shore . . . ": the VOC, the WIC, and Dutch methods of globalization in the seventeenth century', *Renaissance Studies*, **17**, 474–93.

Schofield, R. (1963). 'Parliamentary lay taxation, 1485–1547', University of Cambridge Ph.D. dissertation.

Scholz, C. (2001). 'In fremden Landen Handel treiben – ausländische Händler in Byzanz', *Das Mittelalter*, **6**, 91–107.

Schönfelder, A. (1988). *Handelsmessen und Kreditwirtschaft im Hochmittelalter. Die Champagnermessen*, Saarbrücken-Scheidt.

Schreiner, P., ed. (1991). *Texte zur spätbyzantinischen Finanz- und Wirtschaftsgeschichte in Handschriften der Biblioteca Vaticana*, Città del Vaticano.

Schulte, A. (1900). *Geschichte des mittelalterlichen Handels zwischen Westdeutschland und Italien mit Ausschluss von Venedig*, Leipzig.

Schultze, A. (1908). 'Über Gästerecht und Gastgerichte in den deutschen Städten des Mittelalters', *Historische Zeitschrift*, **101**, 473–528.

Schulz, K. (1985). 'Patriziergesellschaften und Zünfte in den mittel- und oberrheinischen Bischofsstädten', in *Gilden und Zünfte. Kaufmännische und gewerbliche Genossenschaften im frühen und hohen Mittelalter*, ed. B. Schwineköper, Sigmaringen, 311–36.

Schulze, H. K. (1985). 'Kaufmannsgilde und Stadtentstehung im mitteldeutschen Raum', in *Gilden und Zünfte. Kaufmännische und gewerbliche Genossenschaften im frühen und hohen Mittelalter*, ed. B. Schwineköper, Sigmaringen, 377–412.

Schuster, P. (1913). 'Die Schäferstadt Wildberg', *Aus dem Schwarzwald. Blätter des Württembergischen Schwarzwaldvereins*, **21**, 201–4.

Schütt, H.-F. (1980). 'Gilde und Stadt', *Zeitschrift der Gesellschaft für Schleswig-Holsteinische Geschichte*, **105**, 77–136.

— (1985). 'Die dänischen St. Knudsgilden – mit besonderer Berücksichtigung der Gilden in Schleswig und Flensburg', in *Gilden und Zünfte. Kaufmännische und gewerbliche Genossenschaften im frühen und hohen Mittelalter*, ed. B. Schwineköper, Sigmaringen, 231–80.

Schweichel, R. (2001). 'Kaufmännische Kontakte und Warenaustausch zwischen Köln und Brügge. Die Handelsgesellschaft von Hildebrand Veckinchusen, Werner Scherer und Reinhard Noiltgin', in '. . . *in guete freuntlichen nachbarlichen verwantnus und hantierung . . . ': Wanderung von Personen, Verbreitung von Ideen, Austausch von Waren in den niederländischen und deutschen Küstenregionen vom 13.–18. Jahrhundert*, ed. D. E. H. d. Boer, G. Gleba and R. Holbach, Oldenburg, 341–61.

Seabright, P. (2004). *The Company of Strangers: A Natural History of Economic Life*, Princeton, NJ.

Seider, H. (2005). 'Die Wormser Stadtverfassung im Zeitalter des Investiturstreites', University of Frankfurt-am-Main Ph.D. dissertation.

Seifert, D. (1995). 'Der Hollandhandel und seine Träger im 14. und 15. Jahrhundert', *Hansische Geschichtsblätter*, 113, 71–92.

Seland, T. (1996). 'Philo and the clubs and associations of Alexandria', in *Voluntary Associations in the Graeco-Roman World*, ed. J. W. Kloppenborg and S. G. Wilson, London, 110–27.

Sellers, M., ed. (1918). *The York Mercers and Merchant Adventurers 1356–1917*, Durham.

Selzer, S. (2003). 'Trinkstuben als Orte der Kommunikation. Das Beispiel der Artushöfe im Preußenland (ca. 1350–1550)', in *Geschlechtergesellschaften, Zunft-Trinkstuben und Bruderschaften in spätmittelalterlichen und frühneuzeitlichen Städten*, ed. G. Fouquet, M. Steinbrink and G. Zeilinger, Stuttgart, 73–98.

— and U.-C. Ewert (2001). 'Verhandeln und Verkaufen, Vernetzen und Vertrauen. Über die Netzwerkstruktur des hansischen Handels', *Hansische Geschichtsblätter*, 119, 135–62.

— and U.-C. Ewert (2005). 'Die Neue Institutionenökonomik als Herausforderung an die Hanseforschung', *Hansische Geschichtsblätter*, 123, 7–29.

Shephard, J. W. (2005). 'The Rôles d'Oléron: a lex mercatoria of the sea?', in *From Lex Mercatoria to Commercial Law*, ed. V. Piergiovanni, Berlin, 207–54.

Sibalis, M. D. (1988). 'Corporatism after the corporations: the debate on restoring the guilds under Napoleon I and the Restoration', *French Historical Studies*, 15(4), 718–30.

Sicking, L. (1999). 'Die offensive Lösung. Militärische Aspekte des holländischen Ostseehandels im 15. und 16. Jahrhundert', *Hansische Geschichtsblätter*, 117, 39–51.

Simonsfeld, H. (1887). *Der Fondaco dei Tedeschi in Venedig und die deutsch-venezianischen Handelsbeziehungen*, Stuttgart.

Slessarev, V. (1967). 'Ecclesiae Mercatorum and the rise of merchant colonies', *Business History Review*, 41(2), 177–97.

— (1969). 'The pound-value of Genoa's maritime trade in 1161', *Explorations in Economic History*, 7(1), 95–111.

Small, C. (1982). *The Printed World*, Aberdeen.

Smith, A. (1776). *An Inquiry into the Nature and Causes of the Wealth of Nations*, London.

Smith, R. M. (1974). 'English peasant life-cycles and socio-economic networks: a quantitative geographical case study', University of Cambridge Ph.D. dissertation.

Smith, R. S. (1940). *The Spanish Guild Merchant: A History of the Consulado, 1250–1700*, Durham, NC.

Smith, W. D. (1984). 'The function of commercial centers in the modernization of European capitalism: Amsterdam as an information exchange in the seventeenth century', *Journal of Economic History*, 44, 985–1005.

Sobel, J. (2002). 'Can we trust social capital?', *Journal of Economic Literature*, 40(1), 139–54.

Söderberg, J. (2004). 'Prices in the medieval Near East and Europe', Paper presented at the conference 'Toward a global history of prices and wages', Utrecht, 19–21 August.

— (2007). 'Prices and economic change in medieval Sweden', *Scandinavian Economic History Review*, **55**(2), 128–52.

Solow, R. M. (2000). 'Notes on social capital and economic performance', in *Social Capital: A Multifaceted Perspective*, ed. P. Dasgupta and I. Serageldin, Washington DC, 6–10.

Sprandel, R. (1984). 'Die Konkurrenzfähigkeit der Hanse im Spätmittelalter', *Hansische Geschichtsblätter*, **102**, 21–38.

— (1985). 'Handel und Gewerbe vom 6.-11. Jahrhundert', in *Gilden und Zünfte. Kaufmännische und gewerbliche Genossenschaften im frühen und hohen Mittelalter*, ed. B. Schwineköper, Sigmaringen, 9–30.

Spruyt, H. (1994). *The Sovereign State and Its Competitors: An Analysis of Systems Change*, Princeton.

Spufford, P. (1988). *Money and Its Use in Medieval Europe*, Cambridge.

— (1991). 'Spätmittelalterliche Kaufmannsnotizbücher als Quelle zur Bankengeschichte. Ein Projektbericht', in *Kredit im spätmittelalterlichen und frühneuzeitlichen Europa*, ed. M. North, Cologne / Vienna, 103–20.

— (2000). 'Trade in fourteenth-century Europe', in *The New Cambridge Medieval History, Vol. VI: c. 1300–c. 1415*, ed. M. Jones, Cambridge, 155–208.

Stabel, P. (1997). *Dwarfs among Giants: The Flemish Urban Network in the Late Middle Ages*, Leuven / Apeldoorn.

— (1999). 'Venice and the Low Countries: commercial contacts and intellectual inspirations', in *Renaissance Venice and the North: Crosscurrents in the Time of Bellini, Dürer and Titian*, ed. B. Aikema and B. L. Brown, London, 31–43.

— (2004). 'Profiting from collectivity: the costs and benefits of merchant guilds at the Bruges market (13th–15th centuries)', Paper presented at the Fifth European Social Science History Conference, Berlin, 24–27 March.

Staley, E. (1906). *The Guilds of Florence*, London.

Stark, W. (1984). 'Über Platz- und Kommissionshändlergewinne im Hansehandel des 15. Jahrhunderts', in *Autonomie, Wirtschaft und Kultur der Hansestädte*, ed. K. Fritze, E. Müller-Mertens and J. Schildhauer, 130–46.

— (1993). 'Über Techniken und Organisationsformen des hansischen Handels im Spätmittelalter', in *Der hansische Sonderweg? Beiträge zur Sozial- und Wirtschaftsgeschichte der Hanse*, ed. S. Jenks and M. North, Cologne/Weimar/Vienna, 191–201.

Stasavage, D. (2002). 'Credible commitment in early modern Europe: North and Weingast revisited', *Journal of Law, Economics and Organization*, **18**(1), 155–86.

Steensgaard, N. (1973). *The Asian Trade Revolution of the Seventeenth Century: The East India Companies and the Decline of the Caravan Trade*, Chicago / London.

— (1990). 'The growth and composition of the long-distance trade of England and the Dutch Republic before 1750', in *The Rise of Merchant Empires: Long-distance Trade in the Early Modern World, 1350–1750*, ed. J. D. Tracy, Cambridge, 102–52.

Stein, S. J. and B. H. Stein (2000). *Silver, Trade, and War: Spain and America in the Making of Early Modern Europe*, Baltimore.

Stein, W. (1902). 'Über die ältesten Privilegien der Deutschen Hanse in Flandern und die ältere Handelspolitik Lübecks', *Hansische Geschichtsblätter*, 30, 51–136.

Stephenson, C. (1933). *Borough and Town: A Study of Urban Origins in England*, Cambridge, MA.

Stieda, W. (1921). *Hildebrand Veckinchusen. Briefwechsel eines deutschen Kaufmanns im 15. Jahrhundert*, Leipzig.

Stigler, G. J. (1942). *The Theory of Competitive Price*, New York.

— (1968). *The Organization of Industry*. Homewood, IL.

Stiglitz, J. (1999). 'New bridges across the chasm: institutional strategies for the transition economies', Speech delivered at the World Bank in December 1999, [lnweb90.worldbank.org/eca/eca.nsf/0/0ac8adc7b03aca 0885256847004e2b82?OpenDocument&Click-].

— and D. Ellerman (2000). 'New bridges across the chasm: macro- and micro-strategies for Russia and other transitional economies', *Zagreb International Review of Economics and Business*, 3(1), 41–72.

Stöckle, A. (1894). 'Berufsvereine (griechische)', in *Real-Encyclopädie der klassischen Altertumswissenschaft*, ed. A. F. v. Pauly et al., Stuttgart, Vol. 4, cols. 155–211.

Stöckly, D. (1995). *Le système de l'Incanto des galées du marché à Venise (fin XIIIe–milieu XVe siècle)*, Leiden / Boston.

Stolle, D. and M. Hooghe (2003). 'Conclusion', in *Generating Social Capital: Civil Society and Institutions in Comparative Perspective*, ed. M. Hooghe and D. Stolle, New York, 231–48.

Stoob, H. (1995). *Die Hanse*, Graz.

Störmer, W. (1985). 'Vergesellschaftungsformen des Meliorats und des Handwerks in den Städten des bayerisch-österriechischen Raums', in *Gilden und Zünfte. Kaufmännische und gewerbliche Genossenschaften im frühen und hohen Mittelalter*, ed. B. Schwineköper, Sigmaringen, 337–76.

Strayer, J. R. (1969). 'Italian bankers and Philip the fair', in *Economy, Society and Government in Medieval Italy: Essays in Memory of Robert L. Reynolds*, ed. D. Herlihy, R. S. Lopez and V. Slessarev, Kent, OH, 239–47.

Stromer, W. v. (1976). 'Der innovatorische Rückstand der hansischen Wirtschaft', in *Beiträge zur Wirtschafts- und Sozialgeschichte des Mittelalters. Festschrift für Herbert Helbig zum 65. Geburtstag*, ed. K. Schulz, Cologne / Vienna, 204–17.

Stützel, P. (1998). 'Die Privilegien des Deutschen Kaufmanns in Brügge im 13. und 14. Jahrhundert', *Hansische Geschichtsblätter*, 116, 23–63.

Subacchi, P. (1995). 'Italians in Antwerp in the second half of the sixteenth century', in *Minderheden in Westeuropese steden 16de–20ste eeuw. Minorities in Western European Cities Sixteenth-Twentieth Centuries*, ed. H. Soly and K. L. Alfons, Brussels / Rome, 73–90.

Süberkrüb, H. (1951). 'Der deutsche Kaufmann als Gast in den dänischen Städten im 13. Jahrhundert', University of Kiel Ph.D. dissertation.

Sutton, A. F. (2002). 'The Merchant Adventurers of England: their origins and the Mercers' Company of London', *Historical Research*, 75, 25–46.

Szabó, T. (1983). 'Xenodochia, Hospitäler und Herbergen – kirchliche und kommerzielle Gastung im mittelalterlichen Italien (7. bis 14. Jahrhundert)', in *Gastfreundschaft, Taverne und Gasthaus im Mittelalter*, ed. H. C. Peyer and E. Müller-Luckner, Munich / Vienna, 61–92.

Tai, E. S. (1996). 'Honor among thieves: piracy, restitution, and reprisal in Genoa, Venice, and the Crown of Catalonia-Aragon, 1339–1417', Harvard University Ph.D. dissertation.

— (2003a). 'Marking water: piracy and property in the pre-modern West', Paper presented at the conference on 'Seascapes, Littoral Cultures, and Trans-Oceanic Exchanges', Library of Congress, Washington DC, 12–15 February.

— (2003b). 'Piracy and law in medieval Genoa: the consilia of Bartolomeo Bosco', *Medieval Encounters*, **9**(2–3), 256–82.

Talarico, K., ed. (2007). *The ORB: Online Reference Book for Medieval Studies* [www.the-orb.net/textbooks/westciv/medievalsoc.html].

Terrier, D. (1983). 'Mulquiniers et gaziers: les deux phases de la proto-industrie textile dans la région de Saint-Quentin (1730–1850)', *Revue du Nord*, **65**, 535–53.

't Hart, M. C. (1989). 'Cities and statemaking in the Dutch Republic, 1580–1680', *Theory and Society*, **18**(5), 663–87.

— (1993). *The Making of a Bourgeois State: War, Politics and Finance during the Dutch Revolt*, Manchester.

Theuerkauf, G. (1996). 'Binnen- und Seehandel zur Hansezeit an mecklenburgischen Beispielen', in *Zwischen Lübeck und Novgorod. Wirtschaft, Politik und Kultur im Ostseeraum vom frühen Mittelalter bis ins 20. Jahrhundert. Norbert Angermann zum 60. Geburtstag*, ed. O. Pelc and G. Pickhan, Lüneburg, 179–89.

Thirsk, J. and J. P. Cooper, eds. (1972). *Seventeenth-century Economic Documents*, Oxford.

Thomson, E. (1994). *Die Compagnie der Schwarzhäupter zu Riga und ihr Silberschatz*, Lüneburg.

Thomson, J. K. J. (1982). *Clermont-de-Lodève 1633–1789: Fluctuations in the Prosperity of a Languedocian Cloth-making Town*, Cambridge.

— (1996). 'Proto-industrialization in Spain', in *European Proto-industrialization*, ed. S. C. Ogilvie and M. Cerman, Cambridge, 85–101.

Todaro, M. P. (1989). *Economic Development in the Third World*, Harlow.

Torras, J. (1986). 'From masters to fabricants. Guild organization and economic growth in eighteenth-century Catalonia: a case-study', *European University Institute Colloquium Papers*, 30.

— (1991). 'The old and the new: marketing networks and textile growth in eighteenth-century Spain', in *Markets and Manufacture in Early Industrial Europe*, ed. M. Berg, Cambridge, 93–113.

Tracy, J. D. (1990a). 'Introduction', in *The Rise of Merchant Empires: Long-distance Trade in the Early Modern World, 1350–1750*, ed. J. D. Tracy, Cambridge, 1–13.

— (1990b). *Holland under Habsburg rule, 1506–1566: The Formation of a Body Politic*, Berkeley.

— (1991). 'Introduction', in *The Political Economy of Merchant Empires: State Power and World Trade, 1350–1750*, ed. J. D. Tracy, Cambridge, 1–21.

Trakman, L. (1983). *The Law Merchant: The Evolution of Commercial Law*, Littleton, CO.

Trivellato, F. (2007). 'Merchants' letters across geographical and social boundaries', in *Cultural Exchange in Early Modern Europe, Vol. 3: Correspondence, 1400–1700*, ed. F. Bethencourt and F. Egmond, Cambridge, 80–103.

Troeltsch, W. (1897). *Die Calwer Zeughandlungskompagnie und ihre Arbeiter. Studien zur Gewerbe- und Sozialgeschichte Altwürttembergs*, Jena.

Truitt, W. B. (2006). *The Corporation*, Westport, CT.

Tyerman, C. J. (1982). 'Marino Sanudo Torsello and the Lost Crusade: lobbying in the fourteenth century', *Transactions of the Royal Historical Society*, 5th ser., **32**, 57–73.

Udovitch, A. L. (1962). 'At the origins of the western commenda: Islam, Israel, Byzantium?', *Speculum*, **37**(2), 198–207.

United Nations Development Program, ed. (1993). *Human Development Report*, Oxford / New York.

Unwin, G., ed. (1918). *Finance and Trade under Edward III: The London Lay Subsidy of 1332*, Manchester / London / New York.

Van Bavel, B. and J.-L. Van Zanden (2004). 'The jump-start of the Holland economy during the late-medieval crisis, c. 1350 – c. 1500', *Economic History Review*, **57**, 503–32.

Van den Heuvel, D. (2007). *Women and Entrepreneurship: Female Traders in the Northern Netherlands, c. 1580–1815*, Amsterdam.

Van Der Kooy, T. P. (1931). *Hollands Stapelmarkt en haar Verval*, Amsterdam.

— (1970). 'Holland als centrale Stapelmarkt in de Zeventiende en Achtiende Eeuw', in *Van Stapelmarkt tot Welvaartsstaat*, ed. P. W. Klein, Rotterdam.

Van Der Wee, H. (1990). 'European long-distance trade, and particularly in the re-export trade from south to north, 1350–1750', in *The Rise of Merchant Empires: Long-distance Trade in the Early Modern World, 1350–1750*, ed. J. D. Tracy, Cambridge, 14–33.

Van Doorslaer, G. (1907). 'La navigation, l'industrie & le commerce Malinois aux XIIIe, XIVe, & XVe siècles', *Bulletin du cercle archéologique, litteraire & artistique de Malines*, **17**, 29–52.

Van Doosselaere, Q. (2009). *Commercial Agreements and Social Dynamics in Medieval Genoa*, Cambridge.

Van Houtte, J. A. (1953). 'Les foires dans la Belgique Ancienne', *Receuils de la Société Jean Bodin*, 5.

— (1961). 'Anvers aux XVe et XVIe siècles: expansion et apogée', *Annales ESC*, **16**, 248–78.

— (1966). 'The rise and decline of the market of Bruges', *Economic History Review*, 2nd ser., **19**, 29–47.

— (1983). 'Herbergwesen und Gastlichkeit im mittelalterlichen Brügge', in *Gastfreundschaft, Taverne und Gasthaus im Mittelalter*, ed. H. C. Peyer and E. Müller-Luckner, Munich / Vienna, 177–88.

Van Nijf, O. M. (1997). *The Civic World of Professional Associations in the Roman East*, Amsterdam.

Van Tielhof, M. (2002). *The 'Mother of All Trades': The Baltic Grain Trade in Amsterdam from the Late Sixteenth to the Early Nineteenth Century*, Amsterdam.

Van Zanden, J.-L. and M. Prak (2006). 'Towards an economic interpretation of citizenship: the Dutch Republic between medieval communes and modern nation-states', *European Review of Economic History*, 10(2), 11–147.

Vander Linden, H. (1896). *Les Gildes marchandes dans les Pays-Bas au moyen âge*, Ghent.

Vassallo, C. (2002). 'The Maltese entrepreneurial networks from the seventeenth century onwards. A review of the work done so far', Paper presented at the XIII Economic History Congress, Buenos Aires, 22–26 July.

Vázquez de Prada, V. (1960). *Lettres marchandes d'Anvers*, Paris.

Veluwenkamp, J. W. (1981). *Ondernemersgedrag op de Hollandse stapelmarkt in de tijd van de Republiek. De Amsterdamse handelsfirma Jan Isaac de Neufville & Comp., 1730–1764*, Meppel.

Verein für Lübeckische Geschichte (1843). *Urkundenbuch der Stadt Lübeck, Erster Theil*, Lübeck.

Verlinden, C. (1965). 'Markets and fairs', in *The Cambridge Economic History of Europe, Vol. 3: Economic Organization and Policies in the Middle Ages*, ed. M. M. Postan, E. E. Rich and E. Miller, Cambridge, 119–53.

Vitale, V. (1955). *Breviario della storia di Genova*, Genoa.

Volckart, O. and A. Mangels (1999). 'Are the roots of the modern *lex mercatoria* really medieval?', *Southern Economic Journal*, 65(3), 427–50.

Wach, A. (1868). *Der Arrestprozess in seiner geschichtlichen Entwicklung. 1. Teil: Der italienischen Arrestprozess*, Leipzig.

Waley, D. (1969). *The Italian City Republics*, New York.

Waltzing, J.-P. (1895–1900). *Étude historique sur les corporations professionnelles chez les romains*, 4 vols, Louvain.

Wase, D. (2000). 'Die früheste deutsche Ansiedlung auf dem "gotischen Ufer" in Visby', *Hansische Geschichtsblätter*, 118, 9–33.

Watson, I. B. (1980). *Foundations for Empire*, New Delhi.

Weber, F. M. (1955). *Ehingen. Geschichte einer oberschwäbischen Donaustadt*, Ehingen.

Weber, K. (2002). 'The Atlantic coast of German trade: German rural industry and trade in the Atlantic, 1680–1840', *Itinerario: European Journal of Overseas History*, 26(2), 99–119.

— (2004). *Deutsche Kaufleute im Atlantikhandel 1680–1830. Unternehmen und Familien in Hamburg, Cádiz und Bordeaux*, Munich.

Weinryb, B. D. (1945). 'Studies in the Communal History of Polish Jewry II', *Proceedings of the American Academy for Jewish Research*, 15, 93–129.

— (1950). 'Texts and studies in the communal history of Polish Jewry', *Proceedings of the American Academy for Jewish Research*, 19, iii–v, vii–xii, 3–16, 19–73, 77–92, 95–110; Hebrew version: 3–174, 177–218, 221–64.

Wernicke, H. (1999). 'Der preußische Kaufmann und seine Städte in der Hanse', in *'Kopet uns werk by tyden': Beiträge zur hansischen und preussischen Geschichte. Walter Stark zum 75. Geburtstag*, ed. N. Jörn, D. Kattinger and H. Wernicke, Schwerin, 195–200.

White, S. D. (1978). '"Pactum . . . legem vincit et amor judicium." The settlement of disputes by compromise in eleventh-century western France', *American Journal of Legal History*, 22(4), 281–303.

Wiarda, H. J. (1997). *Corporatism and Comparative Politics: The Other Great 'ism'*, Armonk, NY.

Wilflingseder, F. (1969). 'Der Gewandausschnitt. Ein Beitrag zur Linzer Handelsgeschichte vom 15. bis zum 18. Jahrhundert', *Historisches Jahrbuch der Stadt Linz* (1968), 297–319.

Willan, T. S. (1959). *Studies in Elizabethan Foreign Trade*, Manchester.

Williams, D. T. (1931). 'The maritime relations of Bordeaux and Southampton in the thirteenth century', *Scottish Geographical Journal*, 47(5), 270–5.

Winius, G. D. and M. P. M. Vink (1991). *The Merchant-warrior Pacified: The VOC (the Dutch East India Company) and Its Changing Political Economy in India*, Delhi / Oxford.

Winterfeld, L. v. (1955). 'Gründung, Markt und Ratsbildung deutscher Fernhandelsstädte', in *Westfalen, Hanse, Ostseeraum*, ed. L. v. Winterfeld et al., Münster.

Wolff, K. H. (1979). 'Guildmaster into millhand: the industrialization of linen and cotton in Germany to 1850', *Textile History*, 10, 7–74.

Wolff, P. (1954). *Commerces et marchands de Toulouse (vers 1350–vers 1450)*, Paris.

Woodward, R. L., Jr. (2005). 'Merchant guilds', in *Encyclopedia of World Trade from Ancient Times to the Present*, ed. C. C. Northrup, New York, Vol. 3, 631–8.

— (2007). 'Merchant guilds (*Consulados de Comercio*) in the Spanish world', *History Compass*, 5(5), 1576–84.

World Bank, ed. (1994). *The World Bank and Participation*, Washington DC.

—, ed. (2005), *World Development Indicators 2005*, [www.devdata.worldbank.org/wdi2005/cover.htm].

Wrightson, K. (1982). *English Society 1580–1680*, London.

Wubs-Mrozewicz, J. (2004). 'Interplay of identities: German settlers in late medieval Stockholm', *Scandinavian Journal of History*, 29, 53–67.

— (2005). 'The Bergenfahrer and the Bergenvaarders: Lübeck and Amsterdam in a Study of Rivalry c. 1440–1560', in *Das Hansische Kontor zu Bergen und die Lübecker Bergenfahrer: International Workshop Lübeck 2003*, ed. A. Grassmann, Lübeck, 206–30.

Zakharov, V. (2009). 'The communities of foreign merchants in Russia during the 18th century', Paper presented at the XV World Economic History Congress, Utrecht, 3–7 August.

Ziebarth, E. G. L. (1896). *Das griechische Vereinswesen*, Wiesbaden / Leipzig.

Index

agency relationships 325–6, 335–6
see also principal-agent problem
Alberti, Leon Battista, correspondent
   relationship 374
alien merchant guilds 15, 20, 23, 24–5,
   94–159, 202
  barriers to entry 96, 108, 111–13, 115,
   158
  collection of taxes for rulers 173–5
  compulsory staple rights 68–9, 172
  dependence on local 'home' guilds 25,
   108
  efficiency view of 96, 107, 157
  embargoes 213–15
  enforcement of monopolies 132–4,
   137–41, 142, 156–7
   communication between branches
    over penalty enforcement 141
   complaints against 126–30, 132
   inter-guild conflict over monopolies
    134–6, 137
  expansion of privileges 106
  financial contributions from members
   168–9
  financial support for rulers 169–70,
   176–80
  granting of rights by foreign rulers 102,
   105, 107
  guest membership of 108
  and guild/consular courts 253–5, 258
  and 'home' governments 230–2, 233–5
  individual security guarantees 212–13
  limitations on authority 202–3
  monopolistic behaviour 127, 158
   and competition 97–8, 99
   enforcement of legal monopolies 100
   monopsony rights 122–3
   price collusion 115–17, 118–19
   pursuit of legal entitlements 99
   over specific lines of trade 97, 107
   restriction of supply 121–2, 217
   and rivals' trading costs 124–5

political domination of 181
  purchase of licences and exemptions
   142–4
  redistribution of benefits 100
  regulations of 152–3, 154
   German and Spanish merchant guilds
    in Bruges 153–4
   internal regulation and monitoring
    154
   and record-keeping 141–2
  tax advantages 164, 165
  trading at fairs 96–7
  trading privileges 23–4, 97, 106–7
  variation across Europe 155–6
  weakening of 34–5, 183
  see also associate membership, of alien
   merchant guilds; English Merchant
   Adventurers; German Hanse; legal
   monopolies; monopoly power, and
   merchant guilds
Alpert of Metz, Tiel merchant guild 263
American market, and Seville consulado
   143–4, 147
Amsterdam
  antagonism towards merchant guilds
   183, 399
  commercial security in 245
  decline of merchant guilds 32, 34–5
  global entrepôt role 396, 397, 398
  and guild courts 254
  municipal jurisdiction in 307–8
  newsletters from 377
  price stability in 398, 399, 410–11, 412
  sources of information in 366, 368,
   370
   notarial system's role in 369
Antwerp
  bourse in 368, 369
  brokerage system and information 370
  decline of merchant guilds 32
  and guild courts 253
  information places in 368

476